THE OXFORD HANDBOOK OF

ENTREPRENEURSHIP

University of Liverpool

Withdrawn from stock

THE OXFORD HANDBOOK OF

ENTREPRENEURSHIP

Edited by
MARK CASSON,
BERNARD YEUNG,
ANURADHA BASU
AND
NIGEL WADESON

UNIVERSITY PRESS

OXFORD
UNIVERSITY PRESS

Great Clarendon Street, Oxford OX2 6DP

Oxford University Press is a department of the University of Oxford.
It furthers the University's objective of excellence in research, scholarship,
and education by publishing worldwide in

Oxford New York

Auckland Cape Town Dar es Salaam Hong Kong Karachi
Kuala Lumpur Madrid Melbourne Mexico City Nairobi
New Delhi Shanghai Taipei Toronto
With offices in
Argentina Austria Brazil Chile Czech Republic France Greece
Guatemala Hungary Italy Japan South Korea Poland Portugal
Singapore Switzerland Thailand Turkey Ukraine Vietnam

Oxford is a registered trade mark of Oxford University Press
in the UK and in certain other countries

Published in the United States
by Oxford University Press Inc., New York

© Oxford University Press, 2006

The moral rights of the author have been asserted

Database right Oxford University Press (maker)

Reprinted 2009

All rights reserved. No part of this publication may be reproduced,
stored in a retrieval system, or transmitted, in any form or by any means,
without the prior permission in writing of Oxford University Press,
or as expressly permitted by law, or under terms agreed with the appropriate
reprographics rights organization. Enquiries concerning reproduction
outside the scope of the above should be sent to the Rights Department,
Oxford University Press, at the address above

You must not circulate this book in any other binding or cover
And you must impose this same condition on any acquirer

ISBN 978-0-19-954699-2

Printed in the United Kingdom by
Lightning Source UK Ltd., Milton Keynes

Contents

PART III INNOVATION

PART IV FINANCE

PART V EMPLOYMENT, SELF-EMPLOYMENT AND BUY-OUTS

PART VI SOCIAL AND CULTURAL ASPECTS

PART VII SPATIAL AND INTERNATIONAL DIMENSIONS

List of Figures

List of Tables

List of editors and contributors

The editors

Mark Casson is Professor of Economics at the University of Reading. His publications include *The Entrepreneur* (1982; new edition, 2002), *Entrepreneurship and Business Culture* (1995) and *Enterprise and Leadership* (2000). He has contributed articles on entrepreneurship to the *New Palgrave Dictionary of Economics*, the *International Encyclopaedia of Social Science*, the *Fortune Dictionary of Economics* and the *Oxford Encyclopaedia of Economic History*. His most recent work focuses on links between entrepreneurship and theories of the firm.

Bernard Yeung is Abraham Krasnoff Professor of Global Business, Economics and Strategy, Stern School of Business, and Director of China House, New York University. He was Vice-President of the Academy of International Business, 2000–02. He has published widely at the interface of economics, finance and strategy, with special reference to SME performance, family business, corporate finance, capital market functionality, and foreign direct investment. He edited *Small and Medium Sized Enterprises in the Global Economy* (1999) with Zoltan Acs and *Structural Change, Industrial Location, and Competitiveness* with Joanne Oxley.

Anuradha Basu is Professor of Entrepreneurship and Management, Lucas Graduate School of Business, and Director of the Silicon Valley Center for Entrepreneurship, San Jose State University. She was formerly Visiting Scholar, Center for Research on Economic Development and Policy Reform, Stanford University (2002–03) and a faculty member at the University of Reading. She has published widely on Asian entrepreneurship and on ethnic minority and family businesses. Her most recent work focuses on entrepreneurship education and the factors influencing entrepreneurial intentions.

Nigel Wadeson is Lecturer in Economics at the University of Reading. He has published on decision making, the firm, and entrepreneurship in a range of books and journals. He teaches entrepreneurship and small business economics at masters level. He spent several years working in entrepreneurial ventures in the IT industry and has also acted as a consultant involved in high-level government policy work.

The contributors

Zoltan J. Acs is the Doris and Robert McCurdy Distinguished Professor of Entrepreneurship and Innovation, Professor of Economics and Director of the Entrepreneurship Program in the Robert G. Merrick School of Business, University of Baltimore. He is also a census research fellow at the US Bureau of the Census. Previously he was Chief Economic Advisor, US Small Business Administration, Associate Director of CIBER at the University of Maryland, Research Fellow at the Science Center Berlin, and Research Associate at the Institute on Western Europe at Columbia University. Together with David Audretsch, he is the editor and founder of *Small Business Economics: An International Journal*, and the editor of the *Journal of International Entrepreneurship*, and the Kluwer Handbook Series on Entrepreneurship. He has authored over 90 articles on technical change, entrepreneurship, small business economics, regional science and industrial organization in the *American Economic Review*, *Review of Economics and Statistics*, *The Journal of Urban Economics*, *Kyklos*, *Economica and Research Policy* and other leading journals. He has edited, authored or co-authored 18 books.

David B. Audretsch is the Director of the Entrepreneurship, Growth and Public Policy Group at the Max Planck Institute of Economics in Jena, Germany. He is also the Ameritech Chair of Economic Development and Director of the Institute for Development Strategies at Indiana University, and a research fellow of the Centre for Economic Policy Research (London). His research has focused on the links between entrepreneurship, government policy, innovation, economic development and global competitiveness. He is a member of the Advisory Board of ZEW, Mannheim; HWWA, Hamburg; and the Swedish Foundation for Research on Entrepreneurship and Small Business. He has published over 100 articles in leading academic journals, and some 30 books, including *Innovation and Industry Evolution*. He is co-founder and co-editor of *Small Business Economics: An International Journal*. He was awarded the 2001 International Award for Entrepreneurship and Small Business Research by the Swedish Foundation for Small Business Research.

Luca Berchicci is a post-doctoral researcher in management of technology at the Chair of Corporate Strategy and Innovation at the École Polytechnique Fédérale de Lausanne (EPFL). He obtained his Master's degree in Geology at the University of Urbino (Italy) in 1997. In October 2005, he received his PhD in innovation management at the Faculty of Industrial Design Engineering of Delft University of Technology. During his PhD, he carried out practical market-studies, among others for Nike Europe and TNO Industry Research Center. His general research interest is in the area of innovation processes within existing and new organizations and how firms cope with the uncertainties of the innovation process. He is also interested in the effects of new technologies at both industry and firm level.

Candida Brush holds the President's Chair in Entrepreneurship at Babson College, Massachusetts. She conducted the first and largest study of women entrepreneurs in the early 1980s. With four other researchers she founded the Diana Project, a research consortium investigating women's access to growth capital, and published *Clearing the Hurdles: Women Building High Growth Businesses* in 2004. She has published in both management and entrepreneurship journals, including *Journal of Business Venturing, Entrepreneurship Theory and Practice, Journal of Management, Academy of Management Executive,* and *Strategic Management Journal.* A frequent adviser to the US Small Business Administration Office of Advocacy on women's entrepreneurship, she has also been appointed to the Defence Advisory Committee on Women in the Services.

Peter J. Buckley is Professor of International Business and Director of the Centre for International Business, University of Leeds, (CIBUL), UK, and Visiting Professor at the University of Reading. He has published 21 books in English and one in German and over 120 refereed articles in European, American and Japanese journals. His work is heavily cited—the Social Science Citation Index lists over 1,300 citations. He was President of the Academy of International Business 2002–04. His current research interests include the management of knowledge in multinational firms, international alliances and co-operative strategies between firms and foreign direct investment in China.

Andrew Burrows is Director of the Centre for Management Buy-out Research at the University of Nottingham. His research interests include management buy-outs and buy-ins, with special reference to the role of private equity and venture capital. He has made a special study of the funding and development of private buy-outs.

Maria Bytchkova is a doctoral student at London Business School, researching institutional development in transition economies with special reference to SMEs. Her research interests also include institution-building and the political economy of reform.

Martin J. Carter is Lecturer in Economics at the Leeds University Business School. He spent ten years as a manager with Unilever and with Baxter Healthcare before moving into business education where he has taught courses on the economics of marketing and the economics of business and corporate strategy. His published research includes work on the role of information in organization design and on knowledge combination processes in multinational enterprise.

T. A. B. Corley is one of the UK's most senior business historians who has published widely on the history of the oil, consumer goods and pharmaceutical industries. He is an expert on Beechams, Huntley & Palmers, the oil magnates, and Quaker entrepreneurs. He recently provided 90 entries, mostly on entrepreneurs, for the *New Dictionary of National Biography.*

Robert Cressy is Corporation of London Professor of SME Finance at the Cass Business School, City University. He was formerly Professor of Finance and Director of Research at the University of Hull Business School, and Assistant Director of Warwick University Business School's Centre for Small and Medium Enterprises. His research on entrepreneurial finance has consistently emphasized the role of human capital in determining both capitalization of the business and its survival. He is a consultant to the EC Enterprise Directorate and has been a regular contributor to EU reports. He was also a member of the Bank of England's panel on small business finance.

Marina Della Giusta is Lecturer in Economics at the University of Reading. She has published widely on social capital and the influence of trust on economic performance. Her research portfolio includes macroeconomics of international development, and the economics of prostitution. She consults for the United Nations Economic Commission for Latin America and the Caribbean.

Gary Dushnitsky is Assistant Professor of Management at the Wharton School, University of Pennsylvania. His research focuses on the economics of entrepreneurship and innovation, exploring the conditions under which established corporations succeed, or fail, to partner with innovative startups, and the implication to corporate innovativeness. He is the recipient the Heizer Award for the best dissertation by the Entrepreneurship division of the Academy of Management, the Best Dissertation Award by the Technology, and Innovation Management division of the Academy of Management, as well as the Herman Krooss Award for Outstanding Dissertation (Stern School of Business, NYU). His papers received a number of awards including the McKinsey Paper Prize (Honorable Mention) at the Strategic Management Society.

Saul Estrin is Adecco Professor of Business and Society and Research Director of the Centre for New and Emerging Markets at London Business School. His recent publications include *Investment Strategies in Emerging Markets* (with Klaus Meyer), (2004) and papers in *Journal of Comparative Economics*, *Journal of Economic Perspectives* and *Journal of International Business Research.* He is a research fellow of the Centre for Economic Policy Research and associate editor of the *Journal of Comparative Economics.*

Kathy Fogel is Assistant Professor of Finance at the Department of Finance, Sam M. Walton College of Business, University of Arkansas. She holds a PhD in finance from the University of Alberta. The focus of her research is corporate governance, corporate finance, and economic institutions.

Andrew Godley is Professor of Business History at the University of Reading and a former Director of the Centre for International Business History there. He has published an award winning monograph on the relationship between British culture and Jewish entrepreneurship, *Jewish Immigrant Entrepreneurship in London and New York* (2001), together with numerous articles on subjects ranging from the development of the global clothing industry to the earliest multinational manufacturers, and from international retailing to mass migration and ethnic entrepreneurship.

Eleanor Hamilton is Director of the Institute for Entrepreneurship and Enterprise Development at the University of Lancaster Management School. Her research interests focus on the influence and impact of intergenerational learning in family businesses, entrepreneurship education and curriculum, and the interface between entrepreneurship and marketing.

Ashton Hawk is a doctoral student in the Management Department at the Stern School of Business, New York University, with research interests in venture capital and corporate finance.

Carole Howorth is Senior Lecturer in Entrepreneurship in the Institute for Entrepreneurship and Enterprise Development, Lancaster University Management School. She is a director of the Institute for Small Business and Entrepreneurship (ISBE) and an academic advisor to the 2005 ISBE conference. She combines quantitative and qualitative research methods to explore the growth and development of SMEs, the financing of entrepreneurial ventures, and the behaviour of family firms. She has published in national and international journals on entrepreneurship, management buyouts, succession issues, working capital management and credit management.

Max Keilbach is a Max Planck Research Fellow at the Max Planck Institute of Economics, Jena, affiliated to the Entrepreneurship, Growth and Public Policy Group. His main research interests are in the area of innovative entrepreneurship and in its economic impact. He uses empirical, econometric and simulation-based approaches in his analyses. He has published in *Annals of Regional Science*, *Journal of Industrial Organisation*, *Journal of Evolutionary Economics*, *Entrepreneurship: Theory and Practice*, and other leading journals.

Zella King is the Director of the Centre for Career Management Skills and Lecturer in Management at the University of Reading Business School. She has published widely on career-related topics, including several papers on career self-management and the 'bounded' career. She has recently completed an ESRC-funded project exploring the determinants of localized collaborations between scientists from a psychological perspective, and is currently working on a HEFCE-funded project examining the production of human capital in higher education.

Walter Kuemmerle is one of the world's leading experts on international entrepreneurship and private equity. He serves as a researcher, lecturer and consultant at leading institutions of higher learning, companies and non-governmental organizations around the world. He was a professor at Harvard Business School for over 10 years, and has published widely in leading academic and practitioner journals. Recently, he also developed a pioneering MBA course entitled 'International Entrepreneurship: Managing and Financing Ventures in the Global Economy'. He is the author of a case book and instructor's manual with the same title.

Amir N. Licht is Visiting Professor in the Boalt School of Law, University of California, Berkeley. He teaches and researches corporate law and securities regulation at the Interdisciplinary Centre Hezliya, Israel. He has served as Advisor to the Israeli Securities Authority and the Ministry of Justice, and is a research associate of the European Corporate Governance Institute.

Philip McCann is Professor of Economics at the University of Reading, UK, and at the University of Waikato, New Zealand. His research focuses on issues of urban and regional economics, transport economics, international business economics and the economics of technology and innovation. He has published over 50 articles and four books, plus five book translations. Philip received the 2002 Hewings Award for Outstanding Scholarship from the North American Regional Science Association, and he is the only non-North American to win the award.

Stanley Metcalfe is Stanley Jevons Professor of Political Economy and Cobden Lecturer at the University of Manchester. During his career he has lectured at the Universities of Manchester and Liverpool. He has been actively involved in the development of science and technology policy in the UK, being a member first of ACARD and subsequently ACOST. He was until recently a member of the Monopolies and Mergers Commission. His research interests are currently focused upon evolutionary economics and the modelling of evolutionary processes in relation to innovation, competition and economic growth. He is Past President of the International J. A. Schumpeter Society.

Klaus Meyer is a Professor of Business Administration at the University of Reading, and having previously served on the faculty of the Copenhagen Business School (1997–05). His research focuses on the strategies of multinational enterprises in emerging economies and has been published in journals such as *Journal of International Business Studies* and *Journal of Management Studies*. He contributed to the *Oxford Handbook of International Business* (2001) and in 2004 published, jointly with Saul Estrin, *Investment Strategies in Emerging Markets* (Elgar).

Randall Morck is Stephen A. Jarislowski Distinguished Chair in Finance and University Professor at the University of Alberta and a Research Associate of the National Bureau of Economic Research. He has published widely on corporate valuations, business groups, family firms and corporate lobbying in the *Review of Economics and Statistics*, *Journal of Finance*, *Journal of Economic Literature* and other leading journals.

Simon C. Parker is Professor and Head of the Department of Economics & Finance at Durham Business School and Director of Durham's Centre for Entrepreneurship. He is also a research professor at the Max Planck Institute of Economics at Jena, Germany, and an associate editor of Small Business Economics. He has published widely on the economics of entrepreneurship, authoring, *The Economics of Self-employment and Entrepreneurship* (Cambridge University Press, 2004) and editing Volume III of the *Handbook of Entrepreneurship Research*, to be published by Springer in 2006.

Martin Ricketts is Professor of Economic Organisation at the University of Buckingham. His publications include *The Economics of Business Enterprise: An Introduction to Economic Organisation and the Theory of the Firm* (3rd edn) (1987, 2003) and *The Many Ways of Governance: Perspectives on the Control of the Firm* (1999). He has contributed articles on entrepreneurship to the *Journal of Institutional and Theoretical Economics*, the *Journal des Économistes et des Études Humaines* and to symposia on Austrian Economics and the New Institutional Economics.

Mary Rose is Professor of Entrepreneurship in the Institute of Entrepreneurship and Enterprise Development (IEED) in the Management School at Lancaster University, and Research Director of the IEED. She specializes in business history, especially international perspectives on family business and also the history of textiles. She has published widely on the evolution of business values, networking, family firms and the problem of leadership succession, authoring three books and editing another nine. She is Director of the Pasold Research Fund, a charitable trust which provides grants for all aspects of textile history, and General Editor of the *Pasold Studies in Textile History* published by Oxford University Press.

Jordan Siegel is Assistant Professor in the Strategy group at Harvard Business School. One stream of Siegel's research examines how firms in countries with weak and/or incomplete governance institutions access outside finance and technology. Within that stream, one of his studies challenges current views regarding the efficacy of renting foreign jurisdictions through cross-listings and shows that reputational mechanisms are more important. Another stream of Siegel's research focuses on how firms around the world can best manage institutional differences across countries. One study in that stream shows that informal social institutions have major impacts on flows of both finance and mergers and acquisition across countries.

Professor David Storey is Associate Dean (Research) at Warwick Business School and Director of the Centre for Small and Medium Sized Enterprises. His work has focused on small firm growth and on the evaluation of the impact of public policies to assist SMEs. He is the author of several books on small firms, the best known of which is *Understanding the Small Business Sector*. He has two honorary Doctorates and currently holds the title of Visiting Professor at the Universities of Manchester,

Reading and Durham and is an EIM Fellow. In 1998 he received the International Award for Entrepreneurship and Small Business Research from the Swedish Council. He has just completed a four-year appointment as a Member of the Small Business Council, which advises the UK government on small business policy making. He has also undertaken work for several overseas governments and organizations.

Christopher L. Tucci is Associate Professor of Management of Technology at the École Polytechnique Fédérale de Lausanne (EPFL), where he holds the Chair in Corporate Strategy & Innovation. Prior to joining EPFL, he was on the faculty of the NYU Stern School of Business. He is interested in technological change and how waves of technological changes affect incumbent firms. For example, he is studying how the technological changes brought about by the popularization of the Internet affect firms in different industries. He has published articles in *Management Science, Strategic Management Journal, Research Policy, IEEE Transactions on Engineering Management, Journal of Engineering and Technology Management*, and *Journal of Product Innovation Management.* In 2003, he was elected to the leadership track for the Technology & Innovation Management Division of the Academy of Management.

Deniz Ucbasaran is Associate Professor in Entrepreneurship at the University of Nottingham. She has published widely on entrepreneurial types, opportunity identification and exploration, human capital, entrepreneurial cognition and mindsets, entrepreneurial teams, and corporate entrepreneurship. She also researches the relationship between corporate governance and corporate social responsibility.

Paul Westhead is Chair in Entrepreneurship and Director for the Centre of Entrepreneurship, Durham Business School. He has published extensively on habitual entrepreneurs, family businesses, technology-based firms, science parks, the internationalization of small firms and the benefits associated with training programmes for businesses and students.

Mike Wright is Professor of Financial Studies and Founder of the Centre for Management Buy-out Research at the University of Nottingham. He has published numerous papers on management buy-outs and related subjects, including venture capital. His research interests also encompass technology transfer and corporate governance in emerging markets.

CHAPTER 1

INTRODUCTION

MARK CASSON ET AL.

1.1 Objectives of the Book

The modern academic literature on entrepreneurship first appeared in a significant volume about 20 years ago, and it has now reached a reasonable state of maturity (see Shane, 2003). It is therefore an appropriate time to take stock of what has been achieved.

The book is intended to be an authoritative survey of recent academic research into entrepreneurship. It aims to meet the needs of PhD candidates researching in all major academic fields to which entrepreneurship is relevant: industrial economics, business strategy, organizational behaviour, finance and venture capital, and business and economic history. We hope that the contributions will stimulate MBA and doctoral students to investigate outstanding issues, and to open up new research agendas for the future. The book will also provide useful secondary reading for MBA courses on entrepreneurship.

The basic conceptual approach adopted in the Handbook is based upon the entry on entrepreneurship in the *Oxford Encyclopaedia of Economic History* (2003), which was written by one of the editors of this book. These two Oxford reference works will therefore be broadly consistent in their approach to the subject.

The approach taken in this book construes entrepreneurship in terms of arbitrage, innovation, and risk-taking. Entrepreneurs specialize in taking difficult and complex decisions for which other people do not want to take responsibility. The implication is that entrepreneurs make a vital contribution to economic growth. In performing their role in society, entrepreneurs carry out a range of different tasks: they collect information, make judgement calls, raise finance, and develop business organizations. The intensity of entrepreneurial activity is dependent on multiple factors: the volatility of the environment, market structure and institutions, attitudes to risk, the availability of capital, government policy, cultural factors, and social mobility. The arrangement of the chapters follows the conceptualization.

A number of major reference works on entrepreneurship have recently been published, but while these are very valuable, they are mostly reprints of influential papers. The closest competitor to the present book is Z. J. Acs and D. B. Audretsch (eds) *Handbook of Entrepreneurial Research*, Dordrecht: Kluwer, 2003. This work has a strong emphasis on conceptual and methodological issues. It highlights the multi-disciplinary nature of the subject, whereas this book is focused more sharply on the disciplines of economics, finance and business strategy. As a result, we believe that the two Handbooks will be complementary.

Although this Handbook focuses on economic aspects, the contributors to this book survey the field as a whole, and draw on literature from other disciplines as appropriate. Publications in a wide range of journals have been cited. Our contributors are drawn from a wide range of backgrounds, and we have made a deliberate attempt to provide an opportunity for younger scholars to contribute. Our authors therefore include a mixture of leading figures and well-established younger scholars, recruited mainly from Europe and North America. Over-reliance on eminent scholars who have developed mature views based on a lifetime's work can sometimes bias a book like this towards a defensive rather than critical approach to this literature. The selection of contributors is guided by the principle that we should promote an independent and critical perspective. Contributors have been asked to identify the weaknesses, as well as the strengths, of the literature, and to set out a research agenda.

1.2 Basic approach

There is always a risk that a Handbook like this will be little more than a compilation of disparate views. To manage this risk, all contributors were provided with a background 'White Paper' which set out basic definitions, and outlined how the various themes explored in this book related to each other. Also an author conference was held at which contributors were able to discuss preliminary drafts of each other's chapters.

1.2.1 Development of the concept

The 'White Paper' noted that the term 'entrepreneur' appears to have been introduced into economic theory by Richard Cantillon (1759), an Irish economist of French descent. According to Cantillon, the entrepreneur is a specialist in taking risk. He 'insures' workers by buying their output for resale before consumers have indicated how much they are willing to pay for it. The workers receive an assured income (in the short run, at least), while the entrepreneur bears the risk caused by price fluctuations in consumer markets.

This idea was refined by the US economist Frank Knight (1921), who distinguished between risk, which is insurable, and uncertainty, which is not. Risk refers to recurrent events whose relative frequency is known from past experience, while uncertainty relates to unique events whose probability can only be subjectively estimated. Knight thought that most of the risks relating to production and marketing fall into the latter category. Since business owners cannot insure against these risks, they are left to bear them by themselves. Pure profit is a reward for bearing this uninsurable risk: it is the reward of the entrepreneur.

Popular notions of entrepreneurship are based on the heroic vision put forward by Joseph A. Schumpeter (1934). The entrepreneur is visualized as an innovator who creates new industries and thereby precipitates major structural changes in the economy. Schumpeter was concerned with the 'high level' kind of entrepreneurship that, historically, has led to the creation of railways, the development of the chemical industry, and the growth of integrated oil companies. His analysis left little room for the much more common, but no less important, 'low level' entrepreneurship carried on, for example, by firms in the wholesale and retail trades. Alfred Marshall (1919) described the role of these firms in some detail, but omitted them from his formal analysis of supply and demand.

The essence of low-level entrepreneurship can be explained by the Austrian approach of Friedrich A. von Hayek (1937) and Israel M. Kirzner (1973). Entrepreneurs are middlemen who provide price quotations as an invitation to trade. While bureaucrats in a socialist economy have little incentive to discover prices for themselves, entrepreneurs in a market economy are motivated to do so by profit opportunities. They hope to profit by buying cheap and selling dear. In the long run, competition between entrepreneurs arbitrages away price differentials, but in the short run, such differentials, once discovered, generate a profit for the entrepreneur.

The insights of these economists can be synthesized by identifying an entrepreneurial function that is common to all approaches. This is the exercise of judgement in decision-making (Casson, 1982). Thus a middleman who buys before he knows the price at which he can resell must make a judgement about what the future price will be, while an innovator must assess whether a new product will prove attractive to consumers.

1.2.2 Judgement

If information were freely available, and could be processed without cost, then there would be no need for judgement, and no mistakes would ever be made. But access to information differs greatly from person to person. One reason is that sources of information are highly localized: only people 'on the spot' can directly observe an event. Different people in different places will therefore have different perceptions of any given situation. They may therefore make different decisions. The nature of the decision therefore depends on the identity of the person who makes it. The entrepreneur matters because their judgement of a situation is potentially unique.

If a situation recurs frequently, it is worthwhile investigating it carefully in order to derive a suitable decision rule. But where unusual situations are concerned, nobody knows the correct decision rule. To improvize a decision quickly, people have to rely on their intuition and analogy with previous experience. Different intuitions, combined with different experiences, lead to different decisions.

Not all entrepreneurs are successful. There is a strong bias in the literature towards successful entrepreneurs, for fairly obvious reasons: successful entrepreneurs make an impact on the national economy, they are inclined to self-promotion, and the enterprises they create survive long enough to leave good records. The successful entrepreneurs are those whose confidence in their judgement turns out to be well placed. For every high-profile success, however, there tend to be numerous failures. Small start-up businesses are notoriously prone to failure in the first two or three years. Failures are often caused by over-confidence, and also by bad luck. It is not uncommon, in fact, to view entrepreneurial ventures as economic experiments (Harper, 1995).

1.2.3 The supply of entrepreneurial ability

Entrepreneurship is a scarce resource, and so it is important to know whether its supply can be increased. This raises the question of whether entrepreneurs are 'born' or 'made'. There is little evidence that entrepreneurial ability is inherited: for example, the evidence on family firms suggests that sons usually display less initiative than the fathers they succeed. There is some support for the idea that entrepreneurial qualities are incubated in adversity. Fatalistic acceptance of poverty is certainly not an entrepreneurial characteristic, but determination to reverse an economic set-back often seems to be (Brenner, 1983). Many entrepreneurs claim to be 'self-made', but it is impossible to know whether, in making this claim, they are simply unwilling to give credit to parents, teachers and others who have helped them along their way.

The institutional environment is also important. In societies which ascribe high status to noble birth or inherited wealth, the 'self-made man' is regarded with suspicion. Societies that value religious and philosophical speculation over practical experimentation will undervalue education focused on management, and the engineering skills required by artisan entrepreneurs. The supply of able entrepreneurs may therefore be discouraged by institutional constraints which discourage ambitious and talented young people from pursuing business careers. On the contrary, societies that give credit to ability to create and to better one's economic fortunes tend to encourage entrepreneurial development.

1.2.4 Finance

The reputation of an entrepreneur who owns a firm determines how much finance they are able to raise for their business. An owner whom no one trusts cannot attract investors, and so must accumulate all the capital they require for themselves. However good their judgement, an entrepreneur cannot start a large business unless they have sufficient wealth. The main strategies for capital accumulation are as follows.

- *Inheritance.* The entrepreneur's parents or wealthy relatives may die while they are still young. Being the first son under primogeniture, and having elderly parents, is an advantage in this respect. Wealth can be augmented by strategic marriage too—for example, acquiring other people's inheritance from wealthy widows (except when their property is entailed).
- *By working and saving.* This is a slow method, but has the advantage that the entrepreneur may acquire useful skills while in employment, especially if they can obtain a responsible job. They may also make useful contacts with potential customers while in their job.
- *By taking risks.* A merchant may begin on a small scale by smuggling, gun-running, or piracy, and then become legitimate once sufficient capital has been accumulated. Gambling and insurance fraud are other high-risk options (e.g. over-insuring warehouse contents and then committing arson).

Lack of reputation and shortage of capital is a problem that confronts many entrepreneurs from poor backgrounds. The factors identified above are highly relevant to small businesses started by immigrant refugees and members of minority ethnic groups. Yet, in some societies, there may be collective recognition of the need to channel capital to capability risk-takers with sound judgment. Hence, some societies develop capital market devices to bridge savers and entrepreneurs.

1.2.5 Social networks and agglomeration

Judgemental decisions normally require the synthesis of different types of information. The entrepreneur needs to create a network of social contacts that can feed them with the information they require. Location in a major metropolis is a great advantage from this point of view. This is the place where travellers often call first when arriving from overseas; it is where journalists collect information for their stories, and where groups of people assemble to take important decisions—politicians in parliament, business leaders at their headquarters, and so on. This explains why so much high-level entrepreneurial activity in any country is concentrated in the metropolis.

Entrepreneurs will reveal their qualities by the kind of choices they make. Young people have to decide, at some stage, whether to remain in the place where they grew up, or to move on elsewhere. Entrepreneurial people are more likely to move and non-entrepreneurial people to stay. Isolated rural areas where there are few opportunities for profit tend to lose their more entrepreneurial young people and, conversely, large cities tend to attract entrepreneurial people.

Entrepreneurs who are prepared to move long distances have a choice of political regimes under which to operate. The regimes that are most attractive to mobile entrepreneurs are likely to possess the classic institutions of the liberal market economy. They will have some or all of the following characteristics:

- Private property, which is freely alienable, subject to certain minimal restrictions;
- Freedom of movement, and freedom to associate with business partners;
- Confidentiality of specific business information, especially regarding relations with customers and suppliers;
- Protection of creative work through patents, copyright, design protection, and so on;
- Access to impartial courts which will enforce property rights and which have the competence to settle complex commercial claims;
- A stable currency, based on prudent control of the money supply;
- Democratic government, with sufficient balance of power between opposing interests to reduce the risks of draconian interventions in industry and commerce;
- Open-ness to immigration by entrepreneurs and skilled workers (and possibly other groups as well).

The relative mobility of the entrepreneur has implications for the family firm (Church, 1993). 'One day all this will be yours', the father tells the son, and the son feels morally obliged to succeed his father, even though his interests lie elsewhere. A more entrepreneurial son might turn down the offer and set up his own business in a different industry, forcing the father to look outside the family for a successor—possibly with beneficial results for the firm.

Business owners who remain behind in a declining industry or region may join forces to lobby for protective tariffs or industrial subsidies. They harness organizations, such as trade associations, which may originally have been established to provide training, for price-fixing purposes (Olson, 1982). A secretive and conspiratorial business culture develops, reflecting the entrepreneurial weaknesses of the business group. Similarly, craft guilds or trade unions may try to 'protect jobs' by resisting technological change. Inflexible attitudes within a region may deter entrepreneurs in 'sunrise' industries, who move away to areas where they have more freedom of action. This suggests that successive waves of innovation will move around a country, avoiding areas where earlier innovations have stagnated, and ossified the business culture (Pollard, 1981). Only the metropolis will remain vibrant because of its continuing ability to attract young entrepreneurs. If the metropolis too goes into decline, then the outlook for the entire national economy is likely to be bad.

Recent literature has expanded the concept of 'familialism' and linked it to the institutional environment that shapes outside shareholders' property rights. In locations where shareholder rights are upheld, firms can be entrusted to professional managers who can be adequately monitored and disciplined. In this case, succession is based on capabilities and free of blood-line connections. Families provide the basis for highly successful professionalized firms. In an environment where shareholder rights are not well enforced, however, control has value and outside managers cannot be fully trusted. In this environment, family succession matters—capable offspring who can uphold the family's entrepreneurial capability are valuable. At the same time, the literature shows that there could be internal circulation of capital and other resources within the extended family—the high performance of a few successful family firms could mean the deprivation of resources for start-ups. Moreover, large wealthy families can use pyramidal ownership structures to build family empires and possibly use their economic power to lobby for the kind of government policies that preserve their status quo.

1.2.6 Historical significance of the entrepreneur

Early academic writers on British economic and social history employed the concept of the entrepreneur mainly as a social stereotype. The 'Victorian entrepreneur' was a member of an upwardly-mobile lower middle class, imbued with the bourgeois values of proprietary capitalism. The Victorians themselves seem to have been more impressed with their own engineering feats than with their entrepreneurial achievements; thus it was the civil and mechanical engineers, rather than the railway promoters or the company secretaries, that were seen as the heroes of the Railway Revolution (Smiles, 1862). More generally, it was the creation of the

Empire, rather than an entrepreneurial domestic economy, that was the main political preoccupation. Modern interest in Victorian entrepreneurship is more a reflection of a desire to recover something that has been lost than the continuation of a concern that the Victorians themselves expressed. However popular publications such as Smiles' *Self-Help* book (1882), and contemporaneous comments on them, in some ways closely presage modern debates on enterprise culture.

In the United States, a powerful mythology developed around the 'rags to riches' entrepreneur (Sarachek, 1978), but detailed investigations (see for example, Taussig, 1915) highlighted the middle-class professional origins of many successful entrepreneurs.

Schumpeter (1939) provided one of the earliest economic applications of entrepreneurial theory. He identified five main types of 'new combination' effected by entrepreneurs: new products, new processes of production, the development of new export markets, the discovery of new sources of raw material supply, and the creation of new forms of institution—such as the cartel or trust. Schumpeter's classification fits well with the major forms of innovation that occurred in Europe during the 'Age of High Imperialism', 1870–1914. The large-scale entrepreneurial exploits of the 'robber barons' of the late nineteenth century—Vanderbilt, Harriman, Rockefeller, and so on—also conform well to Schumpeter's model. Schumpeter claimed that his schema fitted any economy that made extensive use of credit—from the growth of Mediterranean trade during the Renaissance onwards. He also claimed that he could explain Kondratieff 'long waves' of 50–60 years duration by the periodic clustering of innovations since the Industrial Revolution. Unfortunately, however, the empirical basis of Schumpeter's speculations on long waves has not stood the test of time very well (see Solomou, 1987).

Pursuing the Schumpeterian theme, Hughes (1965) examined the influence of the 'vital few' in promoting economic growth. Hughes's approach is mainly biographical, emphasising the personality factor in entrepreneurship. The great value of his contribution lies in the fact that he recognizes the role of the entrepreneur in the public as well as the private sector, although he sees the public sector entrepreneur as heavily implicated in the growth of bureaucracy. The policy implication of Hughes's study would appear to be that people with entrepreneurial personalities need to be attracted into the private sector where, thanks to competitive markets, the incentives are better aligned with the long-run public interest.

A rather similar conclusion arises from Jones's (1981, 1988) studies of long-term world economic growth. Adopting an international comparative perspective, Jones argues that entrepreneurship is a natural feature of human behaviour which government can either encourage or suppress. Encouragement is provided by a regime of freedom under law, which allows people to carry out experiments in commercial and industrial organization at their own expense. Suppression is effected by governments that fall into the hands of elites, who think they know best which experiments are socially desirable and which are not. They subsidize prestigious experiments out of taxes, and repress ordinary experiments because they are seen as either useless, immoral, or politically subversive.

1.2.7 Entrepreneurship as human capital

Entrepreneurship can be regarded as one of the components of human capital. It is a skill in processing information in connection with judgemental decisions. It includes using social networks to collect information, memorizing and recalling information effectively through association of ideas, and interpreting information using appropriate mental models. Together with other components of human capital—such as skilled manual labour, management and organization—entrepreneurship may be considered as a factor input into a production function. It is an input that improves the allocative efficiency of the economy. It is a substitute for other factors of production such as management. Thus if managers are abundant, but entrepreneurs are scarce, resource allocation decisions that would have been taken by entrepreneurs may be taken by managers instead. This means that a decision that would have been improvised will be taken using imperfect formal procedures.

The demand for entrepreneurship, like the demand for any other factor of production, is a derived demand. Unlike more conventional factors of production, however, the demand for entrepreneurship derives not from the overall level of product demand, but rather from the volatility of such demand. Similarly, it also derives from volatility in supply conditions, such as technological change. Volatility generates novel and complex situations that call for improvised decisions. When volatility increases, there is an increase in the demand for entrepreneurs and a corresponding decline in the demand for managers. This is normally reflected in the formation of more small firms and the restructuring of large firms. The large firms may disappear through bankruptcy, or be split up through management buy-out and 'asset-stripping'; alternatively, they may be re-organized in a more flexible form, as a coalition of entrepreneurs. Greater competition to hire entrepreneurial employees means that the rewards of entrepreneurship will rise. Pay structures will tend to become more flexible, because it will no longer be possible to offer both entrepreneurial employees and non-entrepreneurial employees the same rates of pay.

1.2.8 Enterprise culture

When there is a general perception in a society that volatility has increased, social and political attitudes may change as well. This is what appears to have happened in many Western industrial countries towards the end of the 1970s. Increasing awareness of global competition, and the failure of large-firm 'national champions' to respond effectively, led people to believe that future job-creation would come from small business. Start-up entrepreneurs became popular 'role models', creating a new set of myths about the 'rags to riches' entrepreneur, and encouraging young people to make their careers in the private sector.

Considered as an historical phenomenon, the enterprise culture of the 1980s and 1990s was a natural reaction to some of the anti-entrepreneurial attitudes that had taken root in the West in the early post-war period. It should not be inferred, however, that this enterprise culture was based on a correct understanding of the role of the entrepreneur. The highly competitive and materialistic form of individualism promoted by 'enterprise culture' did not accurately represent the dominant values of successful entrepreneurs of previous generations. For example, the Victorian railway entrepreneurs operated through social networks based in Britain's major provincial towns and cities. The limited amount of evidence that has been collected and analysed in a systematic way suggests that successful entrepreneurship is as much a co-operative endeavour, mediated by social networks, as a purely individualistic and competitive one.

In line with this conceptual approach, the book has been divided into seven parts, dealing respectively with

- I Theory and history
- II Small firms
- III Innovation
- IV Finance
- V Employment, self-employment and buy-outs
- VI Social and cultural aspects
- VII Spatial and international dimensions

The contributions to these parts are summarized in sections 1.3–1.9 below.

1.3 Review of the chapters: Theory and history

Martin Ricketts (Ch. 2) begins by considering the entrepreneur in economic history. In the ancient and mediaeval worlds entrepreneurialism was hampered by the defence of vested interests by landed aristocrats, and by concepts such as just prices and usury. Matters improved somewhat in the mercantilist era, but it was not until the agricultural and industrial revolutions that the modern image of the entrepreneur emerged. Ricketts then moves on to consider the entrepreneur in economic theory. Classical economists such as Ricardo viewed entrepreneurship as a type of skilled labour, and entrepreneurs as providers of capital. The economic system was seen as being 'on a one-way journey to a steady state'. However Adam Smith can be seen as the originator of a theory of economic growth that gives a central role to the entrepreneur. According to Smith, the 'invisible hand' promotes economic progress through the division of labour and the growth of the market.

In addressing the entrepreneur in neoclassical theory, Ricketts contrasts the implications of its rationalist and subjectivist foundations. While the rational foundations have led to a focus on statics, such as in general equilibrium theory, the subjectivist foundations led instead to a view, taken by the Austrian School, of market participants as active bargainers and price setters, leading to a system with more unpredictable and Darwinian characteristics.

Ricketts then moves on to consider key aspects of debates on the role of the entrepreneur. Knight viewed the entrepreneur as uncertainty-bearer, for which service the entrepreneur received a reward of pure profit. Schumpeter, on the other hand, focused on the role of the entrepreneur as an innovator, and hence as the source of 'gales of creative destruction'. Others, such as Casson and Kirzner, have pointed out the role of the entrepreneur as a coordinator of transactions; as intermediator and market-maker. For instance, Kirzner views pure profit as a reward for alertness to opportunities for trade. Neo-Austrians regard resource allocation as an informational rather than a calculation problem.

Finally, Ricketts turns his attention to entrepreneurship in economic development, noting Baumol's suggestion that societies that manage to better channel entrepreneurs into innovative activities, rather than into depredation, crime, and rent seeking are likely to develop faster.

In Chapter 3, Stanley Metcalfe continues the reflective tenor of Chapter 2 by considering how entrepreneurship fits into a long-run evolutionary view of capitalism. He argues that the fundamental historical fact about capitalism is its internal capacity for transformation, and the corresponding transience of the activities and ways of life that it supports. Yet while activities are transient, the institutions of capitalism are remarkably stable; they too evolve, but much more slowly. Heterodox economists, working in a Schumpeterian paradigm, have long recognized market capitalism as a self-organizing system sustaining a spontaneous order; the link between the system and the order, claims the author, is the entrepreneur.

While some writers regard volatility in the economic system as mainly exogenous, Metcalfe argues that it is mostly endogenous. The central analytical problem, he says, is how we analyse change generated within the economic system as distinct from change imposed upon it from outside. Entrepreneurs are the agents of self-transformation: each entrepreneur responds to volatility generated by the activities of other entrepreneurs. To analyse entrepreneurship properly, scholars must recognize the enormous diversity and heterogeneity of attitudes and perceptions within the population of entrepreneurs.

The process of transformation is accelerating, with technological innovation now running at an unprecedented rate. The explanation of this acceleration lies in the progressive accumulation of knowledge. A growing body of public information has been made available that is storable across time and transferable across space, and thus available for the use of future generations and social groups in different locations. As the stock of knowledge grows, so the possibilities for the re-combination of items of information grow faster than an exponential rate. According to Metcalfe, this historical perspective explains the most significant features of the modern entrepreneurial economy.

Nigel Wadeson (Ch. 4) reviews research on cognitive aspects of entrepreneurship. He discusses heuristics and biases, over-optimism, self-efficacy, intrinsic motivation and creativity, counter-factual thinking, intentions-based models, and prospect theory. He then examines in detail the view that entrepreneurship involves an information collection process in which information costs are economized. In some ways the entrepreneur can be viewed rather negatively, as being subject to decision-making biases such as over-optimism. However, in some other respects, the research reviewed paints a positive picture, with the entrepreneur as a creative, motivated, and self-confident individual.

The author refers to both the psychology and entrepreneurship literature. Importantly, the reader is given access to some critiques of theories from psychology which are sometimes treated rather uncritically in entrepreneurship research. Indeed, in the conclusion, Wadeson stresses that psychology is itself an evolving field of study, and that entrepreneurship researchers should take note of criticisms and counter-arguments made by psychologists of theories in their own field.

In Chapter 5, Martin Carter explores the conceptual connections between entrepreneurship and marketing, flowing from the concern of both fields with the organization of market exchange. He examines the relationship from three perspectives: 'market process', mainstream 'marketing' literature, and the literature on the entrepreneurial firm. While the framework for market processes comes from Austrian models of the entrepreneur, marketing literature provides a more detailed account of how entrepreneurs discover and exploit market opportunities. A synthesis of these approaches is suggested by the theory of the market-making entrepreneurial firm.

Market processes may be of more than one type: gradual (Marshallian) or disruptive (Schumpeterian). These have different implications for marketing. The discussion identifies two modes of marketing, a managerial mode and an entrepreneurial mode, each of which can be viewed as adapted to different types of market process. Research on the entrepreneurial mode has focused on the tension between entrepreneurial orientation, when the firm leads the market in the innovation process, and market orientation, when the firm is more concerned with responding to the market's needs. Finally, the author notes that no clear consensus has yet emerged on the marketing needs of the entrepreneurial firm. This remains the area with the greatest opportunities for future research.

Much of the early literature on entrepreneurship consisted of biographies of successful entrepreneurs. Much useful evidence can be gained from these biographies; they can enliven, and assist the interpretation of, statistics relating to firm formation and entrepreneurial behaviour. The strength and limitation of historical biography as a source for the study of entrepreneurship are critically reviewed by Tony Corley in Chapter 6.

Corley notes that the biographical information contained in the business papers, personal correspondence and diaries of entrepreneurs can shed important light on their cognitive capabilities, knowledge, and cultural attitudes. But biographies need to be handled with caution because authors are liable to distort the evidence, especially when the biography has been commissioned by, or written with the co-operation of, the entrepreneur's family or firm. Biographies as a group do not constitute a representative sample of entrepreneurs—they tend to be biased towards certain sectors (e.g. technologically innovative industries), to certain management styles (e.g. paternalism) and to the founders of large successful and long-lived firms. Notwithstanding these limitations, a great deal can be learned by pooling information from different biographies—especially modern biographies, which normally strive for a higher degree of objectivity than did earlier ones.

1.4 Review of the chapters: Small firms

Robert Cressy provides a most valuable service in Chapter 7: he presents a systematic and easily understood framework which explains the relationships between firm size, survival, and the firm's rate of growth. Initial theories of growth, the most famous of which is Gibrat's Law of Proportional Effect, were of a purely statistical nature. However later work modelled entrepreneurship as a learning process, where the entrepreneur gains feedback information on performance following start-up. The chapter also discusses literature on the effects of capital and other constraints on firm growth. It notes that empirical results that identify a strong influence of capital constraints need to be reassessed based on findings on the role of human capital. The chapter also considers the roles of firm and industry life cycles in firm survival and growth.

The modern theory of small firm growth is based on just a few premises. First, individuals choose entrepreneurship over being employed if the expected pay-off of the former exceeds the latter. The higher a person's capabilities, the higher their pay-off to becoming an entrepreneur. Secondly, individuals are *ex-ante* not perfectly sure of their capabilities, but they learn from their experiences. The framework's key prediction is that smaller firms have a higher failure rate and yet surviving ones grow faster than larger firms.

Empirical work gives robust support to the prediction. What is particularly interesting is that the initial capitalization does not prolong survival except in the very short run. The literature also shows that small firms' survival is extended when an industry is in a growing phase and is more knowledge-intensive.

The chapter also summarizes the literature on whether personal wealth affects entrepreneurial entry. The positive relation which is reported, suggests that entrepreneurial entrants face liquidity constraints, although the author considers alternative interpretations too.

The dynamics of populations of firms is key to understanding the aggregate impact of small firm formation on economic growth. In Chapter 8, Zoltan Acs presents a detailed statistical examination of the factors which govern new firm formation. Using US annual data on firm births for 384 labour market areas, in six industry sectors, between 1991–98, he finds that firm birth rate is relatively stable over time but varies across regions. Firm birth rates are positively associated with the lack of presence of large firms, the presence of human capital, population growth and income growth. Moreover, educational attainment has a positive relationship with firm birth, primarily in activities that have higher educational requirement. While some of his findings are controversial, this important chapter should provide a stimulus to further research on this topic.

Many small firms are family firms—though not all family firms are small, as Howorth, Rose and Hamilton make clear in Chapter 9. Family firms are a key component of most economies, accounting for up to 65 percent of GDP. Family firms are diverse, ranging from very small to very large firms, with varying levels and structures of family involvement. Family firms are embedded within societies which differ in their values, attitudes, laws, and business practices, and which are the product of complex path-dependent historical processes.

The diversity of the definitions of family firms suggests that there are multiple types of family firm—founder-owned firms, small family-owned firms passed down through generations, large family-owned pyramidal groups where a family utilizes cross shareholding, super voting shares, and vertically layered ownership to leverage family equity to amass control of multiple corporations. The last type of family controlled firms is very different from the other ones. The entrepreneurial tendency ought to be high in the former while the latter should be more adept at rent-seeking.

The authors point out that family kinship allows family firm groups to overcome institutional deficits at the beginning of industrialization. The family boundary defines the boundary of trust, pooling of capital and managerial resources. In addition, family business owners are able to use paternalistic strategies to create or mould business culture. The chapter also discusses intergenerational succession, noting its association with evolution of ownership structure, and the importance of advance planning and preparation of successors for the transition.

The authors emphasize that culture is an important factor in shaping the evolution of family firms. For example, in the US, the management of family firms is often delegated to professional managers, even where family equity ownership remains sizable, whereas in Europe and many parts of Asia family control is valued, and 'familialism' emerges. The authors also highlight the need to recognize the roles of family members—in particular those of women—who are neither owners nor managers, but mediate relationships between those who are involved directly in the firm.

Government support for small firms has been an important aspect of industrial policy over the last 20 years in many countries. But does such support offer value for money? Are the additional jobs created, and additional profits generated, greater than the costs of the subsidies provided? In Chapter 10, David Storey examines the important issue of evaluating the effectiveness of government support for SMEs. He points to the large sums of public expenditure involved, and points out the weaknesses of some familiar methods of evaluation. He draws on his extensive experience to suggest a number of improvements in the way in which evaluations should be carried out.

Storey distinguishes between 'SME policies' and 'entrepreneurship' policies. The former focus on existing businesses, while the latter focus on start-ups. Both types of policy are normally justified by appeal to alleged market failures, such as asymmetric information and imperfect property rights. In the case of SME policies, such failures, if they existed, could lead, for example, to excessive capital rationing. In the case of entrepreneurship, mis-information may lead to the risks of starting a business being systematically exaggerated. Examples of entrepreneurship policy include 'enterprise-awareness' programmes in schools, colleges and universities. It also includes the provision of information and advice to those considering starting a business, often with a focus upon 'under-represented' groups such as young people, females or those from ethnic minorities.

Storey also distinguishes two ways of implementing policy: by offering subsidies (or subsidized business services), and by improving the general business environment, for example, by reducing 'red tape'. Some policies may be intended to support all firms, whereas others may be targeted on particular types of firm, such as those encountering specific barriers to growth.

The main thrust of Chapter 10 is to urge a more rigorous approach to the evaluation of government support for SMEs and entrepreneurship. Storey argues that evaluation needs to be built in from the outset of programmes, so that those who implement the programmes know that they will be accountable for their impacts, and feel obliged to collect the evidence from which these impacts can be assessed. Modern social cost-benefit analysis, backed by econometric analysis (including panel data techniques) make evaluation much more reliable and cost-effective than it used to be, and so there is no excuse for failing to evaluate. It is possible that rigorous evaluation could save large amounts of public expenditure on entrepreneurship policies which do not address proven market failures.

1.5 Review of the chapters: Innovation

Knowledge supports growth, but the precise mechanism linking knowledge creation to growth is not yet fully understood. In Chapter 11, David Audretsch and Max Keilbach argue that entrepreneurs play the role of transforming new knowledge that is not used by incumbent firms into growth.

They argue that much of the entrepreneurship literature treats entrepreneurial opportunities as exogenous, whereas in fact they are endogenously created. While large firms create much knowledge, they do not exploit all of this knowledge since its exploitation is tainted with uncertainty (which they denote the 'knowledge filter'). This leaves opportunities for new and young firms, which constantly take up a large share of the exploitation of new knowledge and its commercialization. A lot of commercialization of innovation is based on knowledge spillovers to small firms set up and run by individuals who are former employees of large firms. Generally, smaller and younger enterprises, especially in knowledge-intensive industries, experience higher growth and also lower survival.

This pattern is consistent with a *Lamarckian* evolution. Active *Lamarckian* evolution depends on the presence of *entrepreneurship capital* which involves 'a milieu of agents and institutions that are conducive to the creation of new firms.' This involves social acceptance of entrepreneurial behaviour and individuals' willingness to deal with the risk of creating new firms. It also involves the participation of financing agents who are willing to share the risks. Thus, entrepreneurship capital involves possibly many legal, institutional and social factors—some of which are examined later in Chapter 20.

Not all innovations are started by entrepreneurs who create start-ups; large firms also play an important role in innovation, as indicated in Chapter 12, in which Walter Kuemmerle argues that large firms enjoy relative economic stability that can foster investment in innovation. They have more resources than small firms to take on risky, long-term and large-scale development and manufacturing projects. Large firms also train their own technical and managerial talent. However some of their employees later join smaller firms, or start firms on their own.

The author argues that an entrepreneurial climate within a large firm is necessary but not sufficient as a condition for a high rate of innovation. He suggests three approaches that may keep large firms innovative: (1) conceptual approaches, (2) organizational structure and spatial approaches, and (3) leadership and organizational culture approaches. These three approaches are complementary rather than mutually exclusive. The conceptual approach is to distinguish activities that (a) increase the stock of knowledge available to a firm (resources) from (b) activities that make use of this stock of knowledge (opportunities). Managers need to emphasize both. The second approach pertains to making efforts to increase communication across units and layers of the firm, and to locate the authority to make decisions in the hands of those whose knowledge makes them well placed to take them. Finally, organizational leadership is about creating a culture that is conducive to entrepreneurship and innovation; the culture is created through the stimulation and support of certain values on the one hand and through specific quantifiable goals on the other hand.

The theme of innovation is developed further by Berchicci and Tucci in Chapter 13. They reconsider the widely-held view that new entrants are more effective innovators than longer-established incumbent firms. They argue that incumbents are often quite effective innovators, but that they may deliberately delay the commercial exploitation of some of their inventions, giving the appearance that their innovation performance is weak. The authors provide a comprehensive review of the literature, setting out both the strengths and weaknesses of entrants and incumbents with respect to innovation. They then examine some recent empirical evidence that suggests that incumbents on average are neither failing to develop new technologies (even radical/disruptive technologies), nor failing to enter new technology-enabled markets. They argue that incumbents may be quite effective in developing technologies, but that they may deliberately defer their commercialization.

While such delay may be irrational, it need not be so necessarily. A rational innovator will attempt to time the innovation to maximize its net present value. This is not the same thing as innovating as soon as the net present value becomes positive. In the early stages of market growth, it may pay to wait until the market has achieved a critical mass before innovation proceeds, or until more technological information is available. This is particularly the case if incumbents are more able than novice players to compress the time that it takes them to enter. Another factor is that the incumbent firm may already be producing a competitive product. Introducing a new product while continuing to produce the old product may encourage price competition, whereby rents are redistributed to consumers and away from the firm. Such considerations may weigh less heavily with entrants as they fear competitive imitation more than do incumbent firms, and they have no established products with which their innovation will compete. The authors conclude with some interesting implications for entrepreneurial strategy.

1.6 Review of the chapters: Finance

Venture capital (VC) is a key issue in the financing of start-ups and in the expansion of high-growth firms. In Chapter 14, Robert Cressy provides a systematic overview of recent research on this topic. He begins by clarifying the various terminologies employed in the industry.

Cressy suggests that traditional financial market players like banks are not adequately equipped to finance entrepreneurial entries. The reason cited is that bank financing often needs collateral while entrepreneurial entry is based on knowledge and skills, intangibles that are not suitable as collateral. The difficulty may first lie in the mis-match in the term structure between returns to entrepreneurial financing and bank liabilities—banks have to pay interest periodically and regularly while entrepreneurial returns come long after initial investments.

While the mis-match in term structure between assets and liabilities can be dealt with via staggering, there exist other obstacles. One of them is bank regulations—in some countries like the US, commercial banks (until quite recently) were not allowed to own shares or to be involved in investment banking. These restrictions prevented them from providing services that are more useful to entrepreneurs—for example, Initial Public Offerings (IPOs)—and to investors—for example, the use of share ownership to signal their confidence on the quality of an entrepreneurial project.

A more general point is that bridging between investors and entrepreneurs calls for multiple skills: for example, the ability to 'separate the wheat from the chaff' in identifying entrepreneurs to finance, to monitor entrepreneurial behaviour, and to nurture an entrepreneur's business development. These skill requirements lead to the development of venture capitalists who are specialists in bridging between investors and entrepreneurs. VCs construct their dealings with both investors and entrepreneurs using cleverly designed incentive contracts, through which they retain the rights to discipline entrepreneurs. They also utilize syndication and staged release of financing to entrepreneurs.

Finally, the paper discusses the evaluation of VC performance. The critical difficulty is the need to adjust for survival bias and to gauge performance not just on private returns but also social returns.

Another source of venture capital is corporate venture capital. Gary Dushnitsky (Ch. 15) provides a comprehensive discussion of corporate venture capital (CVC). CVC is a minority equity investment by an established corporation in a privately-held entrepreneurial venture. It is not to be confused with corporate venturing. In corporate venturing, a corporation finances corporate employees for venturing initiatives. CVCs are mostly undertaken by large incumbent firms which tend to fund larger start-ups than VCs. CVCs tend to support start-ups in the parent corporations' industry or a related industry. CVCs surge in periods when high expectation of growth are fuelled by rapid technological change; in recent years they have tended to concentrate on the computer and pharmaceutical industries. While CVC activities tend to be concentrated in the US, US companies' share of CVC has declined in recent years, which reflects the fact that non-US companies are forming CVCs that participate in the US market.

The author classifies CVC strategic objectives along a continuum ranging from seeking substitutes to sponsoring complements. 'Substitute' means CVC investment activity is used to identify novel products, services, or technologies that may replace existing corporate products, services, or technologies. Complementary CVC investment activity is used to seek innovations that increase the value of existing corporate businesses.

While CVC-backed ventures experience favourable performance, it is unclear whether this reflects CVC parents' ability to pick winners or to build superior ventures. To understand the contribution of CVCs to entrepreneurial success, it would be useful to investigate how a venture's performance is affected by the technological overlap of the CVC parents and the entrepreneur, the product complementarity or substitutability, and the extent to which business operations are shared. With this in mind, the author suggests a variety of future directions that can deepen our understanding of CVC's impact on the subject both at a micro and a macro level.

1.7 Review of the chapters: Employment, self-employment and buy-outs

Entrepreneurs interact with the labour market in multiple ways. In a very informative chapter, Simon Parker (Ch. 16) presents a systematic examination of these interactions. People make an occupational choice when they decide to become entrepreneurs. They also participate in the labour market when they hire employees. The chapter considers how human capital theory and labour supply models can be used to analyse such behaviour.

Parker first makes it clear that to become self-employed is a labour market choice. An individual compares the outcomes of being self-employed and being an employee. Traditional economic models assume that the former is riskier, but has greater upside potential. A person who is more likely to choose self-employment is more self-confident and less risk-averse. Also, the person derives more non-pecuniary benefits from self-employment and has lower financing constraints. These simple economic considerations can link the propensity to become self-employed with demographic data: for example, age, initial personal wealth, family financial security, education, and previous life experiences.

The author discusses in detail the relationship between entrepreneurs' earnings and education, as compared to the same relationship for the employed. The relationship is complicated because education is a heterogeneous good and there is self-selection in getting an education (e.g. highly capable self-employed people may have deliberately by-passed extensive formal education).

The chapter also reports on the factors that determine firm performance. Experience, formal education, size of the start-up, and access to financing all contribute to survival. High earnings delay retirement decisions. Interestingly, self-employment is often used as a bridge job between 'salaried' employment and actual retirement. While small firms are allegedly important in supporting employment growth, few self-employed actually hire outside workers and the bulk of jobs are created in a few exceptionally dynamic fast growing industries.

There are novice entrepreneurs and there are also habitual entrepreneurs. Habitual entrepreneurs are composed of serial entrepreneurs and portfolio entrepreneurs. Serial entrepreneurs are those who sell or close down a business with significant share ownership and yet maintain a significant ownership stake in a newly started/acquired/inherited business. Portfolio entrepreneurs maintain significant share ownership in multiple businesses that are new/acquired/inherited. In Chapter 17, Deniz Ucbasaran, Paul Westhead and Mike Wright examine the difference between novice and habitual entrepreneurs.

The evidence suggests that habitual entrepreneurs have more managerial human capital but are not necessarily better educated than novice entrepreneurs. Habitual entrepreneurs are more likely to be motivated by 'being their own boss', while novice entrepreneurs are more likely to choose to become an entrepreneur because of financial opportunities, such as family inheritance, or other reactive reasons. Compared with novice entrepreneurs, habitual entrepreneurs are more daring in making financial commitments to their start-ups and yet are also more cautious, for example, they tend to collect more information before starting a business. Habitual entrepreneurs are more able to identify business opportunities, and to capitalize on their organizational capabilities. They therefore invest more in R&D, and put greater emphasis on productivity and efficiency, and on cost and quality control, and so forth. Habitual entrepreneurs sometimes display different cognitive characteristics due to their experiences. However empirical research gives conflicting evidence on the average performance difference between novice and habitual entrepreneurs.

The chapter reviews the policy implications, and then gives detailed advice on directions for future research. It concludes by questioning Jovanovic's view of entrepreneurial learning in which entrepreneurs learn their abilities by engaging in running a business. The authors argue that this fails to explain why habitual entrepreneurs do not necessarily out-perform novice entrepreneurs, and why some failed entrepreneurs choose to try again.

Small firms need not be founded from scratch as 'green-field' enterprises; they can also be created as going concerns through buy-outs of divested activities previously operated by large firms. Management buy-outs of this type are the topic of Chapter 18 by Mike Wright and Andrew Burrows.

Buy-outs have typically been associated with the taking of listed firms into private hands using private equity funds and sometimes debts. The firms are often in industries with mature products and stable cash flows. In a management buy-out, incumbent senior management initiates the transaction and becomes the main non-institutional equity holder. The chapter explains that management buy-out leads to a significant replacement of ownership control and also a significant increase in ownership concentration. The impacts are higher incentives for the new controlling party to seek efficiency improvements, to take risks, and also for close monitoring of performance. Also the new controlling party is more likely to undertake entrepreneurial innovations and strategic changes. The chapter successfully blends together the agency cost reduction and entrepreneurial aspects in deciphering the intricacy of MBOs.

1.8 Review of the chapters: Social and cultural aspects of entrepreneurship

The social dimensions of entrepreneurship are examined by Amir Licht and Jordan Siegel in Chapter 19. The authors use institutional economics and cross-cultural psychology to analyse entrepreneurs as agents of social and economic change. Entrepreneurship reflects personal priorities (e.g. self-enhancement and openness to change) and important personality traits. Inevitably, the level and modes of entrepreneurial activity are affected by the surrounding culture and by legal rules.

The influence of culture has long been recognized. Cultures that maintain high individualism, high masculinity, low uncertainty avoidance and low power distance are conducive to entrepreneurship, the authors claim. The two most important core institutions for encouraging entrepreneurship are well-defined property rights and the rule of law. The literature is rather unsettled on what shapes these institutions. Candidates include colonial past, distribution of economic power, type of industries at the early stage of development, and cultural tradition.

Entrepreneurs have to find ways to overcome institutional deficiencies. It is well known that weaknesses in social institutions create difficulties in raising entrepreneurial finance and in establishing transactional trust. In societies with weak social institutions close-knit networks are developed to overcome the deficiency. The challenge for entrepreneurs is to establish a reputation so as to be allowed into these social networks.

Chapter 20, by Kathy Fogel, Ashton Hawk, Randall Morck, and Bernard Yeung, examines the institutional obstacles to entrepreneurship. The authors point out that entrepreneurship is a composite act, consisting of information gathering and processing, the identification of arbitrage opportunities, risk-taking, managing start-ups and market entry, and procuring financial backing, technological expertise, and other inputs. These activities are inter-temporal in nature and their success depends on intangibles embodied in the entrepreneur. Start-ups are vulnerable to entry deterrence by incumbents, to rent-extraction, and even to outright asset-grabbing by established dominant corporations or government officials.

An interventionist government imposing burdensome rules and market regulations can stifle incentives to be entrepreneurial, while high quality government bureaucracy may actually help. Concentrated control of corporations in the hands of a few rich families may spell trouble for entrepreneurs. Dominant elites may translate their economic power into political influence to protect their status quo—including erecting entry barriers into profitable industries and opposing liberalization measures that would favour start-ups. Based on 1997 to 2001 entry data from 34 European countries, the authors generate preliminary empirical evidence supportive of these ideas.

Their work should be seen as an early contribution. Understanding the interactive dynamic relationship between entrepreneurship and the stages of development, and the associated evolution of institutions, remains a challenging and fruitful topic.

Ethnic minority entrepreneurship has attracted a good deal of attention from researchers. Chapter 21, by Anuradha Basu, provides a comprehensive survey of this field. Basu begins by noting that in most Western industrialized countries, ethnic minorities tend to have high self-employment rates. The significant economic contribution made by minority-owned businesses has led Western policy-makers to regard self-employment as a promising route for ethnic minorities to achieve economic and social advancement, and to be accepted by the majority community. At the same time, there is growing concern about the heterogeneity in the economic performance of ethnic groups. Unfortunately, empirical studies have tended to focus on the experiences of specific ethnic groups, rather than a comparison between them.

Self-employment among minorities can be partly explained by racial discrimination which pushes ethnic minorities into self-employment. But this cannot be the whole story, because starting a business is not an 'easy' option: it may require educational qualifications, skills, and fluency in the host country language, as well as macroeconomic conditions. It also requires access to finance. This leads to another consideration: namely the cultural norms and ethnic resources of immigrant groups. The Gujarati Lohanas, Ismailis, and Marwaris, for example, have a tradition of business and trading, and value entrepreneurship far more than paid employment (Dobbin, 1996). These communities encourage hard work, self-sufficiency, thrift, and provide informal credit institutions too.

Ethnic enclaves can create entrepreneurial opportunities in particular neighbourhoods. They provide a local market, and access to relatively inexpensive labour. However, excessive reliance on family or co-ethnic labour can be detrimental to a business. Ethnic businesses that supply mainstream, non-ethnic products to national and international markets tend to out-perform those who operate purely in local enclaves. Differences in business success between different ethnic groups merit further research, and so too does the process of assimilation: there are still relatively few studies of the way that changing educational attainment influence inter-generational business succession among ethnic minority entrepreneurs.

The migration of entrepreneurs is the subject of Andrew Godley's contribution in Chapter 22. Immigrants have often become successful entrepreneurs—famous historical examples include Nathan Mayer Rothschild, Khwaja Wajid and Greek shipping merchants, among others. The explanation is not simply that they have brought with them outside information and technology. Immigrants are self-selected for their risk-taking and resourcefulness. Because they are new and external members of a society, immigrants have more limited vocational choices. In order to move up the social ladder, they are forced to choose risky activities in which they have a chance to excel. As a result, they are more likely to set up their own businesses, and less likely to choose government jobs and the professions. To manage their risks in an unfamiliar environment, immigrants tend to be closely-knit and to share resources with one another. This allows them to pool financial resources and to avail themselves of supportive social networks, all of which are conducive to entrepreneurial activity.

In Chapter 23, Candida Brush provides a critical review of the literature on women entrepreneurs, and offers suggestions for future lines of research. She notes that studies on women entrepreneurs are sparse in spite of their growing importance over the past decades. Possible explanations are that women's participation in entrepreneurship is a new phenomenon, that there is a presumed similarity between male and female enterpreneurs, and that women entrepreneurs' activities still lack legitimacy and institutional support.

According to Brush, all three explanations are plausible. The limited existing studies suggest that there is a bias in women enterpreneurs' choices of activities—female entrepreneurs tend to enter into businesses which fit the feminine image (e.g. retailing) while male enterpreneurs exhibit no such bias. Female entrepreneurs frequently choose activities that tend to have a higher failure rate and a higher financial barrier. At the same time, women entrepreneurs' businesses seem to experience less growth. It is unclear whether the outcome is due to the characteristics of their chosen activities or whether there exist institutional biases which restrict women enterpreneurs' access to resources.

Another question is whether the observations indicate economic inefficiency. It would be interesting to control for endogeneity in order to distinguish between differences in female and male entrepreneurs' capabilities and the impact of institutionalized biases, as these have different implications for economic efficiency.

In Chapter 24, Marina Della-Giusta and Zella King examine attempts by governments to promote 'enterprise culture', and review the evidence for the success of such initiatives in the UK and elsewhere. The authors refer to 'enterprise culture' as a set of shared values that are conducive to entrepreneurial behaviour.

Britain's lack of entrepreneurial behaviour in the past was attributed to its education system which had no regard for industrial or vocational skills, its financial system which had little concern for small business, and confrontational industrial relations. To tackle these deficits, a wide range of government programmes intended to promote enterprise culture were introduced in the 1980s, targeted at the unemployed, trainees, and school and university students. These programmes were backed up by policies such as the privatization of state-owned enterprises and a push for more cost-accountability in public enterprises.

The results have been mixed. While trade union power has been weakened, there is little evidence to suggest that British workplaces have become more enterprising and innovative. At the same time, there has been a significant decline in satisfaction with working hours. Business start-up rates and numbers of small businesses are rising, but it is unclear whether these changes represent short-term industrial restructuring or a long-term rise in entrepreneurship. The rise in self-employment could reflect reductions in eligibility for unemployment benefit, as well as buoyant macroeconomic demand. Hence, at best, evaluative evidence suggests that policies have a mixed effect. On balance, it seems to be more difficult to change attitudes to entrepreneurship through public policy and 'cultural engineering' than many people believe.

1.9 Review of the chapters: Spatial and international dimensions

Many policy-makers have been impressed with the success of regional clusters in stimulating entrepreneurship—whether in New England, California, or the textile districts on Northern Italy. In Chapter 25, Philip McCann examines recent theoretical developments that explain the way that geographical clustering in industrial districts may encourage new firm developments. Drawing upon the 'contemporary geography of innovation', the author points out four possible explanations for clustering. It may be merely a geographic coincidence; it may be a result of spatial differences in the phases of product or profit cycles; it could be due to variations in the characteristics of locations that lead to differences in the geography of creativity and entrepreneurship; and, finally, it could arise because innovation is most likely to occur in small and medium-sized enterprises, whose spatial patterns happen to be uneven.

The author proceeds to develop a typology of inter-firm relations in centres of agglomeration. In a pure agglomeration, inter-firm relations are inherently transient and firms are essentially atomistic. Some agglomeration centres have industrial complexes characterized by long-term stable and predictable relations between the firms in the cluster. The third type of spatial industrial cluster features a social network where there is mutual trust between key decision-making agents in different organizations; the trust may be at least as important as decision-making hierarchies within individual organizations.

The typologies set up in the paper offer much food for thought. For example, from a policy perspective, the typologies suggest investigation of the type of location-specific institutional characteristics that could induce innovations. Institutional characteristics that induce transactional trust among firms may promote agglomeration. From a firm strategy perspective, the typologies identify important factors in locational choice; for example, firms that experience more spillover outflows to rivals than spillover inflows from rivals would choose to keep their distance from agglomeration centres, while firms in the opposite situation may choose to migrate to them.

Recent years have witnessed a burgeoning literature on 'born global' SMEs. Some writers have challenged the traditional 'Uppsala view' that the internationalization of the firm is an incremental process. This topic is addressed by Peter Buckley in Chapter 26. Recent rapid changes in technologies, faster product development, and large scale globalization of markets have encouraged some SMEs to alter their internationalization strategies—especially where Internet technology can be used to coordinate global marketing and research activities.

While SMEs are constrained in their rate of international growth—both financially and managerially—they could become international by joining a network that is global in scale. To internationalize directly, SMEs have two main alternatives—a simultaneous 'big bang' approach, or an incremental approach. The incremental approach involves learning by doing, and a gradual accumulation of resources. It also provides 'option value': a 'failure' in a specific location may provide a learning opportunity that facilitates future expansion. Although the simultaneous approach offers the prospect of higher profits at an earlier date, and the consolidation of 'first mover' advantage, it also has substantial attendant risks, which mean that it is the appropriate choice for only certain sorts of firm. In particular, it is more appropriate for firms that intend to internationalize through exporting than for those that intend to internationalize through foreign direct investment.

The Handbook concludes with an authoritative survey of issues relating to entrepreneurship in transition economies by Saul Estrin, Klaus Meyer and Maria Bytchkova in Chapter 27. The chapter has five main sections. First, the authors point out that entrepreneurial activities are tied to the stage of development—entrepreneurship in transition economies is different from entrepreneurship in a mature economy. At the beginning of transition, the heritage from planning has its effect on entrepreneurship—former state owned firms were breeding grounds for entrepreneurs and serve as a source of fixed assets. Former party members with connections to political and economic elites are also natural 'entrepreneurs' as they can make things happen in the midst of corruption and chaos, which typically characterize the beginning of transition. Later, as greater political and economic stability is achieved, the price mechanism begins to function, and property rights are defined, a more normal kind of Schumpeterian entrepreneur may emerge. The authors leave us with a puzzle: Is the more successful transition in some Eastern European countries and the lack of progress in some states like Russia related to entrepreneurial development?

The second section examines obstacles to entrepreneurship in transition economies; the list is more extensive than for mature economies. Corrupt government and ineffective regulatory frameworks are certainly significant obstacles. EBRD and World Bank surveys reflect a broad consensus that institutional development is higher in Central European countries than in former Soviet republics, and this may explain the different tracks of development in the two regions. Interestingly, survey results suggest that entrepreneurs are more concerned about governmental obstacles like taxes, financing and policy instability than social and institutional obstacles such as crime and the functioning of the judiciary.

The third section focuses on entrepreneurial entry. The authors point out the need that the growth of a new small-firm sector is not necessarily evidence of an upsurge in entrepreneurship—it may represent the incorporation of enterprises previously operating on grey or black markets. Empirical studies that incorporate this concern suggest no lack of potential entrepreneurs in many transition economies—except, perhaps, in Russia, where people seem to have lower aspirations to self-employment.

The fourth section examines the characteristics of entrepreneurs in transition economies. While some are workers escaping from poverty, others are professionals, former cadres, and returned expatriates. Some of the most successful entrepreneurs are from families with an entrepreneurial tradition, and have had previous exposure to business. Moreover, they have higher economic aspirations (or are greedier) and have a more positive attitude towards the government.

The final section surveys the strategies of entrepreneurs in transition economies. The authors note that entrepreneurs often collaborate to build substitutes for missing markets and institutions—they share trade credits, pool family resources, and form networks to enhance their collective reputation.

1.10 Concluding thoughts

The publication of this Handbook provides a convenient opportunity to take stock of recent progress in the field and to assess the opportunities for future research. The chapters which follow demonstrate that the study of entrepreneurship has progressed remarkably over the last 20 years. Twenty years ago, most theories of entrepreneurship were expressed in very general terms. They are sometimes described as 'Biblical' in their approach. They were concerned with major conceptual issues, such as the nature of economic profit, the difference between risk and uncertainty, and the relation of market process to market equilibrium. These theories were quite successful in explaining long-term historical trends, but were considered to be of little value in analysing the dynamics of small-firm behaviour. Since then the theory of entrepreneurship has been progressively refined, so that there is now a much closer connection between theories of entrepreneurship on the one hand and theories of the firm, and theories of business strategy, on the other.

Empirical work has progressed too. Twenty years ago, much of the empirical work was focused on job creation by SME start-ups. Emerging global competition was destroying jobs in traditional manufacturing sectors dominated by large oligopolistic firms with hierarchical management structures. Encouraging people to start their own business was seen by policy-makers as a useful way of getting the unemployed back to work. It would help to rebuild the economy along more flexible and responsive lines. Recording start-ups and tracking the growth of new firms became a major focus of research, and in the process, some of the wider issues addressed by theory disappeared. Today, however, there is much greater emphasis on testing theories of the formation and growth of firms rather than simply constructing a statistical profile of the SME sector. Shanes' (2003) recent work shows convincingly how theory and measurement have converged; it also shows that entrepreneurship theory has, on the whole, been remarkably successful in explaining the major features of SME behaviour. In contrast to some other areas of applied economic and social research, entrepreneurship theory has proved remarkably successful in interpreting the relevant empirical evidence.

It has always been a central claim of theories of entrepreneurship that entrepreneurship is core and not peripheral to the performance of the economy. Entrepreneurs contribute a scarce and valuable resource: while different authors may give it different names—for example, uncertainty-bearing, exercise of judgement, innovative capability, and so on—they are all agreed that different endowments of this resource can explain the significant differences in economic performance that remain once the impacts of the traditional factors of production—land, labour and capital—have been taken into account. This applies to explaining the differences between countries, between regions, and between cultural and ethnic groups. The pervasive influence of the entrepreneurship can be seen in the great diversity of topics included in this Handbook. There is hardly any aspect of economic and social behaviour which is not affected by entrepreneurship. Indeed, if every possible area of impact had been considered, this Handbook would have been at least twice its present length.

A consequence of the centrality of entrepreneurship is that, while much has already been achieved on the research front, more still remains to be done. The centrality of the entrepreneur within the firm has significant implications for the future modelling of firm behaviour, as well as for empirical research in business and industrial economics. The way that entrepreneurs recognize opportunities for innovation, and the distinctive features of their business judgement, have implications for cognitive economics—an emerging subject at the interface of economics and psychology. Cognition is related to personality—it raises the question of whether different personality types are better suited to entrepreneurship than others, and whether particular types of personality fit a person for a particular type of entrepreneurial activity. This links entrepreneurship to sociology, and thence to social history. However, the theory of entrepreneurship does not yet possess an adequate typology of personalities: although self-confidence and pragmatic problem-solving are widely recognized as entrepreneurial attributes, the way that entrepreneurs frame decisions and deploy heuristics requires further investigation

Personalities can be moulded by culture and institutions. Institutions such as law and contract also influence the ability of entrepreneurs to appropriate a reward from their efforts. A significant amount of recent literature on entrepreneurship highlights the way that institutions can either encourage or inhibit entrepreneurship, and channel it into either socially useful or socially damaging channels. The interface between entrepreneurship and institutions appears to be a particularly fruitful area for future research.

Popular hype on entrepreneurship has tended to emphasize the competitive nature of entrepreneurial behaviour. This view generally derives from placing a disproportionate emphasis on the entrepreneur's strategic decisions on product innovation and pricing. It ignores the fact that in order to set up and grow a business, an entrepreneur needs the active co-operation of investors, bankers, suppliers and employees. Entrepreneurs need to exploit social networks in order to identify potential partners, and they need to 'leverage' the opportunities provided by family and community links in building trust with the other people on whom their success depends. Twenty years ago, some writers on entrepreneurship uncritically accepted the political propaganda surrounding 'enterprise culture', with its emphasis on the competitive nature of the entrepreneur, but nowadays most writers take a more objective, and therefore more critical, view. The successful entrepreneur is not a compulsive competitor, but a person who chooses whom to compete against, and whom to co-operate with, and exercises appropriate judgement when making these choices.

Evolutionary economists have argued that as knowledge of a subject accumulates, a critical mass of knowledge is achieved at which new combinations of existing knowledge generate new results at an accelerating rate. It is quite possible that the study of entrepreneurship has now attained this critical level of knowledge, at which increasing returns to the stock of knowledge are obtained. If so, then the research opportunities in the field are greater than ever before. While much of the necessary groundwork may already have been carried out, and the foundations laid, the edifice itself is far from complete. The field should therefore prove attractive to the next generation of scholars.

Applying the theory of entrepreneurship to this issue predicts a bright future for the study of entrepreneurship. Theory suggests that researchers of high ability will be attracted to the field in increasing numbers to take advantage of the opportunities that it provides. If this analysis is correct, then this Handbook could become obsolete within the next ten years. Nothing would delight the editors more if this prediction were to come true.

References

Aldcroft, D. (1964). 'The Entrepreneur and the British Economy, 1870–1914'. *Economic History Review* (2nd ser.), 17: 113–34.

Brenner, R. (1983). *History: The Human Gamble.* Chicago: University of Chicago Press.

Cantillon, R. (1755). *Essai sur la nature du commerce en generale* (ed. Henry Higgs, 1931). London: Macmillan.

Casson, M. (1982). *The Entrepreneur: An Economic Theory.* Oxford: Martin Robertson.

Church, R. (1993). 'The Family Firm in Industrial Capitalism: International Perspectives on Hypotheses and History'. *Business History*, 35(4): 17–43.

Harper, D. A. (1995). *Entrepreneurship and the Market Process.* London: Routledge.

Hayek, Friedrich A. von (1937). 'Economics and Knowledge'. *Economica* (New ser.), 4: 33–54.

Hughes, J. R. T. (1965). *The Vital Few: The Entrepreneur & American Economic Progress.* New York: Oxford University Press.

Jones, E. (1981). *The European Miracle.* Cambridge: Cambridge University Press.

—— (1988). *Growth Recurring.* Oxford: Clarendon Press.

Kirzner, Israel M. (1973). *Competition and Entrepreneurship.* Chicago: University of Chicago Press.

Knight, F. H. (1921). *Risk, Uncertainty and Profit.* Boston: Houghton Mifflin.

Marshall, A. (1919). *Industry and Trade.* London: Macmillan.

Morck, R. and B. Yeung (2004). 'Family Control and the Rent-Seeking Society'. *Entrepreneurship: Theory and Practice,* (Summer) 28(4): 391–409.

—— and —— (2003). 'Agency Problems in Large Family Business Groups'. *Entrepreneurship: Theory and Practice,* (Summer) 27(4): 367–82.

Olson, Mancur (1982). *The Rise and Decline of Nations.* New Haven, CT: Yale University Press.

Pollard, S. (1981). *Peaceful Conquest.* Oxford: Oxford University Press.

Sandberg, L. G. (1981). 'The Entrepreneur and Technological Change', in R. Floud and D. McCloskey (eds) *The Economic History of Britain Since 1700: 2. 1860 to the 1970s.* Cambridge: Cambridge University Press.

Sarachek, B. (1978). 'American Entrepreneurs and the Horatio Alger Myth'. *Journal of Economic History,* 38: 439–56.

Schumpeter, J. A. (1934). *The Theory of Economic Development* (trans. Redvers Opie). Cambridge, MA: Harvard University Press.

—— (1939). *Business Cycles.* New York: McGraw-Hill.

Shane, S. (2003). *A General Theory of Entrepreneurship: The Individual—Opportunity Nexus.* Cheltenham: Edward Elgar.

Shaver, M. and F. Flyer (2000). 'Agglomeration Economies, Firm Heterogeneity, and Foreign Direct Investment in the United States 2000'. *Strategic Management Journal.*

Smiles, S. (1862). *Lives of the Engineers.* London: John Murray.

—— (1882). *Self-Help.* London: John Murray.

Solomou, S. (1987). *Phases of Economic Growth, 1850–1973.* Cambridge: Cambridge University Press.

Taussig, F. W. (1915). *Inventors and Moneymakers.* New York: Macmillan.

Wiener, M. J. (1981). *English Culture and the Decline of the Industrial Spirit.* Cambridge: Cambridge University Press.

PART I

THEORY AND HISTORY

CHAPTER 2

THEORIES OF ENTREPRENEURSHIP: HISTORICAL DEVELOPMENT AND CRITICAL ASSESSMENT

MARTIN RICKETTS

2.1 Introduction

The historical evolution of ideas about the entrepreneur is a wide-ranging subject and one that can be organized in different ways—theorist by theorist, period by period, issue by issue and so forth. What follows is a compromise between these possibilities. The paper starts with some very broad reflections about economic change over several thousand years and the connections between these changes and the economic thinking of the time. A recognizably 'modern' idea of the entrepreneur begins to emerge in the eighteenth century and the following two sections are devoted to the role of entrepreneurship in classical and neoclassical economic theory. In the next five sections, the paper looks at particular areas that have been associated with debates about the entrepreneurial role—uncertainty, innovation, economic efficiency, the theory of the firm, and economic development. A final section presents a brief summary and comments on the place of the entrepreneur in evolutionary models.

A reader who is already familiar with important distinctions between capitalist, innovator, uncertainty bearer, judgemental decision-maker, market-maker and so forth should be aware that these will be discussed in greater detail as the paper advances. The following section does not examine entrepreneurship through the ages using a constant and clearly defined concept throughout. Rather, it provides some historical context and links this to contemporary attitudes towards trade, economic change and the perceived agents of change. It shows that advances in pure analytical thought were required before helpful definitions of entrepreneurship could be derived, and that without these advances an important ingredient of any theory of economic change was missing.

2.2 The Entrepreneur in Economic History

Entrepreneurship is not a concept that has a tightly agreed definition. In modern common usage an 'entrepreneur' is 'a person who undertakes an enterprise, especially a commercial one, often at personal financial risk'.[1] It is the product of a 'modern' post-enlightenment world in which continual change has become the norm, where 'progress' (technical, social and economic) has become expected and where notions of liberal individualism predominate. The ancient and mediaeval worlds seem not to have developed a concept of entrepreneurship that could plausibly be seen as similar to the modern notion. Philosophers gave only limited attention to economic matters and, in so far as agriculture, industry and trade were discussed, much thinking would have been a sub-branch of politics or ethics. In the Aristotelian tradition, economic thought was highly normative. Trade was a suspect activity liable to undermine the good order of society and sterile in itself. Even if the reality was more complicated, early social thought concerned static societies built upon caste or social position where justice was the outcome of each group faithfully performing its allotted function. In the hierarchy of social esteem, the noble warrior took pride of place, agriculture was respected and compatible with the inculcation of certain virtues, industry in support of military power was too useful to neglect, but commerce was the province of less respected if not completely despised social groups.

[1] The Chambers Dictionary (1993). Curiously, this dictionary definition singles out 'an organizer of musical or other entertainments' for special mention, presumably on the grounds that the entertainment business is particularly individualistic, risky and demanding of novelty.

It is not difficult to understand this early suspicion of commerce and the trader. The landed aristocrat had large, illiquid and specific (to a geographical region) investments to protect. As with a player in a modern game theoretic model of oligopoly, such a person could plausibly commit to fight interlopers. For the widely travelled merchant with access to ships and with assets in liquid and non-specific form, the temptation simply to move elsewhere when the fighting started and to deal with the winners would have been compelling. The aristocrat's position depended upon a willingness to deter others and to fight for what was his. The merchant's position derived from an ability to go where he was treated tolerably and to flee from unrewarding environments. Where violent conflict was endemic or its likelihood significant, nobles and merchants were thus hardly natural allies.

Another reason for the early disapproval of trade, and in particular, the use of money was its association with situations of 'distress'. Where agricultural production dominates and this is mainly accomplished on large estates using slaves or serfs, the economy has many of the features of an extended 'household'. Indeed the modern English word 'economics' derives from the Greek *oikonomiā* or 'law of the household'. Production and consumption in these conditions are largely undertaken locally within the relatively self-sufficient household, and trade with outsiders is limited to luxury goods for high status members, or imports of food and other staple goods at high prices in the event of crop failure. The result would tend to be an association of the merchant with frippery on the one hand and ruthless exploitation on the other.

In the mediaeval era, the authority of St Augustine held that it was unjust to buy below or sell above the 'just price', while 'usury'—interest on the use of money—was condemned in the religious teaching of the era. Each of these doctrines should be seen in the context of the conditions of the time and scholars have argued about their precise interpretation and force, but even allowing for scholarly refinements, the doctrine of the just price would appear to be highly subversive of entrepreneurial activity. When the whole of society is viewed in terms of duty and obligation in the performance of divinely assigned and sanctioned roles; and when preparation for the next life rather than the improvement of material conditions in this one has the higher priority, entrepreneurship could hardly be expected to feature prominently in the prevailing economic thinking.[2]

Absence of a well-developed conception of the entrepreneur in the philosophy of the time in no way implies that economic conditions were completely static, trade suppressed or technology totally unprogressive. Roman law, for example, developed

[2] Gray (1957: 46) sums up as follows: 'No one, under any circumstances, should take advantage of his neighbour. This is the sum and substance of mediaeval economic teaching.' More modern scholarship credits mediaeval economic thought with greater insight than Gray's statement would seem to imply. The relationship between the idea of the 'just price' and a 'competitive market price' has long been debated while certain schools of thought—especially the School of Salamanca—developed sophisticated accounts of trade and prices Grice-Hutchinson (1977).

highly individualistic concepts of private property and contract which permitted the development of an extensive and sophisticated European trading network. Venetian dominance of Mediterranean trade in the early middle ages could not have developed without an environment sufficiently conducive to entrepreneurial activity. Even the mediaeval economy outside the city-states, which in its social stratification and apparent stability is popularly seen as stagnant, is now regarded by historians as having experienced considerable technological advance.[3] Nevertheless, the distinct notion of an entrepreneurial role awaited an era in which success in commerce and the political power of the state were more closely associated.

With the rise of the modern nation states of France, Spain and England from the late fifteenth century onwards, rulers began to take on at least one characteristic of the merchant. No longer able to rely on feudal obligation from the nobility to protect their interests, the accumulation of treasure, and hence the ability to pay armies, became associated with the maintenance and projection of political power. The mercantilist doctrine that emerged from this era was criticized by later classical economists for confounding money with real national wealth although it is doubtful whether mercantilist writers succumbed fully to such a fallacy. For present purposes, however, it is relevant to note that the building of the power and revenue of the state was the central concern. Such a project is unlikely to be conducive to the growth of decentralized and competitive markets and thus might be seen as inimical to the social development of the entrepreneur. Bureaucratic intervention, the selling of monopolies, licensing and taxation are not the most obvious routes to the entrepreneurial society. However, compared with the world that had preceded them, the sixteenth and seventeenth centuries were the more conducive to entrepreneurship.

The state as an economic organization, an idea which underlay mercantilist thinking, and the accumulation of treasure that was seen as a means of building state power, required the input of entrepreneurial and not merely bureaucratic talent, at least in the context of the competitive states of Europe.[4] The whole enterprise may have been statist at heart but it relied on people to develop overseas markets, to build great trading companies, to strengthen domestic industry and to

[3] For example Landes (1999). In all these societies, however, transaction rights were undeveloped and restricted by modern standards. The ability to interact with new entrants and come to novel agreements was circumscribed by established interests that feared competition and private loss. Witt (1987) argues that only innovations that threatened very few losers would find a footing in such societies. Restricted transaction rights might not, however, result in continual pressure towards liberalization. In a context where 'the true potential for individual improvement by innovative competition ... remains unknown, there is no incentive to challenge the restrictions.' (p. 188). On the other hand a sufficient 'critical mass' of innovative behaviour would tend to lead all agents to become more entrepreneurial and innovative, partly because they are more aware of the potential gains and partly as a defensive response to feared losses. The problematic transition from one mutually re-enforcing state to the other is discussed in Witt (1986).

[4] Centralized state control was far more destructive of entrepreneurial endeavour in China than it appears to have been in the context of Europe. European princes were locked into a competitive struggle with other emerging states. This resulted in military conflict but also in commercial,

generate a large tax base. People of energy and talent could migrate between jurisdictions, and the willingness of other places to receive them placed limits on the exploitation that they would tolerate in any given location. English words now often used to describe entrepreneurs such as 'buccaneer' and 'privateer' derive from this period as the state tolerated or even encouraged the piratical disruption of the trade routes of other nations. As the profits of trade increased, the old aristocracy in England began to accept trade as a respectable activity. Money talked. Defoe commented that 'Trade is here so far from being inconsistent with a gentleman, that, in short, trade in England makes gentlemen' while Voltaire observed that 'It is only because the English have taken to trade ... that England can have two hundred men of war and subsidize allied kings'.[5]

It was, however, the agricultural and industrial revolutions of the eighteenth and nineteenth centuries that finally produced the modern multi-faceted image of the entrepreneur. As rulers gradually submitted to constitutional constraints on their power, and property rights became more secure within the nation states, entrepreneurial energy was released at a historically unprecedented rate. In England in particular, major advances in agricultural productivity and innovations in transport, mining, textiles, steel, shipbuilding, engineering and banking became associated with particular names. The Duke of Bridgewater in the construction of canals, Richard Arkwright in the transformation of the cotton industry and the evolution of the factory system, Mathew Boulton, John Roebuck and James Watt in the development of steam power, George Hudson in the promotion of railways—these and others introduced the revolutionary changes that still colour our image of the entrepreneur.

The 'men of business' of the nineteenth century represented a new social phenomenon. Checkland (1964: 103) writes 'It is probably not far from the truth to say that the period from 1815 to 1885 in Britain represents the range of human experience in which individual economic initiative had its greatest opportunity to operate upon men and things, and in so doing to remake an ancient society'. From this period derives the idea of the heroic entrepreneur, a transformer or founder of industries, an undertaker of massive feats of engineering, an opener of continents. Such activities required the raising of enormous quantities of capital, the development of new organizational methods and the coordination of vast numbers of people. The failures could be as spectacular as the successes. Entrepreneurship of this order required as much strategic insight, tactical awareness, personal energy, power of leadership, organizational flair,

industrial and later scientific and cultural competition. China, having suffered grievously from the Mongol invasions, created a centralized monopoly of power that stifled new ideas and rendered her ill-equipped to meet the eventual challenge of the west. Landes (1999: ch. 4) discusses some of the reasons why even Mediaeval Europe was able to introduce and make use of technical developments long known to, but undeveloped in, China. Pomeranz (2002) argues, however, that the economic performance of China was much better than is usually assumed until more recent times. The 'great divergence' did not occur until the late eighteenth century and thereafter.

[5] Defoe, *The Complete Tradesman* and Voltaire, *Lettres Philosophiques*, 'Sur le Commerce', quoted in Mantoux (1964: 134–5).

ruthlessness and determination as military conquest. And like the military commander, the entrepreneur began to be studied and respected.

In the twentieth century, the cult of the entrepreneur initially receded. The large-scale organizations established in the nineteenth century and the corporations developing in the newer electrical, chemical, communications and motor industries began to look more managerial and professional than heroically entrepreneurial. The entrepreneurs having blazed their pioneering trail, it began to be seriously considered that professional scientists, technicians and managers would be able to maintain momentum. By the 1940s Schumpeter (1942) was advancing this view, and others such as Jewkes (1948) were specifically asking the question 'Is the Businessman Obsolete'?[6] Later developments in the century were to redress the balance somewhat. In the UK, for example, the shipbuilding, coal, steel and cotton industries all but disappeared and this substantial and continuing restructuring undermined the notion that change of this degree could be brought about by managerialism alone. The growth of the service sector of the economy, and the development of computer technology, and communications may also have contributed to a rise in self-employment and small-scale entrepreneurship.

From this brief historical review it is apparent that popular conceptions of the entrepreneur have evolved over time. The somewhat varied notions that still prevail reflect this history. The small-scale trader and peddler, the self-employed craftsman, the 'buccaneering' chancer, the innovator and improver as well as the founder of entirely new technologies and industries are all seen as entrepreneurs. It is evident, however, that a coherent theoretical treatment of entrepreneurship is not automatically suggested by the history of economic and social change. The birth of classical political economy coincided with the upheavals of the agricultural and industrial revolutions of the eighteenth century and an interest in 'The Nature and Causes of the Wealth of Nations'. Yet, both in its classical and later neoclassical formulations, economics as a discipline has not found it easy to find a formal place for the entrepreneur.

2.3 The Entrepreneur in Classical Political Economy

Classical economics did not incorporate a systematic treatment of entrepreneurship. The system of economic thought that prevailed during the 'hey day' of the 'men of business' paid no particular attention to them except as a form of skilled

[6] This was the title of ch. 2 in Jewkes (1948).

labour or as providers of capital. The classical system rested upon foundations that subtly drew attention away from the role of the entrepreneur. This is most clearly seen in the work of Ricardo.[7] The three factors of land, labour and capital received rewards in the form of rent, wages and profits. Over time, 'the condition of the labourer will generally decline, and that of the landlord will always be improved' (p. 79) as population growth presses on limited resources of land and rents rise, while 'the natural tendency of profits then is to fall' (p. 98) with capital accumulation. The dynamics of the system were derived from Malthus and a supposed 'natural' tendency of populations to outstrip the means of subsistence. Subsistence might itself afford more than the means to mere survival, if advancing notions about tolerable standards of living could be harnessed to 'moral restraint', but the classical economists never seemed very confident about this. In so far as an entrepreneur can be found in this system he or she is a supplier of the capital required for a one-way journey to the stationary state.

Ricardo recognizes that 'this gravitation as it were of profits, is happily checked at repeated intervals by the improvements in machinery ... as well as by discoveries in the science of agriculture' (pp. 98–9). But his use of the word 'gravitation' indicates an ultimately decisive natural force, one from which no object on earth had escaped at the time Ricardo was writing. It also suggests the Newtonian basis of classical thinking in economics. Objects might move in this system, but they did so 'automatically' in response to natural and impersonal forces. This mind-set was not conducive to a well-developed role for the entrepreneur within classical theory.

Thus, although the work of Ricardo provides a good example of the exclusion of the entrepreneur or the conflation of entrepreneur with capitalist, the same observation has been made of Smith, Senior, Marx and Mill. For Smith, the labour theory of value was an outcome of his 'natural law' preconceptions, and Schumpeter (1949) speculates that these 'led Adam Smith to emphasize the role of labor to the exclusion of the productive function of designing the plan according to which this labor is being applied' (p. 255).[8] It should be recognized, however, that the writings of the classical economists are open to widely differing interpretations and that Adam Smith, perhaps because he offered a much less formal 'model' of the economy than did David Ricardo, can be seen as the originator of an approach to economic growth which implicitly ascribes a central role to the entrepreneur.

Holcombe (2001), for example, contrasts Smithian and Ricardian models of growth and argues that the Smithian approach is completely different from Ricardo's pessimism. Smith's central concern was with the causes of growth and the opening chapter of *The Wealth of Nations*, indeed its opening sentence, ascribes

[7] References are to Ricardo (1817) edited by Gonner (1891).

[8] Rothbard (1995) is particularly critical of the English 'classical' school seeing it as a diversion away from a path running from the School of Salamanca through the French enlightenment tradition of Cantillon (1755), Say (1803) to the Austrian School and the development of subjectivism and marginal analysis.

growing wealth to the division of labour. This division of labour was 'limited by the extent of the market' (ch. III of bk 1) but Smith did not see 'the extent of the market' as a final and limiting constraint leading to a stationary state. Instead, Smith can be interpreted as describing a dynamic process of a continuously increasing division of labour accompanying continuously increasing market size. The motivating force of this expansion is described as follows: 'Every individual who employs his capital in the support of domestic industry, necessarily endeavours so to direct that industry, that its produce may be of the greatest possible value'.[9] This passage is famous for the 'invisible hand' metaphor by which the individual is led 'to promote an end which was no part of his intention'[10]—the enrichment of society as a whole. 'To promote an end' is to encourage movement in a certain direction rather than to achieve a resting point, however, and Smith might therefore be interpreted as offering a theory of growth that has entrepreneurial decision-making at its core. The efforts of people to 'better their condition' will lead to increasing productivity, a more extensive division of labour and an expanding market.

The tension between a Smithian approach to economics based upon the above reading, which is compatible with a process of continuing economic advance, and a more formal Ricardian approach, which emphasizes the nature and inevitability of a final end state, is of continuing relevance and will be discussed further on p. 43 Marx, in his economic analysis, was entirely Ricardian in spite of references to the 'wonders' brought about by the bourgeoisie that reveal a complete awareness of the massive industrial and commercial achievements of his age.[11] This disjunction between a common sense reaction to actual events, which could hardly see the investment of such massive amounts of capital in entirely new industries as 'automatic', and classical Ricardian economic theory, was also apparent in the work of J. S. Mill.

Mill is credited as introducing the word 'entrepreneur' into English economics, although Schumpeter (1949) opines that he did not go much further than including 'superintendence' as a necessary input into production. Gross profits had to be sufficient to provide 'a sufficient equivalent for abstinence, indemnity for risk, and remuneration for the labour and skill required for superintendence' (pp. 245–6). Abstinence reflects the usual classical association of entrepreneur with capitalist. Superintendence makes a portion of the entrepreneur's reward effectively a wage. Even innovation and invention could be seen as a type of labour. 'The labour of invention is often estimated and paid on the very same plan as that of execution'[12]

[9] Smith (1776: 420–1).

[10] Smith (1776: 421).

[11] For Marx these 'wonders' of nineteenth century industrial development were, of course, compatible with the impoverishment and exploitation of the working class—a view held tenaciously by generations of socialist thinkers until shown to be unsustainable by more recent historical scholarship on the 'standard of living controversy'. For a survey see Hartwell (1972).

[12] References are to Mill (1898), The People's Edition.

(p. 26). It was, however, Mill's inclusion of 'indemnity for risk' as part of profit that perhaps lay behind his preference for the word 'undertaker' rather than 'manager' and supports the case that he saw the entrepreneurial function as something qualitatively different from capitalist or worker. Interest is the reward for abstinence 'while the difference between the interest and the gross profit remunerates the exertions and risks of the undertaker' (p. 246).[13]

The association of entrepreneurship with risk bearing is an important strand of thought that survives to this day, and is reflected in the dictionary definition quoted earlier, but it has given rise to substantial controversy. Schumpeter (1954: 556) was sufficiently convinced that this 'served to push the car still further on the wrong track' to devote an extended footnote to explaining the supposed fallacy involved in Mill's position. Because losses can only be experienced by resource owners, and because capital is the only resource under discussion, it is evident that losses are borne by capitalists. If a capitalist lends to an entrepreneur, he or she takes the risk that the debt will not be repaid. If the entrepreneur has sufficient wealth to cover the debt, then 'he too is a capitalist and, in case of failure, the loss again falls upon him as a capitalist and not as an entrepreneur'. For Schumpeter, the supply of capital and the supply of entrepreneurial services were quite distinct, and risk attached to the former not the latter.

Although this argument at first sight seems to have the inescapable force of a syllogism—all losses accrue to resource owners, only capitalists are resource owners, ergo only capitalists experience losses—it is still possible to question the interpretation of the conclusion as well as the validity of the premises. Both Mill and Schumpeter paid tribute to the French tradition in this field and in particular to the work of Cantillon (1755) and Say (1803). Cantillon, who first introduced the term 'entrepreneur', envisaged an agent who contracts with suppliers at known prices in order to produce goods that could be sold later at uncertain prices. Here we have a clear statement that the entrepreneur's profit is a residual. It is what remains after all contractual commitments have been honoured. Schumpeter (1949) remarks approvingly that this conception is 'not infelicitous' as it 'emphasizes the elements of direction and speculation that certainly do enter somewhere into entrepreneurial activity' (p. 254).

This French tradition fits uneasily, however, with Schumpeter's rejection of the entrepreneur as a bearer of risks. The receipt of residual income as conceived by Cantillon, unlike the more modern theory of Israel Kirzner which is discussed below (p. 48), would seem to require the acceptance of risk. If the future residual income is not certain but takes the form, as it were, of a lottery ticket, the holder must be a risk bearer. Schumpeter seems to assume that speculation using other people's money is necessarily riskless. An entrepreneur who starts with nothing

[13] It is in a footnote at this point in the 'Principles' that Mill mentions his 'regrets' concerning the lack of an English equivalent to the French word 'entrepreneur'.

'cannot lose'. But it is still a 'state contingent claim' that the entrepreneur is holding even if the returns are highly geared and negative financial outcomes do not feature. Thus the conclusion 'only capitalists experience losses' is not quite the same as 'only capitalists bear risks'.

An objection might also be raised to the premise that all resource owners are capitalists. We can, of course, always define things this way. But the interpretation of human capital raises problems. An entrepreneur who has persuaded a financier to advance money by means of a fixed interest loan may have used the intangible resources of character, experience, track record and reputation. Failure and bankruptcy would be expected to affect the ability of the entrepreneur to raise similar finance in the future and thus would result in a 'write down' of this entrepreneur's human capital. Viewed in this light it seems reasonable to take the 'common sense' position that the entrepreneur can experience losses. The alternative is to insist that the entrepreneur still loses as a 'capitalist', and that, in spite of the person-specificity of entrepreneurial human capital, it is a distinct entity quite separate from the speculative and organizational skills that he or she supplies. This, however, would seem to open up the possibility of disputes to rival in sophistry those of mediaeval scholasticism.

2.4 The entrepreneur in neoclassical theory

It is sometimes argued that the development of neoclassical analysis beginning with Menger and Jevons in the 1870s, heralded a change of emphasis from the 'magnificent dynamics' of classical theory to 'precise statics'.[14] Robbins (1935: 16) later described this central concern as 'the relationship between ends and scarce means which have alternative uses'. At the heart of this new economics were a clearly stated subjectivism and the systematic application of marginal analysis. Jevons (1871) immediately establishes these foundations with his 'novel opinion' that 'value depends entirely upon utility', by which he meant marginal utility.[15]

An economics based upon subjective value theory and marginal analysis, rather than an objective (labour) theory of value, resulted in some subtle changes in thinking about entrepreneurship. On the one hand, the new discipline was capable of being developed in highly formal and mathematical ways. Rational allocation of

[14] See Collison Black (1970: 9).

[15] Emphasis in original.

any given amount of a scarce resource requires that its marginal benefit should be equal in every potential use. This 'first order condition for maximization' applies to any rational person whether consumer or producer. Working out whether all these individual maximizing decisions could be made mutually compatible was obviously a major interest and it was one of the greatest intellectual achievements of neoclassical economics to show the coordinating role of prices. Walras and other 'general equilibrium' theorists investigated the conditions under which a set of prices existed, in a world of 'price takers', that was compatible with universal market clearing. In this equilibrium, economic rents might accrue to resources such as land or even differential skill, but business profit would be zero. Schumpeter (1953: 893), who greatly admired Walras's work, remarks that his contribution to the analysis of the entrepreneur was 'important though negative'. Walras 'indicated a belief to the effect that entrepreneurs' profits can arise only in conditions that fail to fulfill the requirements of static equilibrium'.

Unfortunately, it was the apparent failure of prices to ensure universal market clearing that was more obvious to observers in the inter-war years than their benign potential as a coordinating mechanism. It was not unnatural, in the face of mass unemployment, to wonder whether alternative resource-allocating mechanisms might produce better results. Such thoughts were not particularly subversive of the calculating, rationalist or marginalist basis of neoclassical economics. Ensuring that resources are allocated rationally to achieve specified ends is the sort of 'scientific' problem that looks suitable for experts, technicians and managers. Refinements of neoclassical theory were thus capable of diverting attention from entrepreneurship entirely—either by a highly static Walrasian formalization of competitive equilibrium, or by conceiving the entire economy as one giant maximization problem. It was the latter view that lay behind the so-called 'calculation debate' about the feasibility of socialist planning during the 1930s and 1940s. The rational, calculating, maximizing, equi-marginal principles of economics could be used by officials to achieve a social optimum—or so it seemed.

Neoclassical thinking was capable of leading in quite a different direction, however. If attention is directed at its subjectivist foundations rather than its calculating rationalism, the problem of reconciling multifarious individual subjective 'ends' with multifarious individually perceived 'means' looks distinctly less of an engineering problem and more of a problem of social institutions and organization. Competitive market processes could be seen as a mechanism by which these ends were revealed, resources discovered and developed, and the various possibilities latent in the resources explored. Participants in this type of market are active bargainers and pricesetters rather than passive Walrasian 'price takers'. Thinking along these lines does not lead so much to 'precise statics' as to 'imprecise dynamics'. Instead of the 'magnificent dynamics' of classical theory leading with Newtonian predictability to the stationary state, we have a dynamics, magnificent or otherwise, of a more evolutionary, unpredictable and Darwinian conception. The modern 'Austrian' school, which includes writers such as Hayek (1945, 1978), Shackle (1972, 1982) and Kirzner (1973, 1979), represents this strand of thought. Clearly, entrepreneurship fits more naturally into this tradition than into static analysis.

The sharp dividing line that has become established since the 1940s between 'Austrian' and 'neoclassical' thinking, however, was much less apparent to writers of the period between 1870 and 1940. The increasing formality of the analysis might be static but the 'vision' was of economic evolution, or 'progress' little different from that of J. S. Mill.[16] This is most clearly seen in the work of Marshall (1912: 165) who emphasized evolutionary change instituted by 'business management' rather than 'entrepreneurship'. Under the heading of 'management', however, Marshall argues that 'the superintendence of labour is but one side and often not the most important side of business work'. In addition, he identifies the accumulation of knowledge about products and processes, the forecasting of market movements, the seeing of opportunities for new commodities and processes, the exercise of judgement, the undertaking of risks and the leadership of people. While therefore clearly stating that there were two 'sides' to business activity, we might now say an administrative side and an entrepreneurial side, Marshall does not feel impelled to distinguish them clearly and to assign separate rewards for each.

2.5 Entrepreneurship and Uncertainty

It was Knight (1921) who effectively proposed to deconstruct the Marshallian business manager and highlight the entrepreneurial element.[17] Starting from the proposition that no profit existed in a Walrasian perfectly competitive equilibrium, it followed that pure profits were related to the existence of disequilibrium.

Disequilibrium must imply unexpected change. Fully anticipated change is quite compatible with sophisticated versions of the Walrasian system in which economic agents trade in futures contracts. Similarly, in a world of complete markets and where probabilities could be assigned to potential outcomes, even risk-bearing could be 'optimized' by trading-in state contingent claims. In such a world it was not clear that 'risk bearing' and profit were related. 'Market' prices would ensure that bearers of risk would be compensated and that risk was distributed optimally

[16] See Schumpeter (1954: 892–3).

[17] Mises (1949) independently developed a view of the market process that is compatible with that of Knight.

across the population. For Knight, profit was related not to risk bearing but to uncertainty bearing. An uncertain situation was one in which probabilities could not be assigned to outcomes so that decision-making was impossible to model in terms of neoclassical optimization. 'It will appear that a *measurable* uncertainty, or "risk" proper, as we shall use the term, is so far different from an *unmeasurable* one that it is not in effect an uncertainty at all'.[18]

A world of true uncertainty gave rise to the possibility of pure profits and losses (*residual* income as distinct from *contractual* income)[19] and a distinct role for the entrepreneur. 'With uncertainty present doing things, the actual execution of activity becomes in a real sense a secondary part of life; the primary problem or function is deciding what to do and how to do it'.[20] This view of entrepreneurship is thus a comprehensive twentieth-century elaboration and refinement of the French tradition. What is required from the entrepreneur is judgement in the face of uncertainty. The entrepreneur, having made a judgemental decision, must be able to implement the decision, which will usually involve hiring other inputs. In this way, Knight's analysis of pure profit leads to a view of the firm with the entrepreneur as the central contractual agent and the residual claimant. In so far as the entrepreneur needs to manage resources in order to implement a plan of action, and in so far as these management activities are 'routine', part of his or her income will be a wage. The rest will be pure profit—a return to good judgement and pure luck.

Schumpeter's objection to the idea that the entrepreneur undertakes 'risk bearing' has already been discussed and would presumably apply to Knight's uncertainty-based theory. Knight specifically discusses these problems when he remarks that 'it is impossible for entrepreneurship to be completely specialized or exist in a pure form' except by imagining a 'rare and improbable case'[21] in which the entrepreneur provides no capital and undertakes no managerial responsibility. Nevertheless, Knight argues that 'judgement of men' is much more pertinent to successful entrepreneurship than 'judgement of things'. Once we admit the possibility that one person might 'have knowledge, or opinions on which they are willing to act, of other men's capacities for the entrepreneur function' then we can envisage a financier being willing to commit resources to a Knightian 'entrepreneur'. Presumably this is what the modern venture capitalist is effectively doing when financing start-ups or management buy-outs, an activity that represents a clearer apparent separation of entrepreneur from capitalist than was common in

[18] Knight (1921: 20).

[19] 'The produce of society is similarly divided into *two kinds of income*, and two only, contractual income, which is essentially a *rent*, as economic theory has described incomes, and residual income or *profit*. Knight (1921: 271).

[20] Knight (1921: 268). Emphasis in original.

[21] Knight (1921: 299).

the classical era.[22] Similarly, the distinction between manager and entrepreneur can be equally problematic in practice even though the theoretical distinction is clear. An entrepreneur has to exercise 'control' in order to put a judgement about resource allocation into effect. This will tend to result in some 'management' activity unless we can imagine a 'pure' case in which the entrepreneur contracts with managers who can be trusted to follow through on his or her judgemental decisions.

2.6 Entrepreneurship and Innovation

Schumpeter's most celebrated contribution to the theory of the entrepreneur did not concern his criticism of J. S. Mill, already discussed, concerning risk bearing. This was ultimately a sub-dispute to his main thesis. His main point is that whether they saw the entrepreneur as a capitalist, a skilled manager or as a risk bearer, the classical economists had overlooked the most important role. The introduction of new products and processes requires organizational skills quite separate from simple management and it is this dynamic task of exploration and innovation that is the distinctly entrepreneurial one. Schumpeter (1912) is particularly associated with this idea of the entrepreneur as a revolutionary innovator.

In a period soon after the 'men of business' in the UK and the 'robber barons' in the US, Schumpeter emphasized the role in economic development of people with the vision and willpower 'to found a private kingdom'. The role of the entrepreneur 'is to reform or revolutionize the pattern of production by exploiting an invention or, more generally, an untried technological possibility ...' (Schumpeter 1942: 132). He coined the now famous metaphor 'gale of creative destruction' to describe the competitive processes of capitalist development. This unceasing gale derives from the energy of entrepreneurs who, through their innovations, undermine the market position of their rivals. Such competitive threats do not simply strike 'at the margins of the profits and the outputs of existing firms but at their foundations and their very lives' (p. 84). Entrepreneurship, for Schumpeter, is the force that prevents the economic system running down and continually resists the approach of the classical stationary state.

Two features of Schumpeter's work on the entrepreneur are particularly distinctive. The first is his view of innovation as revolutionary and discontinuous rather

[22] It will still, in practice, be true that the venture capitalist will be bearing Knightian uncertainty and will also therefore be an entrepreneur. Complete separation of function remains 'rare and improbable' in Knight's framework.

than small-scale, marginal, gradual and cumulative. The second is his (later) view that, as capitalism develops and matures, large firms become the powerhouses of innovation and usurp the entrepreneurial role that was originally so associated with extraordinary and energetic individuals. 'Economic progress tends to become depersonalized and automatized' (Schumpeter 1942: 133) while teams of technicians and specialists eventually receive 'wages such as are paid for current administrative work' (p. 134). The second of these propositions, somewhat paradoxically, is similar to Mill's mid-nineteenth century classical formulation mentioned above, with an additional emphasis on large firms. Both propositions have been subject to re-examination and criticism. Bhidé (2000), for example, uses the history of the microcomputer revolution at the end of the twentieth century to investigate Schumpeter's propositions and concludes that firms of varying sizes play a role in innovation as do large research departments and small-scale enthusiasts. 'Individual entrepreneurs and large companies play complementary roles and (this) helps explain why new combinations evolve in a gradual rather than a discontinuous way' (p. 337).

2.7 Entrepreneurship and Economic Efficiency

Schumpeter's conception of the entrepreneur focuses attention on the process of technological innovation. A complementary approach concerns the process of uncovering and exploiting all the economic possibilities latent in an existing state of technology—the process of diffusion. Here the emphasis is on the discovery of potential gains to trade and hence, by implication, the move from less to more efficient allocations of resources. Casson (1982: 23) for example, presents a theory which is built on Knightian foundations. 'An entrepreneur is someone who specializes in taking judgemental decisions about the coordination of scarce resources'. Over time, opportunities for pure profit are continually occurring and the Walrasian conditions for 'competitive equilibrium' are never achieved. The entrepreneur fulfils the function of an intermediary or 'market-maker' exploiting divergences in the marginal valuations of goods on the part of consumers or marginal opportunity costs on the part of producers to achieve a pure profit. Wherever 'market failure' exists—that is, wherever some re-allocation of resources might conceptually harm no one and benefit at least one person—a profit might be achieved by effecting the re-allocation. Pure profit derives from the 'gains to trade' spotted, or better 'conjectured', by the entrepreneur and is captured by what is essentially a process of arbitrage which, assuming the entrepreneur's judgement is correct, yields a positive residual.

This rather abstract formulation of entrepreneurial activity encompasses simple trading activity, the establishment and growth of firms, the design of suitable incentive contracts, as well as the development of entirely new institutional arrangements. Where perfect Walrasian conditions are contravened and markets do not exist, or property rights in goods and resources are ill defined, entrepreneurial gains will be available to those who can think of ways of overcoming the resulting inefficiencies. Firms subject to external costs or benefits might merge their activities so as to 'internalize' these spillovers. Monopoly restrictions might open possibilities for new entry. Valuable information that cannot be traded in markets because of its 'public good' characteristics might be generated and protected within a firm and used by entrepreneurs to expand the scope of their own activities. Market failure thus implies the possibility of future gain and becomes a generator of entrepreneurial opportunities.

The idea of the entrepreneur as an intermediator, 'market-maker' and hence coordinator of transactions, has resulted in the development of various sub-branches of the literature during the last 30 years. One strand is represented by the neo-Austrian School and the work of Israel Kirzner. A distinctive feature of Kirzner's approach is his emphasis on alertness to currently unexploited opportunities for trade. Pure profit is not a return for bearing uncertainty as much as a reward for pure alertness. The gains from trade have to be noticed before they can be achieved. By spotting potential gains to trade and then arranging the transactions that will capture them, the entrepreneur is the instigator of changes that are efficiency-enhancing. Further, these changes move the economy towards equilibrium. 'The movement from disequilibrium to equilibrium is nothing but the entrepreneurial-competitive process ...' (1973: 218).[23]

It is worth contrasting this view of the entrepreneurial process with that of Schumpeter. For the classical economists, entrepreneurial activities were associated with innovation and thus constituted a force acting against the 'gravitational' attraction of the stationary state. Schumpeter's entrepreneur is clearly of this type—innovative, disruptive and resisting equilibrium. The neoclassical economists had a different problem. No longer in thrall to Malthusian dynamics and the labour theory of value the neoclassical theorists had a sophisticated account of the state of competitive equilibrium but not of the process by which it was approached. Walras introduced a hypothetical 'auctioneer' into his system to adjust prices up or down in response to excess demands or supplies, but although this provided a reasonable theoretical 'model' of a dynamic adjustment process the auctioneer was

[23] For a more extended description and critique of Kirzner's work along with a rejoinder see Ricketts (1992).

still a 'deus ex machina'. To explain equilibrating change without recourse to a fictional outside auctioneer required the introduction of some agent of change within the system. Kirzner's entrepreneur provides this dynamic element and it is generally, though not exclusively, the 'Austrian' tradition that has emphasized its importance.

The 'neo-Austrian' view of entrepreneurship, because it derives from a recognition that resource allocation is an *information* problem and not simply a *calculation* problem, tends to see it as an activity capable of being pursued by virtually any economic agent. Entrepreneurs are not necessarily specialists and they do not necessarily operate on a very large scale. They may make use of very local knowledge—'knowledge of people, of local conditions and of special circumstances'[24]—and some of this knowledge may be 'tacit knowledge',[25] difficult or impossible to communicate to others verbally or in the form of written documents and blueprints. Entrepreneurship moves the system from the bottom up, so to speak, rather than the top down and it does so through the trading activities of market makers. In this, the neo-Austrians are in the tradition of Alfred Marshall whose theory of economic progress is 'an incremental, experimental, evolutionary theory'.[26] It should be apparent, however, that the subjectivism of the neo-Austrian economists is capable of undermining the whole concept of 'equilibrium'. In the absence of any objective set of constraints waiting to be discovered through entrepreneurial alertness, Austrian thinking could lead to a view of economic change that was all process and no particular destination. Once entrepreneurs were conceived to be creative, the economic system, not unlike the natural world, was liable to large Schumpeterian shocks and not merely long periods of incremental adaptation to given underlying conditions.[27]

2.8 Entrepreneurship and the Theory of the Firm

Almost all approaches to the entrepreneur have one thing in common. The entrepreneur contracts with a set of other people and, after all contractual commitments have been honoured, claims the residual. Cantillon, Von Thünen, Schumpeter, Knight, Kirzner and Casson, in spite of very great differences of

[24] Hayek (1945: 20).
[25] Polanyi (1967).
[26] Loasby (1982a: 239).
[27] Shackle (1979: 31) for example refers to 'the anarchy of history'.

emphasis, could at least agree to this basic conception. It is a conception that inevitably places the entrepreneur at the heart of the modern theory of the firm first proposed by Coase (1937). This theory was originally developed without explicit reference to entrepreneurship although Coase was tutored by Arnold Plant at the London School of Economics in the 1930s and there was undoubtedly an LSE tradition in business organization which was well aware of its importance. The tradition can be seen running through to Edwards and Townsend (1967) and in the writings of Jack Wiseman and Basil Yamey.

The problem faced by Coase was the apparent inability of neoclassical economics to explain the structure of firms or indeed their very existence. Then, as now in elementary treatments of the subject, the firm was defined as a technological relationship between inputs and outputs and the details of its internal organization were simply omitted as unnecessary for the purposes of price theory. Any attempt to explain organizational structure thus required adjustments to the Walrasian framework and Coase's contribution was to introduce transactions cost as the key ingredient. For Austrian theorists, the problem with the Walrasian system was its implicit assumption of full information. For Coase, the problem was its assumption of a zero cost of transacting. The two ideas are obviously closely related since transactions cost derives from incomplete information, but Coase's formulation was more suited to the comparative analysis of contractual arrangements and could be approached using standard techniques of rational maximization.

Coase rationalized the firm as the centre of a set of 'internal' employment contracts which substituted for 'outside' market contracts. Other things constant, resources would be administered within the firm when the costs of doing so were lower than the costs of contracting outside. The boundary of the firm was defined in typical neoclassical style such that the transactions cost of the marginal contract was the same in 'the firm' and in 'the market'. If transactions costs are treated as objective and are known to all transactors, the theory can be developed without reference to entrepreneurship. Alchian and Demsetz (1972) for example, present a model in which 'team production' and the impossibility of measuring and rewarding individual contributions to output lead to the requirement for a 'monitor' to detect and punish 'shirking'. This person is a residual claimant in order to provide the incentive to monitor the team which, on the assumption that the monitoring technology is well known, is a purely routine managerial task. The residual will turn out, in equilibrium, to provide a competitive market return to monitoring. Thus firms exist even in a purely neoclassical world once information is no longer perfect and has to be 'produced' but, as would be expected, it is the manager who is the central contractual agent.

If, on the other hand, transactions costs are subjective, conjectural and uncertain the firm as the coordinator of a set of contracts can be seen as an organization inherently associated with the entrepreneurial process. Knight's view of the entrepreneur, the neo-Austrian approach to the entrepreneur and Coase's conception of the firm can therefore be regarded as complementary[28] and the tradition has been developed further in recent years by Casson (2001). The theory of the firm is re-orientated around the analysis of information flows rather than flows of physical inputs and outputs. Casson criticizes neoclassical thinking that tends to ignore 'cultural' factors and is built not simply on methodological individualism but on a particularly desiccated and socially unconnected type of individualism.[29] Some features of the firm can no doubt be explained as a response to predicted opportunism on the part of contractors but entrepreneurs are in the business of reducing transactions costs and improving the quality of information flows by building trust through continuing associations as well as by the power of leadership. Casson prefers a 'theory of the firm centred on the entrepreneur as the founder and prime mover within it.'[30]

The firm is also a significant element in discussions of the finance of the entrepreneur. Knight, as we have seen, thought that pure entrepreneurship could be envisaged only in 'rare and improbable cases'. The entrepreneur will almost always have to provide some capital and labour (managerial) services in addition to pure entrepreneurship. Modern theory, however, has explained several observed financial arrangements as methods of mitigating contractual hazards and directing resources to otherwise 'unqualified' entrepreneurs. One example is the existence of debt contracts with agreed repayment schedules and finance secured upon slowly depreciating and non firm-specific capital. Equity sharing arrangements with venture capitalists can also enable entrepreneurs with very limited access to personal wealth to finance their ideas. These methods can be viable even when contractual performance is completely 'unverifiable'.[31] However, they apply to 'start-ups' and the finance of entrepreneurs without a track record or an established reputation. A further theoretical development makes the long-established corporation itself a mechanism for channelling resources to pure entrepreneurs.

Kirzner (1979: 105) argues that modern corporations represent 'an ingenious, unplanned device that eases the access of entrepreneurial talent to sources of large-scale financing.' The argument is most fully explored by Wu (1989). Wu sees economic development since mediaeval times as leading to the gradual emergence of specialized markets in land, labour and capital. Apparently insuperable contractual hazards prevented a market in entrepreneurship from developing. The non-contractibility of entrepreneurial services leads the entrepreneurs to 'take the

[28] For further discussion see Holcombe and Boudreaux (1989) and Foss (1996). Foss (1993) contrasts the contractual (Coasian) perspective with the competence (evolutionary) perspective. As mentioned in the text, Coase's original approach is neoclassical and Foss argues that 'the firm as a repository of tacit knowledge is neglected in the contractual perspectives, it occupies center stage in the competence perspective'.

[29] See Casson (1991).

[30] Casson (2001: 114).

[31] See, for example, Hart (1995).

initiative to organize production through non market means, that is, by organizing a firm' (p. 232). Although for centuries entrepreneurship was associated with the provision of capital, the modern corporation permits the final stage of specialization to occur. 'The long historical evolution towards functional specialisation among factors of production had reached its destination' (p. 224). The word evolution is important here, for it is the *evolution of reputation* that provides some assurance to capitalists that a return will be provided on their capital. The firm is 'a coalition of entrepreneurs' who share 'pure entrepreneurial profit' between them while paying a market return to the providers of capital. Loss of confidence in the willingness of the entrepreneurs to pay such a return would deprive them of future access to capital and the entrepreneurial profit that might be generated with it. This view of the modern corporation is certainly consistent with business ideas about 'intrapreneurship',[32] 'corporate venturing' and 'corporate entrepreneurship'.

2.9 Entrepreneurship and Economic Development

As Baumol (1968) argued, the omission of the entrepreneur from neoclassical analysis was inevitable given the central place accorded to models of constrained optimization. Even early neoclassical models of economic growth[33] relied upon exogenously given rates of technical change and rates of population growth rather than any discussion of the sources of entrepreneurial initiative. Attempts to make the rate of technical progress endogenous linked it automatically to the rate of capital accumulation or required the introduction of theoretical innovations such as 'invention possibility frontiers' to act as a constraint on entrepreneurial 'choice'.[34] The 'supply of entrepreneurship' did not seem amenable to neoclassical treatment and Schumpeter (1954: 897) explicitly warns against drawing 'supply curves for entrepreneurial services even if we believe in supply curves for any other kind of work'.[35]

[32] A term coined by Macrae (1976)

[33] For example Solow (1956).

[34] For a review see Jones (1975: ch. 8).

[35] Casson (1982) rebels against Schumpeter's injunction and draws the supply curve of 'active entrepreneurs' responding to the expected return to their activity.

One line of enquiry, however, has proved much more amenable to neoclassical treatment. Baumol (1968: 70) suggested that the question of what can be done to encourage the entrepreneur's activity can be approached by examining 'the determinants of the payoff to his activity'. This is a theme to which he returned more than twenty years later. Baumol (1990) treats the overall supply of entrepreneurial talent as given but argues that its allocation to innovation on the one hand or depredation, crime or 'rent-seeking' on the other is a matter of choice. Clearly, societies that manage to encourage entrepreneurial talent to undertake 'productive activities' are likely to develop faster than those societies that give relatively high rewards to 'unproductive' or purely redistributive activities. Historical instances such as the dynamism of the 'High Middle Ages' in Europe and the relative failure of mediaeval China are, argues Baumol, consistent with this thesis.

The theory of rent-seeking was developed initially to explain why the social losses associated with tariff restrictions, quotas, monopoly privileges, taxes and regulations often seemed to be much larger than the simple 'static' efficiency estimates suggested.[36] One straightforward answer was that these interventions were usually beneficial to some partial private interests and permitted monopoly returns (rents) to be made. It therefore made sense for private interests to invest real resources in trying to create these rents—lobbying governments to impose differential costs on their rivals and to erect barriers to entry. These 'rent-seeking' activities were socially wasteful and re-distributive rather than efficiency-enhancing. They represented a form of social loss in addition to, and quite distinct from, the resulting static inefficiency in the allocation of resources. Clearly talents suited to entrepreneurship are likely to be equally well adapted to exploiting potential private gains to rent-seeking.

This approach to entrepreneurship directs attention to political and legal factors such as the security of property rights, the burden and administration of the tax system, the enforcement of contracts, the development of company law, the impact of bankruptcy provisions and so forth. De Soto (1987), for example, argued that workers in the 'extra-legal' sector in Peru were not passive proletarians ripe for revolution but actually represented talented entrepreneurs trying to overcome the institutional barriers that confronted them. This change of view has had a profound impact on development economics. It has led to empirical work such as De Soto (2000) in which poor or non-existent title to property and other legal restrictions are highlighted as inhibitions to entrepreneurship. Conversely, Olson (1982) made growing returns to rent-seeking an important component of his explanation for the gradual ossification of previously dynamic societies. Rent seeking has also played a part in more formal models of economic growth. Murphy et al. (1991) develop a model in which talent is allocated across various sectors

[36] See Buchanan et al. (1980). Anne Krueger (1974) originally coined the term 'rent-seeking' in a study of the effects of Indian trade restrictions.

including a 'rent-seeking' sector. The overall rate of growth of each productive sector depends upon the talent of the best entrepreneur present in the sector because it is his of her ideas that are imitated in future periods. The incentive to enter a sector depends upon the private rate of return available, with high ability individuals able to earn larger returns than lower ability individuals. Where rent-seeking is highly rewarding to the most talented, society loses both by sacrificing immediate output and by experiencing a lower rate of growth because the productive sector is made up of the less talented entrepreneurs. To encourage entrepreneurs to reject rent-seeking it is thus necessary to investigate the determinants of the relative rewards accruing to the two activities.

2.10 Concluding Comments

The central importance of entrepreneurship to economic development and competitive processes is not something that has been discovered just recently. The systematic incorporation of the entrepreneur into economic theory, however, posed enormous methodological difficulties. Economics, whether classical or neoclassical, was primarily concerned with the analysis of long run 'natural' or 'equilibrium' states and this focus tended to divert attention from entrepreneurial activity. Treating entrepreneurship as another 'factor of production' made it difficult to distinguish it from a species of 'management'. Treating entrepreneurship as something qualitatively different from other 'inputs' tended to subvert the calculating rationalism underlying economics and opened up doctrinal disputes that had no solution. Some neoclassical economists such as Alfred Marshall tried to chart a middle way unacceptable to purists on both sides by introducing elements of entrepreneurship informally into their work as a descriptive and interpretative commentary to the theory.

By the mid-twentieth century the divide between the so-called 'Austrian' and neoclassical theorists had become particularly pronounced and inextricably bound up with the dispute over the relative merits of central planning and competitive markets. For the 'Austrians', neoclassical theory in itself had nothing much to say on this fundamental organizational question and could be used to buttress the claims of either side. This was because it ignored the information problem and implicitly assumed that planners were a perfect substitute for entrepreneurs. For the neoclassical economists the Austrians seemed guilty of lack of scientific rigour and even pure ideological bias.

During the later years of the twentieth century, however, these divisions narrowed. Simple observation of the performance of centrally planned systems compared with market economies redirected attention away from the problem of planning flows of physical inputs and outputs to encouraging institutions for generating, transmitting and using information. Whether explicitly recognized or not, this refocusing of attention was about establishing the preconditions for entrepreneurial activity. The 'New Institutional Economics'[37] with its interest in the evolution of rules to govern social inter-action, the development of property rights and the importance of transactions costs is quite consistent with methodological individualism and much neoclassical theory. But it is more open to an investigation of the factors that might encourage or discourage entrepreneurial activities.[38] Further, because many social institutions that neoclassical economics took as 'exogenous' could instead be seen as 'endogenous' and 'unplanned' outcomes of 'repeated co-ordination games' the door opened to a much more explicit evolutionary view of economic change.[39] The simultaneous advances of evolutionary theory in other scientific areas such as animal behaviour perhaps played a part in encouraging its greater acceptance in economics.[40]

In microeconomics, for example, Nelson and Winter (1982) proposed an evolutionary model of the firm. The firm is seen as operating according to an established set of 'routines' and in addition it 'searches' for new ones. Search 'is the counterpart of that of mutation in biological evolutionary theory' (p. 18). Successful routines lead to growth and imitation by others. The entrepreneurial function is here associated with search and 'mutation'. Competitive advantage is not conferred merely by access to special information but also by the ability through the firm's 'routines' to generate a flow of such information. Clearly, entrepreneurial 'mutation' and economic selection through competition are not quite the same as random mutation and natural selection. Nelson and Winters' searchers are not acting randomly and blindly but actively looking ahead at future possibilities. Nevertheless, the system is evolutionary rather than deterministic.

Entrepreneurship is thus gradually finding a somewhat more formal place in economic theory. This does not imply that the methodological disputes discussed earlier have been resolved. Nor does it mean that a general theory of entrepreneurship has become accepted. It does, however, reflect the central importance of the economics of information in the research efforts of the late twentieth and early twenty-first centuries.

[37] See Furubotn and Richter (1997), Kasper and Streit (1998), Klein (1998) and Williamson (2000).

[38] A discussion can be found in Witt (1989).

[39] A classic early example is Carl Menger's account of the evolution of money. See Menger (1871). Sugden (1986) looks more generally at the evolution of social conventions including property rights.

[40] See Smith (1982).

References

Alchian, A. A. and H. Demsetz (1972). 'Production, Information Costs and Economic organization'. *American Economic Review*, 62(5): 777–95.

Baumol, W. J. (1968). 'Entrepreneurship in Economic Theory'. *American Economic Review*, Papers and Proceedings, 58: 64–71.

—— (1990). 'Entrepreneurship: Productive, Unproductive and Destructive'. *Journal of Political Economy*, 98(5): 1, 893–921.

Bhidé, A. V. (2000). *The Origin and Evolution of New Business*. Oxford: Oxford University Press.

Buchanan, J. M., R. D. Tollison and G. Tullock (1980). *Toward a Theory of the Rent Seeking Society*. Texas: A and M University Press.

Cantillon, R. (1755). *Essai sur la nature de commerce en générale*. (ed. H. Higgs, 1931). London: Macmillan

Casson, M. (1982). *The Entrepreneur: An Economic Theory*. Oxford: Martin Robertson.

—— (1991). *The Economics of Business Culture: Game Theory, Transactions Costs and Economic Performance*. Oxford: Clarendon Press.

—— (2001). *Information and Organization: A New Perspective on the Theory of the Firm*. Oxford: Oxford University Press.

Checkland, S. G. (1964). *The Rise of Industrial Society in England 1815–1885*. London: Longmans, Green & Co.

Coase, R. (1937). 'The Nature of the Firm'. *Economica* (New ser.) 4: 386–405.

Collison Black, R. D. (ed.) (1970). *Jevons: The Theory of Political Economy*. London: Penguin Books.

De Soto, H. (1987). *The Other Path: The Invisible Revolution in the Third World*. New York: Harper Collins.

—— (2000). *The Mystery of Capital: Why Capitalism Triumphs in the West and Fails Everywhere Else*. London: Transworld Publishers, Bantam Press.

Edwards, R. S. and H. Townsend (1967). *Business Enterprise: Its Growth and Organization*. London: Macmillan.

Foss, N. (1993). 'Theories of the Firm: Contractual and Competence Perspectives'. *Journal of Evolutionary Economics*, 3: 127–144.

—— (1996). 'The "Alternative" Theories of Knight and Coase, and the Modern Theory of the Firm'. *Journal of the History of Economic Thought*, 18(1): 76–95.

Furubotn, E. and R. Richter (1997). *Institutions and Economic Theory*. Ann Arbor: University of Michigan.

Gray, A. (1957). *The Development of Economic Doctrine*. London: Longmans, Green and Co.

Grice-Hutchinson, M. (1977). *Early Economic Thought in Spain 1177–1740*. London: Allen and Unwin.

Hart, O. D. (1995). *Firms, Contracts and Financial Structure*. Oxford: Clarendon Press.

Hartwell, R. M. (1972). 'The Consequences of the Industrial Revolution in England for the Poor'. *The Long Debate on Poverty*. London: Institute of Economic Affairs.

Hayek, F. A. (1937). 'Economics and Knowledge'. *Economica* (New ser.) 4: 33–54.

—— (1945). 'The Use of Knowledge in Society', *American Economic Review*. 35: 519–30.

—— (1978). 'Competition as a Discovery Procedure'. *New Studies in Philosophy, Politics and the History of Ideas*. London: Routledge and Kegan Paul.

HOLCOMBE, R. G. (2001). 'The Invisible Hand and Economic Progress'. *Entrepreneurial Inputs and Outcomes*, 13: 281–326.

—— and D. J. BOUDREAUX (1989). 'The Coasian and Knightian Theories of the Firm', *Managerial and Decision Economics* (June) 10: 147–54.

JEVONS, W. S. (1871). *The Theory of Political Economy*. (ed. R. D. Collinson Black, 1970). London: Penguin Books.

JEWKES, J. (1948). *Ordeal by Planning*. New York: Macmillan.

JONES, HYWEL. G. (1975). *An Introduction to Modern Theories of Economic Growth*. London: Nelson.

KASPER, W. and M. E. STREIT (1998). *Institutional Economics: Social Order and Public Policy*. Cheltenham: Edward Elgar.

KIRZNER, I (1973). *Competition and Entrepreneurship*. Chicago: University of Chicago Press.

—— (1979). *Perception, Opportunity and Profit*. Chicago: University of Chicago Press.

—— (1989). *Discovery, Capitalism and Distributive Justice*. Oxford: Blackwell.

KLEIN, P. (1998). 'New Institutional Economics', in B. Bouckeart and G. De Geest (eds) *Encyclopedia of Law and Economics*. Cheltenham: Edward Elgar.

KNIGHT, F. (1921). *Risk, Uncertainty and Profit*. Boston: Houghton Mifflin Co.

KRUEGER, A. (1974). 'The Political Economy of the Rent Seeking Society'. *American Economic Review*, 64: 291–303.

LANDES, D. (1999). *The Wealth and Poverty of Nations*. UK/USA: Abacus/Norton.

LOASBY, B. J. (1976). *Choice, Complexity and Ignorance*. Cambridge: Cambridge University Press.

—— (1982a). 'The Entrepreneur in Economic Theory'. *Scottish Journal of Political Economy*, 29(3): 235–45.

—— (1982b). 'Economics or Dispersed and Incomplete Information', in I. M. Kirzner (ed.) *Method, Process and Austrian Economics: Essays in Honor of Ludwig Von Mises*. Toronto: Lexington Books.

—— (1991). *Equilibrium and Evolution: An Exploration of Connecting Principles in Economics*. Manchester: Manchester University Press.

MACRAE, N. (1976). 'The Coming Entrepreneurial Revolution: A Survey'. *The Economist*, 25 December, p. 42.

MANTOUX, P. (1928). *The Industrial Revolution in the Eighteenth Century*. Republished 1964, University Paperback. London: Methuen.

MARSHALL, A. (1912). *Economics of Industry*. London: Macmillan.

MENGER, C. (1871). *Grundsätze der Volkswirtschaftslehre* (trans. and ed. 1950 as *Principles of Economics*). IL: Free Press, Glencoe.

MILL, J. S. (1898). *Principles of Political Economy*, The People's Edition. London: Longmans, Green & Co.

MISES, L. (1949). *Human Action*. London: Hodge.

MURPHY, K. M., A. SHLEIFER and R. W. VISHNY (1991). 'The Allocation of Talent: Implications for Growth'. *Quarterly Journal of Economics*, 106(2): 503–30.

NELSON, R. and S. C. WINTER (1982). *An Evolutionary Theory of Economic Change*. Cambridge, MA: Harvard University Press.

OLSON, M. (1982). *The Rise and Decline of Nations*. New Haven: Yale University Press.

POLANYI, M. (1967). *The Tacit Dimension*. New York: Doubleday Anchor.

POMERANZ, K. (2002). *The Great Divergence: China, Europe and the Making of the Modern World Economy*. Princeton, NJ: Princeton University Press.

Ricardo, D. (1817). *Principles of Political Economy and Taxation* (ed. E. C. K. Gonner, 1891). London: George Bell.

Ricketts, M. (1992). 'Kirzner's Theory of Entrepreneurship—A Critique', in B. J. Caldwell and S. Boehm (eds) *Austrian Economics: Tensions and New Directions*. London: Kluwer Academic Publishers.

Say, J. B. (1803). *A Treatise on Political Economy*. (trans. C. R. Prinsep, 1821). Boston.

Schumpeter, J. A. (1912). *The Theory of Economic Development* (1936 edn). Cambridge, MA: Harvard University Press.

—— (1942). *Capitalism, Socialism and Democracy*. New York: Harper & Brothers.

—— (1949). 'Economic Theory and Entrepreneurial History', in R. V. Clemence (ed., 1989). *Essays on Entrepreneurs, Innovations, Business Cycles and the Evolution of Capitalism*. New Brunswick and London: Transaction Publishers.

—— (1954). *History of Economic Analysis*. London: Allen & Unwin.

Shackle, G. L. S. (1972). *Epistemics and Economics: A Critique of Economic Doctrines*. Cambridge: Cambridge University Press.

—— (1979). 'Imagination, Formalism and Choice', in M. J. Rizzo (ed.) *Time, Uncertainty and Disequilibrium: Exploration of Austrian Themes*. Toronto: Lexington Books.

—— (1982). 'Means and Meaning in Economic Theory'. *Scottish Journal of Political Economy*, 29(3): 223–34.

Smith, A. (1776). *The Wealth of Nations*. (4th edn, ed. E. Cannan, 1925). London: Methuen.

Smith, J. M. (1982). *Evolution and the Theory of Games*. Cambridge: Cambridge University Press.

Solow, R. M. (1956). 'A Contribution to the Theory of Economic Growth'. *Quarterly Journal of Economics*, 70: 65–94.

Sugden, R. (1986). *The Economics of Rights, Cooperation and Welfare*. Oxford: Basil Blackwell.

Thünen, J. H. Von (1826). *Isolated State*. (trans. C. M. Warenberg and ed. P. Hall, 1966). Oxford: Pergamon Press.

Williamson, O. (2000). 'The New Institutional Economics: Taking Stock, Looking Ahead'. *Journal of Economic Literature*, 38: 595–613.

Witt, U. (1986). 'Evolution and Stability of Cooperation Without Enforceable Contracts'. *Kyklos*, 39: 245–66.

—— (1987). 'How Transactions Rights Are Shaped'. *Journal of Institutional and Theoretical Economics*, 143(1): 180–95.

—— (1989). 'Subjectivism in Economics – A Suggested Reorientation', in K. G. Grunert and F. Ölander (eds). *Understanding Economic Behaviour*. Dordrecht: Kluwer.

Wu, Shih-Yen (1989). *Production and Entrepreneurship*. Oxford: Basil Blackwell.

CHAPTER 3

ENTREPRENEURSHIP: AN EVOLUTIONARY PERSPECTIVE[1]

J. S. METCALFE

3.1 Introduction

This chapter suggests that an evolutionary market perspective provides a powerful framework for bringing the entrepreneur back into economic theory precisely because enterprise is the activity of introducing new activities, production methods and products into an economy. Economic variation is the prerequisite for economic transformation and development and this is why enterprise and the entrepreneur are central components of the evolutionary approach to economics. Indeed, the fundamental historical fact about capitalism is its internal capacity for transformation, and the corresponding transience of the activities and ways of life that it supports within a more slowly evolving set of institutions. Economists have for long recognized a capitalist, market economy as a self-organizing system sustaining a spontaneous order; far less well recognized is its capacity for spontaneous transformation, and it is this theme that forms the core of this chapter.

Entrepreneurship is not one-dimensional, the entrepreneur comes in shades of many different kinds, and the wide range of possible entrepreneurial characteristics

[1] This paper is a development of Metcalfe 2003 and draws upon on-going work in the ESRC Centre for Research on Innovation and Competition at the University of Manchester. I am grateful to Mark Casson for helpful guidance on a previous draft.

is normally hidden until they are expressed in action, so that it is presumptuous to conceive of a simple, unifying approach.[2] Moreover, to the extent that the entrepreneur is an 'individual' of some type, he or she is a situated individual working within social as well as economic constraints and fully subject to the framing, instituted rules of the game. Indeed it is difficult to make sense of enterprise without recognizing the explicit role of market institutions as the context that induces and channels entrepreneurial activity. As we shall argue below, what makes market capitalism a restless system is precisely its open nature and the positive inducement it provides to engage in business experimentation. We should remember that methodological individualism is not methodological isolationism, as it so often appears in the discussion of economic agency. Baumol (1993) in his extended discussion of the topic includes, 'the use of imagination, boldness, ingenuity, leadership, persistence and determination' as relevant characteristics of those who engage in novel activities: a list that adequately warns us of difficulties that lie ahead in finding an adequate frame of analysis for these troublesome individuals. No unifying approach is offered here, although we will see how the ability of a theoretical frame to incorporate the entrepreneurial function provides a sharp demarcation test for different kinds of theory of an economy. Moreover, the matter of entrepreneurship has wider implications and here the central problem is not how we deal with economic change but how we deal with change generated within the economic system as distinct from change imposed upon it from outside.

Why do we conceive of entrepreneurial economies as self-transforming economies and of enterprise as the agency of self-transformation? The modern characteristic of ceaseless change is not characteristic of earlier times. What is it about the process of modern capitalism which makes it so revolutionary, perhaps too revolutionary for its own long term good? Our suggested answer is that the dynamic of modern capitalism lies in the combinatorial growth of knowledge and investment opportunities combined with the instituted frameworks of the market economy that taken together simultaneously stimulate and enable entrepreneurial activity. Here there is a paradox, with which any observer of modern economics must contend. Entrepreneurial behaviour is pervasive yet economic theory, with one or two very significant exceptions, has virtually nothing to say about either its significance or about its origins. This is a pity because the failure to treat the entrepreneur seriously cuts off research and advanced teaching in economics from the central dynamic of modern capitalism, its restless, searching, experimental nature; and renders it particularly difficult to teach students of business the significance of the economic institutions that frame the modern world. No theory of growth, let alone economic development can ignore enterprise because it is the motive force of internal economic change. I will explore this conundrum below

[2] Swedberg (2000) and Livesay (1995) are valuable compilations, illustrating the range of approaches to the entrepreneur in the social and management sciences.

and suggest that bringing in the entrepreneur means pushing out several of the cherished methodological stances of modern economics. I will conclude with the claim that only an evolutionary stance on the economic process can give the entrepreneurial function its due place in our thinking. If that is contentious, so be it, the contest between ideas is itself an entrepreneurial, experimental and evolutionary process.

3.2 Enterprise and the Entrepreneur

It will help to begin with a distinction between 'enterprise' and the 'entrepreneur'. By 'enterprise' we mean a pervasive activity that changes the rules within which economic decisions are made. The essential feature is to introduce novelty into the economic structure at any level, new ways of behaving generally based on new beliefs and in many cases new knowledge. Thus we recognize the standard case of the invention that is the basis for new rules of production or the new product or the new pattern of business organization. Enterprise is to be contrasted with simple economic adaptation, changing behaviour within given rules of the game in the presence of invariant beliefs and knowledge.[3] The fact the enterprise connects to novelty, however dramatic or minor, provides important connections with the parallel notion of complexity and emergent behaviour within systems. Hence we will equate enterprise with business experimentation, the implementation of a new business plan either on its own or in the context of a modification of an established larger plan, and ask of any economic system 'How effective is it at generating new and viable business experiments?'

By the 'entrepreneur' we mean the agency that generates the changes in the rules and effects their implementation. In many, but not all, cases business experimentation is reducible to the creation of a new organizational entity, the prototypical small firm. How does the literature treat this phenomenon? Consider first Baumol's (1990) definition of entrepreneurs as, 'Persons who are ingenious and creative in finding ways that add to their own wealth, power, and prestige'. From this follows the idea of the entrepreneur as the agent responsible for conceiving and implementing new business plans, plans to create wealth, power and prestige. Since plans require resources for their activation, we find an easy transition to definitions

[3] The modifier 'simple' is meant to convey the idea that adaptation in reality will normally require some change of knowledge some degree of enterprise as defined. It is a slippery distinction but it serves a purpose.

such as that provided by Mark Casson, who defines the entrepreneur as 'someone who specializes in making judgemental decisions about the allocation of scarce resources' (Casson, 1982: 151). If it is the nature of the judgemental decisions that matters, then, as Ripsas (1998) suggests, they have three principal attributes: their innovative nature, and by implication their connection with new knowledge; the uncertain prospects attached to them, and thus their dependence on partial knowledge; and, finally, the extraordinary profit rewards that can follow from implementing these decisions and thus their connection with radical knowledge.

Such a broad perspective is useful as a starting point but it clearly needs some sharpening if it is to be useful, for any change in business activity falls within this remit; it is, at once, too broad and too narrow. It is too broad because we would want to exclude changes in business arrangements that are purely simple, adaptive responses to changes in the pattern of relative prices within a given framework of rules and beliefs. If when the price of copper increases, makers of electrical cables substitute aluminium as the material of choice, we would not normally consider this to be an act of enterprise, merely good stewardship, economizing on the deployment of existing, familiar economic resources within the existing state of knowledge. Similarly, the founding of any new business stretches the notion of the entrepreneur too far. Many business ventures are copies of existing businesses whose function is to ensure the continuity of economic activities through time; they are based on general knowledge of well-established markets and practices, and in that sense bring nothing new to the economy. While they require resources to be marshalled appropriately, and while they inevitably carry the risks associated with the newness of the venture from the viewpoint of the founder, they are entrepreneurial to a negligible degree. Many small businesses in the retail or catering trades, for example, fall into this category, and the crucial test is that they are devoid of novelty from the wider system perspective. On the other side of the account, definitions of the entrepreneur as individual are too narrow, for they risk excluding entrepreneurial activity based on teams working within existing enterprises, and excluding entrepreneurship in non-economic contexts, and in the context of public enterprise (Baumol, 1990, 1993). The heroic entrepreneur in Schumpeter has an important role to play, but so does the entrepreneurial team developing new business opportunities within an established firm. It is the activity and function that matter not the number of minds involved. We also need to acknowledge that not just the private enterprise business leader can be entrepreneurial. Indeed, to give one example, there is an enormous gap in our thinking about the entrepreneurial role of the consumer in the modern economy, in deciding for what purpose particular goods are used (Gronow and Warde, 2003).

Thus, a working definition needs to go beyond the idea of passive, routine adaptation within known knowledge frames, to focus on the positive element of novel conjectures that bring new knowledge or beliefs into economic application. The point about these conjectures is that while they may have a partial basis in knowledge, they rest in large part on beliefs that are yet to be tested, to be confirmed or falsified. This inevitably brings the definition closer to the Schumpeterian conception of imagined new combinations of resources that include a basis in new technology but are not limited to that. The business conjectures that Schumpeter noted also extend to new markets, new forms of organization and the discovery of new natural materials and they explicitly, and unfortunately, de-emphasized the role of the entrepreneurial consumer. It is not useful to equate enterprise only with technology-based business opportunities even though these are important, and in the case of many famous technology-based entrepreneurs such as Edison (Millard, 1990) or Sperry (Hughes, 1971) central to their achievements. We shall say more about the Schumpeterian dimension in a moment but one or two other preliminary remarks are in order.

3.3 The economic significance of enterprise

It is a familiar theme in the discussion of enterprise that it finds no place in the conventional theories of competition and economic growth (Knight, 1921; Baumol, 1968) and this is surprizing not least because of a widespread recognition that the growth and application of new knowledge is the proximate source of the growth in standards of living for at least two centuries and undoubtedly for longer. In fact the style of modern economic thinking precludes making the connection between enterprise and economic change in any meaningful way. There are two principle reasons for this. The first, and least significant, is the treatment of the connection between new knowledge and economic growth in macroeconomic terms. The devices of steady growth, in which to the extent that different activities are differentiated at all, and that they are all required to expand at the same proportionate rate, undermines any treatment of the enterprise process. The fundamental issue here is that economic growth is never a steady advance, with all activities expanding at the same rate, as the prominent aggregative theories of economic growth would have us accept. In this case, and scale apart, one year is identical to the next, time passes and nothing happens, whether growth is positive or negative makes no difference. By contrast, we know that growth always follows on from development, from changing the economic structure quantitatively and qualitatively. For in this process it is essential that we account for the creation of new activities and the disappearance of established ones and that we account for the differential growth and decline of the continuing activities. What disappears economically is as significant as what emerges as novelty and that which declines in importance is as significant as that which expands. Enterprise and its corollary innovation cannot produce steady growth and we cannot understand its mechanisms at macroeconomic levels of aggregation, for to aggregate is to mask the diversity of growth experience that is the mark of a restless capitalism. Enterprise calls for disaggregated treatment but it also requires calls for methods to track the transmission from the diversity of micro experience to the unfolding of the higher aggregates. There is nothing wrong at all, for example, in enquiring as to the determinants of aggregate productivity growth in an economy, but no merit at all in treating the statistics so generated as if they represent an underlying macroeconomic reality. If we are to connect enterprise, the growth of knowledge and measured economic growth, we need to recognize that growth follows from development and that development is a non-steady state phenomenon.

This takes us to the second, deeper reason, which is that the theory of markets is cast as a theory of equilibrium and in equilibrium, by definition, all internal sources of change have been eliminated. To recognize enterprise is either to force consideration of it outside the market as an exogenous force treatable by the techniques of comparative statics, or to treat it as a property of a system that cannot be in equilibrium. It is this latter possibility that Schumpeter (1934) pointed us towards in his *Theory of Economic Development.* There, his insistence that the capitalist system develops from within must mean that it cannot be a system in equilibrium, otherwise no significance attaches to the claim that that enterprise is an integral element in the market process. How is this conundrum to be settled? The clue is found in another of the subsequent themes of Austrian economics, to the effect that markets generate order but that order is not equilibrium. A market order is a particular pattern of activity and matching allocation of resources that satisfies a test of a balance between production and consumption in a market and in an economy overall. To describe an order as 'an equilibrium' would mean that all agents were entirely satisfied with this pattern of activity and could see no way to improving it in a way that generated greater rewards for them. Schumpeter's considerable legacy is the recognition that ways are always being conjectured by the market participants to improve the use of resources. Thus we recognize that entrepreneurial-led change is based on a process of the internal, self-transformation of the economic system. This process may have no attractors of any kind, it may be truly open-ended, historical and entirely unpredictable in its effects. To understand the basis for this argument is indeed an enormous challenge but, unless we make the effort, the role of the entrepreneur will remain elusive and worse, marginal to economic thinking. Moreover, we will never come to understand the process of economic development or why it is so unevenly distributed around the globe and thus comprehend the reasons behind several of the major moral issues of our times. This needs discussion from two separate viewpoints—that of the nature of the market rules of the game, and that of the connection between enterprise, new beliefs and new knowledge.

3.4 The instituted market frame

In this section, I elaborate on the point that an understanding of the entrepreneurial function cannot be separated from the instituted structure of the economic system in which it is exercised. The nature and consequences of enterprise are embedded in the wider system of market and non-market economic institutions, and the specific features of a market economy encourage a particular spectrum of entrepreneurial activities. In a different set of institutional arrangements, say of labour managed firms, or of stakeholder capitalism, the entrepreneurial spectrum will take on a different hue because those systems give different meanings and content to entrepreneurial activity and provide different incentive systems from shareholder capitalism (Adaman and Devine, 2002). What appears remarkable about the framing institutions of capitalism is not that they generate a particular order but rather their propensity to transform that order. History speaks eloquently to the restless nature of a system that in relatively short periods of time replaces, almost in their entirety, particular ways of carrying out economic activity. The economic world of today bears little resemblance to that of 1960, even less to that of 1903 or 1803, in that the entire pattern of production has changed as new products and methods of making them using new kinds of material and energy appeared, and old ones disappeared. Thus, patterns of resource allocation become radically different over time, the activities and economic ways of life of consecutive generations bear little resemblance to each other, and patterns of consumption include practices and purchases that would be undreamt of by earlier generations. Even in 1960, how many would have imagined, let alone believed, that the desk-top computer would be almost as ubiquitous as the television in the households of a modern economy? Who, in the 1930s, would have foreseen the role of the television in destroying the cinema industry, or would have imagined the effect of the refrigerator on patterns of household living? Few modern homes are lit by coal gas—not so in 1910; a virtually negligible proportion of the population today works directly on the land—not so in 1870; and very few make the trip from Europe to New York by ocean liner—not so in 1920. Indeed, industrial museums proliferate and are an established part of the cultural framework in many advanced economies; and one should reflect on this as a marker of the nature of capitalism. We preserve the past only to remind ourselves that the future will be different. Less happily, whole regions and cities exist with their economic *raison d'être* eliminated by the entrepreneurial process; the negative side of restless capitalism is that it is an uncomfortable system in which to live. The record, in this long-term perspective, appears to be one of radical discontinuity such that any comparison of a single economy over extended time is fraught with difficulty. Growth never happens without development and the ongoing radical redevelopment of the economic structure so that economic change is always uneven within and between countries. As Simon Kuznets (1977) has argued, these economic features partly reflect the role of the scientific revolution in underpinning an entirely new engine of economic change. However, we should not lose sight of the fact that scientific work and entrepreneurship are entirely different, though complementary, and that it is the latter, which gives to science its modern economic significance, not the converse.

What, then, are the instituted features of modern capitalism that create such a strong symbiosis with enterprise and entrepreneurship? They are five in number. The first and most important is the set of rules and traditions enshrined in property rights and the rules of law in which it is the economic weakness of property rights that is the distinctive feature. Strong property rights defined over the ownership and disposal of assets of any kind are essential to any exchange-based economic system. But these provide no guarantee at all of the economic value of the assets in question. The attempts in Feudalism to fix economic values through restrictions on invention or the customary set of prices, for example, are quite incompatible with the rules of restless capitalism. As Hayek pointed out what is protected is the expectation of command not the expectation of economic value (Hayek, 1976: 123–5). Indeed protection of the latter would only be meaningful in a world of stationary beliefs, yet the market process renders that impossible, for it is not the permanence of property rights that matters but their temporary market consequences.[4] This leads directly to the second of our instituted features of restless capitalism.

The effect of these particular rules in relation to property and economic value is to generate open markets in which every established business position is open to competitive challenge, unless temporally protected via a patent, copyright or other statutory limitation. If we see competition not as a state of affairs graded by the structure of the market, but as a dynamic process of rivalry and struggle for a share of the market, then enterprise activity is both necessary and sufficient to create competition. The general rule is that any market can be entered, provided the

[4] No better example of this can be found than the rights attached to a patent for invention. These are rights to exploit in a monopoly fashion but in no way do they prescribe the flow of returns that ensues. Indeed, the fact that the principles of the patent must be placed in the public domain as a condition of its granting is precisely an invitation for other inventors to find alternative routes to the same effect, and thus an incentive to destroy the value of the original patent. Patents are an extremely clever institution, their protection is important but it is not unlimited, and deliberately so, and it is helpless in the face of other genuinely novel entrepreneurial actions.

business idea is good enough and provided incumbents do not create sufficiently onerous, artificial barriers to entry. On the latter, competition authorities in the advanced economies justifiably spend a good deal of effort preventing incumbent firms artificially closing off their markets to entry by rivals. On the former, it is rather obvious that since any entrant incurs costs in establishing a novel business activity there will usually need to be some compensating entrepreneurial advantage in product design and quality, method of production, or scheme for distribution to customers that puts the incumbent at a disadvantage vis-à-vis the new source of competition and which helps circumvent entry barriers. In this sense, entrepreneurship is pervasive because the idea of an open competitive market process is pervasive. Under the rules of restless capitalism a firm never quite knows where the threats to its existence will come from; and frequently they come from such unanticipated directions that their significance is often discounted until it is too late.[5]

Thirdly, markets play fundamental roles in relation to information which guides entrepreneurial behaviour. Enterprise does not occur in a vacuum—it is shaped by the existing order. The prevailing market-based valuations of products and productive services allow the prospective entrepreneur to gauge the potential profitability of a new venture by virtue of its having to fit into the current pattern of production and consumption. Market signals matter not only in the sense of encouraging the efficient use of existing business knowledge, the traditional argument in favour of the competitive organization of industry, but also in the deeper sense of guiding the competitive process of entrepreneurial change. Without knowledge of prices and quantities, no entrepreneur could judge that a business conjecture is potentially viable: he would be doubly blind, not knowing whether either the quantity conjectures or the value conjectures on which the plan depends are plausible. Markets generate this information and thus connect new beliefs with existing patterns of resource allocation. All entrepreneurial conjectures compete with, and are designed to, compete with some existing activity even if the true margins of competition are initially misconceived and revealed in surprizing ways *ex post*. Notice that this remains true even for those radical entrepreneurial conjectures that, for example, introduce products previously unheard of. Even these products must be conjectured to displace existing products in consumers' expenditure and to utilize resources employable elsewhere in the economy. Even if the radical reconfigurations of demand and reallocations of resources that flow from truly radical innovations cannot be foreseen, surely the starting point for the entrepreneurial process can, by virtue of existing market relations. Of course, this is to claim nothing more than the significance, indeed necessity, of an element of

[5] The managerial literature is full of examples of incumbent firms that failed to spot the competitive nature of innovation by unanticipated rivals. See for example, Utterback (1994) and Christensen (1997) for recent discussion of this disruptive aspect of competition.

continuity in the economic process. New activity always builds on an existing base. In this sense, all change is cumulative as Marshall's famous epigram, *natura non facit saltum* reminds us (Marshall, 1920: xiii).

Fourthly, markets are instituted devices for generating low-cost access to consumers and productive services; they are effective ways of reducing the costs of exchange. Markets are not only structures for indicating the terms on which resources and customers are available, they are the channel to gain access to them. Open markets for skilled workers and for free capital are essential to an entrepreneurial economy; without them the possibility of entrepreneurial behaviour will be greatly circumscribed. Equally, markets for outputs play the same role of indicating who and where customers are. Efficient markets, those that establish uniform prices for goods and services with identical characteristics are consequently of great importance to the conduct of enterprise for they indicate the real opportunity costs of innovation. Without them enterprise risks misdirection, which is why getting the prices right is a necessary but not sufficient condition for maximizing the developmental opportunities in any economy.

This takes us to the fifth and final aspect of the institutions of a market economy—the incentives they provide for entrepreneurship. Whether or not profits are the *primum mobile* of the entrepreneur, there can be no doubt that profit is a necessary feature of such activity and that their prospect is essential in the process of attracting risk capital to support conjectures for which there cannot be any basis in fact. Novelty may be its own reward, but novelty is also the signal that what the entrepreneur does is economically superior to already established competing activities. Abnormal profits, far from being an index of the absence of competition, are the very proof that competition is actively pursued, that resources are being reallocated. This is the crucial role that profits and losses play in the mobilization of new economic structures; by focusing on competitive equilibrium we hide this from view. Moreover, one of the key institutions of capitalism, the distinction between contractual returns and residual returns, has no purpose if the system always and everywhere stands in competitive equilibrium. Because the system is never in equilibrium in this sense, the distinction has real force and points to profit not as the consequence of monopoly power but profit as the non-equilibrium consequence of differential, enterprising behaviour.

The conclusion from this is that there is a close correspondence between the institutions of market capitalism and the nature of the enterprise activity that it encourages and rewards. It is perhaps the most remarkable feature of these institutions that they induce the continuing destruction of the orders that they create. Order turns out to be essential for directed change, which cannot emerge out of chaos. But order is not equilibrium, it is the precursor to self-transformation and this is why the institutions noted above frame a restless capitalism. As Schumpeter well understood, capitalism in equilibrium is a contradiction in terms and so devices such as the stationary state, regularly expanding or not, appear from this view to be a particularly unhelpful way to comprehend the processes involved. They hide enterprise whereas the institutions of capitalism bring it to the fore.

To explore this further we turn to the relation between enterprise and the growth of knowledge, the ultimate reason for the restless nature of capitalism. We then outline the relation between enterprise and a population approach to evolutionary dynamics. It will next be helpful in the light of this discussion to provide a brief account of the two principal contrasting theories of economic entrepreneurship associated with Schumpeter and Kirzner respectively. We then turn to an assessment of the characteristics of modern economic theory, which preclude the inclusion of enterprise and the entrepreneur, leading to the claim that the root cause of the difficulty is their underlying approach to the nature of knowledge. We conclude, first, with a brief assessment of how the entrepreneur and the manager can jointly contribute to an understanding of restless capitalism, and secondly, with the claim that the entrepreneurial process is an evolutionary process.

3.5 Discovery, Enterprise and Knowledge

This section explores the claim that the link between capitalism and enterprise is provided by the growth of new knowledge, that the foundations of enterprise are ultimately epistemic. What is unique about each entrepreneur in this view is their formation of a different view of the world, a view that is the basis for differential economic action. Entrepreneurs believe something that nobody else believes, and do so with sufficient strength of mind and purpose as to act upon the belief and commit economic resources to a business plan (Witt, 1998). They lead the way to new dispositions of resources and can do so only on the basis of differential beliefs. These beliefs must be grounded in the understanding of the individual concerned and this understanding must be grounded in that individual's knowledge and beliefs concerning the existing economic world. To say that the entrepreneur is blind to the future consequences of action is not at all the same as saying that the entrepreneur acts randomly. Quite the contrary, for the reasons adumbrated above, entrepreneurs are guided by the market system in respect of the innovations they propose.

All knowledge is, of course, entirely private, it only exists in the form of electro-chemical states in individual minds and brains. Knowledge never appears in the public domain—it is always in this sense entirely tacit and private. What is in the public domain is the representation of that knowledge, almost certainly imperfect, in the form of information whether verbal, sensual or codified in storable written form. That information can be codified and that we, as a civilization, have developed sophisticated languages, including mathematics, to code and decode information is, of course, a central fact in the development of modern entrepreneurial society. A growing body of public information has been made available that is storable across time and transferable across space and thus available for the use of future generations and generations in different locations. The growth in this ensemble of information opens up enormous opportunities for the combination of different pieces of information and thus for the growth of new knowledge in individual minds. Indeed, the significance of this distinction between information and knowledge is fundamental to the growth of the latter. Knowledge always grows through thought experiment in individual minds but this process is greatly influenced by the information to which those minds have access too. The growth in the availability of stored information greatly enriches this process of knowledge growth but is itself insufficient to comprehend the dynamic of the process. What social and economic life in general depends upon is the emergence of correlated knowledge, more safely, correlated understanding across individual minds. Only when individuals understand in common can they act in common. Thus the emergence of social rules, of theories of public action, of theories of nature, of theories of technology, has been central to modern economic growth, as explained above. Every economy depends on high, if localized, levels of correlation of understanding, exactly as Adam Smith described in his account of the division of labour. Moreover, modern societies devote significant resources to the process of correlating understanding through education and of reinforcing these correlations through ideas of law, justice and acceptable rules of behaviour.

However, a world in which every individual knows the same as any other individual would be a world of stationary knowledge. Indeed, it would be a world in which individuality could not be given any substantive meaning. Knowledge grows because it is individually grounded, because individuals react differently to the same information and transmit the new thoughts to others in a continuous process of communication and challenge. Out of this process comes understanding in common, correlated knowledge, of which the processes that generate science are typical examples. Now the chief characteristic of the Schumpeterian entrepreneur, in science as in economic life, is to de-correlate private knowledge, to sow doubt where previously there was understanding in common. Hence, the emphasis on novelty, on challenging existing practices and understandings typical of the Schumpeterian model, and typical of the Kuhnian notion of the paradigm-breaking scientist. The role of the swarm of imitators, and indeed of the Kirznerian entrepreneur discussed below (p. 78), is to re-establish a sufficient degree of correlated understanding around the new activity to ensure its spread into the economic system as the appropriate niche is discovered. Thus, entrepreneurs have a dual role. They claim to know differently from others and they challenge the correlated understanding that others possess. The successful among them generate new patterns of understanding in the use of resources—pattern changes that underpin economic growth. It is on this distinction between knowledge and information that an understanding of the entrepreneur rests: as the individual who dares to act on the basis of thoughts not held by others; who challenges through imagination, not calculation alone, the basis of their economic and social co-operation. No wonder they are rarely thanked for their pains.

That the entrepreneur is the locus of experimentation in the generation of new economic knowledge also helps explain the restless nature of modern capitalism. Economies can never be at rest because knowledge is never at rest and the prevailing pattern of understanding is always being subjected to challenge. By acting entrepreneurially, an individual generates new information that may lead others to see the world differently in a distributed process of knowledge growth. What is distinctive about modern society is its institutionalization of this process of repeated challenge to existing patterns of knowledge correlation (Gibbons et al., 1994). Of course, all economies are knowledge and information economies; they could not be otherwise. What is distinctive about modern times is not only the development of social technologies to correlate understanding but the substantial investment in physical technologies to store and communicate information, greatly widening the number of individuals who can fish in the common pool. In such conditions, contemporary views of the world are challenged on a widespread basis and one would expect the number of entrepreneurs to be increased substantially as a result, as discussions of the acceleration of economic change would suggest. The disruption of existing economic arrangements is thus built into modern capitalism in a fundamental way. Not only do markets act as the context in which knowledge and conjecture lead to new opportunities for enterprise, the establishment of procedures for generating new knowledge independently of the market context has proved a fertile development in the institutions of modern capitalism.

That this creates a problem for connecting the two spheres of knowledge generation should not disguise the remarkable nature of this division of labour. The growth of science and technology in university style organizations, or the research laboratories of corporations, further enshrines the restless nature of capitalism, because a portion of its resources are thereby devoted to finding reasons why the world is not as it seems (Mowery and Rosenberg, 1998). Adam Smith recognized this at the outset of his great work when he pointed out that the principles of the division of labour apply not only to the content of knowledge but to the form of the production of knowledge. No wonder the system is restless or that enterprise is the distinguishing feature of modern capitalism.

3.6 Enterprise, Evolution and the Population Approach

We have given several hints already that the entrepreneur is essential to the process of economic evolution and in this section the connection is spelt out a little more by enquiring into the empirical signatures associated with enterprise. This is a vast topic because it encompasses change within firms and organizations as well as change between them—but it is on the latter that we focus. Leaving aside the narrow question of innovation, the evidence is overwhelming that modern capitalism is always in transition—that market positions are continually being redrawn quantitatively and qualitatively. To facilitate the connection between enterprise and the generation of economic variety, a central unifying device that helps make sense of restless capitalism is that of an evolving population, a set of entities that vary individually and change over time but are subjected to common selective pressures. In our case the entities can be treated as a population of firms constituting an industry and the selective pressures can be read as market forces that stimulate changes in the structure of the population. Two broad selective forces are at work: selective forces proper that result in the differential growth of incumbent firms and the exit of non-viable firms; and, innovative forces, that change the characteristics of incumbent firms (innovation proper, recombination through merger and fission through spin-off activity) and generate entry of new firms into the population. These forces exhaust the possibility of evolution in a population of firms and they provide interesting empirical indicators of the consequences of enterprise.

Thanks to the availability of new micro data sets, the stylized facts on the scale and ubiquity of economic variation are becoming well established and have made it easier to understand the broad sweep of the enterprise dynamic. The wide variations in productivity growth and productivity levels within and between industries (Bartlesmann and Doms, 2000) and the high rates of entry, exit and market share mobility (Audretsch, 1995; Geroski, 1995; Caves, 1998) are typical examples. More recently Baldwin and Gu (2005) in a detailed study of Canadian manufacturing find persuasive evidence for the restless nature of enterprise-driven economic growth expressed in terms of population dynamics. Among their findings we note:

- Of firms in operation in 1989, 70 percent were not in operation in 1999, exits accounted for 46 percent of total output and 50 percent of total employment. Most exits were close-downs, business failures not acquired by another firm.
- About 45 percent of firms active in 1999 entered between then and 1989. Exits on average have 74 percent of the productivity of incumbents and 'Green-field'

entrants 68 percent, but merger entrants are 19 percent more productive than incumbents.

- Turnover among incumbents was far more important than turnover from entry and exit. Over the period 1979–99, growing firms gained 7.5 percentage points of market share per annum and declining firms lost 13.6 percentage points per annum. Entering firms captured 4.2 percent, and exiting firms lost 4.1 percent per annum in market share.

The findings on entry and exit processes are also confirmed by an earlier study on the Canadian data by Baldwin and Rafiquzzaman (1995), which distinguishes entirely new entrants, 'green-field' entrants consisting of a new firm plus new plant, from entry by firms established in some other industry. They find that 6.7 percent of establishments operating in any one year are green-field entrants and that only 3.4 percent of them survive to age ten, although larger firms are relatively more likely to survive at this age. Green-field entrants start with a disadvantage in respect of wages paid, productivity and profitability and it takes eight to nine years for them to improve their performance to approximate to the industry average. However, for the entrants who survive, they find that they are 32 percent of the average industry size at birth, and by ten years they are 48 percent of this figure. By contrast, failed entrants, those not surviving to year ten, are only 20 percent of the average industry size at birth.

The importance of entry and exit phenomena to the market dynamic both in their own right and in relation to productivity growth is incontrovertible, and so a deeper explanation of the two processes and their interconnection is an important aspect of a population dynamics perspective. This is an old theme, traceable back to Marshall and the 'trees in the forest' metaphor and the idea that economic events can follow patterned sequences. Recent work, particularly by Klepper and his co-workers, has thrown a great deal of light on these phenomena under the guise of the 'shakeout' hypothesis.[6] The general observation is that entry and exit patterns follow an ordered sequence over the life of the industry as it gradually evolves towards an oligopoly. The industry becomes as it were an organic whole, subject to growth and development, as it interacts with its environment to establish a supporting niche.

However, at some point in this lifecycle a drastic reduction occurs in the number of viable firms, the 'shakeout', which forms the break between a pre-history and a post-history of the industry. Thus, studies of the auto, television, tyre and

[6] I draw upon the following references in this account. References to earlier work by Klepper are contained within them. Klepper (2002), Klepper and Simons (1997, 2000, 2005), Buenstorf and Klepper (2005). The recent work by Buenstorf and Klepper (2005) puts more emphasis on fission processes in the tyre industry and finds that leading firms disproportionately generate spin-offs. This leads them to an explanation of regional concentration in the industry based on inherited organizational capabilities and their reproduction in other firms. They suggest that this account explains the industry history more accurately than do explanations based on agglomeration economies.

penicillin industries all conform to an entry–exit pattern with several common features:

- All four industries converged to stable oligopolies over a period lasting 30 years or more, with the number of firms dropping by between 77 percent to 97 percent from the peak;
- Entry is concentrated predominantly before the shakeout but exit is distributed across the life of the industry as the forces of selection impose concentration;
- The survival probabilities vary systematically with the age of firm and with the place of a firm in the entry sequence. Early entrants tend to have lower hazard rates than later entrants and it is the timing of entry that most affects the age-to-exit relation;
- Prior experience of an entrant in another industry (compare Baldwin and Gu's findings on diversified entrants relative to green-field entrants, also) significantly improves the probability of survival although this effect decays as ages increase;
- Entrants who draw on core knowledge from other activities also have enhanced prospects of survival (Mitchell, 1989; Helfat and Leiberman, 2002; Thompson, 2002).

Other studies confirm these general findings. For example, Horvath et al. (2001), apply similar methods to the US brewing industry and the shakeout that occurred in the late nineteenth century when the number of firms dropped by 40 percent in a decade. In addition, the pioneering work by organizational ecologists provides important support to these general findings in terms of the connection of firm birth and death rates with the evolving density of the population. These are more ecologically grounded models focusing on the changing carrying capacity of an environment and the age dependence of firm/organizational performance.[7] Since the USA is potentially a special case because of its size and cultural specificity, confirmation of these findings from other economies is particularly significant. Thus a paper by Yamamura et al. (2005) finds essentially the same phenomena in the growth of the Japanese motor cycle post-1945. The shakeout occurs in 1955 when there were 71 producers, whereafter the industry declines towards a four-firm oligopoly. This process is marked by continuous improvements in product quality, a declining trend growth rate in their overall market and a marked shift in the location of the industry in Japan. Innovation by a market leader (Honda) played a key role in establishing a new dominant design around which the industry subsequently coalesced including the three other members of the current oligopoly who entered from a background in other industries.

This field of research has proved remarkably fruitful and is capable of much further extension to other industries and to comparisons of the same industry across different countries. Yet much more can be said conceptually in relation to

[7] See the special issue of *Industrial and Corporate Change* (2004: 13(1)) for a stock-taking of the literature.

entry and exit processes. Exit is not a flow profitability decision but a balance sheet decision and many factors can stand between negative profits and exit, accumulated reserves, public subsidy or support from a different branch of the firm's activities, the prospects for selling on the capital value of the business into new ownership or a different line of production. Optimistic expectations may foster injudicious entry. They may also encourage a firm to hang on irrationally in the hope of better times. Over the longer term, these factors may wash out and leave profit performance as the relevant discriminator between survival and exit on average, if not for explaining the demise of individual firms. Systematic changes in the environment also extend beyond technology. The typical phenomenon that the rate of growth of the market declines as the industry matures will put pressure on margins even though the industry is still expanding. Competition from foreign producers too, and export opportunities are often significant and so we can generalize the population of firms to those located in different countries, as we should for example in relation to the growth of the Japanese motor cycle industry already discussed (p. 74). As we pursue these developments, we see the broad contours of enterprise and economic evolution and the different routes through which selection acts to determine economic fitness and survival. From a system viewpoint it is important that the rules of the game facilitate efficient entry and exit. It matters that when a firm 'dies' the capabilities within it are readily available for other uses including the capabilities of the founders if they are still active. Hence the importance of the market for corporate control in facilitating the takeover of business units that are ailing in their current performance but which can be deployed more effectively in different markets under different management. More generally the role of selection in relation to exit and indeed entry cannot be reduced to the sole role of product markets. Markets for labour and for capital more generally should be part of the explanation of a wider industry dynamics.

3.7 Contrasting theories of the entrepreneur: Destruction and creation

Even among economists who recognize the prime importance of the entrepreneur there are contrasting perspectives to be contended with. The best way to illustrate this is to outline the positions of two of the acknowledged dominant figures, Joseph Schumpeter and Israel Kirzner, Austrian economists of very different persuasions.

Schumpeter's analysis brings together stability in the capitalist *order* with instability in the capitalist *system.* The continuous transformations in economic form are associated with the creation and application of new combinations that arise from within the otherwise relatively more stable order of overarching institutions (Schumpeter, 1928). As he expressed the point,

> ... what we unscientifically call economic progress means essentially putting productive resources to uses *hitherto untried in practice,* and withdrawing them from the uses they have served so far. (p. 378, emphasis in original)

Schumpeter's concept of innovation is supply-oriented, consumers are claimed to be passive elements in the innovation process merely adapting to the offers provided by firms. Innovation occurs in the sphere of production and the new combinations that define innovations express themselves in changes in input–output relations or in production functions, and so redefine cost and productivity relationships. Generally, he argues, this involves the construction of a new plant embodied in a new firm founded for the purpose, and the rise to leadership of new 'men'. Innovations do not typically come from old businesses and when they are associated with established businesses, they involve new forms of internal organization. This process is a competitive process in which old firms either adapt to the new competitive circumstances or decline and die.

The phenomena produced by innovation are quite different from those associated with the growth of population of capital accumulation around existing lines of business activity and cannot be treated as an extension of the accepted theories of economic organization, such as those associated with Walras or Marshall. In response to innovation, the most complete command of routine counts for nothing because the effects of innovation are kaleidoscopic, they render existing views of the world redundant. However, the path to entrepreneurship is never easy and three reasons for this are adumbrated: resistance to new phenomena on the part of the threatened parties, difficulty in acquiring resources or changing consumer behaviour, and the human barriers to committing to a new path of behaviour. However, once an entrepreneur has shown the way, other less entrepreneurial followers imitate the pioneer and establish a competitive process in which the innovation discovers a niche in the economic framework. The effects of this process are distributed unevenly across the system and over time, in many cases, railroads, electrification are favourite examples, imposing major adaptive responses on the economy so that it becomes a different economy. Disharmony is inherent in the very modus operandi of innovation-based evolution, and this cannot be described, let alone understood, in terms of sequences of comparative static adjustments to exogenous changes in economic data.

The deeper economic significance of the entrepreneurial process is that it transforms an economy from within, creating a new pattern of relative prices and thus altering the incentive structure facing subsequent entrepreneurs. It is a process that is irreversible, open and path-dependent in its effects. Innovations are introduced in the context of a prevailing price structure that validates the innovation in terms of profitability. Of those that pass this test and earn economic profits proper, a process of competitive, imitative entry follows which expands supply and destroys the profits as the economy adapts to a new price system. As Schumpeter so graphically expressed the matter, profit 'Is at the same time the child and the victim of development' (1934: 154). Not only are profits uniquely connected to innovation, they also form the principal source of saving and the basis for private family fortunes and the growth of new business dynasties. Entrepreneurial capitalism is clearly an uncomfortable place and it is not surprizing that entrepreneurs should seek to protect their profits from the effects of competition and be willing to sabotage the innovative effects of others.

One of the most important and least explored aspects of Schumpeter's theory is its precise location within the institutions of a monetary economy with its panoply of banks and credit instruments. The entrepreneurial 'new men' do not normally own the means of production—the fixed and working capital to establish the enterprise, and so they must turn to the banks to extend credit, often when no collateral exists. The banks must be independent agents without stake in the gains of the enterprise other than those contracted for in the loans granted, and it is the existence of the need to finance innovation that makes the interest rate positive. At a minimum innovation is a pillar of interest, it is an index of the rate of development after correcting for changes in the general purchasing power of money. That Schumpeter should locate his analysis within the institutions of a monetized, credit economy is of immense importance for it underpins the radical, transformative nature of the entrepreneurial process. Via access to credit, entrepreneurs sidestep the hold on resources of established businesses and are able to prise away those resources and deploy them in the new combinations. It is indeed difficult to see this happening with such ease in a barter economy.

In this sketch of the mature Schumpeter's view, we find many of the themes that have absorbed the time of subsequent scholars of innovation and the entrepreneur. Entrepreneurial activity is the introduction of novel change into the economy, novel meaning not previously known in that context. More than that, it is intrinsic to the idea of novelty that it cannot be foreseen or reduced to an expression of calculable risk; hence the view that the entrepreneur deals in radical uncertainty. Since the consequences of novel ideas cannot be predicted in advance, it follows that all entrepreneurial plans are blind variations in Campbell's sense.

To what extent are entrepreneurs different from artists more generally?—Only in that their conjectures are about business plans. However, there is much more to the entrepreneurial function than having novel thoughts. The entrepreneur must bring the conjecture to fruition in a working business organization for it to be tested by the market, and thoughts must be turned to profitable action if the conjecture is to be of consequence. The entrepreneurial function necessarily extends to the ability to assemble the requisite productive resources, engage with the potential consumers and organize the business. Thus, the idea that what is unique to the entrepreneurial function is business leadership. Here we find the modern emphasis on the new small firm as the prototypical vehicle for entrepreneurial action, and more precisely the new technology-based firm. If entrepreneurship is equated only with business leadership, all business-founding events fall into the net, yet only a few of them will be transformative in the novel sense that Schumpeter meant. Most will be the continuation or minor imitation of established business ideas necessary to preserve the replication of the existing structure of the economy rather than transform it. From a Schumpeterian perspective, these should be excluded from the ambit of entrepreneurship and leadership. We should conclude not that leadership is irrelevant but rather that it is only one component in the Schumpeterian view of the entrepreneur. Schumpeter's aim was to explain the radical self-transformation in the activities and structure of modern capitalist economies as a whole. The entrepreneur as mere business leader does not capture this view at all adequately.

There is a further aspect to Schumpeter's framework, which resonates in the modern world, that of the supply of capital to the prospective entrepreneur; not through the banking system but through capital markets more generally and venture capital markets in particular. The ideas of business angels, of specialized stock markets in which investors can realize their investment exit through an initial public offering, and of corporate venturing by large businesses are newly instituted variations on the Schumpeterian theme that credit markets matter in an experimental economy.

The Schumpeterian perspective on the entrepreneur has provided a compelling framework for many scholars whose central interest is the economics of innovation (Nelson and Winter, 1984; Loasby, 1991, 1999; Andersen, 1994; Metcalfe, 1998; Witt, 1998; Dosi, 2000). However, it is not without its rivals, indeed, an entire School of Austrian inspired thought, associated in particular with Israel Kirzner (1978), stands as a contrast to the innovation-based perspective. Whereas Schumpeter gave the entrepreneur a narrow focus, for the Austrians more generally, the entrepreneur and enterprise are pervasive and fundamental in economic terms, indeed markets cannot work without entrepreneurs. As with Schumpeter there is an emphasis on radical ignorance, a complete unawareness of information that is relevant to choice and action, but the conclusion drawn is rather different. What defines entrepreneurship is alertness to situations where resources are under- or over-valued. *Pace* Schumpeter, the entrepreneur does not create economic uncertainty; rather he/she overcomes the effects of radical ignorance by eliminating market errors. For Kirzner this is the core of the market process. The limited understanding of individuals, arising from the uneven distribution of economic information creates multiple arbitrage opportunities where products and resources are incorrectly valued in their current uses. The alert entrepreneur spots these opportunities and carries out the steps to eliminate the inconsistencies they imply.

Thus, whereas Schumpeter's emphasis is upon the disruption to established economic practices implied by innovation, for Kirzner, entrepreneurship is a non-innovating, cohesive, equilibrating force in whose absence the market economy could not work. Profits accrue to the entrepreneur but these cannot be related to the value of any resources. Instead, they are the reward for alertness, for making the correct conjectures. It follows that economic equilibrium is the end point at which no discoveries remain to be made and this is a highly implausible state of affairs. For perfect knowledge is an unattainable situation precisely because learning processes are individual and idiosyncratic, they have no collective, ultimate limit and the context of learning is the market process itself. Thus, the entrepreneur as innovator is contrasted with entrepreneur as market arbitrager—two quite different takes on what entrepreneurship means; if one is destructive, the other is constructive, yet in construction the conditions for further destruction are created.

It is easy to over-emphasize the differences between these different perspectives; perhaps instead we should recognize that any workable notion of entrepreneurship would have to cover a spectrum of possibilities. Eliminating unexploited gains from trade in the context of existing activities may lack the glamour of the hero entrepreneur, but is equally contingent on the exercise of imagination, equally contingent on the ability to form conjectures about different possible future economic worlds, equally dependent upon a faith in, and commitment to, non- scientific statements that may turn out to be false. Both entail a view of competition as a discovery process that changes the discoverer. For neither Schumpeter nor Kirzner is entrepreneurship a factor that can be supplied in measurable units. It is an attribute of individuals, an attribute of discovering, which is not amenable to rational optimizing calculus (Ripsas, 1998). Finally, they share a common perspective of fundamental importance, the experimenting nature of the economic process. More than anything else, entrepreneurs are the creators of new economic experiments and it is this aspect that enables us to identify the two dimensions of entrepreneurship which make it fit so uncomfortably with modern economic theory, namely, its relation to the growth of knowledge, and the impossibility of fitting it within an equilibrium framework of economic action.

3.8 The market process

The famous definition of economic theory provided by Lionel Robbins (1932), that it is a set of principles to govern the disposition of scarce resources to the satisfaction of unlimited ends, turns out to leave no room for the entrepreneur.

In part, this is a result of the associated emphasis on rational calculation in known circumstances but much more fundamentally, it is because of the role that the idea of equilibrium plays in this scheme of thought. When resources, the preferences of final consumers, and the available productive and organizational knowledge are given, a set of prices are identified that permit all individuals and co-operating teams to fulfill their plans to buy and sell inputs and outputs to the letter. Such an outcome is defined as a market equilibrium relative to the determining data. Now, as Baumol (1968) made clear, such a framework assumes that enterprise has run its course; what it needs is management, the husbanding of the scarce resources in the most economically efficient way as determined by market price signals. Management makes routine decisions within known constraints to meet established objectives, it involves the stewardship of the resources owned or contractually controlled by the firm, and the managers are rewarded according to the value of the productive services they provide, just like any other form of labour. The managerial function is primarily one of rational calculation of the course of action that meets the objectives of the owners of the firm, usually assumed to be the maximization of profits or residual income and to implement policies to achieve this. Clearly, the constraints and objectives considered by managers must be known with sufficient precision to permit these Olympian calculations. Management is quite consistent with the search for incremental improvements in economic efficiency, in response to changes in the economic environment but these responses are passive as distinct from initiatory, they involve mechanical application of established rules to already established activity. A very considerable portion of modern economic theory replicates this simple, adaptive view, however sophisticated the argument may be, the fundamental frame is one of rational optimization in the presence of given constraints or given constraints generating constraints, and adaptation to impose a new optimum when these constraints change. In this scheme, there can be no problem of knowledge per se. From this perspective, the managerial function is everything that entrepreneurship is not. It takes the frame of action as given, and its task is to reduce uncertainty to calculable risk (Schon, 1965). In fact, we can go further, the structure of this kind of economic theory rules out any consideration of enterprise and the entrepreneur as a matter of its logical structure (Loasby, 1991)

The root cause of the difficulty is the notion that markets are in equilibrium in the sense that there is no internally generated scope for change, from which follows the necessity of explaining all economic change by exogenous changes in preferences or resources or technology. If equilibrium means states of rest relative to the given data then all change is without an economic explanation, for if decisions are correct and mutually consistent there can be no internal reason to change them. If this is the core of the theory of market equilibrium, we must immediately recognize it as fundamentally different from the theory of the market process. In the Schumpeterian and Austrian perspectives, markets do not generate equilibrium they generate order, they solve a problem—that of allocating resources to meet needs—but that order necessarily generates its own internal reasons to change. All patterns of order in a modern, entrepreneurial economy are necessarily transient, they are continually destroyed from within, they are naturally restless.

This change in view is not a matter of semantics but a fundamental difference in perspective and understanding of the underpinnings of economic activity; an understanding of the role that the entrepreneur plays in bringing new knowledge into the economic process. Order, a coherent economic structure that 'solves' the resource allocation problem more or less satisfactorily, is not equilibrium because every economic order necessarily generates the means to change that order and does so from within by the creation of new knowledge and the stimuli this gives to new business conjectures. If, following Knight (1946), we accept that human behaviour is inherently 'explorative and experimental' (p. 107), we also must accept that the solving of problems is not a closed process, every problem solved is a new set of problems created, if not for the individual, then for the wider economic system, in a process of action and reaction to the consequences of new understanding. Economic self-organization is the solution to a problem that in its emergence transforms the problem.[8] The day-to-day flow of economic activity necessarily generates flows of new information, which influences the minds of countless individuals, some of whom are then stimulated to conjecture new economic arrangements. Those who are able to act on these conjectures are acting entrepreneurially and their actions change yet again the flow of information generated within the economic process. This is why economic change is fundamentally endogenous. To claim that a market or an economy is in equilibrium, would be to claim that no new conjectures where forthcoming, that new thoughts had ceased to flow everywhere in the economy, that from the epistemological viewpoint the system was perfectly correlated and dead. Thus the fundamental problem; economic order is economic equilibrium only when it is assumed that knowledge is stationary, or when we abstract the economic process for its epistemological underpinnings. To do so is to disassociate the economic process from time and from the nature of human kind and if we do this, we should not be surprized if the entrepreneur and the associated problems of profits, losses, hopes and disappointments, growth and decline disappear from view.

This is the force of the claim above all that economies are knowledge-based economies and could not be otherwise, and that knowledge is never, nor ever could be, stationary. This is the essential point about entrepreneurial activity; it reflects the fundamental nature of human knowledge and the consequence that economic knowledge does not exist separately from an economy. From our evolutionary

[8] Knight (1930), in an essay devoted to explaining why economic development cannot be explained as a tendency towards equilibrium, writes of the self-exciting and cumulative nature of economic progress.

perspective, knowledge and the economy are mutually constituted and they co-evolve; although the system is ordered, it is permanently in a non-equilibrium state precisely because the very operation of the system generates new beliefs, new facts, new correlations in the minds of individuals that lead them to act entrepreneurially. Far from being an optional add-on, enterprise and the entrepreneur are the defining characteristics of the market order. The interesting feature of capitalism in this regard is that it appears to be an instituted frame precisely designed to transform economic activity from within.

Any confusion between order and equilibrium is undoubtedly grounded in the belief that resource allocation has a rational, constrained means, but unlimited ends explanation. Brian Loasby (1999) has captured this point with his usual perspicacity, when he points out that discretionary behaviour is essential to innovation. We cannot allow for the entrepreneur if we seek to pre-programme choice in its entirety. Then there is only the rational, mechanical response, no role for imagining different economic worlds and no escape from the tyranny of optimization.[9] This does not mean that calculation is irrelevant only that the choices and the constraints are not always obvious or perceived in the same way by different individuals. From an evolutionary perspective, what matters is not optimization per se, but differential optimizations in similar circumstances. In short we can find a place for the entrepreneur only if we see economic order as a lived experience in which flows of information are generated to confirm or challenge existing beliefs and thus to change knowledge and its distribution.

The tendency of modern economics to ignore this perspective is reflected in another of its methodological dimensions, that is, the resort to the representative agent as the embodiment of all that is necessary to define an economic equilibrium. It goes without saying that this device eliminates the possibility of the entrepreneur at a stroke, since to act entrepreneurially is to engage in novel economic action, action that is necessarily non-representative. Quite obviously, innovation of any kind is impossible to imagine in such a scheme. To incorporate the entrepreneur is to recognize the immense diversity that characterizes economic action. Such diversity can be captured, as Alchian (1950) suggested, in a statistic such as the mean, median of mode of the relevant distributions of behaviour but, the point is, such representative statistics cannot be defined *ex ante*, they are the emergent outcomes of the economic process. Thus, equilibrium and the representative agent are two of a kind. They are used because the theories in which they are embedded have no role for internally driven change, no role for the entrepreneur, no role for the embedded growth of knowledge.

These difficulties are amplified in a third area, that of an analysis of the path to equilibrium following some exogenous changes in data, the material of many an undergraduate exercise. Here it is essential to know whether the system in view is

[9] Knight (1946: 106).

stable or not—if disturbed, will it follow a path to a new state of rest? Two problems immediately arise. The lesser of the two is that the theory of rational behaviour that defines an equilibrium does not carry over to explain how the agents in the economy respond to being out of equilibrium. The speed of response to out-of-equilibrium circumstances is in this sense arbitrary; it has no rationalization in the underlying theory—nor can it. This is the nature of an equilibrium theory. Kirzner understood this well and we have seen that his class of entrepreneurial theory is designed to explain how non-ordered situations are acted on entrepreneurially. However, limited this explanation might be it does deal with the latent schizophrenia that results from otherwise rational individuals following non-rational adjustment processes. Kirzner's entrepreneurs are rational, not in that they maximize in a narrow sense but that they are alert to profit opportunities. The second difficulty is more fundamental, and it concerns the assumption that the position of equilibrium is invariant to any non-equilibrium motion around it. How can this be? Surely, only if the experience of non-equilibrium situations conveys no new information to the market participants, that is to say, only if we again and quite unjustifiably, separate the generation of knowledge from the economic process. As soon as this assumption that we are dealing with transitions is dropped, we must recognize that all market orders are path-dependent and indeed accept the possibility that the evolution of the market order is entirely open-ended. There may be no economic attractors, for the very process of approaching them will destroy them. Only history and motion remain—but always in the context of market order. Perhaps that is the Faustian bargain made in the evolution of modern capitalism, that we drink at the well of new knowledge but know not where this leads us.

3.9 Managers and entrepreneurs

In the light of this discussion, it is useful to elaborate the distinction drawn in the introduction between entrepreneurs and managers, particularly in view of the possibility that the manager can live quite comfortably in an equilibrium world whereas the entrepreneur cannot. While it is essential to separate the two categories of entrepreneur and manager as functions, in reality it is difficult to do so, and risks obscuring the importance of different kinds of entrepreneurship and of disconnecting the firm from the knowledge through which it is constituted. Thus when Baird (1994) defines the entrepreneur as 'a person who assembles all the resources physically necessary for the production of a good which he then resells to consumers' (p. 144), this risks equating entrepreneurship with management *tout court*. Similarly Mintzberg (1975) in his classic study of what managers do, distinguished three roles, personal, informational and decisional and lumped together enterprise, with allocating resources and responding to disturbances in the environment in the last category.

Not surprizingly, the demarcation of the two activities has been contested terrain. Hartmann (1959), for example, argued that entrepreneurship is a type of management that is pervasive and, *pace* Schumpeter, it cannot be equated solely with the introduction of innovations in the economy. As a species of management within organizations, its distinguishing characteristic is leadership, the making of decisions of strategic importance. What distinguishes the manager with entrepreneurial attributes is its possession of formal, non-functional, ultimate authority associated with the performance of non-routine activities. Here there is a close connection with the Weberian idea of bureaucratic leadership in which authority is linked to charisma, a particular skill at leadership and the motivation of others. In turn, authority is linked to broader cultural traditions including the acceptance of rights in private property. From this perspective, entrepreneurship is distributed through the higher echelons of an organization and is effectively equated with discretionary behaviour to instigate processes of change and set new goals in the organization rather than organize established activity. In this view, there is considerable overlap with Eliasson's idea (1990) of the top management team as the locus of entrepreneurial activity. It is the top team that enjoys discretionary behaviour to create the templates of rules that others in the firm must work too.

Ulrich Witt (1998) has also argued that the entrepreneur's role is to generate a different model of business and to have the leadership skills to ensure that the other members of the firm internalize the model as their correlated framework for understanding. An entrepreneurial theory of the firm presupposes not only organization, but also a sense of purpose and motivation and, indeed, leadership and charisma; not only passive routines but also a conceptual framework in which the business opportunity can be developed further. As Witt rightly suggests, entrepreneurship must be understood in the context of bounded rationality to reflect the judgemental nature of entrepreneurial beliefs and the limiting effect of cognitive frames and their filter effects on information (Fransman, 1994). Members of the firm have to coordinate their actions and this requires a correlated degree of understanding. Not everybody need understand everything that happens in the firm, indeed such a requirement would prevent a division of labour, but these happenings must be connected, again through the role of the top management team. As in the economy more widely, so in the firm, knowledge is not the preserve of any one individual but of the group that is defined as the firm. How to use widely dispersed knowledge reflects the organization as a distributed knowledge system (Tsoukas, 1996). Now, the correlation of knowledge and beliefs is a social process. By interacting and observing others and by sharing experiences together, coordinated, ordered action is made possible. Thus, we may see the organization of the firm as the operator that simultaneously ensures managerial correlation of understanding across its activities while leaving open the possibility of entrepreneurial action to de-correlate those understandings. Not surprizingly, this is exactly the function of the market system as a whole, to permit evolution within order. The higher order correlation required for management requires a shared cognitive frame—the top cognitive frame that must encompass the business plan in all its dimensions. Yet any frame is also a set of blinkers that limits the scope for new thoughts and beliefs. Hence, one of the central problems faced by any firm: how to frame its activities efficiently and effectively while permitting flexibility to external pressures, and simultaneously being open to entrepreneurial conjectures (Nonaka and Toyama, 2002). Thus, just as entrepreneurship and the market process are complements, so are entrepreneurs and managers. From this follows the difficulty of seeing the entrepreneur as an ideal type embodying unique traits, the importance of placing the entrepreneur in social and organizational context, and the need to understand the trade-offs and incentives that result in managerial or entrepreneurial action from the same individuals (Thornton, 1999).

If we take this view of entrepreneurship, what view of the firm follows to parallel the view of the market? As a starting point, it is surely clear that firm and market are not substitutes but complements, and that firms can achieve outcomes that are entirely beyond the scope of markets and vice versa. Markets are about processes of exchange but firms are about the combination of resources for specific productive purposes. The firm is more than an allocating device, it is the locus of decision about what to do and has the unique role of defining and combining the multiple kinds of knowledge required to operate the productive function. Thus, firms have to combine knowledge and resources having first made a decision as to what it is that is to be produced. It is simply an error to imagine that markets can do the same. What is specifically important about the entrepreneur is the vision of new resource combinations and the capacity to articulate such visions in practice through the creation of a productive organization, drawing on markets as necessary. Thus, as Schumpeter argued, and resource-based theorists have subsequently elaborated (Alvarez and Busenitz, 2001), innovations require new combinations of resources—the creation of additional heterogeneity in the economy. Edith Penrose (1961) still provides the best line of advance for this way of thinking about the firm with the view that the managerial team in solving its current problems gains new knowledge and insight from which it may define new opportunities to occupy its attention. Thus, the services of the team are simultaneously managerial and entrepreneurial; both concepts are needed to understand the development of the firm and the productive services that are derived from the bundles of resources under the control of the firm.

In this we can perhaps accept that there is more to enterprise than innovation. It certainly includes changing the rules in many different ways but it also must include responding to those changes via investment or whatever is needed to draw the full potential from an innovation.

3.10 Concluding thoughts

Schumpeter has the distinction not only of placing the entrepreneur at the centre of the process of economic development but of providing a clear articulation of the link between innovation and economic evolution. Innovations are new ways of using and defining resources, they add to the economic variety in the system and the response of the system is the competitive process of growth, decline and structural change. If innovation is variation, then competition is selection, and both are essential to economic change (Nelson and Winter, 1984; Metcalfe, 1998; Cohen and Malerba, 2001). An entrepreneur does not compete by replicating what rivals do but by holding different beliefs and expectations, and having the market assign positive profit to those differences. This is the essential dynamic of economic evolution, it is the economic variety in the system that governs the pace and direction of change. Since the process generates further changes in economic opportunity, we find a place for the Kirznerian idea of the entrepreneur as the agent of the market process, ever alert to new opportunities created by the wider evolution of the system. If one problem leads to further problems then the idea of economic evolution as a cumulative process of unfolding of opportunities falls naturally into place. However, left to itself competition destroys economic variety both absolutely, as some activities disappear, and relatively, as some come to dominate their rivals in economic importance. Without some process to regenerate this variety, economic progress would come to an abrupt end. Here we find the importance of the idea of capitalism as an experimental system, a system that has established instituted frameworks of open market and scientific and technological search to regenerate economic variety (Nelson and Winter, 1982). These instituted frameworks define the nature of modern capitalism as a naturally competitive, knowledge-based system and give substance to the idea that economic change is endogenous, that market economies are strongly ordered but never in equilibrium. From this follows our conclusion about the nature of the entrepreneur as the agent ultimately responsible for changing economic knowledge. In this capacity, the entrepreneur is both destructive—de-correlating existing knowledge—and constructive—bringing new patterns of resource use into existence through the market process and so correlating new knowledge. Knowledge of science and technology is important for the modern entrepreneur but not in itself sufficient, it must be combined with knowledge of market and organization, and it is this, which makes entrepreneurial insight so valuable.

Undoubtedly the wider conditions which influence the extension of enterprise are of great importance, whether in terms of taxation of income and wealth, access to risk capital, regulations to permit the creation of new businesses, or the rules that enforce bankruptcy, and so forth. They define an agenda for entrepreneurial policy. This is the focus of Baumol (1993) when he suggests that policy can influence the payoffs to different kinds of entrepreneurship. However, this may not take us far enough if the question of entrepreneurial opportunity is not addressed. We have suggested that the core of the problem is necessarily defined in relation to the conditions surrounding the creation of new economic knowledge and, while one cannot legislate for creativity, let alone teach it, one can encourage open communication of ideas and the formation of distributed networks of collaborators in the innovation process.

Any approach to the study of the economy which is framed in terms of equilibrium will miss the essential point about modern capitalism: that it is strongly ordered but restless. As a system it can never be in equilibrium because knowledge can never be in equilibrium, and knowledge is not something separate from the economy but rather is intrinsic to its operation. It is because an experimental capitalism is intrinsically restless that the standard of living and the very nature of economic and social life now change so rapidly and so unevenly across the globe with consequences that are both good and bad. Restless capitalism is necessarily uncomfortable capitalism. To understand its restless nature we need to place the notion of entrepreneurship at the heart of the analysis, for the entrepreneur is the crucial agent whose role it is to generate new economic knowledge and thus transform the structure of economic activity. In so doing, new opportunities for entrepreneurial action are created from within the economy. Consequently, the most important aspect of modern capitalism is that just as knowledge creates further knowledge so entrepreneurship creates further entrepreneurship through the institutions of the market economy. That is why economic evolution is necessarily endogenous and could not be otherwise, and why market, firm, competitive process and entrepreneur are indissolubly linked.

References

ADAMAN, F. and P. DEVINE (2002). 'A Reconsideration of the Theory of Entrepreneurship: A Participatory Approach'. *Review of Political Economy*, 14: 329–55.

ALCHIAN, A. (1950). 'Uncertainty. Evolution and Economic Theory'. *Journal of Political Economy*, 60: 211–21.

ALVAREZ, S. A. and L. W. BUSENITZ (2001). 'The Entrepreneurship of Resource-Based Theory'. *Journal of Management*, 27: 755–75.

ANDERSEN, E. S. (1994). *Evolutionary Economics: Post Schumpeterian Contributions.* London: Pinter.

AUDRETSCH, D. B. (1995). 'Innovation. Growth and Survival'. *International Journal of Industrial Organization*, 13: 441–57.

BAIRD, C. W. (1994). 'Profit and Loss', in P. BOETTKE (ed.) *The Elgar Companion to Austrian Economics.* Cheltenham: Edward Elgar.

BALDWIN, J. R. and W. GU (2005). 'Competition, Firm Turnover and Productivity Growth'. *Mimeo.* Micro Economic Analysis Division, Statistics Canada, Ottawa.

—— and M. RAFIQUZZAMAN (1995). 'Selection vs. Evolutionary Adaptation: Learning and Post-Entry Performance'. *International Journal of Industrial Organization*, 13: 501–22.

BARTLESMANN, E. and M. DOMS (2000). 'Understanding Productivity: Lessons from Longitudinal Data'. *Journal of Economic Literature*, 38: 569–94.

BAUMOL, W. J. (1968). 'Entrepreneurship in Economic Theory'. *American Economic Review*, 58: 64–71.

—— (1990). 'Entrepreneurship: Productive. Unproductive. and Destructive'. *Journal of Political Economy*, 98: 893–921.

—— (1993). *Entrepreneurship. Management and the Structure of Payoffs.* Boston: MIT Press.

BUENSTORF, G. and S. KLEPPER (2005). 'Heritage and Agglomeration: The Akron Tire Cluster Revisited'. *Mimeo.* Jena: Evolutionary Economics Group, MPI.

CASSON, M. (1982). *The Entrepreneur: An Economic Theory.* Totowa, N.J.: Barnes & Noble Books.

CAVES, R. (1998). 'Industrial Organization and New Findings on the Turnover and Mobility of Firms'. *Journal of Economic Literature*, 36: 1947–82.

CHRISTENSEN, C. M. (1997). *The Innovator's Dilemma.* Boston: Harvard Business School Press.

COHEN, W. and F. MALERBA (2001). 'Is the Tendency to Variation a Chief Cause of Progress?' *Industrial and Corporate Change*, 10: 587–608.

DOSI, G. (2000). *Innovation. Organization and Economic Dynamics.* Cheltenham: Edward Elgar.

EDQUIST, C., F. MALERBA, J. S. METCALFE and F. MONTOBBIO (2003). 'Sectoral Systems: Implications for European Technology Policy'. *ESSY Working Paper.* Bocconi University.

ELIASSON, G. (1990). 'The Firm as a Competent Team'. *Journal of Economic Behaviour and Organization*, 13: 275–98.

FRANSMAN, M. (1994). 'Information. Knowledge Vision and Theories of the Firm'. *Industrial and Corporate Change*, 3: 713–58.

GEROSKI, P. (1995). 'What do we Know about Entry?' *International Journal of Industrial Organization*, 13: 421–40.

GIBBONS, M., C. LIMOGES, H. NOWOTNY, S. SCHWARTZMAN, P. SCOTT and M. TROW (1994). *The New Production of Knowledge.* Sage: London.

GRONOW, J. and A. WARDE (eds) (2003). *Ordinary Consumption.* London: Routledge.

HARTMANN, H. (1959). 'Managers and Entrepreneurs: A Useful Distinction?' *Administrative Science Quarterly*, 3: 429–451.

HAYEK, F. A. (1976). *Law. Legislation and Liberty: The Mirage of Social Justice*, vol. 2. Chicago: Chicago University Press.

—— (1979). *Law. Legislation and Liberty: The Political Order of a Free People*, vol. 3. Chicago: Chicago University Press.

Helfat, C. E. and M. B. Leiberman (2002). 'The Birth of Capabilities: Market Entry and the importance of Pre History'. *Industrial and Corporate Change*, 11: 725–60.

Horvath, M., F. Schivardi and M. Woywode (2001). 'On Industry Life Cycles: Entry and Shakeout in Beer Brewing'. *International Journal of Industrial Organization*, 19: 1023–42.

Hughes, T. P. (1971). *Elmer Sperry: Inventor and Engineer*. Baltimore: Johns Hopkins University Press.

Kirzner, I. M. (1978). *Competition and Entrepreneurship*. Chicago: Chicago University Press.

Klepper, S. (2002). 'Firm Survival and the Evolution of Oligopoly'. *RAND Journal of Economics*, 33: 37–61.

—— and K. L. Simons (1997). 'Technological Extinctions of Industrial Firms: An Enquiry into their Nature and Causes'. *Industrial and Corporate Change*, 6: 379–460.

—— and—— (2000). 'The Making of an Oligopoly: Firm Survival and Technological Change in the Evolution of the US Tire Industry'. *Journal of Political Economy*, 108: 728–60.

—— and—— (2005). 'Industry Shakeouts and Technological Change'. *International Journal of Industrial Organization*, 23: 23–43.

Knight, F. (1921). *Risk, Uncertainty and Profit*. Boston: Houghton Mifflin.

—— (1930). 'Statics and Dynamics: Some Queries Regarding the Mechanical Analogy in Economics'. Reprinted in *The Ethics of Competition* (ed. R. Boyd, 1997). London: Transaction Publishers.

—— (1946). 'Immutable Law in Economics: Its Reality and Limitations'. *American Economic Review* (May) 36: 93–111.

Kuznets, S. (1977). 'Two Centuries of Economic Growth: Reflections on US Experience'. *American Economic Review*, 67: 1–14.

Livesay, H. C. (1995). *Entrepreneurship and the Growth of Firms*. Cheltenham: Edward Elgar.

Loasby, B. (1991). *Equilibrium and Evolution: An Exploration of Connecting Principles in Economics*. Manchester: Manchester University Press.

—— (1999). *Knowledge. Institutions and Evolution in Economics*. London: Routledge.

Marshall, A. (1920). *Principles of Economics* (8th edn). London: Macmillan.

Metcalfe, J. S. (1998). *Evolutionary Economics and Creative Destruction*. London: Routledge.

—— (2003). 'The Entrepreneur and the Style of Modern Economics'. *Journal of Evolutionary Economics*, 14: 157–75.

Millard, A. (1990). *Edison and the Business of Innovation*. Baltimore: Johns Hopkins University Press.

Mintzberg, H. (1975). 'The Manager's Job: Folklore and Fact'. *Harvard Business Review*, (July–August) 53(6): 49–61.

Mitchell, W. (1989). 'Whither and When? Probability and Timing of Incumbent's Entry into Emerging Industrial Subfields'. *Administrative Science Quarterly*, 34: 208–30.

Mowery, D. and Rosenberg, N. (1998). *Paths of Innovation: Technological Change in 20th Century America*. Cambridge: Cambridge University Press.

Nelson, R. and S. Winter (1982). *An Evolutionary Theory of Economic Change*. Harvard: Belknap Press.

Nonaka, I. and R. Toyama (2002). 'A Firm as a Dialectic Being: Towards a Dynamic Theory of a Firm'. *Industrial and Corporate Change*, 11(5): 995–1009.

Penrose, E. (1961). *The Theory of the Growth of the Firm.* Oxford: Blackwell.

Ripsas, S. (1998). 'Towards an Interdisciplinary Theory of Entrepreneurship'. *Small Business Economics,* 10: 103–15.

Robbins, L. (1932). *The Nature and Significance of Economic Science.* London: Macmillan.

Schon, D. (1965). *Technology and Change: The New Heraclitus.* London: Pergamon.

Schumpeter, J. S. (1928). 'The Instability of Capitalism'. *Economic Journal,* 38: 361–86.

—— (1934). *The Theory of Economic Development.* Oxford: Oxford University Press.

—— (1939). *Business Cycles,* vol. I. New York: McGraw Hill Books.

Singh, J. and J. A. C. Baum (1994). *Evolutionary Dynamics of Organizations.* Oxford: Oxford University Press.

Swedberg, R. (ed.) (2000). *Entrepreneurship: The Social Science View.* Oxford: Oxford University Press.

Thompson, P. (2002). 'Surviving in Ships: Firm Capabilities and Survival in the US Iron and Steel Shipbuilding Industry. 1825–1914'. *Mimeo.* Carnegie Mellon University.

Thornton, P. H. (1999). 'The Sociology of Entrepreneurship'. *Annual Review of Sociology,* 25: 19–46.

Tsoukas, H. (1996). 'The Firm as a Distributed Knowledge System: A Constructionist Approach'. *Strategic Management Journal* (Winter) 17: 11–25.

Utterback, J. M. (1994). *Mastering the Dynamics of Innovation.* Boston: Harvard Business School Press.

Witt. U. (1998). 'Imagination and Leadership – The Neglected Dimension of an Evolutionary Theory of the Firm'. *Journal of Economic Behaviour and Organization,* 35: 161–77.

Yamamura, E., T. Sonobe and K. Otsuka (2005). 'Time Path in Innovation. Imitation and Growth: the Case of the Motorcycle industry in Postwar Japan'. *Journal of Evolutionary Economics,* 15: 169–86.

CHAPTER 4

COGNITIVE ASPECTS OF ENTREPRENEURSHIP: DECISION-MAKING AND ATTITUDES TO RISK

NIGEL WADESON

4.1 Introduction

Currently there is significant interest in the application of theories from cognitive psychology (Barsalou, 1992) to the study of entrepreneurship (Forbes, 1999). Enthusiasts of this approach have claimed that the 'traits approach' to explaining why people choose to become entrepreneurs, in which psychological characteristics such as risk-propensity and need for achievement are studied, has largely failed to produce clear-cut results (Shaver and Scott, 1991; Palich and Bagby, 1995). Shaver and Scott (1991: 31) view achievement motivation as the only trait that seems to have a convincing association with new venture creation. They also make methodological criticisms of traits research. As far as risk is concerned, it appears from the evidence that entrepreneurs consider themselves to be no less risk averse than other people.

Because of the somewhat disappointing results of the traits approach some researchers have turned to studying how entrepreneurs think. If the cognitive processes of entrepreneurs are different from others, then this will affect their assessments of opportunities, and their perceptions of the risks that they involve.

This chapter will review literature on the study of the cognition of entrepreneurs, and how this affects their attitudes to risk. The review begins with the heuristics and biases approach. Various decision-making biases related to over-optimism are then considered. Following this perceived self-efficacy, intrinsic motivation, and intentions-based models are discussed. Some theories dealing specifically with attitudes to risk are then covered. These include prospect theory, Kahneman and Lovalo's model of risk-taking, and Das and Teng's theory of risk horizons and future orientations. Finally, the option value and information cost approach to the analysis of entrepreneurs' decision-making is discussed. Some relevant references to culture research are also given in the conclusion.

4.2 Cognitive heuristics and biases

Kahneman and Tversky laid out the heuristics and biases approach to cognitive psychology in the 1970s. This approach claims that people use heuristics in decision-making. Heuristics are mental shortcuts that are used to reduce information overload, and yield quick decisions. However, according to this approach, the use of heuristics can result in systematic biases. Evidence of the existence of biases is claimed as proof of the use of heuristics. The approach differs from authors such as Simon (1957) and Giegerenzer and Todd (1999), in that it stresses not just the use of heuristics as an effective means of making decisions, but also biases that might result from the use of particular heuristics.

Baron (1998) argues that entrepreneurs make decisions in conditions likely to maximize the impact of cognitive biases. These conditions involve high levels of uncertainty, novelty, emotion, time-pressure, and information overload. Busenitz and Barney (1997) put a positive spin on heuristics and biases in entrepreneurs' decision-making, in particular in the start-up years of a venture. They note that the use of heuristics may be crucial in speeding-up and simplifying decision-making, and that overconfidence may be beneficial both in implementing a decision, and in encouraging enthusiasm in others.

Note that there have been significant criticisms of the heuristics and biases approach, though the approach is nonetheless very popular in psychology. Shanteau (1989) gives a review of the debate. Among the criticisms are:

- A failure to specify when people using heuristics perform well, and when they do not, and not enough attention being paid to the adaptation of heuristics;
- A tendency to overstate the generality of biases;
- Experiments on heuristics and biases deny people the tools they need to arrive at the correct answers;
- To identify a bias in decision-making one must know what the 'correct' decision would have been in each case—researchers measure biases relative to what is correct 'in their view';
- A lack of a general theory, or specific models of the underlying processes;
- Unjustified analogies between perceptual illusions and biases resulting from heuristics;
- Experts may not exhibit the biases observed with naïve subjects;
- If a bias is identified, it is difficult to link it to an individual heuristic, as many heuristics might lead to the same bias.

4.2.1 Heuristics

This section will now discuss some heuristics, and then the next section will deal with some of the biases that can result from their use, and their relevance to entrepreneurship. The three best-known heuristics considered under this approach are the availability heuristic, the representativeness heuristic, and anchoring and adjustment (Tversky and Kahneman, 1974).

Availability heuristic

Under the availability heuristic (Tversky and Kahneman, 1973) people base their probability estimate for an outcome on how easy it is for them to imagine it—in other words how 'available' it is to their perceptions. Some outcomes are more available simply because they were more noticeable when they occurred in the past. So more spectacular outcomes are relatively more available. Outcomes that are hard to picture, or difficult to understand, will be perceived as being less probable. These can include those to which a particular person has had little exposure. For instance, people are often more worried about being involved in an aeroplane crash than a road crash, despite road travel being much more dangerous, partly because an airliner crash is a sensational news story.

Representativeness heuristic

Representativeness is how closely an event or object resembles its parent population in its essential properties, and the degree to which it reflects the features of the process that generates it (Kahneman and Tversky, 1972: 431). Under the representativeness heuristic people make decisions according to comparisons with similar situations already known about.

Grether (1980) notes flaws in experimental evidence in psychology literature. He carried out experiments that confirmed predictions based on use of the representativeness heuristic for inexperienced or financially unmotivated subjects, but found the evidence was less clear for others.

Anchoring and adjustment heuristic

Anchoring refers to a tendency to 'anchor' on some initial reference point, which may be suggested by the way a problem is formulated or by some initial computation. The anchor influences perceptions, so that estimates fail to adjust sufficiently from it. For instance if people are asked if the correct price for a good is less than or greater than £30, and are then asked for their best guess of the correct price, they will tend to give an answer to the latter question that is close to £30.

4.2.2 Resulting biases and entrepreneurs

Over-confidence

Over-confident people attach higher probabilities to particular outcomes than are warranted by what they know (Russo and Schoemaker, 1992; Zacharakis and Sheperd, 2001). Over-confidence is equated to having poor meta-knowledge, which is the case where people do not know what they *do*, or *do not*, know. Evidence shows that people are generally over-confident in their beliefs. For references to general research on over-confidence see Brenner et al. (1996).

According to Russo and Schoemaker (1992) over-confidence can result from the availability heuristic, the anchoring and adjustment heuristic, confirmation bias, and from hindsight bias. The confirmation bias (Klayman and Ha, 1987) is a tendency to seek more, and attach greater weight to information that confirms beliefs, and to tend to fail to seek out, and to ignore disconfirming information. Klayman and Ha suggest that people use a positive test strategy as a default heuristic, and that this heuristic often works well, but leads to problems when used in the wrong circumstances. The hindsight bias is a tendency to see past events as having been more predictable than they actually were.

Note that it is not necessarily a 'bias' to collect less information when confident. It is rational to attach less value to information collection when confidence is high (Hirschleifer and Riley, 1979: 1394–7). However, if the level of confidence is not justified, then this itself will bias information collection, even if the information collected is optimal given the initial level of confidence.

Belief in the law of small numbers

Belief in the law of small numbers refers to people overestimating the degree to which small samples of information resemble the population from which they are drawn (Tversky and Kahneman, 1971, 1983). People do this when they follow the representativeness heuristic. Entrepreneurs may tend not to use large samples because they are not available, and because they often do not have the resources necessary to collect them (Busenitz and Barney, 1997).

It has been claimed that entrepreneurs' start-up decisions may be based on biased information because business failures are less well publicized than successes (Simon et al., 2000), and they exist for a shorter time. Simon and Houghton (2002: 115–16) argue that belief in the law of small numbers may explain why entrepreneurs often overestimate demand. According to Busenitz and Barney (1997) entrepreneurs often use biased samples such as a small number of friends or potential customers.

Evidence of biases among entrepreneurs

Simon et al. (2000), in a survey of MBA students' willingness to start businesses, found support for the view that belief in the law of small numbers, and illusion of control both reduce perceptions of risk. This view is further supported by Keh et al. (2002) in a study of owners of top SMEs in Singapore. They followed a similar research methodology, but also tested for planning fallacy bias. In their study, illusion of control was fully mediated by risk perception while Simon et al. found it was only partially mediated by risk perception. Both studies failed to find support for the significance of over-confidence, and Keh et al. also failed to find support for the significance of the planning fallacy. However Busenitz and Barney (1997), in a study of start-up entrepreneurs, found strong support for the view that the entrepreneurs tended to be over-confident and that they employed the representativeness heuristic.

Note that it is particularly crucial in this field to thoroughly consider the methodologies of studies before deciding how much weight to give to the results of each study. Some of the authors explicitly recognize methodological concerns, but further criticisms are also possible. For instance, both Keh et al. (2002) and Simon et al. (2000) follow the methodology of Russo and Schoemaker (1992) in testing for overconfidence. This involves asking each respondent to give 90 percent confidence limits for ten different statistics such as Singapore's unemployment rate in 1999 (Keh et al., 2002: 142). The respondent is judged over-confident if more than one of the true figures lies outside the confidence limits given. One interpretation of this would be that people place too much weight on their central expectations. However it could be argued that such statistical, general knowledge judgements bear little relation to those concerning entrepreneurial opportunities, and so the relevance of the results to entrepreneurial decision-making remains to be proved. The assumption seems to be that if a person exhibits a cognitive bias in making one type of judgement, then he will exhibit the same bias in making entrepreneurial decisions. Note also that psychologists have found that while people tend to be over-confident in general knowledge over-confidence tests, when asked after a test to estimate the number of questions they have answered correctly the estimate given tends to be correct, or too low (Gigerenzer, 1991; Griffin and Tversky, 1992).

Another possible criticism of some studies is that in presenting people surveyed with short case studies many details are left out about which respondents might make varying assumptions, which they might or might not state in their replies. For example, entrepreneurs might think in terms of employing different strategies in exploiting an opportunity. Some might think, for instance, in terms of investing on a significant scale at the outset to exploit an opportunity quickly; while others might think in terms of making irreversible investments step by step to gather information on likely success. Different strategies would entail different levels of risk and potential returns. Further, as mentioned by Shaver and Scott (1991), in their comments on traits research methodologies when asked to give advice on what someone else should do, a respondent may not necessarily give advice that he/she would follow himself/herself.

Such criticisms probably reflect the inherent difficulty of unambiguously measuring individual cognitive biases in complex and judgemental decision frameworks such as those faced in entrepreneurial opportunity evaluation.

4.3 Over-optimism and related biases

4.3.1 Optimistic bias

Optimistic bias is the tendency to believe things will turn out well. According to Taylor and Brown (1988), optimistic bias has three main forms. These are over-positive self-evaluation, over-optimism about future plans and events, and over-optimism due to the illusion of control bias.

Cooper et al. (1998) found in a survey of entrepreneurs that, while only around 25 percent of new businesses survive for more than five years, 81 percent of the entrepreneurs believed that their chances of success were at least 70 percent, and 33 percent believed they were certain to succeed. The interpretation of such results requires some care however. For instance, such positive statements may partly reflect a need for self-justification. Cooper et al. suggest that entrepreneurs may engage in what psychologists have termed 'post-decisional bolstering', in which decision-makers tend to exaggerate the attractiveness of an option once it has been chosen. Entrepreneurs may also have a natural tendency to speak positively about their efforts due to an incentive to encourage others, such as financiers, employees, and customers to believe that they will be successful. If entrepreneurs are over-optimistic in making the decision to start a venture, and in making initial decisions on the venture, then this has additional implications as compared to a situation in which they only become over-optimistic once an initial commitment has been made.

Note that a number of authors have proposed models that attribute over-optimism and related biases to rational behaviour rather than cognitive factors. For instance Van den Steen (2004) assumes that agents sometimes underestimate, and sometimes overestimate the likelihood of success of an action. In selecting actions with high probabilities of success, they are likely to choose those whose probabilities they have overestimated, and hence they will tend to be over-optimistic. Over-confidence, and illusion of control also form part of his model. Zabojnik (2004) assumes that people have the option to conduct tests of their abilities, and that such tests have opportunity costs. In his model this leads to a tendency for people to have over-positive self-evaluations.

De Meza and Southey (1996) argue that most facts characterizing small businesses can be explained by new-entrants tending to be over-optimistic, and that banks have an important role in deciding which new entrants should be given credit. In their model, banks are more realistic in their estimates of the prospects of entrepreneurs, as the entrepreneurs themselves tend to rate their prospects too highly. Coelho et al. (2004) take a similar view, pointing out that over-optimism implies that governments should not intervene in order to correct what is usually taken as under-provision of finance for start-ups. Another perspective is offered by Bernardo and Welch (2001). They view over-confident entrepreneurs as providing a positive information externality to their social group by being more likely to explore their environment. If such externalities are significant enough then social welfare will be increased through having some over-confident people among the population, even though such people will not be behaving in an optimal fashion with regards to their own private welfare.

4.3.2 Heuristics and biases

Over-confidence, as defined above, leads to incorrect estimates of risks faced, but expectations might be either too favourable or too pessimistic, depending on whether a person's probability estimates are biased towards positive or negative outcomes. However, it may well be that people who are optimistic enough to undertake entrepreneurial ventures have tended to have been biased by over-confidence towards underestimating the risks that they face. Similarly, belief in the law of small numbers may lead to over-confidence if a small sample is used that is biased in a positive direction. Anchoring may lead to over-optimism about a venture as it progresses, in cases where expectations are anchored on forecasts that progress so far suggests are too optimistic.

4.3.3 Illusion of control

The illusion of control is the tendency for people to believe that they can control, or influence, outcomes over which they actually have no control, or to overemphasize the level of control that they do have. It results from two main factors. First, it can be difficult to judge the relative importance of skill and chance. Secondly, people are motivated to control their environments. If entrepreneurs have an illusion of control, then they will perceive less risk because they will believe that they will be able to minimize the occurrence of negative outcomes.

Simon and Houghton (2002: 114–15) suggest that the illusion of control may be associated with entrepreneurs underestimating competitors' responses to their initiatives. They cite Kerin et al. (1992) who argue that pioneers may fail to recognize that competitor responses are beyond their control, and Zajac and Bazerman (1991), who argue that cognitive biases lead to a belief that competitor responses will not affect their chances of success.

4.3.4 Planning fallacy

The planning fallacy (Kahneman and Tversky, 1979a) is a tendency for people to underestimate the amount of time that it will take to complete tasks. It tends to be particularly strong in unique and highly uncertain situations.

The planning fallacy may be partly the result of people focusing on plan-based scenarios rather than relevant past experiences (Buehler et al., 1994). Kruger and Evans (2004) argue that the planning fallacy is the result of a failure of people to break multifaceted tasks down in their minds into their component parts. They find that when people are prompted to unpack the tasks, the planning fallacy is reduced. The planning fallacy leads to risks being underestimated, as it is likely that costs will turn out to be higher than expected.

4.3.5 Self-justification and escalation of commitment

Self-justification is the tendency to justify decisions, even if they had negative outcomes. Feelings of personal responsibility for decisions lead to the need for self-justification. The decision-maker is influenced to justify his actions by his need both to prove his competence and rationality to himself (psychological self-justification), and to others (social self-justification). This can lead to escalations of commitment to failing courses of action (Brockner, 1992). This would increase the risk of entrepreneurs making substantial losses.

4.3.6 Mood

Affect Infusion (Forgas, 1995; Baron, 1998) is the influence of affective states on decision-making. According to the Affect Infusion Model, mood influences decisions when heuristics are employed, and when detailed decisions are being made, for example when mood affects recall from memory. Complexity and uncertainty increase the role of mood in decision-making. People in a good mood are more optimistic about events, so affecting risk perceptions (Johnson and Tversky, 1983). Mood may also to some extent be shared across society (Loewenstein et al., 2001).

4.4 Perceived self-efficacy

Perceived self-efficacy, or simply 'self-efficacy', refers to the degree to which someone believes he/she has the ability to successfully complete a task. There is evidence of a positive correlation between perceived self-efficacy and the decision to be an entrepreneur (Chen et al., 1998; Shane, 2003: 111–2). Entrepreneurs' self-efficacy has also been found to affect their business strategies and performance levels (Westerberg, 1998).

Perceived self-efficacy (Bandura, 1977, 1986, 1995; Gist and Mitchell, 1992) is closely related to the concept of perceived behavioural control, which forms part of the Theory of Planned Behaviour. People with high self-efficacy believe themselves capable of successfully taking adaptive action as challenges unfold. They tend to choose to undertake more challenging tasks, and are less likely to be deterred from them. The latter point makes those with high self-efficacy more likely to succeed in a task, but also carries the risk of over-optimism, and of escalating commitments to failing courses of action (Glen et al., 1997).

The correlation between self-efficacy and actual abilities is imperfect. People who are clearly capable can perceive themselves as having low self-efficacy, while those who objectively clearly have poor capabilities for a task can be very confident.

The strongest sources of self-efficacy perceptions are mastery experiences, which are interpretations of the results of one's own past efforts. Vicarious experiences (observing others) also have an impact, as do social persuasions (the comments of others), and somatic and emotional states. Emotional states impact through the emotional reactions people feel to the prospect of carrying out any specific task, and also through general emotional states, which affect people's overall levels of optimism.

A variety of cognitive factors impact on people's interpretations of information affecting their perceptions of their self-efficacies. For instance people may selectively recall failures. Inaccurate assessments of self-efficacy may also result from past performance having been partly the result of group interdependencies. A further factor is a person's attributional style. Someone with an optimistic attributional style explains negative events in terms of external causes, and explains positive events in terms of internal causes (Baron, 1998).

Stajkovic and Luthans (1998) provide a meta-analysis of research on self-efficacy. There is much evidence showing a link between self-efficacy and success, although there is clearly an issue with causality in interpreting such evidence as success breeds higher self-efficacy, while high self-efficacy can breed success. Note that Hawkins (1992) argues that self-efficacy is a predictor rather than a cause of behaviour.

A further concept refers to the perceived self-efficacy of a group. This is termed collective efficacy (Bandura, 1995). This is the level of collective belief within a team of its own effectiveness in carrying out a task. Teams with high collective efficacy choose more challenging goals, put in more effort, and are more persistent. Studies have found support for a link between perceived collective efficacy and team performance (Sheperd and Krueger, 2002: 171–2).

A problem with the concept of self-efficacy is that it can be used in a way that does little more than simply substitute for the term 'self-confidence', which is already well used in entrepreneurship theory. It would, in fact, be entirely possible to model links between self-confidence, the decision to become an entrepreneur and entrepreneurial behaviour as rational responses to self-knowledge, and self-learning. It is perhaps in the more detailed insights into how self-confidence forms that self-efficacy theory can contribute most.

4.5 Intrinsic Motivation and Creativity

Intrinsic motivation (Deci and Ryan, 1985) is the motivation to do something for its own sake: because it is interesting and enjoyable. This is in contrast to sources of extrinsic motivation such as the receipt of a reward for carrying out an action, or the threat of being punished if results are not favourable enough. Hence intrinsic motivations provide additional incentives to undertake entrepreneurial activities (Delmar, 2000). People may become entrepreneurs in order to follow their interests. Interests may also be a good predictor of entrepreneurial behaviour. Intrinsic motivations may be more effective than extrinsic motivations in leading to creativity (Amabile, 1997). Intrinsic motivation is related to challenge and ability, and so is closely linked to perceived self-efficacy.

Evidence suggests that in some circumstances the introduction of extrinsic rewards can reduce intrinsic motivation. This is known as the overjustification effect (Greene et al., 1976). It would seem to be relevant to incentive systems for encouraging entrepreneurial behaviour within organizations, suggesting that in some cases it may be better to focus on encouraging intrinsic motivation, and to be careful not to damage them through extrinsic motivations. Discussions of economic applications of intrinsic motivation and overjustification (crowding-out) are provided by Frey (1997), and Frey and Jegen (2001).

A link between intrinsic motivation and creativity was mentioned above. Ward (2004) provides an overview of cognition and creativity, noting the importance of analogy, problem formulation, and merging separate ideas. There is evidence supporting the proposition that entrepreneurs tend to be relatively creative (Shane, 2003: 56–8).

4.6 Counterfactual Thinking and Regret Theory

Counterfactual thinking is *ex post* thinking about how things might have been done differently. Counterfactual thinking can lead to regret, which can have the negative effect of lowering perceived self-efficacy. It can also lead to the formation of alternative strategies for the future, so that better strategies can be learned from experience.

Gaglio and Katz (2001), theorizing about Kirzner's concept of entrepreneurial alertness, hypothesized that alert people engage in counterfactual thinking that undoes causal sequences. They are therefore more prone to increase the complexity of their mental schema, and to change those schema, in response to novel events. Gaglio (2004) provides a more in-depth discussion of counterfactual thinking, and its importance in entrepreneurship. Baron (2000) found that entrepreneurs are relatively less likely to engage in counterfactual thinking, have weaker regrets over missed opportunities, and find it easier to admit past mistakes both to themselves and to others.

Note that 'regret' plays a somewhat different role in regret theory (Loomes and Sugden, 1987). In regret theory the overall level of satisfaction gained from following a particular decision option is a combination of the basic utility from the actual consequence, plus an decrement or increment due to regret or 'rejoicing' over avoiding the consequences of alternative decision options. In regret theory, regret is taken into account *ex ante* when making the decision.

4.7 Intentions-based models

Krueger (2000) espouses intentions-based theory as a means of understanding what triggers entrepreneurial activity. He argues that organizations influence attitudes towards entrepreneurial initiatives among their members, that organizational culture helps to determine subjective norms, and that organizations can take steps to improve their members' perceived self-efficacy (which he uses instead of perceived behavioural control) and perceived collective efficacy. For instance, he suggests that organizations should provide their members with multiple low-risk mastery opportunities in order to enhance perceived self-efficacy. Shepherd and Krueger (2002) further consider the cognition of entrepreneurial teams from an intentions-based perspective.

According to intentions-based models, intentions are the best predictor of voluntary behaviour. Fishbein and Ajzen (1975) proposed the Theory of Reasoned Action. According to this theory, intention to act is determined by the decision-maker's attitudes towards the behaviour and by his subjective norms. Attitudes towards the behaviour are its expected consequences. Subjective norms are what the decision-maker believes people whose views he cares about will think about the behaviour. Sheppard et al. (1988) give a meta-analysis of studies on the theory.

The Theory of Planned Behaviour (Ajzen, 1991) is an extension of the Theory of Reasoned Action. It adds a third factor into the determination of intentions. This is perceived behavioural control. It is the decision-maker's beliefs about how much control he will have over carrying out the behaviour.

Tests of these models in psychology have mainly been based on self-reports. However evidence has suggested that self-reports may not be reliable (Ross et al., 1986; Manfredo and Shelby, 1988). See Budd and Spencer (1986), and Evans (1991) for critical assessment of the models, and of tests on them.

Fazio (1986) proposed an alternative intentions-based theory called the Attitude Accessibility Theory. According to this, the faster someone can express an attitude, the stronger it is. The more accessible an attitude is, the more likely it is to guide behaviour.

4.8 Prospect theory and framing: Attitudes to risk

Baron (2004) suggests that entrepreneurs may have a tendency to frame decisions in terms of the gains they will fail to make if they do not become entrepreneurs, rather than the losses they might make if they do, and that this therefore makes them more risk seeking. Baron also suggests that the overweighting of small probabilities may lead people to become entrepreneurs (the weighting function employed in original prospect theory overweights very low probabilities).

Palich and Bagby (1995) found evidence that entrepreneurs frame equivocal business scenarios significantly more positively than others. Entrepreneurs were much more likely to view scenarios as opportunities where others would see them as offering low returns in relation to their risks.

Framing refers to the way in which a decision-maker is presented with, or perceives, a decision problem. For instance a positive way of framing a gamble is to tell a person he has a 55 percent chance of winning, while a negative way of framing it is to tell him he has a 45 percent chance of losing. There is evidence that people are more likely to accept a proposition when it is positively framed (Wang, 1996; Kuhberger, 1998). Prospect theory is often used to explain framing effects. According to prospect theory (Kahneman and Tversky, 1979b), the prospect of a loss is more heavily weighted than the prospect of a gain when making a decision. This is termed loss aversion. Gains yield an increase in the level of utility that is lower than the reduction in utility yielded by losses of the same magnitude. In addition the decision-maker is risk averse when choosing between gains, and risk seeking when choosing between losses. Choosing between gains is subject to what is termed the certainty effect. The certainty effect is where the difference between certain gains and probable gains is given a higher weight by a decision-maker than the same sized difference in uncertainty between probable gains.

Loss aversion is one reason for status quo bias (Kahneman et al., 1991), under which people have a bias towards preferring things as they are. Loss aversion means that people give a greater weight to the negative consequences of change than they do to the positive consequences.

Original prospect theory was modified by Tversky and Kahneman (1992) to create cumulative prospect theory. It employs a modified mathematical model. The exact behaviour predicted by the theory depends on the parameter values employed (Neilson and Stowe, 2002), but citing experimental evidence Tversky and Kahneman claim the following pattern of risk aversion: risk aversion for high probability gains, risk seeking for low probability gains, risk seeking for high probability losses, and risk aversion for low probability losses. Evidence in support of prospect theory was discussed by Camerer (2000). However some studies have produced results that are contradictory to it (Sitkin and Pablo, 1992).

There is some question as to whether prospect theory is applicable to situations in which probabilities are judgemental. Research has suggested that people may have problems reasoning with explicit probabilities. For instance Weber et al. (2004) and Hertwig et al. (2004) find evidence that while decisions based on descriptions may be made as if probabilities of rare events are over-weighted, decisions based on experience are made as if the probabilities of rare events are under-weighted. This brings into question whether empirical results based on decision-making with explicitly stated probabilities are applicable to judgemental decision-making scenarios faced by entrepreneurs. It also suggests that the relevant experience of an entrepreneur may be significant in determining how accurately risk is perceived, as it helps to determine the frequency with which the entrepreneur has experienced different types of events.

4.9 Timid choices and bold forecasts: A further perspective on risk-taking

Kahneman and Lovallo (1993) present a cognitive model of risk-taking. The model is based on risky decisions that are not repeated routinely, and which are not made under severely adverse conditions. In severely adverse conditions, prospect theory predicts that high-risk gambles are likely. There may also be a tendency towards escalation of commitments (Staw and Ross, 1989). The model makes two separate predictions. The first is that people tend to underestimate risk. The second is that when they do recognize risks they tend to be biased towards a greater aversion to them than would be rational.

Forecasts are based on plans. The most likely scenario might be for things to go smoothly according to plan, but there can be a vast number of individually less likely ways for things to diverge from the plan causing less favourable outcomes. The sum of the probabilities of unfavourable scenarios is then large, but according to the model, forecasts are nevertheless based on the optimistic scenario, hence leading people to become subject to the planning fallacy. This is a potential fault in taking an inside view of a problem. Kahneman and Lovallo claim that an inside view is overwhelmingly preferred to an outside view in intuitive forecasting. An inside view focuses on the case at hand, while an outside view focuses on the statistics of a class of similar cases. They claim that an outside view is more likely to yield realistic estimates, giving some protection against wildly unrealistic estimates.

Considering individual decision problems in isolation from others (i.e. using narrow decision frames) leads to sub-optimal decision-making as the advantages of pooling risks are ignored. Hence risk aversion is increased beyond the optimal level. Kahneman and Lovallo claim that it can be inferred from observed preferences that there is indeed a tendency for people to consider problems separately.

4.10 Risk and Time

Das and Teng (1997) claim that neither the traits approach, nor the cognitive approach to entrepreneurship can adequately explain the different attitudes to risk of entrepreneurs relative to non-entrepreneurs. They note that risk is intrinsically embedded in time (Vlek and Stallen, 1980), and argue that the failure to incorporate time is a deficiency in both traits and cognitive research. They put forward the notions of risk horizon, and future orientation to help explain entrepreneurial risk behaviour. Although they adopt a traits approach they suggest that a more sophisticated framework might be developed by incorporating cognitive factors.

Future orientation is a personality trait, which they relate to the further trait of risk propensity. A person's future orientation is whether he is more preoccupied with what will happen in the short term, or with what will happen in the longer term.

They suggest two types of risk horizon: short-range entrepreneurial risk and long-range entrepreneurial risk. Short-range risk is defined as variances in outcomes in the near future. Long-range risk is defined as variances in outcomes in the distant future. Into these concepts they incorporate the concept of missing-the-boat risk and sinking-the-boat risk (Dickson and Giglierano, 1986). Sinking-the-boat risk is particularly evident in new ventures in the short run, due to lack of financial slack and back-up. Missing the boat risk is more long-range, as it is about what the entrepreneur might miss out on in the future. They argue that the same individual may be given to low-risk behaviour with regards to long-range risk, while being given to high-risk behaviour with regards to short-range risk, or vice versa. They also argue that different types of entrepreneurs will tend to have different risk-horizons.

4.11 Option Value and Information Costs

Another approach to analysing behaviour that deviates from full rationality assumes that people are rational in response to the information costs that they face. This begs the question of whether insights drawn from psychology, such as those discussed above, can be brought together with economizing models of entrepreneurship to provide enriched theories, or whether the two approaches are incompatible.

Informational issues are central to entrepreneurship theory. For instance Austrian theorists such as Hayek and Kirzner point out the importance of lack of information about others' plans in leading to profit opportunities within markets (Pasour, 1989), and to the importance of alertness in identifying such opportunities. However neoclassical economics, assuming perfect knowledge, eliminates such possibilities. From an information cost perspective, once the entrepreneur suspects an opportunity may exist, the decision to investigate further depends on the relevant information costs not being too high. Information costs differ among entrepreneurs, depending on their contacts, expertise, the production facilities available to them, opportunity costs, and so on. For instance, some entrepreneurs already in the relevant industry might be able to cheaply trial a new idea, while for others trialling the same idea could be much more expensive. Opportunity identification, investigation, and exploitation can be seen as an information collection process, with the entrepreneur's optimal strategy being closely related to his information costs, and his beliefs.

The 'real options approach' in entrepreneurship theory (McGrath, 1999) gives lessons on how to respond to future information arrival. According to real options thinking, the entrepreneur should value uncertainty, making investments that generate real options. For instance a relatively small investment may generate the information needed to know whether it is worthwhile to invest on a larger scale. Hence high rates of failure of new entrepreneurial firms can be at least partly interpreted as the result of a process of testing the water, or in other words of creating real options. One restriction on the application of this line of reasoning is that sometimes entrepreneurs need to invest on a significant scale at the outset in order to build barriers to entry before others who observe what they are doing, copy their ideas.

However conventional real options theory, in particular theory that is closely derived from financial option models, involves a restrictive assumption. The efficient markets assumption, used in the valuation of options traded on financial markets, means that all currently available information is already reflected in the market price. The result of real option models paralleling this assumption is that it is assumed that there is no endogenous information collection process to go through in valuing a real option, or in deciding whether to exercise it. It is simply assumed that particular information will arrive at particular times, rather than that the decision-maker has to decide what information to collect. The entrepreneur is assumed to be a creator of real options rather than a collector of information.

Note that, when considering what information an entrepreneur will collect, it is a mistake to assume that he will economize on information costs simply by deciding how much information to collect, then collecting it, and then making a decision. This neglects the sequential aspect of economizing on information costs. The collection of information inherently involves option value (Wadeson, 2004). For instance economic search theory involves the derivation of rules to decide when to stop collecting information and make a final decision. There is option value in the decision of how much information to collect. Information collected so far affects the expected value of collecting further information, so the decision of when to stop needs to be made as the information is collected—not before. There is also option value in deciding which information to collect next. Information collected so far changes beliefs, so affecting choices over the subsequent path of information collection.

In order to optimize the information collection process, and hence option value, the correct choices have to be made over what information to collect next. Other things being equal, it is best to collect cheaper information next. However the incentive to collect particular information next is also increased if it is more likely to alter the subsequent path, or lead to rapid abandonment.

Further, information is often collected as a by-product of implementation actions. For instance, in starting a venture the entrepreneur learns more about it, such as the market response. Therefore, as part of optimizing his information collection process, the entrepreneur has to decide how, and in what order, to perform implementation actions. Collecting information as a by-product can reduce the option value that it involves, as reacting to the information in ways that do not build on what has already been done involves a loss of sunk costs. By-product information leads the entrepreneur to adjust his plans after launching a venture, but in ways that are to some degree constrained by his initial investments. Having gained by-product information, the entrepreneur might alternatively decide that he prefers abandonment. For instance, he might have discovered that there is not the market for the product he is producing that he had expected. This need not be seen as 'failure', as it can be the result of an entirely efficient process of information collection. The point is that the entrepreneur needs to collect the right information, in the right sequence, and in the right ways. Further he needs to be willing to abandon at the correct moment, if it is justified by the information that he has collected.

The theories from psychology described in earlier sections do not seem to be contradictory to the essential message of this information cost approach. However it does suggest that entrepreneurs may often collect information and respond to it in less than optimal ways. For instance, anchoring on plans of success, the confirmation bias, and the need for self-justification can all reduce the option value that entrepreneurs gain in the information collection processes that entrepreneurial ventures involve. This can also then lead to increased risk, such as that of escalation of commitment to failing courses of action. It may also be, however, that educating people in the logic of such processes can reduce such biases. For instance, people could find self-justification in having efficiently collected information that leads to abandonment, or by thinking in terms of exercising their real options. Additionally, it is possible that successful serial entrepreneurs, due to selection and experience, tend to be less susceptible to such biases, and are therefore able to more flexibly respond to new information. For instance Baron's (2000) finding that entrepreneurs find it easier to admit past mistakes suggests that they are less susceptible to self-justification bias. However, cognitive biases may also play an important role in decisions of whether to become entrepreneurs in the first place. Hence it may be that successful, and experienced entrepreneurs tend to be less susceptible to cognitive biases relative to novice entrepreneurs. On the other hand, past success may itself increase some biases, such as over-optimism.

There seems to be no reason why some of the theories described in previous sections should not be used alongside, or incorporated into, economic models. For example over-optimism could be analysed by seeing what happens to the entrepreneur's strategies as his initial beliefs become more favourable. This might lead the entrepreneur to decide to launch a venture, to launch it on a larger scale at the outset, and to collect less information before doing so. Such integrations of the two approaches could prove fruitful in allowing further analysis of how entrepreneurs' strategies may be affected by cognitive factors.

4.12 Conclusion

The cognitive approach seems to be a promising line of study, offering interesting insights into entrepreneurship. Some of the literature in this field is rather uncritical of the theories from psychology whose use they promote in the study of entrepreneurship. It is necessary to recognize that psychology is not a fixed body of knowledge but is evolving, and subject to its own debates. Hence, in using its theories, entrepreneurship researchers should recognize criticisms and counter arguments made by psychologists themselves. They should also take account of debates in psychology on the advantages and disadvantages of alternative methodologies for carrying out empirical studies on the theories.

It should also be noted that in many instances there are significant inherent difficulties involved in trying to draw firm conclusions about cognitive processes from evidence of behaviour in making complex decisions, such as those faced by entrepreneurs. For instance, proving a bias means knowing what the optimal behaviour would have been, but this may be very difficult to determine.

In order to understand the decision-making processes of entrepreneurs it is also necessary to consider the lessons of the real options, and information cost economizing approaches. The latter approach stresses the option value involved in processes of information collection inherent in entrepreneurial ventures, and provides insights into how such processes should be sequenced. This view can be combined with effects identified by psychologists in order to better understand how entrepreneurs' strategies may often deviate from optimality.

Finally, some readers will be interested in how culture is related to entrepreneurial cognitions (Mitchell et al., 2002), and to risk-taking (Weber and Hsee, 1998, 2000). Culture would seem to have a significant role. For instance, in the theories from psychology described above, some of the more obvious ways in which culture might have an impact are through subjective norms (intentions-based models), social persuasions (self-efficacy theory), and the role of social self-justification (escalation of commitment theory). Lehman et al. (2004) provide a review of culture research in psychology.

References

AJZEN, I. (1991). 'The theory of planned behaviour'. *Organizational Behaviour and Human Decision Processes*, 50: 179–211.

AMABILE, T. M. (1997). 'Motivating Creativity in Organizations: On Doing What You Love and Loving What You Do'. *California Management Review*, 40(1): 39–58.

BANDURA, A. (1977). 'Self-efficacy: Toward a Unifying Theory of Behavioural Change'. *Psychological Review*, 84: 191–215.

—— (1986). *Social Foundations of Thought and Action: A Social Cognitive Theory*. Englewood Cliffs, NJ: Prentice Hall.

—— (1995). 'Exercise of Personal and Collective Efficacy in Changing societies', in A. Bandura (ed.) *Self-efficacy in Changing Societies*. New York: Cambridge University Press.

—— (1997). *Self-Efficacy: The Exercise of Control*. New York: Freeman.

BARON, R. A. (1998). 'Cognitive Mechanisms in Entrepreneurship: Why and When Entrepreneurs Think Differently than Other People'. *Journal of Business Venturing*, 13(4): 275–94.

—— (2000). 'Counterfactual Thinking and Venture Formation: The Potential Effects of Thinking About "What Might Have Been"'. *Journal of Business Venturing*, 15(1): 79–91.

—— (2004). 'The Cognitive Perspective: A Valuable Tool for Analysing Entrepreneurship's Basic "Why" Questions'. *Journal of Business Venturing*, 19(2): 221–39.

BARSALOU, L. W. (1992). *Cognitive Psychology: An Overview for Cognitive Scientists*. Hillsdale, NJ: Erlbaum.

BERNARDO, A. E. and I. WELCH (2001). 'On the Evolution of Overconfidence and Entrepreneurs'. *Journal of Economics and Management Strategy*, 10(3): 301–30.

BIRD, B. (1988). 'Implementing Entrepreneurial Ideas: The Case for Intention'. *Academy of Management Review*, 13(3): 442–53.

BRENNER, L. A., D. J. KOEHLER, V. LIBERMAN and A. TVERSKY (1996). 'Overconfidence in Probability and Frequency Judgments: A Critical Examination'. *Organizational Behaviour and Human Decision Processes*, 65(3): 212–19.

Brockner, J. (1992). 'The Escalation of Committment to a Failing Course of Action: Toward Theoretical Progress'. *Academy of Management Review*, 17(1): 39–61.

Budd, R. J., and C. P. Spencer, (1986). 'Lay Theories of Behavioural Intention: A Source of Response Bias in the Theory of Reasoned Action?' *British Journal of Social Psychology*, 25: 109–17.

Buehler, R., D. Griffin and M. Ross (1994). 'Exploring the "Planning Fallacy": Why People Underestimate their Task Completion Times'. *Journal of Personality and Social Psychology*, 67: 366–81.

Busenitz, L. W. and J. B. Barney (1997). 'Differences Between Entrepreneurs and Managers in Large Organizations: Biases and Heuristics in Strategic Decision-making'. *Journal of Business Venturing*, 12(1): 9–30.

Camerer, C. F. (2000). 'Prospect Theory in the Wild: Evidence from the Field', in D. Kahneman and A. Tversky (eds) *Choice Values and Frames*. Cambridge: Cambridge University Press.

Chen, C. C., P. Greene and A. Crick (1998). 'Does Entrepreneurial Self-efficacy Distinguish Entrepreneurs from Managers?' *The Journal of Business Venturing*, 13(4): 295–316.

Coelho, M., D. de Meza and D. Reyniers (2004). 'Irrational Exuberance, Entrepreneurial Finance and Public Policy'. *International Tax and Public Finance*, 11(4): 391–417.

Cooper, A. C., C. A. Woo and W. Dunkelberg (1988). 'Entrepreneurs Perceived Chances for Success'. *Journal of Business Venturing*, 3: 97–108.

Das, T. K. and B. Teng (1997). 'Time and Entrepreneurial Risk Behavior'. *Entrepreneurship Theory and Practice*, 22(2): 69–88.

Deci, E. L. and R. M. Ryan (1985). *Intrinsic Motivation and Self-determination in Human Behaviour.* New York: Plenum Press.

Delmar, F. (2000). 'The Psychology of the Entrepreneur', in S. Carter, and D. Jones-Evans, *Enterprise and Small Business: Principles, Practice and Policy.* Harlow: Prentice Hall.

De Meza, D. and C. Southey (1996). 'The Borrower's Curse: Optimism, Finance and Entrepreneurship'. *The Economic Journal*, 106(435): 375–86.

Dickson, P. R. and J. J. Giglierano (1986). 'Missing the Boat and Sinking the Boat: A Conceptual Model of Entrepreneurial Risk'. *Journal of Marketing*, 50: 58–70.

Evans, M. G. (1991). 'The Problem of Analyzing Multiplicative Components'. *American Psychologist*, 46: 6–15.

Fazio, R. H. (1986). 'How Do Attitudes Guide Behavior?' in R. M. Sorrentino and E. T. Higgins (eds) *The Handbook of Motivation and Cognition: Foundations of Social Behaviour. New York: Guilford Press.*

Fishbein, M. and I. Ajzen (1975). *Belief, Attitude, Intention and Behavior: An Introduction to Theory and Research.* Reading, MA: Addison-Wesley.

Forbes, D. P. (1999). 'Cognitive Approaches to New Venture Creation'. *International Journal of Management Review*, 1: 415–39.

Forgas, J. P. (1995). 'Mood and Judgment: The Affect Infusion Model (AIM)'. *Psychological Bulletin*, 117: 39–66.

Frey, B. S. (1997). *Not Just for the Money: An Economic Theory of Personal Motivation.* Cheltenham: Edward Elgar.

Frey, B. S. and R. Jegen (2001). 'Motivation Crowding Theory'. *Journal of Economic Surveys*, 15(5): 589–611.

Gaglio, C. M. (2004). 'The Role of Mental Simulations and Counterfactual Thinking in the Opportunity Identification Process'. *Entrepreneurship Theory and Practice*, 28(6): 533–52.

Gaglio, C. M. and J. A. Katz (2001). 'The Psychological Basis of Opportunity Identification: Entrepreneurial Alertness'. *Small Business Economics*, 16(2): 95–111.

Gigerenzer, G. (1991). 'How To Make Cognitive Illusions Disappear: Beyond "Heuristics and Biases"', in Wolfgang Stroebe and Miles Hewstone (eds) *European Review of Social Psychology*, 2: 83–115. New York: Wiley and Sons.

—— and P. M. Todd (1999). *Simple Heuristics that Make Us Smart*. New York: Oxford University Press.

Gist, M. E. and T. R. Mitchell (1992). 'Self-Efficacy: A Theoretical Analysis of its Determinants and Malleability'. *Academy of Management Review*, 17(2): 183–211.

Glen, W., A. M. Saks and S. Hook (1997). 'When Success Breeds Failure: The Role of Self-Efficacy in Escalating Commitment to a Losing Course of Action'. *Journal of Organizational Behaviour*, 18(5): 415–32.

Greene, D., B. Sternberg and M. R. Lepper (1976). 'Overjustification in a Token Economy'. *Journal of Personality and Social Psychology*, 34: 1219–34.

Grether, D. M. (1980). 'Bayes Rule as a Descriptive Model: The Representativeness Heuristic'. *The Quarterly Journal of Economics*, 95(3): 537–57.

Griffin, D and H. Tversky (1992). 'The Weighting of Evidence and the Determinants of Confidence'. *Cognitive Psychology*, 24: 411–35.

Hawkins, R. M. F. (1992). 'Self-Efficacy: A Predictor but not a Cause of Behaviour'. *Journal of Behaviour Therapy and Experimental Psychiatry*, 23: 251–6.

Hertwig, R., G. Barron, E. U. Weber and I. Erev (2004). 'Decisions from Experience and the Effect of Rare Events in Risky Choice'. *Psychological Science*, 15(8): 534–9.

Hirshleifer, J. and J. G. Riley (1979). 'The Analytics of Uncertainty and Information – An Expository Survey'. *Journal of Economic Literature*, 17(4): 1375–421.

Johnson, E. and A. Tversky (1983). 'Affect, Generalization, and the Perception of Risk'. *Journal of Personality and Social Psychology*, 45(1): 20–31.

Kahneman, D. J. and D. Lovallo (1972). 'Subjective Probability: A Judgment of Representativeness'. *Cognitive Psychology*, III: 430–54.

—— and —— (1979a). 'Intuitive Prediction: Biases and Corrective Procedures'. *TIMS Studies in the Management Sciences*, 12: 313–27.

—— and —— (1979b). 'Prospect Theory: An Analysis of Decision under Risk'. *Econometrica*, 47: 263–91.

—— and —— (1993). 'Timid Choices and Bold Forecasts: A Cognitive Perspective on Risk-Taking'. *Management Science*, 39(1): 17–31.

—— J. L. Knetch and R. H. Thaler (1991). 'Anomalies: The Endowment Effect, Loss Aversion, and Status Quo Bias'. *Journal of Economic Perspectives*, 5(1): 193–206.

Keh, H. T., M. D. Foo and B. C. Lim (2002). 'Opportunity Evaluation under Risky Conditions: The Cognitive Processes of Entrepreneurs'. *Entrepreneurship: Theory & Practice*, 27(2): 125–48.

Kerin, R. A., P. R. Varadarajan and R. A. Peterson (1992). 'First-Mover Advantage: A Synthesis, Conceptual Framework, and Research Propositions'. *Journal of Marketing*, 56: 33–52.

Klayman, J. and Y. W. Ha (1987). 'Confirmation, Disconfirmation, and Information in Hypothesis Testing'. *Psychological Review*, 94(2): 211–28.

Krueger, N. F. (2000). 'The Cognitive Infrastructure of Opportunity Emergence'. *Entrepreneurship: Theory and Practice*, 24(3): 5–23.

Kruger, J. and M. Evans (2004). 'If You Don't Want to be Late, Enumerate: Unpacking Reduces the Planning Fallacy'. *Journal of Experimental Social Psychology*, 40: 586–98.

Kuhberger, A. (1998). 'The Influence of Framing on Risky Decisions'. *Organizational Behavior and Human Decision Processes*, 75: 23–55.

Lehman, D. R., C. Chiu and M. Schaller (2004). 'Psychology and Culture'. *Annual Review of Psychology*, 55: 689–714.

Loewenstein, G. F., E. U. Weber, C. K. Hsee and N. Welch (2001). 'Risk as Feelings'. *Psychological Bulletin*, 127(2): 267–86.

Loomes, G. and R. Sugden (1987). 'Testing for Regret and Disappointment in Choice Under Uncertainty'. *The Economic Journal* (Supp.) 97: 118–129.

Manfredo, M. and B. Shelby (1988). 'The Effect of Using Self-Report Measures in Tests of Attitude-Behavior Relationships'. *Journal of Social Psychology*, 128: 731–43.

McGrath, R. G. (1999). 'Falling Forward: Real Options Reasoning and Entrepreneurial Failure'. *Academy of Management Review*, 24(1): 13–30.

Mitchell, R. K., J. B. Smith, E. A. Morse, K. W. Seawright, A. M. Peredo and B. McKenzie (2002). 'Are Entrepreneurial Cognitions Universal? Assessing Entrepreneurial Cognitions Across Cultures'. *Entrepreneurship Theory and Practice*, 26(4): 9–32.

Neilson, W. S. and J. Stowe (2002). 'A Further Examination of Cumulative Prospect Theory Parameterizations'. *Journal of Risk and Uncertainty*, 24(1): 31–46.

Palich, L. E. and D. R. Bagby (1995). 'Using Cognitive Theory to Explain Entrepreneurial risk-taking: challenging conventional wisdom'. *Journal of Business Venturing*, 10(6): 425–38.

Pasour, E. C. (1989). 'The Efficient Markets Hypothesis and Entrepreneurship'. *Review of Austrian Economics*, 3: 95–108.

Ross, R. M., C. McFarland, M. Conway and M. P. Zanna (1986). 'Reciprocal Relation Between Attitudes and Behavior Recall: Committing People to Newly Formed attitudes'. *Journal of Personality and Social Psychology*, 45: 257–67.

Russo, J. E. and P. J. H. Schoemaker (1992). 'Managing Overconfidence'. *Sloan Management Review* (Winter) pp. 7–17.

Shane, S. A. (2003). *A General Theory of Entrepreneurship: The Individual-Opportunity Nexus*. Cheltenham: Edward Elgar.

Shanteau, J. (1989). 'Cognitive Heuristics and Biases in Behavioural Auditing: Review, Comments and Observations'. *Accounting, Organizations and Society*, 14(1/2): 165–77.

Shaver, K. G and L. R. Scott (1991). 'Person, Process, Choice: The Psychology of New Venture Creation'. *Entrepreneurship Theory and Practice*, 16(2): 23–45.

Shepherd, D. A. and N. F. Krueger (2002). 'An Intentions-Based Model of Entrepreneurial Teams' Social Cognition'. *Entrepreneurship Theory and Practice*, 27(2): 167–85.

Sheppard, B. H., J. Harwick and P. R. Warshaw (1988). 'The Theory of Reasoned Action: A Meta-analysis of Past Research with Recommendations for Modifications and Future Research'. *Journal of Consumer Research*, 15: 325–43.

Simon, H. A. (1957). *Models of Man. Social and Rational*. New York: John Wiley & Sons.

Simon, M. and S. M. Houghton (2002). 'The Relationship Among Biases, Misperceptions, and the Introduction of Pioneering Products: Examining Differences in Venture Decision Contexts'. *Entrepreneurship Theory and Practice*, 27(2): 105–24.

—— S. M. Houghton and K. Aquino (2000). 'Cognitive Biases, Risk Perception, and Venture Formation'. *Journal of Business Venturing*, 15(2): 113–34.

SITKIN, S. B. and A. L. PABLO (1992). 'Reconceptualizing the Determinants of Risk Behavior'. *Academy of Management Review*, 17(1): 9–38.

STAJKOVIC, A. D. and F. LUTHANS (1998). 'Self-Efficacy and Work-Related Performances: A Meta-analysis'. *Psychological Bulletin*, 124: 240–61.

TAYLOR, S. E. and J. D. BROWN (1988). 'Illusion and Well-being: A Social Psychological Perspective on Mental Health'. *Psychological Bulletin*, 103: 193–210.

TVERSKY, A. and D. KAHNEMAN (1971). 'Belief in the Law of Small Numbers'. *Psychological Bulletin*, 76(2): 105–10.

—— and —— (1973). 'Availability: A Heuristic for Judging Frequency and Probability'. *Cognitive Psychology*, 5: 207–32.

—— and —— (1974). 'Judgement Under Uncertainty: Heuristics and Biases'. *Science*, 185 (4157): 1124–31.

—— and —— (1983). 'Extensional Versus Intuitive Reasoning: The Conjunction Fallacy in Probability Judgment'. *Psychological Review*, 90(4): 293–315.

—— and —— (1992). 'Advances in Prospect Theory: Cumulative Representation of Uncertainty'. *Journal of Risk and Uncertainty*, 5(4): 297–323.

VAN DEN STEEN, E. (2004). 'Rational Overoptimism (and Other Biases)'. *American Economic Review*, 94(4): 1141–51.

VLEK, C. and P. J. STALLEN (1980). 'Rational and Personal Aspects of Risk'. *Acta Psychologica*, 45: 273–300.

WADESON, N. (2004). 'Multi-Dimensional Search: Choosing the Right Path'. *International Journal of the Economics of Business*, 11(3): 287–301.

WANG, X. T. (1996). 'Framing Effects: Dynamics and Task Domains'. *Organizational Behavior and Human Decision Processes*, 68(2): 145–57.

WARD, T. B. (2004). 'Cognition, Creativity and Entrepreneurship'. *Journal of Business Venturing*, 19: 173–88.

WEBER, E. U. and C. HSEE (1998). 'Cross-cultural Differences in Risk Perception, but Cross-cultural Similarities in Attitudes towards Perceived Risk'. *Management Science*, 44(9): 1205–17.

—— and —— (2000). 'Culture and Individual Judgment and Decision Making'. *Applied Psychology: An International Review*, 49(1): 32–61.

—— S. SHAFIR and A. R. BLAIS (2004). 'Predicting Risk-sensitivity in Humans and Lower Animals: Risk as Variance or Coefficient of Variation'. *Psychological Review*, 111: 430–45.

WESTERBERG, M. (1998). *Managing in Turbulence: An Empirical Study of Small Firms Operating in a Turbulent Environment*. Lulea, Sweden: Lulea Institute of Technology.

ZABOJNIK, J. (2004). 'A Model of Rational Bias in Self-assessments'. *Economic Theory*, 23(2): 259–82.

ZACHARAKIS, A. and D. A. SHEPERD (2001). 'The Nature of Overconfidence on Venture Capitalists' Decision Making'. *Journal of Business Venturing*, 16(2): 311–22.

ZAJAC, E. J. and M. H. BAZERMAN (1991). 'Blind Spots in Industry and Computer Analysis: Implications of Interfirm (Mis)perceptions for Strategic Decisions'. *Academy of Management Review*, 16(1): 37–56.

CHAPTER 5

ENTREPRENEURSHIP AND MARKETING

MARTIN CARTER[1]

'In the real and living economy every actor is always an entrepreneur.'

(Mises, 1949)

5.1 Introduction

Entrepreneurship and marketing are intimately related. This chapter examines their relationship from three perspectives, the *market process* perspective, the *marketing* perspective, and the perspective of the *entrepreneurial firm*. These provide complementary insights into the connections between the two concepts. This section briefly considers definitions of entrepreneurship and marketing. The

[1] I am grateful for the helpful comments of Mathew Hughes, two anonymous referees, participants at the authors' conference and, of course, the editors. The remaining deficiencies are mine.

following three sections discuss the three complementary perspectives in turn. The final section provides a summary and identifies areas for further research.

Neither concept has a single, universally agreed definition. Theories of the entrepreneur and entrepreneurship are discussed elsewhere in this book, especially in Chapters 1 and 2. The discussion here draws particularly on aspects of entrepreneurship concerned with the discovery of new opportunities for resource allocation (Kirzner, 1997), with innovation (Schumpeter, 1934), with making markets (Casson, 2003) and with the creation of entrepreneurial firms (Gartner, 1990; Casson, 2003). The chapter explores the role of marketing in each of these.

Marketing has been given many definitions. Crosier (1988) reviews more than 50. The main definition adopted here is a functional one, and conceives marketing as the set of activities undertaken by firms for aiding and organizing market exchange. To the extent that entrepreneurs are concerned with organizing market exchange they are carrying out marketing activities, whether or not they describe them as such. The chapter examines the significance of these activities in entrepreneurship.

Marketing is, however, not merely a set of activities. It is also a particular approach to business which determines a firm's priorities. The 'marketing concept' (Kotler, 2000: 19–25) refers to market orientation in the conduct of business which is a focus on satisfying the needs and wants of customers. This approach is based on the premise that greater customer satisfaction enhances the profits of the firm. The chapter will also consider the significance of market orientation in entrepreneurship.

5.2 The Market Process Perspective

Economists have increasingly analysed the processes which take place in markets and not just their equilibrium outcomes (Nelson and Winter, 1982; Langlois, 1986; Krafft, 2000). The strongest contributions to this field have come from the Austrian school of economics, which places entrepreneurship and the discovery and exploitation of new opportunities at the centre of the market process (Kirzner, 1973, 1979, 1997; Boettke and Prychitko, 1994). But aspects of the market process have also been examined in the marketing literature, in Casson's study of the entrepreneur and the market-making firm, and by Loasby (1986, 1999) who suggested an alternative (Marshallian) process of competition. This section considers these four strands in turn.

5.2.1 The Austrian market process framework

In Austrian models of the market process the entrepreneur, usually considered as an individual, initiates change in the market by identifying and introducing new trading opportunities. Possible opportunities are arbitrage between agents who are unaware of each other, improved versions of established commodities or new concepts for products or services. Change depends on the drive and ability of entrepreneurs to discover and to exploit opportunities which are unknown to other agents until they are initiated by the entrepreneur. Hayek (1945, 1948) and Mises (1949) both saw the process as one of dynamic competition between agents in contrast to the neoclassical model of competition as a static equilibrium. Hayek emphasized the need to explain how knowledge is disseminated amongst market participants; Mises stressed the role of profit seeking by entrepreneurs in driving the process.

As Martin Ricketts discusses in Chapter 2 of this Handbook, Austrian theory has proposed several distinct types of market process. Schumpeter (1934) described the entrepreneur as a radical innovator, a disruptor of an existing equilibrium and the instigator of a process of 'creative destruction'. Conversely, Kirzner (1973, 1979, 1997) envisaged a market temporarily stuck in a disequilibrium, with unexploited opportunities for more efficient use of resources. Entrepreneurs are distinguished by alertness to opportunities for change and they 'grasp opportunities for pure entrepreneurial profit created by temporary absence of full adjustment between input and output markets' (1997: 69). Notwithstanding occasional mistakes, their activities move the market towards a potential equilibrium. Shane and Venkataraman (2000) (see also Shane, 2003: 19–22) argue that the Schumpeter's and Kirzner's theories reflect different types of opportunity. Kirznerian opportunities arise from entrepreneurs discovering possibilities inherent in existing information to which entrepreneurs are more alert than others, whereas Schumpeterian opportunities are the result of creation of new information (particularly technology). Kirzner's entrepreneurs move the market towards the equilibrium inherent in current conditions while Schumpeter's creates the prospect of different, more valuable, equilibrium outcomes.

Another distinct type of market process is described in what Littlechild (1986) has called the 'radical subjectivist' approach, drawing on the subjectivist economics of Shackle (1969, 1979) and represented by the work of Lachman (1976, 1977, 1986). In Kirzner's theory, entrepreneurs discover changing opportunities that arise, independently of the entrepreneurs, in an objective world. In the radical subjectivist world, there is no separate reality independent of the actors within the market. Important aspects of the world, which yield opportunities for entrepreneurial activity, depend entirely of the imagination of the entrepreneurs and their ability to create alternatives that do not yet exist. A consequence is that no equilibrium can exist, since the direction taken by the market process depends at least partly on the imaginations of the market participants.

5.2.2 Marketing and the market process

The Austrian view of the market process was motivated by political economy rather than business strategy. Its primary purpose was to explain why the market process could be more effective than socialist planning (Kirzner 1997: 74–8). The means by which entrepreneurs discover and exploit market opportunities do not form a central part of the theory, but the marketing literature is concerned precisely with these questions. Several strands connect directly with the Austrian market process framework.

An author who wrote at length about marketing as a competitive process was Wroe Alderson (1957, 1965). He recognized markets as arenas of dynamic, rivalrous competition in which firms are engaged in a constant struggle to establish and maintain an advantage over competitors.

> Each firm competes by making the most of its individuality and its special character. It is constantly seeking to establish some competitive advantage. ... It is the unending search for differential advantage which keeps competition advancing. A firm which has been bested by competitors according to certain dimensions of value in products or services always has before it the possibility of turning the tables by developing something new in other directions. The company that is in the lead is vulnerable to attack at numerous points. Therein is a strong incentive for technical innovation and other forms of economic progress, both for the leader who is trying to stay out in front and for others who are trying to seize the initiative. (Alderson 1957: 101–2)

Competitive advantage is achieved by engaging in an unending search to differentiate products from those of competitors. Alderson analysed the 'domain of marketing' as a process of sorting heterogeneous supply to meet heterogeneous demand and leading to exchange (1957: 195–228). Unlike economic analysis, which has emphasized the breaking down of supply into homogeneous commodities, marketing theory emphasizes the building up of heterogeneous collections of products—which Alderson called 'assortments'—designed to serve the demands of consumers. Reekie and Savitt (1982) discuss the Austrian character of this process. Information mismatch is a state of ignorance in the sense of Loasby (1976). Managers do not know all the possible outcomes and cannot make decisions by calculation (Alderson, 1965: 60–4). A product is only 'adequately identified' for a consumer if 'the supplier has guessed right' (Alderson, 1965: 61), where 'guessing' stands for entrepreneurial intuition. Heterogeneous markets are not mediated by price, but by continual and unending entrepreneurial innovation.

> A homogeneous market can be cleared by adjustments of price and quantity. A heterogeneous market can only be cleared by information matching two sets, one ranging over heterogeneous demand the other ranging over heterogeneous supply. A discrepant market is only cleared by innovation. ... If strongly motivated problem solvers face each other ... it can never be cleared but only moves in the direction of that equilibrium state. Another state, representing new requirements and new opportunities, has arisen before the last is satisfied. (Alderson, 1965: 207)

Dickson (1992) proposed a synthesis of marketing planning with the Austrian market process. He depicts innovation and entrepreneurial change in the market as the outcome of a continuous two-phase process of 'imperfect procedural rationality', based in firms, but influenced by, and influencing, the market environment. In the external (macro-market) phase, heterogeneous supply and heterogeneous demand are in constant change and constant disequilibrium. In the internal (micro-procedural rationality) phase, sellers conduct market experiments, learn both directly and vicariously from the market and imitate and improve successful innovations. The most competitive firms are those with an insatiable self-improvement drive (experimenting), with acute and less biased perceptions (learning) and who can implement change fastest (imitating/improving). In contrast both with economists' optimization and with Simon's notion of 'satisficing' (Simon, 1978), the drive for experimenting is both the result and the cause of dynamic competition.

Dickson argues that the competitive process forces firms to adopt a customer-oriented approach corresponding to the 'marketing concept'.

> Our theory is that oligopolistic rivalry forces a seller to serve the interests of their customers noticeably better than its competitors. Such customer service improvement is a very conscious, deliberate, relentless process with a clear intended end; it is not incidental, coincidental, accidental, or unintended. In the marketing management literature that idea has been called the 'marketing concept'. (Dickson, 1992: 77)

The 'marketing concept' originated in the 1950s (McKitterick, 1957; Keith, 1960) and has a central place in the marketing management literature (see below; also Kotler, 2000: 19–25; and Baker, 2000: 7–12). A definition offered by Houston indicates how it illuminates the entrepreneurial process:

> The marketing concept states that an entity achieves its own exchange determined goals most efficiently through a thorough understanding of the potential exchange partners and their needs and wants, through a thorough understanding of the costs associated with satisfying those needs and wants, and then designing, producing, and offering products in the light of this understanding. (Houston, 1986: 85)

The marketer understands potential exchange possibilities and the marketing concept incorporates alertness to as-yet-unrealized possibilities that is the hallmark of the Misesian and Kirznerian entrepreneur.

Theodore Levitt (1960) used the term 'marketing myopia' for a lack of such alertness, making recommendations to managers which were consciously Schumpeterian:

> For their own good ... firms will have to destroy their own highly profitable assets. No amount of wishful thinking can save them from the necessity of engaging in this form of 'creative destruction'. I phrase the need as strongly as this because I think management must make quite an effort to break itself loose from conventional ways. (Levitt, 1960: 53)

Levitt also described how successful firms imagine the requirements of their potential customers, often imagining needs that customers have not yet conceived and persuading customers to change as well:

> Nothing drives progress like imagination. The idea precedes the deed. ... The marketing imagination is the starting point of success in marketing. It is distinguished from other forms of imagination by the unique insights it brings to understanding customers, their problems and the means to capture their attention and their custom. ... To attract a customer, you are asking him to do something different from what he would have done in the absence of the programs you direct at him. He has to change his mind and his actions. Hence the seller must distinguish himself and his offering from those of others so that people will want, or at least prefer, to do business with him. The search for meaningful distinction is a central part of the marketing effort. If marketing is seminally about anything, it is about achieving customer-getting distinction by differentiating what you do and how you operate. All else is derivative of that and that only. (Levitt, 1983: 127–128)

The nexus between marketing and entrepreneurship is clear. Firms which successfully identify entrepreneurial opportunities depend on marketing skills to help them understand, influence and, above all, attract customers. Robertson and Yu (2001) examine the problem of attracting customers from a market process perspective. Advertising is, of course, an important tool, which does more than inform. Entrepreneurial firms are more alert than potential consumers and use strongly emphasized messages, such as large billboard campaigns, repeated TV commercials and celebrity endorsement, in order to gain consumers' attention (Kirzner, 1973). Persuasive advertising sets out to change the tastes of consumers.

> Very often, consumers' perceptions of the external world are 'locked in' by their past experience and, therefore, consumers show no interest in new consumption opportunities, even though they may know of their existence. Advertising helps consumers unlock their prior knowledge and perceptions. (Robertson and Yu, 2001: 189)

(See Littlechild (1982) for a deeper analysis of the role of advertising in unlocking customers' perceptions.) Robertson and Yu suggest a dynamic framework for Aldersonian matching of heterogeneous supply with heterogeneous demand in a multi-dimensional attribute space (Lancaster, 1971). A supplier might meet some buyer needs by matching up with those demand space attributes in which it has expertise. Alternatively a firm may use persuasion to move consumer preferences towards the attributes it is able to offer. A richer possibility is that firms actively seek a match by mutual discovery (consumer focus groups for example) to strike a balance between customer needs and technical feasibility.

5.2.3 The market-making firm

A study which links Austrian theory directly with marketing is Casson (2003; first published 1982), whose aim was to construct a theory of the entrepreneur which takes into account 'the difficulties that are inherent in organizing a market'

(Casson, 2003: 14). Casson considered obstacles to trade which the entrepreneur must overcome and the market-making services required to overcome them. Transaction cost arguments imply that some market-making services (although not all) are supplied most efficiently if they are internalized, under the control of the entrepreneur, through the creation of a market-making firm.

Casson's analysis was intended primarily to explain the establishment of new firms as the solution to the market organizing problems of individual entrepreneurs. But all businesses face the problem of market organization, whether they are newly founded by entrepreneurs or long-established joint stock companies. Obstacles to trade exist for all firms, new and old, and these must be dealt with by one or more of the parties to any trade. Many of the Casson's conclusions about market making by the entrepreneurial firm extend to other types of firm and this suggests a promising way of looking at the nature of marketing itself as a business function. Marketing can be identified precisely as that set of activities concerned with overcoming obstacles to trade or with making the market. The mature marketing organization appears to be a natural development of Casson's entrepreneurial market-making firm.

It is thus possible to see Casson's study as the foundation for a general theory of marketing. Although this was not its purpose—for example the list of market-making activities which he discusses (see Casson, 2003: 84 and 148) does not, except in a general sense, include all the tasks and concerns that are found in modern marketing textbooks—it nevertheless provides an explanation, grounded in economics, of why marketing plays such an important role in business. Casson observes that the greatest risks faced by a firm come from market-making (2003: 161). By providing market-making services, a firm effectively insures its potential exchange partners against the risks of entering the market, but the costs of these services are recovered only if, and when, exchange is successfully completed. The focus of marketing on managing the demand side of the market is thus readily understood.

Casson's description of the growth and dynamics of the entrepreneurial firm (2003: ch. 11) captures many aspects of marketing firms in general. Having incurred the set-up costs of a purpose-built, market-making organization it is then in the interests of the business to secure the stability of the organization as far as possible into the future. Firms benefit from information gained by experience, both from the practice of production and other processes and from information about reactions of buyers—and of non-buyers—in the market. Such information helps the firm to maintain its lead over potential imitators and provides both an incentive and a means to enhance demand. Information from the market can reveal further opportunities for entrepreneurial diversification although constrained, eventually, once the firm's indivisible resources are fully utilized. Competitive entry leads, of course, to dynamic competition of the kind already discussed.

5.2.4 Marshallian competition

Loasby (1986, 1999) has explored market competition focusing on the market processes described by Marshall (1919, 1920). Marshall considered that 'the marketing side of the work of a business is an integral process, and not a series of independent transactions' (1919: 270) and provided an elaborate discussion of market-making by merchants and manufacturers (1919: 271–8). A firm's 'external organization'—its involvement with trading partners and competitors in the market—was both a source of knowledge of new opportunities and a place to experiment.

> Each firm's investment in the organization of its particular market was both a source of information which could be used as the basis for new ideas and also an environment in which these ideas could be tested, and discussed and improved before testing; and the intersection of the external organizations of rival firms helped to distribute knowledge within the larger market. Essential to this process, as Marshall observed, were the differences among the market participants in their capabilities, experience, and perception, which together generated the variations from which new combinations of ideas could be formed. (Loasby, 1999: 123)

Innovations are therefore not solely due to discontinuous entrepreneurial discovery but can also result from a continuous process involving established firms enduringly engaged—along with others—in the market. This suggests two types of discovery process, which Loasby called Schumpeterian and Marshallian competition respectively (1986). The gradual Marshallian process resembles Kirzner's equilibrium process in a number of respects, not least in its contrast with the disruptiveness of Schumpeterian change, although while Loasby emphasizes a particular process of learning by established firms within the market, Kirzner leaves the source of entrepreneurial discovery more open. Loasby interpreted these types of competition in the light of contrasting models of scientific discovery. Kuhn (1962) claimed that science advances by means of revolutions in which an accepted framework of ideas (a 'paradigm') is found wanting and displaced by a new paradigm. However, according to Lakatos (1970), progress in science also takes place in scientific research programmes, where core concepts (the 'hard core') do not change, but a 'protective belt' of supporting ideas may be changed and adjusted in the light of experience. Loasby suggested that stable, hard core concepts allow an organization (or a group of organizations linked in the market) to maintain organizational coherence while engaging in a Marshallian research programme of continual discovery. (A similar proposition has been made by Foss and Christensen, 2001). But from time-to-time, a Schumpeterian paradigm-shift takes over, when a rival research programme, perhaps conducted by a different organization, can offer better solutions. Learning in the competitive market depends on both types of process coexisting:

> Somehow or other, we need to maintain both the structured competition between organizations operating within imperfectly specified research programmes, and also the

more fundamental competition between rival programmes. We need both Marshall and Schumpeter. (Loasby, 1986: 56)

The market process perspective emphasizes several themes linking entrepreneurship and marketing. Markets are dynamic and firms' success depends on never-ending alertness to opportunities and competition. Competition is a complex process requiring an intimate understanding and an intricate interchange of information between the supply-side and the demand-side of a market. Suppliers must focus on the wants of buyers, and often imagine them before the buyers do themselves. Exploiting opportunities depends on organizing the market-making services that allow demand to be fulfilled and on influencing demand enough to recover the costs. Two kinds of process, one continuous and gradual, the other discontinuous and disruptive, are both important.

5.3 The marketing perspective

Marketing activities, designed to overcome obstacles to trade, have a long pedigree. Fullerton (1988) places the origins of 'modern marketing' ('pervasive attention to stimulating and meeting demand among nearly all of society') at 1759 in Britain and around 1830 in Germany and USA (Fullerton, 1988: 122). We have seen that Marshall described marketing activities in 1919, but an established literature on marketing, and particularly the identification of marketing as a distinct business function, is much more recent. The 'marketing management school' was initiated in the 1950s and 1960s with the aim of promoting a more entrepreneurial approach to business management, especially through being more deliberately market oriented. It was applied most widely in large firms, and what developed was a framework of rational market planning which was well adapted to conditions of market stability but which, in the view of some, failed when markets were turbulent, the very conditions in which entrepreneurship is needed. A subsequent approach, therefore, has proposed an entrepreneurial mode of marketing. This section first examines the origins and character of marketing management and then the entrepreneurial approach that has grown out of it.

5.3.1 Marketing management

The starting point of the marketing management school was the thesis that the decline of once successful businesses was most often due to a failure of management. The failure was to be too concerned with their products and with selling them in the face of competition and not concerned enough with changing requirements of their markets which would in time make these products obsolete (Levitt, 1960). The answer for firms was to adopt a new business philosophy, in the marketing concept, and a business function, in marketing management (Baker, 2000).

Several authors helped to build the new school of thought, including Drucker (1954), Levitt (1960), McCarthy (1960), Borden (1964) and Kotler (1967). The view of marketing that these and others created was that it was the leading function of business which, applied effectively, would enable any firm to meet the requirements of customers and meet its own goals. Note, for example, the definite article in the American Marketing Association definition:

> Marketing is *the* process of planning and executing the conception, pricing, promotion, and distribution of ideas, goods, services to create exchanges that satisfy individual and organizational goals. (Bennett, 1995, emphasis added)

Marketing management developed as an intellectual discipline which was systematic, analytical and comprehensive. Optimal performance in a given market could be achieved by managing the marketing mix (product, price, promotion, distribution); the needs of different customers could be analysed by identifying market segments; products could be differentiated by positioning; customer tastes could be understood through marketing research; competition could be understood by competitor analysis; economic, technical, social and political trends could be tracked by analysing the marketing environment. Innovation, for Levitt the *raison d'être* of the new ideas, could also be systematized: idea screening, concept testing, product development, test marketing, national launch.

In a review of the development of marketing management Webster (1992) observed how the new approach drew enthusiastically on economics, behavioural science and quantitative methods, in line with the demand from policy analysts of the day for rigorous analysis in business education. The new ideas for professional marketing were adopted most quickly and most extensively by large, hierarchical, integrated corporations, for whom 'responsible marketing management called for careful problem definition, evaluation of multiple alternatives from which a course of action would be chosen that had the highest probability, based on the analysis, of maximizing profit' (Webster, 1992: 3–4). The original advocates of managerial marketing had wanted established firms to anticipate and be the leaders of change (Levitt, 1960, 1983). But it became, in the way it was taught, an 'optimizing paradigm' and was formalized into a set of models and routines.

Did this framework improve the market-making process in the way it was hoped by its authors? Or did it replace one managerial failure, product focus, with another: centralized, bureaucratic marketing which would hold back entrepreneurship? The answer is, cautiously, yes to both. The growth of managerial marketing was well aligned with the relatively stable market conditions of the time in which it developed. Mass consumer markets grew, corporations expanded. The deliberative, formalized approach of marketing management gave firms a sophisticated method for developing their 'external organization' which may have helped to bring about (but at least coincided with) a period of fruitful Marshallian competition and high optimism. But stability and growth did not last. The 1970s were less certain and more turbulent, and the optimizing model of managerial marketing became the subject of critical discussion, some of which sought explicitly to address the role of the entrepreneurial spirit.

5.3.2 The entrepreneurial mode of marketing

In a significant paper Murray (1981) drew on the idea of Ansoff et al. (1976) that firms' behaviour reflected the changing business environment. In a stable environment firms are able to maximize the efficiency of systems which they know and understand, within accepted, unchanging strategic parameters. They can, and do, engage in innovation, but in these conditions they do so continuously (in the sense of incrementally). This environment and this behaviour are what Ansoff et al. and Murray call 'competitive'. 'Competitive' behaviour in this sense corresponds to managerial optimization. An unstable environment however does not permit 'continuous' optimizing behaviour of this kind. When the environment is turbulent, then only discontinuous strategic change will do. This environment and this behaviour are both called 'entrepreneurial'. We therefore have two possible modes of behaviour, and adaptive firms must be able to encompass both if they are to remain competitive in competitive markets and to weather the turbulence of entrepreneurial ones.

Murray's strongest claim, however, is to place marketing at the heart of the entrepreneurial mode, just as the optimizing marketing view sees marketing as the focus of the competitive mode.

> Of all the areas of specialist technical and professional expertise, marketing is uniquely equipped, and indeed should feel uniquely responsible, for analyzing environmental evolution and translating its observations into recommendations for redesign of the corporate resource base and its product-market portfolio. (Murray, 1981: 96)
>
> One requirement is that the marketing manager become something of a professional administrative entrepreneur. ... There is a need therefore for managers who are creative, innovative, skilled in initiating and managing organizational change, and open to radical reconceptualizations of their market and their consumer environment. (Murray, 1981: 97)

The first part of Murray's proposition, that management can adopt different modes with different entrepreneurial character, has been widely explored.

Mintzberg (1973) discussed characteristics of entrepreneurial, adaptive and planning modes, together with the environments and the stages of development of firms in which they are likely to be found. He thought that large firm planning required a relatively stable environment, but acknowledged the possibility of mixed modes, such as entrepreneurial planning. Miller and Friesen studied entrepreneurial behaviour in several types of firms (Miller and Friesen, 1982; Miller, 1983) and the impact of the business environment on entrepreneurial strategy-making (Miller and Friesen, 1983; see also Covin and Slevin, 1989). It has become widely accepted that established, mature corporations and not just new ventures can be entrepreneurial (Stevenson and Jarillo, 1990). Covin and Slevin (1991) proposed a conceptual model of entrepreneurial behaviour in large established firms: entrepreneurial firms are *risk-taking*, *innovative* and *proactive*, and the choice of posture may be influenced by environmental factors and strategic position as well as organization culture, resources and structure.

The second part of Murray's (1981) proposition was that marketing itself is inherently entrepreneurial and should play a central role in the entrepreneurial firm. Several subsequent authors of that period reflected on the same idea. Jain (1983) discussed the evolution of strategic marketing as a stage which can anticipate change and alter the strategic parameters, prior to the optimizing activities of marketing management. More radically, Zeithaml and Zeithaml (1984) suggested that the marketing discipline should be reformulated. Whereas it had traditionally been reactive, in effect a constrained optimization, subject to 'uncontrollable' environmental factors it should develop strategies for proactive, entrepreneurial management of the external environment. Simmonds argued that marketing can be viewed as 'organized rational innovation–a function concerned with identifying the opportunity for change, introducing the action required and monitoring the change once introduced' (1986: 479). Citing Alderson (1965), he saw marketing as 'fundamentally about change' (p. 494) and the problem to be addressed was how to establish and maintain an innovative marketing function within an organizational environment which would resist.

These ideas have been followed by a stream of empirical research examining the relationships between marketing, entrepreneurship, innovation and performance. Morris and Paul (1987) reported a positive association between *entrepreneurial orientation* (measured by attitudes and behaviour reflecting company management's approach to risk, to innovation and demonstrating proactiveness, after Miller and Friesen, 1983) and *marketing orientation* (measured by organization structure, sources of customer feedback and managerial attitudes). Morris et al. (1988) found that marketing managers perceived that entrepreneurial characteristics of firms and individuals are important for the success of a firm and that the marketing department was the strongest source of such expertise. Support for the suggestion that entrepreneurship and innovation matter comes from research into the marketing concept itself. Researchers seeking to establish a simple relationship between market orientation and firm performance have found that increased market orientation alone does appear to be positively related to performance (Kohli and Jaworski, 1990; Kohli, Jaworski, and Kumar, 1993; Narver and Slater, 1990), but that it is not sufficient. Barrett and Weinstein (1998) tested a model in which corporate entrepreneurship, market orientation and flexibility are all connected with performance; Han, Kim, and Srivastava (1998) found evidence that innovation was an important mediating factor; Hult and Ketchen (2001) reported significant contributions from entrepreneurship, innovativeness and organizational learning together with market orientation; Matsuno, Mentzer, and Özsomer (2002) found that entrepreneurial proclivity affected market orientation and the effect of entrepreneurial proclivity on performance was positive only when mediated by market orientation; Weerawarden and O'Cass (2004) found that both entrepreneurial intensity and market focused learning capability are important factors in sustained competitive advantage from innovation.

The close relationship between marketing and entrepreneurship suggested by this research prompted Miles and Arnold (1991) to ask whether marketing orientation and entrepreneurial orientation were the same or whether they were distinct 'business philosophies'. Factor analysis of the responses of a sample of senior managers to multi-item scales for each construct implied that the constructs were positively correlated but measurably different. Atuahene-Gima and Ko (2001) clarify the difference between the two:

> [M]arketing orientation is an adaptive capability by which firms *react* or *respond* to conditions in the market environment. ... Entrepreneurial orientation, in contrast, is an environmental management capability by which firms embark on proactive and aggressive initiatives to *alter* the competitive landscape to their advantage. (Atuahene-Gima and Ko, 2001: 57)

The importance of the distinction is the basis of a recent highly specific claim by Bhuian, Menguc, and Bell (2005) that the relationship between market orientation and business performance is convex with respect to entrepreneurial orientation. When entrepreneurial orientation is too low, firms are risk averse and do not exploit the insights that market intelligence reveals. Innovation is cautious and incremental and the relation between market orientation and performance is weak. When entrepreneurial orientation is too high, then firms use market intelligence only selectively. Innovation is R&D driven and may not be well aligned to market conditions. Again the relation between market orientation and performance is weak. When entrepreneurial orientation is 'just right', firms use the right amount of market intelligence to evaluate their entrepreneurial initiatives and the relation between market intelligence and performance is strong.

While the market process perspective considers market competition as a system, the marketing perspective examines implications for management within the firm. Just as marketing and entrepreneurship are linked in the market, they appear as distinct but complementary components of the management process. Markets exist because market-making is undertaken by firms and market orientation aligns management with the market process. It is therefore not surprizing to find that the mode of marketing management can reflect the type of market process. In stable 'Marshallian' conditions, continuously incremental ('competitive') marketing may yield the best results. But in other conditions, or when an opportunity is identified, discontinuous, Schumpeterian innovation is better. To echo Loasby, there are two types of marketing process and for any firm, over time, there will almost certainly be a need for both.

5.4 The entrepreneurial firm perspective

In much of the entrepreneurship literature the entrepreneur is, by definition, the creator of a new firm (Gartner, 1988, 1990). As discussed above, Casson's (2003) view of the newly created firm is an organization through which the entrepreneur facilitates market exchange. In this respect entrepreneurial firm creation is market-making at its most direct and, although entrepreneurs may not always describe it as such, it is a form of marketing.

The term *entrepreneurial firm* will largely be used in this section to denote a newly founded entrepreneurial business. In part this is because the predominant focus of the entrepreneurship literature is the new firm and the aim of this section is to examine what this literature has to say on the subject of marketing. It is also intended to reflect the idea that firm creation is itself an act of entrepreneurial marketing which is central to the theme of this chapter. However, well-established entrepreneurially oriented firms of the kind discussed in the previous section can also be described as entrepreneurial firms and some ideas discussed here apply to these cases equally well.

Two characteristics of the new entrepreneurial firm have implications for its approach to marketing. One is the novelty and the innovative character of its activities, so that expertise is usually concentrated in a small group or on a single individual. The other is its relatively small size and the consequent limited availability of resources. Tyebjee et al. (1983) proposed that marketing in such firms passes through four definable stages from birth to maturity. The new firm is in the 'entrepreneurial marketing' stage, the least structured and most informal of the four. Entrepreneurial marketing is identified with the person of the founding entrepreneur. Market contacts depend on the entrepreneur's personal network, customers rely on attention of top management and low volumes preclude expenditure on promotion and sales staff. Only as the firm progresses through the subsequent stages, comprising 'gradual delegation', 'specialization' and finally 'professionalization', does the marketing function conform to the managerial model.

Research on marketing in the entrepreneurial firm is comparatively recent and no strong consensus has yet emerged. The remainder of this section examines two strands in which some foundations have been laid. The first is a specific programme of research at the 'marketing/entrepreneurship interface'. The second is of more general work on marketing in small firms.

5.4.1 The marketing/entrepreneurship interface

The most sustained exploration of marketing in the entrepreneurial firm is in the Research at the Marketing/Entrepreneurship Interface Symposia, published to date in fifteen volumes of *Proceedings of the UIC Symposium on Marketing and Entrepreneurship* (Hills, 1987; Hills et al., 1989–2002). Research in this programme examines entrepreneurial activity in fine detail and a review is beyond the scope of this chapter. A common research agenda between marketing and entrepreneurship was described by Hills and LaForge (1992) and Hills (1994) collected together preliminary findings. An early framework was provided by Gardner (1994) who defined the interface between marketing and entrepreneurial behaviour as 'that area where innovation is brought to market' (1994: 38). He identified information as the 'key and principal variable to understand the marketing/entrepreneurship interface' (p. 45), noting Alderson's (1965) emphasis on information flows and Casson's (1982, 1st edn) view (cited in Gardner, 1994) of the entrepreneur as the critical seeker and synthesizer of this information. He pictured the marketing/entrepreneurship interface as a gap between the entrepreneur (including the 'intrapreneur' or the large entrepreneurially oriented firm) on one side and the market on the other. The gap is surrounded by information, but it is to be filled with concepts. He listed what he saw as the major concepts (marketing concept; market segmentation; time, place and possession utility; product life cycle; strategic planning) but concluded that the gap remained to be filled: 'Marketing's role in innovation, then, is to provide the concepts, tools, and infrastructure to close the "gap" between innovation and market positioning to achieve sustainable competitive advantage' (Gardner, 1994: 49).

In a summary of recent conceptual developments at the marketing/entrepreneurship interface Morris et al. (2002) offered some concepts which could fill the gap. They define *entrepreneurial marketing* as 'a proactive, innovative, risk-taking approach to the identification and exploitation of opportunities for attracting and

Table 5.1 Emerging concepts in marketing

Concept	Origin	Characteristics
Guerrilla marketing	Levinson, 1998	Doing more with less, low cost innovative promotion, networking, use time rather than money
Expeditionary marketing	Hamel and Prahalad, 1992	Lead the market rather than follow, continuous search for innovation, tolerate failure
Environmental marketing management	Zeithaml and Zeithaml, 1984	Reduce dependency on external factors, remove constraints, proactive not reactive
Radical marketing	Hill and Rifkin, 1999	Visceral ties with customers, passion drives marketing, CEO 'owns' marketing function
Subversive marketing	Bonoma, 1986	Undermine formal structures, entrepreneurial role models, aggressive, action oriented informal networks
Proactive marketing	Davis et al., 1991	Marketing role to effect and manage change, redefine product and market context, find novel sources of customer value

Source: Morris et al. (2002).

retaining profitable customers' (2002: 22), not merely a stage of marketing but applicable to the new entrepreneurial firm and to the entrepreneurial corporation alike. Drawing on six 'perspectives on the emerging nature of marketing' (Table 5.1) they propose six elements around which marketing's role is to be designed (Table 5.2).

Entrepreneurial marketing, say the authors, represents a 'different approach' from the managerial model of marketing in that 'the firm seeks to lead customers as opposed to reacting to or following them, and attention is devoted to the creation of new markets rather than better serving existing markets' (2002: 22). Here is a clear reflection of the Schumpeterian role for marketing advocated by Levitt, Murray and others. The elements in Table 5.2 capture a number of important entrepreneurial characteristics, and are likely to be found to some degree in most entrepreneurial firms. They do not yet constitute a fully integrated theory of entrepreneurship and marketing, but the ideas reviewed by these authors demonstrate that a relationship can be forged between them.

Table 5.2 Elements of entrepreneurial marketing (Morris, Schindehutte, and LaForge, 2002)

Element	Detail
Customer intensity	'... used to capture a sense of conviction, passion, zeal, enthusiasm and belief in where marketing is attempting to take the firm and the way in which it plans to get there.' (p. 23)
Sustainable innovation	'... involves the ability at an organizational level to maintain a flow of internally and externally motivated ideas, where these ideas are translatable into new products, services, processes, technology applications, and/or markets.' (p. 23)
Strategic flexibility	'... a willingness to continuously rethink and make adjustments to the firm's strategies, action plans, and resource allocations, as well as to company structure, culture and managerial systems.' (p. 23)
Calculated risk-taking	'... reasonable awareness of the risks involved ... and an attempt to manage such risk factors.' (p. 24)
Environmental pro-activeness	Draws on Zeithaml and Zeithaml (1984), discussed earlier
Resource leverage	'... entrepreneurial marketers are not constrained by the resources they currently control' (p. 25). The idea is that entrepreneurs can either stretch resources further than others, or can make use of resources owned by others to pursue their own purpose.

5.4.2 Small firm marketing

Outside the marketing/entrepreneurship interface school, research relevant to marketing in the entrepreneurial firm is to be found mainly in work on marketing in small firms. Not all work in this area addresses the entrepreneurial character of the firm. Recent surveys of marketing theory (Siu and Kirby, 1998) and marketing practices (Coviello et al., 2000) in small firms concluded that, while theory was underdeveloped, 'small firm marketing, although unique in certain aspects, is not fundamentally different from large firm marketing' (Coviello et al., 2000: 541).

Two studies which have considered entrepreneurial marketing in small innovating firms are Carson et al. (1995) and Bjerke and Hultman (2002). The approach by Carson et al. adapts conventional marketing for the constraints and circumstances of the small entrepreneurial firm, proposing additional concepts which should be incorporated in the analysis (Figure 5.1). These are specialized entrepreneurial competencies (such as judgement, knowledge and communication) and entrepreneurial networks (both personal and inter-organizational).

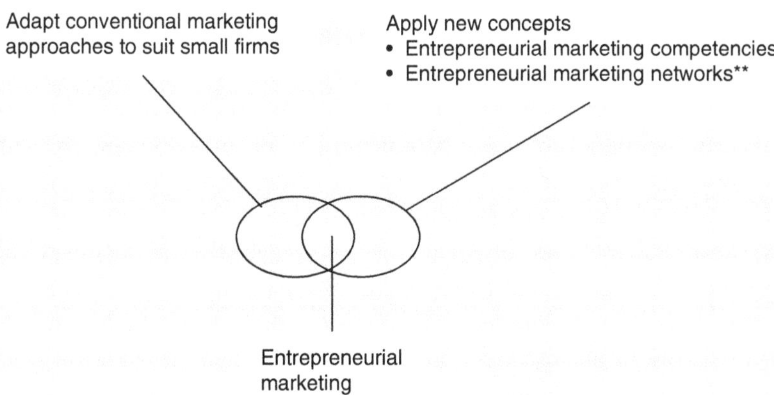

Figure 5.1 Entrepreneurial marketing (Carson et al., 1995)

∗ Entrepreneurial marketing competencies:

Judgement competency, experience competency, knowledge competency, communication competency

∗∗ Entrepreneurial marketing networks:

Personal contact network, inter-organizational relationships: mediated by information, supply and communicate ideas, access resources and skills, fill gaps in the entrepreneurs own competencies.

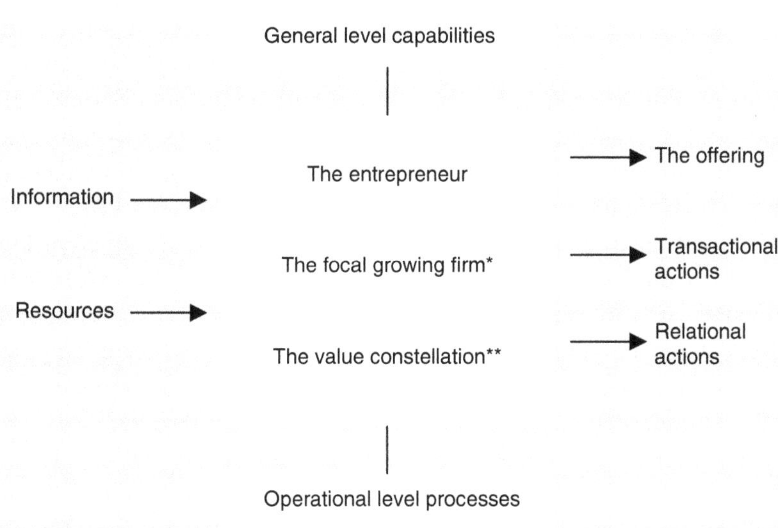

Figure 5.2 Entrepreneurial marketing (Bjerke and Hultman, 2002)

∗ Focal growing firm = owned resources and internal collaborators in value creation

∗∗ Value constellation = network of external collaborators in value creation

Bjerke and Hultman's study sets out a richer and more complex thesis. Entrepreneurial marketing is conceived as the route to 'co-creation' of value with customers in a new, dynamic economic era. In contrast with 'managerial growth' in structured 'focal organizations' of the old era, the new era will be characterized by 'entrepreneurial growth' in 'virtual organizations'. At the centre is entrepreneurial marketing, whose structural components are an entrepreneur, the entrepreneur's market-making firm (the 'focal growing firm') and a network of collaborators (the 'value constellation') (Figure 5.2).

These studies share some of their conclusions, yet they also convey different messages. Both emphasize that entrepreneurial capabilities are distinct and central to the firm and that entrepreneurial organization is likely to be an informal, extended network at personal, and at inter-organizational, levels. However, while the adaptive framework of Carson et al. suggests that the management processes of entrepreneurial marketing are fundamentally similar to those in the managerial firm, Bjerke and Hultman sought to show that the two are fundamentally different.

5.5 Summary and Further Research

Entrepreneurship and marketing are connected in a number of ways. Entrepreneurs reconfigure market exchange and marketing is the functional manifestation of this process. Entrepreneurs are alert to the potential wants of customers and the customer-oriented marketing concept is the managerial expression of this mindset. Entrepreneurs are specialists in judgemental decision-making and marketing provides the framework for applying intuition to heterogeneous markets.

A theme that has run through this chapter is that there are different kinds of process both at the level of the market and at the level of the firm. A Marshallian market process of continuous learning and gradual innovation corresponds approximately with 'competitive' managerial marketing. A Schumpeterian process of discontinuous innovation corresponds approximately with entrepreneurial marketing. Both are needed at different times and in different degrees.

It is evident that a good deal of common ground in the analysis of entrepreneurship and marketing already exists among the approaches explored in this chapter. But there is potential for more work in a number of areas. The market process approach, and in particular the theory of the market-making firm, provides a natural foundation for a general theory of marketing. Consequently the transaction cost approach has a good deal more to contribute to the analysis of entrepreneurial marketing. On the other hand, the marketing perspective also suggests a richer and more detailed view of market processes. Marketing implies that firms seek to survive by continual change and consequently Schumpeterian entrepreneurship commonly takes place within entrepreneurially managed firms. The market process is underpinned by a management process which should be analysed in institutional detail. As yet, models of the entrepreneurial firm are diverse and under-developed and more work is needed to understand the entrepreneurial processes within firms both conceptually and empirically. What marketing practices, for example, are most effective in mediating between the market and the internal entrepreneurial process? Are there limits to the forms and degree of innovation that an organization can achieve, due for example to the need for organizational coherence within the firm?

The interface between marketing and entrepreneurship is a promising field of active research. It is hoped that some of the ideas reviewed here will contribute to its future development.

References

Alderson, W. (1957). *Marketing Behavior and Executive Action: A Functionalist Approach to Marketing Theory.* Homewood, IL: Richard D. Irwin.

—— (1965). *Dynamic Marketing Behavior.* Homewood, IL: Richard D. Irwin.

Ansoff, H. I., R. P. Declerck and R. L. Hayes (1976). *From Strategic Planning to Strategic Management.* New York, NY: Wiley.

Atuahene-Gima, K. and A. Ko (2001). 'An Empirical Investigation of the Effect of Market Orientation and Entrepreneurial Orientation Alignment on Product Innovation'. *Organizational Science,* 12(1): 54–74.

Baker, M. J. (2000). 'Marketing – Philosophy or Function?', in Michael J. Baker (ed.) *Marketing Theory: A Student Text.* London: Business Press, Thomson Learning.

Barrett, H. and A. Weinstein (1998). 'The Effect of Market Orientation and Organizational Flexibility on Corporate Entrepreneurship'. *Entrepreneurship Theory and Practice,* 23(1): 57–80.

Bennett, P. D. (1995). *Dictionary of Marketing Terms.* Chicago, IL: American Marketing Association.

Bhuian, S. N., B. Menguc and S. J. Bell (2005). 'Just Entrepreneurial Enough: The Moderating Effect of Entrepreneurship on the Relationship Between Market Orientation and Performance'. *Journal of Business Research,* 58: 9–17.

Bjerke, B. and C. M. Hultman (2002). *Entrepreneurial Marketing: The Growth of Small Firms in the New Economic Era.* Cheltenham: Edward Elgar.

Boettke, P. J. and D. L. Prychitko (eds) (1994). *The Market Process: Essays in Contemporary Austrian Economics.* Aldershot: Edward Elgar.

Bonoma, T. V. (1986). 'Marketing Subversives'. *Harvard Business Review* (November–December) 64: 113–118.

Borden, N. H. (1964). 'The Marketing Mix'. *Journal of Advertising Research* (June) 4: 2–7.

Carson, D., S. Cromie, P. McGowan and J. Hill (1995). *Marketing and Entrepreneurship in SMEs: An Innovative Approach.* London: Prentice Hall.

Casson, M. (2003). *The Entrepreneur: An Economic Theory* (2nd edn). Cheltenham: Edward Elgar.

Coviello, N., R. J. Brodie and H. J. Munro (2000). 'An Investigation of Marketing Practice by Firm Size'. *Journal of Business Venturing*, 15: 523–45.

Covin, J. G. and D. P. Slevin (1989). 'Strategic Management of the Small Firm in Hostile and Benign Environments'. *Strategic Management Journal*, 10(1): 75–87.

—— and —— (1991). 'A Conceptual Model of Entrepreneurship as Firm Behaviour'. *Entrepreneurship Theory and Practice*, 16(1): 7–25.

Crosier, K. (1988). 'What Exactly Is Marketing?', in Michael J. Thomas and Norman E. Waite (eds) *The Marketing Digest.* Oxford: Heinemann Professional Publishing.

Davis, D., M. Morris and J. Allen (1991). 'Perceived Environmental Turbulence and its Effect on Selected Entrepreneurship, Marketing and Organizational Characteristics in Industrial Firms'. *Journal of Academy of Marketing Science* (Spring) 19: 43–51.

Dickson, P. R. (1992). 'Toward a General Theory of Competitive Rationality'. *Journal of Marketing*, 56(1): 69–83.

Drucker, P. (1954). *The Practice of Management.* New York: Harper and Row.

Foss, N. J. and J. F. Christensen (2001). 'A Market Process Approach to Corporate Coherence'. *Managerial and Decision Economics*, 22: 213–26.

Fullerton, R. A. (1988). 'How Modern is Modern Marketing? Marketing's Evolution and the Myth of the Production Era'. *Journal of Marketing* (January) 52: 108–125.

Gardner, D. M. (1994). 'Marketing/Entrepreneurship Interface: A Conceptualization', in G. E. Hills (ed.) *Marketing and Entrepreneurship: Research Ideas and Opportunities.* Westport, CO: Quorum Books.

Gartner, W. B. (1988). 'Who is an Entrepreneur? is the Wrong Question'. *Entrepreneurship Theory and Practice*, 12(4): 11–32.

—— (1990). 'What Are We Talking About When We Talk About Entrepreneurship?'. *Journal of Business Venturing*, 5(1): 15–36.

Hamel, G. and C. K. Prahalad (1992). 'Corporate Imagination and Expeditionary Marketing'. *Harvard Business Review* (July–August) 69: 31–43.

Han, J. K., N. Kim and R. K. Srivastava (1998). 'Market Orientation and Organizational Performance: Is Innovation the Missing Link?' *Journal of Marketing* (October) 62: 30–45.

Hayek, F. A. von (1945). 'The Use of Knowledge in Society'. *American Economic Review*, 35(4): 33–54.

—— (1948). *Individualism and Economic Order.* London: Routledge and Kegan Paul.

Hill, S and G. Rifkin (1999). *Radical Marketing: From Harvard to Harley, Lessons From Ten That Broke the Rules and Made It Big.* New York: Harper Collins.

Hills, G. E. (ed.) (1987). *Research at the Marketing/Entrepreneurship Interface*, vol. 1. Chicago, IL: University of Chicago Press.

—— (ed.) (1994). *Marketing and Entrepreneurship: Research Ideas and Opportunities.* Westport, CT: Quorum Books.

—— and R. W. LaForge (1992). 'Research at the Marketing Interface to Advance Entrepreneurship Theory'. *Entrepreneurship Theory and Practice*, 16(3): 33–59.

—— ——, B. J. Parker et al. (eds) (1989–2002). *Research at the Marketing/Entrepreneurship Interface*, vols 2–15. Chicago, IL: University of Chicago Press.

Houston, F. S. (1986). 'The Marketing Concept: What It Is and What It Is Not'. *Journal of Marketing* (April) 50: 81–7.

Hult, G. T. M. and D. J. Ketchen (2001). 'Does Market Orientation Matter? A Test of the Relationship Between Positional Advantage and Performance'. *Strategic Management Journal*, 22: 899–906.

Jain, S. C. (1983). 'The Evolution of Strategic Marketing'. *Journal of Business Research*, 11: 409–425.

Kirzner, Israel M. (1973). *Competition and Entrepreneurship*. Chicago, IL: University of Chicago Press.

—— (1979). *Perception, Opportunity and Profit*. Chicago. IL: University of Chicago Press.

—— (1997). 'Entrepreneurial Discovery and the Competitive Market Process: An Austrian Approach'. *Journal of Economic Literature*. (March) 35: 60–85.

Keith, R. J. (1960). 'The Marketing Revolution'. *Journal of Marketing* (January) 24: 35–8.

Kohli, A. K. and B. J. Jaworski (1990). 'Market Orientation: The Construct, Research Propositions and Managerial Implications'. *Journal of Marketing* (April) 54: 1–18.

—— —— and A. Kumar (1993). 'MARKOR: A Measure of Market Orientation'. *Journal of Marketing Research* (November) 30: 467–77.

Kotler, P. (1967). *Marketing Management: Analysis, Planning and Control*. Englewood Cliffs, NJ: Prentice-Hall.

—— (2000). *Marketing Management: The Millennium Edition*. Upper Saddle River, NJ: Prentice-Hall.

Krafft, J. (ed.) (2000). *The Process of Competition*. Cheltenham: Edward Elgar.

Kuhn, T. S. (1962). *The Structure of Scientific Revolutions*. Chicago, IL: University of Chicago Press.

Lachman, L. (1976). 'From Mises to Shackle: An Essay on Austrian Economics and the Kaleidic Society', *Journal of Economic Literature*, 14(1): 54–62.

—— (1977). *Capital, Expectations, and the Market Process*. Kansas City: Sheed, Andrews and McMeel.

—— (1986). *The Market as an Economic Process*. Oxford: Oxford University Press.

Lakatos, I. (1970). 'Falsification and the Methodology of Scientific Research Programmes', in Imre Lakatos and A. Musgrave (eds) *Criticism and the Growth of Knowledge*. Cambridge: Cambridge University Press.

Lancaster, K. (1971). *Consumer Demand: A New Approach*. New York: Columbia University Press.

Langlois, R. N. (ed.) (1986). *Economics as a Process*. Cambridge: Cambridge University Press.

Levinson, C. (1998). *Guerrilla Marketing: Secrets for Making Big Profits From Your Small Business*. Boston, MA: Houghton Mifflin Company.

Levitt, T. (1960). 'Marketing Myopia'. *Harvard Business Review* (July/August), pp. 45–56.

—— (1983). *The Marketing Imagination*. New York: The Free Press.

Littlechild, S. C. (1982). 'Controls on Advertising: An Examination of Some Economic Arguments'. *Journal of Advertising*, 1: 25–37.

—— (1986). 'Three Types of Market Process', in R. N. Langlois (ed.) *Economics as a Process*. Cambridge: Cambridge University Press.

Loasby, B. J. (1976). *Choice, Complexity and Ignorance*. Cambridge: Cambridge University Press.

Loasby, B. J. (1986). 'Organization, Competition and the Growth of Knowledge', in R. N. Langlois (ed.) *Economics as a Process*. Cambridge: Cambridge University Press.

—— (1999). *Knowledge, Institutions and Evolution in Economics*. London: Routledge.

Marshall, A. (1919). *Industry and Trade*. London: Macmillan.

—— 1920. *Principles of Economics* (8th edn). London: Macmillan.

Matsuno, K., J. T. Mentzer and A. Özsomer (2002). 'The Effects of Entrepreneurial Proclivity and Market Orientation on Business Performance'. *Journal of Marketing* (July) 66: 18–32.

McCarthy, E. J. (1960). *Basic Marketing: A Managerial Approach*. Homewood, IL: Irwin.

McKitterick, J. B. (1957). 'What Is the Marketing Concept?' *The Frontiers of Marketing Thought and Action*. Chicago, IL: American Marketing Association.

Miles, M. P. and D. R. Arnold (1991). 'The Relationship Between Marketing Orientation and Entrepreneurial Orientation'. *Entrepreneurship Theory and Practice*, 15(4): 49–65.

Miller, D. (1983). 'The Correlates of Entrepreneurship in Three Types of Firms'. *Management Science*, 29(7): 770–91.

—— and P. H. Friesen (1982). 'Innovation in Conservative and Entrepreneurial Firms: Two Models of Strategic Momentum'. *Strategic Management Journal*, 3(1): 1–25.

—— and —— (1983). 'Strategy-Making and the Environment: The Third Link'. *Strategic Management Journal*, 4(3): 221–35.

Mintzberg, H. (1973). 'Strategy-Making in Three Modes'. *California Management Review*, 16(2): 44–9.

Mises, L. von (1949). *Human Action*. New Haven: Yale University Press.

Morris, M. H. and G. W. Paul (1987). 'The Relationship Between Entrepreneurship and Marketing in Established Firms'. *Journal of Business Venturing*, 2: 247–59.

—— D. L. Davis and J. Ewing (1988). 'The Role of Entrepreneurship in Industrial Marketing Activities'. *Industrial Marketing Management*, 17: 337–46.

—— M. Schindehutte and R. W. LaForge (2002). 'The Emergence of Entrepreneurial Marketing: Nature and Meaning', in G. E. Hills, D. J. Hansen, G. Solomon, T. and E. K. Winslow (eds) *Research at the Marketing/Entrepreneurship Interface*, vol. 15. Chicago, IL: University of Chicago Press.

Murray, J. A. (1981). 'Marketing Is Home for the Entrepreneurial Process'. *Industrial Marketing Management*, 10: 93–9.

Narver, J. C. and S. F. Slater (1990). 'The Effect of Marketing Orientation on Business Profitability'. *Journal of Marketing* (October) 54: 20–35.

Nelson, R. R. and S. G. Winter (1982). *An Evolutionary Theory of Economic Change*. Cambridge, MA: Harvard University Press.

Reekie, W. D. and R. Savitt (1982). 'Marketing Behaviour and Entrepreneurship: A Synthesis of Alderson and Austrian Economics'. *European Journal of Marketing*, 16(7): 55–66.

Robertson, P. L. and T. F. Yu (2001). 'Firm Strategy, Innovation and Consumer Demand: A Market Process Approach'. *Managerial and Decision Economics*, 22: 183–199.

Schumpeter, J. (1934). *The Theory of Economic Development: An Enquiry into Profits, Capital Credit, Interest and the Business Cycle*. Cambridge, MA: Harvard University Press.

Shackle, G. L. S. (1969). *Decision, Order and Time in Human Affairs* (2nd edn). Cambridge: Cambridge University Press.

—— (1972). *Epistemics and Economics: A Critique of Economic Doctrines*. Cambridge: Cambridge University Press.

Shackle, G. L. S. (1979). *Imagination and the Nature of Choice.* Edinburgh: Edinburgh University Press.

Shane, S. (2003). *A General Theory of Entrepreneurship: The Individual-Opportunity Nexus.* Cheltenham: Edward Elgar.

—— and S. Venkataraman (2000). 'The Promise of Entrepreneurship as a Field of Research'. *Academy of Management Review*, 26(1): 13–17.

Simmonds, K. (1986). 'Marketing as Innovation: The Eight Paradigm'. *Journal of Marketing Studies*, 23(5): 479–500.

Simon, H. A. (1978). 'Rationality as a Process and a Product of Thought'. *American Economic Review* (May) 68: 493–512.

Siu, W. and D. A. Kirby (1998). 'Approaches to Small Firm Marketing: A Critique'. *European Journal of Marketing*, 32(1–2): 40–53.

Stevenson, H. H. and J. C. Jarillo (1990). 'A Paradigm of Entrepreneurship: Entrepreneurial Management'. *Strategic Management Journal*, 11(5): 17–27.

Tyebjee, T. T., A. V. Bruno and S. M. McIntyre (1983). 'Growing Ventures Can Anticipate Marketing Stages'. *Harvard Business Review* (January–February) 61: 62–6.

Webster, F. E. (1992). 'The Changing Role of Marketing in the Corporation'. *Journal of Marketing* (October) 56: 1–17.

Weerawarden, J. and A. O'Cass (2004). 'Exploring the Characteristics of the Market-Driven Firms and Antecedents to Sustained Competitive Advantage'. *Industrial Marketing Management*, 33: 419–28.

Zeithaml, C. P. and V. A. Zeithaml (1984). 'Environmental Management: Revising the Marketing Perspective'. *Journal of Marketing* (Spring) 48: 46–53.

CHAPTER 6

HISTORICAL BIOGRAPHIES OF ENTREPRENEURS

T. A. B. CORLEY

6.1 Introduction

'Read no history', declared the novelist and future prime minister, Benjamin Disraeli; 'nothing but biography, for that is life without theory' (Disraeli, 1832). He plainly looked for straight narratives in the biographies he read, without superfluous theorizing to interrupt the flow. Even so, theory is a vital tool for assessing entrepreneurial lives.

Basic theory analyses the entrepreneur's role in the economic system. Of the four conventional factors of production, namely: land, labour, capital and organization (or entrepreneurship), objective demand and supply schedules are possible for the first three. By contrast, a demand curve for entrepreneurship cannot be drawn, as it is for the entrepreneurs themselves to decide whether or not to enter the production process as a free lance. Harvey Leibenstein, a development economist (see p. 143), however, constructed a *supply* curve for entrepreneurs, linking their anticipations of per capita income growth with the rate of expansion of entrepreneurship in terms of their contribution to such growth in incomes (Leibenstein, 1957: 132, 1978: 48–51).

Martin Ricketts, in Chapter 2 of this Handbook, discusses the connections between entrepreneurship and economic development or growth. However,

Frank H. Knight, in 1921, emphasized more static aspects of the entrepreneurial function, such as uncertainty bearing—which he usefully distinguished from insurable risk—organizing a firm's operations and acting as the ultimate decision-maker (Knight, 1921: 237, 275). It was Joseph A. Schumpeter, in his analysis of 'economic development', who linked entrepreneurship with making innovations, namely using a firm's resources in new and more growth-orientated combinations, as well as taking advantage of lucrative 'possibilities' (Schumpeter, 1934: 89, 214). More recently, economists have helped to clarify the topic of opportunities, whether technological, political or demographic—which are objective ones—and entrepreneurs' (subjective) decisions to take advantage of these opportunities, to promote growth (Shane, 2003). Mark Casson defines the entrepreneur as one who 'specializes in taking judgemental decisions about the co-ordination of scarce resources'; to Casson, co-ordination is a dynamic concept, which 'captures the fact that the entrepreneur is an agent of change' (Casson, 2003: 20–1).

Hence many theorists portray the corporate drives of entrepreneurs as forward-looking ones. How, then, can biographies most satisfactorily discuss such drives in a chronological narrative of a life from cradle to the grave? Childhood influences, such as premature responsibilities through a parent's death, and struggles for recognition in early adulthood have to be brought out, as well as the precise explanation of finally winning through. The distinguished Harvard business historian, Henrietta Larson (see p. 142) thereby characterized a good business biography as a 'rounded and balanced treatment of the subject's business career and his qualities which have a bearing on his work'. She found few entrepreneurial biographies that had so far met her criteria by being written with objectivity and also 'an effort to be scientific' (Larson, 1948: 91–2).

Larson's criteria (see section 6.2 to 6.6 below) should be borne in mind when assessing the historical and geographical surveys. Some conclusions will be offered in the last section.

6.2 Britain: The Victorian era

For the remainder of the nineteenth century after Disraeli's pronouncement, entrepreneurs in Britain used their initiatives and skills to transform their economy; as Ricketts has pointed out, 'from this period derives the idea of the heroic entrepreneur', who 'like the military commander, began to be studied and respected'. Paradoxically, even the most powerful industrial magnates of the era, who dominated some of the country's most productive economic regions, were not then commemorated by the full-scale biographies they merited. Sir Titus Salt, the Bradford pioneer in wool, was given a far from perceptive biographical tribute by a clerical friend (Balgarnie, 1877). John Rylands, the most eminent textile manufacturer in Manchester, earned only a few short appreciations of his lengthy career (Farnie, 1993). Neither William, Lord Armstrong nor the Vickers brothers, makers of armaments famous throughout northern England, received proper biographies until decades after their deaths (McKenzie, 1983; Trebilcock, 1977).

Indeed, only one biographer in that era wrote at all 'scientifically' on entrepreneurship. Samuel Smiles (1812–1904) was one who, having enjoyed a successful business career, understood entrepreneurs through and through. His principal subjects were pioneers in the industrial revolution, such as Matthew Boulton and James Watt, while his life of Josiah Wedgwood (Smiles, 1894) analysed Wedgwood's innovations in ceramic technology and also the—often overlooked—essential skill for an entrepreneur of a 'keen insight into the characters of men and women' (Smiles, 1894: 280; Matthew, 2004: 1003). Yet he did not found a genre of entrepreneurial biography in Britain.

The bulk of English people thus had little knowledge of these leading industrialists, an ignorance which publishers scarcely remedied. The three-volume *Fortunes Made in Business* (1884) featured virtually unknown British notables such as the textile innovator, Samuel Cunliffe Lister of Yorkshire. A later work, in parts, concentrated on foreign entrepreneurs such as Edison, Rockefeller and the Krupps armament dynasty, and expired after the eighth part ('Fortunes Made in Business,' 1901–02). Instead, it was the politician or battlefield hero who tended to earn instant biographies in life and two fat 'life and letters' volumes after death (Gosse, 1901: 195).

Neoclassical economists in Britain offered little theoretical guidance, with their static models in which the entrepreneur hardly featured. Only Alfred Marshall, one of the few British academics who had practical knowledge of business, in his *Principles of Economics* wrote a consummate paragraph-long biography of an ideal (imaginary) entrepreneur. It related how his firm would benefit from steadily growing internal economies, derived from specialized machinery and skills alike, overtaking rivals through its competitive advantages, and progressing as long as the business magnate's 'energy and enterprise retain their full strength and freshness' (Marshall, 1890: 315–16).

Marshall's analysis of the entrepreneur (or 'organization'), as the fourth factor of production, did not catch on among his contemporaries, and as an ultimate indignity the entrepreneur's marginal product in the industry was deemed by some leading economists to be negative (Chamberlin, 1962: 217). In that intellectual climate, British authors were unlikely to embark on a scholarly entrepreneurial biography. *The Life of George Cadbury*, for example, was written by a journalist, Alfred Gardiner, who concentrated on Cadbury as a person and underplayed the professional skills that won him the leadership of his industry in Britain, such as innovativeness, efficient industrial organization and astute marketing (Gardiner, 1923).

6.3 The United States and Germany, to 1925

German interest in the topic of entrepreneurship sprang from two sources. The country's rapid industrialization, especially after it was unified in 1870, earned entrepreneurs a public esteem they barely enjoyed in Britain, while theoretical economists in both Germany and Austria assigned a specific role to the entrepreneur. Eugen von Böhm-Bawerk of Vienna linked entrepreneurship to uncertainty, while Friedrich von Wieser stressed the economic importance of the creative and innovative entrepreneur, thereby inspiring Schumpeter's thought in that direction (Schumpeter, 1954: 893).

The German historical school was meanwhile analysing industry along empirical and historical lines. Gustav von Schmoller depicted entrepreneurs as business organizers and risk-takers. Werner Sombart, drawing on Marxian ideas, in his survey of modern capitalism's historical origins emphasized technical progress over time (Larson, 1948: 11–13; Schumpeter, 1954: 809–20; Krooss and Gilbert, 1972).

American authors, on the other hand, had a particular concern with the darker side of entrepreneurship. That country's tycoons were at the zenith of their aggressive fortune-grabbing, so that 'the great wealth of the few has dazzled the imagination of many' (Porter, 1932: 583). The exploits and misdeeds of 'robber barons' such as Cornelius Vanderbilt, J. Pierpont Morgan and Edward H. Harriman inspired any number of propagandist or alternatively 'muck-raking' biographical studies.

Having in their minds 'a case to prove rather than a problem to solve' (Porter, 1932: 596), writers made little attempt to probe deeply into their subjects' personalities or motivation. Only Ida M. Tarbell's *History of the Standard Oil Company* skilfully embedded the life of the founder, John D. Rockefeller, in her account of the corporation's progress, under an epigraph copied from Ralph Waldo Emerson, 'An Institution is the lengthened shadow of one man' (Tarbell, 1904). Academic works, such as a biography of the financier Jay Cooke (Oberholtzer, 1907), were short on analysis and critical judgement. Without a theoretical framework, which would come from Schumpeter and Knight, most biographers failed to capture the idiosyncratic qualities that drove entrepreneurs to such heights and depths of conduct.

6.4 Business history and biography in the United States 1925–2000

Until 1925, the few non-journalistic American contributions to entrepreneurial biography came from economists or economic historians such as Oberholtzer. That year, business history was born at Harvard Business School as an academic discipline, to help train students preparing for industrial or commercial careers.

The world's first professor of business history, Norman S. B. Gras, built his theory of entrepreneurship on Sombart's model of the stages of capitalism, linking them with the rising social status of business people. As Harvard taught by the case study method, some accounts of past entrepreneurial policies and problems were along biographical lines, assembled in a *Casebook in American Business History.* Thus one case discussed how Josiah Wedgwood organized the production and sale of his innovative range of chinaware, and another how John Wanamaker of Philadelphia evolved the concept of the department store (Gras and Larson, 1939). Henrietta Larson, the highly talented but undervalued chronicler of business history in its formative years, wrote a biography of *Jay Cooke, Private Banker,* based on Cooke's personal papers (Larson, 1936). As one of the first outstanding academic works in the genre, it was hailed as marking the dawn of the new and rigorous business history (Krooss, 1958: 469; Yeager, 2001: 744).

Historical studies poured out of Harvard Business School after 1925. Among 19 volumes of *Studies in Business History* was a life of John Jacob Astor of real-estate fame (Porter, 1931). Next year Porter wrote a pioneering survey of American business biography to date. He highlighted the difficulty of how to balance the analysis of business policies with a scrutiny of the 'intangible factors of character and temperament' in entrepreneurs (Porter, 1932: 608–9). From 1926 onwards, a *Bulletin of the Business Historical Society* was published. In 1957, it became the *Business History Review*; both carried biographical articles.

Larson's *Guide to Business History* offered a valuable *catalogue raisonné* of nearly 5,000 books and articles. In a section on biographies, she attributed the meagre number of academic entrepreneurial lives to the current reluctance of businesses to allow access to their records, deterred by the economic slump of 1929 onwards. That negative attitude vanished after 1945, largely thanks to the country's post-war boom and the enhanced reputation of business in general. Allan Nevins set a new standard of objectivity in *John D. Rockefeller: Industrialist and Philanthropist.* Rockefeller might have been personally unsympathetic, but deserved recognition for his first-rate organizational skills (Nevins, 1953).

Partly on Schumpeter's initiative, in 1948 the Research Center in Entrepreneurial History was established at Harvard, together with an associated journal, *Explorations in Entrepreneurial History.* The Center was to be an interdisciplinary one, employing social scientists of every hue, to uncover the roots of entrepreneurial success. With no agreed definition of entrepreneurship behind them, members failed to work out a systematic relationship between the entrepreneur and economic growth, and the Center closed its doors for lack of funds in 1958.

One important project, building on earlier research, was an enquiry into the social backgrounds of American entrepreneurs. F. W. Taussig and C. S. Joslyn had concluded that few in their sample of 7,000 top executives were from low-income families, thereby challenging the 'rags to riches' legend disseminated by the popular author, Horatio Alger (Taussig and Joslyn, 1932). An investigation of the 1,400 entries in the multi-volume *Dictionary of American Biography* likewise revealed that only 4 percent had been born into low-skilled workers' families (Johnson, 1928–36).

On the Center's behalf, Frances Gregory and Irene Neu had, during its lifetime, carried out a more sophisticated enquiry, based on directory entries of America's industrial elite in the 1870s. They found only 8 percent had operatives as fathers; less than a quarter had started work at 15 or younger (Gregory and Neu, 1962: 202–3). William Miller's similar researches for the period 1901–10 concluded that only 2 percent had originated in impoverished families and only a fifth had been working at 15; 'poor immigrants and poor farm boys who became business leaders have always been more conspicuous in American history books than in American history' (Miller, 1962: 328). For Britain, the French scholar François Crouzet surveyed 226 founders of the country's sizeable firms between 1750 and 1850. He discovered that only 7 percent came from a working-class background, of whom 3 percent were from the families of unskilled workmen (Crouzet, 1985: 139).

Barry Supple, when surveying American business history, contrasted trashy biographical works, conveying 'little except homiletic ramblings and unsubordinated platitudes', with 'a hard and growing kernel' of scholarly corporate histories (Supple, 1958: 70–1). The Center's former leading scholar, A. H. Cole, in his valedictory *Business Enterprise in its Social Setting*, maintained that the study of entrepreneurship required a combination of theory and historical data, studied in a dynamic context. Thus economic growth theory suggested how external factors, such as developing information flows, structures and social and economic conditions, stimulated entrepreneurs' motivation and performance; historians could then test that proposition experimentally (Cole, 1959: 225–48).

Cole's thesis found echoes in the new academic discipline of development economics, which geographically extended research on entrepreneurship beyond advanced countries to the whole world. Scholars investigating economic growth in countries from Burma to Peru found the main motive to be the fostering of indigenous entrepreneurs. In 1961–62, two topical works appeared: David C. McClelland's *The Achieving Society* and E. E. Hagen's *The Theory of Social Change.* Based on empirical findings about 'achievers' globally, they stressed the importance of researching into their childhoods, and especially relationships with parents (McClelland, 1961: 68; Hagen, 1962: 342). In 1978, Bernard Sarachek investigated

187 (mostly American) entrepreneurs from biographies and company histories. He found that 56 percent of their fathers had either died, rejected their offspring, deserted the family or were inadequate parents. Most in his sample began to work at an earlier age than those entrepreneurs blessed with supportive parents (Sarachek, 1978: 442–8).

Jonathan Hughes's *The Vital Few: American Economic Progress and its Protagonists* sought to breathe new life into entrepreneurial history and biography. That 'fledgling discipline', he claimed, had so far 'not produced a harvest in proportion to the sowing and cultivation'. He therefore selected eight entrepreneurs, four being 'robber barons' and two (idiosyncratically) William Penn the Quaker and Brigham Young the Mormon, as typical of successive periods (up to about 1910) in the development of the US economy. He provided no theoretical framework, while his often digressive accounts of each subject's career lacked original research and yielded few fresh insights into their personalities or attainments. Hence that work generated more academic interest than it deserved (Hughes, 1973).

From the 1970s onwards, academic entrepreneurial biographies, especially about leaders of the country's technologically advanced industries, became more plentiful in the United States. In automobiles, Anne Jardim's psycho-historical biography of the first Henry Ford expertly dissected his various drives, above all a determination not to relax control of the corporation he had created (Jardim, 1970). Alfred Chandler and Stephen Salsbury wrote on Pierre du Pont and his innovations in modern industrial management, successively as head of General Motors and of the Du Pont chemical corporation (Chandler and Salsbury, 1971). R. E. Olds, founder of Oldsmobile, was given a more conventional biography (May, 1977), while Robert McNamara, before becoming a top politician, had earlier energetically rescued the Ford Motor Company from trouble (Shapley, 1993). Alfred P. Sloan, acknowledged as the country's foremost entrepreneur during the first half of the twentieth century, left his own reminiscences as head of General Motors (Sloan, 1963). His biography has since been written with great skill by David Farber, entitled *Sloan Rules* (Farber, 2002).

However, America's powerful drugs industry still awaits biographies of its principal leaders. A life of Eli Lilly has been published (Madison, 1989), but the innovative entrepreneurs in the world's top pharmaceutical company, Merck, have yet to be chronicled singly or in a full-length corporate history. A lately retired chief executive of Merck, assisted by an economic historian expert in the field, has published a genial and well-constructed autobiography (Vagelos and Galambos, 2004). However, that work was on the whole less useful to historians than the more astringent reminiscences of H. G. Lazell, chairman of the British pharmaceutical giant, Beecham, and pioneer of its semi-synthetic penicillins (Lazell, 1975).

American entrepreneurship over an extensive range of other industries can be illustrated by comparing the life of Henry J. Kaiser, a road and dam builder who turned his hand to mass-producing Liberty ships in the second world war (Foster,

1989) with the innovative family which ran the nation's largest privately-owned company, the grain trader Cargill (Broehl, 1992). The progress of the banking Mellon dynasty, claimed to be the wealthiest in the United States, has been written, but as sponsors of the arts rather than primarily as entrepreneurs (Koskoff, 1978). It may be significant, as one scholar has suggested (Roberts, 2003), that in the 'roaring capitalist 1990s ... massive major new biographies' of the robber barons, Rockefeller (Chernow, 1998), Morgan (Strouse, 1999) and Harriman (Klein, 2000) should have been written. Yet America's doyen in this subject sees the new generation of the country's business historians drifting away from the difficult concepts of big business and entrepreneurship into the more seductive topics of class, gender, race, culture and the environment (Galambos, 2003: 5, 29).

6.5 Britain and entrepreneurship studies 1950s–2000

In Britain's post-1945 period of national recovery from the economic disruption of the second world war, there was little incentive to write entrepreneurial biography or history. The traditional fare from its companies was what Supple called 'puff' stories and histories written by men with no prior (or subsequent) claims to professional competence in the field, namely journalists, public relations officers or in-house authors chosen to enhance the company's image (Supple, 1958: 70). Some time passed before academic business historians could claim to rival their American counterparts.

However, a forerunner had produced some exemplary work a few decades earlier. After a collection of ancient records of a long-defunct cotton manufacturing firm had been discovered, George Unwin, professor of economic history at Manchester, made use of them in *Samuel Oldknow and the Arkwrights.* A chapter on 'The man and his work' attributed Oldknow's success more to 'his creative gifts [as an innovator] than to mere business shrewdness', the absence of which had led to his downfall (Unwin, 1924: 236–42). Henrietta Larson judged that in that book Unwin had arrived at 'the very threshold of business history' (Larson, 1948: 14). His premature death halted that trend, but some associates went on to compose scholarly entrepreneurial biographies: T. S. Ashton on the Warrington file-maker, Peter Stubs (Ashton, 1939), A. P. Wadsworth on the Strutts and Arkwrights (Fitton and Wadsworth, 1958), and R. H. Tawney on the seventeenth-century merchant and politician, Lionel Cranfield (Tawney, 1958).

Two biographies from the 1950s were typical of that decade. *The Life of Lord Nuffield: A Study in Enterprise and Benevolence*, by two economists at Nuffield College, Oxford, contained some useful data on Morris Motors Ltd.'s performance, but appeared while their subject was still alive (Andrews and Brunner, 1955). *The Life of Ludwig Mond*, the chemical entrepreneur, by a general author who admitted to knowing no science (Cohen, 1956) was later superseded by a comprehensive history of Mond's successor company, ICI (see below). Yet it was Charles Wilson's *History of Unilever*, which in 1954 marked Britain's formal entry into academic business history, giving the first full-scale and archive-based account of a surviving British industrial giant, and bringing alive the autocratic personality of its founder, William Lever. Wilson dismissed the notion of the capitalist being 'only a cork bobbing on the economic tide', and rated 'human intelligence, human character, ingenuity and enterprise' as the spur to a nation's economic progress (Wilson, 1954–68: vi, 291).

In 1958, the journal *Business History*, the UK equivalent of America's *Business History Review*, was founded. Two useful collective volumes illustrate the range of its biographical articles. *Speculators and Patriots: Essays in Business Biography* included studies of the notorious company promoter, Ernest Hooley, and the equivocal financier, Sir Ernest Cassel (Davenport-Hines, 1986b), while *Capital, Entrepreneurs and Profits* dealt (among others) with two innovators in very different fields, the poet and designer William Morris and his commercial ventures, and Sir Joseph Whitworth as the pioneer of mass-production engineering (Davenport-Hines, 1990).

One exemplary successor to Wilson's history was *Guinness's Brewery in the Irish Economy 1759–1876* by Patrick Lynch and John Vaizey. Mercifully short and readable, the book comprised a collective biography of a noteworthy family in its corporate and national setting. It found the Guinness entrepreneurs of the period to have mixed innovative drives with an ability to enjoy life outside the brewery (Lynch and Vaizey, 1960: 243–6). A number of heavyweight company histories followed, covering some of Britain's most prestigious enterprises and including T. C. Barker on the glassmakers, Pilkington (Barker, 1960, 1977), D. C. Coleman's history of Courtaulds (Coleman, 1969–80) and W. J. Reader on ICI to 1952 (Reader, 1970–75).

Those and other—usually multi-volumed—blockbusters in a sense defeated their purposes of bringing out for researchers the inner springs of entrepreneurship. Their authors neglected the warning that the public 'is unaccustomed to hacking its way through the *minutiae* which tend to clutter up so many history books' (Barker, Campbell and Mathias, 1971: 19). Barry Supple's *Essays in British Business History* attempted a rescue operation by including extracts from some blockbusters to draw lessons on entrepreneurship and economic policies in the 1870–1945 period of deceleration. He stressed the difference between British business historians' concern with the economic and social context of entrepreneurial activity and the narrower American preoccupation with administrative structures (Supple, 1977: 3). Coleman, having added three Courtauld volumes to the genre, but with a useful study of the money-lender Sir John Banks to his credit (Coleman, 1963), later mischievously opined that company directors viewed the histories they commissioned as 'fairly inexpensive public relations exercises, sitting somewhere between prestige advertising and patronage of the arts' (Coleman, 1987: 144).

By contrast, in a bid to offer an informed public some shortish but authoritative biographies of British entrepreneurs, the European Library of Business Biography published four volumes in the later 1970s, on two motor-car pioneers, Lord Nuffield and Herbert Austin, a shipping magnate and the Vickers armament brothers (Overy, 1976; Trebilcock, 1977; Davies, 1978; Church, 1979). Each volume was enlivened by a copiously documented introduction by Neil McKendrick, who pungently exposed the shortage of objective information available on many entrepreneurs, the consequent difficulty of testing general hypotheses about entrepreneurial behaviour, and the hostility to business and its leaders expressed by many elements in British society, most notably by novelists.

Although that well-intentioned series collapsed prematurely, from 1978 onwards a Business History Unit at the London School of Economics gave hope of invigorating entrepreneurial history through research into broader, especially thematic, issues of concern to historians and economists alike. Under its aegis, four multi-authored books were published, on British multinationals, marketing, technological innovation, and business and religion in Britain respectively (Jones, 1986; Davenport-Hines, 1986a; Jeremy, 1988; Liebenau 1988). These books explored the parts played by the country's entrepreneurs in very diverse categories. Richard Davenport-Hines wrote a highly regarded biography of Sir Dudley Docker, the celebrated promoter of Britain's inter-war merger movement (Davenport-Hines, 1984). W. J. Reader, associated with the Business History Unit, in his history of Metal Box, the packaging materials firm, graphically featured its powerful chairman, Sir Robert Barlow (Reader, 1976) and later chronicled the paper makers Bowater, ruled for 40 years by Sir Eric Bowater whose autocratic rule collapsed in crisis (Reader, 1981).

The most ambitious product to come out of the unit was a five-volume *Dictionary of Business Biography* (Jeremy, 1984–86), of nearly 1,200 entrepreneurs in England and Wales from 1860 onwards. A *Dictionary of Scottish Business Biography* (Slaven and Checkland, 1986–90) contained a further 380 names. Some useful generalizations were drawn from them, but mainly about the subjects' social origins and their educational background (Jeremy, 1984, 1990b; Slaven, 1984: 20–1).

By the final decade of the twentieth century, British business historians appeared to have lost interest in entrepreneurs as such, partly because there seemed to be no usable theoretical models on entrepreneurship; Casson's important book on *The Entrepreneur: An Economic Theory* (Casson, 1982, 2003) was not widely known to them. In 1950, Thomas Cochran of Harvard had pointed out that individual company historians failed to standardize the facts in their histories so as to provide a basis for quantitative research on entrepreneurs and their initiatives over time (Supple, 1958: 69). Four decades later the editors of *Business History*, Charles Harvey and Geoffrey Jones, urged authors to adopt 'a uniform set of definitions, concepts and measures of performance, in their research'. Hence the way forward was to write larger numbers of comparative and thematic studies (Harvey and Jones, 1990: 15).

Indeed, among the more interesting biographical examples of corporate history have been some thematic ones. David Jeremy investigated in depth the influence which devout entrepreneurs had on UK big business. His *Capitalists and Christians: Business Leaders and the Churches in Britain 1900–60* (Jeremy, 1990a) provided much biographical information about those magnates. A second work with a distinctive theme was Robert Fitzgerald's *Rowntree and the Marketing Revolution 1862–1969*. Most unusually, he began his history with a detailed exposition of marketing, which had helped Rowntree to become one of the world's leading confectionery manufacturers. It was not the founder, Joseph Rowntree—earlier covered by Anne Vernon in *A Quaker Business Man* (Vernon, 1958)—but the twentieth-century George Harris who emerged as a top-ranking entrepreneur, having invented and seductively advertised a series of chocolate novelties, from Black Magic to Kit Kat and Aero, that captivated later generations (Fitzgerald, 1995: 284).

Biographies of entrepreneurs in Britain's most successful industries, oil and pharmaceuticals, have so far been patchy. Apart from an earlier life of the founder, Marcus Samuel (Henriques, 1960), there is little of biographical interest on Shell, although a seven-volume history of the company is promised. The three volumes of the history of British Petroleum to 1975, with a further volume in preparation, contain only brief character sketches (Ferrier, 1982; Bamberg, 1994, 2000). By contrast, the historian of the far less prestigious Burmah Oil Company attempted to associate personalities closely with their emerging corporate strategy (Corley, 1983, 1988). As to pharmaceuticals, Allen & Hanburys' history to 1990 expertly covered the contributions of its successive Quaker, and other, leaders (Tweedale, 1990). The history of Glaxo to 1962 (Davenport-Hines and Slinn, 1992) took greater pains to analyse the company's principal characters, most notably Sir Harry Jephcott, than did Edgar Jones's subsequent full-scale history (Jones, 2001).

While not dealing specifically with biographies, in a survey of company and business history during the 1990s Geoffrey Jones criticized those historians for not having achieved any conceptual breakthrough on entrepreneurship, innovation or firm competences, thus failing to match the strides made by other social scientists. The genre had hardly 'moved much beyond the achievements of earlier giants, such as Wilson's *Unilever*' of 1954. 'In some respects', he judged, 'business history has become highly fashionable, so long as it is not written by business historians' (Jones, 1998: 31).

Many recent British biographies of entrepreneurs have indeed been by journalists, often treating their subjects as celebrities whose careers could be presented in a dramatic light. The take-over tycoon, Sir Charles Clore, was an obvious choice (Clutterbuck and Devine, 1987), as was the designer and company founder, Laura

Ashley (Sebba, 1990). Robert Maxwell, publisher and robber of pension funds, had in life pursued his biographer, Tom Bower, with legal actions. Bower took his revenge after Maxwell's death (Bower, 1993a). Bower's biography of Roland Walter (Tiny) Rowland, the financier and founder of Lonrho, was investigative rather than analytical (Bower, 1993b). That of the food tycoon, Sir James Goldsmith, had the disadvantage of being published in his lifetime (Fallon, 1991). Informed and admirably candid entries on all those worthies can be found in the *Oxford Dictionary of National Biography* (Matthew and Harrison, 2004), which contains nearly 7,800 names of entrepreneurs, including many in transport and construction. Lord Hanson, who died in 2004, had earlier been graced with a journalistic biography (Brummer and Cowe, 1994), but a knowledgeable obituary with deadly accuracy captured his significance as Britain's most (in)famous corporate raider and asset stripper (*The Economist*, 2004: 82).

6.6 Biographies of European and Japanese entrepreneurs

In Germany, public interest in the subject of entrepreneurship for more than a century has yielded a healthy number of corporate histories. These have tended to cover the roles of their entrepreneurs at greater length than do equivalent works in Britain or the United States. Horst Wessel's history of the engineering conglomerate Mannesmann AG, which stresses its founders' innovations in steel tubes, is available only in German (Wessel, 1990), as is his history of Germany's largest steel and engineering group, Thyssen & Co., expansively featuring its founder August Thyssen (Wessel, 1991; see also Colli, 2003: 52–3).

The electrical and electronic giant, Siemens AG, is represented in English, no doubt because its products are so widely sold in both Britain and America. Georg Siemens wrote the first volume of a corporate history nearly half a century ago (Siemens, 1957). More recently, Wilfried Feldenkirchen published a biography of the founder, Werner von Siemens (Feldenkirchen, 1994), which he followed up with a history of the company from 1918 to 1945 (Feldenkirchen, 1999). As to motor-cars, the pioneer Franz-Josef Popp appears in Horst Mönnich's *The BMW Story* (Mönnich, 1991). The eventful life of Robert Bosch, founder of the automotive engineering and electrical company of that name, and an innovator in industrial relations, was published under an American imprint (Heuss, 1994).

Dutch entrepreneurship has been ably chronicled by a dedicated team of business historians, for example in a study of the liqueur-maker De Kuyper (Sluyterman and Vleesenbeek, 1995), but the country's reputation has been more in oil and electronics. Henri Deterding, founder of Royal Dutch-Shell, was given a fawning and verbose treatment in F. C. Gerretson's four-volume, *History of the Royal Dutch to 1914* (Gerretson, 1953–57). A later biography by Paul Hendrix, first published in Dutch and then abbreviated for the English market, is adequately researched but over-biased against British and American competitors (Hendrix, 2002). The history of the largest manufacturing company in the Netherlands, Philips of electronics fame, is well covered in A. Heerding's work up to 1922, which explores the complementary characters of the founding brothers, Frederik and Gerard Philips (Heerding, 1986, 1988).

Swedish industry has for many years been celebrated for Electrolux appliances and Volvo motor-cars, and more recently for the IKEA group's furniture and home furnishings, whose founder was Ingvar Kamprad. An earlier noteworthy but controversial entrepreneur was Ivar Kreuger, founder of the Swedish Match Company, who, like Kamprad, has no biography in English. However, the company did sponsor a historical research project, leading to the publication (among others) of Lars Hassbring's account of its international development to 1924 (Hassbring, 1979) and Karl-Gustaf Hildebrand's *Expansion, Crisis, Reconstruction* (Hildebrand, 1985).

French business historians have often concentrated on regional instead of national enterprise. Even so, a number of fairly recent works, all in French, illustrate the range of industries covered. Louis Renault, who founded the motor-car company of that name, was claimed as the country's equivalent of Henry Ford, and like Ford, an 'absolute boss' (Hatry, 1991). André Citröen, whose cars were, and are, adorned with 'chevrons of glory' has an official but scholarly biography (Sabates and Schweitzer, 1985). Two aerospace inovators are likewise commemorated, Pierre-Georges Latécoère, 'aircraft pioneer', (Chadeau, 1990) and Marcel Dessault, 'legend of a century' who invented the Mirage fighter jet (Carlier, 1992). Those authors all chose publicity-seeking sub-titles.

As to Italy, Giovanni Agnelli, the founder of Fiat, appears in two business histories (in Italian), one more personally in the context of the company's growth to 1945 (Castronovo, 1971) and the other in the centenary history of Fiat from 1899 to 1999 (Castronovo, 1999). Another celebrated Italian name, Adriano Olivetti, the typewriter magnate, has been given a wide-ranging biography (Ochetto, 1985). Of late, some newer types of entrepreneurial firm have emerged in the country's industrial districts, being medium-sized, dynamic and usually family-run, resembling the Japanese *zaibatsu* (Colli, 2003: 57). They prospered during the race towards globalization in the 1990s, not only in clothing, footwear, leather and other luxury products, but also in machine tools and machinery. Benetton, the best known of these, and founded in the 1950s by four siblings, had an entrepreneurial structure that combined the advantages of family control with those of delegating operations to its managerially-run subsidiaries (Mantle, 1999; Colli, 2003: 61–5).

Two of Switzerland's most prominent manufacturing industries are represented (in German) with biographical material. Hans Conrad Peyer emphasized the role of the founder Fritz Hoffmann-La Roche in a centenary history of the drug company bearing that name (Peyer, 1996). Henry Nestlé, who established the world's largest food enterprise, was commemorated in his progression 'From pharmacy assistant to pioneering Swiss industrialist' (Pfiffner, 1993).

The phenomenon of entrepreneurship in Japan, which over a few decades played its part in creating a powerful industrial and commercial economy, has stimulated research by business and economic historians throughout the world. A number of good histories are already available in English, yielding valuable biographical information. Konosuke Matsushita, founder of the company which markets Panasonic consumer appliances, is said to be among the most outstanding entrepreneurs in the Japanese 'economic miracle'. A Harvard Business School professor wrote his biography, adopting the Harvard diagrammatic approach to entrepreneurship studies but including no figures to chart the company's progress (Kotter, 1997). Two conglomerates stand out, both former *zaibatsu*, Mitsubishi and Mitsui. The former, active in product areas ranging from food and chemicals to general merchandise, has a history from 1870 to 1914, making much of the founder, Yataro Iwasaki (Wray, 1984). J. G. Roberts' history of Mitsui chronicles the life of Rizaemon Minomura, the architect of that equally wide-ranging conglomerate's prosperity (Roberts, 1973).

Some familiar Japanese corporate names have apparently had to rely on popular works, such as T. Sakiya's account of Honda (Sakiya, 1982). Journalistic exposés include one on the finance house of Nomura and its most famous entrepreneur, Tokushichi Nomura II, sub-titled as 'The inside story of the legendary Japanese financial dynasty' (Alletzhauser, 1991).

This survey of the relevant literature in a number of differing countries has indicated some forms of entrepreneurship that are less common, say, in Britain and the United States but are ideally suited to other societies. The types to be found in industrial districts of Italy have been touched on above, and the family-controlled and diversified *chaebol* of South Korea provide a further example. Some useful lessons could no doubt be gleaned from the structures set up by Asian entrepreneurs in Britain and various other parts of the world, who await their biographies in due course.

6.7 Conclusions

On the basis of the examples from a number of countries, given above, how far can business biography enhance our general understanding of entrepreneurship as a dynamic force in any economy? A problem of method at once arises. On the deductive side, economists formulate hypotheses about the role of the entrepreneur, the demand for, and supply of, entrepreneurship, and so on (see section 1 on p. 138). Inductively, such hypotheses are then tested against the empirical or real-life evidence. Yet workable findings can be drawn only from sufficiently large numbers of observations, whereas biographies are normally about single individuals.

One remedy for this problem might be to combine data from a selection of biographies. Yet all too many entrepeneurs who might be taken as representative of their era, industry or specific expertise, lack usable biographies, while few if any unsuccessful ones have had worthwhile lifestories written about them, so that the reasons for success cannot be adequately balanced against those for failure. Moreover, there is no statistical population of all firms existing at any given time, to allow researchers to take random or stratified samples before seeking biographical information about their noteworthy leaders. Thus, for example, all the surveys presented in section 4 on p. 142–5. about the social origins of entrepreneurs studied only large-scale businesses and neglected the smaller firms where those from impoverished backgrounds would have had greater opportunities to make good.

Even less helpful is that already published lives may have been written by those, such as publicists, general authors or journalists, whose competence in handling archival sources and in objectively interpreting the evidence would have been variable. Yet one cause of optimism is that the quality of biography overall has shown considerable improvement in recent decades. For instance, the best biographers nowadays make considerable efforts to track down all relevant written and oral sources.

To sum up, if in contradiction to Disraeli's judgement theory is a necessary tool, at least for entrepreneurial biographies, perhaps specialist scholars could strive to construct future examples of this genre round specific themes such as innovation, marketing and business networks and alliances. The greater the volume of biographical evidence becoming available in these key areas, the more our overall knowledge of entrepreneurship will be enhanced.

References

Alletzhauser, A. J. (1991). *The House of Nomura.* New York: Little Brown.

Andrews, P. W. S. and E. Brunner (1955). *The Life of Lord Nuffield: A Study in Enterprise and Benevolence.* Oxford: Blackwell.

Ashton, T. S. (1939). *An Eighteenth-Century Industrialist: Peter Stubs of Warrington 1756–1806.* Manchester: Manchester University Press.

Balgarnie, R. (1877). *Sir Titus Salt, Bt. His Life and Times.* London: Hodder and Stoughton.

Bamberg, J. (1994), (2000). *History of the British Petroleum Company* vols. 2 and 3. Cambridge: Cambridge University Press.

Barker, T. C. (1960). *Pilkington Brothers and the Glass Industry.* London: Allen & Unwin.

Barker, T. C. (1977). *The Glassmakers*. London: Weidenfeld & Nicolson.
—— Campbell, R. H. and P. Mathias (1971). *Business History*. London: Historical Association.
Bower, T. (1993a). *Maxwell: The Outsider*. London: Mandarin.
—— (1993b). *Tiny Rowland: A Rebel Tycoon*. London: Heinemann.
Broehl, W. G. (1992). *Cargill: Trading the World's Grain*. Hanover, NH: University Press of New England.
Brummer, A. and R. Cowe (1994). *Hanson: A Biography*. London: Fourth Estate.
Carlier, C. (1992). *Marcel Dassault: Le légende d'un siècle*. Paris: Olivier Orban.
Casson, M. (1982). *The Entrepreneur: An Economic Theory*. Oxford: Martin Robertson.
—— (2003). *The Entrepreneur: An Economic Theory*. Cheltenham: Edward Elgar.
Castronovo, V. (1971). *Giovanni Agnelli: La Fiat del 1899 al 1945*. Turin: UTET.
—— (1999). *Fiat 1899–1999*. Milan: Rizzoli.
Chadeau, E. (1990). *Latécoère, Pierre Georges: aircraft pioneer*. Paris: Olivier Orban.
Chamberlin, E. H. (1962). *The Theory of Monopolistic Competition* (8th edn). Cambridge, MA: Harvard University Press.
Chandler, A. D. and S. Salsbury (1971). *Pierre S. Du Pont and the Making of the Modern Corporation*. New York: Harper & Row.
Chernow, R. (1998). *Titan: The Life of John D. Rockefeller Sr*. New York: Random Press.
Church, R. (1979). *Herbert Austin: The British Motor Car Industry to 1941*. London: Europa Publications.
Clutterbuck, D. and M. Devine (1987). *Clore: The Man and his Millions*. London: Weidenfeld & Nicolson.
Cohen, J. M. (1956). *Life of Ludwig Mond*. London: Methuen.
Cole, A. H. (1959). *Business Enterprise in its Social Setting*. Cambridge, MA; Harvard University Press.
Coleman, D. C. (1963). *Sir John Banks: Baronet and Businessman*. Oxford: Clarendon Press.
—— (1969–80). *Courtaulds: An Economic and Social History*, vols. 1–3. Oxford: Clarendon Press.
—— (1987). 'The Uses and Abuses of Business History'. *Business History*, 29(2): 141–56.
Colli, A. (2003). *The History of Family Business 1850–2000*. Cambridge: Cambridge University Press.
Corley, T. A. B. (1983, 1988). *History of the Burmah Oil Company*, vols. 1–2. London: Heinemann.
Crouzet, F. (1985). *The First Industrialists: The Problem of Origins*. Cambridge: Cambridge University Press.
Davenport-Hines, R. P. T. (1984). *Dudley Docker: The Life and Times of a Trade Warrior*. Cambridge: Cambridge University Press.
—— (ed.) (1986a). *Markets and Bagmen*. Aldershot: Gower.
—— (ed.) (1986b). *Speculators and Patriots*. London: Frank Cass.
—— (ed.) (1990). *Capital, Entrepreneurs and Profits*. London: Frank Cass.
—— and Slinn, J. (1992). *Glaxo: A History to 1962*. Cambridge: Cambridge University Press.
Davies, P. N. (1978). *Sir Alfred Jones: Shipping Entrepreneur Par Excellence*. London: Europa Publications.
Disraeli, B. (1832). *Contarini Fleming*. London: John Murray.

The Economist (2004). '"Lord of the Raiders"', Lord Hanson *The Economist*, (6 November) 373(8400): 82.

Fallon, I. (1991). *Billionaire: The Life of Sir James Goldsmith*. London: Hutchinson.

Farber, D. (2002). *Sloan Rules: Alfred P. Sloan and the Triumph of General Motors*. Chicago, IL: University of Chicago Press.

Farnie, D. A. (1993). 'John Rylands of Manchester'. *Bulletin of the John Rylands Library of the University of Manchester* (Summer) 75(2): 3–103.

Feldenkirchen, W. (1994). *Werner von Siemens: Inventor and International Entrepreneur*. Columbus, OH: Ohio State University Press.

—— (1999). *Siemens 1918–1945*. Columbus, OH: Ohio State University Press.

Ferrier, R. W. (1982). *History of the British Petroleum Company, 1901–32*, vol. 1. Cambridge: Cambridge University Press.

Fitton, R. S. and A. P. Wadsworth (1958). *Strutts and Arkwrights: A Study of the Early Factory System 1758–1830*. Manchester: Manchester University Press.

Fitzgerald, R. (1995). *Rowntree and the Marketing Revolution 1862–1969*. Cambridge: Cambridge University Press.

Fortunes Made in Business (1884). London: Sampson Low.

—— (1901–02). London: Amalgamated Press.

Foster, M. S. (1989). *Henry J. Kaiser: Builder in the Modern American West*. Austin, TX: University of Texas Press.

Galambos, L. (2003). 'Identity and the Boundaries of Business History: An Essay on Consensus and Creativity', in F. Amatori and G. Jones (eds) *Business History around the World*. Cambridge: Cambridge University Press.

Gardiner, A. G. (1923). *Life of George Cadbury*. London: Cassell.

Gerretson, F. C. (1953–57). *History of the Royal Dutch*. Leiden: E. J. Brill.

Gosse, E. (1901). 'The Custom of Biography'. *The Anglo-Saxon Review*, 8: 195–208.

Gras, N. S. B. and H. M. Larson (eds) (1939). *Casebook in American Business History*. New York: Crofts.

Gregory, F. W. and I. D. Neu (1962). 'The American Industrial Elite in the 1870s: Their Social Origins' in W. Miller (ed.) *Men in Business*. New York: Harper & Row.

Hagen, E. E. (1962). *On the Theory of Social Change*. Boston, MA: MIT Press.

Harvey, C. and G. Jones (1990). 'Business History in Britain into the 1990s'. *Business History*, 32(1): 5–16.

Hassbring, L. (1979). *The International Development of the Swedish Match Company 1917–24*. Stockholm: Liber Förlag.

Hatry, G. (1991). *Louis Renault: Patron absolu*. Paris: Éditions JCM.

Heerding, A. (1986–8). *History of NV Philips' Gloelampenfabriken*, vols. 1–2. Cambridge: Cambridge University Press.

Hendrix, P. (2002). *Sir Henri Deterding and Royal Dutch-Shell*. Bristol: Bristol Academic Press.

Henriques, R. (1960). *Marcus Samuel: Founder of Shell 1853–1927*. London: Barrie & Rockliff.

Heuss, T. (1994). *Robert Bosch: His Life and Achievements*. New York: Henry Holt.

Hildebrand, K-G. (1985). *Expansion, Crisis, Reconstruction*. Stockholm: Liber Förlag.

Hughes, J. (1973). *The Vital Few*. Oxford: Oxford University Press.

Jardim, A. (1970). *The First Henry Ford: A Study in Personality and Business Leadership*. Cambridge, MA: MIT Press.

Jeremy, D. J. (1984). 'Anatomy of the British Business Elite 1860–1980'. *Business History*, 26(1): 3–23.

Jeremy, D. J. (ed.) (1984–86). *Dictionary of Business Biography*. London: Butterworth.

—— (ed.) (1988). *Business and Religion in Britain*. Aldershot: Gower.

—— (1990a). *Capitalists and Christians: Business Leaders and the Churches in Britain 1900–1960*. Oxford: Oxford University Press.

—— (1990b). 'The Prosopography of Business Leaders: Possibilities, Resources and Problems'. *Proceedings of Annual Conference of Business Archives Council*, pp. 35–61.

Johnson, A. (ed.) (1928–36). *Dictionary of American Biography*. London: Oxford University Press.

Jones, E. (2001). *The Business of Medicine: The Extraordinary History of Glaxo*. London: Profile Books.

Jones, G. (ed.) (1986). *British Multinationals: Origins, Management and Performance*. Aldershot: Gower.

—— (1998). 'Company History and Business History in the 1990s', in J. Fink (ed.) *Business Records and Business History: Essays in Celebration of the 50th Anniversary of the Danish National Business Archives*. Copenhagen: Erhvervsarkivet.

Klein, M. (2000). *The Life and Legend of Edward H. Harriman*. Chapel Hill, NC: University of North Carolina Press.

Knight, F. H. (1921). *Risk, Uncertainty and Profit*. New York: Augustus Kelly.

Koskoff, D. E. (1978). *The Mellons: The Chronicle of America's Richest Family*. New York: T. Y. Crowell.

Kotter, J. P. (1997). *Matsushita Leadership*. New York: The Free Press.

Krooss, H. E. (1958). 'Economic History and the New Business History', *Journal of Economic History*, 18: 467–80.

—— and C. Gilbert (1972). *American Business History*. Englewood Cliffs, NJ: Prentice-Hall.

Larson, H. M. (1936). *Jay Cooke: Private Banker*. Cambridge, MA: Harvard University Press.

—— (1948). *Guide to Business History*. Cambridge, MA: Harvard University Press.

Lazell, H. G. (1975). *From Pills to Penicillin: The Beecham Story*. London: Heinemann.

Leibenstein, H. (1957). *Economic Backwardness and Economic Growth*. New York: John Wiley.

—— (1978). *General X-Efficiency Theory and Economic Development*. New York: Oxford University Press.

Liebenau, J. (ed.) (1988). *The Challenge of New Technology: Innovation in British Business since 1850*. Aldershot: Gower.

Lynch, P. and J. Vaizey, (1960). *Guinness's Brewery in the Irish Economy 1759–1876*. Cambridge: Cambridge University Press.

McClelland, D. C. (1961). *The Achieving Society*. Princeton, NJ: Van Nostrand.

McKenzie, P. (1983). *The Life and Times of William George Armstrong*. Newcastle: Longhirst Press.

Madison, J. H. (1989). *Eli Lilly: A Life 1885–1977*. Oxford: Oxford University Press.

Mantle, J. (1999). *Benetton: The Family, the Business and the Brand*. London: Little Brown.

Marshall, A. (1890). *Principles of Economics*. London: Macmillan.

Matthew, H. C. G. (2004). 'Samuel Smiles (1812–1904)'. *Oxford Dictionary of National Biography*, vol. 50. Oxford: Oxford University Press.

Matthew, H. C. G. and B. Harrison (eds) (2004). *Oxford Dictionary of National Biography.* Oxford: Oxford University Press.

May, G. S. (1977). *R. E. Olds: Auto Industry Pioneer.* Grand Rapids, MI: Eerdmans.

Miller, W. (1962). 'American Historians and the Business Elite', in Miller, W. (ed.) *Men in Business.* New York: Harper & Row.

Mönnich, H. (1991). *The BMW Story: A Company in its Time.* London: Sidgwick & Jackson.

Nevins, A. (1953). *John D. Rockefeller: Industrialist and Philanthropist.* New York: Scribner.

Oberholtzer, E. P. (1907). *Jay Cooke: Financier of the Civil War.* Philadelphia, PA: G. W. Jacobs.

O'Brien, D. P. (1990). 'Marshall's Industrial Analysis'. *Scottish Journal of Political Economy* (February) 37(1): 61–84.

Ochetto, V. (1985). *Adriano Olivetti.* Bologna: Molino.

Overy, R. J. (1976). *William Morris, Viscount Nuffield.* London: Europa Publications.

Peyer, H. C. (1996). *Roche: Geschichte eines Unternehmens 1896–1996.* Basle: Editions Roche.

Pfiffner, A. (1993). *Henry Nestlé 1814–1890.* Zurich: Chronos Verlag.

Porter, K. W. (1931). *John Jacob Astor: Business Man.* Cambridge, MA: Harvard University Press.

—— (1932). 'Trends in American Business Biography'. *Journal of Economic and Business History,* 4(2): 583–610.

Reader, W. J. (1970–75). *Imperial Chemical Industries: A History.* Oxford: Oxford University Press.

—— (1976). *Metal Box: A History.* London: Heinemann.

—— (1981). *Bowater: A History.* Cambridge: Cambridge University Press.

Roberts, J. G. (1973). *Mitsui: Three Centuries of Japanese Business.* New York: Weatherhill.

Roberts, P. (2003). 'Review of T. M. Collins, 2002. *Otto Kahn, Art, Money and Modern Time*'. *Business History,* 45(2): 119–22.

Sabates, F. and S. Schweitzer (1985). *André Citroën: les chevrons de la gloire.* Paris: EPA.

Sakiya, T. (1982). *Honda Motor: The Man, the Management, the Machines.* Tokyo: Kodansha International.

Sarachek, B. (1978). 'American Entrepreneurs and the Horatio Alger Myth'. *Journal of Economic History,* pp. 439–56.

Schumpeter, J. A. (1934). *The Theory of Economic Development.* Cambridge, MA: Harvard University Press.

—— (1954). *History of Economic Analysis.* London: Allen & Unwin.

Sebba, A. (1990). *Laura Ashley: A Life by Design.* London: Weidenfeld & Nicolson.

Shane, S. (2003). *A General Theory of Entrepreneurship: The Industrial-Opportunity Nexus.* Cheltenham: Edward Elgar.

Shapley, D. (1993). *Promise and Power: The Life and Times of Robert McNamara.* Boston, MA: Little Brown.

Siemens, G. (1957). *History of the House of Siemens,* vol. 1. Freiburg/Munich: Karl Alber.

Slaven, A. (1984). 'The Uses of Business Records: Some Research Trends in British Business History', *Business Archives* (New ser.) 5/1(50): 17–35.

—— and S. Checkland, (1986–90). *Dictionary of Scottish Business Biography 1860–1960.* Aberdeen: Aberdeen University Press.

Sloan, A. P. (1963). *My Years with General Motors.* London: Sidgwick & Jackson.

Sluyterman, K. and H. H. Vleesenbeek (1995). *Three Centuries of De Kuyper.* Schiedam: De Kuyper.

Smiles, S. (1894). *Josiah Wedgwood FRS: His Personal History.* London: John Murray.

Stephen, L. and S. Lee, (1885–1900). *Dictionary of National Biography.* London: Smith Elder.

Strouse, J. (1999). *Morgan: American Financier.* New York: Random House.

Supple, B. (1958). 'American Business History: A Survey'. *Business History*, 1: 63–76.

—— (ed.) (1977). *Essays in British Business History.* Oxford: Clarendon Press.

Tarbell, I. M. (1904). *History of the Standard Oil Company.* New York: McClure & Phillips.

Taussig, F. W. and C. S. Joslyn (1932). *American Business Leaders: A Study in Social Origins and Social Stratification.* New York: Macmillan.

Tawney, R. H. (1958). *Business and Politics under James I: Lionel Cranfield as Merchant and Minister.* Cambridge: Cambridge University Press.

Trebilcock, C. (1977). *The Vickers Brothers: Armaments and Enterprise 1854–1914.* London: Europa Publications.

Tweedale, G. (1990). *At the Sign of the Plough: Allen & Hanburys and the British Pharmaceutical Industry, 1715–1990.* London: John Murray.

Unwin, G. (1924). *Samuel Oldknow and the Arkwrights.* Manchester: Manchester University Press.

Vagelos, R. and L. Galambos (2004). *Medicine, Science and Merck.* Cambridge: Cambridge University Press.

Vernon, A. (1958). *A Quaker Business Man: The Life of Joseph Rowntree 1836–1925.* London: Allen & Unwin.

Wessel, H. (1990). *Kontinuität im Wandel: 100 Jahre Mannesmann 1890–1990.* Düsseldorf: Mannesmann AG.

—— (1991). *Mülheim a.d. Ruhr: Die Geschichte einer Familie und ihrer Unternehmung.* Stuttgart: Franz Steiner Verlag.

Wilson, C. (1954–68). *History of Unilever*, vols. 1–3. London: Cassell.

Wray, W. D. (1984). *Mitsubishi and the NYK 1870–1914.* Boston, MA: Harvard University Press.

Yeager, M. A. (2001). 'Mavericks and Mavens of Business History: Miriam Beard and Henrietta Larson'. *Enterprise and Society*, 2(4): 687–768.

PART II

SMALL FIRMS

CHAPTER 7

DETERMINANTS OF SMALL FIRM SURVIVAL AND GROWTH

ROBERT CRESSY

7.1 Introduction

Several excellent surveys of the literature on business growth and survival have appeared in the last decade. These include Caves (1998) who surveys over 80 theoretical and empirical papers relating to the turnover and mobility of firms (both small and large); Sutton (1997), who summarizes the results of a number of papers on Gibrat's Law of proportionate firm growth and its relationship to industrial concentration; and Geroski (1995), who identifies a number of 'stylized facts' and 'results' in the area of industrial entry. A text by Storey (1994) also summarizes the research on (very) small firms' survival and growth (among other things) until about 1993. In this chapter we shall however focus on the small firm literature on survival and growth, drawing on these largely non-size-specific surveys only when the intersection between their subject matter and that of small firm growth and survival is significant. Our focus (mainly for reasons of space) is moreover primarily on testable or tested theories, implying a neglect of theory, however intrinsically interesting, which offers no (immediately) testable or tested implications.

It is important to note at the outset that the industrial economics literature in general has a rather disparate definition of the term 'small firm' from the small business literature as located in the small business journals. This definition ranges from Hall (1987) who uses quoted companies in her analysis of growth and survival and defines small in terms of sub-median employment size in the US quoted sector in which the median firm has 2,300 employees, down to Cressy (1996b) whose start-up sample from the UK has a mean employment size of 1.5 full-time employees (with about the same number of part-timers) and whose typical firm is much more likely to be unincorporated rather than simply unquoted.

7.2 Definitions

Small firm. There are many definitions of a small firm, but most rely on the numbers of employees of the firm falling below a certain threshold (Bank of England, 2003), sometimes combining this threshold with one on sales (Berger and Udell, 1998).[1] The UK's Bolton Committee report (Bolton, 1971), one of the earliest studies of small firms, attempted to define small in terms of the classically perfectly competitive firm, including reference to absolute employment size. A firm was small if it satisfied four criteria:

1. It was an independent entity, i.e. not a subsidiary of a larger firm
2. It constituted a small proportion of the total market (measured by sales) and so had no power to influence price
3. Its owners and managers were the same people
4. It had less than 100 employees

Bolton was well aware that the definition of *small* might well depend on the characteristics of the industry in which the firm was located and that an employment measure might be more appropriate for service industries where output would be likely to be a function of the number of sales assistants, consultants, service personnel and so on, and less appropriate for highly capital-intensive industries where output would be very much a function of the equipment with which labour worked. Despite these qualifications, most researchers and government departments now work with definitions based on employment.

[1] Berger and Udell, in an important survey of small business finances (Berger and Udell, 1998), define a small firm as one with less than 20 employees and less than $2m in annual sales (in constant dollars). A large firm is thus one either with more than 20 employees or more than US$1m in sales revenues in any one year.

Growth. If one is to adopt a definition of growth consistent with the classical theory of the firm, growth should be measured in terms of the change in (discounted) cash flow profits. Firms in the classical model, be they competitive, oligopolistic or monopolistic in nature were profit-, or more exactly, wealth-maximizers.[2] However, small businesses in practice are notorious for concealing their true profits from the tax authorities for income or corporation tax avoidance reasons. Even sales measures of growth often fall into the same 'errors in variables' problem, as firms seek in practice to minimize their reported sales, to avoid VAT. Thus, despairing of the true economic measures, researchers have sought after alternatives that are robust to manipulations. These generally boil down in practice to measures of employment or asset change and only occasionally sales change.

Of course change can be absolute or proportionate, and for different purposes one might (in theory) use either measure. However, the literature almost exclusively concentrates on the former. Hence the term 'growth' in this chapter will refer to a proportionate change in some firm-level variable like employment, sales or assets expressed as a rate per annum.[3,4]

Firm failure/survival. The following definitions apply to incorporated businesses, small or large. We distinguish first between *exit* and *failure*. A firm exits an industry when it ceases to trade in that industry.[5] It may cease to trade either voluntarily or involuntarily. Voluntary cessation occurs when the firm is sold, merged or closed by its owners. Involuntary cessation or bankruptcy[6] occurs when it is closed by its creditors. The latter happens when the firm *fails* to meet debt obligations as they fall due or violates covenants in the loan agreement. The classical firm, operating in a world of certainty, would always exit voluntarily. Once uncertainty is introduced, however, expected profits and equity maximization is consistent with involuntary exit as the uncertainty is resolved.[7] As pointed out by

[2] Profits convert readily into wealth by the use of discounting.

[3] As noted by Caves (1998) little attention in the literature has been paid to differences that might emerge from empirical work based on alternative definitions of growth variables. It is clear however, that some firms with very few employees grow sufficiently fast to become quoted companies with very little change in employment.

[4] Since our discussion in the chapter concerns failure as well as growth we note that firms that 'fail' under this definition can then be easily accommodated: they can be thought of as having negative growth rates of 100% in the period under consideration (see Dunne, Roberts and Samuelson, 1989 and the next section).

[5] While a firm operating in several industries can exit one industry and still continue to trade in others, small firms tend to be little diversified along the product dimension and we shall, by and large, assume that exit from the industry means cessation of trading generally.

[6] In the US, bankruptcy refers to firms, whereas in the UK to individuals, who fail to meet their debt obligations. In the UK, firms that fail to meet debt obligations are termed *insolvent*.

[7] For example, consider an expected equity maximizer facing two equally likely permanent states of the world—High, when with profits net of debt servicing payments are £10,000, and Low when they are −£5,000. With the relevant discount rate at 10%, and the probability of either state at 50%, equity

Schary (1991), the determinants of these different forms of exit are in principle different. Hence any study of exit should ideally distinguish the alternatives discussed.

What in theory determines whether a firm voluntarily exits? Traditionally, firms were assumed to be profit or equity maximizers and the firm would voluntarily exit the industry if the (known) value of continuing were less than the (known) value of exiting, both being measured in terms of the present discounted value (PDV) of profits or net cash flow from so doing.[8] This kind of exit is a decision made by the firm's equity holders, which in the case of small firms, are its owner-managers. For the definition to be plausible in an applied research context we need to assume a very specific objective on the part of the owner-managers, namely that of wealth maximisation.[9] Exit under this definition does not imply that the firm did not meet its owners' objectives, since during its lifetime it may have yielded a handsome income to its owners. It merely means that 'at this point in time', the value *to* the entrepreneur of continuing is less than the value to him/her of stopping or of switching.[10]

Finally, this model of closure (for it is a model) is embedded not only in an environment of certain knowledge (e.g. of prices, technology and so on) but also one of perfectly functioning capital markets. Once we allow for Knightian uncertainty, or for capital market imperfections, then it becomes possible that a firm may, despite acting optimally with respect to the relevant decision variables, find that it is unable to pay its debt obligations as they fall due and thereby falls into bankruptcy. This event would now be an example of *in*voluntary closure since by definition, the shareholders' wishes would be ignored by creditors (notably the bank) in their desire to recover debts.[11] This outcome is consistent also with low entrepreneurial ability reflected in poor judgement.[12]

value at £50,000 is positive. Future profits should ensure a continuing loan from the bank. However, if future events alter the probabilities, say to 10% and 90% respectively, and these events are *unforeseen* (Knightian uncertainty—see Knight, 1965), the firm may find that the bank will no longer finance its operations at that future date when it defaults on its loan.

[8] See Schary (1991) for a detailed discussion of these conditions.

[9] It also assumes that there is no other asset in the owner-managers' portfolios.

[10] A variant on this definition occurs when the entrepreneur, now allowed to be risk averse rather than risk neutral, maximizes the PDV of expected utility over some horizon. Once again there will exist an exit threshold below which the entrepreneur will exit the industry. See Cressy (1997, 2005) for an example.

[11] On the other hand a rational entrepreneur would recognize that bankruptcy was a possible outcome of the business and one outside her control while perhaps praying for manna from heaven to enable her to continue in business.

[12] The recent literature on the role of optimism in entrepreneurial failure shows that overestimates of one's ability as an entrepreneur for example may lead one to enter business when a more objective assessment would lead one to stay out. Behaviour is still, in a sense, rational, but is skewed by a wrong set of beliefs. See de Meza and Southey (1996).

So, in summary, expected wealth maximization under uncertainty is a possible objective for the entrepreneur and bankruptcy or closure is consistent with this objective. Failure, now due to 'bad luck', and consistent with the entrepreneur's objective, may be the outcome, and is (for borrowers) defined by the event of bankruptcy. In practice, however, for small businesses, particularly unincorporated small businesses, the classical objective of wealth maximization cannot always, and perhaps even in a majority of cases, be assumed to hold. Thus, for example, a Sole Trader may be in business to avoid unemployment or 'to be their own boss', or 'to gain independence' or to achieve a target income. Failure in this case might be defined as the negation of any of these objectives, none of which is necessary or sufficient for wealth maximisation.[13] The concept of firm failure, then, is necessarily relative to the objectives of 'the' entrepreneur. Failure of the firm might in fact therefore simply be defined as 'the inability of the entrepreneurial team to meet the objectives they have set themselves'.[14]

Much of the empirical literature on small business closure, apparently due in the large to data limitations, unfortunately ignores the fine distinctions of definition we have emphasized.[15] In this chapter, we shall therefore define failure pragmatically as either solvent or insolvent closure unless otherwise specified, and use the term closure in instances where there is no way to distinguish voluntary and involuntary closure in the data.

Preamble to the survey

It will soon become clear that the issues of growth and survival are intimately related. Not only is survival an obvious necessary condition for continued growth, but also in the discussion of the empirical work on survival and growth we shall find that estimates of growth, and its relation to size and age of firm, will be influenced by estimates of the survival rates of firms. From an empirical perspective the two are therefore inextricably linked.

The structure of the remaining part of the chapter is as follows. We begin with a discussion of what started as a purely statistical regularity accounting for the observed growth patterns of large firms, namely Gibrat's Law of Proportionate Growth. This alleged law relies on chance to explain a substantial part of the firm's observed growth pattern. However, it also presupposes a constant population of firms and cannot therefore deal with exits, which among small firms are high. Still retaining the role of chance in firm growth we then show that the literature has introduced models attempting to provide theoretical underpinnings for the

[13] Cressy (1996a) found empirical support in UK start-ups for the target income motive for start-up growth.

[14] As we have noted, this might sometimes happen for reasons quite outside the owners' control. In this case we might say that the *business* failed but the *entrepreneur* did not.

[15] Some exceptions include Schary (1991), Cressy (1996b), Everett and Watson (1998), Van Praag (2002).

systematic part of growth and examine their empirical validity. We show that these models still ignore systematic influences on growth that have been identified, namely, age and size effects. This leads on to optimizing theories of firm growth which attempt to explain the stylized facts of growth the previous literature had identified.

7.3 Gibrat's law and its variants

The distribution of firm sizes in an industry is generally positively skewed with large numbers of small firms and a small numbers of large firms. The exact form of the distribution has been variously identified as Lognormal[16] (Hart and Prais, 1956), Pareto (Simon and Bonini, 1958), and Yule (Ijiri and Simon, 1964). While these early studies were based on samples of large quoted companies they recognized that a substantial part of firm growth (and decline) was random in nature. They therefore attempted to provide an underlying parametric stochastic model of firm growth that would 'explain' the observed size distribution and which could in principle be applied to the whole size distribution of firms, quoted and unquoted.[17] The most famous of these models is Gibrat's Law of Proportional Growth (Gibrat, 1931). This alleged law can be written in the following form:

$$\tilde{x}_t = x_{t-1} + \tilde{\varepsilon}_t \tag{1}$$

where x is the log of firm size at time t, and ε a white noise error term. The tildes indicate random variables. This 'law', as the eponymous author saw it, implies that the expected (log) size of a firm in t is simply its size in $t-1$.[18] By successive substitutions into equation 1 we find that the current size under this law is simply the initial size plus a series of random shocks to the firm over subsequent periods:

$$\tilde{x}_t = \tilde{\varepsilon}_t + \tilde{\varepsilon}_{t-1} + \ldots\ldots + \tilde{\varepsilon}_1 + x_0 \tag{2}$$

The law can be shown to result from taking a fixed population of firms of identical initial sizes but each subject to random shocks.[19] It is also clear from equation 2 that, viewed from the present, Gibrat's law implies a constant expected or average firm size in t periods' time given by the initial size x_0. More generally, the expected size of the firm viewed from period t is its current size, i.e. its size in $t-1$.

[16] If a variate X is Lognormally distributed then $\log(X)$ is Normally distributed.

[17] Needless to say, chance is a mere label for our ignorance. Every event necessarily has a cause, and any assertion to the effect that chance underlies growth patterns should be interpreted as meaning that the causes are so complex as to make it impossible to predict their outcome. White noise is the result.

[18] Firm size thus follows a Random Walk (see Feller, 1957).

[19] For a numerical example of this process see Prais (1971).

Empirically speaking, Gibrat produced evidence from French large firms' behaviour to support his hypothesis. A seminal later study by Hart and Prais(1956) on quoted companies in the UK appeared to confirm Gibrat's own finding and to establish a convincing fit to the data. However, whether the law would apply to unquoted firms was left open to later researchers to investigate.

The Gibrat model can be generalized in a very simple and instructive way. Rewrite equation 1 in the following form:

$$\tilde{x}_t = \beta x_{t-1} + \tilde{\varepsilon}_t \tag{3}$$

Where β is a constant. To get an idea of the effect of beta on growth we can rewrite 3 in the form of a growth equation

$$\tilde{g}_t = \tilde{x}_t - x_{t-1} = (\beta - 1)x_{t-1} + \tilde{\varepsilon}_t \tag{4}$$

We can now see that for β a positive fraction this period's expected growth is negatively related to last period's firm size. This implies that small firms grow faster than large:

$$\partial E\tilde{g}_t / \partial x_{t-1} = \beta - 1 < 0 \tag{5}$$

By contrast, for beta equal to one the effect of size on growth is zero and for beta greater than one it is positive. Another implication of Gibrat's law ($\beta = 1$) in addition to the constancy of the unconditional mean is that the unconditional variance increases without limit.[20] By contrast, for $\beta < 1$ the unconditional mean tends to zero, while the unconditional variance tends to a finite limiting value,[21] and for $\beta > 1$ the variance increases even faster over time than under Gibrat's law.

Prais (1981) estimated the relationship (3) for UK manufacturing firms with more than 25 employees firms in three periods: 1885–1939, 1939–50 and 1951–58. He found that in fact Gibrat's law failed to hold in any of these periods, producing betas of 0.98, 0.77 and 1.12. Pre-WW II and during WW II, beta was therefore less than one implying that small (quoted) firms grew faster than large ones. Post-WW II (at least until 1958) beta was greater than one and therefore large (quoted) firms grew faster.[22] Prais was particularly concerned about the effects of such

[20] $\tilde{x}_t = \tilde{x}_{t-1} + \tilde{\varepsilon}_t \Rightarrow \mu_t = \mu_{t-1} = \mu_0, \sigma_t^2 = \sigma_0^2 + t\sigma_\varepsilon^2 \rightarrow \infty$ as $t \rightarrow \infty$

[21] $\tilde{x}_t = \beta\tilde{x}_{t-1} + \tilde{\varepsilon}_t \Rightarrow \mu_t = \beta\mu_{t-1} = \beta^t\mu_0, \sigma_t^2 = \gamma^t\sigma_0^2 + \sigma_\varepsilon^2(1-\gamma^t)/(1-\gamma), \gamma = \beta^2$ and $\lim_{t\rightarrow\infty} \sigma_t^2 = \sigma_\varepsilon^2/(1-\gamma)$.

[22] Other studies by Utton (1974) and by Samuels (1965) found similar values for beta in the post-war periods 1951–65 and 1951–60. The interpretation of Prais' results has been the subject of some controversy. He and Hart (1962) tended to follow the line of Evely and Little (1960) that mergers were relatively unimportant as an explanation of firm growth, whereas Hannah and Kay (1977, 1981) argued that the dominant force in increasing concentration during the post-war period was due to merger activity. A beta greater than one implies that the variance of the underlying lognormal distribution increases over time and this in turn is associated with higher concentration levels measured by e.g. the five-firm concentration ratio.

increasing concentration on the market power of the large companies. Fortunately, however, these trends appear to have been substantially reversed in the post-1971 period. For example, see Hart and Oulton (1997) who examined a very large sample[23] of UK firms in the period 1989–93, including firms with fewer than 17 employees.

Simon and Bonini (1958) argued that one reason why Gibrat's law did not fit the data perfectly (the tail of the distribution was too fat) was that there was no allowance for the effects of birth of firms into the lowest size class: the total number of firms was assumed fixed. They argued that taking births into consideration, Gibrat's law might be resurrected by allowing it to operate above the minimum efficient scale (MES) for the industry. This generated another appropriately skewed distribution of firm sizes but this time described by the parameters of the Yule distribution rather than those of the Lognormal. They did not however, examine the effect of deaths among firms in the initial cohort.

A major variant on the Gibrat process, along with an optimizing model of firm and market behaviour, arrived in 1982 with the publication of what was to be a highly influential[24] article by Jovanovic (Jovanovic, 1982). This paper provided the first stochastic model of firm survival and growth based on individual optimization and market equilibrium.[25] It generates a rich set of predictions about the relationships between firm age and size, survival and growth and about the mean and variance of the size distribution. It also generates Gibrat's law as a special case.[26] Finally, while the model does not account for some aspects of industrial shakeouts[27] and a number of other well-known influences on growth,[28] it is nonetheless a better description of, and explanation for, the process of survival

[23] Some 87,000 independent companies.

[24] A *Google Scholar* search as of today (18 January 2005) reveals this article, published in the highly technical journal *Econometrica*, to have been cited no less than 652 times. This implies an annual citation rate of about 22, extraordinary by most standards for such a journal and for an industrial economics paper.

[25] Earlier models by Lucas (1978) and Kihlstrom and Laffont (1979) preceded Jovanovic in providing optimising models of firm behaviour underlying the growth process, but were non-stochastic in nature and did not produce the range of empirically valid predictions associated with the Jovanovic model.

[26] Under the assumption that technology is Cobb-Douglas with decreasing returns to scale growth is independent of size for mature firms; while under the additional assumption that the distribution of ability in the population is Lognormal, growth is independent of size for firms entering the industry at the same time.

[27] A shakeout is essentially a situation when the number of firms in an industry declines significantly after initial growth in numbers, alongside slowing and eventually declining industry output. See Klepper (2001) for references.

[28] These include: mergers and acquisitions (a large literature finds these important), initial size (by assumption in Jovanovic variations are ruled out), capital constraints (another larger literature supports this factor's role), financial risk (firms have no debt in Jovanovic), learning by doing (firms learn only about their *static* ability), and so on.

and growth than any of its forebears. We therefore devote some time to an exposition of it.[29,30]

Jovanovic imagines an economy in which entrepreneurial ability is dispersed in the population of potential entrepreneurs. This ability is not known to an individual who has no business experience. All individuals know by contrast the distribution of talent in the population. Entrepreneurship itself, however, is a 'learning experiment': you find out just how good (talented) you are at it only by entering the industry and progressively getting feedback from the market. This may lead to higher or lower output than that produced initially, as the estimate of one's ability randomly rises above or falls below the initial value. So the process of learning starts with some prior belief about one's costs or equivalently about one's productivity as an entrepreneur. These beliefs evolve over time. There is a critical level of (estimated) returns as a function of ability defined by the value of an outside alternative to entrepreneurship W, which might be the present discounted value (PDV) of wage employment. Individuals look indefinitely far ahead in their plans (i.e. operate with an infinite time horizon). A cohort of entrepreneurs enters in each period t. Time in the model is identical to the tenure of a continuing entrepreneur.

To understand the optimization procedure and how it impacts on output, growth and exit, note that in period t each entrepreneur behaves as a competitive firm taking the sequence of market prices $\{p_t\}$ as given and choosing an output q_t based on a cost function which depends on his imperfectly known costs (inverse of ability) θ_t. He chooses output to maximize current expected profits π_t (conditional on making subsequent decisions optimally) given by

$$\pi_t = p_t q_t - c(q_t)\bar{\theta}_t \tag{6}$$

where $\bar{\theta}_t$ is the expected value of the cost parameter for period t, updated according to Bayes' rule, and $c(q)$ is convex in q.[31] This output will be positive if the value of staying in, $V(t)$, exceeds the value of quitting entrepreneurship, W. Optimization generates an output

$$q_t = q_t(\bar{\theta}_t) \tag{7}$$

which is decreasing in $\bar{\theta}_t$ the current estimate of costs. This implies that there is a derived distribution of output conditional on the current estimate of costs. Hence, once we know the distribution of theta in any period we know also that of q.

[29] The exposition follows Jovanovic (1982), Brock and Evans (1986) but more closely that of Dunne, Roberts and Samuelson (1989).

[30] Ericson and Pakes (1995) allow for the role of learning by doing in addition to Jovanovic's learning 'pure and simple'.

[31] The entrepreneur in choosing q assumes that he will behave optimally with respect to all future decisions, which obviously depend on the current decision.

All potential entrepreneurs start with the same estimate of their costs, $\bar{\theta}_1$.[32] If the price is high enough they will all enter. Subsequent updating of their beliefs will lead some to revise them upwards and to contract and others to revise them downwards and to expand, even if price is constant. The density of costs evolves over time as ERs update according to Bayes' rule. This rule for a Normal distribution takes the form

$$\bar{\theta}_{t+1} = w_t\bar{\theta}_t + (1 - w_t)\theta_t \tag{8}$$

where θ_t is the current observation on costs and w(t) and 1−w(t) are weights attached to last year's mean estimate $\bar{\theta}_t$ and this year's observation. Bayes' rule implies that as t goes to infinity the weight to last period's mean estimate of costs, w(t), goes to one.

Let the density of expected costs in t+1 given expected costs in t be written

$$h(\bar{\theta}_{t+1}|\bar{\theta}_t) \tag{9}$$

This density has the property that the best estimate of next year's cost is simply today's costs:

$$E(\bar{\theta}_{t+1}|\bar{\theta}_t) = \bar{\theta}_t^{33} \tag{10}$$

Thus, standing in period t viewing his decision for t+1 the entrepreneur is faced with a distribution of costs centred on $\bar{\theta}_t$ and a distribution of q, centred on $q_t = q_t(\bar{\theta}_t)$ (see Figure 7.1).

Jovanovic shows that there exists a failure boundary defined in terms of ability, or equivalently, output or growth such that once the firm's costs rise above the boundary the entrepreneur exits. In Figure 7.1, this is denoted by θ^*_{t+1}. If current costs are estimated to be above θ^*_{t+1} then the ER exits; if below he stays at least one more period. In output terms this implies that for exiting firms, next period's output is zero and growth between this period and next is −100%:

$$g_t^* = (q_{t+1} - q_t)/q_t = -1 \Leftrightarrow q_{t+1} = 0 \tag{11}$$

Several predictions follow from the Jovanovic model and can be seen from a manipulation of Figure 7.1. First, smaller firms fail more frequently as a higher q(t) implies a smaller chance of $q(t{+}1)$ falling below $q^*(t + 1)$. Secondly, younger firms are more likely to fail than older ones as younger firms have fewer observations of costs on which to base their judgement of their true costs. The greater variability of their estimates means that finding that their current output is low (i.e. their current costs

[32] A variation on this assumption has been explored by Frank (1986).

[33] Notice the parallel here with Gibrat's law of equation 1. There the expectation of log(output) in *t*+1 conditional on log(output) in t is simply the latter.

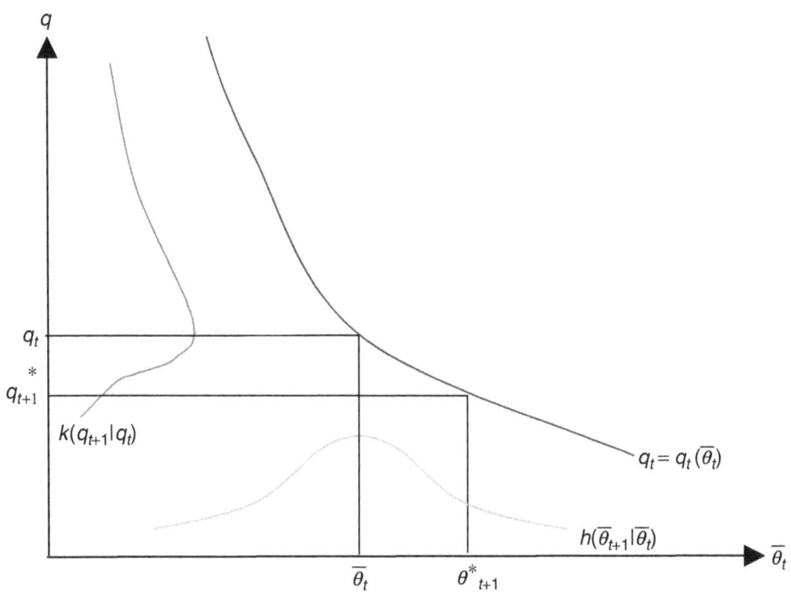

Figure 7.1 Entrepreneurial talent and output in Jovanovic (1982)

are high) they are more likely to quit.[34,35] Thirdly, larger non-failing firms of a given age grow more slowly. This follows from the fact that for fixed t the firm's cost parameter must lie in the interval $[\theta_1,\theta^*_t]$, implying that, output must lie in the interval $[q(\theta^*_t),q(\theta_1)]$. (See Figure 7.1.) Now, while subsequent output may lie above or below the initial level, it is clear that expected growth $E[g^*_t|q_t] = (E[q_{t+1}|q_t] - q_t)/q_t$ must therefore be a decreasing function of $q(t)$.[36] In other words, larger businesses grow more slowly. Finally, the Jovanovic model implies older firms have a smaller variance of growth rates for the same reasons that older firms are less likely to fail: the variance of the ER's estimate of costs is lower for ERs with longer tenure.[37]

[34] This is the case even if their true ability is high. Unfortunately, by the nature of the model, this mistaken (but rational) exit cannot be reversed: the failed entrepreneur by assumption gets no more observations on her ability to make any rational decision to restart.

[35] Note that the current estimate of the mean is a weighted average of the current observation and the previous period's estimate of the mean. The weights reflect the variance of the distribution with more weights being given to the past as the number of observations increases. Hence young firm's will have more fluctuating estimates and more likely to judge themselves failures.

[36] Since the larger this period's output the smaller the possible growth defined by the upper bound to next period's output.

[37] These models assume that entrepreneurs are risk neutral wealth-maximizers. Their focus is in explaining the stylized facts of firm growth and failure. The optimal growth-risk model resulting from this process determines the systematic part of the firm's growth. However, it allows that part of a firm's growth is determined outside the entrepreneur's control by random proportional shocks to the firm's equity value.

7.3.1 Tests of the Jovanovic model

What of the tests of this rich set of predictions? Jovanovic himself provides some evidence for their validity, but many subsequent studies, some of which cover really small firms (defined as those with fewer than five employees), have demonstrated the power of the model.

Hall (1987) while still using quoted company data, with very large 'small' firms, was the first study to examine the potentially important issues of selection out of the sample (by deaths of firms) and unobserved heterogeneity in the estimation of relationship (3), the generalized Gibrat process.[38] Her sample consisted of 1,778 US manufacturing firms in the year 1976. Her sample consisted of two panels selected from this set with employment data for the periods 1972–79 and 1976–83 respectively. Hall identified two types of selection bias that may arise in a panel of firms. The first occurs because selection out of the sample by death is not random; the second occurs because the selection into the sample by births is not random.[39] However, despite the theoretical possibilities she identified, after adjusting for the first of these two effects she found that growth was still negatively related to size as predicted by the Jovanovic model: the 'small firm effect' could not be accounted for either by unobserved heterogeneity or by selection bias. Hall also confirmed Hymer and Pashigans' finding that the variance of growth rates declined with size of firm, again as predicted by the Jovanovic theory.[40,41]

While Hall's study is a landmark in the empirical analysis of growth and survival, her sample, as noted, consisted entirely of quoted companies and her 'small' still means in most people's terminology 'very large'. Evans (1987a, b) by contrast was the first economist to use a panel dataset with seriously small firms included. Evans (1987a) data, was able to remedy some of the defects of her dataset. His sample, again for US manufacturing, and covering the five-year period 1976–80 consisted of a sample of some 20–30,000 firms in 100 industries classified at a rather detailed

[38] Ideally, studies of small firms should be based on a panel of data which allows for the control of unobserved heterogeneity at the firm and time level in the population, and hence avoids biases that may arise from simpler cross-sectional or time series regressions. Most of the datasets studied prior to Hall (1987) (and many since then) unfortunately do not possess this property and studies based on them were therefore subject to potential biases. However, even with a panel of data, biases can still arise and should be controlled for.

[39] Only Hall seems to have noticed both these potential biases, and she like other authors attempts to test for the influence only of potential failure bias.

[40] And because of the positive correlation of size and age, by implication the decline of the variance of growth rates with age of firm.

[41] This fact was first observed by Hymer and Pashigan (1962).They found that on a sample of the 1,000 largest US manufacturing firms that while the Gibrat assumption that firm growth rates are independent of size was supported by the data, the assumption that the variance of growth is independent of size was not: larger firms had less variable growth rates. They concluded that either firms' costs curves were not horizontal as suggested by Simon and Bonini (1958), or that there was monopoly power among the larger firms. However, they, like Simon and Bonini do not provide an optimizing model of the systematic part of the stochastic process.

Table 7.1 Failure rates by size and age of firm (from Evans, 1987b)

Age (years)						
Mean no. employees	0–6	7–20	21–45	46–95	95+	Row average
1–19	40	22	20	17	0	29
20–49	32	14	11	11	16	17
50–99	31	13	10	14	15	15
100–249	25	12	11	7	11	13
250–499	32	13	7	7	6	11
500–999	21	10	6	5	5	8
1000+	–	13	9	2	8	6

level (the two-digit level). His size grouping was furthermore defined to include firms with as few as five employees. Evans' data in a second paper (Evans, 1987b) (See Table 7.1) included firms with as few as one employee. In both of these papers Evans was interested in testing Jovanovic's predictions regarding the relationship between firm size and growth, and that between firm age and growth and the variance of growth. His data also allowed him to examine the effects of failure on both these relationships. Evans found that controlling for selection bias smaller and younger firms grew faster and died more frequently than larger, older firms. The variability of growth also decreased with age. In Evans (1987a), these results held both in aggregate and for upwards of 75 percent of the industries studied.

Evans (1987a) provides a useful conceptual framework to analyse some of the empirical tests of Jovanovic's theory which generates Gibrat's law as a special case.

Write the firm's log size in period t in the form

$$\tilde{x}_t = x_{t-1} + \gamma(x_{t-1}, a_{t-1}) + \tilde{u}_t \tag{12}$$

where $\gamma(x_{t-1}, a_{t-1})$ is a deterministic function of log size x and log age a of the firm and u is a white noise error term. Evans actually writes this model in growth form (derived by re-arranging equation 6):

$$\tilde{g}_t \equiv \tilde{x}_t - x_{t-1} = \gamma(x_{t-1}, a_{t-1}) + \tilde{u}_t \tag{13}$$

The partial derivatives of the growth function with respect to x and a can then be written as γ_x, γ_a and show (conveniently) the elasticity of the expected change in size[42] (or equivalently of the logarithmic growth rate) with respect to the change in the size and age of the firm.[43] Gibrat's law says that gamma and u are independent

[42] To see this note that $\partial Eg_t/\partial \ln(a_t) = \partial\gamma/\partial \ln(a_t) = \partial \ln(S_t/S_{t-1})/\partial \ln(a_t)$ and similarly for x.

[43] Thus an x-derivative of −0.5 shows that a 1% increase in size, holding age constant, lowers growth by .5% per annum.

of x and a or equivalently that these derivatives are identically zero. Evans found from his empirical work on US manufacturing firms between 1976 and 1982 that $\gamma_x, \gamma_a < 0$ consistently with Jovanovic's theory. However, he also found contrary to a Jovanovic special case, that under the assumption of a Cobb-Douglas firm production function with decreasing returns to scale, firm growth was not independent of size for mature firms. Finally, Evans reported that deviations from Gibrat's law were less marked the larger and the older the firm.

7.4 Survival of small businesses

An aspect of the studies reported above is that by and large they deal with small firms of five employees and above and with ages less than six years. However, it is possible to argue that most of the interesting features of firm failure occur within the first six years of trading. The issue of early survival is particularly poignant for the self-employed as most self-employed people in an economy do not have employees and most firms die within the first two to three years of trading (Cressy, 1993). Moreover, researchers in the 1990s inspired by Evans and Jovanovic made some interesting discoveries regarding the survival and closure patterns of seriously small and young firms based on datasets often covering predominantly service industries.

Survival among a random cohort of start-up businesses is remarkably low and varies a great deal in the first two or three years of the firm's life. For example, Brüederl et al. (1992) found that in a cohort of German startups, 24 percent went out of business in the first two years of trading and 37 percent exited in the first five years; Cressy (1996b) found that in a cohort of UK start-ups, 45 percent died in the first two and a half years of trading and 80 percent in the first six years; Mata and Portugal (1994) (as we have seen) found that in a cohort of Portuguese start-ups 20 percent died in the first year and 50 percent in the first four years.[44]

Given the dramatic propensity to demise in the very early stages we might well ask at this point whether the Jovanovic model accounts for the facts of small firm

[44] It is worth noting that the average size of the startups in these samples, unlike the earlier study of Hall, is very small, being always less than five employees. The figures for failure rates of small firms contrast dramatically with those for large firms. For example, Evans (1987b) found that US manufacturing firms with 250–499 employees had a failure (closure) rate of 11.3% per annum rising to 31.9% for plants of six years or less, while DRS found that for manufacturing plants with more than 250 employees exit rates were 19% per annum for all ages of plant rising to 22% per annum for plants of aged five years or younger.

survival. A number of European studies have found that it does. Mata and Portugal (1994), show that in Portuguese manufacturing firms, between one and 100 employees survival rates (failure rates) start at 78 percent (22%) after one year for the new entrants, falling to 52 percent (48%) after four years. But the variation of failure rates with size is also remarkable: after four years, 75 percent of the large firms are still in operation (implying a 25% failure rate) whereas only 44 percent of the smallest (one–two employees) are still around (a 56% failure rate). Likewise, a four-year size transition matrix[45] of these firms shows that among survivors the tendency is to grow rather than to shrink (a finding also echoed in Cressy (1993) and elsewhere), but that post-entry mobility[46] tends to decrease with size. This evidence is consistent with Jovanovic's prediction that growth rates decline with size.[47,48,49] The two key findings of the empirical literature—that small firms are less likely to survive and tend to grow faster than large (controlling for survivorship bias)—have been confirmed in many different country studies. For example, among European countries, we find the two propositions validated in Scotland (Reid, 1991), Germany (Harhoff and Waywode, 1998), the Netherlands (Van Praag, 2003), England (Storey et al., 1987; Cressy, 1996a), Italy (Audretsch et al., 1999) and Austria (Weiss, 1998). By and large, the findings for service industries tend to mirror those for manufacturing.

[45] A size transition matrix shows the proportion of firms starting in a given size class in one year that move to another size class in another year. In this case it is four years.

[46] Defined as the tendency of a firm to switch size classes over time.

[47] It is also consistent they argue with the story of small firms' flexibility.

[48] Evans' methodology, as Hall's, relied on the assumption of a normally distributed and homoskedastic error term in the selection equation for failure. This, as the authors were aware, laid their results open to question, since as we have seen, failure and growth tends to decline with size. A later study by Dunne, Roberts and Samuelson (1989) however, circumvented this methodological issue by using a quite different approach that does not depend on these two assumptions. They examined a sample of US manufacturing plants, some of whom were owned by multi- and others by single-plant companies, and found that smaller plants were more likely to exit than larger ones, and that once failure was allowed for smaller plants owned by single plant firms, they grew faster than larger ones. An important relationship exists between the expected growth of a firm and its survival rate. This is enshrined in the following identity, which comes from the statistical law of total probability:

$$Eg_t = E(g_t|g_t > -100\%)P(g_t > -100\%) + E(g_t|g_t = -100\%)P(g_t = -100\%)$$

where a decline of 100% in size in any given period is defined as failure. This relationship demonstrates that if the probability of survival is not independent of size or age then the using only surviving firms is likely to result in small firms appearing to grow faster than large simply because the −100%s are ignored. Once these are taken into account the empirical validity of Gibrat's law might in theory be restored.

[49] One of the interesting points to emerge from the Evans study is regarding the breakdown of 'failure'. A firm was coded as a 1 if a firm was on the dataset in 1976 and in 1980, and as a zero if not. He notes that the absence of a firm in 1980 may mean (a) it filed for bankruptcy; (b) it voluntarily dissolved itself; (c) it merged with, or was taken over by, another firm. Quoting another study in which M&A accounted for 13% of closures of firms with more than 20 employees, and speculated that such closures accounted for a smaller proportion of firms with fewer than 20 employees. However, Evans' data were not rich enough to establish the facts. He concluded however, that his failure results were not likely to be 'too contaminated' by false accounting.

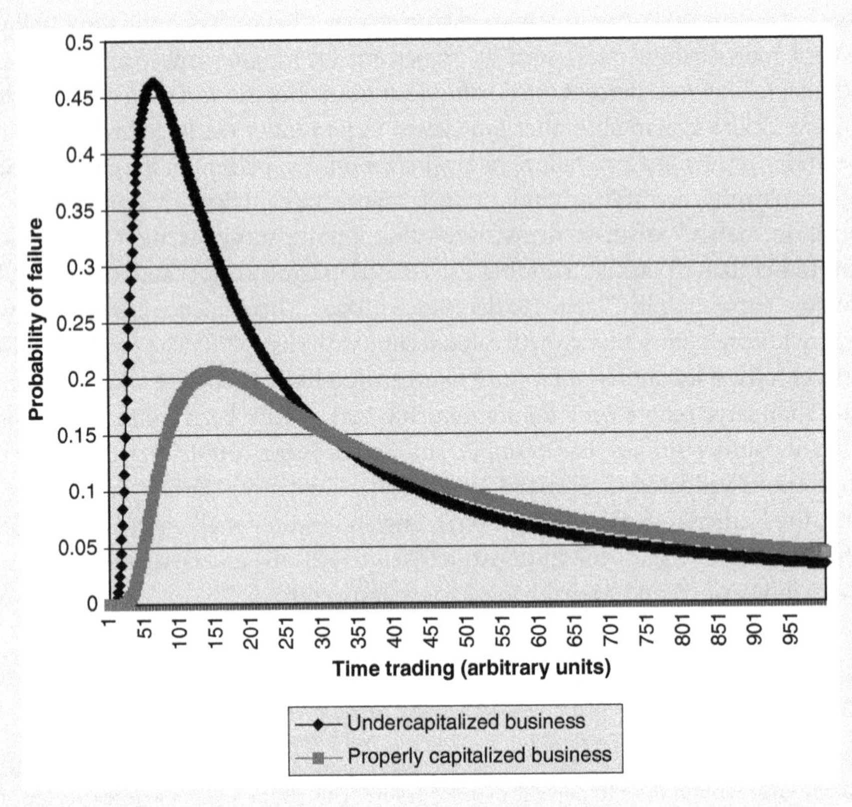

Figure 7.2 Simulation: Young firm failure and capitalization (Cressy, 2005)

These findings have been given a more systematic underpinning in empirical studies of closure rates over the firm life cycle—see Ganguly (1985) and Cressy (1997, 2005) for the UK; Brüederl et al. (1992) for Germany; Van Praag (2003) for Holland and Audretsch and Argarwal (2001) for the US. This research examines the structure and determinants of the failure rate of a given cohort of firms over the first six to ten years of trading. The general finding is that the firm failure distribution over time trading is positively skewed with most firms dying[50] in the first two and a half years of life. However, if a firm survives the first two years ('the valley of death') its long run survival chances are high: the remainder often live to a ripe old age—see Figure 7.2.[51] There are empirically identifiable factors causing the curve to shift. Cressy (1997, 2005) develops a theoretical model which simulates the empirical failure curve and he argues that there are three principal factors influencing the position of the curve:

[50] In this context, by dying we mean closing voluntarily.

[51] Cressy (2005) derives from theoretical considerations an Inverse Gaussian distribution of failure rates. Bruderl et al. (1992) however, fit a log-logistic curve to the German data. The same general pattern of skewness is however apparent in both models.

initial capitalization, growth and risk. He shows that in the case of initial capitalization the curve shifts downwards and to the right as the firm gets more money at start-up. The honeymoon period for the entrepreneur and his business (during which the firm 'cannot' fail) is also lengthened by money (see Figure 7.2). A roughly similar effect is predicted from higher mean growth rate and lower risk associated with it. What is clear from the Cressy model is that in the long run the initial conditions (e.g. start-up size) don't matter: closure rates for initially small and large firms converge.

Extant empirical work, moreover, confirms these predictions. For example, firm exit rates have been found significantly related to both the firm and industry life cycle and to calendar time.[52] Moreover, the advantages to size are short-lived: over time they disappear. The theory is as follows.

Industries are characterized in the early stages of a technology by experimentation with short production runs of experimental designs until in the mature stage a dominant design emerges. In the early, or formative, stage the motivation of entry is innovative skill in producing superior product designs. In this situation small firms have the advantage and enter in large numbers. The larger firms among these entrants have an advantage over the smaller and are more likely to survive over the short run. In the later, or mature stages of the industry, design matters less and there is less entry. Furthermore, knowledge, that in the early stages, is discovered by the small entrant has now been codified and embodied in products, reducing the advantage of the small firm. Furthermore, the surviving small firm will have grown by now and will itself embody some of this knowledge.

Audretsch and Argarwal (2001) (AA) find that the position of the failure curve for new entrants is indeed influenced by the industry's development stage (*formative* vs. *mature*) and by the technological regime (*low* vs. *high* tech). Size of entrant has a short run impact on survival, but this is a function of the stage of the industry and in the longer run, size doesn't matter: the curves converge. AA speculate that this may be due to the influence of growth.[53] Studies relating not to time trading but to calendar time also demonstrate that the form of exit matters. Cressy and Storey (1994), for example, find that the overall exit rate is relatively constant through time, but that, as might be expected, bankruptcies and insolvencies vary counter-cyclically, being much higher in recessions than in booms.[54]

Finally, as mentioned earlier, little empirical work has examined the determinants of different business outcome types. However, a recent paper by Van Praag (Van Praag, 2003), examines the firm-level determinants survival of two outcomes: survival duration and success. Her data is a large sample of American small

[52] The term industry life cycle refers to the passage of the industry through infancy, growth, consolidation and decline and the effects of this are distinguished from those due to the passage of calendar time or history.

[53] In view of the Cressy (2005) model, the relationship may also be influenced by the effects of initial capital constraints and risk which have not so far been controlled for in empirical studies.

[54] Bankruptcy rates among are in fact three times as high in the UK recession of the early nineties as in the boom which preceded it in the late eighties.

businesses and she applies a hazard rate methodology[55] to estimate the determinants of each outcome. Hence she is able to effectively distinguish the determinants of voluntary and involuntary exits. Her research also produces empirical hazard rate curves that mimic the failure distributions derived by Cressy (1997, 2005) its characteristic positive skew over time trading.

Van Praag defines business survival duration as the expected period in business ending in either voluntary or compulsory dissolution.[56] By contrast, success is defined as the expected period in business conditional on involuntary exit.[57] This enables her to estimate a model with 'competing' risks, namely the risk of voluntary closure versus that of involuntary closure, and to examine the factors that determine the two. She finds, as predicted by Schary (1991), that empirically the competing risk model explains the data better than a single (homogeneous) risk model, which ignores the type of exit. The main differences however are not in kind but in quantity: for example, consistently with Bates (1990), Cressy and Storey (1994) and others, start-ups run by older entrepreneurs survive longer in both the voluntary and involuntary senses.[58] However, young starters are more likely to find better outside opportunities than their more mature counterparts and therefore to voluntarily exit entrepreneurship; these youngsters are also more likely to fail due to a lack of leadership or 'knowledge of the world'.[59]

7.5 Survival, Growth and Credit Constraints

A credit constraint exists if an entrepreneur with insufficient wealth cannot obtain debt to fund a viable project, that is, one with a positive net present value

[55] The hazard rate of failure is defined as the probability that a business which has survived to time t should fail in the next instant. Van Praag estimates a log-logistic hazard rate function which is non-monotonic in calendar time and takes the form:

$$\theta(t,x) = k(x)\alpha t^{\alpha-1}/(1 + k(x)t^{\alpha})$$

where x is a vector of explanatory variables, t is time and $k(x) = \exp(x'\beta)$ with beta a vector of parameters.

[56] This is consistent with our definitions of failure above.

[57] In effect this defines success as the ability to stave off bankruptcy for as long as possible.

[58] This means that there are more or longer lasting opportunities available to firms ending in solvent closure, and that managers of older firms can stave off bankruptcy for longer.

[59] This echoes the finding of Cressy (1996b) whose strongest human capital measure predicting survival was the average age of the entrepreneurial team.

(NPV).[60] In such a situation the capital market is inefficient and the wealth of the economy will be lower than it would be with an efficient market. It is commonly believed that credit constraints exist in most economies at most times and that small firms are the most likely to experience them.[61] Credit constraints in turn are expected to have an impact on such firms' survival and growth rates, lowering both. The academic literature in this area is massive. In this section, therefore, we examine a particular subset of this literature that has been subject to intensive empirical testing, namely, the literature on the switching decision—the choice to move into, or out of, self-employment. We first outline the theory to show how it generates a theory of credit constraints and how these in turn affect survival and growth of the afflicted firms. We then examine a number of empirical tests of the theory and finally raise some issues of interpretation of the results.

Evans and Jovanovic (1989) (henceforth EJ) in a now celebrated paper,[62] developed a theory of credit constraints based on the idea that banks lend in proportion to a firm's assets rather than on the basis of its expected cash-flow profits. The result may be that there is insufficient lending and excessive failure of cash-starved businesses. Since collateral tends to fall with business size, a given loan demand is less likely to be supplied the smaller the business. Since under-capitalization will reduce profits, it is expected that small firms will be more likely to fail as a result of credit constraints. Finally, since such constraints cause entrepreneurs to invest a larger proportion of their assets in the business and to reinvest earnings back into the business, smaller firms will have higher rates of return on assets and will be expected to grow faster than large ones.

EJ argued that empirically we should find credit constraints to self-employment (henceforth SE) if, and only if, there was an empirical correlation of assets and switching into SE (or equivalently between assets and SE survival). This is based on the idea of a bank lending rule in which lending is proportional to a fims's assets. A relaxation of the lending rule (or equivalently an unanticipated increase in fixed assets) will, if businesses are constrained, increase switching into SE and increase business survival rates. EJ estimated their model on a sample of 1,949[63] American white males aged between 14 and 24 years in 1966 who were wage workers in 1976 and who were either wage workers of self-employed in 1978.[64] These individuals

[60] This definition assumes that debt is the appropriate financial instrument to fund the project. See Cressy (2002) and the papers contained in the associated symposium for a more detailed discussion of the issues.

[61] Many billions of dollars are spent annually by governments around the world in attempts to alleviate such constraints.

[62] 334 citations were found for this paper as of November 2004.

[63] The actual estimation sample is 1,443 since negative net worth or SE income individuals were deleted from the sample. This is of course a potential source of bias.

[64] And who were not unemployed, out of the labour force, in the military or in school full-time in either 1976 or 1978.

were between the ages of 24 and 34 in 1976, the typical age of entrepreneurial entry. The average SE man in 1978 earned US$15,746 compared with US$16,760 for a wage worker. Net assets of the total sample were about US$20,000. The average work experience and education of the sample individuals was 12 and 14 years respectively. About 4 percent of those who were wage earners in 1976 switched into SE by 1978.

EJ estimated the probability of SE as a function of assets (and its square), wage experience, education, starting wage, income and controls. The coefficient on assets was positive and significant (at the 2 percent level). On the (questionable) assumption of zero correlation of assets and entrepreneurial ability, they concluded that liquidity constraints exist. EJ also estimated SE earnings as a function of the same variables in the switching equation and found that wealthier individuals earned more in SE because they 'will have started businesses with more efficient capital levels' (p. 820). Finally, they found that people with smaller assets are forced to devote a larger proportion of their wealth to their businesses.

7.5.1 Questioning the EJ result

While a growing number of studies have apparently provided support to the EJ finding of credit rationing (see especially Holtz-Eakin et al., 1994a, b; Blanchflower and Oswald, 1998), there are questions about a number of features of their study that have in turn led to extensions of the model and more sophisticated tests of its hypotheses:

(a) How appropriate is the model EJ used? In particular are assets endogenous to the system as they assume, or e.g. are they a function of the human capital of the entrepreneur, thus making the latter the primary constraint? (Cressy, 1996; Astebro and Bernhardt, 2003; Parker and Van Praag, 2003).

(b) How should one interpret the EJ finding of a positive correlation of assets and survival? For example, it has been questioned whether the repeated findings of various studies can 'really' be explained by the existence of uncontrolled-for effects such as control- or risk-aversion of the would-be/actual entrepreneur (Cressy, 1995, 1998) or the existence of sunk costs that differentially affect small and large firms (Cabral, 1995)?

(c) How representative are the datasets used in the EJ-replication studies? For example, the US work by Holtz-Eakin et al. (1994b) examined only the top end of the wealth distribution and found evidence supporting EJ. More recent evidence suggests, however, that the pattern may be radically different for most of the wealth spectrum where the relation between wealth and switching vanishes (Hurst and Lusardi, 2004).

7.5.2 Structure of the EJ model

Cressy (1996b) using a large representative dataset of UK start-ups and a rich vector of entrepreneurial, firm and financial characteristics argued that the true constraint on business survival was not financial, but rather human, capital of the entrepreneur. His evidence showed the correlation between assets and survival was spurious, arising from the correlation of both with the human capital of the entrepreneur. Human capital here was measured by entrepreneurial age ('general experience of life' and greater realism),[65] industry-specific work experience, managerial human capital (measured by team size) and whether the start-up was a business purchase (measuring the existence of economic networks). These same human capital factors were found to explain the provision of bank finance to the firm. Cressy concluded that so far from subsidizing start-ups, governments should focus more on the provision of training to would be entrepreneurs.

Astebro and Bernhardt (2003) (henceforth AB) provide a sophisticated examination of the 'endogeneity of capital constraints' issue raised in Cressy's paper. Working with US self-employment data they they include measures of both transferable human capital (education, etc.) and of entrepreneurial ability (business experience, etc.)[66] They employ a two-stage estimation procedure At the first stage, the relationship between an owner's human capital, entrepreneurial ability and financial wealth are examined; at the second stage the relationship between the firm's start-up capital, entrepreneurial ability, human capital and financial wealth are analyzed, with financial wealth the predicted value determined from the first stage.[67]

At the first stage, wealth is found to increase with both human capital and entrepreneurial ability, suggesting that collateral constraints are indeed endogenous, contrary to EJ. At the second stage, while controlling for financial wealth, start-up capital requirements are found to increase with entrepreneurial ability *and* human capital, implying that better quality entrepreneurs are perhaps more credit-constrained, consistent with the EJ model.[68] The marginal effect of wealth on capital demand diminishes significantly once human capital is added to the equation, whereas adding entrepreneurial ability increases the marginal effect of wealth. This suggests that the human capital does indeed mitigate wealth constraints which bite harder on better entrepreneurs. Capital constraints are thus

[65] The degree of optimism of an entrepreneur decreases with age. See De Meza and Southey (1996).

[66] EJ assumed that human capital in wage and self-employment were independent.

[67] Identification of this instrument is accomplished by using county-level indicators of household income for the owners.

[68] Their model predicts that individuals with greater entrepreneurial ability for *given* wealth will be more credit constrained. AB show that the demand for capital will be higher for better entrepreneurs at any given wealth.

endogenous (as Cressy (1996b) found), but controlling for human capital and entrepreneurial ability does not completely eliminate them.[69]

Parker and Van Praag (2003) (henceforth PVP) also address the important endogeneity issue in EJ using Dutch self-employment data. They employ a different definition of capital constraints loan (down-scaling rather than loan denial) and examine established businesses rather than start-ups, but demonstrate empirically the existence of an 'endogenous triangle' of relationships between human capital, capital constraints and performance among the Dutch self-employed. They too find that credit constraints, measured by the extent of loan downscaling[70] are endogenous, being reduced by human capital of the individual: more educated individuals are less constrained in starting a business because they are better capitalized (possess more initial assets). Capital constraints are found in turn to impede performance (measured by profits from the business) since they constrain it to a sub-optimal initial scale. Finally, human capital enhances business performance directly (via the effect of entrepreneurial ability on productivity) and indirectly (via the relaxation of capital constraints).[71,72]

7.5.3 Sample issues

Other criticisms of EJ-replicative studies revolve around the dataset EJ and others (Holtz-Eakin et al., 1994b) used. EJ's original sample was, as we have seen, of American young white males with an average wealth of US$20,000, a very modest figure indeed. The sample used by a confirmatory study by Holtz-Eakin et al. (1994) (henceforth HE), however, was by contrast, of rather rich US individuals with an

[69] Astebro and Bernhardt are also able to control for the fact that some industries have a larger efficient minimum scale (MES) and for differences in risk across industries, both of which may militate against the decision to enter. Industries with larger MES are entered by wealthier entrepreneurs and firms with greater risk of failure start with less capital, suggesting that credit constraints bite more strongly in these categories. However, using interaction terms between each of these items and wealth they find no marginal impact on capital requirements and hence on credit constraints.

[70] The term downscaling is mine. PVP argue that downscaling of a loan is evidence for the existence of a credit constraint on a firm. This is plausible if one were able to control adequately for other factors that might explain the downscaling. These include the degree of optimism of the borrower. Since younger borrowers are more likely to have their applications downscaled (as optimists they will ask for too much), their entrepreneurial age variable in effect controls for a potential fly in the ointment. However, PVP do in fact implicitly control in their study for this effect with the inclusion of the entrepreneurial age variable. See De Meza and Southey (1996) for some of the theory underlying the optimism hypothesis in entrepreneurship.

[71] This appears to be an average rather than a marginal return, however, and so perhaps overstates the return at the margin.

[72] One point worthy of discussion is PVP's claim that downscaling of a loan is evidence for the existence of a credit constraint on a firm. This is inherently plausible if one were able to control

average wealth of US$72,000 in 1981.[73] While the original HE paper suggested capital constrained entrepreneurs throughout the wealth spectrum, a very recent paper by Hurst and Lusardi (2004) examining a wider sample of US citizens suggests that throughout most of the wealth range there is in fact no correlation of the chances of starting a business with individual wealth levels. They find that it is only at the very top of the distribution that the correlation becomes positive. These high net worth individuals are potentially of high entrepreneurial ability relative to their assets and allegedly credit constrained.[74] Thus studies such as that of HE, that use high net worth individuals to argue more generally for the existence of credit constraints are shown to be much more restrictive in scope than had been imagined.[75]

7.5.4 Contrarian evidence

Other studies of capital constraints from different methodological perspectives have tended to conclude that credit constraints are in general of little importance, for example, Aston (1990) in a survey of potentially fast growth businesses and their financial search procedures found that at most 6 percent of growth potential businesses were constrained. This is a rather small proportion of businesses if capital constraints are as widespread as the empirical work suggests. Likewise,

adequately for other factors that might explain downscaling. Such factors include the degree of optimism of the borrower (see De Meza and Southey, 1996). Thus, it is likely that over-optimistic borrowers are more likely to have their applications downscaled (as optimists they will ask for too much, anticipating faster growth than they achieve, or simply higher survival chances). Although PVP do not discuss this issue explicitly, their inclusion of an entrepreneurial age variable in the capital constraint equation in effect controls for this potential fly in the ointment.

[73] Holtz-Eakin et al. following Blanchflower and Oswald (1998) examined the impact of both the wealth of the individual defined as her liquid assets and her house equity and any inheritance on the decision to enter business and the capitalization of the business once started. In fact, only the inheritance variable had any impact and that impact was quite substantial. For example, a $100,000 inheritance increased the probability of transition into SE by about 15%, proportionately. Importantly, HE also show that the inheritance effect is not due to the inheritance of businesses. If the latter were true then the observed correlation of inheritance and start-up propensity would simply have been the decision by inheritors to continue running their parents' businesses.

[74] This finding is inherently implausible too. The argument for credit constraints is, if anything, about whether relatively poor or cash-strapped individuals can efficiently start their own firms. The fact that it now appears that only the richest individuals in society are 'cash-strapped', surely constitutes a rather exquisite paradox for the theory of credit constraints. It might, of course, be the case that such individuals are indeed the ones to target with loan guarantee schemes and government subsidies, but this seems socially reprehensible to say the least.

[75] To be fair, Holtz-Eakin et al. are aware that their results may not generalize to the broader population, but argue that it is plausible to assume that they do.

Cambridge (1996) also adopting a survey approach found little evidence of constraints in the UK.

7.5.5 Alternative explanations for the findings

The fact that a theory is consistent with the data does not of course prove that it explains it. We need to check that there are no competing explanations available. Thus, in the following sections, we examine alternative explanations, theoretical and empirical, for the correlation of assets and switching/survival.

7.5.5.1 *Risk aversion of the entrepreneur*

Another potential explanation exists for the EJ finding that assets and switching into SE are positively correlated but which does not imply credit constraints. This explanation depends merely on some plausible assumptions and limited evidence about human tolerance of risk. It is commonly believed (and there is evidence to show) that people in general dislike risk. Studies of the stock market show that people need to be offered higher returns to invest in more risky securities. This is consistent with risk aversion. Likewise, most people take out some kind of insurance policy against fire, theft and so forth, which involves the payment of a premium. This also suggests dislike of risk since by the mechanism of insurance the risk is transferred to another party.[76]

Imagine then, that when I increase your assets you become less risk averse, that is to say you become more willing to take risks. For example, if I offer you simultaneously an increase in your wealth W by £1 and a bet which yields +£1 with probability 1/2 and −£1 with probability 1/2, with your additional assets you are now more likely to take the bet than before. In the language of economics, this means your utility of income function displays Decreasing Absolute Risk Aversion (or DARA). Since available empirical evidence suggests that entrepreneurship tends to be more income-risky than wage employment, this means that the marginal entrepreneur (one for whom the expected costs just outweigh the expected benefits) would switch into self-employment should he/she receive a windfall gain. There is, furthermore, some empirical evidence to support the assumption that entrepreneurs have decreasing absolute risk aversion (see Guiso and Paiella, 1999).

[76] There are, of course, counter-examples. The most glaring is the fact that huge numbers (millions) of people, often the poorest, engage regularly in an unfair bet, namely the national lottery. This is inconsistent with risk aversion.

Thus we have the result that higher wealth is associated with greater propensity to enter SE which gives us the EJ result but without capital constraints. No direct test of this proposition is yet available even though it is straightforward to set up.

7.5.5.2 *Control aversion of the entrepreneur*

Entrepreneurs of smaller firms are well known to be *control averse.*[77] Control aversion is defined here as the dislike of perceived interference by outsiders in a business. Control aversion among small firms may in general affect their decision to take on external equity providers or their decision to take on external debt. Empirically there is growing evidence that such aversion does exist and does influence both the capital structure and performance of small firms. (Cressy and Olofsson, 1997; Mueller, 2004). So how can it explain the empirical results on credit constraints?

Entrepreneurs do not like any kind of interference in their operations, in particular by Big Brother in the form of the local bank manager. (Cressy, 1995). For this reason (and for other reasons) they tend to borrow little.[78] In the language of economics, this means that the psychological costs of borrowing outweigh the benefits (at the margin) for the entrepreneur of the smaller firm. As firms get larger, things get less personal, management tends to be rewarded by salaries rather than simply profits, and the aversion to perceived bank interference starts to wane. But at the level of the micro business (one with less than ten employees) control-aversion is likely to restrict borrowing not from the supply—but from the demand-side. The equilibrium trade-off is illustrated in Figure 7.3 (taken from Cressy, 1995) where the red line indicates profits of the firm as a function of borrowing. This represents the utility function of the financial manager of a larger firm. By contrast, the green line represents an indifference curve for the entrepreneur of a small firm. While profits are a 'good' yielding (positive marginal utility), borrowing is 'bad' (yielding negative marginal utility). Thus the indifference curve is upward-sloping—its slope being the ratio of the marginal utility of borrowing to that of profits.[79] Utility is therefore increasing as we move to the north-west of the diagram with higher profits and lower borrowing. The highest indifference curve attainable with the red profit constraint is the green one. The optimum for the larger firm is where profits are maximized, at L*. The optimum of the control-averse

[77] Evidence for this goes back at least 30 years to the UK's Bolton Committee, a landmark in the study of smaller firms (Bolton, 1971). However, of more recent vintage, and referring specifically to aversion to bank control is Cressy (1995).

[78] In Cressy (1993), I showed that only one-third of firms borrowed even on overdraft at start-up. This grew to one-half within three years, but was still a minority of (surviving) firms. Indeed, the attrition rate in the sample was considerable (many businesses closed within three years) but the propensity to borrow among survivors, and the average amount borrowed, increased over time.

[79] The standard formula for the slope of an indifference curve is $-MU_x/MU_y$ where x and y are the two commodities yielding utility to the consumer.

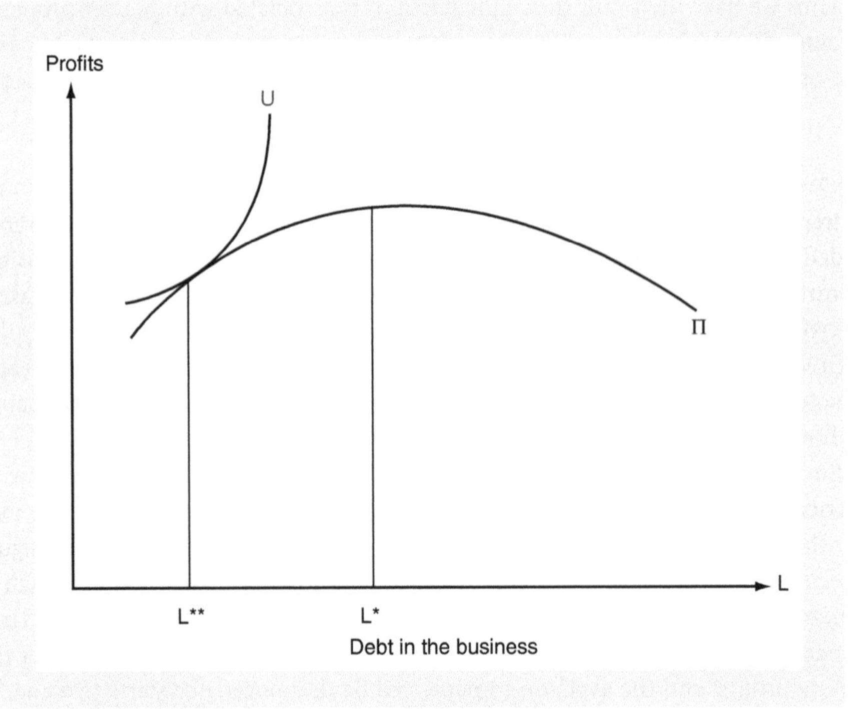

Figure 7.3 Effects of control aversion on the amount of borrowing

entrepreneur, equates the marginal disutility of borrowing with the marginal utility of profits, yielding the smaller borrowing amount L**.

7.5.5.3 *Sunk costs*

Cabral (1995) provides a model of sunk costs which constitutes on the one hand a possible explanation for why small firms grow faster than large ones, and on the other a potentially competing explanation for the alleged role of capital constraints. Cabral argues that the presence of sunk costs together with the well-tested assumption that smaller firms have a lower survival rate implies that small firms will grow faster than large ones. If this claim were true Gibrat's law would be false on theoretical grounds.

Cabral's argument rests on the notion from Jovanovic (1982) discussed on p. 169 above, that entrepreneurs only learn about their efficiency as entrepreneurs after entering the industry. Cabral presents an infinite horizon model, but one in which the significant changes occur only in periods 1 and 2. The remaining periods repeat what happens in period 2. In period 1, firms get a signal about their productivity. In period 2, they learn exactly what their type (productivity) is going to be for that period and for all subsequent periods. Productivity types are one of a triplet: Low, Medium or High. The Low types never make a profit and have no chance of improving productivity; hence they do not invest in capacity and exit once their type is revealed to them. The High types are also 'locked in' to their state and have no chance of declining in quality, so that once their type is revealed they know they will remain with that productivity forever. Therefore, High types install their long run capacity immediately and choose an output constant through time—implying zero growth rate. Only the Medium types may change state, either remaining as they are or rising or falling in efficiency with positive probability between periods 1 and 2. The crucial point is that if the Medium types fail (falling to Low in period 2) viewed *ex ante* of the decision to invest, the owner incurs a loss on the capital invested since he has to quit the industry. Medium types have a survival probability (probability of productivity remaining constant or rising) less than one and hence smaller than that of the High types. This means that Medium types in period 1, in view of their higher expected losses from closure, will install capacity below the long run level. In period 2, when their type is revealed, Mediums will increase capacity and output. Hence their growth rate will be positive and higher than that of the High types. In a word, surviving small firms (Mediums) grow faster than large ones (Highs).[80]

7.6 Control aversion, outside equity and growth

If debt cannot easily be raised by a small firm due to absence of collateral then one might imagine that equity would be the alternative, and indeed more suitable, form of finance. Outside equity funding involves the purchase by an outside organization, or individual, of shares in the firm. However, despite its seeming attractiveness there are insurmountable problems with this as a solution to the provision of small business finance.

First, outside equity is by definition irrelevant to the majority of small businesses who are unincorporated and hence cannot (legally) issue equity. Secondly, even if we confine our interest to small incorporated businesses, control aversion operates even more strongly in the case of equity (by comparison with debt) to discourage

[80] Cabral also uses this model to provide an interesting alternative (possibly complementary) explanation for why allegedly capital constrained businesses grow faster than unconstrained ones. But on that issue, see later.

most small firms from gaining finance this way.[81] The decision not to take advantage of outside equity may well result in more gearing and slower growth for the firms involved, but their owners seem to prefer the disutility of this to the disutility of control-loss (Mueller, 2004).[82] Thirdly, venture capitalists, or Business Angels, the likely source of such finance are not interested in buying equity in the vast majority of small Limited Companies (typical firms) as they offer no prospects of capital gain of the order they are used to and require. Traditionally, VCs have required rates of return (IRRs) of 30 percent plus per annum on their investments. These rates of return are only possible however if the firm grows very fast and in a short time (three–five years) ends up with a stock market flotation or a trade sale. The vast majority of firms, even the majority of sophisticated firms, do not fall into this category.[83]

7.7 Conclusions

Over the last half century, our knowledge of the determinants of small firm survival and growth has evolved substantially in tandem with the data available and the theories used to explain it. Initial theories of growth were purely statistical in nature and offered no intuitive explanation other than constant returns to scale in production for the alleged validity of Gibrat's Law of Proportional Effect. More detailed studies based on data that covered a wider range of firm sizes showed that systematic factors could be identified in growth, namely the role of firm size and age. However, from these studies for statistical and data-based reasons it was initially unclear if size in fact conferred advantage. Subsequent studies dealing with the problems of selection bias arising from the fact that small firms have higher failure rates than large ones, eventually established that, controlling for the difference in survival rates, small is indeed 'beautiful'.

Focus in the literature now shifted from simply identifying survival and growth patterns to explaining them by the construction of optimizing models of firm behaviour. The decision to enter entrepreneurship was modelled as a learning experiment in which the entrepreneur received feedback on his performance only by taking the plunge and setting up. These theories, moreover, could claim to

[81] Cressy and Olofsson (1997) found that some small Swedish firms would rather sell the business altogether than give up a share to an outsider. The aversion to outside equity declined with younger firms in the service industries.

[82] Greater under-diversification of the entrepreneur is also a consequence of not taking on outside equity.

[83] Bhide (1999) found that the vast majority of his fast growth firms grew from retained profits.

explain a number of key stylized facts in the literature, for example, that young firms had more variable growth rates and were more failure prone. In the late eighties, researchers also began to develop theories of, and to empirically identify, the potential role of capital and other constraints on firm growth. Early seminal papers now spawned a huge industry seemingly identifying capital constraints at every turn and in every country where there was data. However, these findings were based on very simple criteria and research now began to question the validity of these assumptions. So, although by and large the findings of the empirical capital constraints literature suggests the widespread existence of capital constraints based on a very simple correlation of assets and survival or state switching, theories were suggesting that capital might even be provided to small firms in surplus. Later empirical contributions with more sophisticated methodologies indeed confirmed that these findings needed to be modified in the light of the role of human capital in the survival and asset accumulation processes. Later theoretical contributions also questioned the interpretation of the findings. A final paradox has now arisen from the most recent American empirical work: capital constraints on the so-called 'switching' criterion seem to exist only in the upper end of the wealth spectrum, implying that it is now the *rich* that need to be subsidized to entice them into entrepreneurial risk-taking!

Alongside this theme there developed a literature that examined how failure evolved along the firm, and industry, life cycle. This curve demonstrated that the first two and a half years of a firm's life were the most risky but that if you, as entrepreneur, survived this initial 'valley of death' your long run chances of failure were rather low. Factors influencing the position of this curve have now begun to emerge but a fascinating finding is that initial size matters only in the short run: in the long run other factors take over and the failure curves of big and small entrants converge on low asymptotic rates—as predicted by theory. Future research promises to both elaborate these findings on new datasets and to refine the underlying economic theory.

References

Audretsch, D. (1991). 'New Firm Survival and the Technological Regime'. *Review of Economics and Statistics*, 68(3): 520–6.

—— (1994). 'Business Survival and the Decision to Exit'. *Journal of the Economics of Businesss*, 1(1): 125–38.

—— and R. Argarwal (2001). *Journal of Industrial Economics* (March) XLIX(1): 24–43.

—— and T. Mahmood (1995). 'New Firm Survival: New Results using a Hazard Function'. *Review of Economics and Statistics* (February) 77(1): 97–103.

Audretsch, D. B., E. Santarelli and M. Vivarelli (1999). 'Startup Size and Industrial Dynamics: Some Evidence from Italian Manufacturing'. *International Journal of Industrial Organisation*, 17: 965–83.

Astebro, T. and E. Bernhardt (2003). 'The Winner's Curse of Human Capital'. *Small Business Economics*, pp. 1–16.

Aston Business School (1990). *Constraints on the Growth of Small Firms.* London: Department of Trade and Industry.

Bank of England (BOE) (2003). *Quarterly Report on Small Business Statistics.* London: Bank of England.

Bates, T. (1990). 'Entrepreneur Human Capital Inputs and Small Business Longevity'. *Review of Economics and Statistics*, LXXII (4): 551–9.

Berger, A. and G. Udell (1998). 'The Economics of Small Business Finance: The Roles of Private Equity and Debt Markets in the Financial Growth Cycle'. *Journal of Banking and Finance*, 22: 613–73.

Bhide, A. (1999). *The Origins and Evolution of Small Businesses.* Oxford: Oxford University Press.

Blanchflower, D and A. Oswald (1998). 'What Makes an Entrepreneur?' *Journal of Labor Economics* (January) 16(1): 26–60.

Bolton (1971). *Report of the Committee of Enquiry on Small Firms*, chaired by Sir John Bolton. London: HSMO.

Brock, W. A. and D. S. Evans (1986). *The Economics of Small Businesses: Their Role and Regulation in the US Economy.* New York and London: Holmes and Meier.

Bruderl, J., P. Preisendorfer and R. Ziegler (1992). 'Survival Chances of Newly Founded Business Organizations'. *American Sociological Review* (April) 57(2): 227–42.

Cabral, L. (1995). 'Sunk Costs, Firm Size and Firm Growth'. *Journal of Industrial Economics* (June) XLIII(2): 161–72.

Cambridge (1995). *The Changing State of British Enterprise.* Cambridge: ESRC Centre for Business Research, University of Cambridge (September).

Caves, R. E. (1998). 'Industrial Organization and New Findings on the Turnover and Mobility of Firms'. *Journal of Economic Literature* (December) XXXVI: 1947–82.

Cressy, R. C. (1993). *The Startup Tracking Exercise: Third Year Report*, prepared for National Westminster Bank of Great Britain (November).

—— (1995). 'Borrowing and Control: A Theory of Business Types'. *Small Business Economics*, 7: 1–10.

—— (1996a). 'Pre-entrepreneurial Income, Cash-flow Growth and Survival of Startup Businesses: Model and Tests on UK Startup Data'. *Small Business Economics* (February, SI) 8(1).

—— (1996b). 'Are Business Startups Debt-rationed?'. *The Economic Journal* (September) 106: 1253–70.

—— (1997). 'Why Do Most Firms Die Young?' report to the Economic and Social Research Council, *ROPA* award number R022250058.

—— (2000). 'Credit Rationing or Entrepreneurial Risk Aversion? An Alternative Explanation for the Evans-Jovanovic Finding'. *Economics Letters*, 66: 235–40.

—— (ed.) (2002). 'Funding Gaps: A Symposium'. *The Economic Journal* (February).

—— (2005). 'Why Do Most Firms Die Young?' *Small Business Economics.*

CRESSY, R. C. and D. STOREY (1994). *New Firms and Their Bank.* National Westminster Bank of Great Britain.

—— and C. OLOFSSON (1997). 'European SME Financing: An Overview'. *Small Business Economics* 9: 87–96.

DE MEZA, D. and C. SOUTHEY (1996). 'The Borrower's Curse, Optimism and Entrepreneurship'. *The Economic Journal* (March) 106(435): 375–86.

DUNNE, T., M. J. ROBERTS and L. SAMUELSON, (1989). 'The Growth and Failure of US Manufacturing Plants'. *Quarterly Journal of Economics*, 104(4): 671–98.

ERICSON, R. and A. PAKES (1995). 'Markov-Perfect Industry Dynamics: A Framework for Empirical Work'. *Review of Economic Studies*, 62: 53–82.

EVANS, D. S. (1987a). 'The Relationship Between Firm Growth, Size and Age: Estimates for 100 Manufacturing Industries'. *Journal of Industrial Economics*, 35: 567–81.

—— (1987b). 'Tests of Alternative Theories of Firm Growth'. *Journal of Political Economy*, 95(4): 657–74.

—— and B. JOVANOVIC (1989). 'An Estimated Model of Entrepreneurial Choice Under Liquidity Constraints'. *Journal of Political Economy*, 97(4): 808–27.

EVELY, R. and I. M. D. LITTLE (1960). *Concentration in British Industry.* Cambridge: Cambridge University Press.

EVERETT, J. and J. WATSON (1998). 'Small Business Failure and External Risk Factors'. *Small Business Economics* (December) 11(4): 371–90.

FELLER, W. (1957). *An Introduction to Probability Theory and its Applications* (3rd edn, vol. 1). New York: John Wiley.

FRANK, M. Z. (1986). 'An Intertemporal Model of Industrial Exit'. *Quarterly Journal of Economics* (May) 103: 333–44.

GANGULY, P. (1985). *UK Small Business Statistics and International Comparisons.* London: Small Business Research Trust, Harper Row.

GEROSKI, P. A. (1995). 'What Do We Know About Entry?' *International Journal of Industrial Organization*, 13: 421–40.

GIBRAT, R. (1931). *Les Inegalités économiques.* Pairs: Librairie du Recueil Sirey.

GUISO, L. and M. PAIELLA (1999). 'Risk Aversion, Wealth and Background Risk'. Manuscript. London: Birkbeck College.

HALL, B. (1987). 'The Relationship Between Firm Size and Firm Growth in the United States Manufacturing Sector'. *Journal of Industrial Economics*, 35(4): 583–606.

HANNAH, L. and J. A. KAY (1977). *Concentration in Modern Industry: Theory and Measurement and the UK Experience.* London: MacMillan.

—— and —— (1981). 'The Contribution of Mergers to Concentration Growth: A Reply to Professor Hart'. *Journal of Industrial Economics* (March) 29(3): 305–13.

HARHOFF, D., K. STAHL and M. WOYWODE (1998). 'Legal Form, Growth and Exit of West German Firms—Empirical Results for Manufacturing, Construction and Service Industries'. *Journal of Industrial Economics* (December) XLVI(4): 453–88.

HART, P. E. 'The Size and Growth of Firms'. *Economica N.S.*, 29(113): 29–39.

—— and S. PRAIS (1956). 'The Analysis of Business Concentration'. *Journal of the Royal Statistical Society* (Ser. A) 119: 150–91.

—— and N. OULTON (1997). 'Growth and Size of Firms'. *The Economic Journal*, 106: 1242–52.

HOLTZ-EAKIN, D., D. JOULFAIAN and H. S. ROSEN (1994a). 'Sticking it Out: Entrepreneurial Survival and Liquidity Constraints'. *Journal of Political Economy*, 102(11): 53–75.

HOLTZ-EAKIN, D., D. JOULFAIAN and H. S. ROSEN (1994b). 'Entrepreneurial decisions and liquidity constraints'. *Rand Journal of Economics* (Summer) 25(2): 342–47.

HURST, E. and A. LUSARDI (2004). 'Liquidity Constraints, Household Wealth and Entrepreneurship'. *Journal of Political Economy*, 112(2): 319–47.

HYMER, S. and P. PASHIGAN (1962). 'Firm Size and Rate of Growth'. *Journal of Political Economy* (December) 70(6): 556–69.

IJIRI, Y. and H. A. SIMON (1964). 'Business Firm Growth and Size'. *American Economic Review*, 54: 77–89.

JOVANOVIC, B. (1982). 'Selection and the Evolution of Industry'. *Econometrica* (May) 50(3): 649–70.

KIHLSTROM, R. E. and J. J. LAFFONT (1979). 'A General Equilibrium Theory of Firm Formation Based on Risk Aversion'. *Journal of Political Economy*, 87: 719–48.

KLEPPER, S. (1996). 'Entry, Exit, Growth and Innovation over the Product Life Cycle'. *American Economic Review*, 86(1): 562–83.

—— (2001). 'Employee Start-ups in High-tech Industries'. *Industrial and Corporate Change*, 10(3): 639–74.

KNIGHT, F. (1965). *Risk, Uncertainty and Profit*. New York: Sentry Press.

LUCAS, R. E. (1978). 'On the Size Distribution of Business Firms'. *Bell Journal of Economics* (August) 9: 508–23.

MATA, J. and P. PORTUGAL (1994). 'Life Duration of New Firms'. *Journal of Industrial Economics* (September) DLII(3): 227–45.

MUELLER, E. (2004). *The Performance of Private Companies: An Empirical Investigation into the Role of Control, Risk and Incentives*. Doctoral thesis, London School of Economics.

National Economic Research Associates (NERA) (1989). *An Evaluation of the Loan Guarantee Scheme*. Research Paper No. 74 (November 1990), Department of Employment, National Westminster Bank of Great Britain.

PARKER, S. (2002) 'Do Banks Ration Credit to New Enterprises? And Should Governments Intervene?' *Scottish Journal of Political Economy*, 49: 162–95.

—— and M. VAN PRAAG (2003). 'Schooling, Capital Constraints and Entrepreneurial Performance: The Endogenous Triangle'. Working Paper, University of Durham, Durham Business School.

PRAIS, S. J., (1971). *The Evolution of Giant Firms in Britain*. London: National Institute of Economic and Social Research.

REID, G. C. (1991). 'Staying in Business'. *International Journal of Industrial Organisation*, 9: 545–56.

SAMUELS, J. M. (1965). 'Size and Growth of Firms'. *Review of Economic Studies* (April) 32: 105–25.

SCHARY, M. (1991). 'The Probability of Exit'. *Rand Journal of Economics* (Autumn) 22(3).

SIMON, H. A. and C. P. BONINI (1958). 'The Size Distribution of Business Firms'. *American Economic Review* 48: 607–17.

STOREY, D. (1994). *Understanding the Small Firms Sector*. London: Routledge.

—— K. KEASEY, R. WATSON and P. WYNARCZYCK (1987). *The Performance of Small Firms*. Beckenham: Croom Helm

SUTTON, J. (1997). 'Gibrat's Legacy'. *Journal of Economic Literature* (March) XXXV: 40–59.

Utton (1974). 'Aggregate Versus Market Concentration'. *The Economic Journal* 84(333): 150–5.

Van Praag, M. (2003). 'Business Survival and Success of Young Small Business Owners'. *Small Business Economics* (August) 21(1): 1–17.

Weiss, C. R. (1998). 'Farm Growth and Survival: Econometric Evidence for Individual Farms in Upper Austria'. *American Journal of Agricultural Economics*, 81: 103–16.

CHAPTER 8

START-UPS AND ENTRY BARRIERS: SMALL AND MEDIUM-SIZED FIRMS POPULATION DYNAMICS[1]

ZOLTAN J. ACS

8.1 Introduction

As the editor of an international journal on small firms (Small Business Economics) I reviewed the last 15 years of literature that we have published, and much to my surprise I found that we have not published one article that deals with barriers to entry (Mc Alfee et al., 2004). While we have plenty of articles that deal with start-ups, self employment, new firm start-ups, new ventures, new technology-based firms, the subject of entry barriers is missing. Perhaps this is explained by the fact that it is relatively easy to enter most industries, and exit, as shown by the high rates of entry and exit in most industries. However, I would argue that the issue is more

[1] The research here is based on joint work with Catherine Armington for the US Small Business Administration. This project originated several years ago while the author was a ASA/NSF/CENSUS research fellows at the Center for Economic Studies (CES) at the US Bureau of the Census, Washington DC, under grant # SBR-980894 with Catherine Armington. This research was also funded

complicated. Most of the entry literature over the years, to which I contributed several times, was about the entry of new plants, not necessarily new firms. Small firm is a subject that does not mix well with the entry literature.

However, I would argue that entrepreneurship is a different subject. It is one where age is the dominant variable and not size. The literature on small business is about firms (Storey, 1994). Entrepreneurship is about people in their roles as identifier of opportunities and the exploiters of opportunities. Moreover, recent theories of opportunity have shed the light on the role of knowledge, knowledge spillovers, human capital, agglomeration of knowledge and similar spatial structures as being the key to entrepreneurship.

This chapter focuses on the age of the establishment as measured by new-firm entry as the operational variable in entrepreneurship and discusses what variables are important in determining entry. Our focus in this chapter is on the role of human capital as a barrier to entry and suggests that the lack of education is the greatest barrier to entry.

8.2 The Business Information Tracking System (BITS)

8.2.1 Brief description of the database

The current Business Information Tracking Series (BITS) file facilitates tracking employment, payroll, and firm affiliation and (employment) size for the more than 13 million establishments that existed at some time during 1989 through to 2001. This database was constructed from the Census Bureau's Statistics of US Business (SUSB) files, which were developed from the microdata underlying the aggregate data published in Census' County Business Patterns. These annual data describing establishments were linked together using the SUSB Longitudinal Pointer File, which facilitates tracking establishments over time, even when they change ownership and identification numbers. The SUSB data beginning in 1988, their

by the National Science Foundation under grant # SES-0080316. We were fortunate to have limited access, through CES to comprehensive US micro data on recent firm formations. Over the years several papers were written using the LEEM (BITS) database at CES. The US Small Business Administration funded the final phase of the project under grant # SBAHQ03M534 under the title, 'Using Census BITS to Explore Entrepreneurship, Geography and Economic Growth'. Finally, the generous financial support of the Doris and McCurdy Distinguished Professorship at the University of Baltimore is acknowledged.

Longitudinal Pointer File, and the BITS files were constructed by Census with substantial support from the Office of Advocacy of the US Small Business Administration.[2]

The basic unit of the BITS data is a business establishment (location or plant). The microdata describe each establishment for each year of its existence in terms of its employment, annual payroll, location (state, county, and metropolitan area), primary industry, and start year. The recorded start year is the year that establishment entered the Census register, which would normally be the year it first hired any paid employees. Additional data for each establishment and year identify the firm (or enterprise) to which the establishment belongs, and the total employment of that firm.

As with most microdata at the Census Bureau, the BITS data are confidential, so the microdata can only be used at the Census Bureau by Census employees, or by approved outside researchers working at one of the Census Centers for Economic Research. These microdata are referred to there as LEEM data (for Longitudinal Establishment and Enterprise Microdata) files. However, many tabulations of these data have been prepared for use by the SBA for other research projects, and these aggregated data are available for further research use.

8.2.2 Longitudinal microdata required to evaluate dynamic theories

In order to test hypotheses about how and why regions differ in their rates of formation of new firms and growth of employment, one needs a database representing all industry sectors, that distinguishes business establishments from firms, identifies start-ups of new firms, and specifies the location and changing employment of each establishment through time. The studies reported here depend crucially on use of the BITS database that the Bureau of the Census has constructed for the Office of Advocacy of the U.S. Small Business Administration for study of entry, survival, and growth in different types of businesses.

This BITS database is a unique by-product of the complex register that Census maintains with information on all businesses in the United States. This Standard Statistical Establishment List, or SSEL, is updated continuously with data from many other sources, but its underlying coverage is based on new business names and addresses from the Master Business File of the Internal Revenue Service. Therefore, every business in the United States that files any tax return is covered by the SSEL, and IRS data from quarterly payroll tax filings (including employment

[2] For documentation of the SUSB files, see U. S. Small Business Administration (1999).

only for the 12 March payroll period) are used to provide comprehensive coverage of all US employment. However, some of the employment numbers are estimated from the payroll numbers, which provide good estimates for establishments that are themselves single-location firms (tax-filing units), but are less reliable for the tax-filing units that represent multiple establishments owned by a single firm.

The data in the SSEL on the individual locations of multi-unit businesses are therefore somewhat less consistent and comprehensive than those for independent, or single-location, firms. All large (i.e. over 250 employees reported) multi-unit firms are surveyed annually (Company Organization Survey), except in Economic Census years, to determine the location, industry, and employment (and predecessor or successor owners) of the individual establishments that are, or were, owned or controlled by each. A sample of the smaller multi-unit firms is also covered each year, on a rotating basis, so that all but the smallest (with less than ten employees) are surveyed at least once between each Economic Census, in addition to their coverage in the quinquenial Economic Census (in each year ending with 2 or 7). The resulting lags in the reporting of the formation, closure, or change in ownership of some locations of smaller multi-unit firms (as well as formerly single-unit firms that have become multi-unit) causes false jumps in some of their establishment employment data, as the temporarily aggregated employment of the covered locations is subsequently correctly distributed to the updated list of actual locations.[3]

Census' annual County Business Patterns (CBP) publication provides aggregations of data on establishments selected from the SSEL and extensively edited at both the establishment level (relative to the previous year's data) and the aggregate level. This CBP subset of the SSEL population represents all active (with positive annual payroll) private sector establishments except those in agricultural production, railroads, large pension, health and welfare funds, and private households. The numbers of establishments, employment, and payroll are classified by state, industry, and employment-size class and then processed to avoid disclosure of confidential data, and published annually as CBP.

The microdata behind the CBP provide the starting point for each annual SUSB file. These are further processed to calculate Metropolitan Statistical Area (MSA) codes, and to improve industry code reporting using the industry codes from the subsequent year SSEL whenever they are more precise. Then firm-level data are constructed by aggregating data from all establishments belonging to each enterprise (industry-wide and country-wide), and these firm-level data are attached to each of the component establishment records. These firm-level data include

[3] For example, if a single-unit retail firm/establishment with 10 employees opens two additional branch stores with another 10 employees in each, the original establishment would appear to have 30 employees until it was surveyed. The more accurate reporting resulting from the survey would lead to its employment being reduced from 30 to ten, and the two new establishments being listed as new formations with 10 employees each.

employment, payroll and receipts (unedited), with the primary state, primary industry division and primary (3-digit SIC) industry within the primary division, based on the largest share of annual payroll. These SUSB data are tabulated and processed for disclosure for a number of standardized tables by firm-size for the Office of Advocacy of the SBA, and for the aggregate SUSB (public) database of the Census Bureau.

A Longitudinal Pointer File is then constructed to link each year's establishment record to the prior year's record for the same establishment, allowing for a change in identity or ownership of continuing establishments. The CFN is the basic Census identification number, which is assigned to each new establishment, and is generally retained consistently over time. However, a change in ownership or legal form, or a change in status between single-unit and multi-unit, will cause a change in CFN. A complex system of computerized matching of records for establishments that might have changed CFNs is used to identify continuing establishments in the SUSB and to update the Longitudinal Pointer File each year. This system examines a wide variety of information, including Permanent Plant Numbers (PPNs), Employer Identification Numbers (EINs), and statistical matching of records for single units, based on such attributes as name, address, zip code, and industry codes. Matches are sought both between years, and within years (mid-year reorganizations).[4] The records that remain unmatched are assumed to represent new establishment formations or closures of existing establishments.

The BITS files are constructed by merging annual SUSB files using the Longitudinal Pointer Files to create a single longitudinal record for each establishment that appears in any of the annual files. Where there has been a mid-year reorganization, the data from the two records representing the same establishment are combined for that year, and both CFNs are retained in the BITS file. Because some establishments with mid-year reorganizations report March employment in both of their records, the aggregate employment from the BITS is slightly lower that that from the SUSB file for each year, since only the employment from the second record for an establishment identified as a mid-year reorganization was used if that employment was non-zero.

The Company Statistics Division of the Census Bureau prepares for the SBA Office of Advocacy an extensive set of tables of aggregated BITS data on annual gross flows (establishment and firm start-ups and closures, employment gains from start-ups and expansions of establishments, and employment losses from closures and contractions) for multi-unit and single-unit firms, by firm size, industry, and location. They also prepare custom tabulations on a contract basis

[4] Taking the match of 1993 to 1992 as a typical example, 5.56 million records matched on CFN, another 32,000 on PPN, and 3,000 on EIN. The remaining unmatched single-unit records were then grouped by zip code, and another 19,000 between years, and 24,000 within 1993 were matched on business name, and another 11,000 across years and 13,000 within 1993 were matched on industry (3-digit SIC) and street number.

for specific research projects. However, many research needs cannot be met by these tabular data designed for public use because they are limited to pre-defined cells representing some minimum number of firms, and do not allow exploration of the data, nor refinement of the specification of variables. Access to the microdata is also necessary to avoid biasing analyses as a result of the necessary suppression of any small cell values and their complementary cells during the disclosure processing for tabular data. These small cells may contribute crucial information to statistical analyses performed within a Census Center for Economic Studies, while avoiding any disclosure problems in the empirical results.

8.3 Using Census' BITS to explore entrepreneurship, geography and economic growth

8.3.1 The theoretical framework

The knowledge-based growth models have three cornerstones: spatially constrained externalities, increasing returns in the production of goods, and decreasing returns in the production of knowledge (Romer, 1986, 1990; Lucas, 1988). New knowledge—in the form of products, processes or organizations—leads to opportunities that agents exploit commercially. Such opportunities are then a function of the distribution of knowledge within and between societies. But opportunities rarely present themselves in neat packages—they have to be discovered and packaged. Precisely for that reason, the nexus of opportunity and enterprising individuals is crucial in understanding economic growth (Shane and Eckhardt, 2003).

However, the ability to transform new knowledge into what Arrow (1962) designated 'economic knowledge' (leading to commercial opportunity) requires a set of skills, aptitudes, insights and circumstances that is neither uniformly nor widely distributed in the population. Moreover, empirical findings support the proposition that entry and entrepreneurship provide important links between knowledge creation and the commercialization of such knowledge, particularly at the early stage when knowledge is still fluid (Audretsch and Keilbach, 2004).

The basic shortcoming of the endogenous growth model is that it fails to recognize that only some of the aggregate stock of knowledge (often associated with R&D costs or products) is economically useful, and that even economically relevant knowledge may not be successfully exploited if the transmission links are missing. Furthermore, much of the general stock of knowledge is not in the public domain, and it may not spill over easily from one carrier to another. Most knowledge, regardless of whether it is in the public or private domain, requires a certain absorptive capacity on the part of the recipients in order for successful transmission to occur. This suggests that there is a filter between the stock of knowledge and the more limited economically useful knowledge. Not only does the level of knowledge vary among countries and regions; the transmission capacity of the filter also varies.

Consequently, despite the gains in terms of transparency and technical ease obtained by imposing strong assumptions in the endogenous growth models, these advantages have to be measured in relation to the drawbacks of deviations from real world behaviour. Hayek (1945) pointed out that the central feature of a market economy is the partitioning of knowledge or information about the economy. The endogenous model fails to incorporate one of the most crucial elements in the growth process; transmission of knowledge through entrepreneurship—new firm formation—and the resulting spatial dimension of growth.

Thus, a closer connection between the endogenous growth models and the models of entrepreneurship seems necessary. The fact that knowledge-producing inputs are not evenly distributed across space implies that regions may not grow at the same rate, not only because they have different levels of investment in knowledge but also because they exploit knowledge at different rates. Even if the stock of knowledge were freely available, including the tacit and non-tacit parts, the ability to transform that knowledge into economic knowledge, or commercialized products, would not be. Moreover, most knowledge is not a free good at everyone's disposal. Often only a few individuals know about a particular scarcity, or a new invention, or a particular resource lying fallow or not being put to best use. This knowledge is both idiosyncratic and local, because it is acquired through each individual's own networks, depending on their occupation, on-the-job routines, social relationships, and daily life. It is frequently this particular knowledge, obtained through a local knowledge network, which leads to profit-making insight (Michelacci, 2003).

The dispersion of information among different economic agents who do not have access to the same observations, interpretations or experiences, has implications for economic growth. Since this is not recognized in the endogenous growth model, we need to extend it with some additional assumptions and outline an alternative structure to improve the model. In order to remedy the limitations of the endogenous growth model and to specify the nature of the transmission mechanism that diffuses knowledge and converts it, via entrepreneurship, to growth, we propose the following assumptions.

1 New firms are assumed to be the primary mechanism to commercialize new knowledge, regardless of whether it is drawn from the stock of existing

knowledge, or is newly discovered, and whether it is scientific knowledge or other. This transformation into economically relevant knowledge often occurs via spillovers that are exploited in new ventures, evidenced in firm formations. When existing firms acquire new economic knowledge, they may create new establishments within the firm, but the majority of such secondary new establishments are replications of other establishments owned by multi-location firms. Thus new firm formations are seen as the primary indicator of knowledge spillovers leading to economic growth.

2 Each new firm embodies a new idea, or innovation, expecting to provide a new, or improved, or more competitive product or service to customers. Schumpeter (1911)[5] suggests that a new idea (innovation) represents any kind of new combination of new or existing knowledge. These new firms are extremely heterogeneous, not only in the size, but also in terms of characteristics such as absorptive capacity, strategy, technology, product range, and performance (profitability, productivity, etc.) Because new entrants, often make mistakes and fail, a very high formation (or gross entry) rate is necessary to sustain long-term growth.

3 Knowledge spillovers are primarily local events; there are few important interregional spillovers. Success in converting available public or private knowledge into economically useful firm-specific knowledge depends on the initiative and skills of the local potential entrepreneurs, and these entrepreneurial conditions vary across regions. Local policy and previous history (path dependence) determines the local entrepreneurial climate, which may be embedded in the local infrastructure, regulation, attitudes, educational policies, networks, technology transfer mechanisms, and so forth.

The combined result of these assumptions, when added to the endogenous growth model, can be characterized as a filter (here defined in terms of entrepreneurship) that determines the proportion of local knowledge that is converted into economically useful firm-specific knowledge (Acs et al., 2004). This suggests that an increasing stock of knowledge (through R&D and education) will lead to higher economic growth only if the knowledge is economically useful and if the economy is endowed with factors of production that can select, evaluate and transform knowledge into commercial use, that is, through entrepreneurs. If these conditions are not fulfilled, an increase in the knowledge stock may have no impact on growth. Similarly, highly entrepreneurial regions with smaller knowledge stocks may experience higher growth than regions more abundantly endowed with knowledge.

The basic structure of the model accommodates both incumbent firms and new firms. Incumbent firms accumulate knowledge over their lifetime, and this accumulated firm-specific knowledge influences their ability to exploit new knowledge

[5] See also Knight (1921), Hannan and Freeman (1989), Acs and Audretsch (1990), Winter (1984), and Williamson (1985).

spillovers—the degree of firm specificity of their existing knowledge constrains their future absorption of knowledge spillovers. Hence, the incumbent firms' ability to exploit spillovers is determined by path-dependence. Furthermore, new establishments that are created by incumbent firms may be located in other regions, since their location decisions are likely to be based on cost-minimizing decisions.

New firms differ from incumbents, in that their economic knowledge is not governed by path-dependence to the same extent, but is built on the local entrepreneurs' ability to exploit opportunities arising from aggregate spillovers. Start-ups entering the market thus provide direct evidence of the conversion of knowledge to growth. They produce genuinely new products and services, or compete using new processes or filling under-served niches.

Both types of firms exploit knowledge spillovers, albeit in different ways. Together their performance determines the share of knowledge spillovers that are commercialized. We can think of θ as the absorptive capacity of incumbent firms and λ as a proxy for entrepreneurship within an economy. Then, in accordance with assumptions 1 and 2, the standard production function has to be modified to account also for entrepreneurship:

$$F(k_i, x, (\lambda + \theta)K)$$

where k_i is new knowledge produced by firm i, x is a vector representing all other inputs, and since each individual firm cannot appropriate all the knowledge they create. Thus, if entrepreneurship is non-existent in an economy (so λ is zero) and θ is constant, then knowledge spillovers will not provide the same solution as in the endogenous growth model with automatic and all encompassing spillovers. In fact, the model will then reduce to the neoclassical growth model.

In addition, it is obvious that it is not only the size of K and the absorptive capacity of incumbent firms that matter, but also the presence of entrepreneurs as captured by λ. Our empirical work was driven by the effort to estimate the size of λ. In Romer's work (1990), λ equals unity, which implies that all knowledge (K) is accessible and convertible into economic knowledge (Acs and Varga, 2002), a very strong and unlikely assumption (Acs and Varga, 2004).

The total amount of entrepreneurial activity (E) in a particular region L—given broader institutional constraints (B)—is a function of the profit (π^*) in excess of wages (w) accruing to the exploitation of new knowledge from (K) the stock of knowledge and the portion of knowledge not commercialized by large firms (θ) and the entrepreneurial culture in a region (C). Thus, the knowledge spillover model of entrepreneurship estimated in this chapter is as follows:

$$E_L = \gamma(\pi^*(K_L, \theta_L, C_L) - W)1/\beta \quad (1)$$

where we expect K_L to be > 0, θ_L to be < 0 and C_L to be > 0.

A rich literature exists in regional economics that sheds some light on how to capture the extent to which pooled labour markets, non-pecuniary transactions, and information spillovers exist. One approach suggests that the infrastructure of services is more developed in regions that are more densely populated. According to Krugman (1991: 484), 'The concentration of several firms in a single location offers a pooled market for workers with industry-specific skills, ensuring both a lower probability of unemployment and a lower probability of labor shortage.' Thus the start-up rate for each industry sector should increase with the existing density of establishments in each sector. Another view is that localized industries tend to support the production of non-tradable specialized inputs. Thirdly, informational spillovers give clustered firms a better production function than isolated producers have. The high level of human capital embodied in their general and specific skills is another mechanism by which new firm start-ups are supported. Thus regions that are rich in this resource should have more start-up activity. University graduates—especially engineers—provide a supply of labour to local firms. New firm start-ups should be positively related to higher average levels of education, and negatively related to the levels of unskilled and semi-skilled workers in the region.

Also associated with studies of new firm formation from the 1980s was the role of industrial restructuring. Industrial restructuring has been associated with (1) the shift from manufacturing employment to services, (2) a reduction in both firm and plant size, and (3) a shift to higher levels of technology. The shift from manufacturing to services, which are usually less capital intensive than manufacturing, could increase the rate of new firm formation. Regions that are dominated by large branch plants or firms will have less new-firm formation (Mason, 1994), in part because such areas have relatively fewer people with the managerial or skilled labour backgrounds that are the source of most firm founders.[6,7]

8.3.2 The construction of variables for empirical examinations

8.3.2.1 *The unit of observation for these studies*

Although the BITS data support analysis at the firm level, these studies focus on the analysis of regional variations within the United States, and seek understanding of

[6] For example, if a single-unit retail firm/establishment with ten employees opens two additional branch stores with another 10 employees in each, the original establishment would appear to have 30 employees until it was surveyed. The more accurate reporting resulting from the survey would lead to its employment being reduced from 30 to ten, and the two new establishments being listed as new formations with ten employees each.

[7] Taking the match of 1993 to 1992 as a typical example, 5.56 million records matched on CFN, another 32,000 on PPN, and 3,000 on EIN. The remaining unmatched single-unit records were then grouped by zip code, and another 19,000 between years and 24,000 within 1993 were matched on business name, and another 11,000 across years and 13,000 within 1993 were matched on industry (3-digit SIC) and street number.

why various levels of economic activity vary across regions. Therefore, after considerable preliminary analysis of the data at the firm level, the scope and definitions of the relevant regional data were carefully defined and the firm-level data were aggregated to create regional data.

The geographic unit of analysis chosen for this study, the Labor Market Areas (LMAs) defined by Tolbert and Sizer (1996), is ideal for our purposes because it identifies economic areas broad enough to contain most of the labour supply and the local market for their business population, while being small enough to substantially avoid the worst of the aggregation problems of larger geographic units. These LMAs are aggregations of the 3,141 US counties into 394 geographical regions based on the predominant commuting patterns (journey-to-work) between them in 1990. Each LMA contains at least one central city, along with the surrounding counties that constitute both its labour supply and its local consumer and business market. Many of the 394 LMAs cut across state boundaries, to better define regionally integrated areas of local economic activity.

Tolbert and Sizer specified these LMAs for the Department of Agriculture, using the Journey-to-Work data from the 1990 U.S. Census of Population. The LMAs are named according to the largest place within them in 1990. Some LMAs incorporate more than one MSA, while others separate some of the larger MSAs into more than one LMA, depending on the commuter patterns. A few smaller independent (usually rural) Commuting Zones have been appended to adjacent LMAs so that each LMA had a minimum of 100,000 population in 1990, which is necessary to avoid possible disclosure of confidential Census data that have been aggregated for LMAs. Alaska and Hawaii each are treated as a single integrated LMA, although they clearly have little mobility across their entire areas. (See Reynolds (1994) for further discussion of why LMAs are the most suitable unit for this type of analysis.)

The LMA unit of observation has the advantage of including both the employment location and the residence location of the population and labour force within the same area. Being based on counties, a wide variety of data collected at the county or Zip-code level can be aggregated to construct LMA-level data. Finally, the 394 LMAs together cover the whole country, so that their data can be aggregated to US totals, and all areas are represented.

8.3.2.2 *Measurement of formation and growth rates*

In the research reported here we are investigating regional differences in gross new firm formation rates, not the net change in numbers of firms or establishments in an area. The factors we are focusing on to account for differences in rates of new firm formation include local differences in educational attainments, entrepreneurship, innovation, and industrial evolution. The factors contributing to explanations of local differences in firm deaths, plant entry and exit, all of which affect the net numbers of establishments, are far beyond the scope of this paper, and generally not strongly related to local human capital.

Firm formation rates are calculated for each of the 394 LMAs, based on new firm formations during the period under study.[8] Single unit firm formations in year t are identified on the BITS as non-affiliated establishments that reported a Census start-year of t or t-1, that had no employment in March of year t-1, and had positive employment below 500 in March of year t. (The Census start-year is the year that the establishment first reported any payroll and therefore entered the Census business register.) This avoids inclusion of either new firms that have not yet actually hired an employee, or firms recovering from temporary inactivity. About 400,000 new firms generally appear in the business register (with some positive annual payroll) the year before they have any March employment, and we postpone their 'birth' until their first year of reported employment. An average of 90,000 older firms each year have no employees in March, but recover some employees the following year. Those new firms that had 500 or more employees in their first year of activity appear to be primarily offshoots of existing companies.[9]

New firm formations include most of the primary locations of the relatively few multi-unit firms (1,500 to 6,000 per year) that appeared to start up with less than 500 employees (firm wide) in multiple locations in their first year. We limited multi-unit firm formations to those whose employment in their new primary location constituted at least a third of their total employment in the first year.[10] This rule effectively eliminated the 600 to 1000 new firms each year which were apparently set up to manage existing locations—relatively small new headquarters supervising large numbers of employees in mainly older branch locations which were newly acquired, or perhaps contributed by joint venture partners.

Because the Labor Market Areas vary greatly in size, the absolute numbers of new firm formations must be standardized by some measure of the LMA size

[8] In fact, birth rates were calculated for each annual period from 1990 through 1998, but these were found to be quite consistent in their rank ordering across LMAs, so the averages of several recent years was used for most of this analysis. Using period averages serves both to smooth out irregularities and to minimize the possibility of disclosure problems with very small numbers of annual births for the smaller LMAs and subsectors.

[9] Annually, there were less than 150 such large apparent births of single-unit firms, with an average of about 1500 employees each. About a third of these larger single unit firms were employee-leasing firms or employment agencies, while the remainder were widely distributed across industries. However, examination of the new firms with 100–499 employees in their first year showed that most seemed to be credible start-ups, frequently in industries that are associated with large business units, such as hotels and hospitals. Since this study is not concerned with the employment impact of start-ups, there is no danger of the bulk of the data on smaller start-ups being swamped by that of a few larger start-ups that might actually be offshoots of existing businesses. Therefore, the start-ups with 100–499 employees were included, if they qualified otherwise.

[10] We tested a similar rule using one-half, and found that the primary difference was in quite small multi-unit firms, where the smaller share was more credible for the first year.

before it is meaningful to compare them across areas. When dealing with the whole service sector, firm formation rates are calculated as the number of new firms per thousand members of the labour force in the LMA in the prior year. This labour force approach has a particular theoretical appeal, in that it is based on the theory of entrepreneurial choice proposed by Evans and Jovanovic (1989). Each worker in the LMA chooses whether to be an employee of an existing business, or to become an entrepreneur and form a new firm. This approach implicitly assumes that the entrepreneur starts the new business in the same labour market where he or she previously worked or sought employment. It also has the added property that there is a clear lower bound of 0.00 (for no new businesses), and a theoretical upper bound of 1.00, which would represent the extreme case where every worker within a region started a new business during a year.

However, when comparing firm formation rates for different industries, or across sub-sectors of the service industry, we need to standardize for the differences in sizes of both areas and sub-sectors. For this purpose we calculate formation rates in terms of the number of new formations per thousand establishments already in existence in that industry or sub-sector in each LMA. This could be termed the ecological approach, because it considers the amount of start-up activity relative to the size of the existing population of businesses in that sector.

Two considerations of the timing of the firm birth rate data should be noted. While new firms enter the business register underlying the BITS file on a nearly continuous basis, their employment data are reported only for a pay period in March of each year. Since we require positive employment before recognizing a new firm, if a firm begins hiring after March, we do not count its formation until the following year. Therefore, each specified year's firm formation counts actually represent firms that hired their first employees sometime between April of the prior year and March of the specified year, for an average of nine months lagged reporting. Further, Reynolds et al. (1995) and others have shown that the time between an individual's decision to create a new firm and the start of the resulting economic activity averages about two years, and is often longer. With such lags in the initialization and reporting of new firm formations, we would not expect to be able to identify a lag structure between differences in their annual rates and the regional factors associated with these differences, even though we have nine years of annual data on new firm formations.

8.3.2.3 *Industry sectors*

We distinguish six broad industry sectors for the analysis of growth, to facilitate analysis of different industries' sensitivities to factors affecting their growth, and to better control for aggregation effects in regions with different shares of weak industries—manufacturing, agriculture, and mining sectors. This expands both the scope and the industrial detail beyond that of previous studies, most of which were limited to manufacturing. Industry codes are based on the most recently reported 4-digit SIC code for each establishment, because the precision and accuracy of the codes tends to increase over time.[11]

Sector	Standard Industrial Classifications
Distributive	4000–5199 (transportation, communication, public utilities, and wholesale trade)
Manufacturing	2000–3999
Business services	7300–7399 and 8700–8799 (incl. engineering, accounting, research, and management services)
Extractive	0700–1499 (agricultural services and mining)
Retail Trade	5200–5999
Local market	1500–1799 and 6000–8999 excl. Business services (construction, consumer and financial services)

These six broad sectors distinguish industries that might differ in their sensitivity to local market conditions. For instance, local consumer services and construction are more dependent on local regional demand than manufacturing and distributive services are, while manufacturing and distributive services may have greater dependence on the supply of semi-and unskilled labour. Growth in extractive industries is limited by the local supply of natural resources and arable land.

8.3.2.4 *Variability in formation in the 1990s*

During the period from 1991 to 1996, US private employment increased over 10 percent, while the employment gains from new establishments during that period contributed over 26 percent. Looking at the comparable growth rates for the six industry sectors we distinguished, in Table 8.1, it is apparent that the greatest growth was in business services (28.7% net increase, with 43.6% gross increase from employment in new establishments), followed by other local market services and construction (12.2%, with 25.8% in new establishments). Employment in manufacturing and extractive industries was virtually constant, although both showed substantial gains in new establishments, indicating that those sectors were continuing to evolve new products and processes to replace those that were discontinued or shrinking.

When we shift from the national totals to looking at the (unweighted) averages of our regional data for the 394 LMAs the mean growth and formation rates are less striking, but the variation across regions is remarkable. Average annual employment growth varies from a small loss to annual growth of 8 percent, while firm

[11] There is a small number (10,000 to 16,000) of new firms each year for which no industry code is ever available. Most of these are small and short-lived. These have been added to the Local market category, which is, by far, the largest of our sectors.

Table 8.1 Establishment employment, gross change in births and firm formation rates 1991–96, by firm type and by industry sector

Establ. class	Employment		91–96 Empl. change		LMA employment growth ratios annualized			LMA firm formation rate per 1,000 labour force		
	1991	1996	Net	Birth	Mean	Min.	Max.	Mean	Min.	Max.
All	92,265,576	102,149,281	10.2%	26.3%	1.03	0.99	1.08	3.67	2.05	10.00
Firm type:										
Single unit	38,532,294	44,811,609	15.1%	31.3%						
Multi-unit	53,731,429	57,324,994	6.5%	22.6%						
Industry sector:										
Bus. services	7,780,445	10,385,762	28.7%	43.6%	1.07	0.94	1.39	0.35	0.11	1.14
Distribution	11,887,375	12,719,155	6.8%	23.4%	1.02	0.95	1.10	0.41	0.20	1.72
Extractive	1,269,551	1,237,600	−2.5%	24.5%	1.01	0.79	1.27	0.09	0.01	0.51
Local market	33,434,183	37,773,144	12.2%	25.8%	1.04	0.98	1.11	1.75	0.94	5.20
Manufactures	18,450,502	18,556,546	0.6%	13.3%	1.01	0.92	1.13	0.19	0.06	0.50
Retail trade	19,443,520	21,477,074	9.9%	33.3%	1.03	0.99	1.09	0.88	0.52	2.61

Note: Change rates are based on the mean of 1991 and 1996 employment for the class of establishments.
Formation rates are 1991–96 annual average new firms in class per 1000 labor force in LMA in 1993.
Type = multi if establishment part of multi-unit firm in either year.

Source: 1989–96 LEEM file tabulations at Census' Center for Economic Studies, and Bureau of Labor Statistics.

Table 8.2 Establishments and 1994–96 firm formations and formation rates: Selected labour market areas, sorted by decreasing 1994–96 formations per 1,000 labour force

LMA	Largest place	State	Formations /1000 LF	1994 Establ.	Avg. ann. formations
	United States		3.85	5,770,090	504,939
Highest 20 LMAs					
287	Laramie	WY	10.18	5,898	887
72	Cape Coral	FL	7.20	14,543	1,782
352	Grand Junction	CO	6.95	4,319	613
71	West Palm Beach	FL	6.84	32,743	4,161
392	Bend	OR	6.61	4,608	625
393	Bellingham	WA	6.60	6,509	735
359	St. George	UT	6.54	3,187	536
70	Miami	FL	6.49	90,179	11,644
345	Missoula	MT	6.47	6,520	817
354	Flagstaff	AZ	6.44	6,037	835
69	Sarasota	FL	6.23	15,683	1,746
344	Bozeman	MT	6.03	5,696	682
353	Farmington	NM	5.92	3,157	417
88	Savannah	GA	5.67	8,734	986
15	Wilmington	NC	5.59	6,805	866
387	Longview	WA	5.57	5,025	514
298	Monett	MO	5.55	2,442	373
348	Santa Fe	NM	5.51	6,801	824
376	Reno	NV	5.38	11,736	1,356
78	Ocala	FL	5.34	6,079	661
Lowest 20 LMAs					
134	Lima	OH	2.54	5,312	333
182	Olean	NY	2.54	4,677	282
213	Mankato	MN	2.53	5,430	353
139	Kokomo	IN	2.52	3,585	235
125	Dayton	OH	2.52	24,505	1,613
237	Galesburg	IL	2.51	2,861	180
165	Erie	PA	2.51	13,602	790
192	Harrisburg	PA	2.50	20,484	1,323
208	Springfield	MA	2.49	13,904	819
224	Sheboygan	WI	2.49	3,717	258
140	Muncie	IN	2.48	7,760	527

(contd.)

Table 8.2 Establishments and 1994–96 firm formations and formation rates: selected labour market areas, sorted by decreasing 1994–96 formations per 1,000 labour force (*contd.*)

LMA	Largest place	State	Formations /1000 LF	1994 Establ.	Avg. ann. formations
	United States		3.85	5,770,090	504,939
133	Findlay	OH	2.47	4,938	313
177	Syracuse	NY	2.46	22,325	1,317
126	Richmond	IN	2.31	2,127	130
178	Oneonta	NY	2.31	3,281	176
187	Sunbury	PA	2.28	3,509	206
183	Watertown	NY	2.28	4,342	246
219	Marshalltown	IA	2.18	2,360	129
179	Binghamton	NY	2.11	5,557	309
181	Elmira	NY	2.06	6,501	346

Source: 1989–96 LEEM file tabulations at Census' Center for Economic Studies.

formation rates vary from two new firms per 1,000 labour force to a high of ten new firms per 1,000 labour force. The local market sector mean firm formation rate accounts for nearly half of the total, although that sector accounted for just over a third of the employment. Similarly, business services, retail trade and even the extractive industries accounted for somewhat more of the firm formations than their shares of employment. Firm formations in the manufacturing and distributive industries both lagged their employment shares.

The considerable variation in firm formation rates is shown in Table 8.2, although it is limited to the two-year average formation rates for 1994 to 1996, but there is little change in the two-year average formation rate rankings throughout the 1990s. Most of the highest-ranking areas were in Florida, the Southwest and Northwest. Miami and West Palm Beach were the only LMAs with large cities included among these. The lowest-ranking areas were predominately found in Pennsylvania, New York, Ohio and Indiana. These included the fairly large cities of Dayton, OH, Harrisburg, PA, and Syracuse, NY.

When we focus on new firm formations in the service sector (SIC 70–89), for a slightly later period (1996 to 1998), we see in Table 8.3 that the areas with the highest formation rates are still concentrated in Florida and the West, but many more areas with large cities are included in the top 20, in addition to Miami and West Palm Beach: Atlanta, Denver, Las Vegas, Orlando and Tampa. The locus of the areas with very low rates of service firm formation is the North-Central, with the addition of

Table 8.3 Regional variation in service firm formation rates (1996–98) ranked by average service firm formations per 1,000 1995 labour force

LMA	Largest place	State	Avg. 1996–98 ann. formation rate	Service firms 1995	1995 labour force
Top 20 LMAs					
287	Laramie	WY	3.28	2,250	90,242
71	West Palm Beach	FL	2.79	12,791	602,263
72	Cape Coral	FL	2.60	4,845	251,563
70	Miami	FL	2.52	36,811	1,794,995
393	Bellingham	WA	2.36	2,244	114,745
69	Sarasota	FL	2.32	5,704	280,316
344	Bozeman	MT	2.28	2,255	113,581
376	Reno	NV	2.26	4,421	254,723
345	Missoula	MT	2.21	2,398	126,036
91	Atlanta	GA	2.19	26,826	1,746,367
352	Grand Junction	CO	2.14	1,628	92,686
289	Denver	CO	2.13	20,972	1,241,321
359	St. George	UT	2.11	1,037	82,660
353	Farmington	NM	2.08	1,137	73,850
354	Flagstaff	AZ	2.07	2,173	139,112
379	Las Vegas	NV	2.06	7,083	613,097
75	Daytona Beach	FL	2.03	3,614	217,087
74	Orlando	FL	2.01	11,732	763,432
67	Tampa	FL	2.01	18,150	1,090,154
392	Bend	OR	1.99	1,492	95,114
Bottom 20 LMAs					
151	Lorain	OH	0.80	2,505	211,001
139	Kokomo	IN	0.80	1,153	95,821
133	Findlay	OH	0.79	1,553	128,032
225	Appleton	WI	0.79	3,497	316,960
224	Sheboygan	WI	0.79	1,147	106,522
183	Watertown	NY	0.78	1,248	105,549
227	Wausau	WI	0.77	2,178	195,815
187	Sunbury	PA	0.77	1,135	89,741
181	Elmira	NY	0.77	2,149	167,177
128	Greensburg	IN	0.77	658	69,562
182	Olean	NY	0.77	1,378	112,608
134	Lima	OH	0.76	1,679	132,715
6	North Wilkesboro	NC	0.76	766	74,383
185	Amsterdam	NY	0.76	652	53,750

(contd.)

Table 8.3 Regional variation in service firm formation rates, 1996–98 ranked by average service firm formations per thousand 1995 labour force (*contd.*)

LMA	Largest Place	State	Avg 1996–98 ann. formation rate	Service firms 1995	1995 labour force
154	Zanesville	OH	0.76	1,033	85,927
237	Galesburg	IL	0.73	878	70,347
219	Marshalltown	IA	0.71	725	59,299
178	Oneonta	NY	0.67	996	75,827
218	Mason City	IA	0.67	1,156	81,392
126	Richmond	IN	0.66	713	55,891

Source: Service establishment records from the 1989–98 LEEM file at Census' Center for Economic Studies and Bureau of Labor Statistics.

several small LMAs in New York. None of these bottom 20 areas has large or medium-sized cities in them. Our analysis seeks to identify some of the important factors that explain these regional variations.

8.4 Empirical results

8.4.1 Regional variation in entrepreneurship[12]

8.4.1.1 *Central hypotheses and model estimated*

A growing literature has sought the determinants of variation in new firm formation on a regional basis (Reynolds, 1994; Keeble and Walker, 1994; Audretsch and Fritsch, 1994; Reynolds et al., 1994). We focus primarily on four determinants of regional variation in the firm birth rate: (1) higher birth rates are promoted by regional spillovers, especially of relevant knowledge; (2) higher unemployment may deter start-ups in some sectors and increase them in others; (3) industrial restructuring should promote new firm formation; and (4) the existence of an entrepreneurial culture should promote start-up activity.

[12] Summary of research reported more fully in Armington and Acs (2002).

To test these hypotheses, we estimate a regression model where the dependent variable is the average annual firm birth rate in year t divided by the labour force in year t (in thousands). This is analogous to the method used by Keeble and Walker (1994).

8.4.1.2 *The explanatory (exogenous) variables*

Establishment size is a proxy for the structure of industry in the region. It is measured as employment in year t divided by the number of establishments in year t in the region. It should be negatively related to regional birth rate since larger average establishment size indicates greater dominance by large firms or branch plants.

In order to assess the potential for positive effects from spillovers, many studies have measured density using the square root of the regional population, or population per square mile. Such measures, however, do not indicate the extent of pooled labour markets very well, since they tell us nothing about the density of similar establishments in the region. Therefore, we introduce a new measure that captures both population density and the number of establishments in a region. *Sector Specialization* is the number of establishments in the industry and region in year t divided by the region's population in year t. The greater the number of establishments relative to the population, the more spillovers should be facilitated (Ciccone and Hall, 1996).

Population growth is the average annual rate of increase in the region in a previous period (calculating the two-year change from the ratio of the population in year t divided by population in t-2, and taking the square root of that two-year change ratio to calculate the annual change ratio). *Income growth* is the average annual rate of increase of personal income in the region similarly calculated. Both of these growth factors from the period preceding our start-up measurement period are expected to promote new firm start-ups in the subsequent period.

The *unemployment rate* is the traditional calculation for the first year of our start-up measurement period—the average number of unemployed in year t divided by the labour force in year t. It is expected to be negatively related to start-ups overall, but probably positively related to new firm start-up rates in industries with low capital requirements, and negatively related to those with high capital requirements. The simple correlation between the unemployment rate and the firm birth rate is close to zero, and is not statistically significant.

The *share of proprietors* in the economy is measured as the number of proprietors in year t divided by the labour force in year t. Proprietors are members of the labour force who are also business owners. It includes both the self-employed who have no employees, and the owners of unincorporated businesses that have employees. The simple correlation between the regional birth rate and the share of proprietors is 0.30, indicating a moderately strong positive relationship between these variables.

To measure the level of human capital in the economy we include two measures of educational attainment in each region. The first is the share of adults with no high school degree, defined as the number of adults without a high school degree in 1990 divided by the number of adults (population 25 years or older). The lack of a high school degree should be a good proxy for the proportion of unskilled and semi-skilled labour, and should be negatively related to the birth rate. The mean percent of the population without a high school degree is 27 percent. In fact, the simple correlation between the percentage of the population without a high school degree and the birth rate is −0.19.

Finally, share of college graduates is defined as the number of adults with college degrees in 1990 divided by the total number of adults. This is a proxy measure of both technical skills needed in the economy, for example engineers and scientists, and skills needed to start and build a business, like finance and marketing and complex reasoning. In 1990 an average of 15.9 percent of the adult population had a college degree. Its simple correlation with the regional birth rates is positive.

8.4.1.3 *Summary of results*

As summarized in Table 8.4, sector specialization and population growth are both strongly positive and statistically significant, as predicted by the theory of regional spillovers. In fact, these coefficients are nearly three times as large as the coefficient on income growth, which is also positive and significant. When analysed separately for each of the industry sectors, we find that both industry specialization and

Table 8.4 Summary of impacts of regional variables on entrepreneurial activity in LMAs in the mid-1990s

Independent variables	Firm formation rates	Sub-sector formation
Establishment size	−	−
Sector specialization	+	+
Business specialization	+	0
High school degree*	−	−
College degree	+	+
Population growth	+	+
Income growth	+	+
Share of proprietors	0	NA
Unemployment rate	0	0

* The coefficient on high-school degree is the negative of that on high-school dropout share.

population growth are positive and significant for each of the six industry sectors. However, the parameters on income growth are very small, and are only significant for business services and local markets.

The coefficient for large firm presence, measured as establishment size, is negative for all industries, and for all sectors by business services and extractive industries, indicating that regions with predominately smaller establishments have a higher start-up rate than regions with more large establishments. This supports the thesis that regions that have already restructured away from large manufacturing dominance have a higher start-up rate than regions that have not.

The coefficient for the unemployment rate is positive, although it is tiny and not statistically significant at the all-industry level. This result is surprising, given that previous cross-sectional studies have generally found a consistently negative result (Storey, 1991). Furthermore, the coefficients on unemployment were positive for all of the six sectors, and significantly so for all but the extractive industries. Perhaps the exceptionally low levels of unemployment and even shortages of labour in the United States in the 1990s account for the prevailingly positive relationship between unemployment and new firm births in this period. The implication here is that as workers shift from being employed to unemployed, the overall entry rate in the region tends to go up slightly, although there is no evidence that it is necessarily the unemployed who are starting the new firms.

The coefficient on the culture variable, measured as the share of proprietors in the region, is negative and statistically insignificant for the all-industry equation, perhaps because the share of proprietors is strongly negatively correlated with establishment size, −0.63. As the average establishment size in a region increases there are fewer opportunities for self-employment, and a smaller proportion of the labour force is made up of owners. When we drop establishment size from the estimated regression, the coefficient on self-employment becomes positive and statistically significant, while the other variables remain virtually unchanged. Within several of the industry sectors—local market, manufacturing, and retail—the share of proprietors is significantly positively related to firm formation rates.

Finally, the coefficient for human capital, as measured by share of college graduates, is positive and statistically significant, suggesting that regions that have higher levels of education will have higher firm formation rates. This is consistent with Anselin et al. (1997), who found that in technologically advanced industries individuals with greater skills, knowledge and expertise are more likely to start businesses. However, for both business services and manufacturing this coefficient is only barely positive, and not statistically significant. Reynolds (1994) found a negative and statistically significant relationship between college education and the new firm birth rate in manufacturing. The results do suggest that manufacturing firms may behave differently from other sectors of the economy.

The positive and statistically significant coefficient for the percentage of the population without a high school degree is at first surprising, but can be easily explained. The correlation between the share with no high school degree and the new firm start-up rate is negative, −19, as expected. However, it is much more strongly negatively correlated with college education, with a coefficient of −0.70. After controlling for the proportion of adults with college degrees, the additional effect of a greater share of less educated workers is to facilitate the start-up process by providing cheap labour for the educated and creative classes. This positive impact of 'no high school degree' after controlling for 'college degree' is consistent across most of the industry sectors, except for business services, with the strongest positive relationship appearing in the distributive industries.

In summary, using annual data on firm births for 384 labour market areas, in six industry sectors, between 1991 and 1998, we find considerable variation in the new firm formation rate across regions, but little variation over time. Variations in the firm birth rates are substantially explained by the lack of large firms, the presence of human capital, regional differences in sector specialization and population growth and income growth, as suggested by the new economic geography.

8.4.2 Human capital and Entrepreneurship[13]

8.4.2.1 *Central hypotheses and model estimated*

It is clear from the data shown earlier in Table 8.4 (in Appendix) that the service firm formation rates vary greatly across local economic areas, and we will seek the determinants of this local variation in the same factors that contributed earlier to the explanation of the differences in formation rates for all industries. The agglomeration effects that contribute to new service firm formation can come both from demand effects associated with increased local population, income, and business activity, and from supply factors related to the quality of the local labour market and business climate.

Among areas with broadly similar regional demand and business climate characteristics, there are further differences in rates of new firm formation and economic growth that are associated with the specific qualities of their human capital, and the propensity of locally available knowledge to spillover and stimulate innovative activity which culminates in new firm formations. Highly-educated populations provide the human capital embodied in their general and specific skills for implementing new ideas for creating new businesses. They also create an environment rich in local knowledge spillovers, which support another mechanism

[13] Summary of research reported more fully in Acs and Armington (2003a).

by which new firm start-ups are initiated and sustained. Thus, regions that are richer in educated people should have more start-up activity, and local new firm formation rates should be positively related to local educational attainment rates. Furthermore, areas that already have relatively intense development of service businesses are likely to have higher levels of service firm formations, resulting in large part from spillovers of relevant specialized knowledge. We would expect that areas with relatively high shares of high-school dropouts would have lower rates of new firm formation.

To test the basic hypotheses that the new firm formation rates are positively related to the level of human capital in a region, we estimate a regression model where the dependent variable is the average annual new service firm formation rate (dividing births by the labour force in thousands) for 1996–98.[14]

8.4.2.2 *The explanatory (exogenous) variables*

The primary explanatory variables are the same measures of the level of human capital and knowledge spillover conditions that were used earlier. Formal education itself does not usually provide either the skills or the inspiration to start a new business. But higher education trains individuals to rationally assess information, and to seek new ideas. Therefore more educated people are more likely to acquire useful local knowledge spillovers from others who are involved in research or in managing some service business. The quantity of potentially useful knowledge spillovers is expected to be a function of the number of similar business establishments, relative to the population of the economic area. *Service-industry intensity* is defined as the number of service establishments in the region divided by the region's population in thousands. The greater the number of establishments relative to the population, the more spillovers should be facilitated due to density of establishments (Ciccone and Hall, 1996).

8.4.2.3 *Summary of results*

Only two of the three human capital variables showed the hypothesized relationships. First, for human capital measured by share of college graduates, are positive and statistically significant for all except the 1993–95 periods, confirming that regions with higher shares of college-educated adults have higher firm formation rates. This positive result on human capital is consistent with previous research (Storey, 1994).

[14] Although we have annual firm formation data for 1990 through 1999, we have chosen not to use pooled cross-section time series regressions, because most of the independent variables describing the characteristics of the LMAs change very little over time, and the errors from omitted variables will be nearly identical for each LMA from year to year, so the diagnostic statistics from such an analysis would be very misleading.

The positive coefficient for high-school dropouts as a share of the non-college adult population is at first surprising—however, it is consistent with our earlier results for the whole economy (Armington and Acs, 2002). There we suggested that after controlling for the proportion of adults with college degrees,[15] the additional effect of a greater share of less educated workers is to facilitate the start-up process by providing cheap labour for the new firms. Even the most sophisticated businesses need some workers who are less educated to do the manual labour. Thus, the relationship between educational attainment and new firm start-ups at the regional level may be U-shaped, with both low levels and high levels of education conducive to firm formation and growth.

Thirdly, the coefficient on intensity of service establishments is positive and statistically significant, suggesting that regions that already have a relatively strong supply of service establishments will have higher rates of new service firm formation, as predicted by the theory of regional spillovers (Jovanovic and Rob, 1989). Indeed, this factor has the strongest relationship of any of our independent variables. The 0.60 value estimated for the standardized coefficient indicates that a locality with a service establishment intensity that is one standard deviation more intense than the mean will be likely to have firm start-up rates that are 0.6 standard deviation higher than the mean.

The unemployment rate is positive and statistically significant for 1990–92, when the economy was undergoing a small recession. However, it is negative and barely significant during the period 1993–95 and insignificant during the years 1996–98, suggesting that this positive effect disappears as the economy improves, or as mean unemployment falls.

Hoping to better distinguish the impacts of our independent variables on the start-up rates of various types of service activities, but limited by data disclosure constraints, we defined 9 service subsectors, using two dimensions that should be relevant to our analysis of variation in start-up rates. The dimensions chosen were the market segment served and the customary education requirement for founder of new firms in each class of service activity. Each of these dimensions was broken into just three categories, so that applying both dimensions resulted in the classification of all services into nine subsectors, within which the service activities were fairly homogeneous with respect to these two dimensions.

We distinguish activities that are most frequently started by people who do not have college degrees (called 'high-school' level for simplicity), from those generally requiring an 'advanced' (graduate, post-graduate, or professional) degree, and assigned the remainder to 'college.' These allocations were based on subjective judgement, using our general knowledge of service industries, supplemented by

[15] Note that when estimated in separate equations for 1996–98 the coefficient for College degree falls to .10 and that for high school dropout falls to .12, while other coefficients remain substantially the same.

detailed descriptions of the 4-digit SIC classes in the 1987 Standard Industrial Classification Manual.[16, 17]

For the nine sub-sectors defined by the education requirement and the market segment together, the firm formation rate was highest, at 14.78, for businesses in non-local markets with founders normally having advanced degrees. The sub-sector requiring the same advanced degree for founders, but serving the local consumer market, had only 5.31 new firms for each hundred existing establishments in that sub-sector. For businesses that normally require a college degree for their founder, the birth rate is quite similar across all three of the market segments. Businesses requiring less educated founders (high school degree) also showed great variation across market segments, with high formation rates for non-local market, and low ones for the local consumer market.

Service firm birth rates were calculated as before for all firms for each of the 394 LMAs, based on new firm formations during each of three recent time periods—1990 through 1992, 1993 through 1995, and 1996 through 1998, and standardizing across different sizes of LMAs by dividing by the size of the labour force (in thousands) in the LMA in the prior year. However, for comparing new firm formation rates for different sub-sectors of the service industry we need to standardize for the differences in size of both areas and sub-sectors. For this purpose we express new firm formation rates in terms of the number of new firms relative to the number of establishments already in existence in that sub-sector and LMA. This could be termed the ecological approach, because it considers the amount of start-up activity relative to the size of the existing population of businesses.

In order to allow for variation in the estimated coefficients of variables that should be sensitive to our sub-sector dimensions, while controlling consistently for other regional characteristics, we expand the independent variables to be subsector-specific for the dimensions we want to test. Naturally, we expected the educational attainment variables to be sensitive to the Education Requirement dimension.

This more detailed pooled estimation model, according to the previous notation, has the following form:

[16] We originally hoped to base this classification on the BLS occupational distribution data for each (three-digit) industry, but we found that many activities requiring academic skills or advanced training for leadership positions, in fact had occupational distributions very heavily weighted toward semi-skilled and unskilled workers. Hospitals and hotels were extreme examples of this contrast between educational requirements for workers and those for the individual responsible for starting the business.

[17] The sub-sector classifications for each 4-digit SIC can be found in the Appendix of the CES Discussion Paper 03-02, where they are ordered by SIC code within each sub-sector. Data on the number of establishments and employees in each 4-digit SIC in 1995, and their net changes to 1998, as well as the total number of new firm formations during 1996 through 1998 per 100 (1995) establishments, are provided for each entry in this table.

$$\text{Birth rate}_{LEM} = f(\text{Coll}_{LE}, \text{Highsch drop}_{LE}, \text{Sub-sector estab intensity}_{LEM}, \text{Pop gro}_{LM}, \text{Income gro}_{LE}, \text{Pop log}_{LEM}, \text{Unempl}_{LE}, \text{Estab size}_{LM}, \text{All-ind estab intensity}_{LM}). \quad (2)$$

In order to estimate this model, we first standardized all of the exogenous and endogenous variables to have a mean of zero and a standard deviation of one, within each of the nine sub-sectors. Therefore, each represents a relative measure for the LMA, within the sub-sector. Then we created dummy variables for each of the three values for each of the sub-sector dimensions—Market and Education. Finally, we multiplied each exogenous variable, times the appropriate dummies to create specialized exogenous variables that distinguished among the dimensions of education and market.

When we look first at the human capital variables in these estimated models for sub-sectors, we see that the share of adults with college degrees is not significant for the formation rate of service businesses requiring only a high school education for the founder. For services businesses requiring a college education, the variation in the local formation rates is much more sensitive than was indicated by either the all-service regression or the pooled sub-sector regression. There is also a significant positive relationship between the share of adults with college degrees and the formation rates of service businesses normally requiring an advanced degree for the founder. This results from the high correlation of the distribution of college degrees with that of advanced degrees.

The positive and statistically significant coefficient for the relationship of shares of high-school dropouts to formation of new service firms that require advanced degrees suggests that such businesses may be more dependent on having a large pool of unskilled labour. The statistically insignificant coefficients for the impact of the share of high school dropouts on formation rates in the sub-sectors of services that require only high school or college degrees suggests that such businesses are not as sensitive to the supply of unskilled labour. They may find that the unskilled labour supply in most areas is adequate for their needs.

The relative intensity of establishments in the same sub-sector of services is a significant explanatory variable for all market segments, but the formation of new firms serving non-local markets is particularly sensitive to the prior existence of similar businesses. This corroborates the many prior case study analyses that addressed the spillover effects of certain rapidly growing local industry clusters, and suggests that these spillover effects are particularly important for businesses that are not focusing on local markets.

Most of the estimated coefficients for regional characteristics crossed with education or market dummies were similar to those estimated without such distinctions. However, the differences that appeared are quite illuminating. The log of population was crossed with all six dummies, and the tiny and insignificant variables crossed with college degree and with non-local markets were later omitted, to strengthen the remaining estimates. These show that, unlike services to local markets, those to non-local markets are not sensitive to the size of the local economic area. Perhaps the high coefficient on sub-sector intensity for non-local services has captured all of the relevant agglomeration effects for that sub-sector. In respect of the education dimension, larger population contributes a bit to the formation rate of services firms requiring founders with advanced degrees, but it reduces the formation rate of firms, normally started by high school dropouts.

The coefficient on unemployment is positive and statistically significant only for service firms normally started by college graduates. This provides some clarification of the conflicting results found in previous studies of the effects of unemployment levels on new firm formation rates. Apparently, after controlling for regional differences in income growth rates, an increase in unemployment tends to lead to an increase in new firm formation by those with college degrees, but not by high school dropouts or those with advanced degrees.

Finally, the negative coefficient on average size of local businesses is strongest for formation of new firms serving local consumer markets, while that on the intensity of all establishments is significant only for formation of new firms serving non-local markets.

In summary, these results suggest that the regional differences in new firm formation rates do indeed depend to a large degree on the educational requirements and the market served by the newly-formed firms. In particular, the local levels of educational attainment impact primarily the firm formation rates of the types of firms that are normally founded by better-educated entrepreneurs, and do not affect start-up rates for those normally founded by individuals with less than a college degree. While formation rates of all service businesses are higher in areas with higher intensities of similar service establishments, new formations of firms serving non-local markets are three times more sensitive to this than those serving local consumer markets, and those serving local business markets are twice as sensitive as those serving local consumers.

8.5. Conclusion

The BITS database constructed for the Office of Advocacy of the U.S. Small Business Administration is uniquely suitable for testing new approaches to explaining regional differences in economic growth rates. Recent theories of economic growth view local externalities, as opposed to scale economies, as the primary engine in generating growth in cities with their closely integrated surrounding counties (Labor Market Areas). While scale economies operate at the plant level, externalities operate at the level of the firm, primarily through entrepreneurial activity.

Using the BITS data we examined the impact of these externalities on regional employment growth from an entrepreneurial perspective by examining the relationship of local economic growth to local entrepreneurial activity. Since higher rates of entrepreneurial activity in an industry sector and region imply lower barriers to birth and greater local competition, this analysis can also be interpreted as an investigation of the impact of local competition on local economic growth. We found that higher rates of entrepreneurial activity were strongly associated with faster growth of local economies.

References

Acs, Z. and C. Armington (2004a). 'The Impact of Geographic Differences in Human Capital on Service Firm Formation Rates'. *Journal of Urban Economics*, 56: 244–78.

—— and —— (2004b). 'Employment Growth and Entrepreneurial Activity in Cities'. *Regional Studies*, 28: 911–27.

—— and —— (2003a). 'The Geographic Concentration of New Firm Formation and Human Capital'. CES-WP- 03-05.

—— and —— (2003b). 'Endogenous Growth and Entrepreneurial Activity in Cities'. CES-WP- 03-02.

—— and —— (2006). *Entrepreneurship, Geography and American Economic Growth.* Cambridge: Cambridge University Press.

—— and D. Audretsch (1990). *Innovation and Small Firms.* Cambridge: The MIT Press.

—— —— P. Braunerhjelm and B. Carlsson (2004). 'The Missing Link: The Knowledge Filter, Entrepreneurship and Endogenous Growth'. Working Paper #4783, London: Center for Economic Policy Research.

—— and A. Varga (2002). 'Geography, Endogenous Growth and Innovation'. *International Regional Science Review*, 25(1): 132–48.

—— and —— (2004). 'Entrepreneurship, Agglomeration and Technological Change'. *Small Business Economics*. 38(8): 911–28.

Agion, P. and P. Howitt (1992). 'A Model of Growth through Creative Destruction'. *Econometrica*, 60: 323–51.

Anselin, L., A. Varga and Z. Acs, (1997). 'Local Geographic Spillovers Between University Research and High Technology Innovation'. *Journal of Urban Economics* 42: 422–48.

Armington, C. and Z. Acs (2002). 'The Determinants of Regional Variation in New Firm Formation'. *Regional Studies*, 36(1): 33–45.

—— and A. Robb (2002). 'Mergers and Acquisitions in the United States: 1990–1994'. CES 98–15.

Arrow, K. (1962). 'The Economic Implications of Learning by Doing'. *Review of Economics and Statistics*, 80: 155–73.

AUDRETSCH, D. and M. FRITSCH (1994). 'The Geography of Firm Births in Germany'. *Regional Studies*, 28(4): 359–65.

—— and M. KEILBACH (2004). 'Entrepreneurship Capital and Economic Performance'. *Regional Studies*, 38(8): 949–60.

BARTIK, T. J. (1989). 'Small Business Start-ups in the U.S.: Estimates of the Effects of Characteristics of States'. *Southern Economic Journal*, 55: 1004–18.

BRAUNERHJELM, P. and B. BOARGMAN. 'Geographic Concentration, Entrepreneurship and Regional Growth: Evidence from Regional Data in Sweden, 1975–99'. *Regional Studies*, 38(8): 929–48.

CICCONE, C. and R. HALL (1996). 'Productivity and the Density of Economic Activity'. *American Economic Review*, 86(1): 54–70.

EVANS, D. and B. JOVANOVIC (1989). 'Estimates of a Model of Entrepreneurial Choice Under Liquidity Constraints'. *Journal of Political Economy*, 95: 657–74.

—— and L. S. LEIGHTON (1990). 'Small Business Formation by Unemployed and Employed Workers'. *Small Business Economics*, 2: 319–30.

FLORIDA, R. (2005). 'The World is Spiky'. *Mimeo.*

HANNAN M. and J. FREEMAN (1989). *Organizational Ecology.* Cambridge, MA: Harvard University Press.

HAYEK, J. (1945). 'The Use of Knowledge in Society'. *American Economic Review*, 35: 520–30.

JAFFE, A. (1989). 'The Real Effects of Academic Research'. *American Economic Review*, 79(5): 957–70.

JOVANOVIC, B. and R. ROB (1989). 'The Growth and Diffusion of Knowledge'. *Review of Economic Studies*, 56: 569–82.

KEEBLE, D. and S. WALKER (1994). 'New Firms, Small Firms and Dead Firms: Spatial Patterns and Determinants in the United Kingdom'. *Regional Studies*, 28: 411–427.

KNIGHT, F. (1921). *Risk, Uncertainty and Profit.* Boston, MA: Houghton Mifflin.

KRUGMAN, P. (1991). 'Increasing Returns and Economic Geography.' *Journal of Political Economy*, 99: 483–99.

KRUGMAN, P. (1998). 'Space: The Final Frontier'. *Journal of Economic Perspectives*, 12: 161–74.

LUCAS, R. (1988). 'On the Mechanisms of Economic Development'. *Journal of Monetary Economics*, 22: 3–39.

MC AFFEE, P., H. M. MIALON and M. A. WILLIAMS (2004). 'When are Sunk Costs Barriers to Entry? Entry Barriers in Economics and Antitrust Analysis. What is a Barrier to Entry?' *American Economic Review*, 94: 461–5.

MICHELACCI, C. (2003). 'Low Returns in R&D due to the Lack of Entrepreneurial Skills'. *The Economic Journal* (January) 113: 207–25.

RAUCH, J. E. (1993). 'Productivity Gains from Geographic Concentration of Human Capital: Evidence form the Cities'. *Journal of Urban Economics*, 34: 380–400.

REYNOLDS, P. (1994). 'Autonomous Firm Dynamics and Economic Growth in the United States, 1986–90'. *Regional Studies*, 28(4): 429–42.

—— B. MILLER and W. MAKI (1994). 'Regional Characteristics Affecting Business Volatility in the United States, 1980–1984', in C. Karlsson, J. Johansson and D. Storey (eds), *Small Business Dynamics: International, National and Regional Perspectives.* London: Routledge.

—— —— and —— (1995). 'Explaining Regional Variation in Business Births and Deaths: U.S. 1976–88'. *Small Business Economics*, 7(4): 387–407.

ROMER, P. (1986). 'Increasing Returns and Long Run Growth'. *Journal of Political Economy*, 94: 1003–37.

Romer, P. (1990). 'Endogenous Technological Change'. *Journal of Political Economy*, 94: S71-S102.

Schumpeter, J. (1911) (1934). *The Theory of Economic Development.* Cambridge, MA: Harvard University Press.

Simon, C. and C. Nardinelli (2002). 'Human Capital and the Rise of American Cities, 1900–1990'. *Regional Science and Urban Economics*, 32: 59–96.

Storey, D. J. (1994). 'The Birth of New Firms—Does Unemployment Matter? A Review of the Evidence'. *Small Business Economics*, 3: 167–78.

Tolbert, C. M. and M. Sizer (1996). 'U.S. Commuting Zones and Labor Market Areas: a 1990 Update'. Rural Economy Division, Economic Research Service, U.S. Department of Agriculture, Staff Paper No. AGES-9614.

U.S. Small Business Administration (1988a). *Uses and Limitations of USEEM/USELM Data*, Office of Advocacy, Washington, DC.

U.S. Small Business Administration (1988b). *Handbook of Small Business Data*, Office of Advocacy, Washington, DC.

U.S. Small Business Administration (1999). *Statistics of U.S. Business—Microdata and Tables of SBA/Census Data.* Washington, DC: Office of Advocacy.

Van Stel, A. J. and D. Storey (2004). 'The Link Between Firm Births and Job Creation: Is there an Upas tree effect?' *Regional Studies*, 38(8): 893–910.

Villalonga, B. (2001). 'Diversification Discount or Premium? New Evidence from BITS Establishment-Level Data'. (December) CES-WP-01–13.

Williamson, O. (1985). *The Economic Institutions of Capitalism.* New York: The Free Press.

Winter, S. (1984). 'Schumpeterian Competition in Alternative Technological Regimes'. *Journal of Economic Behavior and Organization*, 5: 297–320.

CHAPTER 9

DEFINITIONS, DIVERSITY AND DEVELOPMENT: KEY DEBATES IN FAMILY BUSINESS RESEARCH

CAROLE HOWORTH, MARY ROSE AND ELEANOR HAMILTON

9.1 Introduction

Family firms are a crucial dimension of modern economies world wide and they contribute significantly to employment and wealth generation. They represent between 75 and 95 percent of firms registered world wide and account for up to 65 percent of GDP (Neubauer and Lank, 1998; Colli, 2003; Colli et al., 2003; IFERA, 2003). Clearly, a high percentage of entrepreneurs founded their businesses in the form of family firms, and many more find families an important source of resources and especially of human capital (Aldrich and Cliff, 2003). Entrepreneurship researchers are beginning to acknowledge the valuable insights provided by family firms research across a broad range of relevant areas including the interaction of family and business, entrepreneurial learning, continuing innovation and the longevity, development and growth of firms.

Very small family firms are often embedded in industrial clusters and these have proved important sources of innovation, flexibility and competitive advantage as, for example, in northern Italy since the 1970s (Colli, 1998). Family businesses have also been the basis of the wave of entrepreneurship and Chinese capitalism, which has transformed many of the economies of South East and East Asia over the last three decades (Redding, 1990).

Some family businesses are giants including Ford, Levi Strauss, W. L. Gore and Walmart in the United States; and in Europe, IKEA (Sweden), Lego (Denmark), Fiat, Benetton and Ferrero (Italy). In South and East Asia family firms are also the norm and include firms such as Samsung. In India, the Marwari, Parsee and other ethnic or caste groups dominate private sector business and without exception, they operate family businesses. The largest of these family houses, such as the Tatas and Birlas, have survived several generations (Bagchi, 1972; Timberg, 1978; Ray, 1979). Family ownership has also remained almost universal in the Arabian peninsular since the early 1970s (Field, 1984). In Japan, the Zaibatsu were powerful family groups and even though they were swept away by the Americans following the Second World War, small family firms continue to be important in Japan today, accounting for 99 percent of all businesses (Fruin, 1980). Family groups also predominated in South Korea, at least until the Asian business crisis of the late 1990s (Hattori, 1984; Amsden, 1989). Since family firms of one kind or another were the norm until after the Second World War, many long-lived, large corporations—such as the American chemicals giant, Du Pont, also have family roots. Indeed, it has been suggested that family firms are especially worthy of study precisely because they are so often dynastic (Casson, 1999).

The very diversity of family businesses and their behaviour make them an important field of study and one which is naturally multidisciplinary, involving sociology, economics, management, culture and history. Understanding family firms requires the analysis of the complex interaction of family and firm, the forces underlying family values and the way these shape the business culture, behaviour, and capabilities of firms. Yet some would question the extent to which family businesses are entrepreneurial and hence how far the study of family firms can be embedded within the study of entrepreneurship and included in a Handbook of Entrepreneurship. After all, family firms, through time, have been seen to mitigate agency problems as a reaction to risk and uncertainty and they are associated with securing continuity, rather than being necessarily entrepreneurial (Pollak, 1985; Randoy and Goel, 2003). Nevertheless the founders of a family business would be classified as entrepreneurs within any perspective that defines entrepreneurship as synonymous with new venture creation (Gartner, 1985, 1988; Bygrave and Hofer, 1991; Shaver and Scott, 1991). Increasingly the study of family firms has been proposed as a field distinct from, but overlapping with, the study of entrepreneurship (Hoy and

Verser, 1994) and there is a growing consensus that family businesses are of contemporary interest for researchers in entrepreneurship (Brockhaus, 1994; Hoy and Verser, 1994; Baines and Wheelock, 1999). Clearly, the founders of family firms may be described as entrepreneurs, but it is the transfer of entrepreneurial learning between family members and the revitalization of entrepreneurial spirit through intergenerational succession which provides particularly rich insights for entrepreneurship researchers.

Intergenerational succession lies at the very heart of the family firm. Any institution and particularly a family firm can be likened to 'the lengthening shadow of one man [or woman].' However, 'a shadow is a fleeting thing... and if the firm is to persist beyond the lifetime of its founder, [its leadership] must pass from one generation to the next' (Davis, 1968: 407). Succession has in it the potential for change and regeneration of the firm, albeit based upon a bedrock of shared experience and history. It is this potential for change and regeneration described as 'interpreneurship ... intergenerational entrepreneurship leading to transformation' (Hoy and Verser, 1994: 19), which powerfully links family business with the study of entrepreneurship. The future prosperity of any family business, and indeed its ability to survive, is inextricably linked to the succession process and the way it is handled. This interplay between the continuities of past experience and the need for change lie at the heart of the family business. They mean that the decisions to innovate and change, made by later generations, are every bit as entrepreneurial as the original decision to found the business. Discontinuity and difference rather than continuity are a necessary part of succession given that the business must operate in the social, technological, economic and cultural climate of a new generation (Hamilton, 2002).

Family business founders bequeath an entrepreneurial legacy to their successors—a kind of intangible asset (or liability) which is as crucial to the firm's future as buildings, machinery, technology, goodwill, contacts, and standing (Rose, 1993: 134). Given the intimate intertwining of family and firm, this legacy provides the foundation on which future generations may build or destroy the firm. It encompasses attitudes to successors—both insiders and outsiders—and may embrace experience within the family as well as within the firm. It also includes knowledge and understanding passed between generations of the firm. It thus contributes to a dynamic learning process and also, of course, to failures in understanding.

Thus, we can see that the founding and development of family businesses are important dimensions of entrepreneurship. Insights from research on family businesses can be transferred into alternative entrepreneurial contexts and aid understanding of, for example, interaction between family and business; discontinuity as well as continuity; change and development of firms; and entrepreneurial learning. From being on the periphery of entrepreneurship, family business has moved to the very heart of new research. The aim of this chapter is to provide an insight into the key debates in the family business literature and to highlight implications for future research within family firms and within entrepreneurship more widely. The key debates are related to three overlapping themes, which can be summarized as definitions, diversity and development.

The next section begins with an examination of definitions of family firms. The debate about what constitutes a family firm is every bit as complex as the definition of an entrepreneur. This chapter explores the range of definitions but shows that any definition needs to be interpreted in its economic, social, institutional and cultural context. An explanation for the multiplicity of definitions is provided in the section that follows, which explores the diversity in scale, scope, organization and longevity of family firms, and shows differences through time in different societies and between families. It demonstrates the strong path dependency of family firm development, with change (or lack of it) underpinned by the foundations of the past. This leads us on to consider the development of family firms and, in particular, intergenerational succession. We analyse the range of ways family businesses handle succession and the impact of contrasting family experiences. Factors associated with successful development and the performance of family firms pre- and post-succession are examined. The chapter then explores research which compares the performance of family firms with non-family firms and this highlights the potential policy implications of family business research. These are developed in the conclusion alongside recommendations for the direction of future research.

9.2 Defining the Family Firm

There are a multitude of definitions of the family firm (Litz, 1995; Westhead and Cowling, 1998; Chua et al., 1999; Colli, 2003; Colli et al., 2003; Sharma, 2004). Definitions include aspects of one or all of the following: percentage of family ownership, percentage/number of family managers/employees, family controlling interest, multi-generation, family objectives, family intentions, for example, succession to a family member. Different definitions clearly affect the level of inclusion/exclusion and Westhead and Cowling (1998) attempt to quantify this using a variety of permutations of definitions. Definitions are often based on the percentage of ownership of the firm that is in the hands of members of the same kinship group. Different studies have employed percentages from 50 percent to 100 percent but the most commonly used definition is that of a majority, or more than 50 percent, of the ownership of the firm being in the same family. However, researchers studying the largest family firms argue that the majority ownership definition is inappropriate in their context as a very small percentage of family ownership (e.g. 3–5%) can give one family a high level of influence within a firm. In Italy, for instance, family influence over large corporations has been maintained through the use of holding companies, agreements, cross shareholdings and the issuing of stocks carrying multiple voting power. This allows the founders and their families to raise resources on financial markets, while also controlling the company with only a small fraction of the share capital (Colli, 2003).

Others insist that firms must be at least second generation before they can be labelled as family firms. Westhead and Cowling (1998) recommend the use of definitions that incorporate multiple criteria and they highlight that definitions should take into account whether the firm is perceived to be a family business by the owners and employees. Following their work there has been a growing tendency towards using the dual definition of family firms being firms which have a majority of family ownership (>50 %) and which also perceive themselves to be family firms. However, many variations still occur and this makes it very difficult to compare results and build up a body of empirical evidence and predictive models.

The absence of consensus is potentially damaging for moving the study of family business forward and there is a case for using a more general, less precise definition as a starting point. One broad general definition of the family firm emphasizes family influence: that is that the family owns enough of the equity to be able to exert control over strategy and also that it is involved in top management positions. This definition does transfer through time and space, and is today one of the most used and most quoted. So it can be considered a useful benchmark and a starting point for examining the rich diversity of family firm structure, behaviour and capability.

9.3 Diversity: Culture, society and why history matters

Family firms are hard to define because they are not homogeneous. They range from the micro to the giant and their behaviour and capabilities vary through time, internationally, and regionally. Family firms are also inseparable from the families that own and control them, and therefore differences in family values and objectives can lead to variations in the way family firms are structured and managed (Church, 1993; Poutziouris and Chittenden, 1996; Colli and Rose, 1999; Rose, 2000;

James and Kobrak, 2004). To understand variety in the strategy and the structure of family firms, their attitudes to risk and uncertainty, inheritance and community need to be assessed. These issues can vary internationally, culturally and historically.

The evolution of family business behaviour in different countries, and even between regions, shows strong evidence of path dependency (Rose, 2000). Path dependency can be defined as:

> The influence of past events and of the states they bring about must be communicated—like the deepening of wheel ruts by each successive vehicle—through some definite chain of intervening causal events, effects and resultant states—down to the present state, whence they can be passed on to future events. (David, 1997: 123)

Often seen as synonymous with 'learning by doing', path dependency takes on a very particular meaning when applied to the family business. The family firm is embedded within societies with a peculiar array of values and attitudes as well as laws and business practices which vary internationally precisely because of being moulded by differing historical experience. Equally, at the level of the individual firm, shared family experience leads to shared understandings and perceptions which shape the evolution of the firm. This is not the same as saying that the development of family firms is in some way pre-determined. Instead history matters in the change and innovation process as it affects choices and informs development. Without an understanding of history, the variation in capabilities and peculiarities of family firms is hard to appreciate.

Family firms have always lain at the heart of industrialization in most countries. Whether discussion is of eighteenth-century Britain or twenty-first century developing countries, the owners of mainly small scale firms have seen the family as the ideal interface between the market and the firm (Natziger, 1969; Ben-Porath, 1980). The boundaries of the family firm have usually lain within a rather large group with shared culture and values (Casson, 1982, 1991, 1993; Pollak, 1985). The family, widely defined to include that extended kinship group of cousins, in-laws and connections in the local business community or religious groupings, therefore represented more than just a reservoir of skill, an internal labour market or a source of finance as suggested by resource-based views of the firm. It was a network of trust, the use of which reduced the transaction costs and the dangers and uncertainties of business activity.

In the hazardous and uncertain environment of early industrialization from the eighteenth to the twenty-first century, family firms represent a reaction against business hazards, distrust and the danger of failure. Established businesses normally choose to reinforce their position and reduce exposure to uncertainty by diversification. For the family business, operating within a localized business community, in the early stages of industrialization or in a modern developing country, such insurance strategies often involved externalization rather than internalization. This was facilitated by a common culture and often reinforced the founding families' standing within the community. In labour markets too, family business owners have sometimes used paternalist strategies to create or mould community culture, in an effort to reduce conflict and uncertainty. This is not to say that competition is not intense in developing communities. Rather, it is to highlight that in a volatile environment, family business owners looked for ways of protecting their firms and their families.

The characteristics of family firms generally evolve through time, while for individual family firms strategy often shifts in line with the life cycle of the firm (Gersick et al., 1997). Similarly, changes in the legal, demographic, social, cultural, educational and economic environment mean that family businesses in any country change through time. Recent work by Colli, Fernandez Perez and Rose comparing British, Spanish and Italian firms from the eighteenth to the twentieth century shows how differing legal frameworks for business affected the types of family business that emerged. They also show that distinctive national and even regional family firm behaviour stemmed from the interplay between the institutional, cultural, economic and social environments through time (Colli and Rose, 1999; Colli et al., 2003).

The institutional and legal environment is the product of a complex historical process, underpinned by cultural forces at both the regional and national level. Geert Hofstede has defined culture 'as the interactive aggregate of common characteristics that influence a human group's response to its environment' (Hofstede, 1980). His more recent work takes the notion of culture further, describing it as a form of mental programming. Accordingly, he suggests that 'culture is learned not inherited. It derives from one's social environment, not from one's genes'. As a result of the differing mental programming of societies, there are, therefore, significant variations in behaviour and social norms which impact on all forms of business, including family business (Hofstede, 1994). Howorth and Ali (2001) showed that culture affected the values emphasized and the strategies and relationships within family firms. Aspects of culture which have been shown to be important include the size of families; inheritance traditions; the relative importance of family or business values; attitudes towards elders and the status of retired people within the community; cognitive biases and prevalence of emotional or rational decision-making criteria; importance of specific traditions, for example, preference for male successors; relative value placed on education and outside experience; and tradition of in-firm training.

Inevitably, international differences in values and attitudes impact on family business behaviour. There are striking contrasts in values and attitudes between the United States and Europe which relate to enterprise, to firms, to innovation and to technology. In the United States, enterprise is viewed as a commodity which can be bought or sold, whereas in Europe it is associated with community (Albert, 1991; Hau, 1995). In a recent book, Mary Rose demonstrated that differing histories and values led to sharp contrasts in the behaviour of family firms in the British and

American cotton industries in the nineteenth and twentieth centuries. The United States' position as a country of recent settlement impacted on attitudes towards the family. Since the objectives of families and family firms are inseparable, this also affected family business policies. For example, the British desire to found a family dynasty meant that 'British entrepreneurs ... viewed their businesses in personal rather than organizational terms, as family estates to be nurtured and passed on to their heirs. In the United States, high geographical and social mobility are thought to have weakened family ties and certainly ties to specific localities' (Rose, 2000). The long-term ties between family and enterprise are not confined to Britain, for in essence they are typically European—particularly in Italy and Greece which are strong family-based cultures. The enterprise is established for future generations and the result is a type of familialism, where the allocation of power, resources and responsibilities is strictly on a kinship basis (Colli, 2003). Familialism has sometimes been associated with Mediterranean societies. However, there is a need to distinguish between the Mediterranean countries concerned. A recent article showed that when Spanish and Italian family business behaviour was compared, national, cultural and institutional forces created distinct variations in behaviour (Colli et al., 2003). In Italy, for instance, 'outsiders' may be fired for failing to give family interests pre-eminence over economic considerations. In addition, family insiders have been preferred to outsiders as a matter of course in several leading Italian businesses. Indeed, the concept of family business in Italy should be used in a relatively strict way. Usually—and especially among the largest private groups in the country—families retain a significant proportion (often the majority) of the capital and have their members among the top executives (Colli and Rose, 1999).

In India, the family lies at the very core of culture. 'The centre of the Indian social identity is the family. Family businesses are not merely an economic structure, for most ... individuals, they are the source of social identity. There is a strong social obligation to continue one's father's work.' (Dutta, 1997). Japanese and Chinese family firms contrast illustrating the danger of assuming common culture where countries are close geographically. In China, the family is the basic survival unit and people exist only in terms of their immediate family network and exhibit a high level of distrust of outsiders (Redding, 1990). Intricate stem networks of families have emerged, especially where Chinese communities have migrated overseas, as in the ASEAN countries such as Hong Kong, Singapore, Indonesia, Malaysia, the Philippines and Thailand (Ampalavanar Brown, 1995). Family ownership and low trust of outsiders leads to an autocratic management style and close family control of diversification. In large East Asian firms, from Indonesian conglomerates to Korean *chaebols*, key management positions were, and still are, reserved for relatives and family members. In Japan, social values and attitude to the family is different from China and is not defined in biological terms. Instead, there is a far stronger influence of Confucian philosophy where family is defined as those who contribute to the economic welfare of the group or 'ie' (Morikawa, 2001).

The variety in the motivations and behaviours found internationally within family firms is further reflected in the range of ownership and management structures adopted. Family objectives predominate in the stereotypical family firm which is closely-held, family owned, and managed with little outside influence or representation, and family objectives predominate. It has already been shown that trust and distrust, of people and of information, lie at the heart of family business research. These notions are captured by both Agency and Stewardship theory, though with differing emphases. Agency theorists would argue that this provides less potential for agency problems than in a firm where ownership and management are separate. However, there is evidence that some family firms employ strategies and procedures which would normally be used to control agency problems. A high percentage of family firms award performance-related pay incentives (Schulze et al., 2001), family firms employ non-executive directors (Westhead et al., 2001) and studies have highlighted family firms with distant/poor relationships between owners and managers and high information asymmetries (Howorth et al., 2004). This indicates that some family firms do experience agency problems and that the stereotypical family firm may occur less frequently than popularly expected.

One very simple model that is frequently used to throw some light on the information flows within family firms, is the widely accepted 'three circles model' (Gersick et al., 1997). In this model, the ownership, management and family influences within family firms are represented as three overlapping circles. Individuals who influence a family firm may belong to one or more of the three circles. Entrepreneurs who founded the family firm are usually members of all three groups and they are placed at the centre of the model where all three circles overlap. However, some individuals could be members of only one group and they will be placed in one of the outer segments of the model. This provides potential for information asymmetries and agency problems (Randoy and Goel, 2003). For example, if decisions regarding the firm are discussed by the family around the dinner table, owners and/or managers who are not family members will have an informational disadvantage. Howorth et al. (2004) provide evidence of exclusion from information and decision-making, in different family firms, for individuals in all three of the outer segments of the three circles model: owners, managers or family members. In some cases individuals were members of two of the groups (e.g. owner and family member) and still suffered from information asymmetries.

This highlights that agency theory is not as 'silent' (Arthurs and Busenitz, 2003) in family firms as might popularly be assumed and in fact examination of agency issues assist in understanding variations in ownership and management structures. Agency theory is based on assumptions of financial motivation and individuals who are self-serving. And yet, in family firms there may be motivations that cannot be measured financially as well as individuals who put the organization (either the family or the family firm) before their own interests. Recent studies have highlighted that stewardship theory may be a helpful framework within which to explore private family firms (Zahra et al., 2003). Stewardship theory is underpinned by assumptions of non-financial objectives and individuals that are organization-serving. Specifically, stewardship theory suggests managers' and employees' motives are aligned to those of the organization (Davis et al., 1997), but it does not assume financial goals or economic rationality. Of particular relevance to family firms is the way in which altruism is handled. Schulze et al. (2003) suggest that altruism is a major characteristic of relationships within family firms. Where the agency theory assumption of economic rationality would predict that altruism carries an expectation of some return, stewardship theory can encompass pure altruism, which is selfless. Thus, in the stereotypical family firm, stewardship theory would expect behaviour which puts the organization first, a strong psychological ownership of the family firm (Pierce et al., 2001), and a high occurrence of altruism (Casson, 1999).

Westhead and Howorth (2004) argue that agency and stewardship theories are complementary and they use them together in a conceptual framework to identify different types of family firms based on ownership structure, management structure and objectives. Westhead and Howorth (2004) empirically identify seven different 'types' of family firms. Approximately half of the family firms in their sample conform to the stereotypical picture of a firm, which has closely held ownership, is family managed and focuses on family objectives. The remaining family firms had varying degrees of family ownership and management, and showed different patterns of objectives that were important to them. The stereotypical or 'average' family firms, not unsurprisingly, showed average levels of performance based on various indicators including measures of financial performance, sales and growth and a weighted average performance measure, which assesses satisfaction with performance against objectives. Better and worse performances were associated with small groups of outlying family firm types. However, the types of family firms identified by Westhead and Howorth have not yet been tested in a wider context. Our earlier discussion indicates the importance of further research to assess the validity of their model in different cultural, national and development contexts.

As not all family firms conform to the stereotypical image this confirms that different types of family firms exist. There may be variations in the level of family ownership and control. Poutziouris (2001) identified that 65 percent of family firms in his sample held 100 percent of the ownership within a single family. Dilution of ownership will provide a different dynamic as non-family members are allowed to shape development of the firm and its objectives. The diversity seen in family firms is therefore closely linked to patterns of development. Earlier conceptualizations suggested that family firms were a stage in the development of firms (Chandler,

1977). However, we have shown that family firms exist in all sizes and different types. It is therefore imperative that the development of family firms is examined and, in particular, the succession from one generation to the next. Multi-generation family firms may differ considerably from first generation family firms (Westhead et al., 2002a) as motivations change with each generation. For example, later generations may be less motivated towards business growth in comparison to the founder generation. On the other hand, a new generation of owners may inject new life into the family firm and/or take it in a different direction. Succession can thus provide an important motivation for the identification and exploitation of new entrepreneurial opportunities.

9.4 Development of the Family Firm: Intergenerational Succession

Intergenerational succession represents a crucial inflexion point in the history of any family firm and as such has been a primary focus for research. Succession is closely linked to objectives of continuing survival and independent ownership. Many studies cite the fact that the majority of family firms do not survive into second or third generations of the family. It should be noted, however, that family firms are not extraordinary in this, as the majority of firms generally do not survive the equivalent of one generation, for example, 25 years. Nevertheless, there are notable exceptions where family firms have survived for many generations, some of which, like Ford, are household names and have a long history of pursuing innovation and new opportunities. It is useful to study these exceptional cases to determine factors that may encourage their longevity and good performance. In this way theory can be developed which may then be tested more generally on entrepreneurs outside the family firm context. Qualitative research methods have proven very useful in this respect. In particular, business historians have been able to track the performance and development of individual family firms over time and they have explored why a few family firms survive. They have demonstrated the way in which accumulated wealth could allow established family business owners to diversify, allowing them to build a portfolio of investments which reduced risk (Rose, 1986, 1994).

Succession can take family firms in different directions so that structures will vary and objectives might change. For example, there is compelling evidence that family firms vary in the way the ownership structure changes as it goes through different stages of succession. Three main forms of family firms' ownership structure have been identified and labelled 'controlling owner' (usually represented by a mother and/or father figure), 'sibling partnership' (ownership is shared between brothers and/or sisters) and 'cousin consortium' (ownership is shared among cousins who may be sons and daughters of members of a sibling partnership) (Gersick et al., 1997; Lansberg, 1999). The most common succession route is evolutionary wherein the ownership structure of the family firm evolves from a 'controlling owner' to a 'sibling partnership' to a 'cousin consortium'. Obviously the complexity of the ownership structure increases at each stage of evolutionary succession as ownership of the firm is diluted and a larger number of individuals become involved. However, not all family firms follow this succession route. In the 'recycled business form', ownership changes but stays in the same form, for example, from one sibling partnership to another sibling partnership. 'Devolutionary succession' occurs where ownership becomes more concentrated and complexity is reduced, for example, from a cousin consortium to a sibling partnership. As in any firm, moving from a diluted to a more concentrated ownership structure requires a high level of liquidity and this is one of the major reasons why succession is less frequently observed to occur in this direction. While these are the three main succession routes, over a number of stages or generations any permutation of movements in any direction between and along the three routes is possible, providing potential for wide diversity in the influences on development and structure of the family firms.

Firms that are more successful at negotiating the succession hurdle plan for succession well in advance, train and prepare successors and successees for the transition, and have good communication channels between all the various parties, that is, the three 'circles' involved in ownership, management and family decisions. Researchers commonly seek to identify the managerial analysis, strategies and tactics that support transition (Barach et al., 1988; Handler, 1991; Fox et al., 1997; Morris et al., 1997; Stavrou, 1999). Dyer and Handler (1994) explore the overlap between entrepreneurship and family business at various nexus points: early experiences in the entrepreneur's family of origin, family involvement and support in early start-up, employment of family members in the new venture and the involvement of family members in ownership and management succession. They propose 'entrepreneurial succession' as an area for research and theory development. After consideration of possible research approaches to 'a complex dynamic process like succession', they suggest in-depth case studies to generate theories that are well grounded and which can take into account the unique characteristics of succession processes.

In some of the literature, the succession process and therefore the survival of the firm are perceived to be threatened by family values and goals (Davis, 1968; Levinson, 1971). Clearly, the fact that family firms' goals can be broad and legitimately encompass family as well as business objectives (Donckels and Frohlich, 1991;

Chua et al., 2003; Leenders and Waarts, 2003) is one of the main differentiators between family and non-family firms, and it is what makes family firms such an interesting topic of study. In the stereotypical family firm, it is expected that objectives will focus on maintaining family control and independence, rather than establishing ownership and management structures that encourage superior firm performance (Upton et al., 2001). Where members of the same family wholly own a firm, it is perfectly legitimate to allow objectives relevant to the family system, rather than the business, to take precedence (Chua et al., 2003; Leenders and Waarts, 2003). Where there is an element of ownership by outside investors (i.e. non-family members) there may be less emphasis on family objectives and greater emphasis on business performance. Similarly, where the board of directors are all family members, family agendas may predominate (Morris et al., 1996) but where more of the directors and managers are non-family members there may be less emphasis on family objectives. Successful leadership succession may involve change in attitudes as well as leader, while building upon past foundations. This can involve bringing in outsiders which can affect both the chemistry and the dynamics of the firm and may affect the flow of information within the firm. Outsiders will provide the family firm with additional resources, especially access to different networks and expertise, which may lead to new opportunities and improved performance. Nevertheless, in the majority of family firms the CEO is a family member (Kelly et al., 2000) and only a small percentage employ non-executive directors (Westhead et al., 2001).

9.5 Women, succession and the development of the family business

A further aspect of the family dynamic in family firms, one which was alluded to earlier, is the influence of individuals who are family members but not part of the ownership or management groups. Research by Hamilton (2005) has highlighted in particular, that women frequently play a powerful role behind the scenes in developing family businesses. Her research also showed that women are often involved in founding and running family businesses. And yet, the role of women in family business is relatively under-investigated. Consequently, the term 'invisible' or 'hidden' is often used to describe the role of women in family businesses (Marshack, 1994; Mulholland, 1996a, 1996b; Dhaliwal, 1998; Baines and Wheelock, 1999; Ogbor, 2000; Poza and Messer, 2001; Colli et al., 2003). The relative silence and invisibility of women in family business research is a product of social, economic and historical factors. The majority of the entrepreneurship and family business literature assumes that understanding processes of founding and leading a business should focus on an individual 'owner manager' who is assumed to be the entrepreneur. The individual, usually identified as male, is most commonly the focus of research. The 'invisibility' of the women contributes towards, and reinforces, a dominant discourse of entrepreneurship, which has been described as individualistic, gender biased and discriminatory (Ogbor, 2000; Hamilton and Smith, 2003; Nicholson and Anderson, 2005). This discourse is dominated by the narrative of the heroic male. Ogbor (2000) argues that the traditional discourse in entrepreneurship acts as a technique of sustaining the power and domination of a 'monolithic' knowledge (p. 629). It prevents any understanding of entrepreneurial diversity by remaining uncritical of the social, cultural, and institutional forces shaping the pattern and development of entrepreneurship in contemporary society. Women do exert great influence on the development of family businesses, both behind the scenes and in founding and running family businesses (Colli et al., 2003; Hamilton, 2005). Gendered and stereotypical assumptions about women participating in family business serve to reinforce and perpetuate entrepreneurship as a male construct and limit our understanding of entrepreneurship and entrepreneurial behaviour in its many forms and contexts.

Others recognize the complex dynamic between the family and the business from an intergenerational perspective (Stavrou, 1999; Le Breton-Miller et al., 2004; Hamilton, 2005). Succession, some say, involves forms of intergenerational learning leading to an entrepreneurial legacy passed from one generation to the next, a core element of which is the shared values of the family (Rose, 1993; Hamilton, 2002).

9.6 So are family firms really different?

This chapter has surveyed the state of family business research exploring the nuances of definition, the diversity of family business behaviour through space and time and the process of change captured through intergenerational transition. All elements are intertwined and, ironically, the route through succession chosen by some family firms can disqualify them from being defined as family firms. This highlights the blurring of boundaries between family and non-family firms and the difficulties in defining family firms. In some cases, potential successors are not interested in continuing the family firm. In other cases, there are no potential family successors, and in some family firms there is no intention to pass the firm on to members of the family. Alternatives to intergenerational succession include selling the company through a trade sale, management buy-in or management buy-out, listing the company, or liquidation. While family firms research has traditionally focused on intergenerational succession, recent studies have highlighted the adoption of alternatives (Howorth et al., 2004) although frequencies have yet to be quantified.

The inconclusive and often convoluted discussion of definition has slowed down the progress of family business research. Yet the broad benchmark definition given at the beginning of this chapter is unequivocal—family firms are owned and controlled by families who may, to a greater or lesser degree behave differently from other firms. Recently, Westhead and Howorth (2004) have examined the performance of family firms and their evidence indicates that it is closely associated with the balance of family and non-family objectives alongside the ownership and management structures of family firms. Also, the three factors may be inter-related. While all firms are likely to have multiple objectives, family firms are generally thought to be less likely to place a high priority on profitability or increasing shareholder wealth in comparison to non-family firms. Some family firms place greatest emphasis on keeping the firm within the family and will focus their efforts on ensuring intergenerational succession and employment of family members. Other family firms are more interested in the size and/or status of the firm. Still others focus on maintaining independent ownership of the firm (Poutziouris, 2001). And we have seen that, contrary to popular belief, a significant number of family firms do focus on improving indicators of their financial performance (Smyrnios and Romano, 1994).

This highlights that the reason researchers have found it difficult to compare the performance of family firms against non-family firms could be due to the wide diversity within the population of family firms. Clearly the objectives of family firms vary and this will affect their performance. For example, family firms which focus on financial performance indicators are likely to have better financial results. Family firms that focus on family objectives may have less impressive financial results in the short term but may perform better in terms of longevity. Family firms that focus on independence objectives may constrain the growth of the firm by avoiding external sources of equity. Moreover, there may be differences depending on the stage of the family firm's development. Owners of multi-generation firms may not have the same entrepreneurial drive as first generation founders of the family firm and this may result in poorer performance for multi-generation family firms. Clearly, the issues of diversity, definition and development underpin any attempt to assess the performance of family firms. Family firms may be efficient, but they are not efficient per se, as much depends on the specific national context and surrounding conditions (Church, 1993; Poutziouris and Chittenden, 1996; Colli and Rose, 1999; Whitley, 2000; James and Kobrak, 2004).

The key to the difference between family and non-family business lies less in performance than in the overlapping culture of family and business. Family firms are not alone in laying emphasis on their history and tradition—for tradition lies at the core of many modern food and drink brands. Indeed perusal of modern websites demonstrates that a number of past or non-family firms place considerable emphasis on their heritage. Some firms—including, for instance, Du Pont—perpetuate the legends of the family long after family ownership has ceased. It is, however, the genuine overlap between family and business that makes family firms different. Families, with their shared histories and experience, are often inseparable from their businesses, and the failure of the business is rather like a death in the family. It is the coincidence of family and business attitudes that makes succession so traumatic in family firms, magnified as it can be by the emotional and psychological pressures of family life.

The conflict sometimes accompanying succession sits somewhat uneasily with the altruism often associated with family business. This stems from loyalty and commitment between family members and, it is expected that parents will be altruistic towards their offspring (Becker, 1981). However, the very features that make family firms different—the centrality of family—can undermine altruism, turning it to conflict. Information flows in an altruistic environment may also be compounded by biases and filters (Bergstrom, 1989). Biases occur when information is interpreted in a biased manner depending on the preconceptions of the receiver. Filters occur when information which is contrary to the receiver's preconceptions is either ignored or given lower credence. Biases and filtering of information is quite commonly observed within the relationship of parents and their offspring and thus also within family firms. Balancing family and business values is therefore crucial to the development of, and identity of, family firms. Problems can arise because ownership and management are performance-driven systems whereas the family is a relationship-based system. Thus, decisions may be made based on family values and emotional ties rather than on financial or economic performance criteria. To understand the development of the family firm and what makes it different we really need to understand the family dynamic.

9.7 Conclusions and the Way Ahead

Family business research has progressed massively in the last 20 years. This is illustrated by the launch of the journal *Family Business Review* in 1988, its emergence becoming a core area in business history; and the appearance of Special

Issues on family firms in the two journals, the *Journal of Business Venturing* and *Entrepreneurship: Theory and Practice* in 2003, 2004 and 2005. A recent article by Sharma surveyed 217 refereed articles relating to the subject of family business. The article concluded that while considerable progress had been made in the rigorous use of theory, attention had been given to family firms and their performance but their internal organization had been relatively neglected (Sharma, 2004). There are, however, other potential areas for future progress. This chapter has revealed that family firms are not a homogeneous group; they look and behave differently in different cultures and even different families. This suggests that an important way forward for family business research is the analysis of the sources and consequences of these differences.

A research agenda based on diversity has methodological and disciplinary implications. We have shown that family firm behaviour is moulded not just by business considerations but also by the institutional and value systems which surround it. These in turn are underpinned by a range of historical, sociological, economic and political forces. The wider use of multidisciplinary approaches to family business, combined with internationally comparative studies, drawing heavily on the wide business history literature, would enormously increase our understanding of the evolution of contemporary family business and its capabilities. Interestingly, the first issue of *Family Business Review* was prefaced by a historical article by Peter Hall, signalling an awareness that history matters to family business studies. Yet this proved to be short-lived and there has been remarkably little interaction between the many business historians working on family business and those engaged in mainstream work in either entrepreneurship or family business.

We have already learned a lot about family business which can be transferred into alternative contexts, for example, factors associated with successful succession. There is still much more to learn. We have highlighted that understanding influences on the longevity of some family businesses would be valuable to entrepreneurship researchers as well as more widely. This includes an understanding of success factors associated with knowledge transfer between successors and successees and the development of entrepreneurial learning through the generations. Family business research also recognizes the value of learning which occurs within the family and outside the business context. A focus on intergenerational aspects of succession invites questions about the nature of the influences between the generations in terms of learning about the business, ways of working, understanding how to operate—the 'practice' of the family business. The potential for exploring theoretical links suggests that it would be useful to examine the engagement of the two generations in the same business, and the process of succession in the light of recent work in entrepreneurial learning (Costello, 1996: Deakins, 1996; Gibb, 1997; Deakins and Freel, 1998; Rae and Carswell, 2000; Rae, 2000; Cope, 2003, 2005). For example, early work in the entrepreneurship field highlighted that entrepreneurs were more likely to have a family background of entrepreneurship. It would be useful to examine how this is associated with entrepreneurial learning occurring within the family and transfer of key skills such as opportunity alertness between generations. Hoy and Verser (1994) highlight a number of key research areas linked to the concept of intergenerational learning and influence. For example, they point to the transfer of the owner's vision to other family members, sustaining the innovativeness of the founder, intergenerational strategic thinking, and the influence of the family's values and priorities on the nature of the firm.

Family business research can have a sustained impact on the wider field of entrepreneurship but it is vital to confirm where family firms are really different from non-family firms and how far such differences impact on performance. Comparisons and contrasts between firm culture, objectives and values appear to be more relevant than arbitrary degrees of family ownership and management, but these are more difficult concepts to tie down and lend themselves less easily to measurement.

Some have proposed a broader view of family and enterprise, a stronger link between the dynamics of the family and the workplace (McCollom, 1988; Baines and Wheelock, 1997; Fletcher, 2000; Johanisson and Huse, 2000). Stafford et al. (1999) proposed what they call a research model of sustainable family business which recognizes that both the family and business systems are critical. The key feature of the model is that it draws attention to the overlap between the family and the business, and the importance of the interface between the two. Emotional relationships and relational goals are as important as business and economic goals in the family firm (Cramton, 1993). There have been calls for more studies 'connecting family systems and entrepreneurial phenomena' (Aldrich and Cliffe, 2003: 575) acknowledging that the family, the business and entrepreneurship are inextricably linked.

References

Albert, M. (1991). *Capitalisme contre capitalisme.* Paris: Editions du Seuil.

Aldrich, H. E. and J. E. Cliffe (2003). 'The Pervasive Effects of Family on Entrepreneurship: Toward a Family Embeddedness Perspective'. *Journal of Business Venturing*, 18(5): 573–8.

Ampalavanar Brown, R. (ed.) (1995). *Chinese Business Enterprise in Asia.* London: Routledge.

Amsden, Alice H. (1989). *Asia's Next Giant.* New York and Oxford: Oxford University Press.

Arthurs, J. D. and L. W. Busenitz (2003). 'The Boundaries and Limitations of Agency Theory and Stewardship Theory in the Venture Capitalist/Entrepreneur Relationship'. *Entrepreneurship Theory and Practice*, 28(2): 145–62.

Bagchi, A. H. (1972). *Private Investments in India, 1900–1939*. Cambridge: Cambridge University Press.

Baines, S. and J. Wheelock (1999). 'A Business in the Family: An Investigation of the Contribution of Family to Small Business Survival, Maintenance and Growth'. *Institute for Small Business Affairs*, Research Series, Monograph No. 3.

Barach, J. A., J. Gantisky, J. A. Carson and B. A. Doochin (1988). 'Entry of the Next Generation: Strategic Challenge for Family Business'. *Journal of Small Business Management* (April), pp. 49–56.

Becker, G. S. (1981). *A Treatise on the Family*. Cambridge, MA: Harvard University Press.

Ben Porath, Y. (1980). 'The F-Connection: Families, Friends and Firms and the Organisation of Exchange'. *Population and Development Review*, 6(1): 1–30.

Bergstrom, T. C. (1989). 'A Fresh Look at the Rotten Kid Theorem and Other Household Mysteries'. *Journal of Political Economy*, 97: 1138–59.

Brockhaus, Sr., R. H. (1994). 'Entrepreneurship and Family Business Research: Comparisons, Critique, and Lessons'. *Entrepreneurship: Theory and Practice*, 19(1): 25–38.

Bygrave, W. and C. W. Hofer (1991). 'Theorising About Entrepreneurship'. *Entrepreneurship: Theory and Practice*, 15(4): 13–22.

Casson, M. (1982). *The Entrepreneur*. London: Mark Robertson.

—— (1991). *The Economics of Business Culture: Game Theory, Transaction Costs and Economic Performance*. Oxford: Oxford University Press.

—— (1993). 'Entrepreneurship and Business Culture', in J. Brown and M. B. Rose (eds) *Entrepreneurship, Networks and Modern Business*. Manchester: Manchester University Press.

—— (1999). 'The Economics of Family Firms'. *Scandinavian Economic History Review*, XLVII: 20–3.

Chandler, Sr., A. D. (1997). *The Visible Hand: The Managerial Revolution in America*. Cambridge: Cambridge University Press.

Chua, J. H., J. J. Chrisman and P. Sharma (1999). 'Defining the Family Business by Behavior'. *Entrepreneurship: Theory and Practice*, 23(4): 19–39.

—— J. J. Chrisman and L. P. Steier (2003). 'Extending the Theoretical Horizons of Family Business Research.' *Entrepreneurship: Theory and Practice*, 27(4): 331–8.

Church, R. (1993). 'The Family Firm in Industrial Capitalism : International Perspectives on Hypotheses and History'. *Business History*, XXXV, (4): 17–43.

Colli, A. (1998). 'Networking the Market: Evidence and Conjectures from the History of the Italian Industrial Districts'. *European Yearbook of Business History*, 1: 75–92.

—— (2003). *The History of Family Business, 1850–2000*. Cambridge: Cambridge University Press.

—— and M. B. Rose (1999). 'Families and Firms: The Culture and Evolution of Family Firms in Britain and Italy in the Nineteenth and Twentieth Centuries'. *Scandinavian Economic History Review*, 47: 24–47.

—— P. Fernadez Perez and M. B. Rose (2003). 'National Determinants of Family Firm Development? Family Firms in Britain, Spain and Italy in the Nineteenth and Twentieth Centuries'. *Enterprise and Society*, 4(1): 28–64.

Cope, J. (2003). 'Entrepreneurial Learning and Critical Reflection: Discontinuous Events as Triggers for "Higher-level" Learning'. *Management Learning*, 34(4): 429–50.

—— (2005). 'Understanding Entrepreneurship through Phenomenological Inquiry: Philosophical and Methodological Issues.' *International Small Business Journal*, pp. 163–89.

COPE, J. (2005). 'Towards a Dynamic Learning Perspective of Entrepreneurship'. *Entrepreneurship: Theory and Practice*, XXX: 373–97.

COSTELLO, N. (1996). 'Learning and Routines in High-Tech SMEs: Analysing Rich Case Study Material'. *Journal of Economic Issues*, 30(2): 591–7.

CRAMTON, C. D. (1993). 'Is Rugged Individualism the Whole Story? Public and Private Accounts of a Firm's Founding'. *Family Business Review*, VI(3), 233–61.

DAVID, P. (1997). 'Path dependence: Putting the past into the Future of Economics', L. Magnusson and J. Ottosson (eds) *Evolutionary Economics and Path Dependence.* Cheltenham: Elgar.

DAVIS, S. M. (1968). 'Entrepreneurial Succession'. *Administrative Science Quarterly*, 13: 402–16.

DAVIS J., F. D. SCHOORMAN and L. DONALDSON (1997). 'Toward a Stewardship Theory of Management'. *Academy of Management Review*, 22(1): 20–47.

DEAKINS, D. (1996). *Entrepreneurship and Small Firms.* Maidenhead: McGraw-Hill.

—— and M. FREEL (1998). 'Entrepreneurial Learning and the Growth Process in SMEs'. *The Learning Organisation*, 5(3): 144–55.

DHALIWAL, S. (1998). 'Silent Contributors: Asian Female Entrepreneurs and Women in Business'. *Women's Studies International Forum*, 21(5): 463–74.

DONCKELS, R. and E. FRÖHLICH (1991). 'Are Family Businesses Really Different? European Experiences from STRATOS'. *Family Business Review*, 4(2): 149–60.

DYER, Jr., W. G. (1986). *Cultural Change in Family Firms: Anticipating and Managing Business and Family Transitions.* San Francisco: Jossey-Bass.

—— and W. HANDLER (1994). 'Entrepreneurship and Family Business: Exploring the Connections'. *Entrepreneurship: Theory and Practice*, 19(1): 71–83.

DUTTA, S. (1997). *Family Business in India.* New Delhi: Response Books.

FIELD, M. L. (1984). *The Merchants.* London: John Murray.

FLETCHER, D. (2000). 'Family and Enterprise', in S. Carter and D. Jones-Evans (eds) *Enterprise and Small Business: Principle, Practice and Policy.* Harlow: Pearson Education.

FOX, M. V. NILAKANT and R. T. HAMILTON (1997). 'Managing Succession in Family-Owned Business'. *International Small Business Journal*, 15(1): 15–25.

FRUIN, W. M. (1980). 'The Family as Firm and the Firm as a family: The Case of Kikkoman Shōyu Company Limited'. *Journal of Family History*, 5(4): 432–49.

GARTNER, W. B. (1985). 'A Conceptual Framework for Describing the Phenomenon of New Venture Creation'. *Academy of Management Review*, 10(4): 696–706.

—— (1988). '"Who is an entrepreneur?" Is the wrong question'. *American Journal of Small Business*, 13(1): 11–32.

GERSICK, K. E., J. A. DAVIS, M. MCCOLLOM HAMPTON and I. LANSBERG (1997). *Generation to Generation: Life Cycles of the Family Business.* Cambridge, MA: Harvard Business School Press.

GIBB, A. A. (1997). 'Small Firms' Training and Competitiveness. Building upon the Small Business as a Learning Organisation'. *International Small Business Journal*, 15(3): 13–29.

HAMILTON, E. (2002). 'One lifetime is not enough: stories of intergenerational influence and succession in family business', 25th Institute for Small Business Affairs National Small Firms Policy and Research Conference, Brighton.

—— (2005). Situated Learning in Family Business: Narratives from Two Generations. Unpublished PhD Lancaster University.

Hamilton, E. and R. Smith (2003). 'The Entrepreneuse: A Silent Entrepreneurial Narrative', in *Small Business and Entrepreneurship Development Conference*, University of Surrey, 4 March to 4 April, pp. 183–92.

Handler, W. C. (1991). 'Key Interpersonal Relationships of Next-Generation Family Members in Family Firms'. *Journal of Small Business Management* (July), pp. 21–32.

Hau, M. (1995). 'Traditions comportamentales et capitalisme dynastique. Le cas des "grandes familles"'. *Entreprises et Histoire*, 9: 43–59.

Hattori, T. (1984). 'The Relationship Between Zaibatsu and Family Structure: The Korean Case', in A. Ochochi and S. Yasuoka (eds) *Family Business in the Era of Industrial Growth*. Tokyo: Tokyo University Press.

Hofstede, G. (1994). *Cultures and Organizations: Intercultural Co-operation and its importance to Survival: Software of the Mind*. London: Harper Collins.

Howorth, C. and Z. A. Ali (2001). 'Family Business Succession in Portugal'. *Family Business Review*, 14(3): 231–44.

—— P. Westhead and M. Wright (2004). 'Buyouts, Information Asymmetry and the Family-Management Dyad'. *Journal of Business Venturing*, 19(4): 509–34.

Hoy, F. and T. G. Verser (1994). 'Emerging Business, Emerging Field: Entrepreneurship and the Family Firm'. *Entrepreneurship: Theory and Practice*, 19(1): 9–23.

IFERA (2003). 'Family Businesses Dominate: International Family Enterprise Research Academy (IFERA)'. *Family Business Review*, 16(4): 235–40.

James, H. and C. Kobrak (2004). 'Persistent Traditions: Family Business in Germany'. Working Paper quoted with permission of authors.

Johannisson, B. and M. Huse (2000). 'Recruiting Outside Board Members in the Small Family Business: And Ideological Challenge'. *Entrepreneurship and Regional Development*, 12: 353–78.

Kelly, L. M., N. Athanassiou and W. F. Crittenden (2000). 'Founder Centrality and Strategic Behavior in the Family-Owned Firm'. *Entrepreneurship Theory and Practice*, 25(2): 27–42.

Lansberg, I. (1999). *Succeeding Generations: Realizing the Dream of Families in Business*. Boston, MA: Harvard Business School Press.

Le Breton-Miller, I., D. Miller and L. P. Steier (2004). 'Towards and Integrative Model of Effective FOB Succession'. *Entrepreneurship: Theory and Practice*, 28(4): 305–28.

Leenders, M. and E. Waarts (2003). 'Competitiveness and Evolution of Family Businesses: The Role of Family and Business Orientation'. *European Management Journal*, 21(6): 686–97.

Levinson, H. (1971). 'Conflicts that Plague Family Businesses'. *Harvard Business Review* (March–April), pp. 90–8.

Litz, R. A. (1995). 'The Family Business: Towards Definitional Clarity'. *Proceedings of the Academy of Management*. Best papers, Entrepreneurship, pp. 100–104.

Marshack, K. J. (1994). 'Copreneurs and Dual-Career Couples: Are They Different?' *Entrepreneurship: Theory and Practice*, 19(1): 49–69.

McCollom, M. E. (1988). 'Integration in the Family Firm'. *Family Business Review*, 1(4): 399–417.

Morikawa, H. (2001). *A History of Top Management in Japan: Managerial Enterprises and Family Enterprises*. Tokyo: University of Tokyo Press.

Morris, M. H., R. O. Williams, J. A. Allen and R. A. Avila (1997). 'Correlates of Success in Family Business Transitions'. *Journal of Business Venturing*, 12: 385–401.

MORRIS, M. H., R. W. WILLIAMS and D. NELL (1996). 'Factors influencing family business succession'. *International Journal of Entrepreneurial Behaviour & Research*, 2(3): 68–81.

MULHOLLAND, K. (1996a). 'Gender and Property Relations within Entrepreneurial Wealthy Families'. *Gender, Work and Organisation*, 3(2): 78–102.

—— (1996b). 'Entrepreneurialism, Masculinities and the Self-made Man', in D. L. Collinson and J. Hearn (eds) *Men as Managers, Managers as Men, Critical Perspectives on Men, Masculinities and Managements*. London: Sage.

NATZIGER, E. W. (1969). 'The Effect of the Nigerian Extended Family on Entrepreneurial Activity'. *Economic Development and Cultural Change*, 18(1): 25–33.

NEUBAUER, F. and A. G. LANK (1998). *The Family Business: Its Governance for Sustainability*. Basingstoke: Macmillan Press Ltd.

NICHOLSON, L. and A. R. ANDERSON (2005). 'News and Nuances of the Entrepreneurial Myth and Metaphor: Linguistic Games in Entrepreneurial Sense-making and Sense-giving'. *Entrepreneurship: Theory and Practice*, 29(2): 153–72.

OGBOR, J. O. (2000). 'Mythicizing and Reification in Entrepreneurial Discourse: Ideology-Critique of Entrepreneurial Studies'. *Journal of Management Studies* (July) 37(5): 605–35.

PIERCE, J. L., T. KOSTOVA and K. T. DIRKS (2001). 'Toward a Theory of Psychological Ownership in Organizations'. *Academy of Management Review*, 26(2): 298–310.

POLLAK, R. A. (1985). 'A Transaction Cost Approach to Families and Households'. *Journal of Economic Literature*, 23: 581–608.

POUTZIOURIS, P. Z. (2001). 'The Views of Family Companies on Venture Capital: Empirical Evidence from the UK Small to Medium-size Enterprising Economy'. *Family Business Review*, 14(3): 277–91.

—— and CHITTENDEN, F. (1996). 'Family Businesses or Business Families?', *ISBA Research Series Monograph 1*. Leeds: The Institute for Small Business Affairs.

POZA, E. J. and T. MESSER (2001). 'Spousal Leadership and Continuity in the Family Firm'. *Family Business Review*, XIV(1): 25–36.

RAE, D. (2000). 'Understanding Entrepreneurial Learning: A Question of How?' *International Journal of Entrepreneurial Behaviour and Research*, 6(3): 145–59.

—— and M. CARSWELL (2000). 'Using a Life-story Approach in Researching Entrepreneurial Learning: The Development of a Conceptual Model and its Implications in the Design of Learning Experiences'. *Education and Training*, 42(4/5): 220–7.

RANDOY, T. and S. GOEL (2003). 'Ownership Structure, Founder Leadership, and Performance in Norwegian SMEs: Implications for Financing Entrepreneurial Opportunities'. *Journal of Business Venturing*, 18(5): 619–37.

RAY, R. (1979). *Industrialisation in India*. New Delhi: Oxford University Press.

REDDING, S. G. (1990). *The Spirit of Chinese Capitalism*. Berlin: de Gruyter.

ROSE, M. B. (1986). *The Gregs of Quarry Bank Mill: The Rise and Decline of a Family Firm*. Cambridge: Cambridge University Press.

—— (1993). 'Beyond Buddenbrooks: The Management of Family Business Succession' in J. Brown and M. B. Rose (eds), *Entrepreneurship, Networks and Modern Business* 9. Manchester: Manchester University Press.

—— (1994). 'The Family Firm in British Business, 1780–1914' in M. W. Kirby and M. Rose. *Business Enterprise in Modern Britain: From the Eighteenth to the Twentieth Century*. London: Routledge.

—— (2000). *Firms, Networks and Business Values: The British and American Cotton Industries since 1750*. Cambridge: Cambridge University Press.

SCHULZE, W. S., M. H. LUBATKIN and R. N. DINO (2003). 'Toward a Theory of Agency and Altruism in Family Firms'. *Journal of Business Venturing*, 18(4): 473–90.

—— —— —— and A. K. BUCHHOLTZ (2001). 'Agency Relationships in Family Firms: Theory and Evidence'. *Organization Science*, 12(2): 99–116.

SHARMA, P. (2004). 'An Overview of the Field of Family Business Studies: Current Status and Directions for the Future'. *Family Business Review*, XVII(1): 1–36.

SHAVER, K. G. and L. R. SCOTT (1991). 'Person, Process, Choice: The Psychology of New Venture Creation'. *Entrepreneurship, Theory and Practice*, 16(2): 23–45.

SMYRNIOS, K. and ROMANO, C. (1994). *The Price Waterhouse/Commonwealth Bank Family Business Survey 1994*. Sydney: Department of Accounting, Monash University.

STAFFORD, K., K. A. DUNCAN, S. DANES and M. WINTER (1999). 'A Research Model of Sustainable Family Business'. *Family Business Review*, XII(3): 197–208.

STAVROU, E. T. (1999). 'Succession in Family Business'. *Journal of Small Business Management*, 37(3): 43–61.

TIMBERG, T. A. (1978). *The Marwaris: From Traders to Industrialists*. Bombay: Asia Publishing House.

UPTON, N, E. J. TEAL and J. T. FELAN (2001). 'Strategic and Business Planning Practices of Fast Growth Family Firms'. *Journal of Small Business Management*, 39(1): 60–72.

WESTHEAD, P. and M. COWLING (1998). 'Family Firm Research: The Need for a Methodological Rethink'. *Entrepreneurship Theory and Practice* (Fall) 23: 31–56.

—— and (2004). 'Ownership and management structure, company objectives and performance: an empirical examination of family firms'. Paper presented at the International Family Enterprise Research Academy 4th Annual Research Conference. Jönköping International Business School, Sweden.

—— M. Cowling and C. HOWORTH (2001). 'The Development of Family Companies: Management and Ownership Issues'. *Family Business Review*, 14(4): 369–85.

—— —— and M. COWLING, (2002). 'Ownership and management issues in first and multi-generation family firms'. *Entrepreneurship and Regional Development*, 14(3): 247–69.

WHITLEY, R. (2000). *Divergent Capitalisms: Social Structuring and Change in Business Systems*. Oxford: Oxford University Press.

ZAHRA, S. A. (2003). 'International Expansion of U.S. Manufacturing Family Businesses: The Effect of Ownership and Involvement'. *Journal of Business Venturing*, 18(4): 495–512.

CHAPTER 10

EVALUATING SME POLICIES AND PROGRAMMES: TECHNICAL AND POLITICAL DIMENSIONS[1]

DAVID J. STOREY

10.1 Introduction

It is now recognized that governments spend considerable sums of taxpayers' money in seeking to enable Small and Medium-sized Enterprises (SMEs) to come into existence and to grow. For example, DTI (2002) shows that, in the UK, the annual total financial support for small business is equivalent to a public expenditure of £7.9 billion, the details of which are provided in Table 10.A1 in the Appendix. This comprises £5.3 billion of direct expenditure by government departments and their agents and £2.6 billion in terms of favourable tax

[1] An earlier version of this paper was produced for the OECD SME Working Party and presented at the Ministerial conference in Istanbul in June 2004. The author wishes to acknowledge the contributions made by country representatives to the development of that paper. Thanks go to the OECD

treatment for small firms. To contextualize that expenditure, each year the UK spends more taxpayers' money on small businesses than it spends on the police force.[2]

The simple justification for such expenditure is that SMEs are major sources of job creation, innovation and competitiveness in a modern economy and that it is governments' task to promote these characteristics in order to enhance the welfare of its citizens. However, this is not a sufficient justification since, if markets work perfectly, this will lead to a socially optimal number of smaller firms. Indeed government intervention to promote small firms could have undesirable consequences such as 'crowding out' or to taxes being raised to pay for bureaucrats to administer 'assistance' programmes that are ineffective. Instead, government intervention has to be justified on the grounds of market failure, four of which have been identified by the current author (Storey, 2003). The four are: imperfect information on the private benefits of starting a business; imperfect information on the private benefits of obtaining external advice; the inability of financial institutions to accurately assess the risks of SMEs; the presence of externalities.

In practice, governments throughout the world have many different policies to address these market failures. Some provide finance directly[3] and/or indirectly;[4] some provide, and others finance the provision of, business advice to SMEs. Some governments also try to increase the rate of start-up of new firms, through measures such as grants, tax relief and educational programmes.[5] Many examples of these policies are provided by the current author in an earlier work (Storey, 2003).

The current chapter is primarily focused on further developing one of the themes of the above paper—that of the political economy of evaluating the impact of SME policies. It reaches five key conclusions. First, that evaluation needs to become more central to the policy-making process. Evaluation should not be undertaken solely as a historic accounting exercise to determine whether public

Secretariat staff, particularly Marie-Florence Estime. The current version of the paper has benefited considerably from the many helpful comments received from Mark Casson and those attending the workshop at Reading, 22–3 April, 2005. The views expressed in the paper, however, remain those of the author alone.

[2] Because DTI (2002) correctly seeks to include all public funding to SMEs, this estimate is orders of magnitude higher than previous estimates. For example, according to the European Commission State Aid Scoreboard in 2004, EU Member Sates spend approximately 6 billion Euros on state aid to SMEs, where state aid is defined by article 87(1) of the Treaty (EIM, 2004). The EU figure is clearly a huge underestimate of the scale of taxpayers funds devoted to SMEs.

[3] Examples include loans and grants.

[4] The best-known examples are Loan Guarantee Schemes in which government acts as part guarantor for loans made by commercial banks to SMEs that lack access to collateral (OECD, 1995).

[5] In the UK, Small Business Service (2004) has clearly sought to link market failures to policy intervention. It is also clear both about the objectives of policy and how the impact of the policy is to be assessed.

money has been spent wisely, although that role is of value. Instead of being, 'at the end of the line', evaluation should be used to inform current policy, so that current objectives and targets may be modified in the light of evidence of policy effectiveness. Hence considerations of how policy is evaluated should therefore be incorporated into policy formulation when new ideas are being developed. They could even influence the choices made by governments about how best to engage with SMEs. Specifically, evaluation has to be incorporated as a key element in policy development. Evaluation therefore cannot be undertaken in isolation; instead it has to be part of a package which comprises a clear justification for the policy, clear statements about the programme targets and clear statements about what constitutes success, and failure.

Second, all programmes and policies, rather than merely some, have to be assessed. This paper is however less clear about whether all programmes should be assessed with the same level of sophistication. The key argument in favour of a consistent level of sophistication is that this enables valid comparisons to be undertaken between one programme and another. The argument against it is that it is inappropriate to have similar evaluation budgets for programmes of widely differing scales.

Third, the paper demonstrates that it is now technically possible to provide accurate measures of programme impact. It shows, through its 'Six Steps to Heaven' approach that, although there are examples of the most sophisticated approach being used, these continue to be the exception rather than the rule. The cause for concern is that the less sophisticated approaches tend to provide misleading answers, most frequently over-estimating policy impact. There is, therefore, a concern that those favouring certain programmes have an incentive to ensure the cheaper and less sophisticated approaches are adopted.

Its fourth key conclusion is that, where appropriate, the most sophisticated—Step V or Step VI—approaches are to be used. The key limitation of the 'Six Steps' approach—that it is appropriately applied to assessing the impact of individual programmes and policies rather than that of SME and Entrepreneurship policy in total—is also recognized.

Finally, in undertaking SME policy evaluations, it is necessary to be aware of the potential for conflict between the interested parties. Ideally, those undertaking the evaluations need to be independent of those responsible for the programmes, as in any audit role. But, if a key role of the evaluation is to contribute to making continuous improvements in policy, then the evaluators need the active co-operation and involvement of both policy-makers and deliverers. This may be more difficult to achieve if the evaluator is viewed as an 'outsider'. On balance, the paper concludes that the independence of the evaluator is of the greater importance, but this is a close call.

Prior to reviewing how SME policy initiatives are evaluated, it is helpful to understand why SME policy exists and why the policies pursued clearly vary from one economy to another. This is covered in the next section of the paper. We then move on to the key theme of evaluation, beginning with a case study of how this process has evolved in the UK.

10.2 SME and Entrepreneurship Policy

Lundstrom and Stevenson (2005) make an important distinction between SME policy and Entrepreneurship policy. SME policy instruments are focused upon existing businesses, so they include loans and grants or business advice. In this sense, SME policy is conventional, industrial or sector-based policy targeted towards smaller firms. Entrepreneurship policy, however, is focused on influencing the creation of new firms, so it focuses not on businesses but on individuals or groups of individuals. Examples of Entrepreneurship policy include 'enterprise-awareness' programmes in schools, colleges and universities. It also includes the provision of information and advice to those considering starting a business, often with a focus upon 'under-represented' groups such as young people, females or those from ethnic minorities.

While the distinction between SME and Entrepreneurship policy is an important one, the rationale for the existence of either policy must be based on evidence of market failure. For example, those seeking to persuade governments to use tax-payer's money to fund 'enterprise-awareness' campaigns need to show that, for some reason, the market provides a sub-optimal number of enterprises, and that intervention will lead to a cost-effective move towards optimality. The distinction between policies is clearly shown in Table 10.1 below. It takes examples or elements of both SME and Entrepreneurship policy.

Table 10.1 Elements common to SME policy and entrepreneurship policy

SME policy	Entrepreneurship policy
• Reducing red-tape and paperwork burden	• Reducing red-tape and paperwork burden
• Access to capital/financing	• Access to micro loans and seed funds
• Provision of information services	• Provision of information about start-up
• Export and marketing services	• Highlighting entrepreneurs as role models
• Provision of training and consultancy	• Entrepreneurship education
• Technology transfer	• Facilitating networking services

Source: Derived from Lundstrom and Stevenson (2005).

From Table 10.1 it is clear that a number of elements are common to both SME and Entrepreneurship policy, so the distinction made by Lundstrom and Stevenson is less clear cut than might initially appear. For example, both SME policy and entrepreneurship policy are concerned to minimize bureaucratic and paper-work burdens, although the precise nature of these burdens does vary sharply between start-ups and established businesses.

One illustration is that the bureaucratic burdens of establishing a limited company vary considerably from one country to another. As Djankov et al. (2002) show, the entrepreneur in Italy seeking to establish a new business, has to follow 16 different procedures, pay nearly US$4,000 in fees, and wait at least 62 days to acquire the necessary permits. In contrast, an entrepreneur in Canada can finish the process in two days by paying US$280 fees and completing only two procedures. Entrepreneurship policy may therefore legitimately focus upon seeking to lower these barriers to starting a business. In contrast, SME policy, which focuses upon established businesses, may seek to reduce regulatory burdens such as employment regulation on established firms. The World Bank (2005) shows, on an index of 100 with higher values implying more rigid regulation, Spain scores 69 and France 66, compared with the USA scoring 3 and Canada 4. This implies that the bureaucratic burdens on established small firms are considerably higher in Spain/France than in USA/Canada.

Nevertheless, although there is some overlap between SME and Entrepreneurship policies, the distinction made by Lundstrom and Stevenson does have validity. This is because taxpayers' funding for policies can either focus upon seeking to ease the process by which businesses are started—entrepreneurship policy—or on enhancing the performance of assisted firms—SME policy. Unsurprizingly, different

	LIMITING	COMPETING
Low direct assistance	[Developing Countries]	[USA]
	COMPENSATING	NURTURING
High direct assistance	[EU]	[US Minority]
	High impediments	Low impediments

Figure 10.1 A typology of public policy toward small business

Source: Dennis (2004).

countries make different choices about this balance of policies.[6] They also make different choices about the extent to which policies focus upon providing direct assistance and on lowering the 'burdens' or impediments. Dennis (2004), in Figure 10.1, makes the interesting distinction between the provision of assistance and the lowering of impediments.

He argues that policy-makers have four options. Most EU countries choose to have, by world standards, comparatively high impediments[7] to starting a business, as illustrated by Djankov et al. (2002). On the other hand, they also spent considerable sums of public money on supporting smaller enterprises, which can be considered as compensating for the impediments. For this reason, this box is labelled 'compensating'. These countries also seem to place relatively more emphasis on SME rather than Entrepreneurship policy.

A very different approach is adopted in the USA. Here the direct assistance is low, but so also are the barriers to starting a business. Competition is therefore seen as the focus of US policy and this box is labelled 'competing'. The US however, does have some exceptions to this—its programmes to promote the interests of

[6] Countries also change the focus of their policies over time, the clearest example being the UK. Greene et al. (2004) identify three periods of Enterprise policy in the UK. The 1970s can be considered as a 'policy-off' period; the 1980s can be considered as an active Entrepreneurship policy period in which the apparent objective was to convert the unemployed into small business owners. In contrast, the 1990s was an SME policy period in which attention focused upon identifying and helping small businesses with growth potential. Currently it appears that the UK is undergoing another policy change which might be called the 'Third Way'. As referred to in the next section, the UK government (Small Business Service 2004) has identified seven key areas of policy on which it wishes to focus. These areas combine both SME and Enterprise policy. Interestingly, however, the justification for Entrepreneurship policy is now very different from that in the 1980s. Then, it was that facilitating business creation would lead directly to lower unemployment. In the middle of the first decade of the twenty-first century, the social and economic justifications are very different. The social justification is based on the observation that some social groups—the young, women and some ethnic minorities—are less likely to be self-employed than mature white males. Policy therefore focuses on reducing barriers to enterprise amonge these low participation groups. The economic argument is that that new firms constitute a credible threat to existing business, leading to the exit of the inefficient, so enhancing productivity in the economy. Some evidence, at least for the manufacturing sector, is provided by Disney et al. (2003). They show that between 1980 and 1992 single-establishment firms experienced no productivity growth among survivors; instead all productivity gains came because the entrants were more productive than those that exited.

[7] The term 'impediments' is used, because it is the one used by Dennis. However the term clearly has negative connotations, implying perhaps that individuals are prevented from starting a business without good reason. Governments in countries with high 'impediments', however, justify these policies on the grounds that this provides protection for the consumer. For example all countries impose 'impediments' that prevent unqualified individuals establishing a business as a doctor or surgeon, whereas only some countries have similar restrictions on those wishing to start a business as an electrician or a driving instructor. 'Impediments' to entry into the medical profession are justified on the grounds that unqualified, and presumably incompetent, doctors could cause serious damage to patients/consumers. However, errors or incompetence on the part of an electrician or a driving instructor could also clearly endanger human life, yet the extent to which these individuals are 'impeded' from starting a business varies considerably from one country to another, depending upon the extent to which emphasis is placed on the desire to protect the consumer.

technology-based firms, and in the promotion of minorities. Here again the barriers are low but there is a high level of direct assistance provided. This is shown in the box labelled 'nurturing'.[8]

Finally, there are many countries where the barriers to starting a business are high, but where public assistance is low. This box is labelled as 'limiting' but contains often large numbers of less developed countries in Africa, South America and some former communist countries.

The above illustrates policy-makers do indeed have a wide choice on how, if at all, they wish to promote new and smaller enterprises. The interested reader can find more information on the US policies from Anderson (2004), Anglund (2002) and Bean (2001) for the US, and for Europe the EU Green Paper, (European Commission (2003)).

10.3 SME policy evaluation in practice: The UK context

We now move from a cross-country review of SME and Entrepreneurship policy to a case study of the UK, but with a clear focus on how evaluation has slowly become more central to policy formulation.

As noted earlier, a necessary, but not sufficient, condition for government intervention is evidence of market failure. In Storey (2003), the current author set out four market imperfections most relevant to SME policy. The first three relate to imperfect information, and the final one to a divergence between social and private returns.

1 Individuals do not realize (are ignorant of) the private benefits of starting a business. This is frequently used to justify 'entrepreneurship policies' such as the raising of enterprise awareness amongst young people.[9]
2 Owners of small firms do not fully appreciate the private benefits to their business of taking certain courses of action. Examples here include public

[8] The UK would also be in this box since, by the international standards of Djankov et al. (2002) it has low barriers to starting businesses, yet it has considerable sums of public money directed towards the SME sector.

[9] For a review see Davies, H (2002). This is certainly not to imply that the Davies review is an illustration of 'good practice' in evaluation, but merely that it does provide a recent review of the topic.

subsidies to promote SMEs to undertake more workforce training[10] or obtaining external advice from specialists or consultants.[11]

3 Financial institutions are unable to accurately assess the risk of lending to small firms, so denying some small firms access to funds and constraining their growth. To respond to this problem governments in many countries have introduced Loan Guarantee Schemes in which the state agrees to reimburse about 80 percent of bank losses.[12]

4 There are some SME policies that reflect the divergence between private and social benefits. The best examples relate to policies to promote innovation in small firms. Here it is argued that, without subsidies, there would be a socially sub-optimal formation and growth of technology-based firms.[13]

These generally-recognized market failures, at least in the academic literature, provide a helpful context to understanding the evolution of UK SME policy since the Labour Party came to power in 1997.[14] Perhaps inevitably, policy was characterized by an initial lull, subsequently followed by the need to be seen to be taking action. The House of Commons Trade and Industry Committee memorably summed up the position in 1999:

From the situation as we saw it a year ago, where there seemed to be something of a policy vacuum on SMEs, we have moved to one where there is some risk of an excess of loosely connected and apparently uncoordinated policy initiatives shooting off in all directions, generating noise and interest but not commensurate light. The annual SME debate [in the House of Commons] is a welcome opportunity for the Minister responsible [to give] the House reassurance that there is in fact some overarching strategic thinking behind them.

The Committee's irritation at the absence of 'overarching strategic thinking' may well have stemmed from the following exchange when the Minister was questioned by Mr Berry, a Member of the Committee:

Question from Mr Berry: '*You are absolutely right to say there are lots of exciting things that have been happening in recent times and we are all anxious to do more, but I have to confess I am really uncertain about this particular initiative and the fundamental thinking behind it because I do not know precisely what it is going to do. Unless we know precisely what it's about, how do we know whether the £100,000,000 is the right figure or not?*'

[10] See, for example, the justifications for Small Firms Training Loans (Fraser et al. 2002) or Investors in People (Fraser 2003).

[11] See the review by Wren and Storey (2002) of the Enterprise Initiative.

[12] Examples include Netherlands, Canada, France and the UK. In all countries an interest rate premium is charged to cover administration costs and defaults incurred. Fairly typically where the proportion guaranteed is high—such as Canada—the interest rate premium is also high. The reverse is the case for France—where only 65 percent guarantee is provided, but the interest rate premium is only 0.5 percent. (OECD, 1995).

[13] This is the justification for the Small Business Innovation Research Program in the US. See Lerner (1999).

[14] For a review of the earlier periods see Greene (2002).

Reply from the Minister: '*When I run through the budget for the extra money, the additional money, you will get some idea of where our priorities are going to lie in the first instance*.' (Minutes of Evidence taken before the Trade and Industry Select Committee, 17 March 1999; Trade and Industry Committee, Thirteenth Report 'Small Businesses and Enterprise', HC 330)

In short, those formulating active enterprise policies were much clearer in their own minds about the 'what' question than the 'why' question. The 1999 Committee report re-emphasized the recommendations of their earlier report in which they said:

We recommend that, as a matter of urgency, the government define the objectives of SME policy. The objectives chosen must be accompanied by measurable targets, with a timetable for their attainment. (Trade and Industry Committee, *Small and Medium Enterprises*, 9 June 1998)

In practice the development of strategic thinking on SME policy-making, as recommended by the Committee, took time to come to fruition. Despite the Committee's call for urgency, it was six years[15] before the UK government was able to be demonstrate clear policy coherence. This demonstration is found in *A Government Action Plan for Small Business: The Evidence Base* (SBS 2004). For the first time, the UK government identifies priority areas that draw clearly upon a careful review of evidence. It sets measurable targets which means that evaluation can then be undertaken

The seven key priority areas—called 'strategic themes'—for UK policy are:

(i) Building an enterprise culture
(ii) Encouraging a more dynamic start-up market
(iii) Building the capability for small business growth
(iv) Improving access to finance
(v) Encouraging more enterprise in disadvantaged communities and under-represented groups
(vi) Improving small businesses experience of government services
(vii) Developing better regulation and policy

Besides identifying its strategic themes, the document has two other important qualities. First, it clearly recognizes that SME policy emerges directly from market failure. It says:

The government approach to helping small businesses does not seek to favour small businesses over larger ones. It recognizes that wealth is primarily created by the action of businesses operating in free markets, and it is not the role of government to either duplicate or substitute for private sector activity. In particular it recognizes market forces have a crucial role to play in generating business 'churn' and in creating the competitive forces that

[15] And several changes of Minister and Chief Executive of the Small Business Service.

provide the link between new business formation and productivity growth in the economy as a whole. But the government's enterprise policy also recognizes that the market mechanism is weak or incomplete in a number of important areas affecting the formation and development of small businesses. Left to themselves, markets cannot always be relied upon to deliver outcomes which are optimal from society's perspective, or to achieve important equity objectives that ensure prosperity for all. Where this is the case, there is a role for government to intervene.

The document then goes on to also identify four broad types of market failure, which differ somewhat from those of Storey (2003). The four types identified are:

(i) Imperfect and asymmetric information;
(ii) Externalities and incomplete property rights;
(iii) Imperfect market structures; and
(iv) Poor regulation

Given this identification of policy priorities that emerge from recognizing the role of market failure, each of the seven strategic themes in turn is then reviewed under the same three headings:

1. Rationale: why is action needed?
2. Nature and extent of the problem: what does the evidence say?
3. Measuring success: what are the plans to monitor and evaluate success?

Given that context it can be seen that it is possible to formulate a framework in which SME policy evaluation can take place. It is the political economy of developing that framework to which the remainder of this paper is directed.

10.4 Undertaking Evaluation

In their review of policy evaluation in innovation and technology, Papaconstantinou and Polt (1997) provide a very helpful definition of evaluation. They say:

> Evaluation refers to a process that seeks to determine as systematically and objectively as possible the relevance, efficiency and effect of an activity in terms of its objectives, including the analysis of the implementation and administrative management of such activities.

Several words or phrases in this definition merit strong emphasis. The first keyword is *process*. A central theme of this paper is that evaluation is not a 'one-off' activity, undertaken once a particular programme has been completed. Instead evaluation is an integral element of a 'process' of improved policy or service delivery.

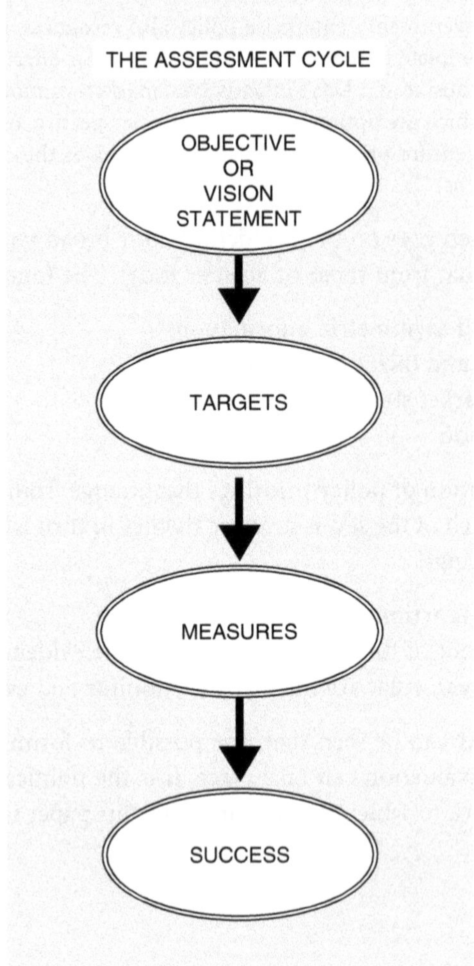

Figure 10.2 The assessment cycle: Evaluation at the end of the line

To illustrate this definition of evaluation, Figure 10.2 shows a highly simplified way in which policy is delivered. It assumes a linear process, beginning with a 'Vision Statement', resulting in the formulation of legislation. The second and third stages, shown as Targets and Measures, occur when legislation is 'interpreted' by public servants, to make it applicable to the practical circumstances they face.

Figure 10.3 assumes that, once the policy has been in operation for a period of time, it will be subject to a 'review' or an 'evaluation'. This may be considered as the fourth stage and is often conducted when there is a proposal to change the legislation, either to increase its scale, to reduce it or to abolish it.

The observation that evaluation is the fourth and, in Figure 10.2, the last stage in this linear process leads to the expression that evaluation is at 'the end of the line'.

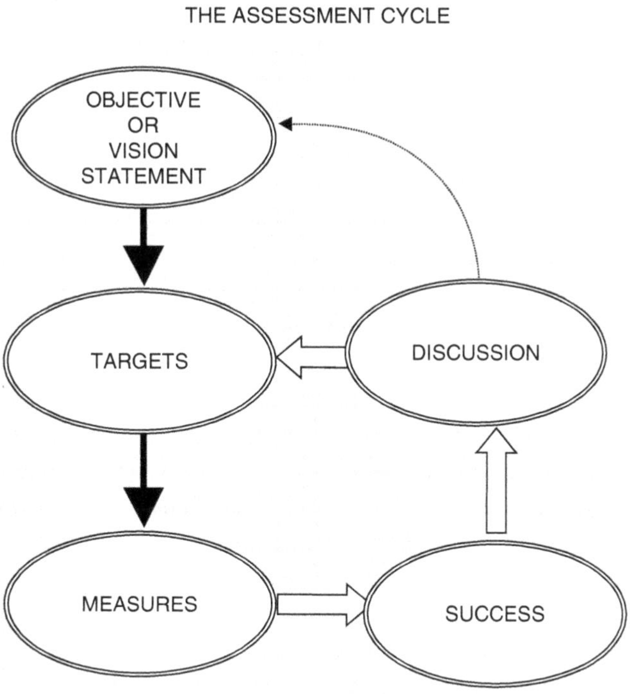

THE ASSESSMENT CYCLE

OBJECTIVE OR VISION STATEMENT

TARGETS

DISCUSSION

MEASURES

SUCCESS

Figure 10.3 The assessment cycle: Evaluation as part of the policy process

However, it is then difficult to square this with the definition of evaluation above that refers to 'a process'. Where evaluation takes place to simply provide guidance on the scale of budget allocated to a programme, or to determine whether money in the past has been wisely spent, it is difficult to view this as a 'process'.

Instead, for this to become a 'process' two changes are needed, both involving an additional stage. This is shown as the box called 'Discussion' in Figure 10.3. The first type of Discussion recognizes that when an evaluation is conducted, the most likely outcome is that the programme will have performed better in some respects than others. It is also the case that programmes frequently perform well in aspects that either were not anticipated by those developing them, or where such aspects were thought to be of low importance when the programme was being framed.[16] The

[16] An example of this is the evaluation of the Shell Technology Enterprise Programme (STEP). This scheme provides work placement experience for undergraduates, and it was expected that it would lead to students being more likely to subsequently work in an SME. The evaluation however showed that, while STEP enhanced entry into the labour market upon graduation, it made them much less likely to get a job in an SME on graduation (Fraser, Storey and Westhead, 2006). But, as a result of these findings, a greater emphasis was placed upon recognizing more widely the value of work placements to undergraduates.

conduct of the evaluation provides the opportunity for the objectives of the programme to be discussed. Those responsible for the programme have to decide whether the programme should focus more heavily upon those areas where it was clearly being effective, and place less emphasis upon those where impact is less. Alternatively, they could assert the continued importance of the original objectives and re-fashion the programme accordingly.

The example above shows that implementing evaluation as a 'process' can be achieved, by feeding even provisional results from the evaluation back into the debate. A second, and perhaps even more powerful contribution to the 'process', is to incorporate the expertise of those who are to conduct the evaluation into the 'Objectives and Vision' statement when legislation is being framed. This is shown as the thin arrow in Figure 10.3. The role of the evaluator would be to confirm that the legislation was framed in such a way as to enable a satisfactory evaluation to be conducted. The presence of the evaluator would ensure the objectives and targets of the legislation were sufficiently clear to enable an evaluator to undertake their work, at a future time. The evaluator would also ensure that a process of data collection is established to enable the evaluation to be conducted, ideally prior to the policy being implemented. Finally, a budget for the evaluation, reflecting the scale and complexity of the programme, has to be set aside, together with a framework statement on how the evaluation is to be conducted.

Incorporating the evaluator into the earliest stages of legislative development in this way addresses three key problems. The first, as will be discussed in more detail later, is that the objectives of programmes are frequently expressed in terms that are not sufficiently specific to enable evaluators to assess the effects of the programme. Incorporating the evaluator at the stage when legislation is being formulated requires legislators to address two important questions:

1 How will we know if this legislation/programme is successful?
2 How will we know if this legislation/programme has failed?

A second problem faced by evaluators is the absence of suitable data. Sometimes there is not even data on the firms that participate in the programme, but this is comparatively rare. Much more frequently the evaluator is hampered by the absence of data on firms that did not participate in the programme and so could be used as a 'control group' to estimate policy impact. Finally, as will be shown later, the evaluation would also benefit from data on firms that applied to participate in the programme but were rejected, or those that were unaware of the programme but were eligible to apply, or those that were aware but chose not to apply. By including the evaluator at 'the front end', data collection at or even before the programme is implemented, enables better quality evaluations to be undertaken.

The third problem is that, because consideration is not given to evaluation until, or sometimes long after, the programme begins, those managing the programme feel evaluation is being imposed upon them. A debate then begins about the nature, scale and budget for the evaluation. If those responsible for delivering such programmes find an evaluation unexpectedly imposed upon them, it is understandable that their response can be one of irritation. The evaluation is inevitably time-consuming, particularly for 'front line' staff, who will argue that their opportunity cost of forgoing providing services to firms is high. Where the commitment to the evaluation is funded from the programme's own budget there is likely to be an even more strident response. It is hugely beneficial to all parties to address all these issues when the legislation is being framed, so that all parties are aware that the evaluation will take place, and understand the grounds on which it will be conducted and how it will be funded. For all these reasons it is critical for evaluation to be considered as part of a 'process', with all parties being aware that evaluation is incorporated at all stages.

A second key phrase in the definition of evaluation by Papaconstantinou and Polt is: *as systematically and objectively as possible.* Given that evaluation traditionally takes place 'at the end of the line' there are likely to be strong entrenched interests in place once a programme has been in existence for a number of years. These entrenched interests include the direct beneficiaries of the programme, such as the businesses receiving funds, but they will also include those who are responsible for initiating and administering these programmes. All else held equal, it is to be expected that all these groups will choose the programme to continue or expand. The task of the evaluator, however, is to 'systematically and objectively' assess the merits of the programme. In this task, the evaluator is likely to conflict with those committed to the programme per se. Only through the use of objective techniques discussed later in the paper can the evaluator demonstrate their independence to those delivering programmes.

Nevertheless, while objectivity is vital, the evaluator's task is best conducted by drawing on the support of those delivering the programme. While the evaluator is expected to be knowledgeable about evaluation, those delivering the programmes have valuable insider knowledge of how the programme actually works. They will often be able to provide simple but unexpected explanations for the 'associations' identified by the evaluators. Without their knowledge and support there is the risk of ill-informed inferences being derived. Hence there is a fine line between the need for the evaluator to exhibit objectivity and independence, yet also to gain the support and inside knowledge of those delivering the programmes. This support is much more likely to be forthcoming if, when the programme is devised, it is made clear to those delivering programmes that an evaluation will take place.

The third key phrase in the Papaconstantinou and Polt definition is: *the relevance, efficiency and effect of an activity in terms of its objective.* The implicit assumption in this statement is that the policy has clear objectives and that these are stated in sufficiently clear terms for them to be used by the evaluator. In practice this is often not the case. Objectives are often specified in generic terms, such as a desire to make an economy more 'enterprising', but this is of limited value to the evaluator. By taking a simple example, i.e. the objective of making an economy 'more enterprising', the evaluator could consider a possibly bewildering range of measures to assess policy impact. These might include, the number of new firms started, those started by young or disadvantaged people, those started by people who have not been in business before, the increase in the total number of firms, whether these firms grow, whether they internationalize and of course whether they survive. All could be considered as measures of whether a country is 'enterprising', but some may be regarded as more appropriate measures than others. Where there are a wide range of possible measures, on some of which the policy performs well and on others less well, there is an inevitable tendency for those favouring continuation of the policy to select the measures or targets on which it has performed well. In contrast, those favouring policy closure or contraction will select their chosen measures. Richard Harrison and Claire Leitch (1996) delightfully encapsulate this in an essay entitled, 'Whatever You Hit Call the Target: An Alternative Approach to Small Business Policy', in which they emphasize the importance of being clear on the targets that most closely reflect the objectives of the policy.[17]

The reality is, however, that the measures by which the effectiveness of the programme is assessed are often not specified. The evaluator therefore has to 'second guess' what the original objectives of the legislator were when framing the programme. This then leads inevitably to a range of performance measures being chosen, probably in conjunction with those responsible for implementing the programme. It also means that those delivering the programme at the time are likely to emphasize measures on which they feel the programme is likely to be concurrently performing well, even if these measures correspond only weakly to what appear to be the objectives of those originally framing the legislation.

In principle, such a discussion could be of real value and does reflect the role of evaluation as a 'process'. In practice, unfortunately, it leads to those responsible for the programme identifying those measures upon which they have performed relatively well as being those upon which the programme should be evaluated. Frequently this leads to a somewhat unseemly debate from which neither the evaluators nor the programme managers emerge with credit.

The central conclusion from this review of Evaluation context is the integral role it has to play in the policy 'process'. Evaluation cannot be left 'at the end of the line'. Instead, it has to be a key element of initial policy formulation. Once the policy is operational, all organizations and individuals responsible for delivery have to be

[17] This is, of course, not to imply that targets cannot be changed. Indeed a frequent, and highly desirable, outcome from an evaluation is that it can lead to a change in targets. This is shown as the Discussion Box in Figure 2. What, however, is undesirable is for a number of targets to be selected and for policy-makers to claim programmes to be successful whichever target they happen to hit at a particular time. It emphasizes the importance of being clear on the criteria for unsuccessful policy.

aware that evaluation is to take place. Once the evaluation has been undertaken, and sometimes as it is taking place, it should be used as the basis for dialogue with policy-makers, with the objective of delivering better policy. The outcome of the evaluation can then become an input into a philosophical debate on the appropriate ways for governments and SMEs to interact.

(i) The evaluation framework

SME and Entrepreneurship policies can be assessed on a number of criteria[18], but the key to effective assessment is the issue of Additionality. This is defined as the true impact of the scheme/programme. While it is not always easy to quantify, it is likely to be reflected in measures such as additional output, employment, sales or export activity that can be attributed to the existence of the programme. In other words, it is activity that would not have taken place without the programme, and is attributable to the firm participating in the programme. This is shown diagrammatically in Figure 10.4 below taken from Oldsman (2002).

It shows, for any given outcome, that policy impact can be considered as the difference between the observed outcome with the intervention, and what would have happened without the intervention. The Figure shows these two outcomes diverging after the time when the policy is implemented.

While this is a simple concept, identification of the programme impact 'as systematically and objectively as possible' can be challenging. This is because programme impact cannot be easily observed for a number of reasons. The first is that it is not always clear what changes might have occurred in the firms as a

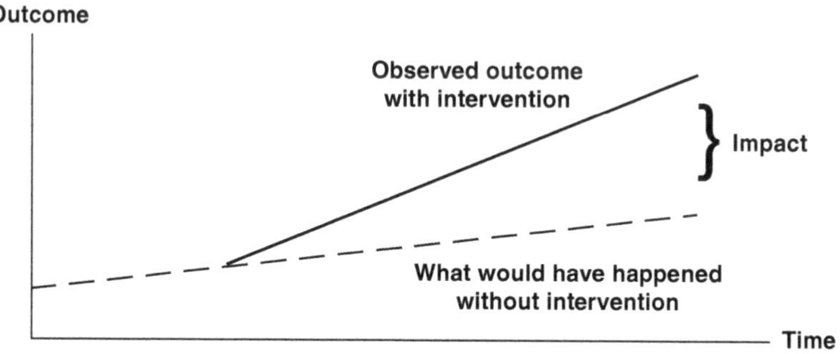

Figure 10.4 The impact of an intervention

Source: Oldsman (2002)

[18] The OECD SME Working Party identified seven headings under which policies can be assessed. These are: Rationale, Additionality, Appropriateness, Superiority, Systemic Efficiency, Own Efficiency and Adaptive Efficiency (OECD, 2000).

result of participation; in other words the Outcome measures are unclear. Some programmes might be expected to lead to a greater likelihood of firm formation or survival, others to growth in sales, profits or employment, others to a greater likelihood of innovating or selling into overseas markets. Other programmes might be expected to enhance all these characteristics, and in other cases it is unclear what firm characteristics are expected to show improvement. Evaluation therefore requires a decision on appropriate Outcome measures.

A second problem is that participation in the programme will precede improvement. Using the example of Figure 10.4, the point at which the lines diverge will not necessarily be immediately after the programme is delivered. Some programmes will have their impact possibly years before others. As an example, a programme in which SMEs are subsidized to participate in an international Trade Fair so as to encourage them to internationalize,[19] might be expected to have a quick impact upon sales. In contrast, a programme to fund Research and Development in SMEs would be expected to have little impact for several years.

A third problem is the myriad of influences upon the performance of an SME, other than that of programme participation. These include the skill of the owner, the sector and location of the business, macro-economic conditions and the role of chance. In principle, only when account is fully taken of these 'exogenous' factors can the impact of the programme be estimated. The next section shows the various ways in which these issues have been addressed.

(ii) The Six Steps approach

Many approaches to the challenge of impact assessment have been adopted, but it is possible to characterize them within the 'Six Steps to Heaven' framework, Storey (2000). This is shown in Table 10.2.

Table 10.2 Six Steps to Heaven: Methods for assessing the impact of SME policy

Monitoring:		
STEP I	*	Take up of schemes
STEP II	*	Recipients Opinions
STEP III	*	Recipients' views of the difference made by the Assistance
Evaluation:		
STEP IV	*	Comparison of the Performance of 'Assisted' with 'Typical' firms
STEP V	*	Comparison with 'Match' firms
STEP VI	*	Taking account of selection bias

[19] 'Access to International Markets', a presentation by the Delegation of Greece, OECD Working Party on Small and Medium-Sized Enterprises, Athens, 26–8 April, 1998.

The 'Six Steps' procedure recognizes that there is a gradation of sophistication in assessment procedures. The six steps show a gradation, with Step I being the least sophisticated procedure and Step VI being the most sophisticated. Here sophistication is intended to reflect the confidence the policy-maker has in being able to attribute changes in businesses supported under the programme—often called the 'treatment group'—to participation in the programme. Alternatively expressed, it may be considered as the confidence the policy-maker has that all other influences are held constant.

Table 10.2 shows that a distinction is made between Monitoring and Evaluation. Steps I to III are not considered to be Evaluation, but instead are referred to as Monitoring. The difference between Monitoring and Evaluation is that the former relies exclusively upon the views of the recipients of the policy. Evaluation however seeks, by some means, to contrast these views or actions with those of non-recipients in order to present the 'counter factual'. The difference between actual changes and the 'counter factual' is viewed as the impact of the policy—or its 'additionality'. In terms of Figure 10.4, Monitoring is the continuous line, and it is only the inclusion of the control group that enables the dotted line to be identified and hence policy to be evaluated.

A full review of Steps I to IV are provided in Storey (2000), but for current purposes it is sufficient to note that, despite the frequency with which they are used, these approaches either do not attempt to make a comparison with a 'control group', or do so in a clearly inadequate manner. It is not until Step V that an attempt is made to compare 'treatment' with 'non-treatment' firms, where the latter do not differ in terms of observable factors such as ownership, size, sector and geography. This is normally undertaken through a matching process. Once the matching is complete then differences in the performance of the two groups is attributed to participation in the programme.[20]

While the Step V approach reflects a real attempt to address the issue of the counter-factual, it cannot be considered as 'best practice'. The results are still somewhat ambiguous because observed differences in performance may also reflect the presence of 'un-observables'. The most obvious of these may be dynamism or motivation of the SME owner, with this leading to various forms of selection bias in the estimation techniques.

Two examples of selection bias are self-selection and committee selection. Self-selection bias may occur where, for example, programmes seek to provide support for rapidly growing businesses. Here those businesses that are seeking growth may be more likely to apply to become participants in the programme than those with only modest, or no growth ambitions. The problem arises where this is only partly reflected in 'observable' factors, since the latter underestimate how the firm would have got on

[20] Examples of Step V approaches include Lerner (1999) for the United States and Eshima (2003) for Japan.

even if the programme had not existed. The 'counter-factual' dotted line in Figure 10.4 is specified too low, and the programme impact is consequently over estimated.[21] The clearest example is where applicant firms, although apparently no different from non-applicant firms in terms of the 'controls',[22] in fact have more motivated owners.[23] These differences in owner motivation—which is very difficult to observe—mean these firms would be expected to perform better than the 'matches', even if there had been no programme. It is therefore unreasonable to attribute all differences in performance between the programme firms and the matches to programme participation. Failure to take account of selection, however, leads to precisely this error.

A second example is committee selection.[24] This refers to programmes where only a proportion of applicants is successful. Here a committee or similar group makes a judgement, with the 'better' firms/applicants obtaining the funding. If the committee is effective it will eliminate those firms likely to perform poorly, so that the programme participants are clearly non-randomly drawn from applicants. As before, even if the programme did not exist, the selected firms would be expected to have outperformed the other firms. Hence observed differences in performance between programme participants and matched firms cannot be attributed solely to programme participation.[25]

There are now a number of statistical techniques that address the issue of selection bias with these being closely associated with James Heckman (Heckman et al. 1997; Heckman, 2001). It is a curiosity that, although these techniques are now well established in the evaluation of labour market and welfare programmes, they are much less frequently used in estimating the impact of business support. A helpful review of these techniques is provided by Smith (2002), who identifies five statistical techniques to identify programme impact when users differ from non-users. These begin with tests to control for observable differences but then move on, using greater sophistication, to account for both programme selection

[21] This issue is addressed by Wren and Storey (2002) in their review of the UK Enterprise Initiative and by Roper and Hewitt-Dundas (2001).

[22] Here typical 'controls' might be business sector, location, age and ownership.

[23] This is because the focus of assistance programmes is clear in the way in which they are promoted. Thus programmes seeking to attract growing businesses are unlikely to have as high a proportion of 'life-stylers' as in the SME population as a whole.

[24] An example of where Committee selection is addressed is in the evaluation of the support provided by the Princes Trust by Meager, Bates and Cowling (2003) discussed later. Their Step VI approach contrasts with the Step V approach used by Lerner (1999) in his review of the SBIR programme in the United States.

[25] It is of course possible that the Committee may not be good at selecting the good from the bad firms. In this instance the Committee may serve no useful function. Alternatively the Committee might play a different role in ensuring that a quota of certain types of firms receives funding. These might be firms from certain geographical areas or whose owners are disadvantaged in some respect. If that role is clear, than the Step V procedure would address this. However, if it is not explicitly the role of the Committee then this could lead to the programme effects being mis-estimated using a Step V approach.

and self-selection. He concludes that using some instrumental variables that predict programme use, but are uncorrelated with the observable values that affect the economic outcomes of the programme, is ideal (Angrist and Kruger, 2001). The problem, of course, is that good instruments are hard to find.

(iii) An illustration of a Step VI evaluation: Princes (Youth Business) Trust

The Princes Youth Business Trust (PYBT)—currently named 'The Prince's Trust'—was established by Princes Charles in 1976, but was considerably expanded in scale following the urban riots in England in the early 1980s. Its purpose was to support enterprise among disadvantaged young people. The programme provides funding for those wishing to start a business but who were unable to access funds from other sources; it also provides advice and mentoring for clients. More than 90 percent of participants received a start up grant, with 60 percent receiving between £1,500 and £3,000. Although it began without government funding, a 'matching' agreement meant that between 1999 and 2005, PYBT, or Prince's, Trust as it had become, received £27.5 million of taxpayers money.

A Step VI evaluation of PYBT was undertaken by Meager et al. (2003). They identified 2,000 individuals supported by the Trust between 2000 and 2001 and whose progress was then tracked on two later occasions. These individuals were then matched with 1,600 otherwise similar non-participants. The matching was based on age, gender, region and employment status. The 'matches' were also contacted on a total of three occasions. Sample selection was significant and taken into account, making this a Step VI approach.

The purpose of the evaluation was to examine whether, in terms of subsequent employment status and earnings, PYBT participants out-perform the otherwise similar match group. Meager et al. find no evidence of either. They found that individuals whose business was supported by the Trust were no more likely to be in (some form of) work than the match group. In terms of earnings, the Trust business owners had higher incomes while in business but, on leaving self employment, their income levels returned to that of the match group.

The interesting point, noted by Greene and Storey (2005) about the Meager et al. Step VI evaluation, is that the Prince's Trust/PYBT has been subject to four previous evaluations, over the period 1993–2003. Two of these evaluations could be considered to be Step I, and two of them could be considered to be Step IV. Both the Step I evaluations appear to demonstrate considerable 'added value' provided by the Trust; in contrast, the Step IV evaluations show some impact, while the Step VI evaluation shows no impact at all. This is consistent with the view that the more sophisticated the evaluation (the higher the step number) the lower is the apparent impact of the programme.[26]

[26] Other interpretations are of course possible, the most important of which is that the other PYBT studies were conducted on different cohorts at different periods of time, when different results might have been obtained using a Step VI approach. Arguably, the only valid test would be to undertake, on the same group of Trust participants, an evaluation using all six approaches.

While other interpretations are possible, the most likely interpretation of these reviews of PYBT is that the Step VI method ensures that more factors are held constant than is the case with the less sophisticated approaches. This means that only those benefits that are genuinely attributable to the programme are identified, rather than incorporating other benefits that may or may not reflect the specific contribution of the programme.

(iv) Some modifications to, and limitations of, the 'Six Steps' approach

So, should a Step VI approach be adopted in all evaluations? The argument in favour of a consistent Step VI approach in all cases is that, if some programmes are evaluated in a less comprehensive manner than others, this causes problems in comparing effectiveness across all programmes. Assume SME policy has only two programmes. Programme A provides Grants and Programme B provides Training. If policy is delivered efficiently the marginal impact per unit of currency will be identical for the two programmes. However, such a judgement would be impossible to reach if Programme A were assessed in one way and Programme B in another.

This is a very important point since the PYBT example above shows that it is the more sophisticated approaches that are the most likely to specify accurately the 'counter-factual'. In most instances, inaccurate specification of the counter-factual leads to the programme's impact being overestimated. As was seen by Greene and Storey (2005), programmes evaluated using the low numbered Steps approach consistently imply a bigger impact than those using the higher numbered Steps approach. Unfortunately, the studies using the more sophisticated approaches—those with higher Step numbers—are also much lengthier and more expensive to conduct. Conducting small numbers of interviews with programme participants is easy, quick, cheap and requires almost no analysis. This contrasts starkly with the more sophisticated approaches where evaluation needs to be built-in from the start, where non-programme participants as well as programme participants need to be monitored, and where the statistical expertise needed to conduct the analysis is likely to be rare and expensive. It is also fair to say that 'a good case study is worth a thousand equations' in terms of media and political impact. For all these reasons the 'cheap and cheerful' approach is popular.

The central problem therefore is that if some programmes were evaluated in a less challenging manner than others, it would lead to problems in allocating funds between programmes within the SME and Entrepreneurship policy area. Equally, however, it is difficult to justify the same level of sophistication, and hence evaluation budgets, being applied to small as to large programmes. This is illustrated in Figure 10.5, taken from Bartik (2002). It shows that impact accuracy increases with budget.

This highlights an important trade-off in evaluation. Ideally all programmes within SME and Entrepreneurship policy should be assessed using the same

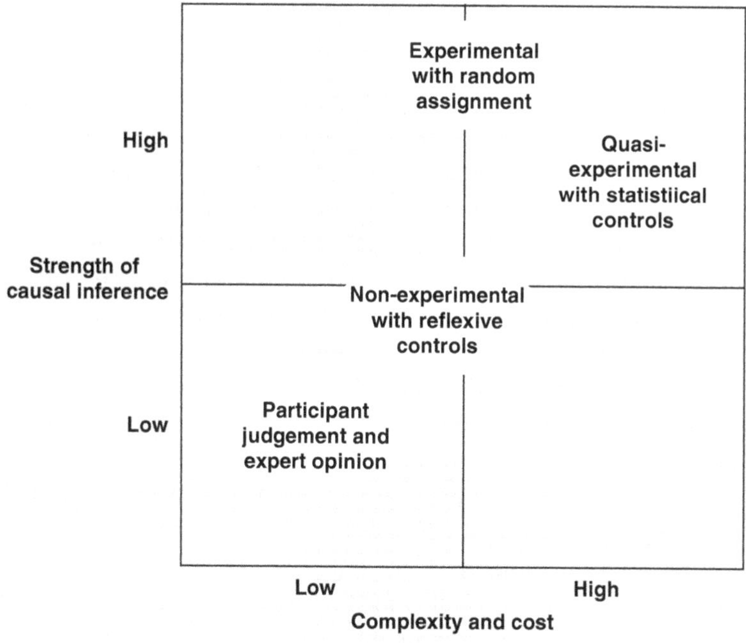

Figure 10.5 Trade-offs in evaluation design

methods in order to validly compare their marginal effects. In this way it may be possible to transfer resources from Programme A to Programme B and enhance the overall impact of SME policy. The problem, however, is that it is difficult to justify the same level of analytical sophistication for small, as for large programmes. But, if the smaller programmes are less rigorously assessed, then they may appear to have a larger impact and so justify budget increases to the detriment of larger programmes/projects.

Finally, it is also important to emphasize that the 'Six Steps' approach is designed to examine the impact of individual programmes and policies. Since it operates by comparing firms that participate in programmes or policies with those which do not, it cannot be used to examine policies that apply equally to all firms in the economy simultaneously. Hence tax incentives that are taken up by all SMEs are not appropriately examined using this approach. It is equally true that the totality of the impact of enterprise programmes could be underestimated using this approach where there was strong inter-dependency of programmes. Essentially the 'Six Steps' approach estimates the marginal effects of individual programmes, but the sum of the marginal effects could be less than the total effects. It would be, however, unwise for these rather technical arguments to obscure the need for taxpayers to be satisfied that impacts of individual programmes were being assessed by the most technically sophisticated means.

10.5 Lessons

Funding for public programmes to assist SMEs comes from the taxpayer. Those responsible for developing and delivering such programmes therefore have a responsibility to ensure that value for money is provided. The sums of money are not trivial, and the total public budget devoted to funding SME and Entrepreneurship policy is rarely quantified, primarily because there are so many of these public programmes, and they are delivered by a multitude of different agencies.

An exception is a recent study, summarized in the Appendix which reported that the total annual UK government expenditure on providing services to Small Businesses for the most recent year available was approximately £8 billion. To place this in context, the UK public expenditure on police was £7 billion. This emphasizes the importance of being aware of the total budget and of ensuring that value for money is derived from programmes. Evaluation is expected to play a key role in informing politicians and taxpayers.

The example above demonstrates not only that the sums of public money are substantial, but also that responsibility for that money is widely distributed among different departments within government. This constitutes a major policy challenge because, while Departments may have 'budget lines' for small businesses, their overall Departmental priorities may lie elsewhere. This means that, while the total public expenditure on small firms may be substantial, there is a strong risk that it lacks coherence and focus.

Given the goal of policy coherence, this paper has emphasized that evaluation has to be an integral part of the policy process. It is not an optional 'add-on'. Instead, considerations of evaluation need to be incorporated in all stages of policy development. This means that, when legislation is being framed, objectives should be specified in a manner that evaluation can be conducted. It may also mean that an evaluation methodology is formulated, and budget set aside to enable data collection to begin.

The paper also makes it clear that the last few years have seen major statistical advances that mean it is now possible to undertake much more accurate assessments of programme impact than was the case only a few years ago. It is no longer valid to argue that assessment procedures are very imperfect. Quite simply, the technology is there and is used extensively in many other aspects of public programmes, such as labour markets. It is curious that these techniques have been slow to develop in SME and Entrepreneurship policy assessment, but there is now experience of them being developed for several types of such programmes.

Nevertheless there remain important issues for discussion and debate. First, while current statistical techniques are able to assess policy much more accurately than has been the case in the past, politicians, public servants and many academics are nervous about their widespread adoption. This is partly because the mathematical and quantitative skills needed even to understand the outcomes are not available to all; it is also partly because of a widely-held mistrust of attempts to quantify policy impact on the grounds that this leads to the 'softer' aspects of policy delivery being ignored. For some groups, therefore, no matter what improvements are made in the accuracy of quantitative techniques, there will always be entrenched resistance to their widespread adoption.

Others have less of a 'root and branch' objection, but continue to have misgivings about the implementation of more sophisticated evaluation, for four groups of reasons: (i) there is clear evidence that the more sophisticated evaluations, in general, identify lower programme impact; (ii) it is also clear that the more sophisticated evaluations are also more lengthy and more expensive, primarily because more items are held constant, rather than being attributed to the programme; (iii) this could easily lead to a conflict of interest since, if those responsible for the programme are also responsible for setting the budget and timing for the evaluation, there may be pressure for favoured programmes to be evaluated using less sophisticated procedures; (iv) a priori, it would seem that this type of discretion is undesirable, and implies responsibilities between evaluators and programme managers need to be separated.

Secondly, it is clear that in almost all countries some programmes are evaluated, sometimes more than once, and others are never evaluated.[27] As noted above, it is also the case that some programmes are evaluated using considerably more sophisticated techniques than others. In part, this understandably reflects governments choosing to link evaluation budgets to programme scale.[28] The problem, however, is that this makes comparisons difficult between the results of small and large scale evaluations. Yet, if SME policy is to be economically efficient, then the marginal efficiency of all policies should be identical, but this information will not be available if policies are evaluated using different methods. The pragmatic response may be, as a minimum, to agree that all programmes should be evaluated, so that none slips through the net. It also seems appropriate to broadly link the scale of the evaluation budget to the scale of the programme. Moreover, to facilitate the broadest comparisons, it might be suggested that no programme be evaluated

[27] A UK example is the Loan Guarantee Scheme which has had five 'external' evaluations, since being introduced in 1981 as a pilot. In contrast, the wide range of schemes, which began at about the same time, to provide tax relief to wealthy individuals to encourage them to act as Angels, appears to have escaped almost all evaluation. Since the general view is that the LGS has been broadly effective, and the tax relief schemes have clearly been the subject of widespread abuse, this would appear to be the opposite of what might be expected in a rational policy regime.

[28] Even this is however an imperfect argument judging from UK experience. As shown in Table 10.A1, p. 276, favourable tax treatment of small businesses accounts for £2.5 billion out of the total £7.9 billion public expenditure on SMEs. However, as far as this author is aware, there have been no evaluations, in the public domain, that have evaluated the impact of, for example, the 10p rate of Corporation Tax for small businesses.

using less than Step IV, and that the larger the programme the greater the expected use of Step V and Step VI approaches.

Thirdly, a judgement has to be reached about whether programmes should be evaluated by the departments responsible for delivering them, by other organs of government, or by external organizations. There are arguments favouring evaluators from all of these groups. The departments responsible for delivering the programme clearly have unique inside knowledge and understanding, which will not be available to any outsiders. Also they may be more likely to engage the support of those delivering the programme. Finally, because of their 'insider' status, any recommendations for change that they make are more likely to be accepted and implemented since they are making them to their colleagues with whom they have had prior discussions. On the other hand, however, there is the risk that their 'independence' may be impaired through this closeness, and the real risk of the evaluators being subject to 'capture' or political influence.

An alternative would be for evaluations to be conducted by a specialist part of government, independent of the programme delivery department. The advantage here is that they would have greater specialist evaluation skills, and be seen to be more independent than the department delivering the programme. Their detailed programme specialism would however, be less and so they would rely more heavily upon the co-operation of the programme deliverers. They would also be likely to be influenced by political considerations than specialists from outside government.

Another option would be to engage specialist 'outsiders' such as consultants or academics. Both these groups have the advantage of being less clearly subject to 'capture', and being likely to be specialists within their subject.[29] The central disadvantage of the employment of outsiders is that if evaluation is viewed as one element in the 'process' of policy improvement then this has to lead, as in Figure 10.3, to discussion. That discussion risks being less engaging when it is led by outsiders, who may be viewed as less well informed, than when it follows from an Evaluation conducted by those responsible for the programme. A judgement therefore would be needed which would review these conflicting arguments and reach the important decision on who should conduct evaluations.

Thirdly, since evaluation is not 'the end of the line', experience of where evaluation has led to policy modifications is critical. These modifications may be either changes in the objectives of the programme or to changes in the way that

[29] A case could be made that consultancy practices are not wholly independent, since their business depends upon a future flow of contracts, probably from the same department of government. A highly critical report, which was not what the sponsor wanted, could therefore risk jeopardising future income streams with its associated business consequences. It might be argued that future revenue consequences are a less serious consideration for academics. As Kuusisto et al. (1999) pointed out, it is fair to say that in the UK context the most powerful critiques of SME programmes have been from academics rather than from private sector consultants. However it is also appropriate to point out that, from the perspective of those commissioning research, consultants have a reputation for jobs being completed on time—this not always being a characteristic of academics.

programmes are implemented or delivered. For example, programmes may be extended to include businesses in sectors that were previously excluded; changes in the terms and conditions of the programme or changes in the desired outcomes.[30]

The process by which any programme changes are implemented is likely to vary depending on the scale and profile of the programme, and according to political processes. Nevertheless the key purpose of conducting evaluations is for them to be an influence upon policy. In some countries, particularly for high profile programmes, it may be valuable for information stemming from the evaluation to enter the public domain. This is more likely to occur where 'outsiders' have conducted the evaluation.

One way to achieve this is for all programmes to have only a fixed 'life', with continuation depending upon a satisfactory evaluation. This could be considered as a variation on 'sun-setting' legislation. It has the advantage of ensuring when the programme is first developed, that all participants agree its objectives, and how it will be assessed. It would also enable programmes to be reoriented to reflect any changed economic circumstances.

10.6 Conclusions

This paper has provided an extensive review of the methods used to evaluate elements of SME and Entrepreneurship policy. The key conclusion of the paper is that Evaluation needs to become more central to the policy-making process, and that in the UK there is evidence of this happening. Evaluation should not be undertaken solely as a historic accounting exercise to determine whether public money has been spent wisely, although that role is of value. Instead of being 'at the end of the line', evaluation should be used to inform current policy, so that the objectives and targets may be modified in the light of evidence of policy effectiveness. Hence considerations of how policy is evaluated should therefore be incorporated into policy formulation when new ideas are being developed.

Ensuring that evaluation is given a higher priority means that all, rather than merely some, programmes are assessed. The paper is however less clear about the extent to which all programmes should be assessed with the same level of sophistication. The key argument in favour of a consistent level of sophistication is that this enables valid comparisons to be undertaken between one programme and

[30] A clear example is the UK governments acceptance of the key recommendations from the Graham report on the Loan Guarantee Scheme (Graham, 2004).

another. The argument against is that it is inappropriate to have similar evaluation budgets for programmes of widely differing scales.

Nevertheless, the paper makes it clear that it is now technically possible to provide accurate measures of programme impact. It shows, through its 'Six Steps to Heaven' approach that, although there are examples of the most sophisticated approaches being used, these are the exception rather than the rule. The cause for concern is that the less sophisticated approaches tend to provide potentially misleading answers, most frequently overestimating policy impact. Despite these reservations, the paper concludes that, where appropriate, the most sophisticated—Step V or Step VI—approaches are to be used.

In undertaking these evaluations it is necessary to bear in mind some potential conflicts. The first is that ideally those undertaking the evaluations need to be independent of those responsible for the programmes, as in any audit role. But, if a key role of evaluation is to contribute to making continuous improvements in the policy, then the evaluators need the active co-operation and involvement of both policy-makers and deliverers. This may be more difficult to achieve if the evaluator is viewed as an 'outsider'. On balance, the paper concludes that the independence of the evaluator is of the greater importance, but this is a close call.

However, it would be misleading to infer that the only important issue in SME policy is persuading policy-makers and public servants of the importance of evaluation. While this is, in the judgement of the current author, the top priority, there also remain a number of unresolved scholarly issues. The first is the extent to which the 'type' of evaluation influences the apparent impact of the policy. In simple terms, if the same policy were evaluated using Step II, Step V and Step VI approaches, what difference would it make? Our evidence from an examination of one programme—The Prince's Trust—is that policy impact is lower simply because more factors are 'controlled' in the sophisticated approaches, but all these evaluations were undertaken on different cohorts at different times so making comparability imperfect. There is, therefore, a strong case for evaluating the same cohort using different approaches. The value of such work would then be to see which Steps yield the greatest gains in accuracy. This could provide invaluable help in setting a minimum threshold evaluation approach.

A second area of policy uncertainty is whether there are greater benefits from initiatives in certain policy areas than others. For example, Loan Guarantees exist in many countries and are generally thought to be a success, whereas strategies to encourage more owner or workforce training in SMEs have generally modest take-up. The ability to make these comparative evaluations would also be of real value. If SME policy is cost effective, the impact of the taxpayer's marginal pound should be identical for all programmes. There is, therefore, a major research opportunity in making these types of cross-programme comparisons.

Thirdly, the same policy can often be implemented or administered in a very different manner in different countries, or in the same country at different points in time. For example, in most countries, there is some form of subsidized advice and information services for small firms. However, the way this is 'rationed' to small firms varies considerably. In some instances it is rationed on grounds of time, so that no firm can obtain more than a specified number of day's assistance; in others it is rationed because only certain groups or firms in certain sectors are able to access it for free. Other forms of rationing include initial free use but then subsequent use being fully charged, while in others, there is a fixed subsidy, irrespective of use. While these are real issues which policy-makers encounter, there remains little research upon which they can draw.

Finally, the 'six steps' approach is most suited to the assessment of individual programmes or policies. But, as is clear from this review of SME and Entrepreneurship policies, these are frequently delivered in 'clusters'. Some countries may have different combinations of policies and the key challenge for evaluators is to identify the impact of the full cluster—which may be less, or more than, the summation of individual policies.

APPENDIX

Table 10.A1 United Kingdom support for small businesses (2001), in £m Sterling

Expenditure		5,342
of which		
Small Business Service budget	349	
Other expenditure by Department of Trade and Industry and its agencies	275	
BTI	44	
DCMS and agencies	332	
DPES and agencies	138	
RDA's	274	
DWP	71	
Local authorities	300	
Tax agencies (support services)	81	

(*contd.*)

Table 10.A1 United Kingdom support for small businesses (2001), in £m Sterling (*contd.*)

Expenditure		5,342
DEFRA (Agriculture Department) grants, advice in-kind support	3,120	
DTLR and agencies	107	
EC and EIB	246	
Favourable tax treatment (R&D Tax Credit; 10p Corporation Tax; 20p Small company corporation tax rate; Venture Capital Trusts; Enterprise Investment Scheme)		2,590
Total		7,932
(as a percent of GDP)		(0.8)

Source: 'Cross-cutting review of government services for small businesses', Department of Trade and Industry, September 2002, URN 02/1324.

References

Anderson, R. E. (2004). *Just Get Out of the Way: How Governments Can Help Businesses in Poor Countries.* Washington, DC: CATO Institute.

Anglund, S. M. (2002). *Small Business Policy and the American Creed.* Westpoint CT: Praeger.

Angrist, J. D. and A. B. Krueger (2001). 'Instrumental Variables and the Search for Identification: From Supply and Demand to Natural Experiments'. *Journal of Economic Perspectives*, 15(4): 69–85.

Bartik, T. (2002). 'Evaluating the Impacts of Local Economic Development Policies on Local Economic Outcomes: What has Been Done and What is Doable?' Paper presented at Evaluating Local Economic and Employment Development Conference, OECD, Vienna, 20–1 November.

Bean, J. A. (2001). *Big Government and Affirmative Action: The Scandalous History of the Small Business Administration.* Lexington, KY: University of Kentucky Press.

Davies, H. (2002). *A Review of Enterprise and the Economy in Education.* London: HM Treasury, HMSO.

Dennis, Jr., W. J. (2004). 'Creating and Sustaining a Viable Small Business Sector'. Paper presented at School of Continuing Education, University of Oklahoma, 27 October.

Department of Trade and Industry (2002). *Cross Cutting Review of Government Services for Small Businesses* (September) URN 02/1324.

Disney, R., J Haskel and Y. Heden (2003). 'Restructuring and Productivity Growth in UK Manufacturing'. *Economic Journal* (July) 113(289): 666–94.

Djankov, S., R. La Porta, F. López-de-Silanes and A. Shleifer (2002). 'The Regulation of Entry'. *The Quarterly Journal of Economics* (February) CXVII(1): 1–37.

EIM (2004). *Review of Methodologies to Measure the Effectiveness of State Aid to SMEs.* EIM: Netherlands.

Eshima, Y. (2003). 'Impact of Public Policy on Innovative SMEs in Japan'. *Journal of Small Business Management* (January) 41(1): 85–93.

European Commission (2003). *Entrepreneurship in Europe.* Brussels: European Commission.

Fraser, S. (2003). 'The Impact of Investors in People on Small Business Growth: Who Benefits?' *Environment and Planning C* (December) 21(6): 793–812.

—— D. J. Storey, J. Frankish, and R. Roberts (2002). 'The Relationship Between Training and Small Business Performance. An Analysis of the Barclays Bank Small Firms Training Loans', *Environment and Planning C* (April) 20(2): 211–33.

—— —— and P. Westhead (2006). 'Student Work Placement in Small Firms: Do they pay off or shift tastes?', *Small Business Economics*, 26(2): 125–44.

Graham, T. (2004). *Review of the Small Firms Loan Guarantee.* London: HM Treasury.

Greene, F. J. (2002). 'An Investigation into Enterprise Support for Younger People, 1975–2000'. *International Small Business Journal*, 20(3): 315–36.

—— and D. J. Storey (2005). 'Evaluating Youth Entrepreneurship: The Prince's Trust'. CSME, Warwick Business School (unpublished).

—— K. Mole and D. J. Storey (2004). 'Does More Mean Worse? Three Decades of Enterprise Policy in the Tees Valley'. *Urban Studies* (June) 41(7): 1207–28.

Harrison, R. T. and C. M. Leitch (1996). 'Whatever You Hit Call the Target: An Alternative Approach to Small Business Policy', in M. Danson (ed) *Small Firm Formation and Regional Economic Development.* London: Routledge.

Heckman, J. J. (2001). 'Micro Data, Heterogeneity and the Evaluation of Public Policy–Nobel Lecture'. *Journal of Political Economy* (August) 109(4): 673–748.

—— H. Ichimura and P. Todd (1997). 'Matching as an Econometric Evaluation Estimator: Evidence from Evaluating a Job Training Programme.' *Review of Economic Studies*, 64(4): 605–54.

Kuusisto, J., R. Berney and R. Blackburn (1999). 'A Critical Evaluation of SME Support Policies in the United Kingdom and the Republic of Ireland—An In-depth Delphi Study of Selected SME Support Policies and their Evaluation'. Finland: Ministry of Trade and Industry, Studies and Reports 6/1999.

Lambrecht, J and F. Pirnay (2005), 'An Evaluation of Public Support Measures for Private External Consultancies to SMEs in the Walloon Region of Belgium'. *Entrepreneurship and Regional Development*, 17(2): 89–108.

Lerner, J. (1999). 'The Government as Venture Capitalist: The Long Run Impact of the SBIR Program'. *Journal of Business*, 72(3): 285–318.

Lundstrom, A. and L. A. Stevenson (2005). *Entrepreneurship Policy: Theory and Practice.* New York: Springer

Meager, N., P. Bates and M. Cowling (2003). 'An Evaluation of Business Start Up Support for Young People'. *National Institute Economic Review* (October) 186: 70–83.

Oldsman, E. (2002). 'Evaluating Business Assistance Programme'. Paper presented at 'Evaluating Local Economic and Employment Development conference', OECD, Vienna, 20–1 November.

OECD (1995). *Best Practice Policies for Small and Medium-sized Enterprises.* Paris: OECD.

OECD (2000). *Small and Medium Enterprise Outlook.* Paris: OECD.

Papaconstantinou, G. and W. Polt (1997). 'Policy Evaluation in Innovation and Technology: An Overview'. *Policy Evaluation in Innovation and Technology: Towards Best Practices.* Paris: OECD.

Roper S. and N. Hewitt-Dundas (2001). 'Grant Assistance and Small Firm Development in Northern Ireland and the Republic of Ireland.' *Scottish Journal of Political Economy,* 48(1): 99–117.

(Small Business Service) SBS (2004). *A Government Action Plan for Small Business: The Evidence Base.* London: Department of Trade and Industry.

Smith, J. A. (2002). 'Evaluating Active Labour Market Policies', Paper presented at OECD Conference: 'Evaluating Local Economic and Employment Development'. Vienna, 20–1 November.

Storey, D. J. (2000). 'Six Steps to Heaven: Evaluating the Impact of Public Policies to Support Small Businesses in Developed Economies' in H. Landstrom and D. L. Sexton (eds) *Handbook of Entrepreneurship.* Oxford: Blackwells.

—— (2003). 'Entrepreneurship, Small and Medium Sized Enterprises and Public Policies', in Z. J. Acs and D. B. Audretsch (eds) *Handbook of Entrepreneurship Research.* Dordrecht: Kluwer Academic Publishers.

World Bank (2005). *Doing Business in 2005.* Washington, DC: World Bank.

Wren, C. and D. J. Storey (2002). 'Evaluating the Effect of "Soft" Business Support Upon Small Firm Performance'. *Oxford Economic Papers,* 54: 334–65.

PART III

INNOVATION

CHAPTER 11

ENTREPRENEURSHIP, GROWTH AND RESTRUCTURING

DAVID B. AUDRETSCH AND MAX KEILBACH

11.1 Introduction

Economic growth has been a major preoccupation of economists, dating back at least to Adam Smith. William Stanley Jevons, for example, posited a growth theory based on the activity of sunspots. Robert Solow took a less exotic approach to explaining economic growth. Writing in the post-war era, Solow was awarded the Nobel Prize for his model of economic growth based on what became termed as the neoclassical production function. In the Solow model two key factors of production—physical capital and (unskilled) labor were econometrically linked to explain economic growth.[1]

[1] Solow, of course, did acknowledge that technical change contributed to economic growth, but in terms of his formal model, it was considered to be an unexplained residual, which 'falls like manna from heaven.' As Nelson (1981: 1,030) points out, 'Robert Solow's 1956 theoretical article was largely addressed to the pessimism about full employment growth built into the Harrod-Domar model .... In that model he admitted the possibility of technological advance.' Solow's pathbreaking research inspired a subsequent generation of economists to rely upon the model of the production function as a basis for explaining the determinants of economic growth. This approach generally consisted of relating various measures representing these two fundamental factors of production, physical capital

While economic growth policy seemingly fell squarely within the domain of macroeconomics, the primacy of capital as a factor of production had implications at the microeconomic level for the organization of both the enterprise and the industry or market. There were both theoretical arguments and empirical insights suggesting that the organization of economic activity to efficiently utilize the factor of physical capital might, in fact, not be consistent with the assumptions needed for perfect competition, and therefore economic welfare. In particular, capital seemed to be deployed most efficiently in large organizations capable of exhausting significant economies of scale, resulting in a concentrated industry or market, consisting of just a few main producers. The emergence and ascendancy of the applied field of industrial organization in economics reflected the importance of this concern.

During the post-war period, a generation of scholars galvanized the field of industrial organization by developing a research agenda dedicated to identifying the issues involving this perceived trade-off between economic efficiency on the one hand and political and economic decentralization on the other (Scherer, 1970). Scholarship in industrial organization generated a massive literature focusing on essentially three issues: (i) What are the gains to size and large-scale production? (ii) What are the economic welfare implications of having an oligopolistic or concentrated market structure, that is economic performance promoted or reduced in an industry with just a handful of large-scale firms? and (iii) Given the overwhelming evidence that large-scale production resulting in economic concentration is associated with increased efficiency, what are the public policy implications?

A generation of scholars had systematically documented and supported the conclusion of Joseph A. Schumpeter (1942: 106): 'What we have got to accept is that the large-scale establishment or unit of control has come to be the most powerful engine of progress'; and in particular, of Oliver Williamson's classic 1968 article 'Economies as an Antitrust Defense: The Welfare Tradeoffs', published in the *American Economic Review.* It became something of a final statement demonstrating what appeared to be an inevitable trade-off between the gains in productive efficiency that could be obtained through increased concentration, and gains in terms of competition—and implicitly, democracy, that could be achieved through decentralizing policies. But it did not seem possible to have both, certainly not in Williamson's completely static model.

It would be a mistake to think that knowledge was not considered as a factor influencing economic growth prior to the 'new endogenous growth theory'. As already explained, one of the main conclusions of the Solow model was that the traditional factors of capital and labour were inadequate in accounting for

and unskilled labour, in trying to explain variations in growth rates. It must be emphasized that the unexplained residual, which typically accounted for a large share of the (unexplained) variance in growth rates, was attributed to technological change.

variations in growth performance. Indeed, it was the residual, attributed to reflect technological change, that typically accounted for most of the variations in economic growth.

Still, the introduction of knowledge into macroeconomic growth models was formalized by Romer (1986) and Lucas (1988). Romer's (1986) critique of the Solow approach was not with the basic model of the neoclassical production function, but rather what he perceived to be omitted from that model—knowledge. Not only did Romer (1986), along with Lucas (1988) and others argue that knowledge was an important factor of production, along with the traditional factors of labour and capital, but because it was endogenously determined as a result of externalities and spillovers, it was particularly important.

That entrepreneurship in the form of new and small enterprises could play an important role in a knowledge-based economy seems to be contrary to many of the conventional theories of innovation. This conventional wisdom had been shaped largely by scholars such as Alfred Chandler (1977), Joseph Schumpeter (1942) and John Kenneth Galbraith (1962) who had convinced a generation of scholars and policy-makers that innovation and technological change lie in the domain of large corporations and that small business would fade away as the victim of its own inefficiencies.

At the heart of this conventional wisdom was the belief that monolithic enterprises exploiting market power were the driving engine of innovative activity. Galbraith (1956: 86) echoed Schumpeter's conclusion: 'There is no more pleasant fiction than that technological change is the product of the matchless ingenuity of the small man forced by competition to employ his wits to better his neighbor. Unhappily, it is a fiction.'

The conventional wisdom about small and new firms was that they were burdened with a size-inherent handicap in terms of innovative activity. Because they had a deficit of resources required to generate and commercialize ideas, this conventional wisdom viewed small enterprises as being largely outside of the domain of innovative activity and technological change. Thus, even after David Birch (1981) revealed the startling findings from his study that small firms provided the engine of job creation for the US, most scholars still assumed that, while small businesses may create the bulk of new jobs, innovation and technological change remained beyond their sphere.

The purpose of this paper is to suggest that a more recent literature has emerged which identifies how and why entrepreneurship in the form of new and small firms is a driving engine of industrial restructuring and economic growth. The starting point of this literature is the consideration of entrepreneurial opportunities and how they relate to opportunities generated by incumbent corporations. Entrepreneurship is distinguished from incumbent organizations with respect to both opportunity creation and exploitation. According to the 'Knowledge Spillover Theory of Entrepreneurship' (see Audretsch et al., 2006), entrepreneurial opportunities are not exogenous to the economy, but rather systematically created by incumbent organizations investing in new knowledge and ideas but unable to fully commercialize that new knowledge.

Thus, while Romer and others in the endogenous growth literature assume the spillover of knowledge to be automatic, the existence of the knowledge filter impedes the spillover and commercialization of knowledge. By serving as a conduit of knowledge spillovers, entrepreneurship not only triggers industrial restructuring but also provides the missing link in models of economic growth.

11.2 Where does opportunity come from?

Where do opportunities come from? Hebert and Link (1989) have identified three distinct intellectual traditions in the development of the entrepreneurship literature that addresses this question. These three traditions can be characterized as the German Tradition, based on von Thüenen and Schumpeter; the Chicago Tradition, based on Knight and Schultz; and the Austrian Tradition, based on von Mises, Kirzner and Shackle. The general view in these contributions is that entrepreneurial opportunities arise from a continuous stream of (exogenous) shocks due to changes in the physical environment (e.g. due to changes in relative factor prices) or in the knowledge base (e.g. due to innovation). However, this literature does not offer an endogenous view of how these shocks are actually generated, that is the formation of new opportunities is taken as exogenous.

The view taken by the contemporary literature on entrepreneurship is no different. There, it is a virtual consensus that entrepreneurship revolves around the recognition of opportunities and the pursuit of those opportunities (Venkataraman, 1997). But, in this literature, the existence of those opportunities is, in fact, taken as given. The focus has been on the cognitive process by which individuals reach the decision to start a new firm. This has resulted in a methodology focusing differences across individuals in analyzing the entrepreneurial decision (Stevenson and Jarillo, 1990). Krueger (2003: 105) has pointed out that, 'The heart of entrepreneurship is an orientation toward seeing opportunities,' which frames the research questions, 'What is the nature of entrepreneurial thinking and what cognitive phenomena are associated with seeing and acting on opportunities?'

Thus, the traditional approach to entrepreneurship essentially holds the opportunities constant and then asks how the cognitive process inherent in the entrepreneurial decision varies across different individual characteristics and attributes (McClelland, 1961; Shaver, 2003). As Shane and Eckhardt (2003: 187) summarize this literature in introducing the individual-opportunity nexus, 'We discussed the process of opportunity discovery and explained why some actors are more likely to discover a given opportunity than others.' Some of these differences involve the willingness to incur risk; others involve the preference for autonomy and self-direction, while still others involve differential access to scarce and expensive resources, such as financial capital, human capital, social capital and experiential capital.

Stevenson and Jarillo (1990) assume that entrepreneurship is an orientation towards opportunity recognition. Central to this research agenda are the questions, 'How do entrepreneurs perceive opportunities and how do these opportunities manifest themselves as being credible versus being an illusion?' Krueger (2003) examines the nature of entrepreneurial thinking and the cognitive process associated with opportunity identification and the decision to undertake entrepreneurial action.

To say that the literature has treated opportunities for entrepreneurs as being exogenous does not mean that all opportunity for a broader range of economic actors has been considered to be exogenous. For example, the most predominant theory of the firm does not assume that opportunities are exogenous to the firm. Rather, innovative opportunities are the result of systematic effort by firms and the result of purposeful efforts to create knowledge and new ideas, and subsequently to appropriate the returns of those investments through commercialization of such investments (Griliches 1979; Cohen and Levin 1989; and Chandler, 1990). In what Griliches formalized as the model of the knowledge production function, incumbent firms engage in the pursuit of new economic knowledge as an input into the process of generating the output of innovative activity. Such efforts to create opportunities involve investments in research and development (R&D) and the enhancement of human capital through training and education.

Thus, according to the model of the knowledge production function (Griliches, 1979) opportunities are endogenously created by purposeful and dedicated investments and efforts by firms. This is a stark contrast to the intellectual tradition in the entrepreneurship literature where opportunities are taken as being exogenous, but the decision to become an entrepreneur is endogenous.

11.3 Opportunity exploitation

Who exploits, or takes advantage of opportunities? Different literatures have undertaken different approaches to provide different answers to this question.

The entrepreneurship literature has not treated this as being exogenous, but rather as the central question in the literature.

The focal point of this research is on the cognitive process identifying the entrepreneurial opportunity along with the decision to start a new firm. Thus, a perceived opportunity and intent to pursue that opportunity are the necessary and sufficient conditions for entrepreneurial activity to take place. The perception of an opportunity is shaped by a sense of the anticipated rewards accruing from, and costs of, becoming an entrepreneur. Some of the research focuses on the role of personal attitudes and characteristics, such as self-efficacy (the individual's sense of competence), collective efficacy, and social norms. Shane (2000) has identified how prior experience and the ability to apply specific skills influence the perception of future opportunities.

The concept of the entrepreneurial decision resulting from the cognitive processes of opportunity recognition and ensuing action is introduced by Shane and Eckhardt (2003) and Shane and Venkataraman (2001). They suggest that an equilibrium view of entrepreneurship stems from the assumption of perfect information. In contrast, imperfect information generates divergences in perceived opportunities across different people. The sources of heterogeneity across individuals include different access to information, as well as cognitive abilities, psychological differences, and access to financial and social capital.

This approach focusing on individual cognition in the entrepreneurial process has generated a number of important and valuable insights, such as the contribution made by social networks, education and training, and familial influence. The literature certainly leaves the impression that entrepreneurship is a personal matter largely determined by DNA, familial status and access to crucial resources. For example, Sarasvathy et al. (2003: 142) explain the role of entrepreneurial opportunity in the literature, 'An entrepreneurial opportunity consists of a set of ideas, beliefs and actions that enable the creation of future goods and services in the absence of current markets for them'. Sarasvathy, Dew, Velamuri and Venkataraman provide a typology of entrepreneurial opportunities as consisting of opportunity recognition, opportunity discovery and opportunity creation.

In contrast, a very different literature, associated with the model of the knowledge production function looked for opportunity exploitation for the unit of observation of the firm. This literature implicitly assumed that opportunity exploitation takes place within the same organizational unit creating those opportunities in the first place—the firm. By explicitly modelling and specifying the econometric estimation of the knowledge production function as linking firm innovative output to firm investments in new knowledge (Griliches, 1984), such as R&D and human capital, this literature assumed that the creation and exploitation of new opportunities occurred within the same organizational unit. Just as the firm is viewed as providing the organizational unit for the creation of the opportunities, through purposeful investments in R&D, it is also viewed as appropriating the returns to those investments through innovative activity, such as patented inventions creating new intellectual property.

However, the empirical evidence from systematic empirical testing of the model of the knowledge production function contradicted the assumption of singularity between the organization creating the opportunities and the organization exploiting the opportunities. For example, Acs and Audretsch (1990) found that the most innovative US firms are large corporations that account for most of the country's private R&D investments. However, large firms did not account for the greatest amount of innovative activity in all, or even most of the innovative industries. For example, in the pharmaceutical preparation and aircraft industries the large firms were much more innovative, while in computers and process control instruments small firms contributed the bulk of the innovations.

Acs and Audretsch (1988, 1990) found a small-firm innovation rate in manufacturing of 0.309, compared to a large-firm innovation rate of 0.202. Their findings, along with others, suggested an organizational discordance between the creation and exploitation of opportunities.

A third literature concerning the exploitation of opportunity was provided by evolutionary economics (Nelson and Winter, 1982). Nelson and Winter suggested that opportunity exploitation was shaped by two distinct knowledge regimes underlying each industry context. What they term as the routinized technological regime reflects knowledge conditions where the large incumbent firms that have created the opportunities through purposeful R&D and other knowledge creating efforts are also the firms that exploit the opportunities they created. Thus, the routinized technological regime essentially corresponded to the assumption implicit in the model of the knowledge production function that the firm exploiting opportunities is the same firm that created those opportunities in the first place. In contrast, in the entrepreneurial technological regime the knowledge conditions bestow the capacity to exploit the opportunities in a different organizational context, a small enterprise (Winter, 1984). Thus, the empirical evidence from testing the model of the knowledge production function actually seemed to support the evolutionary view more than the assumption of organizational homogeneity for opportunity creation and exploitation.

There are, however, two important distinctions to emphasize. The first is the view that, in the entrepreneurial regime, the small firms exist and will commercialize the new knowledge or innovate. In the lens provided by the spillover theory of entrepreneurship, the new firm is endogenously created via entrepreneurship or the recognition of an opportunity and pursuit by an economic agent (or team of economic agents) to appropriate the value of their knowledge. These knowledge-bearing economic agents use the organizational context of creating a new firm to attempt to appropriate their endowments of knowledge.

The second distinction is that the knowledge will be commercialized, either by large or small firms. In the lens provided by the 'Knowledge Spillover Theory of

Entrepreneurship', which is explained in the following section, the knowledge filter will impede and pre-empt at least some of the spillover and commercialization of knowledge. Only certain spillover mechanisms, such as entrepreneurship, can to some extent permeate the knowledge filter. But this is not a foregone conclusion, but rather will vary across specific contexts, and depends on a broad range of factors, spanning individual characteristics, institutions, culture, laws, and is characterized by what Audretsch et al. (2006) denote as *Entrepreneurship Capital.*

11.4 The 'Knowledge Spillover Theory of Entrepreneurship'

The discrepancy in organizational context between the organization creating opportunities, and those exploiting the opportunities that seemingly contradicted Griliches' model of the firm knowledge production function, was resolved by Audretsch (1995), who introduces the 'Knowledge Spillover Theory of Entrepreneurship', 'The findings challenge an assumption implicit to the knowledge production function—that firms exist exogenously and then endogenously seek out and apply knowledge inputs to generate innovative output ... It is the knowledge in the possession of economic agents that is exogenous, and in an effort to appropriate the returns from that knowledge, the spillover of knowledge from its producing entity involves endogenously creating a new firm' (pp. 179–80).

What is the source of this entrepreneurial opportunity that endogenously generated the start-up of new firms? The answer seemed to be through the spillover of knowledge that created the opportunities for the start-up of a new firm, 'How are these small and frequently new firms able to generate innovative output when undertaken a generally negligible amount of investment into knowledge-generating inputs, such as R&D? One answer is apparently through exploiting knowledge created by expenditures on research in universities and on R&D in large corporations' (p. 179).

The empirical evidence supporting the 'Knowledge Spillover Theory of Entrepreneurship' was provided from analyzing variations in start-up rates across different industries reflecting different underlying knowledge contexts. In particular, those industries with a greater investment in new knowledge also exhibited higher start-up rates than those with less investment in new knowledge. This evidence suggests one conduit for transmission of knowledge spillovers.

Thus, compelling evidence was provided suggesting that entrepreneurship is an endogenous response to opportunities created, but not exploited, by the incumbent firms. This involved an organizational dimension involving the mechanism transmitting knowledge spillovers—the start-up of new firms. In addition, Jaffe (1989), Audretsch and Feldman (1996) and Audretsch and Stephan (1996) provided evidence concerning the spatial dimension of knowledge spillovers. In particular, their findings suggested that knowledge spillovers are geographically bounded and localized within spatial proximity to the knowledge source. None of these studies, however, identified the actual mechanisms which actually transmit the knowledge spillover; rather, the spillovers were implicitly assumed to automatically exist (or fall like manna from heaven), but only within a geographically bounded spatial area.

As section 2 of this chapter emphasized, while in the recent literature much has been made about the key role played by the recognition of opportunities in the cognitive process underlying the decision to become an entrepreneur, relatively little has been written about the actual source of such entrepreneurial opportunities. The 'Knowledge Spillover Theory of Entrepreneurship' identifies one source of entrepreneurial opportunities—new knowledge and ideas. In particular, the 'Knowledge Spillover Theory of Entrepreneurship' posits that it is new knowledge and ideas created in one context but left uncommercialized or not vigorously pursued by the source actually creating those ideas, such as a research laboratory in a large corporation or research undertaken by a university, that serves as the source of knowledge generating entrepreneurial opportunities. Thus, in this view, one mechanism for recognizing new opportunities and actually implementing them by starting a new firm involves the spillover of knowledge. The organization creating the opportunities is not the same organization that exploits the opportunities. If the exploitation of those opportunities by the entrepreneur does not involve full payment to the firm for producing those opportunities, such as a licence or royalty, then the entrepreneurial act of starting a new firm serves as a mechanism for knowledge spillovers.

Why should entrepreneurship play an important role in the spillover of new knowledge and ideas? And why should new knowledge play an important role in creating entrepreneurial opportunities? In the Romer (1986) model of endogenous growth, new technological knowledge is assumed to automatically spill over. Investment in new technological knowledge is automatically accessed by third-party firms and economic agents, resulting in the automatic spillover of knowledge. The assumption that knowledge automatically spills over is, of course, consistent with the important insight by Arrow (1962) that knowledge differs from the traditional factors of production—physical capital and (unskilled) labour—in that it is non-excludable and non-exhaustive. When the firm or economic agent uses the knowledge, it is neither exhausted nor can it be, in the absence of legal protection, precluded from use by third-party firms or other economic agents. Thus, in the spirit of the Romer model, drawing on the earlier insights about knowledge from Arrow, a large and vigorous literature has emerged obsessed with the links between intellectual property protection and the incentives for firms to invest in the creation of new knowledge through R&D and investments in human capital.

However, the preoccupation with the non-excludability and non-exhaustibility of knowledge first identified by Arrow and later carried forward and assumed in the Romer model, neglects another key insight in the original Arrow (1962) article. Arrow also identified another dimension by which knowledge differs from the traditional factors of production. This other dimension involves the greater degree of uncertainty, higher extent of asymmetries, and greater cost of transacting new ideas. The expected value of any new idea is highly uncertain, and as Arrow pointed out, has a much greater variance than would be associated with the deployment of traditional factors of production. After all, there is relative certainty about what a standard piece of capital equipment can do, or what an (unskilled) worker can contribute to a mass-production assembly line. In contrast, Arrow emphasized that when it comes to innovation, there is uncertainty about whether the new product can be produced, how it can be produced, and whether sufficient demand for that visualized new product might actually materialize.

In addition, new ideas are typically associated with considerable asymmetries. In order to evaluate a proposed new idea concerning a new biotechnology product, the decision-maker might not only need to have a PhD in biotechnology, but also a specialization in the exact scientific area. Such divergences in education, background and experience can result in a divergence in the expected value of a new project or the variance in outcomes anticipated from pursuing that new idea, both of which can lead to divergences in the recognition and evaluation of opportunities across economic agents and decision-making hierarchies. Such divergences in the valuation of new ideas will become greater if the new idea is not consistent with the core competence and technological trajectory of the incumbent firm.

Thus, because of the conditions inherent in knowledge—high uncertainty, asymmetries and transactions costs—decision-making hierarchies can reach the decision not to pursue and try to commercialize new ideas that individual economic agents, or groups or teams of economic agents think are potentially valuable and should be pursued. The basic conditions characterizing new knowledge, combined with a broad spectrum of institutions, rules and regulations impose what Acs et al. (2004) term the 'knowledge filter'. The knowledge filter is the gap between new knowledge and what Arrow (1962) referred to as economic knowledge or commercialized knowledge. The greater the knowledge filter is, the more pronounced is this gap between new knowledge and new economic, or commercialized, knowledge.

The knowledge filter is a consequence of the basic conditions inherent in new knowledge. Similarly, it is the knowledge filter that creates the opportunity for entrepreneurship in the 'Knowledge Spillover Theory of Entrepreneurship'. According to this theory, opportunities for entrepreneurship are the duality of the knowledge filter. The higher the knowledge filter is, the greater are the divergences in the valuation of new ideas across economic agents and the decision-making hierarchies of incumbent firms. Entrepreneurial opportunities are generated not just by investments in new knowledge and ideas, but in the propensity for only a distinct subset of those opportunities to be fully pursued by incumbent firms.

Thus, the 'Knowledge Spillover Theory of Entrepreneurship' shifts the fundamental decision-making unit of observation in the model of the knowledge production function away from exogenously assumed firms to individuals, such as scientists, engineers or other knowledge workers—agents with endowments of new economic knowledge. As Audretsch (1995) pointed out, when the lens is shifted away from the firm to the individual as the relevant unit of observation, the appropriability issue remains, but the question becomes: 'How can economic agents with a given endowment of new knowledge best appropriate the returns from that knowledge?' If the scientist or engineer can pursue the new idea within the organizational structure of the firm developing the knowledge, and appropriate roughly the expected value of that knowledge, she has no reason to leave the firm. On the other hand, if she places a greater value on his ideas than do the decision-making bureaucracy of the incumbent firm, he may choose to start a new firm to appropriate the value of his knowledge.

In the 'Knowledge Spillover Theory of Entrepreneurship', the knowledge production function is actually reversed. The knowledge is exogenous and embodied in a worker. The firm is created endogenously in the worker's effort to appropriate the value of his knowledge through innovative activity. Typically an employee from an established large corporation, often a scientist or engineer working in a research laboratory, will have an idea for an invention and ultimately for an innovation. An expected net return from the new product accompanies this potential innovation. The inventor would expect to be compensated for his/her potential innovation accordingly. If the company has a different, presumably lower, valuation of the potential innovation, it may decide either not to pursue its development, or that it merits a lower level of compensation than that expected by the employee.

In either case, the employee will weigh the alternative of starting his/her own firm. If the gap in the expected return accruing from the potential innovation between the inventor and the corporate decision-maker is sufficiently large, and if the cost of starting a new firm is sufficiently low, the employee may decide to leave the large corporation and establish a new enterprise. Since the knowledge was generated in the established corporation, the new start-up is considered to be a spin-off from the existing firm. Such start-ups typically do not have direct access to a large R&D laboratory. Rather, the entrepreneurial opportunity emanates from the knowledge and experience accrued from the R&D laboratories with their previous employers. Thus the knowledge spillover view of entrepreneurship is actually a theory of endogenous entrepreneurship, where entrepreneurship is an endogenous response to opportunities created by investments in new knowledge that are not commercialized because of the knowledge filter.

As investments in new knowledge increase, entrepreneurial opportunities will also increase. Contexts where new knowledge plays an important role are associated with a greater degree of uncertainty and asymmetries across economic agents evaluating the potential value of new ideas. Thus, a context involving more new knowledge will also impose a greater divergence in the evaluation of that knowledge across economic agents, resulting in a greater variance in the outcome expected from commercializing those ideas. It is this gap in the valuation of new ideas across economic agents, or between economic agents and decision-making hierarchies of incumbent enterprises, that creates the entrepreneurial opportunity.

As already discussed, a vigorous literature has identified that knowledge spillovers are greater in the presence of knowledge investments. Just as Jaffe (1989) and Audretsch and Feldman (1996) show, those regions with high knowledge investments experience a high level of knowledge spillovers, and those regions with a low amount of knowledge investments experience a low level of knowledge spillovers, since there is less knowledge to be spilled over.

The 'Knowledge Spillover Theory of Entrepreneurship' analogously suggests that, *ceteris paribus*, entrepreneurial activity will tend to be greater in contexts where investments in new knowledge are relatively high, since the new firm will be started from knowledge that has spilled over from the source actually producing that new knowledge. A paucity of new ideas in an impoverished knowledge context will generate only limited entrepreneurial opportunities. In contrast, in a high knowledge context, new ideas will generate entrepreneurial opportunities by exploiting (potential) spillovers of that knowledge. Thus, the knowledge spillover view of entrepreneurship provides a clear link, or prediction that entrepreneurial activity will result from investments in new knowledge and that entrepreneurial activity will be spatially localized within close geographic proximity to the knowledge source. Systematic empirical evidence consistent with the 'Knowledge Spillover Theory of Entrepreneurship' has been provided by Audretsch et al. (2006) and Acs et al. (2004). Both studies find that entrepreneurship rates tend to be greater in the context of greater investments in new knowledge.

11.5 Growth

The 'Knowledge Spillover Theory of Entrepreneurship', which focuses on how new knowledge can influence the cognitive decision-making process inherent in the entrepreneurial decision and links entrepreneurship and economic growth, is consistent with theories of industry evolution (Jovanovic, 1982; Lambson, 1991; Hopenhayn, 1992; Ericson and Pakes, 1995; Audretsch, 1995; and Klepper, 1996). While traditional theories suggest that small firms will retard economic growth, by imposing a drag on productive efficiency, these evolutionary theories suggest exactly the opposite—that entrepreneurship will stimulate and generate growth. The reason for these theoretical discrepancies lies in the context of the underlying theory. In the traditional theory, new knowledge plays no role; rather, static efficiency, determined largely by the ability to exhaust scale economies dictates growth. In contrast, the evolutionary models are dynamic in nature and emphasize the role that knowledge plays. Because knowledge is inherently uncertain, asymmetric and associated with high costs of transactions, divergences emerge concerning the expected value of new ideas. Economic agents therefore have an incentive to leave an incumbent firm and start a new firm in an attempt to commercialize the perceived value of their knowledge. Entrepreneurship is the vehicle by which (the most radical) ideas are sometimes implemented and commercialized.

A distinguishing feature of these evolutionary theories is the focus on change as a central phenomenon. Innovative activity, one of the central manifestations of change, is at the heart of much of this work. Entry, growth, survival, and the way firms and entire industries change over time are linked to innovation. The dynamic performance of regions and even entire economies, that is the *Standort*, is linked to the efficacy of transforming investments in new knowledge into innovative activity.

Why are new firms started? The traditional, equilibrium-based view is that new firms in an industry, whether they are start-ups or firms diversifying from other industries, enter when incumbent firms in the industry earn supranormal profits. By expanding industry supply, entry depresses price and restores profits to their long-run equilibrium level. Thus, in equilibrium-based theories, entry serves as a mechanism to discipline incumbent firms. In contrast, the new theories of industry evolution develop and evaluate alternative characterizations of entrepreneurship based on innovation and costs of firm growth. These new evolutionary theories correspond to the disequilibrating theory of entrepreneurship proposed by Shane and Eckhardt (2003).

For example, Audretsch (1995) analyzes the factors that influence the rate of new firm start-ups. He finds that such start-ups are more likely in industries in which small firms account for a greater percentage of the industry's innovations. This suggests that firms are started to capitalize on distinctive knowledge about innovation that originates from sources outside of an industry's leaders. This initial condition of not just uncertainty, but greater degree of uncertainty vis-à-vis incumbent enterprises in the industry is captured in the theory of firm selection and industry evolution proposed by Jovanovic (1982). Jovanovic presents a model in which the new firms, which he terms *entrepreneurs*, face costs that are not only random but also differ across firms. A central feature of the model is that a new firm does not know what its cost function is, that is its relative efficiency, but rather discovers this through the process of learning from its actual post-entry performance. In particular, Jovanovic (1982) assumes that entrepreneurs are unsure about their ability to manage a new-firm start-up and therefore their prospects for success. Although entrepreneurs may launch a new firm based on a vague sense of expected post-entry performance, they only discover their true ability—in terms of managerial competence and of having based the firm on an idea that is viable on the market—once their business is established. Those entrepreneurs who discover that their ability exceeds their expectations expand the scale of their business, whereas those discovering that their post-entry performance is less than commensurate with their expectations will contact the scale of output and possibly exit from the industry. Thus, Jovanovic's model is a theory of 'noisy selection', where efficient firms grow and survive and inefficient firms decline and fail. The links between entrepreneurship on the one hand, and growth and survival on the other, have been found across a number of social science disciplines, including economics, sociology and regional studies.

A series of survey articles by Sutton (1997), Caves (1998) and Geroski (1995) summarize the findings from a plethora of empirical studies examining the relationship between firm size and growth within the North American context. The early studies were undertaken using data from the US. These studies (Mansfield, 1962; Hall, 1987; Dunne, Roberts and Samuelson, 1989; and Audretsch, 1991) established not only that the likelihood of a new entrant surviving is quite low, but that the likelihood of survival is positively related to firm size and age. A 'stylized result' (Geroski, 1995) emerging from this literature is that, when a broad spectrum of firm sizes is included in samples of US enterprises, smaller firms exhibit systematically higher growth rates than their larger counterparts. The growth advantage of small and new firms vis-à-vis large enterprises has been shown to be even greater in high technology industries (Audretsch, 1995).

These so-called stylized results between firm size and age on the one hand, and growth and survival on the other, were subsequently confirmed for a number of European countries. A wave of studies have confirmed these findings for different European countries, including Portugal (Mata et al., 1995; and Mata, 1994), Germany (Wagner, 1994), Norway (Tveteras and Edide, 2000; and Klette and Mathiassen, 1996) and Italy (Audretsch et al., 1999).

Using a large comprehensive panel data set from the ZEW-foundation Panel (West), 'Gibrat's Law' is rejected for the group of young firms belonging to technology intensive branches as well as those operating in non-technology intensive branches (Almus and Nerlinger, 2000), indicating that the smaller enterprises grow faster than their larger counterparts.

Heshmati (2001) has examined the relationship between firm size, age and growth for a large sample of small firms in Sweden between 1993 and 1998. The results indicate that, in Sweden, firm size and age are negatively related to employment growth, which is consistent with the findings for the US. However, in terms of sales growth, a positive relationship emerges, suggesting that, at least over this period, larger firms generated more growth in terms of sales than in terms of employment.

Wagner (1994) tracked the performance of small (and large) firms prior to exit. He used a longitudinal data base identifying the pre-exit performance of cohorts of firms exiting in 1990, 1991 and 1992. One striking result he found was that more than half of the exiting firms (between 53 percent and 61 percent) were founded prior to 1979, making them over 11 years old. He also found that young firms, which were classified as being younger than five years old, accounted for about a third of all exits. At the same time he found that the likelihood of survival increases with firm size.

Almus and Nerlinger (2000) also use a large panel data base to examine how the post-entry performance of new firms varies across sectors. In particular, they find that the growth rates of new firms tends to be greater in very high-tech industries than in high-tech industries and other manufacturing industries. This mirrors the results found in the North American context.

Using firm-level data from Italy, Audretsch et al. (1999) find that growth rates are negatively related to firm size. In addition, they find that the likelihood of survival is greater in the start-up year than in the second year, but subsequently increases over time. Similarly, Tveteras and Eide (2000) provide evidence for Norwegian manufacturing using the estimation technique of a semi-proportional Cox Model that the likelihood of survival is lower for smaller and younger establishments. Bruederl and Preisendoerfer (1998) examine a data base consisting of 1,700 new-firm start-ups in Germany and find that the subsequent performance, measured in terms of likelihood of survival and growth, is greater for those entrepreneurs that (1) participate in a network with other entrepreneurs, (2) receive active help from their spouse, and (3) receive emotional support from their spouse. In addition, they find that entrepreneurial success is positively influenced by the ethnic background of the entrepreneur, educational background, type of work experience, and whether the entrepreneur already had entrepreneurial experience. Their most striking finding is that entrepreneurial success is the highest within the context of a network with other entrepreneurs.

Thus, while there is somewhat more ambiguity in the studies linking growth and survival to firm size and growth, the results for Europe generally mirror the so-called 'stylized results' found within the North American context:

1 Growth rates are higher for smaller enterprises;
2 Growth rates are higher for younger enterprises;
3 Growth rates are even higher for small and young enterprises in knowledge-intensive industries;

4 The likelihood of survival is lower for smaller enterprises;
5 The likelihood of survival is lower for younger enterprises; and
6 The likelihood of survival is even lower for small and young enterprises in knowledge-intensive industries.

What emerges from the new evolutionary theories and corroborative empirical evidence on the role of entrepreneurial firms is that firms are in motion, with a lot of new firms entering the industry and a lot of firms exiting out of the industry. The evolutionary view of entrepreneurship is that new firms typically start at a very small scale of output. They are motivated by the desire to appropriate the expected value of new economic knowledge. But, depending upon the extent of scale economies in the industry, the firm may not be able to remain viable indefinitely at its start-up size. Rather, if scale economies are anything other than negligible, the new firm is likely to have to grow to survival. The temporary survival of new firms is presumably supported through the deployment of a strategy of compensating factor differentials that enables the firm to discover whether or not it has a viable product.

The role of learning in the selection process has been the subject of considerable debate. On the one hand there is what has been referred to as the *Larackian* assumption—that learning refers to adaptations made by the new enterprise. In this sense, those new firms that are the most flexible and adaptable will be the most successful in adjusting to whatever the demands of the market are. As Nelson and Winter (1982: 11) point out, 'Many kinds of organizations commit resources to learning; organizations seek to copy the forms of their most successful competitors'. On the other hand there is the interpretation that the role of learning is restricted to discovering if the firm is producing a good, or offering a service that is compatible with market viability. Under this interpretation, the new enterprise is not necessarily able to adapt or adjust to market conditions, but receives information based on its market performance with respect to its fitness in terms of meeting demand most efficiently vis-à-vis rivals. The theory of organizational ecology proposed by Michael T. Hannan and John Freeman (1989) most pointedly adheres to the notion that, 'We assume that individual organizations are characterized by relative inertia in structure'. That is, firms learn not in the sense that they adjust their actions as reflected by their fundamental identity and purpose, but in the sense of their perception. When viewed from this evolutionary perspective, the start-up of a new firm injects diversity into the market. The process of entrepreneurship, or starting a new firm, is therefore a mechanism generating diversity and the spillover of knowledge. As a result of the start-up, knowledge is transformed into new approaches that otherwise would have remained unexplored.

As a result of the diversity of new approaches, entrepreneurship is a vital force fostering industrial restructuring. In his 1911 classic treatise, *Theorie der wirtschaftlichen Entwicklungen* (Theory of Economic Development), Schumpeter proposed a theory of 'creative destruction', where new firms with the entrepreneurial spirit displace less innovative incumbents, ultimately leading to a higher degree of economic growth. Even in his 1942 classic, *Capitalism, Socialism and Democracy*, Schumpeter still argued that entrenched large corporations tend to resist change, forcing entrepreneurs to start new firms in order to pursue innovative activity: 'The function of entrepreneurs is to reform or revolutionize the pattern of production by exploiting an invention, or more generally, an untried technological possibility for producing a new commodity or producing an old one in a new way.... To undertake such new things is difficult and constitutes a distinct economic function, first because they lie outside of the routine tasks which everybody understands, and secondly, because the environment resists in many ways' (1942: 13). By pursuing opportunities that otherwise would not have been pursued by the incumbent organizations, entrepreneurship plants the seeds for entire new industries and is, thus, a driving force of industrial restructuring.

The systematic and empirical evidence described above supports such an evolutionary view of the role of new firms in manufacturing, because the post-entry growth of firms that survive tends to be spurred by the extent to which there is a gap between the minimum efficient scale (MES) level of output and the size of the firm. However, the likelihood of any particular new firm surviving tends to decrease as this gap increases. Such new sub-optimal scale firms are apparently engaged in the selection process. Only those firms offering a viable product that can be produced efficiently will grow and ultimately approach or attain the MES level of output. The remainder will stagnate, and depending upon the severity of the other selection mechanism—the extent of scale economies—may ultimately be forced to exit the industry. Rather, by serving as agents of change, entrepreneurial firms provide an essential source of new ideas and experimentation that otherwise would remain untapped in the economy. The impact of entrepreneurship is therefore manifested by growth—at the levels of the firm, the region and even at the national level.

But is this motion horizontal, in that the bulk of firms exiting are comprised of firms that had entered relatively recently? Or is it vertical, in that a significant share of the exiting firms had been established incumbents that were displaced by younger firms? In trying to shed some light on this question, Audretsch (1995) proposes two different models of the evolutionary process. Some contexts can be best characterized by the model of the conical revolving door, where new businesses are started, but there is also a high propensity to subsequently exit from the market. Other contexts may be better characterized by the metaphor of the forest, where incumbent establishments are displaced by new entrants. Which view is more applicable apparently depends on three major factors—the underlying technological conditions, scale economies, and demand. Where scale economies play an important role, the model of the revolving door seems to be more applicable. While the rather startling result that the start-up and entry of new businesses is apparently not deterred by the presence of high scale economies, a process of firm selection analogous to a revolving door ensures that only those establishments successful enough to grow will be able to survive beyond more than a few years. Thus the bulk of new start-ups that are not so successful ultimately exit within a few years subsequent to entry. By serving as agents of change, new firms provide an essential conduit of knowledge spillovers exploiting new opportunities through experimentation that otherwise would remain untapped in the economy.

The likelihood that the new idea spawning the entrepreneurial start-up is not compatible with market viability and sustainability is high. Thus, the evolutionary interpretation linking knowledge to entrepreneurship and ultimately economic growth suggests that the entrepreneurial act is to learn from the market about the viability and compatibility of a new idea that was rejected, or undervalued by incumbent organizations. The new start-up serves as a conduit for knowledge spillovers from the source producing that knowledge to commercialization in a new firm.

One of the important findings of Glaeser et al. (1992) and Feldman and Audretsch (1999) is that economic growth is promoted by knowledge spillovers. However, their findings, as well as the corroborative results from a plethora of studies, focused on a spatial unit of observation, such as cities, regions and states. For example, Glaeser et al. (1992) found compelling empirical evidence suggesting that a greater degree of knowledge spillover leads to higher growth rates of cities. If the existence of higher knowledge spillovers bestow higher growth rates for cities, this relationship should also hold for the unit of observation of the (knowledge) firm. The performance of entrepreneurial firms accessing knowledge spillovers should exhibit a superior performance. Thus, the 'Entrepreneurial Performance Hypothesis' states that 'The performance of knowledge-based start-ups should be superior when they are able to access knowledge spillovers through geographic proximity to knowledge sources, such as universities, when compared to their counterparts without a close geographic proximity to a knowledge source'.

The 'Entrepreneurial Performance Hypothesis' has been subjected to empirical scrutiny. Evidence supporting the 'Entrepreneurial Performance Hypothesis' at the firm level has been provided by Gilbert (2004), Audretsch et al. (2006), and Gilbert et al. (2005).

However, the 'Entrepreneurial Performance Hypothesis' and supporting empirical evidence cannot be interpreted as attributing the entire impact of entrepreneurship on growth to be restricted to the growth of entrepreneurial firms themselves. Such an extreme assumption of no external impacts is implicit in the analyses of new and small enterprises found in the pathbreaking Birch (1979) study, as well as the more recent Davis et al. (1996a, b) update. While there is severe methodological disagreement between the Davis et al. and Birch approaches to measuring the impact of small firms on economic performance, both implicitly agree in an absence of external impact. Thus, in a type of statistical apartheid or segregation, in the Birch and Davis et al. studies, the impact of small and new firms is measured only within that set of firms.

In contrast, the impact of entrepreneurship on economic growth is not constrained to be limited to manifest itself solely in those entrepreneurial firms, but rather has an external impact of far greater significance. The link between entrepreneurship and economic growth should also exist at the more aggregated level of economic activity. A location, or *Standort*, endowed with a higher degree of what is Audretsch et al. (2006) term as 'Entrepreneurship Capital', will facilitate knowledge spillovers and the commercialization of knowledge, thereby generating greater economic growth. The 'Growth Hypothesis' states, 'Given a level of knowledge investment and severity of the knowledge filter, higher levels of economic growth should result from greater entrepreneurial activity, since entrepreneurship serves as a mechanism facilitating the spillover and commercialization of knowledge.'

In introducing the model of the production function, Robert Solow (1956) argued that economic growth is determined explicitly by the stocks of capital and labour. Technical change entered the production function exogenously as a shift factor. More recently Romer (1986), Lucas (1993) and others extended the neoclassical model of growth by suggesting that not only is knowledge an important factor generating growth, but because it spills over for use by third-party firms it is actually the most potent factor.

The 'Knowledge Spillover Theory of Entrepreneurship' explained in the previous section suggests that this assessment of the role of knowledge overlooks some of the most fundamental mechanisms driving the process of economic growth. The spillover process that Romer and the endogenous growth theory assume to be automatic is not at all automatic. Rather it is a process that is actively driven by economic agents. According to Audretsch et al. (2006), 'Entrepreneurship Capital' serves as a mechanism facilitating the spillover of knowledge.

While Romer and Lucas added the factor of knowledge capital to the traditional factors of physical capital and labour, Audretsch et al. (2006) do not dispute the importance of the traditional factors, but suggest an additional factor as well—the degree of entrepreneurship capital specific to a *Standort*, or location. By entrepreneurship capital Audretsch et al. (2006) mean the capacity for the *Standort*, that is the geographically relevant spatial units of observation, to generate the start-up of new enterprises.

While the neoclassical tradition identified investment in physical capital as the driving factor of economic performance (Solow, 1956), the endogenous growth theory (Romer 1986, 1990; Lucas 1988) put the emphasis on the process of the accumulation of knowledge, and hence the creation of 'knowledge capital'. The concept of 'social capital' (Putnam, 1993; and Coleman, 1988a,b) could be considered as a further extension because it added a social component to those factors shaping economic growth and prosperity. According to Putnam (2000: 19):

Whereas physical capital refers to physical objects and human capital refers to the properties of individuals, social capital refers to connections among individuals – social networks and the norms of reciprocity and trustworthiness that arise from them. In that sense social capital is closely related to what some have called 'civic virtue.' The difference is that 'social capital' calls attention to the fact that civic virtue is most powerful when embedded in a sense network of reciprocal social relations. A society of many virtues but isolated individuals is not necessarily rich in social capital.

Putnam also challenged the standard neoclassical growth model by arguing that social capital was also important in generating economic growth, 'By analogy with notions of physical capital and human capital – tools and training that enhance individual productivity – social capital refers to features of social organization, such as networks, norms, and trust that facilitate coordination and cooperation for mutual benefits.'

A large and robust literature has emerged trying to link social capital to entrepreneurship (Aldrich and Martinez, 2003; and Thorton and Flynn, 2003). However, while it was clear that Putnam was providing a link between social capital and economic welfare, this link did not directly involve entrepreneurship. The components of social capital that Putnam emphasized the most, included associational membership and public trust. While these may be essential for social and economic well-being, it was not obvious that they involved entrepreneurship, per se.

Social capital and entrepreneurship capital are distinctive concepts that should not be confused. According to Putnam (2000: 19), 'Social capital refers to connections among individuals – social networks and the norms of reciprocity and trustworthiness that arise from them. In that sense social capital is closely related to what some have called "civic virtue." ... Social capital calls attention to the fact that civic virtue is most powerful when embedded in a sense network of reciprocal social relations.... Social capital refers to features of social organization, such as networks, norms, and trust, that facilitate coordination and cooperation for mutual benefits'.

Audretsch et al. (2006) argue that what has been called social capital in the entrepreneurship literature may actually be a more specific sub-component, which we introduce as *entrepreneurship capital.* Entrepreneurship has typically been defined as an action, process, or activity. Entrepreneurship involves the start-up and growth of new enterprises. Entrepreneurship capital involves a milieu of agents and institutions that is conducive to the creation of new firms. This involves a number of aspects such as social acceptance of entrepreneurial behaviour; but also, of course, individuals who are willing to deal with the risk of creating new firms,[2] and the activity of bankers and venture capital agents who are willing to share the

[2] As Gartner and Carter (2003) state, 'Entrepreneurial behavior involves the activities of individuals who are associated with creating new organizations rather than the activities of individuals who are involved with maintaining or changing the operations of on-going established organizations.'

risks and benefits involved. Hence entrepreneurship capital reflects a number of different legal, institutional and social factors and forces. Taken together, these factors and forces constitute the entrepreneurship capital of an economy, which creates a capacity for entrepreneurial activity (Hofstede et al., 2002).

It should be emphasized that entrepreneurship capital should not be confused with social capital. The major distinction is that, in our view, not all social capital may be conducive to economic performance, let alone entrepreneurial activity. Some types of social capital may be more focused on preserving the status quo and not necessarily directed at creating challenges to the status quo. In contrast, entrepreneurship capital could be considered to constitute one particular sub-set of social capital. While social capital may have various impacts on entrepreneurship, depending on the specific orientation, entrepreneurship capital, by its very definition, will have a positive impact on entrepreneurial activity.

Audretsch et al. (2006) include a measure of entrepreneurship capital, along with the traditional factors of production of labour, physical capital and knowledge capital, in a production function model to estimate economic growth. Their evidence suggests that entrepreneurship capital exerts indeed a positive impact on economic growth. This finding holds for different measures of entrepreneurship capital, ranging from the more general to the more risk oriented. While the findings by Audretsch et al. (2006) certainly do not contradict the conclusions of earlier studies linking growth to factors such as labour, capital, and knowledge, their evidence points to an additional factor, entrepreneurship capital, that also plays an important role in generating economic growth.

The results from including measures of entrepreneurship capital in the context of estimating economic growth in a production function model, are consistent with other studies also finding a positive relationship between various measures of entrepreneurship and economic growth. For example, Acs et al. (2004) find a positive relationship between entrepreneurship and growth at the country level. Wennekers and Thurik (1999) provided empirical evidence from a 1984–94 cross-sectional study of the 23 countries that are part of the Organization for Economic Co-operation and Development (OECD), that increased entrepreneurship, as measured by business ownership rates, was associated with higher rates of employment growth at the country level. Similarly, Audretsch et al. (2002) and Carree and Thurik (1999) find that OECD countries exhibiting higher increases in entrepreneurship also have experienced greater rates of growth and lower levels of unemployment.

In a study for the OECD, Audretsch and Thurik (2002) undertook two separate empirical analyses to identify the impact of changes of entrepreneurship on growth. Each one uses a different measure of entrepreneurship, sample of countries and specification. This provides some sense of robustness across different measures of entrepreneurship, data sets, time periods and specifications. The first analysis uses a data base that measures entrepreneurship in terms of the relative share of economic activity accounted for by small firms. It links changes in entrepreneurship to growth rates for a panel of 18 OECD countries spanning five years to test the hypothesis that higher rates of entrepreneurship lead to greater subsequent growth rates. The second analysis uses a measure of self-employment as an index of entrepreneurship and links changes in entrepreneurship to unemployment at the country level between 1974 and 1998. The different samples including OECD countries over different time periods reach consistent results—increase in entrepreneurial activity tends to result in higher subsequent growth rates and a reduction of unemployment.

The Global Entrepreneurship Monitor (GEM) Study (Reynolds et al., 2000) also established an empirical link between the degree of entrepreneurial activity and economic growth, as measured by employment, at the country level. Thus, not only are there theoretical arguments but also there is empirical evidence suggesting that the growth of countries is positively associated with an entrepreneurial advantage.

Figure 11.1 shows that those countries exhibiting a greater increase in entrepreneurship rates between 1974 and 1986 also tended to exhibit greater decreases in unemployment rates between 1986 and 1998. This would suggest a negative relationship between entrepreneurial activity and subsequent unemployment. Unemployment is used here because of its importance as a policy goal. A similar relationship between entrepreneurship and growth rates for a broader spectrum of countries, including both OECD and non-OECD countries, is shown by the Global Entrepreneurship Monitor (GEM) Study (Reynolds et al., 2000).

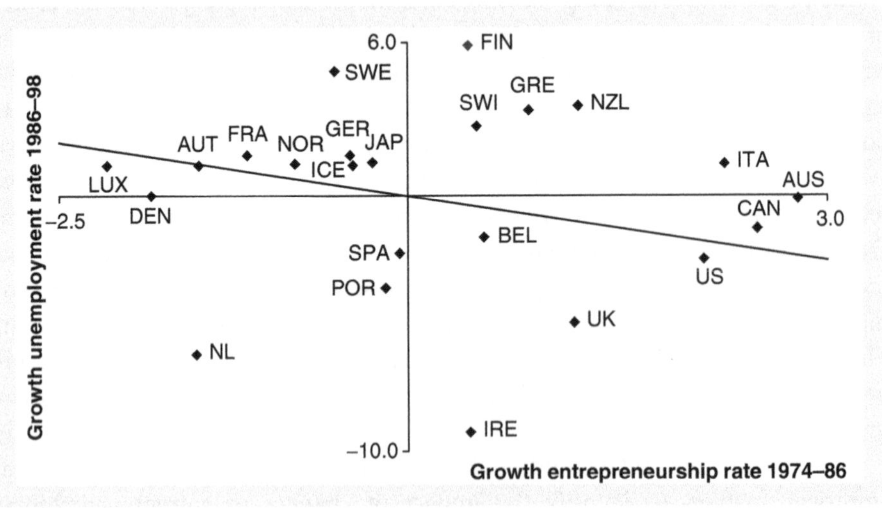

Figure 11.1 Changes in entrepreneurship and unemployment rates in OECD countries

Source: Audretsch et al. (2002)

Several studies have attempted to link entrepreneurship to regional growth. The unit of observation for these studies is at the spatial level, either a city, region, or state. The most common and most exclusive measure of performance is growth, typically measured in terms of employment growth. These studies have tried to link various measures of entrepreneurial activity, most typically start-up rates, to economic growth. Other measures sometimes used include the relative share of SMEs, and self-employment rates.

For example, Holtz-Eakin and Kao (2003) examine the impact of entrepreneurship on growth. Their spatial unit of observation is for states. Their measure of growth is productivity change over time. A vector autoregression analysis shows that variations in the birth rate and the death rate for firms are related to positive changes in productivity. They conclude that entrepreneurship has a positive impact on productivity growth, at least for the case of the United States.

Audretsch and Fritsch (1996) analyzed a database identifying new business start-ups and exits from the social insurance statistics in Germany to examine whether a greater degree of turbulence leads to greater economic growth, as suggested by Schumpeter in his 1911 treatise. These social insurance statistics are collected for individuals. Each record in the database identifies the establishment at which an individual is employed. The start-up of a new firm is recorded when a new establishment identification appears in the database, which generally indicates the birth of a new enterprise. While there is some evidence for the United States linking a greater degree of turbulence at the regional level to higher rates of growth for regions (Reynolds, 1999), Audretsch and Fritsch (1996) find that the opposite was true for Germany during the 1980s. In both the manufacturing and the service sectors, a high rate of turbulence in a region tends to lead to a lower, and not a higher, rate of growth. They attribute this negative relationship to the fact that the underlying components—the start-up and death rates—are both negatively related to subsequent economic growth. Those areas with higher start-up rates tend to experience lower growth rates in subsequent years. Most strikingly, the same is also true for the death rates. The German regions experiencing higher death rates also tend to experience lower growth rates in subsequent years. Similar evidence for Germany is found by Fritsch (1997).

Audretsch and Fritsch (1996) conjectured that one possible explanation for the disparity in results between the US and Germany may lie in the role that innovative activity, and therefore the ability of new firms to ultimately displace the incumbent enterprises, plays in new-firm start-ups. It may be that innovative activity did not play the same role for the German *Mittelstand* as it does for SMEs in the US. To the degree that this was true, it may be held that regional growth emanates from SMEs only when they serve as agents of change through innovative activity.

The empirical evidence suggested that the German model for growth provided a sharp contrast to that for the US. While Reynolds (1999) had found that the degree of entrepreneurship was positively related to growth in the United States, a series of studies by Audretsch and Fritsch (1996) and Fritsch (1997) could not identify such a relationship for Germany. However, the results by Audretsch and Fritsch were based on data from the 1980s.

Divergent findings from the 1980s about the relationship between the degree of entrepreneurial activity and economic growth in the US and Germany posed something of a puzzle. On the one hand, these different results suggested that the relationship between entrepreneurship and growth was fraught with ambiguities. No confirmation could be found for a general pattern across developed countries. On the other hand, it provided evidence for the existence of distinct and different national systems. The empirical evidence clearly suggested that there was more than one way to achieve growth, at least across different countries. Convergence in growth rates seemed to be attainable by maintaining differences in underlying institutions and structures.

However, in a more recent study, Audretsch and Fritsch (2002) find that different results emerge for the 1990s. Those regions with a higher start-up rate exhibit higher growth rates. This would suggest that, in fact, Germany is changing over time, where the engine of growth is shifting towards entrepreneurship as a source of growth. The results of their 2002 paper suggest an interpretation that differs from their earlier findings. Based on the compelling empirical evidence that the source of growth in Germany has shifted away from the established incumbent firms during the 1980s to entrepreneurial firms in the 1990s, it would appear that a process of convergence is taking place between Germany and the US, where entrepreneurship provides the engine of growth in both countries. Despite remaining institutional differences, the relationship between entrepreneurship and growth is apparently converging in both countries.

The positive relationship between entrepreneurship and growth at the regional level is not limited to Germany in the 1990s. For example, Foelster (2000) examines the employment impact not just within new and small firms but on the overall link between increases in self-employment and total employment in Sweden between 1976 and 1995. By using a Layard-Nickell framework, he provides a link between micro behaviour and macroeconomic performance, and shows that increases in self-employment shares have had a positive impact on regional employment rates in Sweden.

Callejon and Segarra (1999) use a data set of Spanish manufacturing industries between 1980 and 1992 to link new-firm birth rates and death rates, which, taken together, constitute a measure of turbulence, to total factor productivity growth in industries and regions. They adopt a model based on a vintage capital framework in which new entrants embody the edge technologies available and exiting businesses represent marginal obsolete plants. Using a Hall type of production function, which controls for imperfect competition and the extent of scale economies, they find that both new-firm start-up rates and exit rates contribute positively to the growth of total factor productivity in regions as well as industries.

11.6 Conclusions

The prevalent and traditional theories of entrepreneurship have typically held the context constant; and then have examined how characteristics specific to the individual, impact the cognitive process inherent in the model of entrepreneurial choice. This often leads to the view that is remarkably analogous to that concerning technical change in the Solow model—given a distribution of personality characteristics, proclivities, preferences and tastes, entrepreneurship is exogenous. One of the great conventional wisdoms in entrepreneurship is 'Entrepreneurs are born not made.' Either you have it or you don't. This leaves virtually no room for policy or for altering what nature has created.

This paper has presented an alternative view. The 'Knowledge Spillover Theory of Entrepreneurship' holds the individual attributes constant and rather focuses on variations in the context. In particular, we consider how the knowledge context will impact the cognitive process underlying the entrepreneurial choice model. The result is a theory of endogenous entrepreneurship, where (knowledge) workers respond to opportunities generated by new knowledge by starting a new firm. In this view, entrepreneurship is a rationale choice made by economic agents to appropriate the expected value of their endowment of knowledge. Thus, the creation of a new firm is the endogenous response to investments in knowledge that have not been entirely or exhaustively appropriated by the incumbent firm.

In the endogenous theory of entrepreneurship, the spillover of knowledge and the creation of a new, knowledge-based firm are virtually synonymous. Of course, there are many other important mechanisms facilitating the spillover of knowledge that have nothing to do with entrepreneurship, such as the mobility of scientists and workers, and informal networks, linkages and interactions. Similarly, there are certainly new firms that have nothing to do with the spillover of knowledge. Nevertheless, the spillover theory of entrepreneurship suggests that there will be additional entrepreneurial activity as a rationale and cognitive response to the creation of new knowledge. Those contexts with greater investment in knowledge should also experience a higher degree of entrepreneurship, *ceteris paribus*. Perhaps it is true that entrepreneurs are made. But more of them will discover what they are made of, in a high-knowledge context than in an impoverished knowledge context. Thus, we are inclined to restate the conventional wisdom and instead propose that entrepreneurs are not necessarily made, but are rather a response—and in particular a response to high knowledge contexts that are especially fertile in spawning entrepreneurial opportunities.

By endogenously facilitating the spillover of knowledge created in a different organization, and perhaps for a different application, entrepreneurship may provide what could be considered to be the missing link to economic growth. Confronted with a formidable knowledge filter, public policy instruments emerging from the new growth theory, such as investments in human capital, R&D, and university research may not adequately result in satisfactory economic growth. One interpretation of the European Paradox, where such investments in new knowledge have certainly been vigorous and sustained, is that the presence of such an imposing knowledge filter chokes off the commercialization of those new investments, resulting in diminished innovative activity and ultimately stagnant growth.

By serving as a conduit for knowledge spillovers, entrepreneurship is the missing link between investments in new knowledge and economic growth. Thus, the spillover theory of knowledge entrepreneurship provides not just an explanation of why entrepreneurship has become more prevalent as the factor of knowledge has emerged as a crucial source for comparative advantage, but also why entrepreneurship plays a vital role in fostering industrial restructuring and generating economic growth. Entrepreneurship is an important mechanism permeating the knowledge filter to facilitate the spillover of knowledge, create new industries and move out of old ones, and ultimately generate economic growth.

References

Acs, Z. and D. Audretsch (1988). 'Innovation in Large and Small Firms: An Empirical Analysis'. *American Economic Review*, 78: 678–90.

—— and —— (1990). *Innovation and Small Firms.* Cambridge: MIT Press.

—— —— P. Braunerhjelm and B. Carlsson (2004). *The Missing Link: The Knowledge Filter and Entrepreneurship in Endogenous Growth.* (Discussion Paper). Stockholm: Center for Economic Policy Research.

Aldrich, H. and M. Martinez (2003). 'Entrepreneurship, Networks and Geographies', in *Handbook of Entrepreneurship Research.* New York: Springer Publishers.

Almus, M. and E. Nerlinger (2000). 'Testing Gibrat's Law for Young Firms–Empirical Results for West Germany'. *Small Business Economics*, 15: 1–12.

Arrow, K. (1962). 'Economic Welfare and the Allocation of Resources for Invention'. *The Rate and Direction of Inventive Activity.* Princeton: Princeton University Press.

Audretsch, D. (1991). 'New Firm Survival and the Technological Regime'. *Review of Economics and Statistics*, 73: 441–50.

—— (1995). *Innovation and Industry Evolution.* Cambridge, MA: MIT Press.

—— (2006). *The Entrepreneurial Society.* New York: Oxford University Press.

—— and M. Feldman (1996). 'R&D Spillovers and the Geography of Innovation and Production'. *American Economic Review*, 86: 630–40.

—— and M. Fritsch (1996). 'Creative Destruction: Turbulence and Economic Growth'. *Behavioral Norms, Technological Progress, and Economic Dynamics: Studies of Schumpeterian Economics.* Michigan: University of Michigan Press.

—— and —— (2002). 'Growth Regimes over Time and Space'. *Regional Studies*, 36: 113–24.

—— and P. Stephan (1996). 'Company-Scientist Locational Links: The Case of Biotechnology'. *American Economic Review*, 86: 641–52.

AUDRETSCH, D. and R. THURIK (2002). *Linking Entrepreneurship to Growth* (STI Working Paper) 2081/2 OECD.

—— E. SANTARELLI and M. VIVARELLI (1999). 'Start-up Size and Industrial Dynamics: Some Evidence from Italian Manufacturing'. *International Journal of Industrial Organization*, 17: 965–83.

—— et al. (2002). 'Impeded Industrial Restructuring: The Growth Penalty'. *Kyklos*, 55: 81–98.

—— M. KEILBACH and E. LEHMANN (2006). *Entrepreneurship and Economic Growth.* Oxford: Oxford University Press.

BIRCH, D. (1979). 'The Job Creation Process', 1979. Unpublished Report, MIT Program on Neighborhood and Regional Change.

—— (1981). 'Who Creates Jobs?' *The Public Interest*, 65: 3–14.

BRUEDERL, J. and P. PREISENDOERFER (1998). 'Network Support and the Success of Newly Founded Businesses'. *Small Business Economics*, 10: 213–25.

CALLEJÓN, M. and A. SEGARRA (1999). 'Business Dynamics and Efficiency in Industries and Regions: The Case of Spain'. *Small Business Economics*, 13: 253–71.

CARREE, M. and R. THURIK (1999). 'Industrial Structure and Economic Growth'. *Innovation, Industry Evolution, and Employment.* Cambridge: Cambridge University Press.

CAVES, R. (1998). 'Industrial Organization and New Findings on the Turnover and Mobility of Firms'. *Journal of Economic Literature*, 36: 1947–82.

CHANDLER, A. (1977). *The Visible Hand: The Managerial Revolution in American Business.* Cambridge: Belknap Press.

—— (1990). *Scale and Scope: The Dynamics of Industrial Capitalism.* Cambridge: Harvard University Press.

COLEMAN J. (1988a). 'Social Capital in the Creation of Human Capital'. *American Journal of Sociology*, 94: 95–121.

—— (1988b). 'The Creation and Destruction of Social Capital: Implications for the Law'. *Notre Dame Journal of Law, Ethics and Public Policy*, 3: 375–404.

COHEN, W. and R. LEVIN (1989). 'Empirical Studies of Innovation and Market Structure'. *Handbook of Industrial Organization*, vol. 2. 'Amsterdam: North Holland.

DUNNE, T., M. ROBERTS and L. SAMUELSON (1989). 'The Growth and Failure of U.S. Manufacturing Plants'. *Quarterly Journal of Economics*, 104: 671–98.

DAVIS, S., J. HALTIWANGER and S. SCHUH (1996a). *Job Creation and Destruction.* Cambridge, MA: MIT Press.

—— —— and —— (1996b). 'Small Business and Job Creation: Dissecting the Myth and Reassessing the Facts'. *Small Business Economics*, 8: 297–315.

ERICSON, R. and A. PAKES (1995). 'Markov-Perfect Industry Dynamics: A Framework for Empirical Work'. *Review of Economic Studies*, 62: 53–82.

FELDMAN, M. and D. AUDRETSCH (1999). 'Science-Based Diversity, Specialization, Localized Competition and Innovation'. *European Economic Review*, 43: 409–29.

FOELSTER, S. (2000). 'Do Entrepreneurs Create Jobs?' *Small Business Economics*, 14: 137–48.

FRITSCH, M. (1997). 'New Firms and Regional Employment Change'. *Small Business Economics*, 9: 437–48.

GALBRAITH, J. (1956). *American Capitalism: The Concept of Coutervailing Power.* Boston: Houghton Mifflin.

GALBRAITH, J. (1962). *Economic Development in Perspective.* Cambridge: Harvard University Press.

GARTNER, W. and N. CARTER (2003). 'Entrepreneurial Behavior and Firm Organizing Processes'. *Handbook of Entrepreneurship Research.* New York: Springer Publishers.

GEROSKI, P. (1995). 'What Do We Know About Entry?' *International Journal of Industrial Organization*, 13: 421–40.

GILBERT, B. (2004). *Clusters and New Venture Performance* (PhD Dissertation). Bloomington: Indiana University.

—— P. McDOUGALL and D. AUDRETSCH (2005). 'Clusters, Knowledge and New Venture Performance: An Empirical Investigation'. (Unpublished Manuscript).

GLAESER, E., H. KALLAL, J. SCHEINKMAN and A. SHLEIFER (1992). 'Growth of Cities'. *Journal of Political Economy*, 100: 1126–52.

GRILICHES, Z. (1979). 'Issues in Assessing the Contribution of Research and Development to Productivity Growth'. *Bell Journal of Economics*, 10: 92–116.

—— (1984). *R&D, Patents and Productivity.* Chicago: University of Chicago Press.

HALL, B. (1987). 'The Relationship between Firm Size and Firm Growth in the U.S. Manufacturing Sector'. *Journal of Industrial Economics*, 35: 583–605.

HANNAN, M. and J. FREEMAN (1989). *Organizational Ecology.* Cambridge, MA: Harvard University Press.

HEBERT, R. and A. LINK (1989). 'In Search of the Meaning of Entrepreneurship'. *Small Business Economics*, 1: 39–49.

HESHMATI, A. (2001). 'On the Growth of Micro and Small Firms: Evidence from Sweden'. *Small Business Economics*, 17: 213–28.

HOFSTEDE, G. et al. (2002). 'Culture's Role in Entrepreneurship: Self-employment Out of Dissatisfaction'. *Innovation, Entrepreneurship and Culture: The Interaction Between Technology, Progress and Economic Growth.* Brookfield, VT: Edward Elgar.

HOLTZ-EAKIN, D. and C. KAO (2003). *Entrepreneurship and Economic Growth: The Proof is in the Productivity.* Syracuse: Syracuse University, Center for Policy Research.

HOPENHAYN, H. (1992). 'Entry, Exit and Firm Dynamics in Long Run Equilibrium'. *Econometrica*, 60: 1127–50.

JAFFE, A. (1989). 'The Real Effects of Academic Research'. *American Economic Review*, 79: 957–70.

JOVANOVIC, B. (1982). 'Selection and the Evolution of Industry'. *Economica*, 50: 649–70.

KLEPPER, S. (1996). 'Entry, Exit, Growth, and Innovation over the Product Life Cycle'. *American Economic Review*, 86: 562–83.

KLETTE, T. and A. MATHIASSEN (1996). 'Job Creation, Job Destruction and Plant Turnover in Norwegian Manufacturing'. *Annales d'Economie et de Statistique*, 41/42: 97–125.

KRUEGER, N. (2003). 'The Cognitive Psychology of Entrepreneurship'. *Handbook of Entrepreneurship Research.* New York: Springer Publishers.

LAMBSON, V. (1991). 'Industry Evolution with Sunk Costs and Uncertain Market Conditions'. *International Journal of Industrial Organization*, 9: 171–96.

LUCAS, R. (1988). 'On the Mechanics of Economic Development'. *Journal of Monetary Economics*, 22: 3–42.

—— (1993). 'Making a Miracle'. *Econometrica*, 61: 251–72.

MANSFIELD, E. (1962). 'Entry, Gibrat's Law, Innovation, and the Growth of Firms'. *American Economic Review*, 52: 1023–51.

MATA, J. (1994). 'Firm Growth during Infancy'. *Small Business Economics*, 6: 27–40.

—— P. Portugal, and P. Guimaraes (1995). 'The Survival of New Plants: Start-up Conditions and Post-entry Evolution'. *International Journal of Industrial Organization*, 13: 459–81.

McClelland, D. (1961). *The Achieving Society*. Princeton: Van Nostrand.

Nelson, R. (1981). 'Research on Productivity Growth and Differences: Dead Ends and New Departures'. *Journal of Economic Literature*, 19: 1029–64.

—— and S. Winter (1982). *An Evolutionary Theory of Economic Change*. Cambridge: Belkap Press.

Putnam, R. (1993). *Making Democracy Work*. Princeton: Princeton University Press.

—— (2000). *Bowling Alone: The Collapse and Revival of American Community*. New York: Simon and Schuster.

Reynolds, P. (1999). 'Creative Destruction: Source or Symptom of Economic Growth?', in *Entrepreneurship, Small and Medium-sized Enterprises and the Macroeconomy*. Cambridge: Cambridge University Press, 97–136.

—— et al. (2000). *Global Entrepreneurship Monitor: 2000 Executive Report*. Wellesley: Babson College.

Romer, P. (1986). 'Increasing Returns and Long-Run Growth'. *Journal of Political Economy*, 94: 1002–37.

—— (1990). 'Endogenous Technological Change'. *Journal of Political Economy*, 98: 71–102.

Sarasvathy, S., N., Dew, R. Velamuri and S. Venkataraman (2003). 'Three Views of Entrepreneurial Opportunity'. *The International Handbook of Entrepreneurship*. Dordrecht: Kluwer Academic Publishers.

Scherer, F. (1970). *Industrial Market Structure and Economic Performance*. Chicago: Rand McNally.

Schumpeter, J. (1911). *Theorie der wirtschaftlichen Entwicklung. Eine Untersuchung über Unternehmergewinn, Kapital, Kredit, Zins und den Konjunkturzyklus*. Berlin: Duncker und Humblot.

—— (1942). *Capitalism, Socialism, and Democracy*. New York: Harper and Brothers.

Shane, S. (2000). 'Prior Knowledge and the Discovery of Entrepreneurial Opportunities'. *Organization Science*, 11: 448–71.

—— and J. Eckhardt (2003). 'The Individual-Opportunity Nexus'. *Handbook of Entrepreneurship Research*. New York: Springer Publishers.

—— and S. Venkataraman (2001). 'Entrepreneurship as a Field of Research: A Response to Zahra and Dess, Singh, and Erickson'. *Academy of Management Review*, 26: 13–17.

Shaver, K. (2003). 'The Social Psychology of Entrepreneurial Behaviour'. *Handbook of Entrepreneurship Research*. New York: Springer Publishers.

Solow, R. (1956). 'A Contribution to The Theory of Economic Growth'. *Quarterly Journal of Economics*, 70: 65–94.

Stevenson, H. and J. Jarillo (1990). 'A Paradigm of Entrepreneurship: Entrepreneurial Management'. *Strategic Management Journal*, 11: 17–27.

Sutton, J. (1997). 'Gibrat's Legacy'. *Journal of Economic Literature*, 35: 40–59.

Thorton, P. and K. Flynne (2003). 'Entrepreneurship, Networks and Geographies'. *The International Handbook of Entrepreneurship*. Dordrecht: Kluwer Academic Publishers.

Tveteras, R. and G. Eide (2000). 'Survival of New Plants in Different Industry Environments in Norwegian Manufacturing: A Semi-Proportional Cox Model Approach'. *Small Business Economics*, 14: 65–82.

Venkataraman, S. (1997). 'The Distinctive Domain of Entrepreneurship Research'. *Advances in Entrepreneurship, Firm Emergence and Growth* vol. 3. Greenwich: JAI Press.

Wagner, J. (1994). 'Small Firm Entry in Manufacturing Industries: Lower Saxony, 1979–1989'. *Small Business Economics*, 6: 211–24.

Wagner, J. (1995). 'Exports, Firm Size, and Firm Dynamics'. *Small Business Economics*, 7: 29–40.

Wagner, J. (2001). 'A Note on the Firm Size-Export Relationship'. *Small Business Economics*, 17: 229–37.

Wennekers, S. and R. Thurik (1999). 'Linking Entrepreneurship and Economic Growth'. *Small Business Economics*, 13(1): 27.

Williamson, O. (1968). 'Economies as an Antitrust Defence: The Welfare Tradeoffs'. *American Economic Review*, 58: 18–36.

Winter, S. (1984). 'Schumpeterian Competition in Alternative Technological Regimes'. *Journal of Economic Behavior and Organization*, 5: 287–320.

CHAPTER 12

INNOVATION IN LARGE FIRMS

WALTER KUEMMERLE

12.1 Introduction

Large firms are anchor tenants of every developed economy.[1] In the real estate industry, understanding the characteristics of anchor tenants and their evolution over time is crucial for successful property development, but the significance of large firms in the world economy goes beyond anchor tenants in real estate. Large firms have a long-term impact on their economic and social environment and their leases cannot simply be cancelled or extended. Large firms typically house sizeable amounts of product and process knowledge. This influences not just current economic output but, through innovation, also the long-term prosperity of an economy.

Young firms started by entrepreneurs represent a significant share of total employment. In the United States, for example, 40 percent of total employment in 1995 was in firms less than ten years old (Acs and Armington, 2003). However, there is little doubt that large firms such as Pfizer, Toyota or Siemens make an important contribution on several dimensions. To start with they generate economic output in a relatively stable manner, which is beneficial for managing the

[1] The term 'anchor tenant' comes from the commercial real estate industry and describes one or two large tenants in a commercial real estate project such as a shopping mall or office building. The characteristics of the anchor tenant, for example whether it is an upscale department store operator or not, has a significant impact on the overall nature of the shopping mall, on the type of other stores the mall will attract and on the clientele who will shop at the mall.

economy and for fostering innovation. In addition, their typically substantial financial means and favourable credit ratings enable large firms to take on risky, long-term and large-scale development and manufacturing projects that could not be taken on by smaller firms. And thirdly, large firms serve as a training ground for technical and managerial talent. Many of these engineers, scientists and managers will later on join smaller firms or start firms on their own. Gompers, Lerner and Scharfstein (2003), for example, in a study of the likelihood that former managers of public companies in the US would themselves start venture-capital backed companies found that this event was particularly likely if the publicly listed firm had a large stock of technology. Finally, large firms are often more effective at lobbying and can thus influence the national and local context for innovation more significantly than a diverse group of small firms could.

Students of entrepreneurship typically focus on young firms. But they are well-advised to examine large firms in more detail for at least two reasons. First, large firms play an important role in entrepreneurship ecology and in the genesis of new firms. These new firms are often in the same or related industries, based on similar technologies or in the same geography. Xerox and its PARC laboratory in Palo Alto is one example. Engineers at PARC were influential in the creation of the first personal computer, new graphics interfaces and the laser printer (Hiltzik, 1999). Based on these innovations at PARC a broad range of independent firms were created in Silicon Valley and elsewhere.

Secondly, as firms grow larger they tend to lose much of the flexibility and agility that characterize resource allocation and managerial execution in small firms.[2] Some large firms, however, stay more entrepreneurial and innovative than others. While entrepreneurship is often associated with small but fast-growing firms, this need not be the case. I define entrepreneurship as opportunity-driven behaviour cognizant of the resources required to pursue the opportunity. The kernel of entrepreneurship is to identify a potential opportunity, match the opportunity and resources optimally, and keep adjusting that match as the opportunity materializes.[3] Opportunities and resources are thus intertwined and entrepreneurs must be mindful of constraints on access to resources. My definition of entrepreneurship does not pertain to firms of a certain size, industry or nationality. In fact, there are large firms that display remarkably entrepreneurial resource allocation processes; 3M has been cited as an example (Bartlett and Mohammed, 1994).

[2] Continued dominance of the same large firms might not be optimal for economic growth. A recent study has shown that continued dominance of large firms hurt economy-wide growth, especially productivity growth (Fogel et al., 2005).

[3] The literature has devoted considerable attention to the definition of entrepreneurship. Among other definitions there are those that focus on innovation (Schumpeter, 1942), attitude towards risk (Knight, 1921; Cantillon, 1931), and pursuit of opportunity (Stevenson and Gumpert, 1985). The argument of this paper is not affected by which definition one adheres to most closely. The reader should accept, however, that entrepreneurship implies the identification and management of opportunity in some way or form.

Students of entrepreneurship should pay close attention to large firms that are particularly entrepreneurial and successful at innovation and to those that are not. The above-mentioned Xerox PARC site has been described as an organization within Xerox that was productive at invention but was eventually unable to innovate and create handsome profits for Xerox itself (Hiltzik, 1999: 395).

This chapter provides a discussion of the complex relationship between large firms and innovation with particular attention paid to entrepreneurial mechanisms in large firms that foster such innovation. Note that while my definition of entrepreneurship covers all types of opportunity-seeking behaviour, in this chapter I focus exclusively on the sub-set of entrepreneurship that results from technological progress and on the innovations associated with such progress. The next section (12.2) surveys the relationship between size and innovation. The section that follows (12.3) elaborates on distinct barriers to innovation in large firms. I then discuss (12.4) factors and processes that help foster and sustain innovation in large firms before concluding with some avenues for further research (12.5).

12.2 Innovation and Firm Size

Innovation is the process of converting technological advances or inventions into new products or product attributes with the goal of creating demand and increasing market share. Successful innovations have been described as requiring intra-firm processes that are quite different from the processes leading to successful inventions (Burgelman and Sayles, 1986). Innovations require the timely combination of information from technical and non-technical sources, such as knowledge about a new technology, about current demand patterns, competitors and market dynamics as well as about manufacturability and logistics. As a firm grows larger, it becomes increasingly difficult for managers pursuing innovations to manage and combine organizationally dispersed information of such diverse categories. Even if all the knowledge required for a particular innovation was available within the boundaries of the firm, the difficulty of pulling it all together at the right time would increase with firm size. In essence it is the mastery of this combinatorial challenge that makes some large firms more innovative than others.

Both invention and innovation are broad terms. While invention output is relatively easy to measure through patents, the quantification of innovation output is an empirical challenge. There are not many large-sample studies that convincingly document a relationship between firm size and innovation output. Schumpeter hypothesized that large firms with monopoly power would innovate more than small firms since small firms would be deterred by the prospect of their rents from innovation being competed away before they could recuperate innovation costs (Schumpeter, 1942). Empirical evidence shows the opposite to be true. Scherer (1984: ch. 11) found that smaller firms were more likely to introduce major innovations. Acs and Audretsch (1988) identified innovations at the firm level from published articles. They found that, controlling for size, small firms innovated more. Lerner (2004), in an analysis of innovations by financial service firms, found that smaller firms were more likely to introduce innovations and that firms with stronger academic ties were more likely to introduce innovations.

The large-firm disadvantage on innovation at the firm level seems to linger on even in the case of a spin-off. This is probably due to the persistence of organization-specific processes and organization culture. One study of 35 spin-offs from Xerox found that spin-offs where Xerox maintained a high equity position, and where the CEO came from Xerox, performed worse than spin-offs where Xerox equity stake was low and where the CEO was an outsider (Chesbrough, 2003).

Other studies focus on input measures, particularly R&D expenditures. Cohen, Levin and Mowery (1987) studied line-of-business data and found that business unit size had no effect on R&D intensity. A study by Mansfield (1984) suggests that the largest firms devote a bigger share of their total R&D budget to basic R&D than smaller firms, but that these largest firms rarely carry out risky product or process R&D. A study of Korean firms by Lee (1999) found a largely negative relationship between firm size and R&D intensity.

While the overall evidence suggests that innovation slows down as firms become larger, large firms appear not to regain the innovativeness when their growth slows or when sales decline. Corollary evidence comes from a study that found that managers were particularly likely to leave large firms in order to start out on their own if sales in the large firm had been lagging in the previous quarters (Gompers et al., 2003).

While firms appear to lose their innovation efficiency as they grow, and while this process seems to be mostly irreversible, large firms located within clusters appear to spawn more young firms than outside of clusters. Large firms in California and Massachusetts were on average 35 percent more likely to spawn than firms in other parts of the US (Gompers et al., 2003). A study of a UK sample also points to spatial heterogeneity in innovation: firms within clusters innovated more than firms outside of them (Baptista and Swann, 1998).

In summary, while large firms do play an important role in economy and society, their own ability to innovate seems to decline as they grow larger. This suggests that unless there is a steady rate of new firm creation, a region can experience a dramatic decline in its capacity to innovate. The intriguing question is, of course, why innovation declines with size and what can be done by managers and public policy-makers to work against this tendency.

12.3 Barriers to innovation in large firms

Intra-firm barriers to innovation fall into two categories, general behavioural barriers exacerbated by the growing size of an organization and context-specific barriers. Behavioural barriers are created by layers of corporate hierarchy. These lead to noise in the decision-making process, to organizational inertia, as well as to a lack of transparency and appropriate incentives. Context-specific barriers can be caused by the industry context as well as by the regional and national economic and social context.

12.3.1 Behavioural barriers

As a firm grows larger, it invariably has to devote an increasing amount of resources to administering its own hierarchy. A study by the Conference Board found that business units with between 1,200 and 4,500 employees had on average six layers of decision hierarchy, meaning that the firms owning these business units had at least seven layers of hierarchy (Janger, 1989). This implies an average of about five to six directly reporting co-workers for each boss.[4]

Each layer of hierarchy acts like an additional cushion in processes of intra-firm information gathering, decision-making and execution. Bower, in his landmark study of the resource allocation process, extensively examined the role of middle management layers. He found that these layers could either be energizers or inhibitors of investment projects that had been hatched at various levels within the organization. Bower (1970) coined the term 'impetus' for the role that various intermediate layers of management played during the resource allocation process. In a study of corporate entrepreneurship, Burgelman (1983), found that autonomous strategic initiatives within a firm were a key component of corporate entrepreneurship. He also found that such autonomous efforts encountered major difficulties in large, diversified firms, and that middle managers often were part of the problem.

Thick layers of management do not only introduce noise into the signals from operating managers to top management they also reduce the speed of these signals. This creates organization inertia that can lead companies to take a narrow focus

[4] Assuming a control span of five direct reports and six layers of hierarchy (five layers and a CEO) there will be 3,125 employees at the lowest level. Including the superiors at each level this leads to a total of 3,125 + 781 = 3,906 employees.

and miss critical market information (Hannan and Freeman, 1984). In a study of a technologically intensive industry, Henderson (1990), found that leading firms became so focused on improving their existing model range that they missed out on what Henderson calls 'architectural' innovations. Christensen (1997) demonstrated that leading firms in the hard disc drive industry lost their market leadership by focusing on the needs of their best customers. A firm's current best customers typically wanted disc drives of the same physical size but with higher storage capacity or at lower cost. Physically smaller disc drives were initially inferior in performance. Over time, however, the performance of these smaller drives would surpass the larger ones. Even though the incumbents were quite capable of designing and marketing smaller drives, top management did not make the critical resource allocation decisions soon enough to develop and bring these smaller drives to market. In one instance, development engineers at an incumbent firm had developed working prototypes of a smaller drive a full two years before a competitor became the first to introduce these drives to the market (Christensen, 1997: 20). Christensen attributes the slowness of incumbents primarily to the resistance of powerful marketing organizations within incumbent firms and states: 'The evidence is quite strong that formal and informal resource allocation processes make it very difficult for large organizations to focus adequate energy and talent on small markets, even when the logic says they might be big someday.' (Christensen, 1997: xxi).

The phenomenon of information being distorted and slowed down as it travels through corporate hierarchies in large firms is often known to the managers involved. The root cause of the coordination problem in large firms typically lies in an incentive system that is not sufficiently dynamic to make managers act in the best interests of the firm. In a recent paper, Kaplan and Henderson (2005) have argued that in order to explain why established firms fail in the face of radical or discontinuous technological change one must simultaneously consider cognition problems and incentive problems because cognition and incentive-response behaviour of mangers co-evolve. In my view, the same argument about interdependence of cognition and incentive problems can be extended to understanding the more general question why large firms are less innovative.

While the issue of incentives has been understood theoretically and empirically for a long time, it is apparently very hard to design a good incentive system in practice (Jensen and Meckling, 1976). Incentives are often designed in one of two ways: they are either tied to dimensions at the operating level and within the zone of influence of a manager, or tied to dimensions at a very high level (such as the firm level or divisional level) and thus can only be influenced minimally by the manager. In the former case, the fact that the incentive system is not sufficiently dynamic can become a significant problem. For example, managers will sell more large disk drives if this will increase their next monthly paycheck and yearly bonus, even though they might fully realize that it would make sense for firm profitability and survival in the long-run to focus on selling smaller drives instead. In the latter case (if incentives are driven primarily by a firm-wide parameter) managers might not increase their personal efforts at all since they feel that such efforts have little effect on their compensation.

While real-life incentive systems in large firms are often not sufficiently dynamic, there are other challenges, too. Some processes, such as innovation processes, require intense team efforts where accurate measurement of an individual's contribution is close to impossible. Team leadership and intra-firm transparency play a critical role under such circumstances. If those who make critical compensation and promotion decisions are far removed from the operating level, it is likely that their decisions are based on second-hand information. Smaller firms appear to suffer less from this problem.

Finally, one can also explain the lower rate of innovation in large firms as a result of behavioural information search barriers. An employee working on an innovation is often faced with the need to collect additional information and with several possible locations inside the firm where he or she could search for such information. The employee will typically have a strong hypothesis as to where such a search might be most fruitful. The locations where the employee expects to succeed in obtaining information, however, might not be the locations that actually yield the most accurate and useful information. A recent paper by Hansen and Nohria (2004) classified some of the information search problems in the innovation process in large firms by distinguishing seekers of help and potential providers of help, and also by distinguishing those who are unwilling and those who are unable on either dimension. This resulted in four information search problems: the 'not-invented-here' syndrome, the 'hoarding of expertise' problem, the 'needle in a haystack' problem and the challenge of weak social ties—'stranger' problem. All four problems are less of an obstacle to innovation in smaller firms than in large ones.

Differences in the rate of innovation between small and large firms can also be explained by the allocation of property rights. Acs, Morck, Shaver and Yeung (1997) have argued that in large firms innovators often have very limited property rights to their innovations because the new product or process typically belongs to the firm. Thus, the innovators must share the pay-off from their innovation with many other stakeholders. As a consequence, employees in large firms might put less effort into innovation than employees in small firms.

12.3.2 Contextual barriers

Innovation in large firms can also be hampered by barriers other than general behavioural ones. Since these other barriers pertain to the broad context in which a firm operates, I will call them contextual barriers. They include industry structure, the immediate regional context and the national context.

Mansfield (1984) found that relatively concentrated industries tended to devote a smaller, not larger percentage of sales to R&D. A likely explanation is that higher industry concentration entails lower intensity of competition among large players and, as a consequence, a reduced interest in innovating aggressively.

Other industry specific characteristics might also act as barriers to intra-firm innovation. When new technologies impact the products or services offered by an industry in radically new ways or when the innovation context changes, large firms seem to be at a particular disadvantage. In the pharmaceutical industry, for example, research for new drugs has become increasingly complex over the years. Research endeavours now require a broader set of expertise than just chemistry and biology. Some of the new drug discovery techniques, such as high-throughput screening (a method to more quickly assess the viability of a large number of chemical compounds), only have a short track record. As a consequence, large pharmaceutical firms have been slow in adopting these techniques even though the same large firms struck alliances with small biotechnology firms to get access to these techniques (Thomke and Kuemmerle, 2002). In essence, the life-sciences industry as a whole maintained a high pace of innovation, but the locus of innovation shifted to some degree away from large pharmaceutical firms to smaller biotechnology firms because certain innovation capabilities developed faster outside of large firms than inside them.

The immediate regional context can also act as a barrier to innovation in large firms. If a large firm seeks to enter a technologically intensive industry in which the firm has no deep expertise, it might face bigger problems than a start-up firm in that industry not just because its absorptive capacity is lower for reasons described above but also because firms in the immediate geographic vicinity might treat the large firm differently than they would treat other small firms. Abrahamson and Fairchild (2001) have argued that there is co-evolution between innovative ideas and the communities in which they are developed. Also, von Hippel (1994) has described the importance of organizationally and spatially sticky knowledge for innovation processes. If many members of an innovation community such as Silicon Valley work for small firms, they might view large firms and their employees with some caution or even aversion.

First, there is a competitive threat. Managers in large firms with ample resources could potentially take advantage of early-stage ideas hatched in small firms, develop these ideas faster into new products than the small firm could, and gain a large market share. As mentioned earlier, evidence suggests that large firms are not very good at executing such a technology adaptation strategy, but the perceived threat of such a strategy toward a small firm remains. Secondly, perceived differences in the culture of small and large firms might lead to self-selection in employment. Managers and engineers in large technology firms have been described as being inflexible and narrowly-focused in their thinking (Christensen and Bower, 1996). Those who choose to work for small firms in technologically intensive industries might do so in part to avoid negative traits of a large-firm culture and might thus be less than enthusiastic in welcoming employees of a large firm into an innovation community within a geographic cluster. The regional context can be particularly hostile towards a large firm if the large firm has not previously had any company presence in a cluster and is establishing a new greenfield operation there. This combination of being new to the cluster and being a large firm might seriously limit the large firm's capacity to innovate at that location.

The national context also can have an impact on large firms' ability to innovate. As mentioned earlier, the rate of innovation in a large firm depends critically on a manager's ability to combine, in a time-sensitive and effective way, information from different sources that are dispersed within the firm. The quality of managerial talent and training has a big impact on this ability. In some countries, it is more likely that the brightest university graduates in science and technology join large firms than in other countries. Japan is one example (Kuemmerle, 2001). In the US, by contrast, many outstanding university graduates will join start-up firms or start their own firms.

This difference across the two countries is rooted in a complex web of relationships that makes up each country's innovation system. In the US, the stigma of entrepreneurial failure is lower than in Japan. At the same time, entrepreneurial success in the US is more celebrated, and successful entrepreneurs often become role models for entire generations of university graduates.[5] Also, in the US, venture capital is available and universities do a considerable amount of research with potential commercial value. In Japan, by contrast, there are few currently successful entrepreneurs, there is very little venture capital and universities for the most part do not do research that could quickly be commercialized. On 31 December 1999, private equity (including venture capital) under management in the US amounted to about 1.5 percent of GDP, while the corresponding figure for Japan on 31 December 1998, was only 0.05 percent or about one-thirtieth of the figure for the US.[6] As a result of these conditions, it is likely that established firms in Japan will continue to attract outstanding university graduates in science and technology, while entrepreneurial careers will continue to attract mediocre talent and misfits.

If large Japanese firms are able to attract more qualified entry level engineers and scientists than large US firms, and if engineers in Japan are willing to stay with their firm longer than in the US, it is likely that large firms in Japan will be more innovative over time than large firms in the US. Of course, this does not necessarily mean that the US and its innovation system (including universities, and small and

[5] Venkataraman points out the importance of local entrepreneurial role models for a flourishing entrepreneurial culture (Venkataraman, 2004).

[6] Figures for Japan for 31 December 1999 were not available. Figures were calculated by the author based on data in: (Kuemmerle, 2001).

large firms) will be less productive than the Japanese innovation system. On the contrary, since small firms have to deal with fewer of the behavioural barriers described earlier, all else being equal, the US innovation system should be more productive than the Japanese innovation system.

In summary, there are both behavioural and other contextual barriers, such as industry-specific, regional or national ones, to innovation in large firms. In a theoretical paper Holmstrom (1989) has argued that firms can be modelled as carrying out two activities, innovation (for example new product development) and routine (for example manufacturing or sales), and that these activities require different forms of organization and management. Therefore, the cost of carrying out both tasks within one firm might be higher than relegating innovation to small firms and routine to large ones.

12.4 Approaches to Sustain Entrepreneurship and Innovation in Large Firms

The empirical evidence cited in the section 2 of this chapter overwhelmingly suggests that large firms are less innovative than small firms. The obvious question then is how some large firms succeed at being more innovative than others. In this section I suggest that an entrepreneurial climate inside the firm is a necessary condition for high levels of innovative output. I then discuss management approaches that have been reported to make and keep large organizations innovative.

As discussed earlier, innovation results from (a) combining dispersed knowledge available inside the firm, and (b) co-ordinating the process of delivering a product or a service based on this newly combined knowledge before competitors do so. Innovation for a specific product or service often involves some knowledge that is not available inside the firm at the start of the innovation process. I consider the process of bringing such knowledge into the firm through licensing or hiring of specialists as an integral part of the innovation process.

From my own research on the geographic organization of R&D in large firms, as well as on the genesis and expansion of entrepreneurial firms, I conclude that an entrepreneurial climate within the firm is a necessary but not sufficient condition for a high rate of innovation (Kuemmerle, 1999, 2002). In the first section of this paper, I defined entrepreneurship as opportunity-driven behaviour cognizant of the resources required to pursue the opportunity. It is this tendency to start with consideration of an opportunity, rather than with the resources currently available, that leads managers to excel at mastering the challenge of combining dispersed knowledge and skills within the firm and, if necessary, seeking knowledge from out-side the firm. By contrast, managers in large firms often start an innovation process by considering the resources currently available to them. Stevenson and Jarillo (1990) have argued that the culture and budgeting process in large firms tend to reinforce resource-driven, as opposed to opportunity-driven, behaviour.

At the same time, an entrepreneurial climate alone is not sufficient to sustain a high rate of innovation over time. To start with, a firm might devote more resources to innovation projects than it can afford and become illiquid before it can financially benefit from the innovation. Also, uncertainty is an inherent part of any innovation process and this exposes even a large firm with a circumspect management team to the possibility of serious financial and organizational distress. Finally, it is important to note that highly innovative firms do not necessarily survive over long periods of time. In fact, a successful firm that is entrepreneurial, has a high innovative output, and is efficient at creating this output, might break apart rather than survive because it did not devote enough resources to creating lasting cohesiveness or 'organizational glue'.[7]

Essentially, there are three categories of approaches that keep large firms innovative. They are (1) conceptual approaches, (2) organizational structure and spatial approaches, and (3) leadership and organizational culture approaches. These three approaches are complementary rather than mutually exclusive. Also, the pursuit and success rate of these approaches is dependent on the disposition of the leadership of a firm, on the firm's size, its history and its tangible and intangible resources. Constraints in material resources, however, appear to be more often an excuse for lack of innovation in a firm than a true constraint. For example, the case of Infosys, a pioneering Indian firm in the customized software industry, demonstrates how entrepreneurial firms can succeed even if their material resources are tightly constrained (Kuemmerle and Coughlin, 2000).

(I) A conceptual approach

An important conceptual approach to making and keeping a large firm entrepreneurial is to distinguish activities that (a) increase the stock of knowledge available to a firm, and (b) activities that make use of this stock of knowledge. In order to be successful the firm also needs to manage the link between knowledge accumulation and use of knowledge. The conceptual distinction between exploration and exploitation has been noted by J. G. March, and has been shown to apply to

[7] The phenomenon of firms dissolving despite a high rate of efficient innovation and strong financial performance can be observed quite frequently in service industries where firm survival depends not on the nature and size of fixed assets but on top management's ability to manage a growing pool of creative talent over time. Advertising agencies, venture capital firms and specialized law firms are examples.

firms' investment abroad by Thomas Wesson and to firms' R&D activities by Walter Kuemmerle (March 1991; Wesson 1993; Kuemmerle 1999). In fact, much of the literature on technology management focuses either on activities through which firms create new knowledge, or on downstream activities through which firms exploit such knowledge. Cohen and Levinthal (1990) have argued that firms typically absorb knowledge from the outside but that firms' capacity to absorb such knowledge is limited.

Since small firms, especially those headed by entrepreneurs, typically have small stocks of knowledge, managers are keenly aware of their firm's need to increase the stock of knowledge. At the same time, small firms are typically watching their cash balances carefully and managers in these firms are also keenly aware of the importance of each additional technology application and new product for their firm's financial position. Large firms that mimic such behaviour by creating and maintaining strong intra-firm awareness of the need to build up new knowledge on the one hand, and the need to efficiently exploit the firm's stock of knowledge on the other, are more likely to be entrepreneurial and innovative.

A study of 3M, one of the most consistently innovative large firms over the last seven decades, describes how 3M used several very specific measures focused on creating new knowledge (Bartlett and Mohammed, 1994). First, firm policy suggested that employees should devote '... up to 15% of their time to non-program activities that were related to innovative ideas they believed could be of value to the company.' (Bartlett and Mohammed, 1994: 2). Among other things, this rule intended to keep researchers alert to any technological developments outside 3M that could be developed further and that might eventually result in innovative products. The highly successful 3M 'Post-it' notes were the result of continued development of a malfunctioning glue by a 3M researcher (Nayak and Ketteringham, 1994). At the same time, 3M placed a strong emphasis on bringing new products to the market. This was achieved by specific renewal rules: 30 percent of sales had to come from products introduced within the previous four years. Also, the firm incited its business unit managers to try products out in the marketplace. The credo 'Make a little, sell a little' was well accepted within 3M (Bartlett and Mohammed, 1994: 2). The company also involved sophisticated potential or current customers, called lead users, in the actual product development process (Von Hippel, Thomke and Sonnack, 1999). Finally, the company sought to make sure that there was a direct link between the firm's increasing stock of knowledge and its product divisions. Often researchers would move with a specific product they developed from a research lab position into a commercial position. There was also a widely-supported credo 'Products belong to the divisions, but technology belongs to the company' that sought to ensure that divisional rivalry did not affect the size and free intra-firm sharing of the firm's technology stock (Bartlett and Mohammed, 1994: 3). The approaches of letting researchers work on their own projects for part of their time and of introducing products in small launches early in the life of a product were particularly straightforward in 3M's businesses such as abrasive materials and optical systems, because product launches in these industries are not necessarily very costly, but the lessons from 3M can also be applied to other industries.

Top management in a large firm can emphasize the distinction between opportunities and resources and raise the awareness among middle managers about the link between these two. This should happen simultaneously in various ways: via the firm's daily routines and resource allocation processes, via training of employees, via management of divisional P&L statements and via creation of a firm culture open to innovation and renewal. If top management of a large firm emphasizes the importance of both opportunities *and* resources, its innovation processes will exhibit more similarity to innovation processes in small entrepreneurial firms than would otherwise be the case.

(II) Approaches pertaining to organizational structure and spatial distribution of innovation activities

Beyond the conceptual distinction and linkage of opportunities and resources, there are a number of specific organizational measures that have been described as conducive to innovation in large firms. These are (1) matrix structures; (2) organizing for permeable middle management layers; (3) organizational; and (4) spatial separation.

Matrix structures are organizational structures that involve separate but overlapping decision hierarchies within the firm. An example would be a firm that is organized by product divisions (e.g. pumps, valves and pipes) but also by function (e.g. applied research, product development, manufacturing, marketing, sales, after-sales service). A typical unit manager in such a firm will report to two managers: a division head and a functional head. The up-side of a matrix organization is that the manager will be exposed to two separate knowledge and decision streams within the firm. Since innovation most likely results from the combination of knowledge available in separate locations within the firm, a matrix organization is more likely to result in innovations than a one-dimensional hierarchy. At the same time, a matrix organization creates challenges. Managers need to be willing, and able, to report to at least two superiors and to constantly make trade-off decisions between the requirements from both superiors. At the same time, the superiors need to be aware of the multiple demands placed on the unit manager and assess the unit manager's ability to make successful trade-off decisions during performance evaluations. Bartlett and Ghoshal have argued that effective matrix organizations require not just the creation of a matrix organization chart and structure but a deep awareness among managers at all levels about the benefits and demands of a matrix organization. Bartlett and Ghoshal call this 'creating a matrix in managers' heads' (Bartlett and Ghoshal, 1989: 175).

Independent of whether a firm is organized along a one-dimensional decision hierarchy or along a matrix, each decision hierarchy needs to be permeable. This means that ideas from managers in direct contact with customers, or from bench

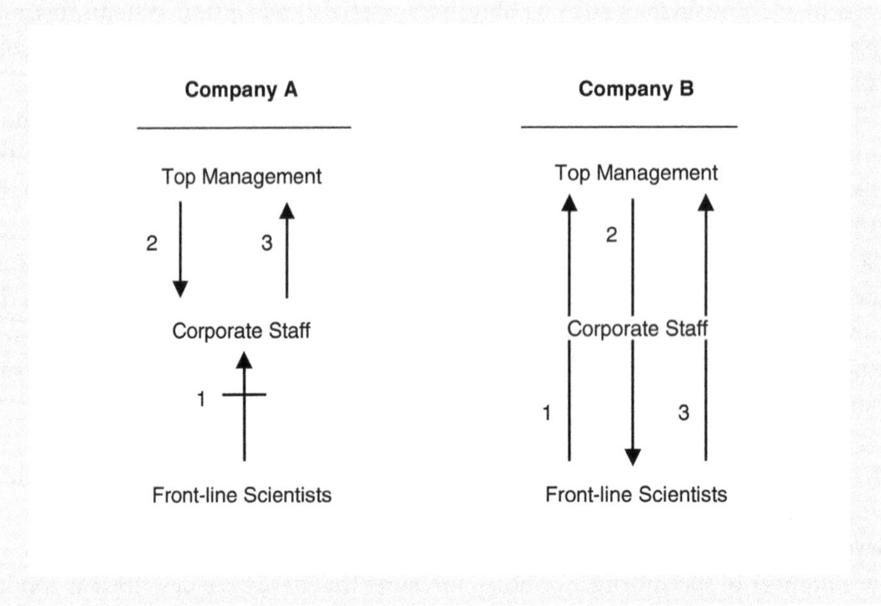

Figure 12.1 An example of resource allocation in two established firms

Source: Kuemmerle, Walter (2005). The Process of International Expansion: Comparing Resource Allocation in Established Firms and Entrepreneurial Start-ups. In *Strategy as Resource Allocation* (eds) J. L. Bower and C. Gilbert: Oxford University Press.

researchers in direct touch with leading edge science, need to reach the top decision-makers within the firm in relatively unaltered form. At the same time, top management decisions need to reach the operational level without too much 'editorial influence' from middle management. Since the number of middle management layers grows as the size of a firm increases, the permeability of these layers naturally declines. In a study of resource allocation processes to R&D in large firms, I found differing levels of hierarchical permeability across a pair of matched case studies (Kuemmerle, 2005); Figure 12.1 illustrates this.

In Company A, front-line scientists suggested an investment in a new R&D site based on their intimate knowledge of the invention landscape. Middle managers inhibited the flow of information. They did so partially inadvertently and partially advertently because incentives were misaligned. A short time later a similar investment was suggested by an alert top manager, but instead of involving front-line scientists in the decision and securing their organizational support for the investment, it was discussed only with corporate staff and middle management. Front-line scientists were surprized and felt that their expertise had been disregarded. The investment in the new R&D site turned into a failure because the new site and ideas that came from there were never really accepted at the firm's home base. Company B made a very similar investment around the same time. Since middle management layers in Company B were permeable, a proposal from front-line scientists was discussed by top management with input from middle management. The proposal was approved with some reasonable alterations. As a consequence, front-line scientists were committed to a speedy and effective implementation of the investment. It turned out to be a success.

In addition to growing with size, middle management layers also have a tendency to become less permeable over time and structural inertia increases. In an empirical test of Hannan and Freeman's (1984) structural inertia hypothesis, Ruef (1997) found that larger California hospitals were less likely to successfully modify their services in order to increase their survival chances. Ruef also found that generalist hospitals with a broader scope of service offerings were better able to adapt to a changing environment. For firms in technologically intensive industries these findings suggest that frequent reshufflings of middle managers across firm functions and across locations can help to keep middle management layers permeable both for ideas from operating managers and for directives from top management. In a set of in-depth case studies, Ghoshal and Bartlett (1997) showed that several successful large firms have recently taken a more proactive approach than in the past to empower individual managers and to enable these managers to pursue new opportunities with the boundaries of the firm.

For some innovations, especially discontinuous ones, which change the basis of competition in an industry, neither matrix organizations nor permeable decision hierarchies appear to be sufficient. O'Reilly and Tushman (2004) have argued that such innovations are more likely to emerge and succeed if top management sets up the project team charged with the innovation as a structurally independent unit with its own resources and processes. Such an independent unit will be linked to the rest of the firm only at the very top of the organization. In very large firms, 'top' could mean the divisional top management; in smaller firms, 'top' could mean the top management of the firm overall. O'Reilly and Tushman call organizations that pursue existing and emerging businesses in separate organizational units linked to the rest of the firm only at the top 'ambidextrous organizations'.

Organizational separation to overcome the pitfalls of a large firm might go even a step further, with part of the innovation being farmed out to a separate firm. Design firm IDEO, for example, is often used by established firms to achieve breakthrough designs that might be difficult to accomplish within the firm's own design department (Hargadon and Sutton, 1997).

In addition to or instead of organizational separation, there is also the possibility of geographic separation of teams and units in charge of innovation activities. Even geographic separation over small distances can create a sufficient level of independence and distinctive culture to spur innovation (Allen, 1977). Geographic separation by large geographic distances, and especially by country borders, often creates a very distinct organization and results in distinct products. A remarkable example is the Mazda Miata, the car that re-started the boom for two-seated roadster cars in 1989 after a long industry hiatus. The Miata was conceived around 1980 not in Hiroshima, the location of Mazda's headquarters and R&D home base, but in Mazda's Irvine, CA research facility (Wilson, 1989). Only a few years later, after concept development was already fairly complete, did the project get moved to Mazda's Hiroshima home base. In addition to having been conceived away from Mazda's R&D home base, the car was not conceived by a team of Mazda engineers but was largely the brainchild of a former US auto journalist who had been hired by Mazda.

Organizational and spatial separation of innovative projects and units does create a significant challenge over time. The question becomes how such autonomous units in charge of specific innovation projects should later be reintegrated into the firm. Leaders must determine not just how to accomplish this feat but also what the optimal level of initial separation of a unit should be and when, if at all, the move towards re-integration should start.

(III) Approaches pertaining to leadership and firm culture

It is unlikely that conceptual approaches or specific organization design measures alone can make and keep a large firm innovative. The firm's leaders must also create a culture that is conducive to entrepreneurship and innovation. It appears that such a culture is created through the stimulation and support of certain values on the one hand, and through specific quantifiable goals on the other. Burgelman (1983) has described autonomous strategic initiatives by operating managers and engineers as an important component of corporate entrepreneurship and innovation. At the same time he suggested that while top management will rarely get involved directly in such strategic initiatives, it needs to provide the right intra-firm structures and reward mechanisms for these initiatives to occur.

Brown and Eisenhardt (1997) studied how six business units in the computer industry adapted to change and found that successful managers used improvisation techniques that were confined by very few but specific rules. These rules provided strict guidelines in an otherwise relatively free-wheeling environment. Also, managers used specific product interval rules to guide the process of innovation. The role of leaders is to develop such rules and monitor their appropriateness over time. Top management at 3M had a long-standing specific rule that 25 percent of sales should be derived from products introduced within the previous five years. In 1992, that rule was raised by a new CEO to 30 percent of sales coming from products introduced within the previous four years (Bartlett and Mohammed, 1994: 2). In 2002, yet another new CEO took over and raised 3M's target to doubling sales over a period of ten years while the previous doubling of sales had taken 15 years. At the same time, the new CEO commented about his challenge and the culture at 3M: 'My job is to add scale in a fast-moving entrepreneurial environment. If I end up killing that entrepreneurial spirit, I will have failed.' (Arndt, 2002). The three CEOs at 3M described in this example needed to assess both the culture of the firm and the specific quantitative goals set at the time in order to assess how far the goals could be stretched while maintaining or even improving the entrepreneurial culture of a firm.

This example points to another important role of leaders in large firms. In order to keep a firm's climate entrepreneurial and innovative, leaders must monitor the appropriateness of quantitative goals and must be ready to reset such goals as the firm grows, as its technology base and product range changes and as the external context evolves. Iterative innovation planning inside the firm can be helpful in this regard not just because it points to specific innovations that a firm should target but also because top managers learn about a firm's ability to meet more ambitious future goals during the planning process (Wheelwright and Clark, 1992).

King and Tucci (2005) examine radical innovation in the disk drive industry, just like Christensen did. In contrast to Christensen, they find that incumbents fared better than new entrants and spin-offs. Two possible explanations for King and Tucci's findings are sample selection and model specification issues. An alternative explanation is that managers in established firms might have recently become more alert to the threats posed by radical innovations. As a result, these managers are taking more decisive action in order to recognize radical innovations early and are successful in leading their employees towards a cohesive response strategy.

12.5 Avenues for Future Research

The question of how large firms can achieve and sustain high levels of innovation over time is likely to become even more relevant in the future. Mansfield (1998) found that the average interval between academic research and the first commercial introduction of a product had shrunk from about seven years (from 1975 to 1985) to about six years (from 1986 to 1994). In other words, it took less time than before to turn an invention into an innovation. One explanation for this could be contextual changes such as faster dissemination of research results through electronic publishing and increased university efforts to commercialize technology. In section 3 of this chapter I suggested that small firms have a relatively higher absorptive capacity than large firms. If this is true, small firms would benefit disproportionately from contextual changes that make it possible to access inventions earlier than before. As a consequence, the gap in innovation rates between small and large firms might grow further. This should be of great concern to large firms. After all, early decline is not something that large and currently powerful firms aspire to.

There are at least three interesting areas that deserve attention by researchers: (i) size thresholds; (ii) the role of context for innovation; and (iii) organizational approaches to sustaining innovation. Size thresholds are distinct firm sizes at which the rate of innovation of a firm slows down in a non-monotonous way. Academic knowledge of such thresholds is primarily theoretical in nature, even though practitioners seem to be keenly aware of such thresholds.[8] It would be of high interest, for example, to predict when Google Inc. will reach a size beyond which its innovativeness will decline markedly. Knowledge about thresholds could lead to focused research about behavioural reasons for their existence and about management practices that keep firms innovative even as they grow beyond thresholds. For example, does innovation slow down when the founders of a successful firm do not know every employee personally anymore? How can this issue be moderated? Also, it is likely that thresholds are impacted by industry, firm age and other aspects of firm history such as mergers. Empirical research designs need to control for other such influences on innovativeness. Finally, an important question is how firm size should be measured. Since the decline of innovative behaviour appears to be closely related to behavioural issues, headcount might be the most appropriate measure of firm size, but there might be other highly correlated measures such as sales level or product range.

The external context for entrepreneurship and innovation in large firms is another broad area that offers considerable room for additional research. As countries around the world increasingly embrace the idea of entrepreneurship as an engine for economic growth, national and local governments are concerned with creating the right framework for start-up firms in order to generate a large number of fast-growing companies. It seems that this current drive in public policy neglects large firms and their importance as anchor tenants. An intriguing question, for example, is the relationship between the location of large firms in technologically intensive industries and the innovativeness of these firms over time. One hypothesis is that large firms inside a cluster that are surrounded by many small firms in the same industry will be more innovative over time than large firms outside such a cluster. The reason for this is that large firms inside a cluster spawn many entrepreneurial firms but also that the cluster attracts skilled workers who will first seek entry level positions in large firms before moving on to smaller ones. Also, large firms might acquire small firms and successfully absorb their employees and technologies.

Regarding contextual factors, it also seems likely that the nature of market competition has an impact on large firms' propensity to innovate. For example, in countries where capital markets work well (that is, where asset prices are informed and guide resources towards firms with growth opportunities, and where corporate governance mechanisms are effective) large firms can be expected to be more agile and innovative than in countries where capital markets do not work well.

[8] Specialty textiles manufacturer W. L. Gore & Associates, for example, has been reported to intentionally limit the workforce at each manufacturing plant to 200 people to accentuate a close-knit and interpersonal atmosphere that suits the firm's flat management hierarchy and pay-for-performance compensation schemes (Industry-Week, 1983).

Finally, there is the perennially interesting question how large firms can be kept innovative through specific management approaches pertaining to firm structure and intra-firm processes. For example, we need to develop a much better understanding how autonomous units in a large firm should be structured. What is the optimal profile of the leader of such a unit and what type and level of resources should the unit receive at the outset? How should it be governed and when is the optimal time to reintegrate it into the firm? Does some management experience in an independent fast-growing firm help or hinder the leader of such an autonomous unit? Can this kind of entrepreneurship expertise and innovation management skill be acquired through training or creativity management techniques? These questions offer a rich agenda for academic researchers and several generations of doctoral students.

References

Abrahamson, E. and G. Fairchild. (2001). 'Knowledge Industries and Idea Entrepreneurs: New Dimensions of Innovative Products, Services, and Organizations', in C. B. Schoonhoven and E. Romanelli (eds.) *The Entrepreneurship Dynamic.* Stanford CA: Stanford University Press.

Acs, Z. and D. B. Audretsch. (1988). 'Innnovation in Large and Small Firms: An Empirical Analysis'. *American Economic Review,* 78: 678–90.

—— and C. Armington. (2003). *Endogenous Growth and Entrepreneurial Activity in Cities* (Working Paper). Baltimore: University of Baltimore.

—— R. Morck, J. M. Shaver and B. Yeung. (1997). 'The Internationalization of Small and Medium-Sized Enterprises: A Policy Perspective'. *Small Business Economics,* 9: 7–20.

Allen, T. J. (1977). *Managing the Flow of Technology.* Cambridge, MA: MIT Press.

Arndt, M. (2002). '3M: "A Lab for Growth?" ' *Business Week,* 21 January, pp. 50, 51.

Baptista, R. and P. Swann (1998). 'Do Firms in Clusters Innovate More?' *Research Policy* 27(5): 525–40.

Bartlett, C. and S. Ghoshal (1989). *Managing Across Borders: The Transnational Solution.* Boston: HBS Press.

—— and A. Mohammed (1994). *3M Optical Systems: Managing Corporate Entrepreneurship (9–395–017).* Boston: Harvard Business School Publishing.

Bower, J. L. (1970). *Managing the Resource Allocation Process: A Study of Corporate Planning and Investment.* Boston: Harvard Business School Press.

Brown, S. L., and K. M. Eisenhardt (1997). 'The Art of Continuous Change: Linking Complexity Theory and Time-based Evolution in Relentlessly Shifting Organizations'. *Administrative Science Quarterly* (March) 42: 1–34.

Burgelman, R. A., and L. R. Sayles (1986). *Inside Corporate Innovation.* New York: The Free Press.

—— (1983). 'A Process Model of Internal Corporate Venturing in the Diversified Major Firm'. *Administrative Science Quarterly,* 28: 223–44.

Cantillon, R. (1931). *Essai Sur la Nature du Commerce.* London: Macmillan.

Chesbrough, H. (2003). 'The Governance and Performance of Xerox's Technology Spinoff Companies'. *Research Policy*, 32(3):403–21.

Christensen, C. M. (1997). *The Innovator's Dilemma: When New Technologies Cause Great Firms to Fail.* Boston: Harvard Business School Press.

—— and J. L. Bower. (1996). 'Customer Power, Strategic Investment and the Failure of Leading Firms'. *Strategic Management Journal*, 17: 197–218.

Cohen, W. and D. Levinthal (1990). 'Absorptive Capacity: A New Perspective on Learning and Innovation'. *Administrative Science Quarterly*, 35: 128–52.

Cohen, W. M., R. C. Levin and D. C. Mowery (1987). 'Firm Size and R&D Intensity: A Re-examination'. *Journal of Industrial Economics*, 35: 543–65.

Fogel, K., R. Morck and Bernard Yeung (2005). 'Corporate Stability and Economic Growth: Is What's Good for General Motors Good for America? Highland Heights', KY.

Ghoshal, S. and C. A. Bartlett (1997). *The Individualized Corporation.* New York: HarperCollins.

Gompers, P., J. Lerner and D. Scharfstein (2003). *Entrepreneurial Spawning* (Working Paper). Boston: Harvard Business School.

Hannan, M. and J. Freeman (1984). 'Structural Inertia and Organizational Change'. *American Sociological Review*, 49:149–64.

Hansen, M. T. and N. Nohria. (2004). 'How to Build Collaborative Advantage'. *MIT Sloan Management Review*, 46(1): 22–30.

Hargadon, A. and R. I. Sutton (1997). 'Technology Brokering and Innovation in a Product Development Firm'. *Administrative Science Quarterly*, 42: 716–39.

Henderson, R. (1990). 'Architectural Innovation: The Reconfiguration of Existing Product Technologies and the Failure of Established Firms'. *Administrative Science Quarterly* (March) 35: 9–30.

Hiltzik, M. (1999). *Dealers of Lightning: Xerox PARC and the Dawn of the Computer Age.* New York: Harper Business.

Holmstrom, B. (1989). 'Agency Costs and Innovation'. *Journal of Economic Behavior and Organization*, 12: 305–27.

Industry-Week. (1983). Wilbert L. Gore. *Industry Week*, October 17, pp. 48–9.

Janger, A. (1989). *Measuring Managerial Layers and Spans*, vol. 237, *The Conference Board Research Bulletin.* New York: The Conference Board.

Jensen, M. C. and W. H. Meckling (1976). 'Theory of the Firm: Managerial Behavior, Agency Costs, and Ownership Structure'. *Journal of Financial Economics*, 3(4): 305–60.

Kaplan, S. and R. Henderson (2005). *Organizational Rigidity, Incentives and Technological Change: Insights from Organizational Economics* (Working Paper).

King, A. and C. L. Tucci (2005). 'Can Old Disk Drive Companies Learn New Tricks? Entrepreneurship, Technology and Schumpeterian Innovation', in M. Casson, B. Yeung, A. Basu and N. Wadeson (eds) *Oxford Handbook of Entrepreneurship.* Oxford: Oxford University Press.

Knight, F. H. (1921). *Risk, Uncertainty and Profit.* Boston: Houghton Mifflin.

Kuemmerle, W. (1999). 'The Drivers of Foreign Direct Investment into Research and Development'. *Journal of International Business Studies*, 30(1): 1–24.

—— (1999). 'Foreign Direct Investment in Industrial Research in the Pharmaceutical and Electronics Industries–Results from a Survey of Multinational Firms'. *Research Policy*, 28(2–3):179–93.

—— (2001). 'Comparing Catalysts of Change: Evolution and Institutional Differences in the Venture Capital Industries in the U.S., Japan and Germany', in R. Burgelman and H. Chesbrough (eds) *Research on Technological Innovation, Management and Policy.* Greenwich, CT: JAI Press.

—— (2002). 'Home Base and Knowledge Management in International Ventures'. *Journal of Business Venturing*, 17: 99–122.

—— (2005). 'The Process of International Expansion: Comparing Resource Allocation in Established Firms and Entrepreneurial Start-ups', in J. L. Bower and C. Gilbert (eds) *Strategy as Resource Allocation.* Oxford: Oxford University Press.

—— W. and W. J. Coughlin (2000). *Infosys: Financing an Indian Software Start-up.* Boston, MA: Harvard Business School Publishing.

Lee, D-S. (1999). 'A Study of Firm Size and Technological Innovation'. *Journal of Economic Research*, 4: 61–85.

Lerner, J. (2004). *The New Financial Thing: The Origins of Financial Innovations.* Boston: Harvard Business School.

Mansfield, E. (1984). 'R&D and Innovation: Some Empirical Findings', in Z. Griliches (ed.) *R&D, Patents and Productivity.* Chicago: University of Chicago Press.

—— (1998). Academic Research and Industrial Innovation: An Update of Empirical Findings. *Research Policy*, 26: 773–76.

March, J. G. (1991). 'Exploration and Exploitation in Organizational Learning'. *Organization Science*, 2: 71–87.

Nayak, P. R. and J. M. Ketteringham (1994). *Breakthroughs!* San Diego, CA: Pfeiffer.

O'Reilly, C. A. III and M. L. Tushman. (2004). 'The Ambidextrous Organization'. *Harvard Business Review*, 82(4): 74–81.

Ruef, M. (1997). 'Assessing Organizational Fitness on a Dynamic Landscape: An Empirical Test of the Relative Inertia Thesis'. *Strategic Management Journal*, 18: 837–53.

Scherer, F. M. (1984). *Innovation and Growth: Schumpeterian Perspectives.* Cambridge, MA: MIT Press.

Schumpeter, J. (1942). *Capitalism, Socialism, and Democracy.* New York: Harper&Row.

Stevenson, H. H. and D. E. Gumpert (1985). 'The Heart of Entrepreneurship'. *Harvard Business Review* (March–April), pp. 85–94.

—— and J. C. Jarillo (1990). 'A Paradigm of Entrepreneurship: Entrepreneurial Management'. *Strategic Management Journal*, 11: 17–27.

Thomke, S. and W. Kuemmerle (2002). 'Asset Accumulation, Interdependence and Technological Change: Evidence from Pharmaceutical Drug Discovery'. *Strategic Management Journal*, 23: 619–35.

Venkataraman, S. (2004). 'Regional Transformation through Technological Entrepreneurship'. *Journal of Business Venturing*, 19(1): 153–67.

von Hippel, E. (1994). ' "Sticky Information" and the Locus of Problem Solving: Implications for Innovation'. *Management Science*, 40(4): 429–39.

—— S. Thomke and M. Sonnack. (1999). 'Creating Breakthroughs at 3M'. *Harvard Business Review* (September–October), pp. 47–57.

Wesson, T. (1993). 'An Alternative Motivation for Foreign Direct Investment' (Unpublished Dissertation). Cambridge, MA: Harvard University.

Wheelwright, S. and K. C. (1992). *Revolutionizing Product Development.* New York: The Free Press.

Wilson, K. A. (1989). 'Horse Play with Mazda'. *AutoWeek*, 20 March, p. 18.

CHAPTER 13

ENTREPRENEURSHIP, TECHNOLOGY AND SCHUMPETERIAN INNOVATION: ENTRANTS AND INCUMBENTS

LUCA BERCHICCI AND
CHRISTOPHER L. TUCCI

13.1 Introduction

The question of how incumbency status relates to the ability and propensity to innovate has been widely examined by a large body of empirical literature inspired by two contrasting statements of Schumpeter (Schumpeter, 1934, 1942). The first one states that entrepreneurship is a mechanism to create changes in the system through innovation and entrepreneurs are the agents of creative destruction (Schumpeter, 1934). The second one states that large firms will be (more than) proportionately more innovative than small firms (Schumpeter, 1942). The existence of such a large literature does not seem to guarantee a clear interpretation of the findings due to the difficulties of measuring innovative activity (Cohen, 1995).

Nevertheless, conventional wisdom suggests that young, entrepreneurial firms have a greater advantage in innovation (e.g. Ács and Audretsch, 1990; see also Kuemmerle's Ch. 12 in this Handbook). In general, conventional wisdom suggests that these entrepreneurial entrant firms possess capabilities as niche-filling and flexibility, seeking out protected market niches that are too small for larger organizations (e.g. Chen and Hambrick, 1995). Moreover, these organizations are also seen as being quicker than incumbents due to structural simplicity, streamlined operations, lack of structural inertia, faster decision-making processes and targeted innovation (e.g. Dean et al., 1998). The result is a quicker response to the dynamics of industry environments.

These arguments seem to be supported by many recent studies, which tend to find that young firms have introduced a proportion of innovations larger than their share of employment (e.g. Acs and Audretsch, 1988). This finding has frequently been interpreted as showing that young firms are more innovative than incumbents, or more efficient innovators, achieving greater output per unit of R&D input (Acs and Audretsch, 1991; Cohen, 1995). Further, many scholars argue that incumbents are so hampered by their bureaucracy that they fail to introduce the next generation of new products (Ghemawat, 1991; Utterback, 1995; Christensen and Bower, 1996). Moreover, some scholars claim that incumbents are slow to introduce not only radical technologies but also what appear to be 'minor' changes (Henderson and Clark, 1990).

Several scholars have extended the argument by suggesting that incumbent organizations fail following an innovation not because of some fatal inherent flaw, but because managers fail to spot market opportunities (Tushman and Romanelli, 1985; Christensen, 1997). For example, Christensen and colleagues have argued that managers pay so much attention to their existing customers and existing technological suppliers that they miss out on future opportunities (Christensen and Rosenbloom, 1995; Christensen and Bower, 1996). They recognize too late the potential of emerging markets. Henderson (1993) argues that efforts of incumbents in developing radical technologies are characterized by 'incompetence and underinvestment,' given their inclination to 'technological inertia' (Ghemawat, 1991: 161).

In this chapter, we review the literature on the (lack of) innovativeness of incumbents both in creating new products and entering new markets. We then present some non-anecdotal evidence as counter-argument to the alleged curse of incumbency. First, we use as illustration a cross-sectional study by Chandy and Tellis (2000) of a large number of radical product innovations. Secondly, we explore to what extent the story of incumbents' inability to enter new markets matches the history of the computer rigid hard drive industry. This industry is particularly suited to this analysis since its technological generational changes have been described by scholars as 'radical' and 'disruptive,' and because its history

(Christensen, 1993) served to inspire Christensen's recent theories. We do not find persuasive evidence that incumbents are too late into new technologies and technology-created market niches. In the remainder of the chapter, we discuss rational non-entry vs. irrational non-entry and develop managerial implications.

13.2 Entrants, incumbents and innovation in the literature

Innovation at the organizational level is governed by a set of organizational routines and search strategies (Hannan and Freeman, 1984). Organizational routines are repositories of organizational knowledge and through the combination of these routines organizations generate outcomes (Sorensen and Stuart, 2000). The potential of incumbents to perform well in the generation of innovations and entering new markets reflects a combination of their ability to refine and coordinate their organizational routines, here referred to as organizational competences,[1] and the extent to which these routines are well-suited to the state of the external environment (Sorensen and Stuart, 2000). There is a cycle between the creation of new knowledge and the accumulation of existing knowledge within incumbents, which tend to be reinforcing (Cohen and Levinthal, 1990). Henderson (1993) argues that incumbents possess information processing routines that facilitate incremental innovations along existing technological trajectories. Furthermore, the accumulation of knowledge enhances an organization's ability to recognize and assimilate new ideas and opportunities as well as to convert this knowledge into further innovations. Through the knowledge cycle, incumbents are able to create new innovations and recognize new markets.

13.2.1 Developing new technologies

13.2.1.1 *Incumbents' inability to develop new technologies in two broad categories*

Many scholars argue that incumbents may have trouble innovating in the sense of creating new knowledge (e.g. Abernathy and Utterback, 1978) and are less likely

[1] Organizational competence refers to the capacity to generate innovation and environmental fit refers to the match between organizational competence and the state of the environment (Sorensen and Stuart, 2000).

Table 13.1 The liabilities and advantages of incumbents in the process of innovation (entrants generally have disadvantages where incumbents have advantages, and vice versa).

	Disadvantages	Advantages
Incumbents	Few perceived incentives	Organizational routines
	Organizational rigidities Inertia	Technological and market capabilities
	Rigid formalization	Market power and position
	Cognitive barriers	Available internal resources
	Technological myopia	R&D investment
	Organizational filters	Managerial knowledge
	Interpretative schemes	Reputation/Legitimacy

than non-incumbents to introduce radical innovations. They claim that the very strength of organizational routines that allow incumbents to exploit existing knowledge may turn into a liability when exploring new knowledge (see Table 13.1). In the 1970s, scholars clarified and extended this practical approach. Highlighting a couple important factors from Table 13.1, two rationales suggested by this literature for the lack of innovativeness of incumbents are organizational rigidities/routines and cognitive barriers (Berchicci, 2005; see Walter Kuemmerle in Ch. 12 in this Handbook for much more detail on these rationales).

13.2.1.2 *Organizational rigidities/routines*

Organizational routines allow incumbents to exploit the current product category because they enable the team to focus efficiently on current activities (Chandy and Tellis, 2000). The organizational capabilities that are well suited in current challenges easily turn into organizational rigidities when facing new challenges (Leonard-Barton, 1995), according to this line of thinking. The organizational rigidities are the flip side of organizational capabilities or competences and are built on the same activities that create core capabilities. Moreover, as organizations age and grow large, they are prone to inertia (Hannan and Freeman, 1984) which may reduce the innovativeness of the firms (Chandy and Tellis, 2000). Complex organizational structure, organizational formalizations and rigid communication channels may also provoke information loss (Arrow, 2000). Therefore, according to this logic, inertia, formalization of routines and internal process, and institutionalization of power structure may increase organizational rigidity and reduce the likelihood of adaptation and change for innovation.

13.2.1.3 *Cognitive barriers*

Incumbents are believed to be subject to 'technological myopia' (Foster, 1986), which inhibits their ability to perceive the potential of newly-emerging technologies and overestimating existing ones. This is because organizational competences serve to direct managers' attention to maximize the utility of the current technology for current customers filtering any information that is not relevant for that purpose. This organizational filter (Chandy and Tellis, 2000) may work between the external environment and the organization, and also within organizational boundaries. Moreover, organizational routines and interpretative barriers strongly affect the development of a market understanding, which hinders the development of new products for new markets (Dougherty, 1990).

13.2.2 Not all is lost for incumbents, however

However, not every technological change will sweep away incumbents as new entrants rise to dominate. Most scholars would agree that incumbents, in fact, are more adept at producing 'incremental' or 'competence-enhancing' innovation (cf. Tushman and Anderson, 1986). Therefore, the argument primarily hinges around whether incumbents are capable of pursuing new technologies that might be more damaging to them in the market, and whether later entry is *prima facie* evidence of incompetence. There is some literature to suggest that incumbent firms may be able both to develop radical technologies and to adapt to radical technological change. The opportunities of incumbents to develop and introduce radically new products may be considered to be in terms of financial, technological and market capabilities (Srivastava et al., 1998) and ability to handle uncertainty (e.g. Aldrich and Auster, 1986; Cohen, 1995).

13.2.2.1 *Financial capabilities*

Financial capabilities refer to available resources for risky R&D projects because of the availability—and stability—of internal funds (Arrow, 2000). Moreover, the returns from R&D activities are higher when a larger sales volume allows the innovator to amortize the fixed costs of innovation. Moreover, the resources to undertake the process of innovation allow incumbents to tolerate an occasional unsuccessful R&D project (Damanpour, 1992).

13.2.2.2 *Technological capabilities*

Technological capabilities refer to a system comprising (1) technical abilities in the form of employees' skills; (2) managerial systems, supporting and reinforcing the growth of knowledge; and (3) values that serve to encourage or discourage the accumulation of different kinds of knowledge (Leonard-Barton, 1995). It is assumed that R&D intensity positively influences a firm's technological competence and the rate of new technologies created by it. For example, higher R&D investment increases the level of research activity within the organization and permits it to engage in basic research, which is essential for generating proprietary scientific information (Nelson and Winter, 1982), that results in specialized scientific/technological expertise (Rosenberg, 1990). The tangible outcome of basic research is the ability to develop several significant product technologies[2] (Hambrick and Macmillan, 1985). The coupling of basic (R&D) and applied (product development) research provides higher firm performance (Buderi, 2000).

13.2.2.3 *Market capabilities*

Market capabilities refer to how well incumbents know their current customers and possess market power giving customers preferential access to distribution channels (Mitchell, 1989) and sustaining market presence (Chandy and Tellis, 2000). Thus by exploiting existing knowledge, incumbents build up experience in production, in workforce, in stronger relationships with vendors and customers (Hannan and Freeman, 1984; King and Tucci, 2002). Moreover, incumbents often have external relationships and contacts, and reputation and legitimacy, which facilitate further market transactions and new relationships (Damanpour, 1992).

Besides external communication, internal communication is crucial for the exploitation of knowledge. Communication patterns within the organization allow incumbents to use existing knowledge for further innovation (Cohen and Levinthal, 1990). Thus incumbents have polished the routines, structures, incentive programmes and other infrastructure that are needed to develop new products and bring them to market. The more incumbents have significant competitive strengths in terms of available internal resources, technological and market capabilities, managerial knowledge and ability to handle uncertainty in R&D, the better they are able to generate innovation through well-defined organizational routines.

On the other hand, incumbents may adapt and even embrace technological shifts that may threaten their very survival. For example, given the radical nature of the Internet for firms in computer industry, incumbents like IBM are emerging as leading e-business infrastructure providers (Rothaermel, 2001a). Market capabilities (Abernathy and Clark, 1985), prior collaborative relationships (Mitchell and Singh, 1996), and complementary assets (Tripsas, 1997) allow incumbents to take advantage of technological discontinuities, or at least not stumble from them.

[2] A product technology is an engineering diagram or prototype that demonstrates the product's functionality. To become a marketable product, it must undergo several stages of refinement and verification involving product architecture, parts assembly, aesthetics, and production feasibility (Wheelwright and Clark, 1992).

For example, Tripsas (1997) demonstrates how complementary assets protected incumbents in the typesetter industry from the effects of technological changes thought to be 'radical'. Moreover, incumbents may form strategic alliances with new entrants as a response to technological change, improving new product development and firm performance, as in the case of the biotechnology industry (Rothaermel, 2001b).

13.2.3 Entering new markets

Waves of technological change may open up new market opportunities within an existing industry. Conventional wisdom suggests that newcomers typically develop niche innovations, while incumbents are more likely to be followers than to be the first to enter new product areas (Scherer, 1980). Scholars have used economic and organizational arguments to 'explain' late entry by incumbents, but in many cases the late entry is seen as a negative.

13.2.4 Some problems incumbents might encounter in exploiting new markets

13.2.4.1 *Perceived incentives*

An incumbent with a large share in existing markets may have few incentives to develop products for a niche market (Ali, 1994). Although new markets provide opportunities for growth (Foster, 1986), they may cut sales of existing products (Reinganum, 1983; Utterback and Kim, 1985) and diminish the value of existing capabilities and physical assets (Tushman and Anderson, 1986). In the case of familiar markets, new products may represent a threat of cannibalization with the current business model. This threat may cause new projects to be managed sub-optimally or to be even avoided because of inertia provided by mainstream operating units (McDermott and O'Connor, 2002). An incumbent's choice of product development is sensitive to the degree of uncertainty in the process of innovation. When innovation is highly uncertain, an incumbent with a large market share (Ali, 1994) and with a risk-adverse attitude (Singh, 1986) may be reluctant to invest. This is because the incumbent gains profits for existing products based on current technology. When innovation is less uncertain, the opposite may be true. The incumbent is willing to invest regardless of what the necessary resources are, if the innovation is perceived to be a potential success (Ali, 1994) and if the new product addresses current customers (Chandy and Tellis, 2000).

More recently, scholars have proposed that managers often miss identifying new markets. This lack of recognition of a technological change can damage incumbent companies. For example, Christensen (1997) and Christensen et al. (1995, 1996) argue that incumbent firms can survive from generation to generation, but that managers fail to recognize the potential new market and so fail to effectively use their existing capabilities to the best advantage in entering the new market. They argue that incumbents enter late and only with a token response. Thus, according to Christensen, the problem lies not predominantly with the existing firm, but with the managers of that firm. The solution, he argues, is to improve managerial foresight and tactics. Drawing on previous studies of firm reorientation and recreation in response to new technologies, (e.g. Tushman and Romanelli, 1985) Christensen (1997) argues that wise managers can proactively meet the challenges of the new market by creating external and autonomous spin-off entities. These entities will then have the advantage of the incumbent's experience and resources, but the flexibility and freedom of new entrants. Other scholars have proposed that managers could mitigate the destructive effect of radical innovations if they recognized that fundamental organizational change were required and if they acted in time to reorient or recreate the organization to fit the new environment (Tushman and Romanelli, 1985; Brown and Eisenhardt, 1998).

13.2.5 Incumbents may be able to exploit technology-created markets

However, inertia, lack of recognition, and cannibalization arguments do not explain why some incumbents enter eventually (and sometimes are relatively early entrants), even in markets based on technology that may be somehow damaging to the competitiveness of the firm's current products or services. For example, some scholars claim that an incumbent's quick response will occur when an overlap exists between its core capabilities and those needed to endure in the new market (Brittain and Freeman, 1980; Lambkin, 1988).

Similarly, industry incumbents are more likely to enter early if their core products have been threatened but their experience and complementary assets have preserved their value in the new technology wave (Mitchell, 1991; King and Tucci, 2002). To put it another way, if the firm has control over some important asset whose diminished value in the market has been created by the new technology, it might make sense to move into the new market before the value of the asset completely deteriorates. Thus there are several pressures competing against the incentives and other problems outlined above. Timing of market entry should (and often does) take these competing objectives into consideration.

13.3 Evidence of incumbent ineptitude, or lack thereof[3]

13.3.1 Incumbency and inventiveness

Are incumbents unable to introduce radical innovation? Answering this question was the main goal of a paper by Chandy and Tellis (2000), which has mainly been cited in the marketing literature rather than in management. That is a pity, because Chandy and Tellis present some very interesting and far-reaching results. Instead of using case studies of highly specialized innovations, they perform a cross-sectional study of a wide range of product categories within consumer durables and office products. Through an historical analysis of a large number of radical innovations in the last century, Chandy and Tellis test whether the incumbent's were 'cursed', that is, were unable to introduce radical product innovations. Chandy and Tellis' results are summarized in Table 13.2.

The results shown in Table 13.2 suggest that incumbents may be as likely as entrants to introduce radical innovations. Taking into account firm size, it seems

Table 13.2 Incumbency product innovativeness

		Incumbents	Non-incumbents
Are incumbents less likely than entrants to introduce radical innovation?	Number of innovations	47%	53%
Are large firms less likely to introduce radical innovation than small firms?	Small and medium firms	17%	42%
	Large firms	30%	11%
Has the incumbency status of radical innovators changed over time?	Pre-World war II	27%	73%
	Post-World war II	74%	26%
Has the size of radical innovators changed over time?		Large firms	Small-medium firms
	Pre-World war II	17%	83%
	Post-World war II	74%	26%

Source: Chandy and Tellis (2000).

[3] We realize that our presentation of 'evidence' in this debate is a bit one-sided. However, we feel the burden of proof should be on the other side: by providing counter-examples, we refute the most general claims that incumbents are by and large not very innovative (especially when confronted with potentially damaging technology).

that smaller non-incumbents are almost four times as likely to be radical innovators as large non-incumbents. In contrast, large incumbents are almost twice as likely to come up with something radical as are small/medium incumbents. Therefore, size seems to benefit incumbents more than entrants.

To continue with the results, when the time dimension is considered in the analysis, it can be seen there is a big gap in innovation patterns before and after the Second World War. The results indicate that (large) incumbents significantly outnumber (small) non-incumbents for recent radical innovations. These findings suggest that small firms or entrants were more 'radically' innovative prior to the Second World War, while more recently, large firms and incumbents account for the majority of radical innovation. One of the possible explanations for the innovativeness in recent years of incumbents and large firms may lie with instituted organizational features that better support radical innovation (cf. Williamson, 1975). Chandy and Tellis's paper, bucking 'conventional wisdom', suggests therefore that incumbents and large organizations introduced a majority of the radical product innovations in the last 60 years.

13.3.2 Incumbency and market entry

Where market entry is concerned, the disk drive industry provides an excellent setting in which to explore incumbent reaction to new technologies and new markets. Moreover, Christensen, in developing his theories, seems to have been most inspired by the history of the disk drive industry. Unlike other industries where new technology, potentially damaging to incumbents, often occurs decades apart, innovation in the disk drive industry has come in several overlapping waves, thereby allowing researchers to study such innovations and their 'effect' on firm technology and market strategies. Thus, this industry provides a good place to investigate both the effect of innovation and incumbent entry.

From 1965 to 1995, the industry went through several changes in both technology and markets (Christensen, 1993). The original 14″ hard drives were largely used in mainframe computers. The emergence of minicomputers inaugurated the 8″ market. The 5.25″ drives became popular for use in desktop machines. Finally, 3.5″ and smaller drives found use in desktop and portable systems. Since 1995, drives that are made for cell phones, portable music players, and even watches have come on to the market.

For the earlier generations of disk drives, scholars have argued that for incumbents, the 'problem' was not one of incumbents' failure to develop new technologies, but one of recognizing new technology-created markets. Certainly, each succeeding disk drive 'form factor' (diameter) went into a vastly larger market, with maximum sales per year of 368,000 units for 14″ drives, to 427,000 for 8″

drives, to 8.7 million for 5.25″ drives, to 77.4 million (by 1995) for 3.5″ drives.[4] The technology has been argued to be 'off-the-shelf' in terms of the basic components of a motor, although King and Tucci (2002) point out that some of the transitions required extensive re-tooling. However, for the most part, most scholars agree that subsequent form factor represented an entirely new market opportunity, albeit enabled by unique combinations of technologies.

Let us first dispel the notion that these new market niches completely destroyed incumbents in the rigid hard drive industry. While it is true that several firms went out of business, or exited the disk drive market during each transition phase, it is a plain fact that more incumbents survived to produce drives in the new niche than died off or exited. From the 14″ to 8″ transition, 21 incumbents survived it, while 17 did not. For the 8″ to 5.25″, 27 incumbents survived, while 12 did not. For the 5.25″ to 3.5″ transition, 38 survived, while 28 did not. Furthermore, as King and Tucci (2002) point out, among those incumbents, the incumbents with the most experience tended to survive to the next niche and indeed enter it earlier.

Table 13.3 provides some information about the transitions in rigid hard drives. First, we see that incumbents going on to be one of the top players in the next transition never entered before the first non-incumbent, which is entirely consistent with most scholars' views of technological change. However, once the forecast for the category exceeded zero, at least one major, market-leading incumbent entered within one year for all transitions. Furthermore, by the time sales peaked in the form factor, the average year of entry was certainly not higher for incumbents; in fact, if anything it is lower on average. This comparison is a little problematic because we do not know which incumbents wanted to enter but could not, nor do we know which entrants wanted to enter but did not. However,

Table 13.3 Entry timing for non-incumbents and incumbents in rigid hard drives

Transition	First year forecast > 0	First non-incumbent entry year	First 'major' incumbent entry year	Average non-incumbent entry year*	Average incumbent entry year*
14″ to 8″	1978	1977	1978	1981.2	1980.8
8″ to 5.25″	1979	1978	1979	1982.6	1982.2
5.25″ to 3.5″	1982	1980	1983	1987.7	1985.8

* Before and including peak sales year in that form factor.
Source: Kashima and Tucci (2003).

[4] All statistics from the rigid hard drive industry are based on the *Disk/Trend Report*, a highly reliable and complete compendium of all business activity in that industry compiled by James Porter and published annually over a 24-year period.

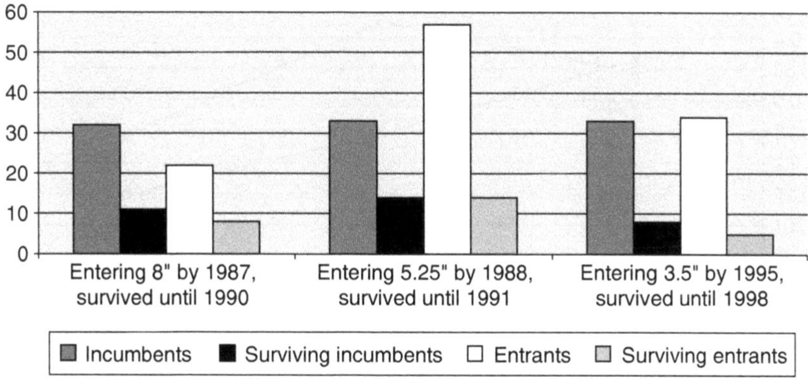

Figure 13.1 Survival (count) by incumbency status within three years of peak

conditional on entry itself, entrants are definitely not faster on average, despite one of their ranks being first.

Further, if we examine survival counts for a conservative three years[5] after the peak sales year[6] (as shown in Figure 13.1), we see several things. First, the sheer number of surviving incumbents as pointed out above. Secondly, the large number of firms entering the 5.25″ transition with almost 60 entrants joining over 30 incumbents in the market. Thirdly, the difference between survival rates certainly looks to be in incumbents' favour, or at least not in their disfavour.

To get at this last point directly, Figure 13.2 plots the survival rates across the three transitions. One thing that jumps out from Figure 13.2 is that incumbents do not appear to have a greater incidence of exit than entrants; if anything, incumbents appear to survive at a greater rate. Thus we have some counterfactual examples, based on decades' worth of data, that in many cases, incumbents are not hesitant to develop new technology—even potentially damaging technology—and, while not first to the markets created by that technology, not afraid to eventually enter and survive.

[5] Conservative because shorter survival periods favour entrants, who rarely last for very many years.

[6] The reason we keep using peak sales year is that (1) some industry insiders propose that the strategy of companies can shift after the peak sales year to one of servicing old markets intentionally rather than trying to enter new ones; and (2) there are certain statistical issues with the universe of incumbents left after the peak year. King and Tucci (2002) give more information on both of these factors.

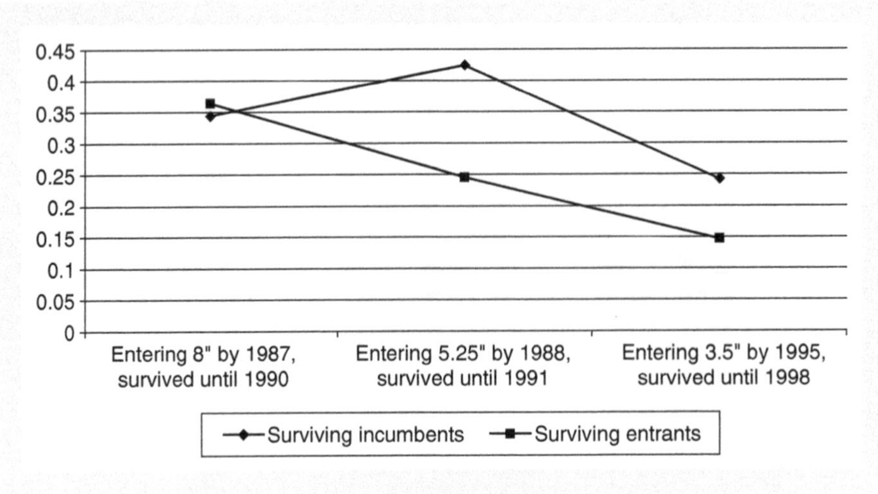

Figure 13.2 Survival (%) by incumbency status

13.4 Rational vs. Irrational Non-Entry

What accounts for the above findings? We have documented that incumbents do in fact develop new technologies, even those that might be damaging to them. However, they may enter the market later than the first wave of entrants, and, depending on when the study was done, may be seen as slow or even incompetent in reacting to the new technology. We feel that past research in management of technological innovation implicitly overlooks the distinction between the development of a new product and its release into the market with regard to incumbent-entrant dynamics. Tushman and Anderson (1986), for example, discuss how a technological discontinuity has the possibility of overturning existing firms. They propose that when innovations are competence-destroying for incumbents, incumbents will be less likely to adopt them. One implication of this, proposed by Tushman and Anderson, is that incumbents do not develop innovations that render their own capabilities irrelevant. Another interpretation of this is that incumbents may develop but not release the innovation until a more auspicious time. Note that these two interpretations are difficult to unpack given Tushman and Anderson's data.

In a similar vein, Christensen and Bower (1996) examine response of rigid hard drive manufacturers to various form factor changes. The newer form factors (pioneered by entrants) were smaller and their capacities lower, but technological progress in capacity ensured that the smaller form factors eventually became acceptable to the broader market. Christensen and Bower claim that incumbents were slow to enter these new form factors. However, another interpretation of this is that incumbents already developed the technology and were withholding the release of the products from the market.

Other papers dealing with entry timing of incumbents into new technologies could similarly be re-interpreted as a strategic choice between entering immediately and waiting. The technology could be thought of as an 'option' to enter the new market if it ends up being promising (Trigeorgis, 2001; Schwartz and Kashima and Tucci, 2003). It is difficult to determine whether the waiting was 'irrational' (as many researchers have claimed) or 'rational'. Thus we may say that some of conventional wisdom may be based on confusing irrational vs. rational non-entry.

The economics of innovation literature does discuss the issue of a 'sleeping patent', in which an incumbent invests in a patent to forestall or block entry into its own market. In this case, the patent does represent the development of technology embodied in a new product, but the firm has no intention of releasing the technology to market. Gilbert and Newbery (1982) propose a model in which incumbents and entrants bid (invest) to develop a new product that will 'cannibalize' the incumbent's current market, with the completion date deterministically based upon the amount invested. The result of the model is that the incumbent always has the incentive to outbid the entrant and thus preemptively patents the technology.

Gilbert and Newbery did not explicitly study the timing of when to release the product based on new technology, but the timing implications are evident. The entrant would release the new product immediately, and the incumbent would never release the product. However, these results are an artifact of one major assumption: demand is static and completely known (Reinganum, 1983). Kashima and Tucci (2003) relax this assumption, and allow both the entrant to delay release and the incumbent to expedite it.

13.5 Managerial implications for incumbents

Play to your strengths. Take full advantage of the wide range of R&D afforded by already being in business and already being in the market. Keep scanning for new technologies and developing technological options, even with small investments. There are several well-known examples of companies 'stockpiling' technology for future use, either because other complementary technologies are not defined, or the eventual product is not defined (e.g. Hitachi and biotechnology), competitors have not entered, or demand is unknown (e.g. Intel and Pentium processors)

(Conner, 1988; Garud and Nayyar, 1994). Garud and Nayyar (p. 375) note, however, that investments must be made continuously and they cite the example of Xerox, which was unable to 'reactivate' its personal computer business despite having developed it quite early. Xerox stopped its own efforts and 'gaps' were created in its knowledge. Thus, maintain and keep an inventory of technology for later use.

Protect your complementary assets. Be aware of technologies that may cripple not only your core products and services, but also your complementary assets, such as distribution, marketing, manufacturing, or other important assets. Value continuously your complementary assets in different markets, and examine the trajectory of their value. If their value is predicted to decline precipitously in the current market, put them to their next best use.

Don't be afraid to exploit your assets in new technology-based markets once the market is proven. Don't be afraid to exploit your assets in new technology markets where the new market might cannibalize the old one. This has been said many times in the strategic management literature but it bears repeating here. For example, in disk drives, most of the new markets were much larger than the old ones. For example, 5.25″ disk drives sold more than 20 times the quantities per year as did 8″ disk drives. Most rigid hard drive incumbents made the decision to go on, eventually, and it paid off for them to do so (King and Tucci, 2002).

Enter when the time is right and with correct force. On the other hand, it was not obvious in the first year or so after a 5.25″ drive was produced that the new market would take off. As discussed above, once the market is shown to be growing, and perhaps dominating the current market, that is the time to 'activate' the technology and enter quickly. King and Tucci (2002) demonstrate that production and sales experience in a technology-created niche might be beneficial in understanding, surviving, and prospering in the next one (in addition to being beneficial by reaping current sales), thus we recommend entry on as large a scale as possible, once the decision has been made.

13.6 Conclusions

In summary, there has been a confusion in the literature in the field of management. This confusion centres around the timing of technological and market entry and the investment that allowed the entry, as shown in Figure 13.3. This confusion

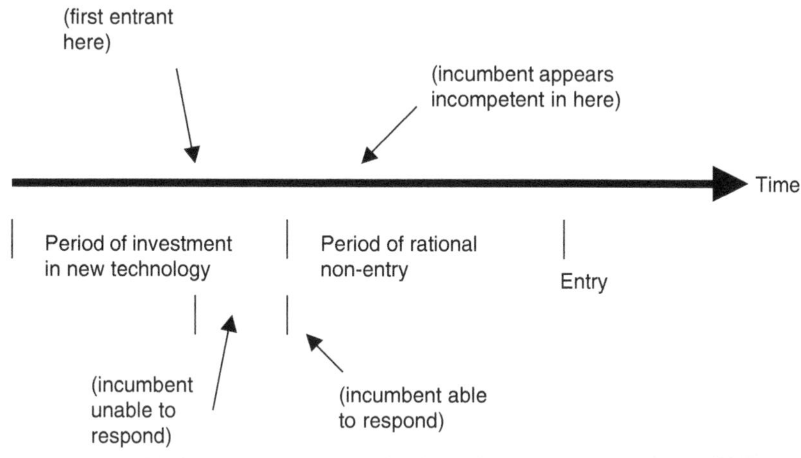

Figure 13.3 Incumbent investment and response: Some possibilities

has worked its way into innovation management, where we often examine the release of new technologies into the market as shorthand for technological capabilities. This confusion also pervades the strategy literature, in which evidence of dynamic capabilities is sought only in the release of products to new markets. Theoretically speaking, dynamic capabilities have nothing to say about market entry timing, only about whether entry ever occurs. As discussed above (p. 344–5, rational delays or non-entry are entirely feasible and not a cause to dismiss the routines that might make up an incumbent's market-entry mechanisms. The most difficult challenge to analyzing the period between the time that the first non-incumbent enters and the time the incumbent enters is: wondering whether the non-entry is rational or irrational. Before writing off the incumbent as an incompetent, irrational loser, this chapter would suggest that in many (if not most) cases, such a judgement would be (a) overly harsh from a theoretical point of view, and (b) a mistake of underestimation from a practical point of view. We are sure that the ranks of the corporate graveyards are littered with the bodies of entrants who made just such a judgement!

References

Abernathy, W. J. and K. B. Clark (1985). 'Innovation: Mapping the Winds of Destruction'. *Research Policy*, 14: 3–22.

—— and J. M. Utterback (1978). 'Patterns of Industrial Innovation.' *Technology Review*, 80(7): 40–7.

Acs, Z. J. and D. B. Audretsch (1988). 'Innovation in Large and Small Firms–an Empirical-Analysis'. *American Economic Review*, 78(4): 678–90.

—— and—— (1990). *Innovation and Small Firms*. Cambridge, MA: MIT Press.

—— and—— (eds) (1991). *Innovation and Technological Change: An International Comparison*. Ann Arbor: University of Michigan Press.

Aldrich, H. and E. R. Auster (1986). 'Even Dwarfs Started Small: Liabilities of Age and Size and their Strategic Implications'. *Research in Organizational Behavior*, 8: 165–98.

Ali, A. (1994). 'Pioneering Versus Incremental Innovation–Review and Research Propositions'. *Journal of Product Innovation Management*, 11(1): 46–61.

Arrow, K. J. (2000). 'Innovation in Large and Small Firms', in R. Swedberg (ed.) *Entrepreneurship*. Oxford: Oxford Management Reader.

Berchicci, L. (2005). *The Green Entrepreneur's Challenge*. Delft: University of Technology Press.

Brittain, J. and J. J. Freeman (1980). 'Organizational Proliferation and Density-dependent Selection', in J. R. K. and R. Miles (ed.) *The Organizational Life Cycle*. San Francisco: Jossey-Bass.

Brown, S. L. and K. M. Eisenhardt (1998). *Competing on the Edge Strategy as Structured Chaos*. Boston: Harvard Business School Press.

Buderi, R. (2000). *Engines of Tomorrow: How the World's Best Companies are Using Their Research Labs to Win the Future*. New York: Simon and Schuster.

Chandy, R. K. and G. J. Tellis (2000). 'The Incumbent's Curse? Incumbency, Size, and Radical Product Innovation'. *Journal of Marketing*, 64(3): 1–17.

Chen, M. J. and D. C. Hambrick (1995). 'Speed, Stealth, and Selective Attack—How Small Firms Differ from Large Firms in Competitive Behavior'. *Academy of Management Journal*, 38(2): 453–82.

Christensen, C. M. (1993). 'The Rigid Disk Drive Industry: A History of Commercial and Technological Turbulence'. *Business History Review* (Winter), 531–88.

—— (1997). *The Innovator's Dilemma, When New Technologies Cause Great Firms to Fail*. Boston: Harvard Business School Press.

—— and R. S. Rosenbloom (1995). 'Explaining the Attackers Advantage—Technological Paradigms, Organizational Dynamics, and the Value Network'. *Research Policy*, 24(2): 233–57.

—— and J. L. Bower, (1996). 'Customer Power, Strategic Investment, and the Failure of Leading Firms'. *Strategic Management Journal*, 17(3): 197–218.

Cohen, W. M. (1995). 'Empirical Studies of Innovative Activity', in P. Stoneman (ed.) *Handbook of the Economics of Innovation and Technological Change*. Oxford: Blackwell.

—— and D. A. Levinthal (1990). 'Absorptive Capacity: A New Perspective on Learning and Innovation'. *Administrative Science Quarterly* 35(1): 128–52.

Conner, K. R. (1988). 'Strategies for Product Cannibalization'. *Strategic Management Journal* (Summer SI) 9: 9–26.

Damanpour, F. (1992). 'Organizational Size and Innovation'. *Organization Studies*, 13(3): 375–402.

Dean, T. J., R. L. Brown and C. E. Bamford (1998). 'Differences in Large and Small Firm Responses to Environmental Context: Strategic Implications from a Comparative Analysis of Business Formations'. *Strategic Management Journal*, 19(8): 709–28.

Dougherty, D. (1990). 'Understanding New Markets for New Products'. *Strategic Management Journal* (SI) 11: 59–78.

FOSTER, R. N. (1986). *Innovation: The Attacker's Advantage.* New York: Summit Books.

GARUD, R. and P. R. NAYYAR (1994). 'Transformative capacity: Continual Structuring by Intertemporal Technology Transfer'. *Strategic Management Journal* 15(5): 365–85.

GHEMAWAT, P. (1991). *Commitment: The Dynamic of Strategy.* New York: The Free Press.

GILBERT, R. and D. M. G. NEWBERY (1982). 'Preemptive Patenting and the Persistence of Monopoly'. *American Economic Review,* 72(3): 514–26.

HAMBRICK, D. C. and I. C. MACMILLAN (1985). 'Efficiency of Product R-and-D in Business Units—the Role of Strategic Context'. *Academy of Management Journal,* 28(3): 527–47.

HANNAN, M. T. and J. FREEMAN (1984). 'Structural Inertia and Organizational-Change'. *American Sociological Review,* 49(2): 149–64.

HENDERSON, R. (1993). 'Underinvestment and Incompetence as Responses to Radical Innovation—Evidence from the Photolithographic Alignment Equipment Industry'. *Rand Journal of Economics,* 24(2): 248–70.

—— and K. B. CLARK (1990). 'Architectural Innovation: The Reconfiguration of Existing Product Technologies and the Failure of Established Companies'. *Administrative Science Quarterly,* 35: 9–20.

KASHIMA, K. L. and C. L. TUCCI (2003). A discussion on new product release timing: Real option and project divestiture effects. (Working paper). École Polytechnique Fédérale de Lausanne, College of Management of Technology.

KING, A. and C. L. TUCCI (1999). 'Can Old Disk Drive Companies Learn New Tricks?' Proceedings of the Product Development Management Conference, Cambridge, July.

—— and —— (2002). 'Incumbent entry into new market niches: The role of experience and managerial choice in the creation of dynamic capabilities'. *Management Science,* 48(2): 171–86.

LAMBKIN, M. (1988). 'Order of Entry and Performance in New Markets'. *Strategic Management Journal,* 9: 127–40.

LEONARD-BARTON, D. (1995). *Wellsprings of Knowledge: Building and Sustaining the Sources of Innovation.* Boston, MA: Harvard Business School Press.

MCDERMOTT, C. M. and G. C. O'CONNOR (2002). 'Managing Radical Innovation: An Overview of Emergent Strategy Issues'. *Journal of Product Innovation Management,* 19(6): 424–38.

MITCHELL, W. (1989). 'Whether and When—Probability and Timing of Incumbents Entry into Emerging Industrial Subfields'. *Administrative Science Quarterly,* 34(2): 208–30.

—— (1991). 'Dual Clocks–Entry Order Influences on Incumbent and Newcomer Market Share and Survival when Specialized Assets Retain their Value'. *Strategic Management Journal,* 12(2): 85–100.

—— and K. SINGH (1996). 'Survival of Businesses Using Collaborative Relationships to Commercialize Complex Goods'. *Strategic Management Journal,* 17(3): 169–95.

NELSON, R. R. and S. G. WINTER (1982). *An Evolutionary Theory of Economic Change.* Belknap Press of Harvard University Press.

REINGANUM, J. F. (1983). 'Uncertain Innovation and the Persistence of Monopoly'. *American Economic Review,* 73: 741–48.

ROSENBERG, N. (1990). 'Why Do Firms Do Basic Research with Their Own Money'. *Research Policy,* 19(2): 165–74.

ROTHAERMEL, F. T. (2001a). 'Incumbent's Advantage through Exploiting Complementary Assets via Interfirm Cooperation'. *Strategic Management Journal,* 22(6–7): 687–99.

ROTHAERMEL, F. T. (2001b). 'Complementary Assets, Strategic Alliances, and the Incumbent's Advantage: An Empirical Study of Industry and Firm Effects in the Biopharmaceutical Industry'. *Research Policy*, 30(8): 1235–51.

SCHERER, F. M. (1980). *Industrial Market Structure and Economic Performance*. Chigago: Rand McNally.

SCHUMPETER, J. A. (1934). *The Theory of Economic Development*. Cambridge, MA: Harvard University Press.

—— (1942). *Capitalism, Socialism, and Democracy*. New York: London: Harper and Brothers.

SCHWARTZ, E. and L. TRIGEORGIS (2001). *Real Options and Investment under Uncertainty*. Cambridge, MA: MIT Press.

SINGH, J. (1986). 'Performance, Slack and Risk Taking in Organizational Decision Making'. *Academy of Management Journal*, 29: 562–85.

SORENSEN, J. B. and T. E. STUART (2000). 'Aging, Obsolescence, and Organizational Innovation'. *Administrative Science Quarterly*, 45(1): 81–112.

SRIVASTAVA, R. K., T. A. SHERVANI and L. FAHEY (1998). 'Market-based Assets and Shareholder Value: A Framework for Analysis. '*Journal of Marketing*, 62(1): 2–18.

TRIPSAS, M. (1997). 'Unraveling the Process of Creative Destruction: Complementary Assets and Incumbent Survival in the Typesetter Industry.' *Strategic Management Journal*, 18: 119–42.

TUSHMAN, M. L. and P. ANDERSON (1986). 'Technological Discontinuities and Organizational Environments'. *Administrative Science Quarterly*, 31(3): 439–65.

—— and E. ROMANELLI (1985). 'Organizational Evolution: A Metamorphosis Model Of Convergence And Reorientation', in L. L. Cummings and B. M. Staw (eds) *Research in Organizational Behavior*, Greenwich, CT: JAI Press.

UTTERBACK, J. M. (1994). 'Radical Innovation and Corporate Regeneration'. *Research–Technology Management*, 37(4): 10.

—— (1995). *Mastering the Dynamics of Innovation*. Boston: Harvard Business School Press.

—— and W. J. ABERNATHY (1975). 'Dynamic Model of Process and Product Innovation.' *Omega-International Journal of Management Science*, 3(6): 639–56.

—— and KIM, L. (1985). 'Invasion of a Stable Business by Radical Innovation', in P. R. Kleindorfer (ed.) *The Management of Productivity and Technology in Manufacturing*. New York: Plenum.

WHEELWRIGHT, S. C. and K. B. CLARK (1992). *Revolutionizing Product Development; Quantum Leaps in Speed, Efficiency, and Quality*. New York: The Free Press.

WILLIAMSON, H. F. (1975). *Evolution of International Management Structures*. Newark, DE: University of Delaware Press.

PART IV

FINANCE

CHAPTER 14

VENTURE CAPITAL

ROBERT CRESSY

14.1 Introduction

Venture capital has, in recent years become a substantial and growing area of academic research.[1] This florescence has emerged from the pioneering work of Bygrave, Timmons, Sahlman, Gompers, Lerner and others together with the build-up and final bursting of the stock market bubble of the 1990s, regarded by many as fuelled by venture capital (see Gompers and Lerner, 2001). However, it is still a comparatively young field and several of the fundamental questions raised by scholars working within it remain to be answered. These fundamental questions include the following:

- *Why do venture capital firms exist (or persist)?* In other words, what is different (if anything) about venture capital as compared with other types of finance that creates a need for it as a separate entity?
- *How important is venture capital to an economy?* This question raises issues of the monetary value of venture capital and the contribution of enterprises financed by venture capital to national product.

[1] A brief interrogation of the SSRN database shows that there are some 225 papers now available from SSRN members, and the more important of these papers are highly cited in the literature. A search of the Business Source Premier database on the string venture capital or private equity yields X published papers and a Google Scholar search shows that the most cited paper in this area has no fewer than 268 citations (27 per year). This newness of the field also means that many of the research papers we shall discuss have not yet been published other than in Working Paper form.

- *Who are the main recipients of venture capital and why?* The answer to this question involves an exploration of the types of firm funded by venture capital and an examination of what makes them 'special'.
- *What is the nature of and motivation for the kinds of contracts governing the relationship between venture capital fund providers (e.g. financial institutions) and fund disbursers (Venture Capitalist investors?)* The answer to this question involves an exploration of the agency problems engendered by the venture capital relationships and their proposed solution in the contractual conditions governing them.
- *Do venture capitalists (VCs) have superior investment selection skills and do their post-investment activities add value to the ventures they fund?* In other words, do VCs add value to companies in which they invest by being better at selecting investments and in monitoring and advising these firms or are they simply an addition to the firm's costs and a deduction from investors' returns?
- *Why do VCs syndicate (invest with other VCs) and stage investments (invest in tranches rather than all at once)?* The answers to these two questions relate to two relatively unique characteristics of VC investment behaviour that require explanation.
- Finally, there is the key investor question: *What are the returns to and the risk of venture capital as an investment?* This question is surprisingly difficult to answer because of the availability of reliable data and statistical problems of interpreting it. However, recent work has provided some interesting findings worthy of report.

So what are the aims of the current survey? The survey aims to provide the postgraduate student and the interested layperson with an overview of the current scholarly answers to the questions we have just outlined. In doing so it attempts as far as possible to cut through the jargon and hyperbole endemic to the subject and to provide convenient access to the main issues. A basic knowledge of economics and finance is presupposed. For the reader considering embarking upon research in this area we shall attempt at the end of the chapter to indicate promising directions for future research. Finally, surveys that use a different approach, or cover earlier periods than the current one, the reader may wish to consult include Fried and Hisrich (1988), Mason and Harrison (1999) and Gompers and Lerner (2001). Text books on the subject include Gompers and Lerner (1999) and Smith and Smith (2004).

14.1.1 Definitions

Winston Churchill once described Britain and America as 'two countries separated by a common language.' This linguistic quip certainly applies to the term 'venture capital investment' which in the US refers only to investment in the shares of privately-held companies at an early stage of a company's development, whereas in the UK and continental Europe it refers to investment at all stages of a company's development. However, it is useful for our purposes to specify the term in greater detail than is commonly done in the literature, with an emphasis on its American connotation.

Venture capital investment consists in the purchase of shares of young, privately held companies by outsiders for the primary purpose of capital gain.

This definition of course presupposes subsidiary definitions of the terms 'young', 'privately held', 'company' and 'capital gain', terms which are themselves not without ambiguity. We shall use the component terms as follows:

- *Young* means typically less than 5 years old[2]
- *Privately held* means unquoted on a stock market (including the so-called 'secondary' markets such as NASDAQ and AIM)
- *Company* distinguishes the business from an unincorporated business, and presupposes the existence of shares in the company which can in principle be sold
- *Outsider* means an individual or company who is not, prior to the first purchase event, a member of the board of directors of the company in question.
- *Capital gain* means the investor's gain (loss) from any appreciation (depreciation) in the share price of the investee company.

The advantage of using this tight definition of the term is that it immediately raises some of the major issues associated with venture capital. Venture capitalists can realize a capital gain from an investment (via a strategy of 'buying cheap and selling dear') only if there is ultimately an *exit route* from their investment; in other words, an opportunity (that needs to be seen in general outline in advance) when they can convert their shares into cash. Unlike a publicly-quoted company's shares, a private company's shares are *illiquid*: They can (before flotation) be sold to only a limited number of potential buyers, and often only at a great discount to their purchase price, unless the company has grown and developed into a viable business that others will wish to purchase. Such purchasers will typically be other companies (trade sale/acquisition) or the general public (via a stock market floatation).

Interestingly, and perhaps unique to venture capital backed companies, a significant proportion of such companies that are floated on the stock market are done so, but without having made a profit. This makes their valuation problematic since it must, by definition, be substantially dependent on future as yet unrealised surplus. The confidence and reputation of the venture capitalist backers and

[2] For example, in the biotech industry the average age of a company at first round was 2.6 years; however, this mean conceals considerable variation: the standard deviation of the distribution is almost three times the mean figure.

underwriters is therefore central to the public's decision to buy the company's shares (Booth and Smith, 1986; Megginson and Weiss, 1991). The traditional stock exchanges require a track record of profitability before a company can be floated on them, making the creation of new kinds of stock markets in which these rules are relaxed (the so-called *secondary* markets) crucial for the effective *flotation* of many venture capital-backed firms and, working backwards, for the provision of venture capital funding to them.[3]

Venture capitalists (individuals and institutions that make venture capital investments) are alleged to be experts at fostering company development, and in addition to offering money, they are often regarded as pivotal in providing advice, support, contacts and preparation for a flotation to their investee companies (see Smith and Smith (2004) for references). Being part of a network is central to doing this (Bygrave, 1987, 1988). They also need to make sure that the large sum(s) of money they have invested is/are being used for the purposes specified in the venture capital contract. This involves *monitoring* of the investment, or more specifically of the entrepreneurs using the VCs' money. To make a floatation (an exit generally considerably more profitable than a trade sale)[4] in which a proportion (commonly 10%) of a company's shares are offered to the public, the company should have been chosen well from the alternatives at the outset. Thus venture capitalists are alleged to have superior skills in investment *selection*, the superiority consisting in being able to spot the potential in a company and to be able to do so before the competition (other VCs) do so. Moreover, this should be done consistently rather than randomly. In the absence of specialist knowledge VCs may call upon others for a second opinion on the venture. (Sah and Stiglitz, 1986; Brander et al., 2002). The role of the VC's network may also be crucial in obtaining high quality companies for investment.

Venture capitalists' desire for capital gain rather than dividends means that as investors they are interested in potentially fast growth companies with large-market potential and sustainable competitive advantage, factors seen as yielding the maximum capital gain to the investor. Often these companies are in the high tech sectors (Telecoms, IT, Biotechnology, etc.) Venture capitalists therefore reject a very high proportion of propositions for funding that they receive (99% at least according to industry practitioners), many of which may be quite unsuited to their investment strategy even if they may potentially yield positive economic value (i.e. positive *net present value* or *NPV*).[5] Some VCs quote a required *ex ante* return of

[3] In Europe, these secondary markets include AIM in the UK, Neuer Markt in Germany (until 2003), the Nouveau Marche in France in North America the NASDAQ. Such markets have not yet developed in Asia and many Asian companies (e.g. Chinese companies) are floated on the American NASDAQ instead.

[4] However, see Fredriksen et al. (1997) for a contrary view from Swedish experience.

[5] Because much of the profitability of such companies lies in the future, it is often more appropriate to use *real option* techniques for valuing such companies. The real option approach allows for the fact

30 percent per annum and argue that half of their investments fail (though perhaps not all completely, in the sense of yielding zero return). This suggests an average return across all investments of some 15 percent per annum. We come back to this issue in some detail later.

14.1.2 The importance of venture capital finance

How important is venture capital to the economy? As a form of funding, venture capital certainly possesses a certain glamour, being associated in the public mind with the financing of young, small, innovative high tech firms that in some cases have gone on to become 'tech stars' and household names—the Apples, Genentecs, eBays, and Amazons of this world. It is also associated with considerable risk, as anecdotes abound regarding the proportion of such ventures that fail (as mentioned, 50% is an oft-quoted figure). In the cold light of day, the value of such innovation is difficult to measure[6] and even more difficult is the issue of whether the high tech stars funded by VCs would have gone on to be successes even in the absence of venture capital support.[7] Most fast-growth businesses (only about a quarter of which are high tech) seem to grow by the use of retained profits and bank borrowing—but more on this later.

For our purposes a more prosaic, if less satisfactory, approach to the examination of the importance of venture capital is to look not at the output/profit side of the equation but instead at the input side and to ask how much venture capital is invested across the globe and how fast this amount is growing. Statistics on the global value of funds invested and their growth rates are now readily available. Not surprisingly, these statistics reveal that North America and Western Europe, home to the oldest venture capital industries in the world, currently provide the largest investment in venture capital. Specifically, America followed by Great Britain, provide the largest amounts of venture capital to the world economy. However, more interestingly, these countries are by no means home to the fastest growth in venture capital investment. Age brings with it a certain sluggishness[8] and inertia in firms in general and of the venture capital partnerships in particular: while the

that the NPV may be currently negative but has a positive probability of becoming positive at some stage in the future when an investment may be made. Using the well-known Black-Scholes option pricing model, one can then judge whether the right to invest at some date in the future has positive value now, net of any initial costs of purchasing this right.

[6] This is a subject of current research in progress.

[7] This is the issue of the economic value-added of venture capital which we shall come on to later in the chapter.

[8] See the chapter on the growth and survival of small firms for a discussion of this characteristic of firm growth.

'elephants' of the venture capital industry are the United States and the United Kingdom, the 'cheetahs' of the industry are China, Indonesia and India, countries whose economies are 'taking off' and are now attracting venture capital at phenomenal rates.

Price Waterhouse Coopers (henceforth PWC) data reveal that Global venture capital funds raised (the supply side of the equation) reached a peak of US$262 billion in the year 2000 (the zenith of the high tech equity bubble) falling to US$82 billion in 2003 (Arundale, 2005). By comparison, global funds invested (the demand side) reached a peak of US$192 billion in 2000 falling to a trough of US$86 billion in 2002, rising again to US$115 billion in 2003.[9] The PWC data show that in value terms of the global investments made in the period 1998–2003 half were made in the United States and another 30 percent in Europe (of which half was in Britain), followed by 15 percent in the Asia Pacific countries of China (US$1.67 bn), India (US$0.86 bn), Indonesia (US$0.65bn) and Singapore (US$0.45 bn). On the other hand, Asia Pacific now dominates the growth league, taking 5 of the top 10 places in the world and recording astronomic growth rates ranging from 81 percent to 35 percent per annum (ranks 1 to 5 in the league table). The US and the UK on this criterion are now ranked a mere 16th and 14th in the world respectively.

As regards industrial sectors for venture capital investment, the PWC data show, as mentioned, that most are made in high technology (IT, Telcomms, Biotech, etc.) However, since the year 2000 there may be the beginnings of a trend away from high tech investment, its share falling from 63 percent in that year to 33 percent in 2003. It is also worth noting here a geographical difference in investment focus: the vast majority (75%) of funds raised in Europe go into *buy-outs,* which in general involve established businesses wishing to restructure and change management rather than young high tech firms with huge growth potential. In Europe, around 4.5–6 percent of venture capital goes into high tech at the early stage of a company's development. (This kind of funding encompasses *seed capital*[10] and *start-up* finance). In the States, this fraction has traditionally been much larger at around 20 percent. Our interest in this chapter is precisely in this small, but potentially important, fraction of total venture funds flowing into early stage funding. These funds assist the development of young, dynamic, high tech companies rather than permit the restructuring of industrial megaliths. The companies they fund generate potentially huge externalities to an economy. Moreover, such firms would be significantly capital constrained without the availability of venture capital.

[9] The observant reader will have noted that investment in the year 2003 exceeded funds raised. This is because the cumulative amount of funds raised in the past exceeded the cumulative amount of investment made in the past, i.e. in the year 2003, VCs had reserves from which they were able to invest.

[10] Seed capital is capital to fund the very early stages of a company's development, e.g. for the construction of a prototype for a product.

In terms of the size of the typical investment it is worth noting that even at the early stage, amounts relative to the size of business are large: in the United States, the typical initial investment[11] is of the order of US$2–3m. In the UK, it is slightly smaller at US$2m. If one compares these figures with the few hundred dollars used by the typical startup business in the United States or in Europe one can appreciate that the scale of funding of VC-backed companies is massive.

Finally, despite the large aggregate sums of money invested in venture capital across the globe, we must note, contrary to public perception, that the incidence of venture capital investment among small firms in general is extremely low, with typically less than one percent of start-ups being funded from this source (Cressy, 1993). However, when this form of funding is infused it naturally constitutes the overwhelming majority of a firm's funds.

14.2 Venture Capitalists

Measured in terms of personnel, venture capitalists are organizations that can range in size from a single high net worth individual (the so-called *Angel* investor) up to very large organizations employing hundreds or even thousands of staff, for example, the UK's 3i or Apax partners (see Denny (2000) for an overview of the UK industry). Typically however, the venture capital partnership (for they are generally arranged as partnerships rather than limited companies) has only a handful of investment managers and support staff. As with most industries, the distribution of venture organization size is almost certainly lognormal implying a positively skewed distribution with a small number of large firms, and a large number of small firms.[12]

14.2.1 Business angels

Business angels are high net worth individuals, usually successful entrepreneurs wishing to plough back some of their wealth into the community and wishing to

[11] Initial investment refers here to the first investment done by a VC in a firm, regardless of the stage of the firm's development. The figures from Gompers (1995) for the United States show that this increases steadily from Seed capital at US$921 to Bridge finance at US$2,702.

[12] If a variate log(X) is Normally distributed, then by definition X is Lognormally distributed. A lognormal distribution of firm sizes is positively skewed implying that there is typically a large number of small firms and a few large firms in the industry. See Chapter 7 on Survival and Growth of Small Firms in this Handbook for more detailed discussion.

help develop the managerial skills of young, potentially fast growth entrepreneurs. They are much larger in number than institutional VCs and make smaller, faster investments that involve the day-to-day involvement of the investor in strategy and implementation. Their investment decisions can be faster than institutional VCs because they are less bureaucratic organizations and often do not require *due diligence*[13] to be performed before 'taking the plunge'. However, they also complement the activities of VCs acting in tandem with them, for example, by providing *seed capital* (funding for a prototype or proof of concept) and leaving any larger follow-on investments to the bigger VC firms. The total contribution of Angels to external equity investment is estimated to be equivalent to that of aggregate institutional venture capital (see Mason and Harrison (1999) for the UK; and Wetzel (1987), van Osnabrugge and Robinson (2000), for the US. For more global empirical coverage see Reynolds et al., 2001).

14.2.2 Institutional venture capital

14.2.2.1 *Limited partnerships*

In the US and the UK, institutional venture capital organizations tend to be Limited Partnerships (Gompers and Lerner, 1999; Smith and Smith, 2004). Such partnerships involve aspects of both limited liability (for the investors or fund providers) and of unlimited liability (for the venture capitalists). There are two kinds of 'agency' relationships in venture capital:[14] one between the Investors (fund providers) and the VCs, and one (or strictly several)[15] between the VCs and the investee companies (companies in which VCs invest the Investors' money). These relationships are subject to various conflicts of interest arising from the fact that one party to the agreement has privileged information that it can potentially take advantage of. Investors are invited to participate in a fund, for example, 'The

[13] *Due diligence* is a strict and detailed check carried out by professionals on the quality of the investment covering finance, legal matters, technology, management quality etc. and is intended to protect the investor against obvious deficiencies in the investment, e.g. poor quality management or dubious technology.

[14] An *agency* relationship is one that involves a *principal* who commissions work from an *agent*. For example, outside venture capital I may employ a builder to construct an extension to my home, I am then the principal, the builder, the agent. The agent's effort is assumed not to be observable by the principal and hence the agent has an incentive to shirk (do less work than she or he agrees to). The principal delegates this task and then has the job of monitoring what the agent does. Continuing the tradesman example, most people who have employed builders will know the difficulty of getting them to appear on time to work continuously on your job rather than jointly with other projects, and so on. Therefore, their actions need to be monitored, but this may be difficult, or in some circumstances impossible. See Hart (1995) for an excellent discussion of these and related issues.

[15] As there are many investments made from a given fund of money.

Guangdong Telecomms fund II', with an obvious *sector* or *stage* focus, and often will meet to hear presentations from its organizers (the VCs). The fund size is normally fixed (e.g. US$1bn). Once this sum has been raised, investments will be made, usually being completed within three years of the money being raised. Limited partnerships take the form of a *closed end funds* (Gompers and Lerner, 2001) which are investment vehicles quoted on a stock exchange and allowing the investor to liquidate his investment even if the investments made by the VC have not yet been harvested.

14.2.2.2 *Dependents, independents and corporates*

Institutional VCs are divisible into *independents, dependents* and *corporations.* Independents are partnerships investing their own money. 'Dependent' or 'captive' VCs are partnerships that are subsidiaries or affiliates of another financial institution, for example, a bank. (E.g., Barclays Ventures of the UK are a subsidiary of Barclays Bank plc.) Finally, 'Corporate' VCs are corporations who invest in the equity of private companies while remaining involved in industrial or commercial activity as their main business. Intel Inc of the United States is the most successful corporate VC in the world and has made more than X investments in spin-offs from the parent company (see Cressy and Koppelkamm, 2006).

In some countries, venture capital is organized quite differently from the Anglo-Saxon limited partnership. For example, in Canada, most VC investment takes place via Labour Sponsored Venture Capital Organizations (LSVCCs) which are run by labour unions and have objectives in general different from maximizing the returns to investors, for example the direct generation of employment. The Canadian government provides generous tax incentives to investors in such organizations who have over CA$4 billion capital under management and have funded over 60 percent of new capital investment in Canada in recent years (Cumming and Mackintosh, 2002).

14.3 Fund providers ('investors')

Firms that do not exclusively rely on their own retained profits for investments periodically raise funds from Investors, typically big financial institutions (the banks, pension funds or insurance companies), government or the universities. Pension funds make up a very large proportion of quoted equity ownership in Europe and North America and it is argued that despite some of the apparent problems associated with venture capital (e.g. illiquidity and 'excess' risk) they offer a suitable investment vehicle for them (e.g. British Venture Capital Association, 2000; henceforth BVCA). BVCA suggests that the problems of risk can be overcome by the use of venture capital as a small proportion of a diversified portfolio. This would, it is claimed, reduce the 'excess' firm-specific risk associated with it. Likewise, the problem of the illiquidity of venture capital investments could be circumvented by the use of quoted investment vehicles in which venture capital is embedded, thus obviating the need to sell individual shares should the need arise.

Governments provide assistance to venture capital investment in many European countries, for example, the UK's setting up of Regional Venture Capital funds to plug the so-called regional equity gaps or the German government's *BioRegio* Program providing incubator environments for biotech start-ups. (Murray, 1994, 1998).

Universities often generate spin-off companies from their science departments, companies that are often based on patents from university inventions from which academics then attempt to make money (see Shane, 2004; Tang et al., 2004). For example, the Scottish Wolfson Microelectronics company was a spin-off from Edinburgh university's computing department. ARM arose from the association of a team of software design engineers at the university of Cambridge, England. Anticipating these developments, universities have some incentive to provide funds in support of such companies, taking a share in their equity in compensation to help reduce their dependence on government funds. Harvard university is an illustrious example, with the largest endowment of the American universities, estimated currently to be US$22.6 billion (US$22,600 million).[16] A significant proportion of this is spent on equity investment in high tech spin-offs from that university.[17]

14.3.1 What drives venture capital fundraising?

This question was posed and answered for the special case of the United States by Gompers and Lerner in their eponymous paper (Gompers and Lerner, 1998 henceforth GL) and has subsequently been extended to cover a range of other countries (Jeng and Wells, 1998).

GL, using aggregate national and state-level data for the period 1972–1994, concluded that the main determinant of fundraising was demand from entrepreneurs for funds. Because of data limitations, GL used single equation modelling

[16] The top ten universities range from US$22.6 bn down to US$4 bn in size.

[17] Interestingly, however, Harvard is not the top of the league table for university licensing income, ranking only 16th with US$16.6 m in revenues from this source in 1999–2001. Perhaps much of the return is received in the form of capital gain from the sale of equity held in these businesses.

techniques in their analyses rather than a simultaneous equation approach which would in principle enable one to isolate supply and demand effects. They argued that demand from entrepreneurs was the primary determinant of funding growth, with demand in turn being stimulated by (i) a growing economy; (ii) technological change; and (iii) reductions in taxation (specifically the capital gains tax rate.) All these factors they argue made it more attractive for entrepreneurially-minded individuals to start their own businesses—and hence generate an increase in the demand for venture capital funds. On the supply side they argue that changes in regulation of the United States pension funds allowed large amounts of venture capital to be channelled into their investments. Finally, at firm level, the role of VC reputation for success also contributed to the availability of venture capital funds.

If true, the idea that demand determines the size of the VC industry would be novel as it has often been argued that in venture capital the situation is most commonly one of 'too much money chasing too few good businesses' and therefore that it is the supply of venture capital that is responsible for VC industry growth. However, the subsequent discussion of their paper by Blair and Hellmann (see Gompers and Lerner, 1998, following), showed that there are serious methodological flaws in their paper: (a) Given the often substantial time from start-up to cash-in and the uncertainties associated with the outcomes, few if any entrepreneurs are likely to have started with capital gains tax (CGT) advantages dominant in their minds, thus questioning the interpretation of their negative coefficient on CGT; (b) econometrically speaking the price of VC funds is not observable and there are no instruments to distinguish demand from supply of funds that enable one to properly distinguish the two; (c) in the capital gains tax regressions (key to their argument) GL have too few observations with which to work, reducing the power of their tests; (d) some of their variables were too crude to allow with any certainty the isolation of even the pension fund effects from other concomitant events; and so on.

We must conclude from the above discussion that although it is possible that the GL hypothesis is correct, the US data and analysis certainly do not enable us to infer this at the present time.

14.4 Why do venture capitalists exist?

What does venture capital offer that the more conventional methods of finance do not? In practical terms, the obvious reasons for the existence and persistence of venture capital are the following.

14.4.1 Financial intermediary

As a financial intermediary (an institution that channels funds between consumers who save and businesses that need to invest), VCs would seem to have competition: most notably the banks—but less obviously the finance houses (hire purchase), friends and relatives (love money) and owner savings. There is plenty of evidence that the last two options are used to finance the high tech start-up by the owner–manager (henceforth OM) (e.g. Cressy, 1993, 2006; Bhide, 2000). But why not the banks?

14.4.2 What's wrong with banks?

The main source of external finance for the typical small firm in the United States and Europe—those that do borrow mainly for purposes of working capital (Cressy, 1993, 2006)—is the banking system. The problem for the young high tech business is that banks typically require collateral or a track record, together with business propositions they can understand. Young, high tech firms with growth potential (we shall refer henceforth to as NTBFs or New Technology Based Firms) do not fit into this category well, lacking both. Their assets are both intangible—patents and copyrights—and specific—possessing negligible liquidation value—and they offer products or services at the cutting edge of technology that often are recondite to the lay-person and often generate positive net cash flows only some years down the line. Nor do these businesses want the worry of needing to meet regular debt service payments required by a loan or even an overdraft (line of credit) facility.[18] Although most fast-growth businesses grow by the use of retained profits (Bhide, 2000) high tech start-ups generally do not have this privilege.

14.4.3 Advantages of venture capital to the company

First, as already indicated, outside equity has the advantage that it involves no collateral requirement on the user. Most high tech start-ups have little by way of tangible assets that banks like to use as security for loans. Secondly, VCs from the US and the UK usually offer funding to investee companies chiefly in the form of *preference shares.* These shares are usually (a) *convertible* to ordinary equity (offering

[18] Overdraft (line of credit) financing has the advantage of flexibility as to what is drawn down (borrowed) and when this is paid back. However, the overdraft is in principle repayable on demand and is usually collateralized on accounts receivable.

upside potential to the investor should the company succeed and he convert his shares into equity), and (b) *cumulative* in that the dividends they require to be paid can be paid according to a very flexible schedule, thus allowing the company to match its payments to its cash flows to some degree. Thirdly, if your VC is chosen correctly, he or she will have expertise in the area of your business (e.g. telecommunications experience in China for a Chinese telecom start-up) and be at the centre of a network of contacts that facilitates the provision of services useful to your business and offers of future funding that your growth will almost certainly need. Fourthly, by facilitating growth, you as owner will own shares which may make you very rich rather quickly—though initially only on paper.[19]

14.4.4 Disadvantages of venture capital to the company

We can set against these advantages the following disadvantages.

The fractional share of the original owners in the company necessarily declines. This means three things: (a) at a given value of the company the wealth of the owners declines;[20] (b) some control is relinquished to outsiders (at least initially), since the VC will normally require a majority of voting shares; and (c) the owner-manager (OM) with high probability will be replaced over time as his skills are recognized as inadequate to the task confronting him (Hannan et al., 1996; Cressy and Hall, 2005). The OM will also find that if he fails to meet certain specified milestones conditional for funding his share and likely control of the company will decrease further.

14.4.5 Advantages to the VCs

VCs stand to make considerable financial gains from investing their clients (or their own) money. The VC's monetary return consists of two components: the annual management fee that the VC charges investors and which covers primarily the salaries of its investment managers, and its share of the capital gain from the eventual

[19] A relative of mine was a paper millionaire in this way when his business was taken over by a NASDAQ quoted company. He was made a director of that company and was paid in the company's shares. Unfortunately the price of those shares then proceeded to halve over the next year. He could not sell immediately for obvious reasons and therefore had to patiently watch his wealth decline by the same fraction.

[20] Hopefully however, the value of the company actually increases as a result of the additional funding.

sale of the firm's shares should they be sold profitably (see Gompers and Lerner, 1999).

The VC's management fee averages at about 2–3 percent of the value of the fund, and is paid annually for the duration of the fund. Thus a US$1 billion[21] fund would attract an average management fee for the VC firm of US$20–30 million per annum over a ten-year period—the typical duration of the fund under which the money is invested. The total cost of VC management over the life of the fund is therefore of the order of US$250 million. It is important to note that this fee is independent of the firm's current performance, though a poorly performing fund might find it difficult to raise money for future investments thus exerting some discipline on performance, but only over the longer term.

Performance-related pay or 'carried interest' for the VC comes in at 20–30 percent of any capital gain on the shares. It is paid only after investors' money has been returned to them. Thus, if the investments made by the VC under our US$1 billion fund double the value of the fund overall, then the VC will in addition to the management fee earn US$200–300 million in carried interest. If we add these figures together, we can see that the VC in our example would earn US$500 million over a ten-year period, averaging out at US$50 million per annum, for its services. However a more accurate average return of 15 percent per annum on its investments[22] would bring this total up to US$1.01 billion over ten years or about US$100 million per annum.

14.4.6 Disadvantages to VC

The VC needs to monitor and advise investee management on a regular basis. Thus she/he will pay the company regular visits, sit in on board meetings, make regular phone calls to the directors, and so forth. However, she/he will also have to draw on the services of external advisors like accountants, lawyers, recruitment consultants and others on behalf of the company.

Venture capital contracts are written in the context of great uncertainty implying that an exhaustive specification of the outcomes of the investment is impossible. This means that the environment is one of 'incomplete contracting' (see Aghion and Bolton, 1992; Hart, 1995; Hellmann, 1998). In lieu of a complete contract stating who owns what when a given event happens, the parties agree as to who has control of key variables in key circumstances, for example, bankruptcy of a limited company means that the control of the firm is turned over to bondholders who then have the right to sell off the firm's assets to retrieve their debts. The right of the

[21] US$1 followed by nine zeros.

[22] See section on the returns to venture capital investment for the choice of this figure.

VC to replace the owner-manager can in fact be considered an optimal control right, and one in principle voluntarily agreeable to by the entrepreneur (Hellmann, 1998).[23]

Replacement of underperforming or inappropriate CEOs and other senior management is in fact commonplace in the venture capital industry. It has been estimated that in Silicon Valley in the United States during the first 20 months 10 percent of managers of VC-backed young high tech companies are replaced, rising steadily to 80 percent in the first 80 months. (Hannan et al., 1996). In Europe, matters are little different (Cressy and Hall, 2005). The main determinants of the decision to replace in this latter study were found to be (a) the track record of the incumbent manager and the firm (managerial experience and the oversight of commercially useful patents were important), (b) the return to the replacement manager, (c) the costs of monitoring. It is worth noting that the oversight of private firms is an important consumer of VCs' time. Time spent in directing, monitoring and recruiting is estimated at about 60 percent of available hours (see Smith and Smith, 2004).

14.5 Venture capital contracts

As already mentioned, there are two agency relationships in venture capital: the first is between the fund-providers and the VCs and the second between the VCs and the owner-managers of the investee firm. Each involves an asymmetry of information and an associated agency problem, namely the issue of motivating the agent to perform in alignment with the interests of the relevant principal. Several papers have modelled these relationships theoretically. For example, Admati and Pfleiderer (1994) examine an environment in which a capital-constrained entrepreneur needs funds for a business. Only the entrepreneur observes the interim results of the business before the next round of funding is proposed. Under outside equity financing the entrepreneur gets only part of the return to the business if it is successful and hence has an incentive to continue the business even if he knows it is going under. AP show that under these circumstances, if the funding is provided by a knowledgeable insider (VC) instead of by an

[23] Hellmann curiously admits in one part of his paper that typically entrepreneurs will not voluntarily relinquish control rights to the VC but then proceeds to derive a theory that assumes the opposite. The reality is of course that the VC will often have a considerably greater bargaining power than the entrepreneur and be able to push through a contract over the provisions of which the latter has little choice.

outsider, then unless the contract is structured appropriately the insider too has an incentive to 'excessive' continuation. This contract incidentally also motivates the syndication of later round investments.

14.5.2 Syndication of investments

The syndication of an investment occurs when a VC selects (is selected by) another VC to co-invest in a given round of funding for a venture.[24] Partnerships of this kind are temporary associations, and over a number of rounds of investment in the same company, several different syndicates may play a role. This makes them rather different from more permanent associations between firms (e.g. joint ventures, mergers). Theory suggests several reasons for the syndication of investments:

1 *Resource constraints* (financial, managerial etc.) Thus if a firm lacks expertise or funds to carry on an investment on its own, it may combine with others who have the expertise or funds to do so. (Bygrave, 1987, 1988; Lerner, 1994; Lockett and Wright, 1999). By so doing the firm may not only complement its skills, it may also learn new skills (engaging in learning by doing) for future investing. (For an application to biotech in three European countries see Remer, 2005).
2 *Risk reduction.* The portfolio approach to investment involves spreading risk by dividing one's initial capital amongst a range of investments. If the returns to such investments are not perfectly positively correlated, risk reduction may be obtained. (Wilson, 1968; Bygrave, 1987, 1988).
3 *Reduction of competition.* If there is 'too much' competition for a given deal, VCs may combine to keep down the price of the company's shares. This involves the setting-up of a syndicate. Venture capitalists themselves sometimes quote this as a reason for choosing to invest cojointly. No studies have been devoted to exploring this factor in syndication to the current author's knowledge.
4 *Solution to agency conflicts.* Admati and Pfleiderer (1994) argue that syndication in second rounds and above will occur as a device to prevent insiders (early-round VCs) who have private knowledge of the company's fortunes exploiting outsiders (the later-round VCs and investors) who do not. The VC, who has inside information, has an incentive to either (a) overprice the company's issue of shares to fund investment (thus hurting outside investors but benefiting her or him as an existing—first period—shareholder), or (b) to underprice the issue (thus benefiting the VC who gets the new shares cheaply

[24] Since investments in venture capital tend to come in tranches or rounds, so that the total invested is the sum of the amounts over the several rounds, the focus of activity is often at the round level.

but at the expense of the entrepreneur whose wealth is reduced). Only if the early VCs' share of the firm is kept constant through subsequent rounds of funding they argue will the interests of the VC and investors (later VCs) be aligned, since only then are the advantages of overpricing to the VC as an 'old' shareholder exactly offset by the advantages of underpricing to the VC as a 'new' shareholder. This implies syndication must occur as new funds are added—otherwise the early VCs' share will increase and with it his incentive to exploit.[25]

5 *Superior selection of investments.* Canvassing opinion from independent observers (common enough in the medical and building worlds) may improve one's decision-making skills. The same logic applies to venture capital investments (Sah and Stiglitz, 1986; Amit et al. 2002).

6 *Economies of scale.* There are certain fixed costs associated with venture capital investments. These include most notably the cost of *due diligence* (a very detailed investment quality check) which may run into millions of dollars. A syndicate enables the VCs to reduce unit costs from this source, since the cost of due diligence is independent of the number of investors in the round. Little attention has been paid to this motive in the literature. (But see Valliere and Petersen, 2004 for an exception).

7 *Window dressing.* Lakonishok et al. (1991) argue that pension funds window-dress, adjusting their portfolios by buying shares that have appreciated and selling those that have depreciated. This makes their portfolio look attractive even if the returns are in fact low. The same logic can be applied to venture capitalists who may make investments in the late rounds of promising ventures even if the price is high and the returns low. Lerner (1994) on a sample of US investments found evidence in support of this hypothesis: when experienced VCs invested for the first time in later rounds, the company was usually 'doing well' and likely to go public.

One may also enumerate certain reasons for *not* syndicating an investment. These include:

(a) *Difficulties of partner co-ordination.* Clearly the Lead VC in a syndicate has the problem of co-ordinating the views of other members in making decisions. This can create management problems in some cases.

(b) *Potential reduction in VC profits.* By definition, sharing an investment provides a smaller share of (given) profits than investing alone.[26]

So these are the pros and cons of syndication. What of the empirical facts and explanations? A high proportion of venture capital investments in the US are

[25] Lerner (1994) finds evidence in support of the constancy of VCs' shares in later rounds of funding.

[26] The counter-argument is that although the share of the pie falls automatically, the size of the pie will be likely to increase and with it the total return to the participating VC.

syndicated, suggesting that the benefits of syndication in general outweigh the costs. (Bygrave, 1987). A smaller, but still highly significant proportion, are syndicated in the UK (Lockett and Wright, 1999, 2001). Can we identify the factors behind the VC syndication decision?

Bygrave (1987) in an early empirical study of American syndication activity examined the networking of 464 American VCs who invested in 1,501 portfolio ventures in the period 1966–82. He examined the plausibility of two of the competing motives for syndication identified above: risk reduction and complementary skills. Identifying the odds of syndication with the ratio of the total number of paired investments (an investment was paired if two or more VCs engaged in it) to lone investments (done by single VCs)[27] he subdivided his sample into high- and low-innovative companies, high- and low-tech industry of origin, early- and late-stage of investment and large and small venture capitalists. Although Bygrave did not perform a multivariate regression, his analysis effectively holds the investment amount constant.

Bygrave found that the odds of syndication were higher for early-than late-stage investments, for more- rather than less-innovative companies and for high- rather than low-tech industries. Finally, he found that there was no difference in the odds of syndication for small and large VCs. These findings he argued were more plausibly explained by partners' need for resources than by their need to reduce risk. (In particular, he argued that large VCs being more diversified already would have a very limited marginal diversification advantage from syndication).[28] We note in passing that Bygrave's methodology fails to control for the whole range of possible alternative motives for syndication outlined above. Lockett and Wright (1999, 2001) examine the empirical determinants of syndication.

Remer (2005) using a broad set of controls and 9,560 investments in 1,500 biotech companies explores the role of VC financial constraints, risk reduction and knowledge (proxied by the cumulative number of investments the VC has done) in the syndication decision. Controlling for market conditions, sector and stage of investment they find that the round amount is an important determinant of the decision to syndicate, suggesting the presence of risk and capital constraints are indeed important in the syndication decision. However, they also find that the experience of the VC is negatively related to the decision to syndicate. This relationship is stronger the more specialized (by stage and sector) the VC's knowledge is. They conclude that the better matched is a VCs knowledge to the venture under consideration the less need he has to take on partners, and given the costs of syndication mentioned above, the less likely he will trade off skill acquisition with monetary discount.

[27] This is a positive monotonic function of the probability of syndication.

[28] Criticisms of the Bygrave study include the fact that he did not employ a direct measure of VC experience or skills and would have been better able to control for a range of other factors (not simply investment size) had he employed a regression approach. I find the results compelling nonetheless.

14.5.3 Staging of investments

Venture capitalists do not invest all of their money in a company in one go. Faced with an environment of uncertainty they prefer a wait-and-see approach to investing, further funds at any given 'round' being injected only if a firm is judged worthy at that stage of its development. To put some numbers on this concept, the typical biotech firm in the US, UK or Germany for example, has some five rounds of funding during its lifetime (Remer, 2005). However, the number of rounds such a firm experiences varies considerably around the mean figure with some companies getting no more than the first tranche and others receiving up to 20 rounds. In the case of biotech, failure to receive funding implies almost certain and immediate failure, unless there happens to be a trade buyer willing to 'pick up the tag'—too often an unlikely occurrence.

Several recent theoretical papers have explored the rationale of investment staging, Admati and Pfleiderer (1994), Bergemann and Hege (1998, 2000), Neher (1999), Wang and Zhou (2003), Cornelli and Yosha (2003) and Kockesen and Ozerturk (2002).

Cornelli and Yosha (2003) argue that the use by VCs of staging and convertible securities together provides a solution to the conflict of interest between the VC and the entrepreneur regarding 'the continuation decision'—whether or not to continue providing funds to the business. This conflict arises because funds are provided by an outsider (the VC) and the insider (the entrepreneur) would always like to continue the business when the VC would prefer to terminate it. The entrepreneur therefore has an incentive to window-dress, providing excessively rosy interim reports on the progress of the business with the purpose of misleading the VC. Since the VC as outsider cannot observe the quality of the project but merely this 'signal' of quality the strategy of window-dressing results in her or him making decisions based on faulty information and in terminating the business too late. The use of traditional debt-equity financing does not solve the window-dressing problem but the use of convertible debt[29] does. With convertible debt the entrepreneur's gain from reducing the likelihood of liquidation is more than offset by the increased likelihood of debt conversion by the VC (conditional on refinancing) thereby reducing the entrepreneur's share of the company. This is because although window-dressing makes low quality projects more difficult to identify, by its nature it also makes high quality projects easier to identify. This in turn increases the probability that in the event of refinancing the VC will convert and become the owner of a considerable fraction of the company.

What of the empirical evidence on staging? Gompers (1995) provides early evidence of investment staging by American VCs. He argues, following Jensen

[29] Cornelli and Yosha (2003) consider the use of convertible debt rather than the more common convertible preference shares, but the principle remains the same.

(1986), that the 'discipline' of debt reduces agency costs: a higher proportion of debt in a firm's capital structure will mean that the entrepreneur has less free cash to play with since surplus funds will be eaten up by larger, regular debt servicing payments. Debt requires collateral and collateral value is lower the more intangible or specific the assets of the company are. Real growth options also imply less use of debt by the firm.

The degree of intangibility and specificity of assets is proxied empirically by the ratio of industry R&D to sales. The presence of real growth options is proxied empirically by the market-to-book ratio.[30] Because lower debt levels are likely to result in less effort on the entrepreneur's part and more monitoring from the VC, empirically we should expect to find more frequent staging of VC investments in companies with more intangible or specific assets or growth options as VCs devise methods to deal with these problems.

Gompers uses a sample of 794 American companies receiving 2,143 rounds of investment over the period 1961–92 to test these hypotheses. He notes the following empirical regularities: (a) the average time a business experiences until funding at the next round falls, from 1.63 years to 0.97 years as the stage of investment goes progressively from Seed capital to Later-stage funding; (b) along with this decline in round length he finds the average amount of funding rises from US$921 to US$2,702; (c) at the same time cash utilization rates (*cash burn*, or the rate at which money invested is spent by the entrepreneur) rise from $565 to $2,785 per annum. The explanation for these patterns is straightforward: frequency of rounding falls, and cash invested rises, as the uncertainty associated with the business declines. Likewise, since funds are committed for the purpose of funding business expansion or development and these are greater as we move towards exit, the rate of cash burn rises for this reason also. Gompers also performs a multivariate analysis of the duration and size of the financing round and for the number of rounds a business has. Using *hazard rate* techniques, which show the probability of getting the next round of funding at time t, given that one has not received it to date,[31] he regresses duration against a number of theoretical variables and controls. The former include the stage of investment, the amount of funds injected to date, the industry ratio of tangible to intangible assets, R&D expense ratios, the age of the firm and the amount of financing to be offered in the current round. He finds that shorter round lengths are associated with larger previous investments in the firm, greater use of intangible assets, higher R&D expense ratios and younger firms at the time

[30] A value of the market to book ratio greater than one suggests that there are growth options present in the firm that are not picked up in the traditional accounting valuation.

[31] We note that simple hazard rate analysis (rather than *competing* hazard rate analysis) presupposes that the firm will get funding in any given round. This requirement is imposed by the Venture Economics data since it excludes information on firms that did not get funding. However, the penalty of using this data is that it overstates the duration of rounds of early stage firms who are more likely to fail to get funding than their later stage counterparts.

of funding. Likewise, in the size regressions, Gompers finds that larger sums are invested in later stage ventures, in companies that have larger previous investments or more tangible assets in place and who are older at the time of the current round.

Gompers does not explore the role of convertible securities in the continuation decision but from the empirical work of Trester (1998) and Hege et al. (2003) we know that in the United States the usage of convertibles is high and may have some secular influence on the hazard rate. Using a questionnaire-based approach Hege et al. (2003) find that in Europe 10 percent of VC contracts involve the use of convertibles, whereas in the US a much larger 68 percent do. In multiple regressions for investment success however (success being defined as the sale of the company), Hege et al. (2003) find an insignificant sign for the use of convertibles, suggesting that their use may in practice have no (upside) performance impact.[32] However, they do find a weak impact of convertibles use on the duration of liquidation in the case of failure, with greater usage reducing the time to liquidation.

Davila et al. (2003),with the agency issues discussed in Admati and Pfleiderer (1994) (henceforth AP) in mind examine the differential role of early- and late-round staging in a sample of 170 Silicon Valley companies in the period 1994–99. They argue that the first round of investment is aimed primarily at removing the cash constraint the entrepreneur faces. Follow-on rounds however, are concerned with mitigation of the agency costs associated with relationship of entrepreneur and venture capitalist. They test two hypotheses, namely (i) cash constraints limit firm growth more in earlier than in later rounds, (ii) the signalling value of funding events is larger in earlier than in later rounds. In their dataset, the authors have 4,155 event months in 268 of which financing occurs. Variables include employee-level information such as hiring and firing dates and salaries, and company-level information such as dates and amounts of funding received. By using an event study approach, they find that growth in early rounds is delayed (not significantly different from zero) until funding is received (the event) and becomes positive in succeeding months; whereas in later rounds this is not the case—growth is both significant much higher before and after the funding event. Thus, early rounds do indeed seem subject to funding constraints whereas later rounds do not. Likewise, the salary regressions for first round funding show that in the months preceding the funding event salaries that are lower than for non-funding months rise as the event date approaches, and thereafter remain constant. For later round events, salaries are constant both before and after the funding event indicating that the funding event no longer impacts on salary.

[32] It should be noted that their sample size at 171 observations across Europe and America is rather small.

14.6 Performance of Venture Capital

The performance of venture capital should be understood in the context of a set of investments forming a portfolio, to which the concepts of risk and return can be applied. Firm-specific risk of a portfolio can in general be virtually eliminated if the size of a portfolio is sufficiently large and diversified—it should ideally mimic the composition of the market for quoted securities. If one were then to apply the Capital Asset Pricing model (CAPM) the VC would choose a risk-return combination that best suited the investors whose money one invested. The only risk to which such investors would be subject would be market-wide risk—the risk associated with the stock market as a whole.[33]

What of the VC's portfolio? As we have seen, a VC's portfolio (investments made in a series of funds raised over time) is not necessarily fully diversified in this way, being concentrated in high tech businesses. It is substantially illiquid to boot, making valuation particularly difficult.[34]

Although the majority of the promotional literature from the VC industry seems to suggest that the returns to venture capital exceed well-known benchmarks (like the NASDAQ and the FTSE All Share indices), little has really been known about the returns to venture capital. However, the academic literature seems to assume that since venture capital is 'special' it should attract higher than average returns from the stock market. Recently, however, it has been argued (Cochrane, 2004) that there are really only three reasons why the risk and return of venture capital might in practice differ from that of traded stocks even holding constant their *betas* (beta is a measure of systematic or market wide risk) or other characteristics (e.g. size and industry). These are (1) *liquidity*: a higher return may be required by investors to compensate for the illiquidity of private equity; (2) *diversification*: private equity has typically been a high proportion of an investors net wealth implying that they do not hold fully diversified portfolios and hence have high firm-specific risk associated with them; (3) *costs of monitoring and governance*: VCs often provide services of monitoring and control over investments made on behalf of their clients (see above for details) and this additional cost must be accounted for in the returns these investments yield. Cochrane argues, however, and provides compelling evidence in support of the claim, that VC returns, even when the lower risk of the VC's portfolio approach is ignored, are little different from those of similar traded stocks and are highly volatile. This finding is confirmed in a recent study of VC returns to companies going to IPO (Initial Public Offering) in the UK (Cressy and Lembergs, 2006).

[33] To diversify away international risk, this portfolio in theory would contain every quoted stock in the world.

[34] Firm-specific risk (assumed to be eliminated by the investor in the CAPM model) will in practice play a role in pricing of such portfolios and so the CAPM cannot strictly be applied to price them. This has however, not prevented economists from attempting to use it for that purpose (See Cochrane, 2004).

14.6.1 Measures of performance

We have talked about performance of VC investments but have not yet defined what we mean by the term. In finance, the typical measure of performance is the return on a quoted security, which consists of both a dividend yield (dividends expressed as a proportion of the current value of the stock) and a capital gain yield (ditto, capital gains). We emphasized above that only the latter is practically relevant to the return on venture capital. However, as we shall see later, we do not observe the value of a venture capital investment much of the time. In fact we observe it only if (a) the company receives a further round of investment from a VC; or (b) its shares become part of an IPO; or (c) it is sold to another company (trade sale or acquisition). If on the other hand, the company does not receive more money in the current period but remains on the VC's books, or becomes bankrupt and disappears from the books, no such value is typically observed. This presents the econometrician with a potential sample selection problem since the sample of observed values is generally unrepresentative of the population of values.

Consider, for example, the relationship between one source of observation of value, the IPO, and the true value of the firm in any period. It turns out that empirically the chances of an IPO increase with a firm's value (Cochrane, 2004). This means that if we include in our estimate of returns only those investments with high (and hence observable) values we end up with a potentially gross overestimate of the returns to venture capital—gross because IPOs are a small proportion of the total number of VC investments and make up a disproportionately large fraction of the total value.

Potential biases do not stop at selection however. For example, if one were to ignore the fact that the true distribution of VC returns is highly skewed (approximately lognormal according to Cochrane, 2004) and were to take *arithmetic* mean returns rather than *geometric* mean returns as our measure, this would again overstate the returns to venture capital.[35] Both these errors have, unfortunately, been perpetrated in the academic and practitioner literature in this area.[36] So how does one deal with this problem?

Cochrane (2004) wishes to estimate the joint distribution of company returns and IPO status (defined as reaching IPO or not).[37] The estimated joint distribution will then give him the returns to venture capital as a whole, including the return to those investments that never reach IPO. Previous studies simply estimated the returns to IPO (and sometimes trade sale) treating these as the

[35] The average of ln(x), a concave function of x, is always less than the average of x.

[36] Early empirical studies of the returns to venture capital include Moskowitz and Vissing-Jorgenson (2000), Reyes (1997), Gompers and Lerner (1997), Smith and Smith (2004).

[37] More generally, sale status, since a company may be sold either through a trade sale or an IPO. However, we shall refer to IPO status rather than sale status here.

Table 14.1 Numbers by value and IPO outcome

V	IPO=1	IPO=0	
50	2	18	20
500	4	1	5
	6	19	25

returns to venture capital as a whole, thereby providing a very rosy picture of industry profitability.

To understand Cochrane's method we use a simple numerical example. Suppose there are only two firm values, US$50 and US$500 (million), Low and High. The number of Low firms is much larger at n=20 than the number of High firms, n=5. Suppose that the distribution across categories (IPO=0, 1 and V=50,500) is as in Table 14.1.

We shall assume for simplicity that there is one observation on a firm's value if it does an IPO and none if it does not. In other words, firm value is observed if and only if it does an IPO. We wish to estimate the joint probability that a firm will have value V and an IPO outcome (IPO=1 if it goes to IPO; IPO=0 if not).

Note that from Table 14.1 the joint probability of an IPO and a value of 50 is 2/25, while the probability of an IPO conditional on a market value of 50 is the larger number 2/20. However, the joint probability of an IPO and a value of 500 is 4/25, *much* smaller than the probability of an IPO conditional on a value of 500 which is 4/5. Since the unadjusted estimate of the probability of an IPO is the conditional probability (V is observed only at an IPO) we estimate the conditional probability distribution as in Table 14.2.

The joint probabilities of IPO and value are, however, in Table 14.3.

Thus for each value V, the conditional probabilities overestimate the joint probabilities very substantially because the probability of an IPO declines with firm value. These would seem to be the only values we have to work with however, and previous estimates were based on the conditional distribution. This clearly

Table 14.2 Conditional probabilities of an IPO

V	$p(IPO = 1 \mid V)$
50	2/6=33%
500	4/6=67%
	6/6=100%

Table 14.3. Joint probabilities

V	$p(IPO = 1, V)$
50	2/25=8%
500	4/25=16%
	6/25=24%

leads to sample selection bias. Cochrane adopts a procedure to circumvent this bias.

Using the identity

$$p(IPO,V) = p(IPO\,|\,V)p(V) \tag{1}$$

where p(IPO|V) is the conditional probability and p(V) is the marginal probability, it would seem possible that we could estimate the joint probability p(IPO, V). From Table 14.4 we might imagine that we could calculate the marginal probabilities of value as

Table 14.4 Marginal probabilities of value

V	$p(IPO = 1 \text{ or } IPO = 0)$
50	20/25=80%
500	5/25=20%
	25/25=100%

However, this cannot be done, since we cannot count the number of firms *at each V*. We can only count the total number of firms and deduce the total number of non-IPOs since value is observed only at IPO. So how does Cochrane calculate the joint probabilities we are interested in?

His solution to this problem appears to be roughly the following. If there is a relation between the distribution of a firm's value at IPO and its age, and the age of non-IPO firms is known we can estimate the conditional distribution of value for IPOs as a function of age and then extrapolate this to non-IPO firms. Given that we know the total distribution of firm ages (IPO and non-IPO firms) we can use the rule

$$p(V) = p(V\,|age)p(age) \tag{2}$$

to calculate the marginal distribution of V for all firms. Plugging this back into Equation (1) above we get the joint distribution desired. Thus we need a function

$p(V \mid age)$ which can be estimated on a sample of IPOs and then applied to all firms. We also need the age distribution $p(age)$ for all firms. Then we can calculate the joint density despite the fact that the value of non-IPO firms is not observed.[38]

14.6.1.1 *Analysis of success outcomes*

Another way to examine the performance of venture capital investments is to look at the determinants of the chance that one of them will end in a sale (trade sale or IPO). Several studies have used this empirical approach which has the obvious advantage that it does not presuppose a market model to value companies—the choice of which offers no consensus.

For example, Hege, Palomino and Schweinbacher (2003) (henceforth Hege et al. 2003) examine the determinants of success in a large sample of European venture capital investments. They combine a database (VentureXpert) with a questionnaire approach to venture capital firms and use both discrete measures of success (high, medium and low represented by IPO, Trade Sale and Bankruptcy respectively) and continuous measures (reported valuation data). Three main findings emerge from their study. First, VCs in the US are more likely than those in Europe to use control rights in their contracts and to enforce them when the need arises. For example, US VCs make much greater use of convertible securities (an extraordinary ratio of 7:1) which in the event of bankruptcy is associated with a shorter time to liquidation.[39] Control also appears in the statistic that American VCs are three times as likely to replace an underperforming manager as their European counterparts and this reduces the time to liquidation in the event of bankruptcy.[40] Secondly, a higher proportion of total investment in the American is invested in first rounds; Europeans seem to have a preference for later rounds (MBOs, etc.) However, Hege et al. (2003) regressions show that these investments are also more likely to fail. Controlling for post-investment monitoring (the other main function of the VC) along with other factors, the negative informational deficiencies associated with first round investments may reduce their chances of success below those of later stage investments.[41] Thirdly, American syndicates are on average significantly larger than those in Europe. This may be for several reasons (as noted above), but it is

[38] This is slightly different from Cochrane's actual technique which uses not firm age but intertemporal information on the distribution of returns (variation in the horizon) to identify the parameters of the distribution. Our exposition has the advantage of simplicity.

[39] In the United States according to Hege et al. (2003), at the median 68% of VCs' investments make use convertibles whereas only 10% of European VCs' investments do. Curiously, however, in regressions the use of convertibles has no effect on success measured by the chances of an IPO when other factors are controlled for.

[40] An American VC is three times more likely to replace an owner-manager than a European VC.

[41] The potential gains from such investments in the United States are arguably larger than in Europe because of the effective size of the market. (See Cochrane (2004), who likens venture capital investment to an option.) It would therefore seem that the option variance is somewhat higher in the United States than in Europe or that the Americans are more gambling-prone.

apparently not because larger syndicates are associated with greater success, since the authors' regressions show that greater syndicate size has no impact or even a negative impact on IPO success.

Remer (2005) has a possible explanation for the seemingly paradoxical outcome on syndication. As we have already seen, Remer finds, on examining the outcomes of specifically biotech investments in three countries—the US, the UK and Germany—in a sample of about 1,700 biotech ventures funded between 1970 and 2002, that controlling for industry-wide, economy-wide and financial factors the probability of syndication is negatively related to the experience of the VC, which is in turn positively related to performance (probability of an IPO). The better that experience is matched to the project under consideration the stronger this relation is. This suggests that the motivation for syndication is partly to gain experience: that is to say, less experienced VCs tend to syndicate, and such VCs are more likely to be associated with failure than with success. Thus allowing inexperienced VCs to join your syndicate is a liability in the short-run, whatever the long run gains that might be envisaged and/or materialize.

14.6.1.2 *Comparative growth approaches*

The venture capital industry often highlights the alleged superior performance of venture capital backed firms in terms of profits, turnover, employment and other measures of company growth. However, these claims are certainly unreliable because they typically involve only the more successful companies in the VCs' portfolios and are therefore subject to the selection bias discussed above in the discussion of Cochrane's paper. Academic studies are now offering more scientific results on the relative growth performance of VC-backed firms and these are not subject to the selection biases of earlier attempts.

In a recent study of the population of VC-backed firms in Spain, Alemany and Martí (2005), finds that VC-backed companies do indeed perform better in terms of the growth of those key variables listed above.

14.6.1.3 *Studies of returns*

Cochrane (2004) uses company level data to estimate returns to venture capital. This means that risk-adjusted returns will include firm-specific risk and therefore be larger than the fund level returns reported by previous writers, given allowance for selection bias. He is thus providing an upper bound estimate of the returns to venture capital. Cochrane notes that company value is observed in any given period only when three conditions are satisfied: (a) when another round of funding is planned;[42] (b) when the company is acquired; or (c) when an IPO occurs

[42] We observe company value in this round as the post-money value defined as the pre-money value (its value at the last round) plus the new injection of funds. Thus if the company's first round

(company is partially sold). These three events are encapsulated in the omnibus term 'new financing round'. If, on the other hand, in any period (i) the company fails (becomes bankrupt, etc.), or (ii) remains private without additional funding in that period, company value is not observed. Ignoring these factors will therefore lead to biases that overstate the returns to venture capital.

In his empirical model, Cochrane assumes (without loss of generality) that true initial company values V_0 are set at US$1 for all companies.[43] In period 1 and after, however, they are determined by the equation

$$\ln(V_{i,t+1}/V_{i,t}) = \gamma + \ln R_t^f + \delta_i(\ln R_{t+1}^m - \ln R_t^f) + \varepsilon_{i,t+1}; \varepsilon_{i,t+1} \sim N(0,\sigma 2) \quad (3)$$

where V_t is observed only if the company has a new financing round. Note that this is similar to a dynamic version of the *capital asset pricing model* (CAPM) which in unlogged form says that the expected return to an asset in period t to t+1 is $ER_{it} = V_{i,t+1}/V_{i,t}$ and this in turn breaks down into the safe rate R_{ft} plus a company specific constant $\beta_i \equiv \delta_i$ times the market risk premium $(ER_{mt} - R_{ft})$:

$$ER_{it} = R_{ft} + \beta_i[ER_{mt} - R_{ft}] \quad (4)$$

where E is the expectations operator and *Rmt* is the return to the market portfolio (portfolio of all the shares in the market). Given the first period values of US$1 Cochrane then models the second and later period values taking into account the selection occurring for the reasons mentioned above. The crucial assumptions of his empirical analysis are that (i) the probability of a new financing round is a *logistic* function of current firm value (he shows this to be in fact an increasing function of value), and (ii) the probability of a firm going out of business is a declining *linear* function of current value. Cochrane then estimates this model using Maximum Likelihood methods. The distribution of returns turns out to be lognormal with a mean of about 15 percent per annum (rather than 108% from the unadjusted estimates) and a standard deviation of 89 percent (rather than the unadjusted estimate of 135%). This implies that the frequently calculated *arithmetic* means of the distribution are, because of the extreme skewness of the distribution, much higher than the correctly chosen (log) mean estimates. He concludes that venture capital investments are rather like call options, offering low average returns with a very small probability of very high ones.

Other recent studies broadly confirm Cochrane's findings even if they do not control as accurately as he does for selection biases. Thus Hege et al. (2003) find

value is US$1 and its second round injection is US$2 m, then the PreMV=US$1 and PostMV=US$1,000,001. This is equivalent to the price of the new shares issued at funding being used to revalue all the shares in the company.

[43] Scaling like this has no effect on the *rates* of return since the ratio of any two periods' value V_{t+1}/V_t is unaltered.

that in their sample of European and American companies the average log (1+IRR) in 1997 is 18 percent per annum rising to 29 percent in 1999 and falling to −12 percent in the year 2000. Cressy and Lembergs (2006) on a sample of UK-based VCs from the Private Equity Intelligence and Venture Economics databases find an average fund IRR of some 15 percent. They, like Cochrane, find that the distribution of returns is Lognormal, but because their sample is of IPO companies only (companies much less likely to fail), it has a much smaller standard deviation.

14.7 Venture capitalist value-added and compensation

We have seen that the secular returns to venture capital seem to be rather low given the very high risks associated with it. We have also noted that returns to venture capital estimated in the most reliable study to date (namely that of Cochrane) overestimate the true returns since they are (a) individual rather than portfolio returns, and (b) they ignore the costs of VC salaries and carried interest. It is conceivable that the correct estimates will find them to be below those of the relevant risk-adjusted benchmarks. One is therefore entitled to ask: Are the payments made by investors to their VCs justified?

As mentioned in the Introduction to this chapter, we do not as yet know the answer to this question. The reason for this is that we do not have enough data to weigh up the social costs and benefits of this kind of finance. The important issue is in fact not so much the level of private returns to VC investments but the extent of positive externalities generated by their activities. If VCs indeed finance some of the most innovative companies on the planet, companies that would not otherwise have been brought into existence, even if the private returns from these investments are less than their costs, it may still be the case that the public returns exceed the costs. As measured by the spillover advantages that society as a whole receives from the innovations generated by 'the few', we may still be better off with, than without, venture capital.[44]

[44] There is in fact quite a large literature on the spillover effects of innovative SMEs. See Andretsch and Feldman (2003).

14.8 Directions for future research

Crystal ball gazing is an activity that rational people naturally shun. However, this review of the literature on venture capital suggests a few avenues that the interested researcher may wish to explore.

One of the most exciting areas for future research in venture capital lies in examining the impact of investee companies on innovation and economic growth. The goal of this research would be to quantify the extent of the overall contribution, direct and indirect, of venture capital to society, including the important spillover effects of innovation. There is a considerable literature on the spillovers from innovation in general but little has yet emerged on the spillovers from specifically venture capital-financed enterprises.

Another area of considerable interest is the effects of cycles in the macro-environment on venture capital and innovative activity. Recent case study research (Cressy and Remer, 2004) indicates the adverse impact of cycles in venture capital activity on the viability of VC-backed firms and whole industries. Long term investments in firms (e.g. biotech) with no immediate products or sales find it impossible to survive in a market in which IPO activity can dry up almost overnight. VCs will not invest in such a market unless trade sales are a prospect but it is possible (witness the aftermath of 2000) that both exit routes are closed. Given that biotech for example is an industry that we shall all need in the next decades to solve a myriad of problems, regulation of the markets is a live issue. Do we need to regulate stock market speculation in the interests of preserving such nascent industries (not to mention protecting ignorant investors from themselves)?

References

Admati, A. and Pfleiderer, P. (1994). 'Robust Financial Contracting and the Role of Venture Capitalists'. *The Journal of Finance*, 49: 371–402.

Aghion P. and Bolton P. (1992). 'An Incomplete Contracts Approach to Financial Contracting'. *Review of Economic Studies*, 59: 437–94

Alemany, L. and J. Martõ (2005). 'Unbiased estimation of economic impact of venture capital backed firms'. Working Paper. ESADE Business School, Madrid, Spain; European Finance Association Conference Paper, Moscow, August.

Amit R., J. Brander and Ch. Zott (1998). 'Why do Venture Capital Firms Exist? Theory and Canadian Evidence'. *Journal of Business Venturing*, 13: 441–66.

—— L. Glosten and E. Muller (1990). 'Entrepreneurial Ability, Venture Investments, and Risk Sharing'. *Management Science*, 38(10): 1232–45.

Arundale, K. (2005). 'Private Equity and Venture Capital Investment Trends', Lecture Notes for the MSc Finance Elective in Entrepreneurial Finance. London: Cass Business School.

AUDRETSCH, D. B. and M. P. FELDMAN (2003). 'Knowledge Spillovers and the Geography of Innovation', in J. V. Henderson and J-F. Thisse (eds) *Handbook of Regional and Urban Economics*, Vol. 4. Amsterdam: North-Holland.

BERGEMANN D. and U. HEGE (1998). 'Venture Capital Financing: Moral Hazard and Learning'. *Journal of Banking and Finance*, 22: 703–35.

—— and—— (2000). 'The Financing of Innovation: Learning and Stopping'. Mimeo. Yale University

BHIDE A. (2000). *The Origin and Evolution of New Businesses*. New York: Oxford University Press.

BOOTH, J. R. and R. L. SMITH, (1986). 'Capital Raising, Underwriting and the Certification Hypothesis'. *Journal of Financial Economics*, 15: 261–81.

BRANDER, J. A., R. AMIT and W. ANTWEILER (2002). 'Venture Capital Syndication: Improved Venture Selection vs. the Value-added Hypothesis'. *Journal of Economics and Management Strategy* (Fall) 11(3): 423–52.

British Venture Capital Association (2000). *Private Equity – The New Asset Class: Highlights of the London Business School Report 'UK Venture Capital and Private Equity as an Asset Class for Institutional Investors*. Available at www.bvca.co.uk.

BYGRAVE W. (1987). 'Syndicated Investments by Venture Capital Firms: A Network Perspective'. *Journal of Business Venturing*, 2(2): 139–55.

—— (1988). 'The Structure of the Investment Networks of Venture Capital Firms'. *Journal of Business Venturing*, 3(2): 137–57.

—— J. TIMMONS (1992). *Venture Capital at the Crossroads*. Boston, MA: Harvard Business School Press.

CHAN Y.-S., D. SIEGEL and A. THAKOR (1990). 'Learning, Corporate Control and Performance Requirements in Venture Capital Contracts'. *International Economic Review*, 31(2): 365–81.

COCHRANE, J. H. (2004). 'The risk and return of venture capital'. Working Paper, University of Chicago, 19 March. (Published in 2005 under the same title in *Journal of Financial Economics*, 75(1): 3–52).

CORNELLI, F. and O. YOSHA (2003). 'Stage Financing and the Role of Convertible Securities'. *Review of Economic Studies*, 70: 1–32.

CRESSY, R. (1993). *The Startup Tracking Exercise*. London: National Westminster Bank of Great Britain.

—— (2006). 'Debt Finance and Credit Constraints on SMEs', in Parker (ed.), *International Handbook of Entrepreneurship*. London: Kluwer.

—— and T. HALL (2005). 'When should a venture capitalist replace an owner-manager? Theory and empirics'. Working Paper. London: Private Equity Research Centre, Cass Business School.

—— and D. KOPPELKAMM (2006). 'Managing and financing corporate spinouts: The case of Intel'. Working Paper No. 17, London: PERC, Cass Business School.

—— and S. REMER (2004). 'UrGenT' and 'CardioGenix': The early development of two German Biotech ventures, and the impact of venture capitalists and the financial markets on them, European Commission's *Gate2 Growth* project: *Academic Network in Entrepreneurship, Innovation and Finance*, European Commission, Brussels.

—— A. LEMBERGS and S. REMER (2005). 'Venture capital God favours the big battalions but also the SAS. Working Paper No. 15. London: Private Equity Research Centre, Cass Business School.

Cumming, D. and J. C. Mackintosh (2002). 'Comparative venture capital governance: Private versus labor sponsored venture capital funds'. Working Paper. University of Alberta, November.

Davila, A., G. Foster and M. Gupta (2003). 'Staging venture capital: Empirical evidence on the differential role of early versus late rounds'. Working Paper. Stanford University, February.

Denny, M. (2000). 'The UK Venture Capital Industry and Investment in Smaller Companies and Technology Startups'. *Venture Capital Journal* (April–June) 2(2): 155–164.

Fredriksen O., Ch. Olofsson and C. Wahlbin (1997). 'Are Venture Capitalists Firefighters? A Study of the Influence and Impact of Venture Capital Firms'. *Technovation*, 17(9): 503–11.

Fried V. H. and R. D. Hisrich (1988). 'Venture Capital Research–Past, Present and Future'. *Entrepreneurship Theory and Practice* (Fall), pp. 15–28.

—— and—— (1994). 'Toward a Model of Venture Capital Investment Decision Making'. *Financial Management*, 23: 28–37.

—— and—— (1995). 'The Venture Capitalist: A Relationship Investor'. *California Management Review*, 37(2): 101–13.

Gompers P. (1995). 'Optimal Investment, Monitoring, and the Staging of Venture Capital'. *Journal of Finance*, 50: 1461–89.

—— (1996). 'Grandstanding in the Venture Capital Industry'. *Journal of Financial Economics*, 42(1): 133–56.

—— and J. Lerner (1997). 'Risk and Reward in Private Equity Investments: The Challenge of Performance Assessment'. *Journal of Private Equity* (Winter) pp. 5–12.

—— and—— (1998). 'What Drives Venture Capital Fundraising?'. NBER Working Paper 6906, Available at www.nber.org/papers/w6906

—— and —— (1999). *The Venture Capital Cycle*. Cambridge, MA: MIT Press.

—— and—— (2001). 'The Really Long-Run Performance of Initial Public Offerings: The Pre-NASDAQ Evidence'. *NBER* Working Paper 8505, Available at www.nber.org/papers/w8505

—— and—— (2001). 'The Venture Capital Revolution'. *Journal of Economic Perspectives*, 15(2): 145–68.

Gorman, M. and W. A. Sahlman (1989). 'What do Venture Capitalists Do?' *Journal of Business Venturing*, 4: 231–48.

Hannan, M. T., J. N. Barron and M. D. Burton (1996). 'Inertia and Change in the Early Years: Employment Relations in Young, High-technology Firms'. *Industrial and Corporate Change*, 5: 503–35.

Hart, O. (1995). *Firms, Contracts and Financial Structure*. Oxford: Oxford University Press.

Hege, U., F. Palomino and A. Schweinbacher (2003). 'Determinants of venture capital performance: Europe and the United States'. RICAFE Conference Paper, London School of Economics, July.

Hellmann T. (1998). 'The Allocation of Control Rights in Venture Capital Contracts'. *RAND Journal of Economics*, 29(1): 57–76.

Jeng, L. A. and Wells, P. C. (1998). 'The Determinants of Venture Capital Funding: Evidence across Countries', May. Available at SSRN: http://ssrn.com/abstract=103948 or DOI: 10.2139/ssrn.103948

Jensen, M. (1986). 'Agency Cost of Free Cash Flow, Corporate Finance and Takeovers'. *AER Papers and Proceedings*, 76: 323–29.

Klofsten, M., P. Lindell, C. Olofsson and C. Wahlbin (1988). 'Internal and External Resources in Technology-Based Spin-Offs: A Survey'. *Proceedings: Babson Conference on Entrepreneurship Research*, pp. 430–43.

Kockesen, L. and S. Ozerturk (2002). 'Staged financing and endogenous lock-in: A model of startup finance', Working Paper. Columbia University, New York.

Lakonishok, J., A. Shleifer, R. Thaler and R. W. Vishny (1991). 'Window Dressing by Pension Fund Managers'. *American Economic Review Papers and Proceedings* (May) 81: 227–31.

Lerner, J. (1994). 'The Syndication of Venture Capital Investments'. *Financial Management*, 23(3): 16–24.

Lockett, A. and M. Wright (1999). 'The Syndication of Private Equity: Evidence From the UK'. *Venture Capital*, 1(4): 303–24.

—— and—— (2001). 'The Syndication of Venture Capital Investments'. *Omega*, 29(5): 375–90.

Mason, C. and R. Harrison (1999). 'Venture Capital: Rationale, Aims and Scope, Editorial Article'. *Venture Capital: An International Journal of Entrepreneurial Finance*, 1(1): 1–46.

Megginson, W. and K. Weiss (1991). 'Venture Capitalist Certification in Initial Public Offerings'. *Journal of Finance*, 46: 879–903.

Moskowitz and Vissing-Jörgenson (2000). 'The private equity premium puzzle'. Manuscript, University of Chicago.

Murray, G. (1994). 'The Second "Equity Gap": Exit Problems for Seed and Early Stage Venture Capitalists and their Investee Companies'. *International Small Business Journal*, 12: 59–76.

—— (1998). 'A Policy Response to Regional Disparities in the Supply of Risk Capital to New Technology Based Firms in the European Union: The European Seed Capital Fund Scheme'. *Regional Studies*, 32: 405–19.

—— (1999). 'Early-stage Venture Capital Funds, Scale Economies and Public Support'. *Venture Capital*, 1(4): 351–84.

Neher, D. (1999). 'Staged Financing: An Agency Perspective'. *Review of Economic Studies*, 66: 255–74.

Remer, S. (2005). 'Smart money? The role of venture capitalists' knowledge in the financing of new biotechnology-based ventures'. Doctoral thesis. Cass Business School, City University, London.

Reyes, (1997). 'Industry Struggling to Forge Tools for Measuring Risk'. *Venture Capital Journal.*

Reynolds P., M. Camp, E. Autio, et al. (eds), (2001). *GEM – Global Entrepreneurship Monitor–2001 Executive Report.* London: Babson College, Kauffman Center, London Business School.

Robinson D., T. Stuart (2000). 'Network Effects in the Governance of Strategic Alliances in Biotechnology'. Working Paper. Graduate School of Business, University of Chicago, pp. 1–54.

Sah, R. K. and J. E. Stiglitz (1986). 'The Architecture of Economic Systems: Hierarchies and Polyarchies'. *American Economic Review*, 76(4): 716–27.

Sahlman, W. A. (1990). 'The Structure and Governance of Venture-capital Organizations'. *Journal of Financial Economics*, 27(2): 473–521.

Shane, S. (2004). *Academic Entrepreneurship: University Spinoffs and Wealth Creation* (New Horizons in Entrepreneurship Series). Cheltenham: Edward Elgar.

Smith, R. L. and J. K. Smith (2004). *Entrepreneurial Finance.* New York: John Wiley & Sons.

Tang, K., A. Vohora and R. Freeman (2004). *Taking Research to Market: How to Build and Invest in Successful University Spinouts.* Euromoney Books.

Trester, J. (1998). 'Venture Capital Contracting under Asymmetric Information'. *Journal of Banking and Finance,* 22: 675–99.

van Osnabrugge, M. and R. J. Robinson (2000). *Angel Investing—Matching Start-up Funds with Start-up Companies.* California: Jossey-Bass.

Wang, S. and H. Zhou (2004). 'Staged Financing and Venture Capital: Moral Hazard and risks'. *Journal of Corporate Finance,* 10(1): 131–55.

Wetzel, Jr., W. E. (1987). 'The Informal Risk Capital Market: Aspects of Scale and Efficiency'. *Journal of Business Venturing,* 2: 299–313.

Wilson R. (1968). 'The Theory of Syndicates'. *Econometrica,* 40(6): 119–32.

CHAPTER 15

CORPORATE VENTURE CAPITAL: PAST EVIDENCE AND FUTURE DIRECTIONS

GARY DUSHNITSKY

15.1 Introduction

In May 1999, an entrepreneurial provider of wireless multimedia software for mobile applications, PacketVideo, received a financing round of $4m from an investment syndicate consisting of Intel Corporation and two venture capital funds. At the time of the investment, the market capitalization of the semiconductor incumbent was about 1.25 million times bigger than the post-round valuation of the year-old venture it financed. This observation raises a number of questions. What is the magnitude of corporate venture capital investments? Why do industry incumbents pursue equity investments in small entrepreneurial ventures? And when will entrepreneurs seek corporate backing? The answers to these questions can advance our understanding of entrepreneurial success, corporate innovativeness and economic growth.

This chapter reviews the academic literature on corporate venture capital, that is minority equity investments by established corporations in privately-held entrepreneurial ventures. We start with a detailed definition of the phenomenon. An historical background of Corporate Venture Capital (CVC) is presented, followed by an extensive review of CVC investment patterns. We then present scholarly findings beginning with firms' objectives, through the governance of their CVC programmes and the relationships with the portfolio companies and ending with a review of corporate, venture and CVC programme performance. The chapter concludes with directions for future research.

15.2 Definition

For the purpose of this chapter, CVC is defined as a minority equity investment by an established corporation in a privately-held entrepreneurial venture. Three factors are common to all CVC investments. First, while financial returns are an important consideration, there are often strategic objectives that motivate CVC activities. Second, the funded ventures are privately held considerations and are independent (legally and otherwise) from the investing corporation. Third, the investing firm receives a minority equity stake in the venture. Later, I highlight the main terms in the corporate venture capital literature. A brief discussion of corporate actions that do not fall within the above definition follows.

Three decades and a similar number of CVC waves have left the field with many, often overlapping, terms. To avoid confusion, Figure 15.1 summarizes the terminology used in this chapter. In doing so, I build on the terminology of recent work by Block and MacMillan (1993), Chesbrough (2002), Gompers and Lerner (1998), and Maula (2001). The main players include the *Parent Corporation* (e.g. Motorola) that launches a *Corporate Venture Capital Program* (e.g. Motorola Ventures), which in turn invests in *Entrepreneurial Ventures* (e.g. Cedar Point Communications, E-Ink, and IceFyre Semiconductor, Inc.). Scholars investigate the activities in which these players engage, focusing mainly on *Governance* and *Investment Relationship.* The former refers to the relationship between a parent corporation and its CVC programme (e.g. the relationship between Motorola and Motorola Ventures). Study topics include the organizational structure of the CVC program, CVC objectives, the compensation scheme, and so forth. The investment relationships between a CVC programmes and its portfolio companies (e.g. Motorola Ventures and E-Ink) are characterized by a certain level of fit. The issues that fall under this rubric include the monetary and non-pecuniary support provided by the corporation, the knowledge and information that flows back from the venture as well as the level of relatedness between the products, services or technologies of the two.

The practice of corporate venture capital should not be confused with other corporate activities that are aimed at enhancing firm innovativeness, growing

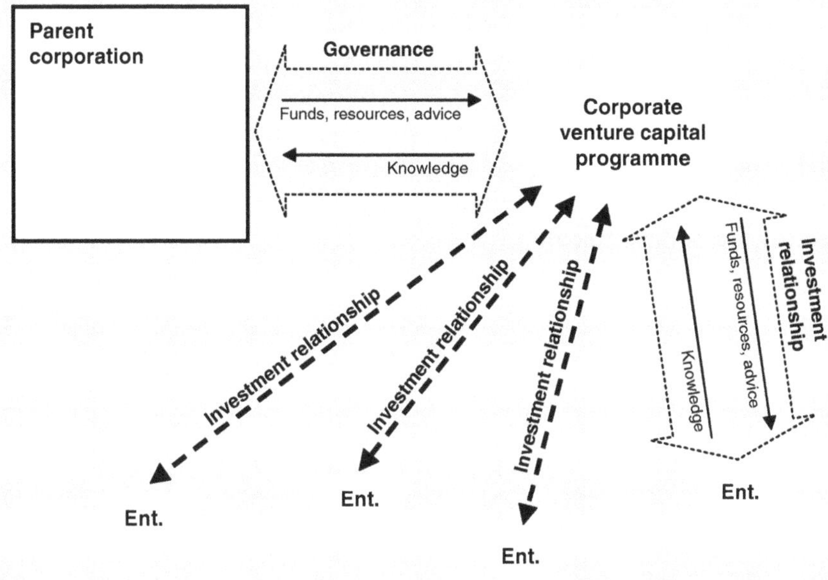

Figure 15.1 Corporate venture capital: Terminology

revenues, or increasing profits. The definition excludes: (i) non-equity-based inter-organizational relationships; (ii) other equity-based forms of inter-organizational relationships (e.g. joint ventures or investments in public companies); (iii) internal corporate venturing; and (iv) spin-outs (i.e. independent businesses started by departing employees). In addition, investments by financial firms aimed solely at diversifying their financial portfolios, as well as investments by independent VC funds, are not a part of CVC activities.

While often used synonymously, the term 'corporate venture capital' differs from either 'corporate venturing' or 'corporate spawning'. The latter is associated with the study of corporate spin-outs, when an individual leaves his or her employer and opens a related business (e.g. Klepper, 2001; Gompers et al., 2004). It focuses on employees who walk away from corporate positions in order to start their own businesses (i.e. corporate outflow), whereas CVC is interested in harnessing entrepreneurial knowledge or products (i.e. corporate inflow). The term 'corporate venturing' (also known as 'corporate entrepreneurship' or 'corporate intrapreneurship') addresses different activities, including investment in internal corporate divisions, business development funds, and so on (for a review see Guth and Ginsberg, 1990; Thornhill and Amit, 2001). The origin of the entrepreneurial team differs between the two: corporate employees are being funded by corporate venturing initiatives, whereas corporate venture capital commonly targets entrepreneurs with no prior relationship to the corporation. Another key distinction is the fact that both the CVC investor and the entrepreneurial venture are participating in the market for entrepreneurial financing, along with independent VCs and angel investors. In the case of corporate venturing, however, employees are provided with corporate funds and do not consider competing sources of capital. Finally, it is important to note that a few CVC programmes have been mandated by their parent corporation to engage in venturing activity, in addition to venture capital investment.

15.3 Historical background

Historically, corporate venture capital investment has been highly cyclical. To date, we have witnessed three waves of corporate venture capital. As a collective, established corporations are regarded as an important source of funding in the markets for entrepreneurial financing. They are second only to independent venture capital funds in dollar amount invested, and lead other investor groups such as angels and Small Business Investment Corporations (Prowse, 1998; Timmons, 1994).

The first wave of corporate venture capital started in the mid-1960s. Three factors are associated with the substantial increase in corporate funding for new ventures at that time. The overall corporate diversification trend of the 1960s, combined with excess cash flow experienced by many of the investing firms constitute two of the main factors (Fast, 1978). The financial success of pioneering independent venture capital funds and the stellar performance of their portfolio companies constitute the third driving factor (Gompers and Lerner, 1998).[1] About one-fourth of Fortune 500 firms experienced venturing programmes during that period, including such firms as American Standard, Boeing, Dow, Exxon, Heinz, Monsanto, and W. R. Grace.

These early programmes invested in either external start-ups, employee-based ventures or both. Externally focused programmes funded start-ups with the goal of addressing or extending corporate needs. They pursued venture capital investments either directly (e.g. GE's Business Development Services) or indirectly through independent venture capital funds (Gompers, 2002). A few firms

[1] The first VC fund, American Research and Development, was formed in 1946. Digital Equipment, Memorex, Raychem, and Scientific Data Systems are only some of the first success stories of the venture capital industry.

attempted to reinvent their business by encouraging employees, mostly those in technical roles, to start new ventures. These efforts were supported by parent corporations (e.g. DuPont's Development Department and Purina's New Venture Division), which provided funding as well as non-monetary support (Gompers, 2002). During these early days, many CVC programmes invested in external as well as internal ventures. For example, Exxon Enterprises, an affiliate of Exxon Corporation, initiated and funded some 37 high technology ventures during the 1970s. About half of these ventures were internally grown ventures, while the other half were external ventures (Sykes, 1986).

The first wave ended in the early 1970s. The attractiveness of venture capital investment decreased dramatically with the collapse of the market for IPO in 1973. Many independent funds suffered lower returns and difficulties in raising new funds (Gompers and Lerner, 1998). Macroeconomic changes and the oil shock of the time meant that many of the investing corporations no longer experienced excess cash flows, thus drying off available resources for investment. Finally, frictions within the CVC programmes and between the programmes and their parent corporations resulted in inferior financial and strategic performance, ultimately leading to the termination of CVC efforts.

The second wave took place in the first half of the 1980s. Changes in legislation, significant growth in technology-driven commercial opportunities, and favourable public markets stimulated the venture capital market as a whole.[2] Again, many leading firms in the chemical and metal industries launched CVC programmes. Technology firms (e.g. Analog Devices, Control Data Systems, and Hewlett-Packard) and pharmaceutical companies (e.g. Johnson & Johnson) also initiated new venture financing efforts during that time. The market crash of 1987 led to a sharp decline in independent, as well as CVC investments.

The third wave took place during the 1990s. The period was characterized by technological advancement, explosion in internet-related new venture creation, and a surge in venture capital investing. The number of CVC programmes has soared to more than 400. Diverse multinational corporations such as News Corp. (E-Partners), Smith Kline Beecham (S. R. One), Texas Instrument (TI Ventures), Dell (Dell Ventures), and Novell (Novell Ventures) established CVC funds. A handful of corporations such as Intel created multiple funds. Inflation-adjusted CVC investment levels during this time far exceeded previous waves. By the year 2000, established corporations have become important players in the venture capital industry participating in rounds well in excess of US$16 billion, approximately

[2] Gompers and Lerner (1998) summarize the causes for the venture capital revival in the 1980s. The 'prudent man' amendment to the Employee Retirement Income Security Act of 1979 led pension funds to funnel a fraction of their portfolios towards VC investments. A year earlier, capital gains tax rates were lowered effectively increasing the returns on investments. Finally, the emergence of technological opportunities, for example biotechnology and personal computers, stimulated a further investment.

15 percent of all venture capital investment. This marked a sharp incline from the meagre US$0.5 billion invested by corporations in 1996 (Venture Economics).

As with previous waves, a crisis in the public markets has driven many corporations to fold their venturing activities. Yet, a number of leading corporations remain committed to CVC investment even during the current period of sharp declines and significant financial losses (Chesbrough, 2002). A testament to the increased role of CVC is the fact that dozens of firms have joined the Corporate Venture Group within the National Venture Capital Association (NVCA) since late 2003. Moreover, CVC investment remains well above historical levels despite the downturn in the market for venture capital.

To conclude, the historical overview highlights three key drivers of corporate venture capital activity. At the macro level, the emergence of novel technologies is an important precursor to CVC investment. Established firms often leveraged their CVC programmes to identify, learn, and invest in attractive technologies. The financial markets played a key role as well. Not only did they serve as catalysts for entrepreneurial activity to begin with, but also they facilitated the transformation of technological advancement and commercial power into high financial returns. Further research is warranted to establish whether corporations can, or should, mimic successful venture capital funds, yet it is undeniable that CVC activity has closely paralleled the expansions and contractions of the financial markets in general, and the venture capital market in particular. At the firm level, we observe that CVC investment is undertaken predominantly by incumbent firms. Whether it is agency considerations or value creation that drive firms' behaviour is unclear. Consistent with the former, early CVC waves involved established firms that operate in stable industries and enjoy significant free cash flows. During later waves however, CVC was pursued mainly by incumbents in turbulent industries potentially as a response to Schumpeterian competition.

15.4 Investment patterns

This section provides an overview of the main patterns in CVC activity. It focuses on various facets of established firms' investment, including industry affiliation and geographic location, dollar amount invested, and ventures' characteristics. A brief comparison between CVC and independent VC investment patterns is presented. Data on investment activity is drawn from Venture Economics VentureXpert database. Venture Economics collects data through multiple sources including the investment banking community, surveys of general partners and their portfolio companies, government filings and industry associations (European Venture Capital Association, National Venture Capital Association, etc.). Venture Economics representatives often contact investors and companies to verify and supplement their records. Previous academic studies on the venture capital industry have used the Venture Economics database (Bygrave 1989; Gompers, 1995 and 2002; Gompers and Lerner, 1998; Sorenson and Stuart, 2001). Because each investment generates a unique record in the database, the data contain the full history of investors' investments in each venture. While the data is not without limitations, it is among the most comprehensive record of private equity activities in general, and venture capital investments in particular.

Figures 15.2a and b (Panels A, B) presents a summary of total annual investment in new ventures by corporations and independent venture capital funds during the period 1969 to 2003. The amounts represent dollar volume of rounds and are adjusted to 2003 dollars.[3] We observe that CVC activity has gone through three waves in the last 30 years. The first wave peaked in the early seventies. Activity declined until approximately 1978, when changes in legislation led to an increase in venturing investments by independent venture capitalists as well as established firms. This second wave peaked around 1986 with total annual investment at

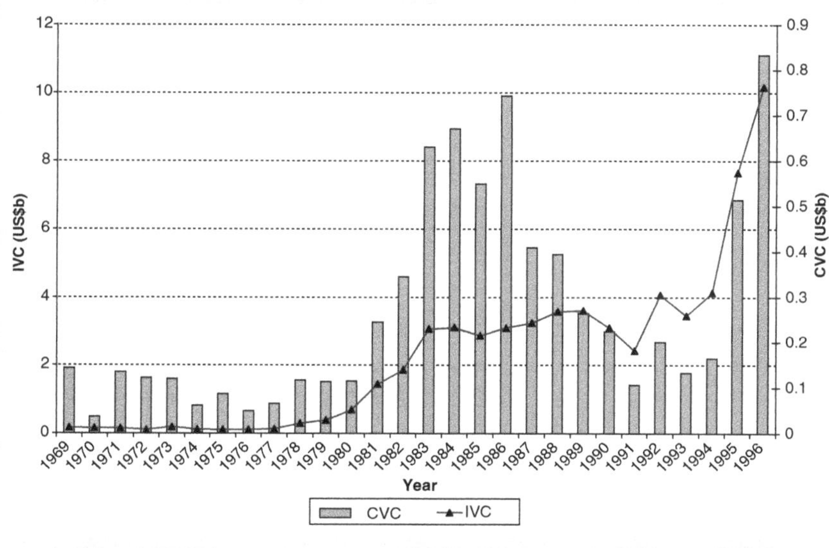

Figure 15.2a Panel A: Annual IVC and CVC investments (1969–96) (CPI-adj)

[3] A round may consist of several investments by different investors, some of which may be corporate investors while others may be independent VC funds. The amounts are adjusted to 2003 dollars using US annual CPI.

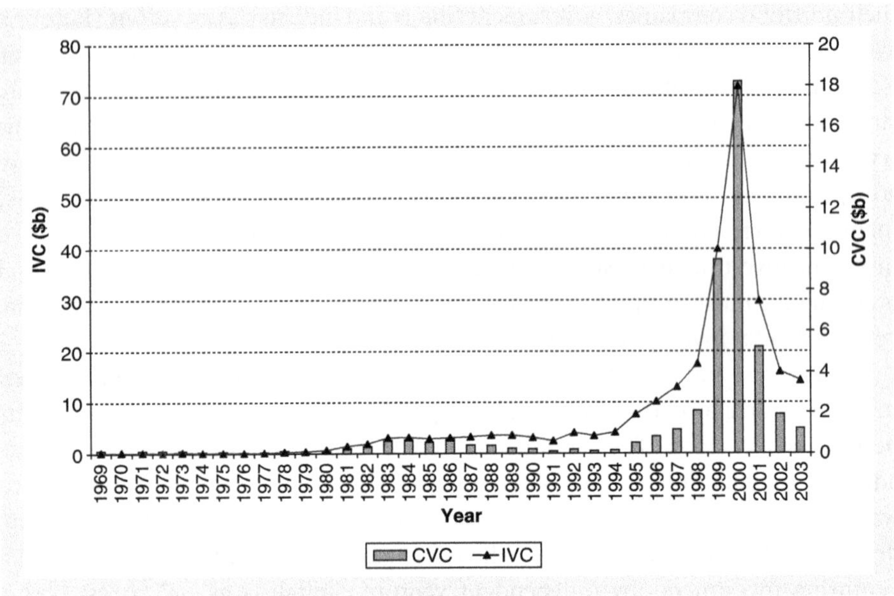

Figure 15.2b Panel B: Annual IVC and CVC investments (1969–2003) (CPI-adj)

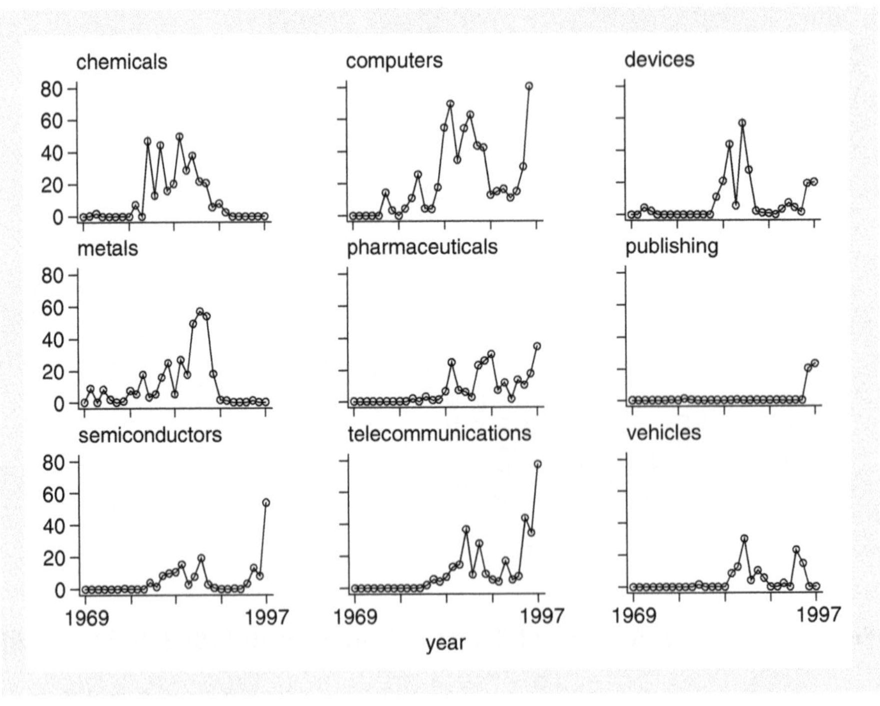

Figure 15.2c Panel C: Annual CVC activity by sectors (1969–97)

approximately US$750 million. Investment levels declined sharply after the stock crash of 1987 to a level of US$130 million in 1993. The third wave began with the rise of the Internet in the mid-nineties. At its peak in the year 2000, the dollar volume of rounds in which corporate investors participated exceeded US$18 billion, about 15 percent of all venture capital investments that year.

Table 15.1 presents a summary of the investment activity of the 20 largest venturing firms in our sample in terms of total cumulative round volume. Intel leads the list with total investments approaching US$1.5 billion since 1992. The top-20 list is dominated by the largest electronics and computer concerns such as Microsoft, Sony, Motorola, AOL, and Dell. Johnson & Johnson is the first pharmaceutical firm to appear in the list at the 13th position with cumulative investments approximating US$196 million. The majority of these firms have started their

Table 15.1 Activity summary of 20 largest venturing firms (1969–99)

Firm	Year began investing	Maximum annual ventures	Total US$ invested[a]	Maximum annual invested[a]	Average annual rounds	Total venture funds
Intel	1992	179	1,486	771	57	5
Cisco	1995	55	1,056	730	19	1
Microsoft	1983	29	713	436	7	1
Comdisco	1992	70	554	334	24	2
Dell	1995	48	502	395	26	1
MCIworld.com	1996	11	495	410	8	1
AOL	1993	39	333	169	10	2
Motorola	1963	33	315	177	11	1
Sony	1984	30	313	169	7	6
Qualcomm	1999	5	262	207	5	1
Safeguard	1983	21	231	118	6	3
Sun Micro	1999	31	204	180	19	1
J & J	1961	21	196	80	5	2
Global-Tech	1999	13	188	122	11	1
Yahoo	1997	5	186	163	3	1
Xerox	1960	30	184	24	13	6
Compaq	1992	21	182	113	5	3
Citigroup	1999	11	156	93	9	1
Ford Motor	1951	22	146	125	8	4
Comcast	1996	16	144	84	11	1

Note: [a] in US$ millions.

corporate venturing funds after 1993. A few have been engaged in corporate venturing since the sixties including Xerox, Johnson & Johnson, and Motorola. A handful of firms including Intel, Sony, and Xerox operate a number of funds with which they invest in new ventures.

Figure 15.2c (Panel C) presents a summary of total annual corporate venture capital activity by sectors during the period 1969–97.[4] Consistent with Table 15.1, we observe that firms in the information technology sectors and the pharmaceutical industry actively engage in corporate venture capital. The chemical industry and the metals industry had lively CVC investment during the 1980s that was not matched during the CVC wave of the 1990s. We may speculate that much of the run-up in CVC investment in the late 1990s was driven by the Internet. For example, starting in 1995, the publishing industry experienced a surge in CVC activity which was mainly a result of established media moguls such as News Corp. investing in Internet start-ups that provided news and other information online.

Detailed analysis of the last CVC wave finds substantial cross-sector variation in firms' investment behaviour. Some firms invest in ventures that operate in their own sector while others invest in neighbouring sectors, report Dushnitsky and Lenox (2005a) based on a large panel of US public firms during the period 1990–99. For example, nearly 50 percent of all CVC investment by chemical and pharmaceutical companies went into ventures within those sectors, while only 18 percent of all CVC investment by semiconductor firms went into semiconductor ventures. The authors attribute these patterns to firm-level, and venture's industry-level (as opposed to firm's industry) factors. The likelihood of investing CVC increases in industries with rich technological opportunities (e.g. up to 93% of the annual amount of CVC is channelled into industries that experience the highest levels of patenting), weak intellectual property protection, and where complementary capabilities are important to appropriate the returns to innovation. Corporate cash flow is also found to be significantly and positively associated with a firm's CVC behaviour. Finally, the greater the firm's absorptive capacity, the more it invests corporate venture capital.

Figures 15.3a to c present a breakdown of global CVC activities by country for the period 1990–99. According to Venture Economics, the majority (approximately 71%) of CVC-investing firms are based in the United States (Panel A). Asian and European firms are also among the leading CVC investors, particularly those in Japan (e.g. Sony, Mitsubishi and Sumitomo), United Kingdom (e.g. Reuters, Reed Elsevier and News Corp.), Germany, South Korea, and France. The figure may downplay the role of these firms, as many of them are coded as US-based though

[4] We excluded investments post-1997 as they were clearly dominated by firms in the information sector (see Panel B) and overshadow variance in prior activity. Sectors were defined by SIC code as follows: chemicals (28** excluding 2834 and 2836, 29**, 3080), pharmaceuticals (2834, 2836), devices (38**), and information (357*, 367*, 48**, 3663).

the parent corporation is not headquartered in the United States (e.g. Panasonic Ventures or Mitsui & Co. Venture Partners). As for venture's country affiliation, we find, not surprisingly, that US-based ventures constitute about 75 percent of all CVC-backed ventures (Panel B). Other CVC-backed ventures tend to operate in countries with substantial CVC headquarters, with Israel being the only exception. Again, the data may over-emphasize the role of US-based ventures. Recent surveys suggest that the weight of American ventures is lower, and stands at 61 percent (Birkinshaw, Murray and van Basten-Batenburg, 2002), or even as little as 38 percent (Ernst & Young, 2002). These surveys cover a small number of globally leading corporate investors and thus may not represent the geographical distribution of the population of corporate funds. Finally, the fact that corporate venture capital, in aggregate, tends to originate and reach the same countries does not necessarily mean that funds invest domestically. As we discuss below, CVC is used at times to access foreign technologies or learn about and enter geographically distant markets.

A closer investigation reveals that while the identity of CVC-originating and CVC-receiving countries greatly overlaps, the level of CVC inflows and outflows correlates to a lesser extent. The differences may be explained by cross-country variation in national innovative capacity. At the national level, innovative activity is often associated with the existence of technological capabilities, a strong legal regime, an effective capital market, and competitive product markets (Jeng and Wells, 2000; Furman, Porter and Stern, 2002). Consistent with previous research, countries with greater technological capabilities, larger capital markets and stronger legal protection have a larger number of CVC-backed ventures. However, the number of CVC investors in a country is mainly associated with the presence of an effective financial market, and to a lesser extent with its technological advancement.[5] Both the number of ventures and CVC investors increase in a country's gross domestic product (GDP), yet they are not correlated with national-level measure of competition. These observations should be taken with caution due to data limitation, measure validity, and the fact that they represent simple pair-wise correlations. Nonetheless, they highlight contextual differences in the factors that stimulate entrepreneurs and CVC activities.

Corporate investors and independent venture capital funds often exhibit different investment practices. One dimension on which they differ is the stage of investment. Figure 15.4a (Panel A) illustrates that mature ventures constitute a higher fraction of established firms' portfolios in the period 1990–2003, compared to independent VCs' portfolios. Start-up stage ventures, defined as companies still undergoing R&D and with no commercial operations, are more than 10 percent of

[5] Results are for a sample of 44 different countries (excluding the US) and are based on pairwise correlations at the ($p < .1$) significance level. Venture Economics is a source of CVC in- and out-flows. The World Bank (WDI online) and La-Porta et al. (La Porta et al., 1998; Djankov et al., 2002) provide technological, legal, financial indexes at the national level.

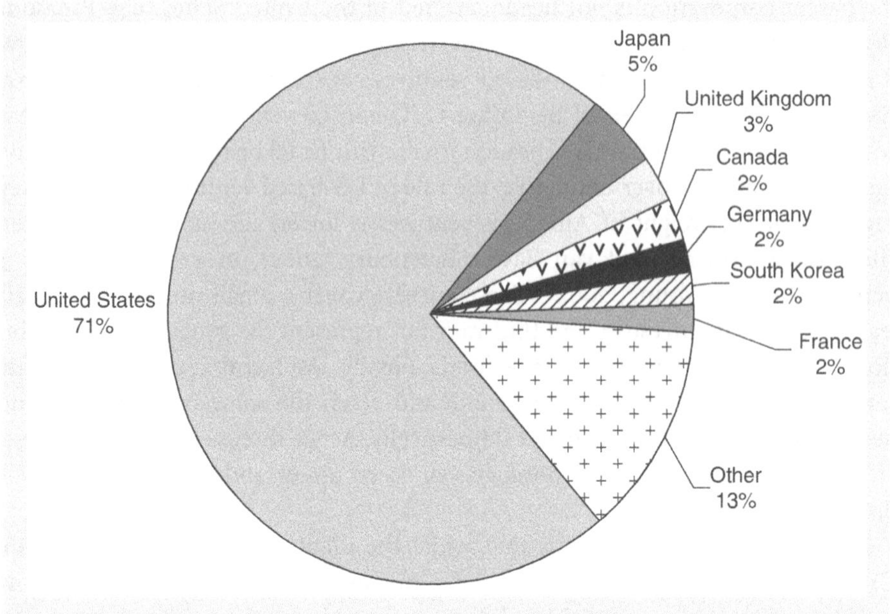

Figure 15.3a Panel A: CVC investments by corporate location (1990–2003)

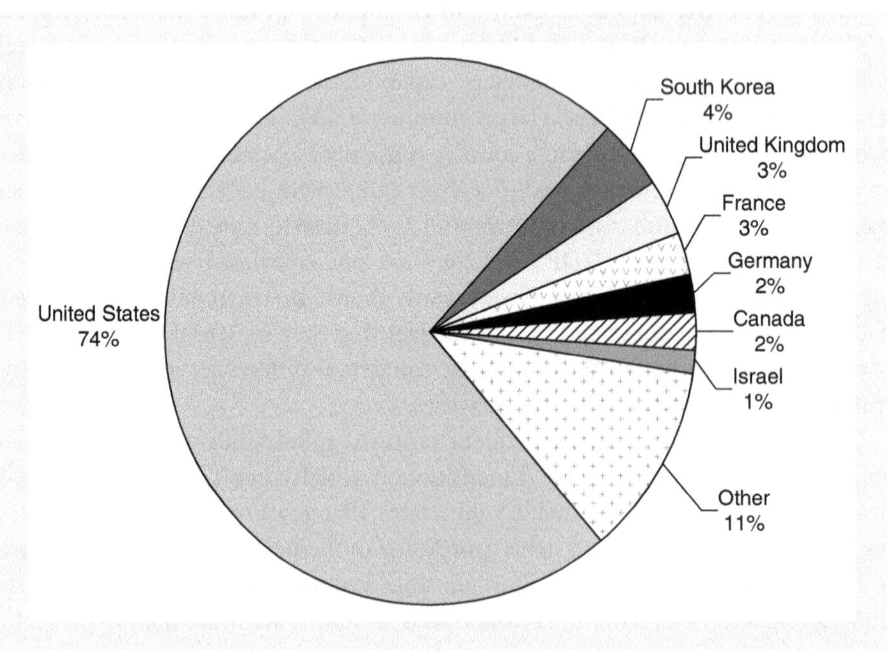

Figure 15.3b Panel B: CVC investments by nation (1990–2003)

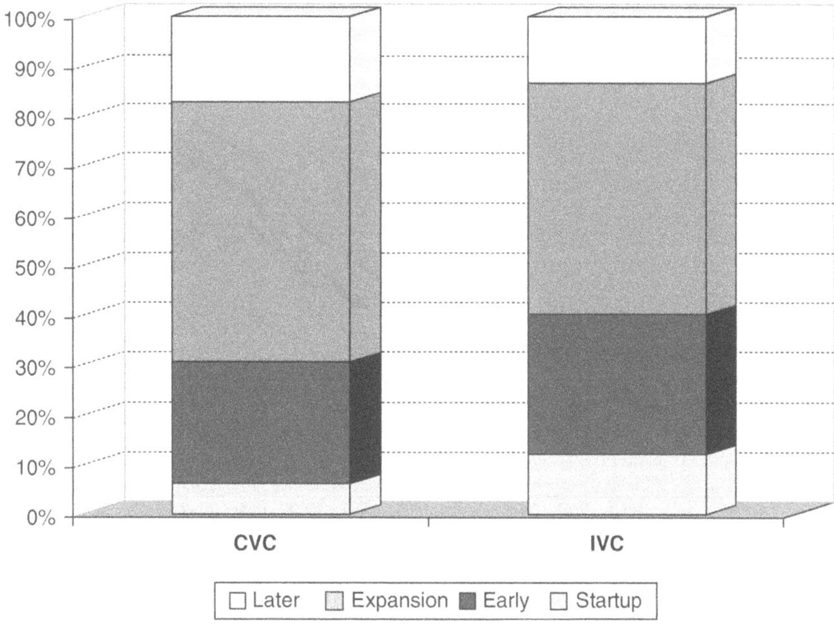

Figure 15.4a Panel A: CVC and IVC investment patterns by venture stage for 1990–2003

independent VC portfolios, but less than 5 percent of that of CVC investors.[6] These patterns are consistent with the analysis of Gompers and Lerner (1998) of CVC and IVC investments between 1983 and 1994. Interestingly, Dushnitsky (2004) reports that this disparity cannot be explained by investors' stage-preferences, as declared and documented in Venture Economics and the Directory of Corporate Venturing. Most CVC programmes pursue a balanced strategy investing in both early- and late-stage ventures, and among the remaining programmes the number of those focused on late stage financing is equal to that interested solely in early-stage ventures.

Shifting from the stated preferences to the actual investment patterns, we observe that as the market for venture capital grew over the last decade, corporate funding of later stage ventures grew more rapidly (Figure 15.4b, Panel B). The figure

[6] Investment stage is defined based on venture's development, ranging from Startup, through Early, and Expansion to Later (based on National Venture Capital Association definitions). The term 'Early stage' describes ventures which are undergoing product development and initial marketing, manufacturing and sales activities. Ventures in the Expansion stage usually have developed products and have a developed consumer base. These ventures experience increasingly growing revenue, but are not likely to be profitable. Later stage ventures are beyond expansion stage and exhibit consistent growth. Later stages include private equity investment such as acquisition or LBO, which are not considered as venture capital investments.

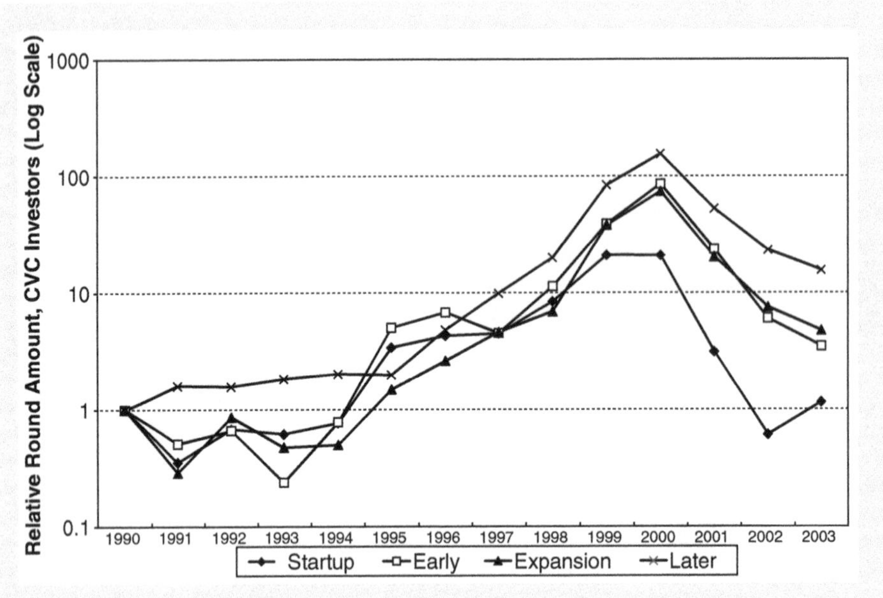

Figure 15.4b Panel B: Relative CVC investment by venture stage 1990–2003

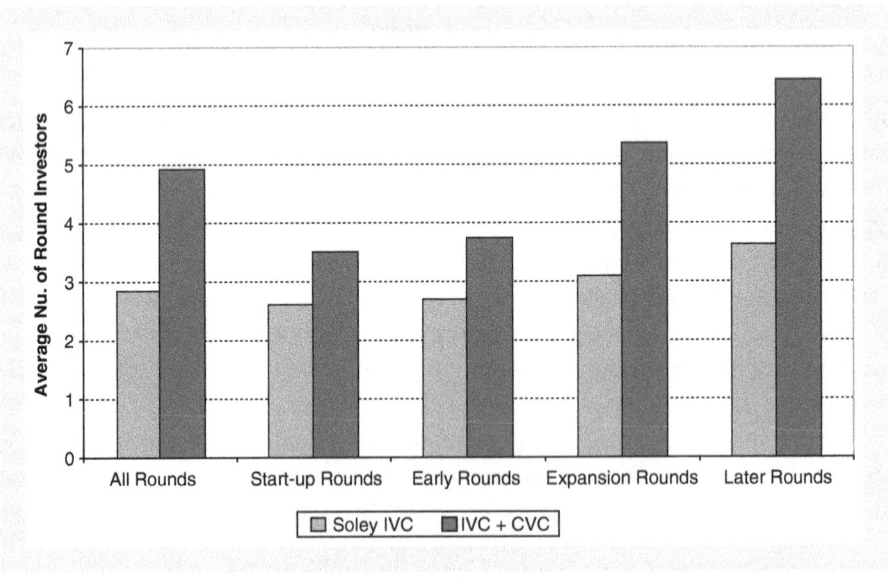

Figure 15.5a Panel A: Syndicate size by venture stage (1990–99)

tracks the evolution of CVC investment by stage, pegging 1990 investment level as the origin point. It demonstrates that the explosion in expansion and late-stage activity was met by a substantial, yet smaller, increase in corporate funding for start-up and early-stage ventures.

Combined, the evidence reviewed in the two paragraphs above suggest that in the face of 'willing' corporate investors, young entrepreneurial ventures may be less inclined to seek corporate backing while mature ventures are more interested in doing so. Interestingly, an early-stage round is more likely than a start-up stage round to involve a firm and a venture operating in a related industry. However, later stage rounds (e.g. expansion, or later) are less likely to have a firm-venture pair in the same industry, in comparison to start-up stage rounds (Gompers, 2002).

The two investor groups also differ in their syndicate size. Figures 15.5a and b show that the average syndicate size is significantly larger when one of the investors is a corporate venture capitalist. The larger syndicate membership is not merely a feature of greater CVC involvement in later stage rounds. It is clear that corporate investors' participation is associated with higher average syndicate size, irrespective of the round in which investment is taking place (Panel A). Moreover, the observation is not a mere artifact of heterogeneity in the valuation of ventures. We define ten strata, such that in each stratum, IVC-backed and CVC-backed ventures received similar round valuations. Within each stratum, we continue to observe that syndicates involving corporate investors exhibit higher membership size (Panel B).

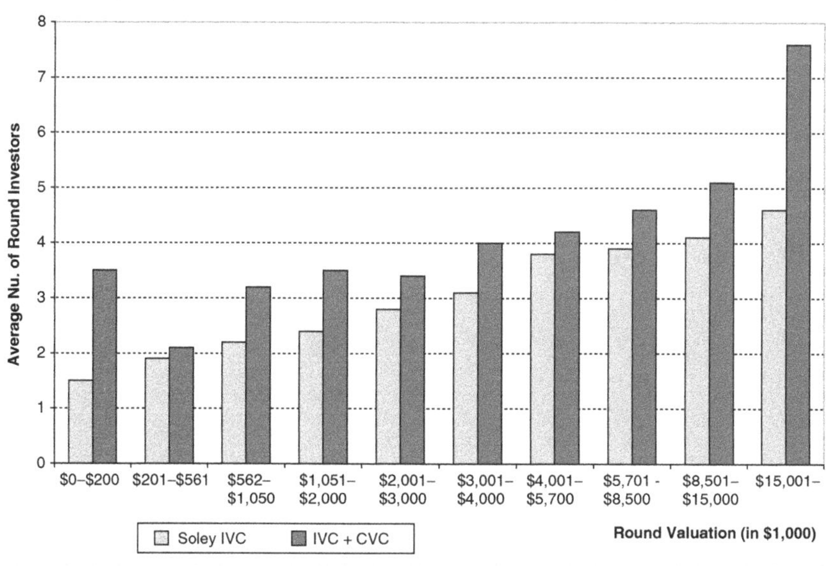

Figure 15.5b Panel B: Syndicate size by round valuation (1990–99)

15.5 The corporate venture capital literature

This section summarizes the academic work on corporate venture capital. Building on more than 15 years of scholarly work, we present evidence on the key characteristics of CVC programmes, their parent corporations, their portfolio companies and the relationships between them. The performance implications are discussed next. Figure 15.6 summarizes the topics.

A caveat is warranted here, however. Much of the existing literature relies on case studies or descriptive surveys. The generalizability of any one study may be limited due to the small number of companies being covered and the cross-sectional nature of the sample.[7] A number of important causal factors such as firm size or industry choice are often not controlled for. Other important issues, such as unobserved heterogeneity and temporal precedence, cannot be addressed using cross-sectional

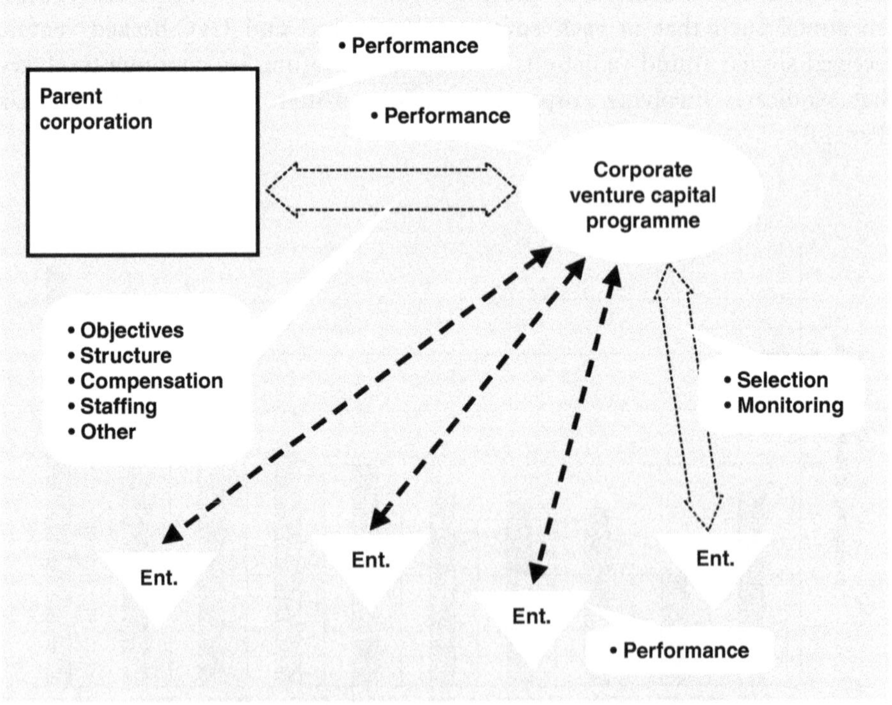

Figure 15.6 Corporate venture capital: Performance

[7] The most comprehensive survey (Birkinshaw et al., 2002) covers less than a hundred corporate venture capital programmes across three continents (Asia, Europe and North America).

Table 15.2 Primary data on corporate venture capital: Overview of major scholarly surveys

Author(s)	Survey (Study) Year	Subject	Response Nu.	Response Rate	Industries	Geo. Focus
Block and Ornati	(1987)	CVC	42	7%	*NA*	USA[a]
Siegel, Siegel and MacMillan	(1988)	CVC	52	35%	*NA*	*NA*
Sykes	(1990)	CVC	31	36%	Industrial, Communication	*NA*
Sykes	(1992)	CVC	8	*NA*	NA	NA
McNally	1992–95	• CVC • C-IVC[b] • CVC-backed Ventures	• 28 • 39 • 48	• 26%[c] • 80% • 73%	• Elec. (18%), Utilities (22%), Other (60%) • Med./Bio., Elec., Other	• UK[d] • *NR* • UK • *NR*
Maula	2000	CVC-backed Ventures	91	17%[e]	Internet (50%), Computers (18%), Comm. (15%), Semi./ Elec. (10%), Med./Bio. (7%)	USA
Ernst & Young[f]	2002	CVC	40	*NA*	*NA*	Global (*NA)*
Birkinshaw, Van Basten-Batenburg and Murray	2001–02	CVC	95	29%[g]	Hi-Tech (37%), Med./Bio. (12%), Other (51%)	Europe (51%), N.America (46%), Asia (2%)

Notes: NR – not relevant. NA – not available

[a] Survey sent to Fortune 500 companies, implying only US-based firms were included.

[b] Independent VC firms that raised money and managed a fund for a non-financial corporation.

[c] Initially 109 firms were identified and 73 responded (67%), but only 28 (i.e. 26%) engaged in CVC.

[d] Among the respondents, 19 were UK firms and 9 foreign subsidiaries operating in the UK.

[e] Maula identified 856 CVC-backed ventures of which only 810 had continued operations. There were 135 respondents (17%), and lack of information on CVC investors, as well as not meeting various criteria, further dropped the sample to 91.

[f] Professor Thomas Helmann was the academic representative on the advisory board.

[g] Birkinshaw et al. identified 447 CVC units of which only 327 were still active–95 (29%) responded.

samples. Therefore, when interpreting the results given in the table below, the reader should be cognizant of the context from which they were drawn. To that end, Table 15.2 summarizes the main properties of the major CVC surveys.

15.6 Investors' objectives

The motivation for firms' corporate venture capital is the subject of substantial study. Independent Venture Capital funds invest in early- and late-stage business endeavours with the sole purpose of capital appreciation through lucrative exits (usually via an Initial Public Offering or a trade sale). Why do established corporations choose to invest in young ventures? The literature suggests some firms pursue CVC to secure financial gains, while others seek strategic benefits. Yet, others pursue both (Block and MacMillan, 1993; Chesbrough, 2002).

In the first comprehensive survey of CVC practices, Siegel, Siegel and MacMillan (1988) find that CVC programmes rank 'Return on Investment' as the most important objective. The authors assert caution in interpreting this result because almost 42 percent of the respondents ranked financial returns as less than essential, while emphasizing various strategic objectives. Combined with the fact that many programmes seek financial returns along with strategic objectives, this implies that CVC is not solely a financial exercise. Among the strategic benefits, 'Exposure to New Technologies and Markets' was ranked significantly higher than any other strategic objective. Other objectives, by order of importance, were 'Potential to Manufacture or Market New Products', 'Potential to acquire Companies', and 'Potential to Improve Manufacturing Processes'.

Winters and Murfin (1988) point at international business opportunities and expansion of corporate contacts as additional strategic benefits. Corporate venture capital offers multinational firms with 'International Business Opportunities', specifically the opportunity to license entrepreneurial venture's technologies or products and market them overseas. The authors further stipulate that CVC activity expands a firm's 'contacts' beyond its common network, thus opening it to many new business opportunities. Finally, the authors are skeptical of CVC role in facilitating acquisitions. Not only can a corporation seek acquisition targets independently of its venture capital activities, but also 'There are no cheap acquisitions to be obtained by this venture capital involvement since professional venture capital investors always seek the maximum financial returns for their early-stage investment.'

Sykes (1990) conducts a survey of strategically driven corporate venture capitalists. He reports 'Identify New Opportunities' and 'Develop Business Relationships' top the list of strategic objectives. Other objectives, by order of importance, are 'Find Potential Acquisitions', 'Learn How to do Venture Capital', and 'Change Corporate Culture'. The lowest ranking objective, as reported by the 31 firms that responded to the survey, is 'Assist Spin-Outs from the Corporation'.

McNally (1997) sheds light on the objectives of corporate venture capitalists in the United Kingdom. Only 36 percent of the firms in his sample cite financial returns as the primary reason for their investment activity. However, 'Financial

Return on Investment' is a prominent goal when considering either primary or secondary CVC objectives. As with US-based programmes, 'Identification of New Markets' is the top strategic objective (68%). Other primary strategic objectives include 'Exposure to New Technologies' (43%), 'Develop Business Relationships' (38%), 'Identification of New Products' (38%), and 'Assess Potential Acquisition Candidates' (21%).[8] The study offers a unique perspective into the decisions of firms that considered, but did not pursue, corporate venture capital. McNally's survey covers 73 firms, of which 45 did not invest in new ventures but partially considered doing so.[9] The most common motivation for contemplating such activity among the non-investors was to gain a window on technology. This finding holds, irrespective of whether the firms considered investing directly or through independent VC funds. The decision not to pursue CVC was motivated either by the lack of corporate resources (i.e. capital and managerial time; see also Dushnitsky and Lenox, 2005b), or by the preference towards more conventional mechanisms for knowledge acquisition (i.e. internal R&D or acquisitions) that offer greater control.

A more recent account of CVC objectives is presented by Kann (2000).[10] Focusing solely on programmes with a strategic objective, she reports that 'External R&D' is the most common objective (45%), followed by 'Accelerated Market Entry' (30%), and 'Demand Enhancement' (24%). Kann (2000) defines these objectives as follows: 'External R&D' programmes seek to increase internal R&D capabilities through entrepreneurial technologies, with the ultimate goal of filling gaps in corporate technological portfolios or enhancing awareness to strategic blindspots. Firms threatened by rapid changes to their core businesses often pursue 'Accelerated Market Entry' in an attempt to leverage entrepreneurial technologies and reinvent themselves. Finally, some programmes pursue a 'Demand Enhancement' strategy by sponsoring ventures with complementary technologies, products, or services.[11]

Two surveys target the CVC population post-2000 market decline. The first, conducted by Ernst & Young (2002), includes 40 global leaders that engage in venture capital investments. A total of 56 percent of the respondents state strategically driven activity, 33 percent declare financially driven investment, and 11 percent

[8] A firm may list a number of objectives in its response, thus primary objectives are not mutually exclusive.

[9] The decision not to pursue CVC is not due to lack of opportunity on the firms' part: about 67 percent of the 45 companies were approached either by an entrepreneurial venture or an independent VC fund. Of the firms that were approached only 44 percent (29%) entertained the idea of direct investment (investing through a VC fund).

[10] Kann's (2000) results are based on interviews and secondary data for 152 CVC programmes operated by 120 corporations. All CVC programmes were listed on the *Directory of Corporate Venturing* (AssetsAlternatives) or *MoneyTree* (Price Waterhouse Coopers).

[11] Kann (2000) argues that such a goal is common in industries that experience (1) technologies that are at the early stage of their life cycle; (2) emergence of standards; or (3) saturated demand.

claim to pursue both. That being said, the report notes that 'most strategic investors would argue that a sound strategic investment is likely to produce sound financial returns ....' Again, 'Window on Technology Developments' is ranked as the leading strategic objective. Other goals, by ranking, include 'Importing/Enhancing Innovation with Existing Business Units', 'Leveraging Internal Technological Developments', 'Tapping into Foreign Market', and 'Corporate Diversification'.

Birkinshaw et al. (2002) survey 95 CVC programmes from around the world. More than half of the programmes are affiliated with European firms, and the remainder are mainly North American corporations. 'Learning and Developing Strategic Relationships' tops the list, with 'Increasing Demand for our Products and Services' in second place. Other reasons, such as 'Investing in External Start-ups for Financial Returns', and 'Development of Internal Business' were ranked much lower. However, the ranking conceals heterogeneity in CVC objectives. The authors analyze response patterns and identify four clusters, each associated with a different objective. Based on their cluster analysis, they conclude that 32 percent of the programmes invest in external start-ups in order to gain high financial returns, and 31 percent pursue a strategic window on technology. The remaining 37 percent invest primarily in internal ventures, rather than external startups. Some seek to cultivate internal growth (26%), while others aim to leverage corporate intellectual property and spin out businesses (11%).

To conclude, established firms pursue investment in new ventures for various reasons. Some firms seek to cash-in on their incumbent industry position and enjoy high financial returns. Their goal is capital appreciation through lucrative exits, such as an IPO or a trade sale of their portfolio companies. Most firms pursue CVC for a variety of strategic objectives. Perhaps the most common objective is the pursuit of novel technologies that are relevant to core corporate activities, often referred to as 'Window on Technology' (also 'External R&D' or even 'Potential to Improve Manufacturing Processes'). In the same way, spotting potential acquisition candidates is an oft-cited objective. Another common CVC objective is the development of strategic relationships, most often with the intent of learning or engaging new markets. Recent surveys indicate that investment in ventures with the intent to create demand for corporate products or services is an alternative role of corporate venture capital. Less common is the view of CVC investment as an opportunity to enter foreign markets (e.g. 'International Business Opportunities,' or 'Tapping into Foreign Markets'). Similarly, a few firms point at 'Exposure to Entrepreneurial Spirit' and an effort to 'Change Corporate Culture' as an important, yet not primary, objective.

In an attempt to understand the motivation behind CVC investment, the literature proposes a number of typologies of CVC objectives (e.g. Siegel et al., 1988; Chesbrough, 2002). However, these typologies bundle CVC objectives along with at least one other facet of CVC operations (e.g. structure). We propose a different classification of the seven strategic objectives mentioned above. Our typology is guided solely by CVC objectives, specifically the intended effect of a venture's success on existing corporate businesses. The classification places CVC strategic objectives along a continuum ranging from seeking substitutes to sponsoring complements. On the one hand, investment activity may be used to identify novel products, services, or technologies to replace existing corporate products, services, or technologies, that is, targeting potential substitutes. For example, CVC may serve as an early alert system allowing the corporation to identify threatening entrepreneurial technologies. Some of the objectives that fit here include 'Exposure to New Technologies' (McNally, 1997), 'External R&D', 'Accelerated Market Access' (Kann, 2000), and potentially 'Identification of Acquisition Candidates' (Siegel et al., 1988). On the other hand, investment activities may seek to complement corporate businesses by funding ventures that increase the value of existing corporate businesses (Brandenburger and Nalebuff, 1996). The two may complement each other along different dimensions: technologically (e.g. 'Develop Business Relationships', Birkinshaw et al., 2002), in the product market (e.g. 'Demand Enhancement', Kann, 2000), as well as geographically (e.g. 'Tapping into Foreign Market', Ernst & Young, 2002).

15.7 Programme governance

The governance of CVC activities is a multi-faceted topic. It covers the structure of the CVC programme, the degree of autonomy it possesses, and the compensation of the personnel in charge of making these investments. Past work provides excellent documentation of each facet of CVC governance. However, it pays less attention to the inter-dependencies between them, which we highlight in this sub-section.

We review the work on CVC governance chronologically. By presenting the studies in chronological order, rather than addressing the issues of structure, autonomy, and compensation separately, we highlight the evolution of governance practices between the second and third Corporate Venture Capital waves. The reader, however, is asked to be cautious in interpreting the results. The observed patterns may reflect temporal evolution of governance mechanisms, but may also be a product of the intentionally selective sampling employed by some studies.[12]

[12] Governance practices may be over, or under, reported to the extent that different facets of CVC governance are correlated. For example, a study focusing on CVC of a particular structure (e.g. wholly-owned subsidiary) may emphasize compensation practices that might not be common across all programs.

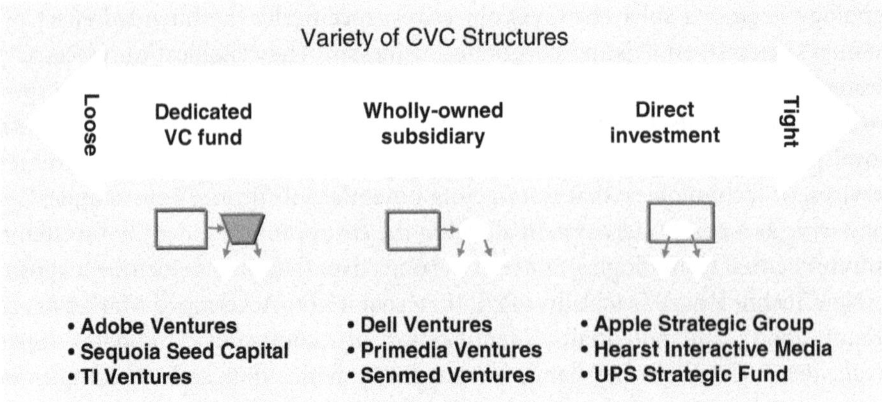

Figure 15.7 Variety of CVC structures

The review of the work on programme structure poses a particular challenge. It is often the case that studies use a similar label to describe dissimilar programme structures. To avoid unnecessary confusion, we assign labels to each structure (see Fig. 15.7). Some firms choose to invest in entrepreneurial ventures indirectly by joining existing VC funds as limited partners. We label this practice, 'CVC as LP'. Other firms choose to establish CVC programmes. In contrast to the independent venture capital funds, which are structured almost exclusively as a limited partnership, we observe heterogeneity in programme structures. These range from tight structures to loose ones. Programmes where current operating business units are responsible for CVC activities are denoted as having a tight structure. This is a 'Direct Investment' structure (e.g. Nortel Networks). Other programmes are organized as 'Wholly-Owned Subsidiaries', which are separate organizational structures set up for the sole purpose of pursuing corporate venture capital (e.g. Nokia Ventures). 'Dedicated Funds' constitute the last, and least common, structure where a firm and an independent VC fund co-manage the investment activity. Examples include Sequoia Seed Capital, a joint venture between Sequoia Capital and Cisco Systems, and TI Ventures in which Texas Instrument is the sole limited partner.[13]

Siegel et al. (1988) provide detailed information regarding programme autonomy levels and compensation practices. About 66 percent of the respondents stated that they undergo a thorough review by corporate headquarters prior to each investment. Only 11 percent of the respondents are free to pursue investments without prior corporate approval, and another 21 percent are subject to only formal approval process. Interestingly, about half of the CVC programmes (48%) report

[13] The VC firm that manages TI Ventures, Granite Ventures, heads yet another dedicated fund, Adobe Ventures.

that a dedicated pool of funds is made available to them on a one-time basis.[14] Other programmes are either assigned smaller funds on a periodic basis (27%), provided with funds on an ad hoc basis (19%), or did not respond (6%). Using cluster analysis, the authors identify two CVC types: programmes characterized by a high degree of autonomy and permanent financial commitment (denoted 'pilots'), and programmes that are highly dependent on corporate approval and capital commitment (denoted 'co-pilots'). As for the compensation scheme of CVC personnel, they find that linking pay to a venture's performance is common practice. This is achieved either by a bonus based on the venture's performance over the short or long term (29%, 14%, respectively), or direct participation in the venture fund (10%). Nonetheless, a substantial number of CVC programmes offer only base salary (31%).

Winters and Murfin (1988) observe four different structure types.[15] Two of the structures they identify (invest in funds and direct investment in companies) map directly onto 'CVC as LP' and 'Direct Investment' discussed on the previous page. They go on to discuss two types of CVC subsidiaries. Both are similar in terms of their structure (consistent with the 'Wholly-Owned Subsidiary' label) but differ in their investment objectives (i.e. financial vs. strategic). The authors note that a CVC subsidiary is more likely to have funds dedicated for investment activity. Furthermore, a subsidiary structure is advantageous because it attracts the co-operation of VCs by signalling corporate commitment to venture investing. It also mitigates entrepreneurs' concerns of malfeasant corporate behaviour, and offers flexibility in locating the programmes in a state with low capital gains taxes.

In a study of strategically driven CVC programmes, Sykes (1990) finds that 84 percent of the programmes invest as limited partners, 81 percent act as direct investors, and 64 percent pursue both.[16] The differences in structure do not reflect dissimilarity in objectives. The two groups rank a list of strategic objectives similarly with one exception: direct investors also seek to change corporate culture whereas limited partners see their investment as an opportunity to learn about venture capital markets. The study is also witness to an evolution in governance practices: 'In the past few years "focused" VCLPs, dedicated to serving the specific business area interests of a sole corporate investor, have made an appearance. This is almost like having a direct investment portfolio, except independently managed' (Sykes, 1990: 46).

[14] The majority of the respondents state a large pool of funds was specifically earmarked for venture capital investment on a one-time basis. This practice is common among independent VC funds. Each limited partner commits to provide a certain amount of money, and transfer the funds based on VC's 'capital calls'.

[15] The authors mention a fifth programme structure which invests solely in internal ventures.

[16] Unfortunately, the study does not clarify whether direct investors includes investment by a CVC subsidiary or is limited solely to investment by corporate business units.

Block and Ornati (1987) focus on the compensation practices firms undertake when they establish new venture divisions. In their study of 42 Fortune 500 companies, they find many firms recognize the importance of pay-for-performance. Yet, in practice corporate venture managers are paid no differently than other corporate personnel.[17] Sykes (1992) conducts a related study and reports similar findings: the need for 'equity-based' compensation for venture managers is acknowledged but not always practised.[18] Among the main reasons for the lack of 'equity-based' compensations are: (i) a need for pay-equality vis-à-vis other corporate employees (especially those in direct contact with the venture); (ii) an effort to align the venture's goal with corporate interests; (iii) an inability to determine venture performance or manage complex compensation systems; and (iv) an attempt to avoid problems when transferring employees to and from the venture. Finally, career concerns may drive CVC personnel to shun potentially profitable ventures that pay over the long haul (Rind, 1981). Specifically, CVC managers are wary that they will not be in their positions to enjoy the fruits of such investments, but will be held accountable for the losses in the short run.

McNally (1997) presents a careful study of the structure of programmes in the UK. He reports that 82 percent of the respondents provide funds to entrepreneurial ventures, 43 percent invest through independent VC funds, and 25 percent do both. Moreover, the evidence suggests wholly-owned CVC subsidiaries invest in ventures directly as well as through independent VCs. This may suggest that the 'CVC as LP' and the other three structures are not necessarily mutually exclusive. Shifting from structure to degree of autonomy, McNally finds that programmes experience a moderate level of flexibility. This is especially true of investment in independent VCs, where a third of the programmes were not subject to headquarter's approval. In contrast, only 9 percent of the programmes investing directly in new ventures did not require any headquarter's approval. As for the interaction between the CVC structure and its objectives, there is little evidence to indicate the two are correlated. Both the programmes that invest through VC funds, and those that fund ventures directly, rank the search for new technologies, establishment of business relationships and high financial gains as their top objectives.[19] The author also notes the growing salience of dedicated funds, reporting that 46 percent of the independent VC funds that had non-financial firms as limited partners, had a sole limited partner. The majority of these funds are managed by Advent International.

Kann (2000) reports the vast majority of strategically-driven programmes are controlled by their parent corporations. She distinguishes between three structures:

[17] They found that 69 percent are not compensated any differently than their corporate peers.

[18] Sykes (1992) reports that only two corporate ventures received stock-like compensation and two others received standard corporate pay. The other four had a bonus based on long or short term performance.

[19] McNally notes that ad hoc investments directed at entrepreneurial ventures (rather than through VCs) are likely motivated by strategic, not financial, objectives.

'CVC as LP', 'Dedicated Fund' and a third category of corporate-managed-programmes which aggregates 'Direct Investment' and 'Wholly-Owned Subsidiary'.[20] Seventy-eight percent of the programmes fall in the last category, whereas each of the first two accounts for 11 percent. Further analysis reveals a significant correlation between CVC structure and objectives. Univariate tests suggest that firms that seek to sponsor complementary ventures are more likely to pursue 'CVC as LP'. In contrast, firms that aim to increase internal R&D capabilities are more likely to employ a corporate-managed programme structure. Unfortunately, the analysis does not allow us to determine whether CVC objectives differ between programmes structured as 'Direct Investment' and those structured as 'Wholly-Owned Subsidiary'.

The Ernst & Young survey finds that 32 percent of the programmes are structured as a CVC subsidiary and 59 percent pursue some variation of 'Direct Investment', either as an independent unit (5%) or a fully integrated part of a corporate business unit (55%).

Birkinshaw et al. (2002) offer an insight on the governance of CVC programmes. They report that 90 percent of the programmes are owned solely by the parent corporation, but do not distinguish between 'Direct Investment' and 'Wholly-Owned Subsidiary'. They, too, present evidence that the CVC programmes are only moderately autonomous: about 35 percent of the programmes do not have a dedicated pool of funds and seek approval for each investment. The authors find CVC governance and objectives are correlated. Programmes that invest externally for strategic gains are more likely to have their funds subject to corporate approval (35% of programmes with such objective), in comparison to programmes that seek only financial gains (25% of programmes with such objective). Interestingly, strategically-driven programmes experience less autonomy with respect to management of their portfolio companies, but greater autonomy in making decisions regarding the CVC programme itself.[21] Finally, they find that standard corporate salary is the common compensation scheme among CVC personnel, mainly due to concerns over pay-inequality and attempts to align a programme's interests with that of the parent corporation. Bonus based on either financial or strategic performance is used occasionally and, to a lesser extent, carries interest in CVC portfolio companies.

To summarize, three important facets of CVC governance are explored. As for programme structure, we observe four distinct categories: 'Direct Investment' (i.e. a corporate business unit manages CVC activity), 'Wholly-Owned Subsidiary'

[20] Kann refers to investment *channel* rather than *structure*. The third group consists of CVC investment '... either through an internal venture capital business unit, a wholly owned venture capital subsidiary, an existing business development group or through the operating business units' (Kann, 2000: 15).

[21] In comparison to financially-oriented programmes, strategically-oriented programmes report lower levels of decision autonomy with respect to establishment of investment criteria and hiring, but higher levels of decision autonomy in making US$1M–US$5M investments or pursuing an IPO.

(i.e. a subsidiary is set up to handle investments), 'Dedicated Fund' (i.e. a fund co-managed by the firm and a venture capitalist), and 'CVC as LP' (i.e. capital allocated to a venture capital fund). Interestingly, we witnessed an evolution in CVC governance practices with the emergence of the 'Dedicated Fund' over the past decade. As for programme autonomy, we observe substantial variation along two dimensions: capital allocation and decision autonomy. Some programmes are allocated a large amount of capital upfront while others receive the necessary funds on an ad hoc basis. In some firms, the ability to make investments (i.e. fund a particular venture), and exit (i.e. sell a venture or take it public), is fully delegated to the CVC programme. In other firms, it is subject to scrutiny and corporate approval. As for the compensation of CVC personnel, we observe a growing propensity to provide high power incentives to CVC managers. These include bonuses based on financial or strategic milestones and, seldom, participation in venture success (e.g. carried interest). Standard corporate salary was the prevailing compensation scheme among CVC personnel in the past and remains the practice in a substantial minority of programmes, nowadays.

The inter-dependencies between the three governance facets have received little attention in the literature. Yet, there is some evidence to suggest that these facets are partially correlated. Tightly structured programmes (e.g. 'Direct Investment') are more likely to be subjected to rigorous corporate scrutiny. Also, they are more likely to employ corporate-wide compensation to avoid inequality concerns and ensure alignment with corporate interest. In contrast, loosely structured programmes (e.g. 'Wholly-Owned Subsidiary' and 'Dedicated Fund') are likely to have a dedicated pool of funds and enjoy decision autonomy. Moreover, the compensation schemes employed in these programmes often have a substantial upside. Finally, the literature indicates that passive investment through VC funds (i.e. 'CVC as LP') is associated with specific governance mechanisms. However, there is little evidence to suggest that CVC governance, and particularly CVC structures, differ across programmes' objectives, for the group of corporate managed programmes (i.e. Direct Investment, Wholly-Owned Subsidiary, and Dedicated Fund).

15.8 Investment relationships

Information, capital and commercial assets flow between CVC programmes and entrepreneurial ventures. From the CVC's perspective, selection and monitoring are the fundamental building blocks of a successful investment relationship.[22] The latter has to do with the mechanisms through which the CVC manages its portfolio companies once a funding deal has taken place (e.g. board seats), whereas the former addresses the ways in which a CVC programme identifies, selects and attracts prospective portfolio companies in the first place (e.g. *deal flow, due diligence*). Many of the selection and monitoring mechanisms also allow the firm to leverage, or learn about, entrepreneurial inventions.

On the issue of venture selection, R. Siegel et al. (1988) find that ties to independent venture capitalists, direct contacts to entrepreneurs and referral from departments within the corporation are the main sources of deal flow. The more autonomous programmes (i.e. 'pilots') rank ties to independent VCs as the main source of deal flow, whereas referral from a firm's own departments is more important for 'copilots' (programmes that are more dependent on corporate approval and capital). An inadequate deal flow is experienced when the ventures operate in an industry that is attractive to the parent firm.[23] The authors also find that CVC programmes and independent VC funds employ similar investment criteria. Accordingly, they attribute great importance to entrepreneurs' experience and personality as well as ventures' product or market potential. On the issue of post-deal investment relationship the study describes a number of impediments to effective relationships. It reports that incompatibility between corporate and entrepreneurial cultures is a leading obstacle to an effective relationship.

A study of 31 strategically-driven programmes finds that ties to the venture capital community, and to a lesser extent referral from corporate personnel, are important *deal-flow* sources (Sykes, 1990). The author documents different aspects of the post-deal relationship including monitoring activities (e.g. attending board meetings, receiving periodic reports) and provision of value-added services to the venture (e.g. awarding expert advice). He also finds a portfolio company may be leveraged to the advantage of the parent firm (e.g. seeking advice from the venture, identifying other investment opportunities, forming business relationships). When the investment channel is one of 'CVC as LP' there is negligible interaction between the corporation and the venture. In these cases, the focus shifts to the role of the venture capitalist as a broker and facilitator of corporate-venture interaction.

[22] Equally important is entrepreneurs' perspective. From their perspective the investment relationship is an opportunity for monetary and non-pecuniary support. Because the majority of the work on the topic builds on survey of CVC programmes we have only limited account of entrepreneurs' viewpoint, and most of it is framed in the context of ventures' overall performance. Therefore, it is presented in the 'ventures' performance' section.

[23] This counter-intuitive observation may be explained by the fact that entrepreneurial concerns of potential imitation are particularly high in such circumstances, thus shifting deal flow away from corporate investors and towards alternative sources of funding (e.g. VC funds). See also *Directions for Future Research* section.

Investment relationships in the UK are described in detail by McNally (1997). The sources of *deal flow* vary as firms approach potential portfolio companies either directly, or through intermediaries such as venture capitalists. Often a business relationship (i.e. customer–supplier linkages or contractual alliances) predates the investment relationship. As for the investment criteria, contrary to Siegel et al. (1988), McNally finds that CVCs assess ventures' products and market first, and only then evaluate entrepreneurs' experiences. The selection process is strict, and CVC investors fund less than 10 percent of the potential targets.[24] Once an investment is made, corporate investors closely monitor the ventures: 96 percent of them take a seat on the board and communicate with their portfolio companies on a monthly or weekly basis. The interaction is not limited to unidirectional monitoring. A vast majority of the ventures view CVC board presence positively and particularly commend (a) corporate assistance in solving short-term problems, and (b) corporate role as a sounding board to management team. These observations do not apply to firms that pursue 'CVC as LP'. These firms have little interaction either during the pre- or post-deal phases. For example, none of the firms associated with a 'CVC as LP' programme has ever taken part on ventures' boards.

Firms' monitoring practices are at the centre of a few recent surveys on both sides of the Atlantic. Maula (2001) surveys 91 US-based ventures in the computer and communication industries during the late 1990s. He finds that in 31 percent of the cases, the corporate investor holds a board seat and in 40 percent of the cases it holds passive observer rights rather than an active board position. These results echo a recent study of European venture capital practices (Bottazzi, DaRin and Hellmann, 2004).[25] The authors find that CVC investors serve on portfolio companies' boards (68%) and conduct close monitoring and monthly site visits (70%) almost as frequently as independent venture capitalists do (78%, 76% respectively). According to a survey by Ernst & Young (2002), VC referral and direct entrepreneur referrals are the main sources of new investments, each accounting for about 30 percent of CVC deal flow. Other sources include, by order of importance, internal employees and professional service firms.

Birkinshaw et al. (2002) find substantial variation in selection and monitoring practices across programmes' objectives. Venture capitalists are the main source of deal flow for externally-focused programmes investing either for financial or strategic reasons. Other external sources include direct contact by entrepreneurs (ranked 2nd) and referral by corporate employees (ranked 3rd). The reverse rank-order holds for internally-focused programmes. As for the acceptance rates, most

[24] The investment amount and the CVC's industry affiliation are reportedly the leading criteria in entrepreneurs' investor choice (McNally, 1997).

[25] Based on the Survey of European Venture Capital (SEVeCa). The survey was sent to all registered European venture capital firms operating between 1998 and 2001, and reached a 15% response rate.

internally-focused programmes and all externally-focused ones screen out about 85–90 percent of all the incoming ideas and fund only 2–3 percent of the initial proposal pool.[26] With respect to post-deal practices, the majority of the programmes take a full board seat (50%) or an observer seat (39%).[27] The evidence suggests only a limited communication between the venture and the corporation; while CVC personnel interact with the venture on a weekly or monthly basis, other corporate personnel seldom do so.

To conclude, CVC programmes are highly active in selecting and managing their investment relationships. Much like independent venture capitalists, corporate investors rely on referrals from other venture capital investors for the majority of their deal flow. Employees and business partners constitute an important, yet smaller, source of prospective targets. There is only cursory evidence regarding CVC selection processes. It suggests that corporate investors and venture capitalists employ similar investment criteria, evaluating the individual entrepreneur as well as the underlying opportunity. Moreover, CVC programmes fund a small percentage of the initial deal pool. While this observation implies rigorous screening and *due diligence* practices, we know little about the specific steps CVC investors take. Future work should study if and when do firms leverage their skilled R&D personnel, market familiarity, and unique industry outlook to select superior ventures. Further insight might be gained by comparing the process of choosing a portfolio company with the organizational routines that are involved in selecting an alliance partner or an acquisition target.

Moreover, corporate investors are actively involved with their portfolio companies. Most programmes communicate with the ventures more than twice a month and more than two-thirds of the programmes have a board seat, or at least hold observer rights. The relationships, however, are not limited to monitoring activities. The entrepreneurs benefit from corporate advice, and at times, the ventures educate the parent corporation about new technologies or business opportunities. Again, we need further insight regarding the type of advice and support afforded by the corporation. Do firms leverage their skilled R&D personnel, manufacturing capabilities, or industry outlook to assist portfolio companies? Detailed case studies may provide an answer to this question. These studies should recognize that the nature and magnitude of such support mechanisms may vary greatly by CVC objectives.

[26] Programmes that invest internally with the goal of spinning out ventures are the exception. These programmes consider about 30 percent of the incoming ideas and invest in approximately 15 percent of all proposals.

[27] These proportions may be understated as internally-focused programmes can exert monitoring in other forms.

15.9 Performance implications

The performance implications of CVC receive much attention in the literature. Common topics include the link between the programme's objective (financial or strategic) and its success, or the impact of the programme's structure on its performance. Unfortunately, the lack of agreed-upon measures of strategic and financial outcomes, and to a greater extent the ambiguity regarding whose performance is being measured, resulted in much confusion. To avoid the confusion, we break the discussion into three parts (see Fig. 15.6). The first part addresses the success of entrepreneurial ventures that are backed by corporate investors. The performance of CVC programmes is the focus of the second part. Finally, the third part addresses the implication to the parent corporation. The distinction is necessary as some ventures, and even CVC programmes, may experience benefits at the expense of their parent firm, and vice versa.

Again, a few caveats are warranted. The existing literature relies predominantly on case studies or descriptive surveys that cannot control for a number of competing causal factors such as firm size, industry attributes, or macroeconomic conditions. Even when a multivariate analysis is presented, it is often based on a cross-sectional sample and thus cannot effectively address issues of unobserved heterogeneity and temporal precedence. Moreover, the evidence is often based on surveys where participants were asked to rank their own achievements. Self-reported measures are subject to biases and misrepresentations and should be interpreted with caution. While the study of CVC objectives or governance is also liable to self-report problems, these problems are of special concern when it comes to measuring performance.

Performance of the entrepreneurial venture. There are reasons to believe that corporate backing may increase a venture's success rate. An established firm may contribute to a venture on a number of dimensions (see Table 15.3). First, a corporate venture capitalist may provide value-added services similar to those provided by quality VC funds (Block and MacMillan, 1993). Secondly, it can extend unique services, which capitalize on corporate resources and complementary assets. For example, a venture may gain access to corporate laboratories, it can employ the corporation as a readily available beta site, or leverage a firm's network of customers and suppliers as well as domestic and foreign distribution channels (Teece, 1986; Pisano, 1991; Acs et al., 1997; Maula and Murray, 2001). A corporate investor can also offer unique insights into industry trends.[28] Lastly,

[28] Many ventures appreciate CVCs' expertise, as Rosenstein et al. (1993) find in a survey of 162 ventures. One entrepreneur shared his opinion of corporate investors, '[they] had a better understanding of operating business—hands-on versus venture capitalists whose experience is often

the fact that a focal venture is chosen by an industry incumbent, acts as an endorsement effect toward third parties and/or the capital markets (Stuart, Hoang and Hybels, 1999).

McNally (1997) investigates 23 corporate-backed ventures located in the UK.[29] As expected, most ventures experience substantial non-pecuniary benefits in the form of help with short-term problems (83%), and access to corporate management (70%) and technical (49%) expertise (see discussion of the investment relationship). Other benefits include the ability to leverage corporate assets and access to corporate marketing and distribution networks (39%). In almost two-thirds of the cases, the firm and the venture entered a business relationship at a later date (e.g. buyer–supplier relationships, licensing agreements, or research contracts). The most important indirect advantage to the ventures (70%) is the increase in their credibility, consistent with the endorsement effect. A small, yet substantial, group of ventures experienced pricing benefits (42%) and lower performance targets (39%), which might have come at the expense of the corporate investor. Finally, among those ventures that received indirect CVC investment (i.e. 'CVC as LP'), almost half were not aware of the corporate investor. The only benefit they report was the enhanced opportunity for future business relationships.

Gompers and Lerner (1998) employ secondary data on more than 30,000 investment rounds in US-based ventures during the period 1983–94. They define venture success as an IPO or an acquisition at high valuation, and find that CVC-backed ventures are at least as likely to succeed as VC-backed ventures, particularly when there is a fit between the venture and the corporation.[30] They also report that CVCs invest at a premium in comparison to similar investments by independent VCs. The premium, however, is not sensitive to the degree of fit between the venture and the corporation. While CVC premium is advantageous from the venture's viewpoint (it is able to raise funds at lower cost), it may imply lower returns to the corporate investor.

Maula (2001) explores in depth the mechanisms through which 91 US-based ventures benefit from their corporate backers. Building on the responses of

obtained vicariously'. A more recent testimony was voiced by a founder of a software venture: 'Lane15 Software ... needs advanced warning of trends and technologies in microprocessors and computer systems. Investments from Intel Capital and Dell Ventures ... ensure [it] has an insider's knowledge' (*Entrepreneur* magazine, 7/2002).

[29] We focus on the benefits associated with corporate-backing. However, corporate investment is also associated with some difficulties: two ventures (9%) experienced difficulties in obtaining further financing.

[30] A venture and a corporate investor exhibit 'direct fit' when their lines-of-business overlap, and 'indirect fit' when the venture is a customer or a supplier of the corporation. Gompers and Lerner utilize observed investments to label a CVC programme 'strategic'. This is fundamentally different from classifying a programme according to its declared goals. The latter is an *ex ante* measure of firms' intent while the former is an *ex post* measure collapsing firm's intended behaviour along with entrepreneurs' preferences and actions.

Table 15.3 Benefits to entrepreneurial ventures from CVC-backing

Activity	Benefits
Financing	• Access financial resources: equity, royalties, R&D funding, etc.
	• Reduce costs
R&D / New product development	• Utilize market intelligence
	• Access to extensive publications library
	• Obtain technological insights
	• Leverage core competencies
	• Access complementary technologies
	• Access to labs and test facilities
Manufacturing	• Receive manufacturing knowledge and capabilities
	• Capitalize on component purchasing power
	• Access quality assurance capabilities
Marketing / distribution	• Improve market access (distribution channels, global networks)
	• Access and establish loyal customer base
	• Acquire market research and personal insights
	• Reduce cycle time
	• Increase credibility
	• Ties to a partner capable of driving industry standards
Legal / Regulatory	• Advise on regulatory or patent approvals
service / Support	• Establish warranty, service and customer support procedures
reputation	• Exploit 'Halo effect', large company's endorsement to clients, within industry and during financing

Note: Adopted from Kelly et al. (2000).

ventures' CEOs, he studies the role of related resources (either production or distribution), knowledge acquisition, and endorsement in value creation.[31] Consistent with previous studies, Maula finds that all channels, except the acquisition of distribution-related resources, are significantly associated with value-added experience. It further indicates that the ability to leverage corporate resources is a function of complementarities between the two, as well as prior social interaction.

[31] The value created, or value-added, to the venture is operationalized using CEO response to three items: 'This investor has provided us with valuable value-sharing support in addition to the financing,' 'The value-adding support provided by this investor has been critical to our success,' and 'We are very happy about having this investor.'

The prominence of the corporate investor, venture's age, and customer switching cost are associated with increases in the endorsement effect.

Maula and Murray (2001) study 325 IT and communication ventures that IPOed on NASDAQ between 1998 and 1999. Focusing on CVC investment by members of the Global Fortune 500, they report that ventures co-financed by CVC investors receive higher valuations than comparable ventures funded solely by independent VCs. Moreover, ventures that are co-financed by multiple CVC investors earn even higher valuations. Note, while Gompers and Lerner (1998) study the probability of an IPO as a function of corporate backing, Maula and Murray investigate the valuation conditioned on going through an IPO. Both studies find that corporate backing has a positive impact on a venture's performance.

In sum, prior work suggests that CVC-backed ventures experience favourable performance. These benefits are evident both in absolute terms (McNally, 1997; Maula, 2001) as well as in comparison to VC-backed ventures (Gompers and Lerner, 1998; Maula and Murray, 2001). However, we do not know whether the benefits to the venture come at the expense of the corporation (e.g. inflated valuations). Further, it is unclear whether a venture's favourable performance should be attributed to the firm's ability to pick winners, or its ability to build superior ventures. A comparison between two groups: ventures funded by a single corporate investor, and those funded by a syndicate of corporate and independent venture capitalists—may shed light on the issue. If corporate investors excel in venture selection, the two groups should command similar round valuations and experience similar probability of success (e.g. an IPO event). If, however, firms are good at building strong ventures, the two groups should experience similar probability of success, yet ventures backed by a sole CVC may experience lower round valuation (i.e. at time of selection and investment they were not yet of superior quality).

Finally, we need to map the mechanisms through which corporate backing enhances the value of ventures. Future research should explore the effect of technological overlap (e.g. cross-citation of patents), shared manufacturing operations (e.g. the venture, or the firm, are listed as a major supplier of the other), joint marketing efforts (e.g. listings of the other products in own marketing material, use of similar third-party marketing channels), or product complementarities (e.g. product offering in related Corp-Tech categories) on ventures' performance (e.g. probability of IPO or growth in sales).

Performance of the CVC programme. Evaluating the performance of the CVC programme is a challenging task. There is no agreed-upon list of strategic benefits on which programmes are measured. This is further complicated by the fact that measuring programmes solely on their strategic contribution may hide financial losses, and vice versa. Yet, the difficulties did not deter scholars from addressing this issue. The work relies predominantly on surveys of CVC executives who rate the performance of their own programme. The responses inform us as to the spectrum of benefits associated with corporate venture capital, and the degree to which each was met. The benefits broadly fall into the following categories, echoing the list of CVC objectives: Internal Rate of Return (financial), window on technology (strategic), identifying acquisition candidates (strategic), strategic relationships development (strategic), demand enhancement (strategic), foreign market entry (strategic), change to corporate culture (strategic), and leverage internal technological developments (strategic).

R. Siegel et al. (1988) request corporate venture capitalists to rate their satisfaction with the programme's performance. The authors find that other than 'opportunities to improve manufacturing processes' all CVC objectives were reportedly met with above-satisfactory levels, with 'exposure to new technologies and markets' receiving the highest rating. Further analysis links programme attributes to ultimate performance, comparing the performance of 'pilot' (high degree of autonomy, permanent financial commitment) and 'co-pilot' (highly dependent on corporate approval and capital commitment) programmes. While 'pilots' attached greater weight to financial objectives, they reported higher satisfaction in achieving both financial and strategic objectives. The only exception was the higher satisfaction of 'co-pilots' with identification of acquisition opportunities.

Sykes (1990) investigates the overall strategic value generated by CVC programmes, using a sample of 31 firms that pursue strategically-driven investment. About 40 percent of the respondents report very high value creation, while 24 percent report nil or negative value. The magnitude of CVC value creation varies by investment structure and programme objective. In particular, roughly 50 percent of the respondents state strategic value is more likely to be generated through direct investment rather than investment as limited partners. Programme longevity, however, is similar for both groups: a median age of four years. Programmes motivated by the need to 'identify new opportunities' and 'develop business relationships' were associated with strategic value creation, while those seeking potential acquisition targets scored unsatisfactory levels. Interestingly, this pattern holds irrespective of the programme's structure. Finally, programmes that rated higher on strategic value creation are also associated with higher return on investment.

McNally (1997) surveys CVC programme directors in 28 UK-based organizations. He reports significant differences in the performance of programmes that follow a 'CVC as LP' structure versus those that invest directly. About 50 percent of the 'CVC as LP' programmes terminated their investment activity, and all of them did so due to unsatisfactory performance. In contrast, only 39 percent of the programmes that directly fund ventures no longer pursue investment activity, of which only 33 percent state poor performance as the reason for termination. None of the benefits associated with investment as limited partners is strategic. Rather, the benefits consist of the opportunity to learn about venture capital, gain financial returns, as well as enhance social responsibility. In contrast, programmes that directly invest in entrepreneurial ventures report high satisfaction with strategic goals, such as the opportunity to develop business relationships and exposure to new markets and technologies.[32]

The study by Gompers and Lerner (1998) may also shed light on programme performance. To the extent that programme longevity is a proxy of its success, CVC programmes do not fare as well as independent VC funds: a mean of 2.5 years (and 4.4 investments) for the former compared to 7.1 years (and 43.5 investments) by the latter. Interestingly, investment in ventures operating in the same line of business, which they denote 'strategic fit', is associated with greater programme stability. If a strategic fit exists in at least half of a programme's investments, its life-span is equivalent to that of independent VC funds. Furthermore, the authors report that the likelihood of a CVC-backed venture success is similar to that of a VC-backed venture, and increases when there is a fit between the venture and the corporation. They also find that CVC investments are made at a premium compared to similar investments by independent VC funds.

Birkinshaw et al. (2002) survey CVC executives as well. They find that internal rate of return (IRR) and financial gains are the most common measures used by firms to evaluate their CVC programme. In terms of delivering on objectives, the results suggest programmes fare better with respect to strategic goals. Gaining a window on technology was at the top of the list. The ability to deliver financial returns was ranked fourth after 'better use of existing corporate assets' and 'increased visibility/awareness of corporation'. Interestingly, programmes of different objectives exhibit similar performance along the financial, strategic, and internal motivation dimensions.

Hill et al. (2004) utilize the same database in a rigorous investigation of the determinants of CVC performance. In a multivariate regression analysis, they find that programmes that aggressively pursue syndication with independent VCs experience greater perceived strategic value, higher investment output per year and lower closure rate among portfolio companies.[33] The positive effect of syndication on investment output per year is particularly strong for programmes seeking investment in external ventures. They find that the degree of CVC governance (i.e. having pre-allocated capital and minimal corporate review) does not affect

[32] McNally reports the ability to assist spin-out from the corporation is associated with the highest satisfaction level. However, he notes only two out of the 23 respondents pursued this strategy.

[33] Birkanshaw et al. (2002) define 'perceived strategic value' as survey response to questions regarding programmes' ability to: (1) increase the demand for corporate products or technologies; (2) enhance corporate visibility; (3) create spin-outs; and (4) generate internal recognition for new venture creation. Investment output is defined as the number of programme's investments divided by its age. Lower closure rate is the percentage of investments in programme's portfolio that have been closed down.

perceived strategic value for externally focused programmes. It is, however, significantly associated with a decrease in portfolio companies' closure rates. A decrease in closure rates is also associated with the use of VC-like compensation (i.e. carried interest) for externally focused programmes.

To conclude, there is mixed evidence regarding the performance of corporate venture capital programmes. Nonetheless, a few consistent observations emerge. The lifespan of CVC programmes is no longer than that of independent VC funds. The degree to which firms experience strategic and financial benefits varies by programme objectives and governance structure. That being said, programmes that perform well strategically also report favourable financial returns. The ability to experience strategic benefits diminishes substantially for firms investing as limited partners in an existing VC fund (i.e. CVC as LP).

Our understanding of programme performance can be advanced in a couple of ways. First, there is a need for a universal performance metric. Currently, the strategic performance of a CVC programme is either collapsed into a single measure (Sykes, 1990), or evaluated using eighteen different components (McNally, 1997; Birkinshaw et al., 2002). A useful metric is one that offers a parsimonious, yet meaningful, evaluation of CVC contribution. Along these lines, it may be useful to summarize the programme's performance along three dimensions: (a) technology, (b) the product market, and (c) geography.

Secondly, the design and measurement of CVC performance should be revisited. The evidence we present above is almost exclusively based on executives' accounts of their programme performance. The measures have many advantages, yet they are also subjective and liable to various single source biases. Future work should triangulate these informative, yet individual, assessments with quantitative measures such as a count of patent cross-citation patterns, count of joint marketing efforts, and so on. Separately, to the extent that CVC executives construe their own performance favourably, we may overestimate programme success. These concerns may be alleviated by soliciting evaluations from other, non-CVC personnel (e.g. CEO, CFO, COO and head of business units).

Performance of the parent corporation. The parent corporation does not necessarily experience favourable outcomes when its portfolio companies, or even the CVC programme, report positive performance. As we state above, benefits to the entrepreneurial venture may come at the expense of the corporate investor (e.g. inflated valuations). It is difficult to assess the contribution of corporate venture capital even when interests are aligned. A programme aimed at enhancing demand may affect revenue and profits in the short term, whereas the contribution of a window on technology strategy is expected to occur over a longer period of time. In spite of these challenges, a handful of scholars explore the performance implications to the investing corporations. These studies employ pooled cross-sectional time-series samples, as opposed to survey responses. They mostly centre on the effect on firm innovation rates (e.g. patenting output), implicitly focusing on the role of CVC as a window on technology.

Dushnitsky and Lenox (2005c) explore investing-firms' value creation using a panel of about 1,200 US public firms during the period 1990–99. They compare investing firms' value creation to that experienced by non-investing firms in the same industry during the same year. The main advantage of their proxy for firm value creation, Tobin's q, is the fact it captures both the narrow financial returns to CVC investment and the long-term strategic benefits.[34] The results of multivariate regression analysis suggest that CVC is associated with the creation of firm value, but that this relationship is conditional on both temporal and sectoral factors. The positive relationship between CVC and firm value is greatest within the devices and information sectors. Moreover, the marginal contribution of CVC rises when firms explicitly pursue strategic objectives.

Chesbrough and Tucci (2004) investigate the research activities of 270 US and foreign CVC investing firms, during the period 1980 to 2000. They explore variations in the level of corporate R&D expenses prior to, and immediately after, the onset of the CVC programme. A multivariate regression analysis indicates the existence of a CVC programme is significantly associated with increases in corporate R&D, even after controlling for firm factors and industry affiliation. Building on these findings, the authors state that corporate venture capital is of strategic value to the parent corporation, and may supplement other R&D efforts.

Dushnitsky and Lenox (2005a) analyze a large unbalanced panel of US public firms during the time period 1975–95. The authors study the innovation implications of CVC, using a count of citations to each firm's patents. By utilizing panel data analysis and controlling for unobserved, time-variant heterogeneity, they find that increases in CVC investment are associated with subsequent increases in citation-weighted patenting rates. This finding is consistent with the view of CVC as a window on novel technologies. Further, the magnitude of this effect depends on the industry's Intellectual Property (IP) regime and firms' absorptive capacity. It is in weak IP regimes that CVC is associated with greatest contribution to firms' innovativeness. This finding is consistent with the view that ventures resort to secrecy in such industries and CVC provides the corporation with a unique opportunity to conduct due diligence and participate on board meetings thus allowing it to pierce the veil of secrecy and learn about the venture's closely-held technologies.

Schildt et al. (2004) study the venturing activities of the largest 110 US firms in the information and telecommunication sectors during the period 1990–2000. The authors compare the inclination to perform explorative learning through CVC, strategic alliances, joint ventures, and acquisitions. They define explorative innovation activity as investing-firm patents citing portfolio companies, and

[34] The authors define Tobin's q as the market valuation over the value of tangible assets.

exploitative innovation as patents citing both firm's prior patents and portfolio companies. In comparison with acquisition, corporate venture capital is found to be only weakly associated with explorative behaviour. The results suggest that exploitative activity is as important a part of CVC investment as it is for other forms of inter-organizational learning.[35]

To conclude, a growing body of work investigates the contribution of CVC programmes to the parent corporation. The evidence suggests that investment is associated with firm value creation. The benefits are likely to be higher for strategically-driven programmes. More importantly, the ability to enjoy an effective window on technology is a function not only of the investment activity per se, but also of the parent firm's absorptive capacity as well as other, industry-level factors.

Future work may expand on these studies in a number of ways. First, one should recognize the disconnection between venture and parent firm success. As we mentioned above, a venture may command inflated valuations which could have an adverse effect on parent firm performance. On the other extreme, an outright failure of the venture may be associated with substantial strategic benefits. These benefits may accrue to the investing firm when technologies remain viable after the originating venture has dissolved (Hoetker and Agarwal, 2004) and failure itself carries informational weight (McGrath, 1999).

Secondly, scholars should go beyond firm-innovation-rates and study the impact of CVC on other facets of firm performance. It is all the more important to do so given that some of the more salient CVC objectives (e.g. enhancing demand or building strategic partnerships) are not aimed at supporting a firm's R&D effort. Admittedly, a programme aimed at enhancing demand (i.e. financing ventures with complementary products or services) may in turn increase the demand for corporate innovations and ultimately result in an increase in firm innovation rate. Nonetheless, more direct impact may be recorded on firm market share, number of strategic partners and so on.

Finally, the field of corporate venture capital may benefit from, as well as contribute to, an explicit discussion of players' bargaining power. For example, Gompers and Lerner (1998) observe corporate venture capitalists tend to invest at a premium. They speculate that existing investors, or the ventures themselves, bargain away some of the value. Future work should continue to explore whether CVC creates value to begin with, and if so, what proportion is appropriated by the investing firm. To address the latter question, scholars need to identify events that affect bargaining power. A softening of the market for IPO, or a variation in CVC

[35] The authors find only seven out of 998 CVC investments result in investing-firms' patents citing portfolio companies. The dependent variable may fail to reflect the learning benefits associated with CVC due to (1) a citation lag that averages three-to-four years (Hall et al., 2001), and (2) the fact that CVC has boomed in 1999 and 2000.

prominence in the venture capital community may prove useful instruments in such future exploration.

15.10 Directions for Future Research

We know much more about corporate venture capital today. Nonetheless, there are a number of issues that merit future research. First, a careful documentation of corporate venture capital practices is called for. Such work may constitute a sound basis for a comparison with previous work and rigorous analysis of CVC governance, investment activity, and performance. Birkinshaw, Murray and van Basten-Batenburg (2002) provide a good starting point, offering detailed insight into corporate objectives, the governance of the programmes, the relationship with the portfolio companies and so on. Future work faces a few challenges. It should construct comprehensive databases and avoid convenience sampling of CVC programmes (e.g. hastily identifying only subsidiary-based programmes or narrowly focusing on financially-oriented programmes). Future studies could also benefit from the development of parsimonious metrics which sufficiently describe each aspect of CVC activity. Not only would it elucidate the role of each aspect and the inter-dependencies between them, but also it would facilitate building a cumulative body of knowledge about corporate venture capital. Another challenge is to move away from cross-sectional studies and towards longitudinal samples that allow one to disentangle firm factors from macroeconomic or industry effects (e.g. Dushnitsky and Lenox, 2005a; Chesbrough and Tucci, 2004; Gompers and Lerner, 1998).

Secondly, the antecedents to corporate venture capital have not received appropriate attention in the literature. Current work identifies the factors that affect firm decision not-to-pursue investment activity (McNally, 1997) as well as the industry and firm level factors that drive CVC investment (Dushnitsky and Lenox, 2005b). Further investigation of the factors that motivate firms to invest in entrepreneurial ventures may shed light on the strategic role corporate venture capital plays. For example, we need to learn the identity of those within the organization who decide to launch a CVC programme and the processes involved in this decision. These insights, in turn, can help explain variation in programme objectives, structure and performance. Other opportunities exist in advancing our understanding of corporate governance mechanisms (at the firm level) and their impact on the practice of corporate venture capital.

Thirdly, the study of CVC antecedents should go beyond a firm-centric investigation to explain why some CVC-venture pairs form an investment relationship, while others do not. To that end, there is a need to consider corporate and entrepreneur perspectives in tandem. Dushnitsky (2004) provides initial evidence to that effect. He argues that many investment relationships do not materialize because the corporation will not invest unless the entrepreneur discloses her invention, and the entrepreneur is wary of doing so, fearing imitation. As a result, Dushnitsky predicts that a firm is more likely to exploit entrepreneurial disclosure and thus relationships are less likely to be formed when (a) the invention is a potential substitute of corporate products, and (b) a corporate business unit manages investments that potentially substitute their own products. The author also conjectures investment relationships are more likely to form when the products are complements. Analyses of start-up stage investment during the 1990s support these hypotheses and suggest that, at times, CVC programmes aimed at enhancing demand may flourish while those seeking a window on technology may meet substantial hurdles.[36] In particular, firms that view their investment activity as a window on novel and potentially substituting entrepreneurial technologies may find such entrepreneurs the least likely to seek direct corporate backing.

More empirical and theoretical work on the topic is warranted. If imitation concerns are driving investment patterns, CVC-venture investment relationships should seldom occur at the start-up stage. To the extent that mature ventures are better equipped to preclude imitation (e.g. they have developed products that can be patented), investments in potential substitutes may become more common during the expansion and later stages. Indeed, the probability of an investment relationship between a firm and a venture of the same industry (i.e. potential substitutes) is low at the start-up stage and increases as a venture matures (Gompers, 2002).[37] By studying corporate and entrepreneur perspectives concurrently, future work can deepen our understanding of demand-enhancing and technology-seeking corporate venture capital, and the success rate at various stages of investment.

Fourthly, the inter-dependencies between independent venture capitalists and corporate investors constitute a fertile area for future research. While both players seek to invest in entrepreneurial ventures, there is little theory and even less empirical evidence regarding the indirect effect one group of investors has on the other. One exception is the work by Dushnitsky (2004) who speculates IVCs exert

[36] Some of the earlier work on CVC provides anecdotal evidence of entrepreneurs' dis-inclination to approach firms in a competing line of business (Rind, 1981; Hardymon, DeNino and Malcolm, 1983).

[37] Gompers (2002) investigates the probability of an investment between a firm and a venture in related industry (which he defines as a 'strategic fit'). He sets the earliest stage, the start-up-stage, as a benchmark and reports that development- and beta-stages are more likely to see an investment involving a firm and a venture of the same industry, but shipping-stages, profitable-stages, and restart-stages are equally likely to see such an investment. Note, these patterns may be consistent with Dushnitsky (2004) but may also result due to heterogeneous investor stage preferences or measurement errors.

externalities on corporate investors, as highly sought-after entrepreneurs may opt for IVC backing and away from corporate funding. The externalities are attributed to the differences in the propensity of investors to expropriate entrepreneurial invention and its effect on entrepreneurs' investor choices. Additional empirical efforts are needed to document these externalities. The researcher can potentially exploit cross-industry and cross-national variations in the size and salience of the IVC and CVC communities to gauge the magnitude and direction of these externalities. Such empirical efforts should then be used to identify additional mechanisms through which externalities—be that positive or negative—take effect.

There is also room to explore the direct relationship between IVCs and CVCs. Anecdotal evidence regarding direct collaboration between the two investor groups is widespread. Yet only limited work on joint syndication practices or other forms of co-operation exists. A couple of recent studies address these questions. Maula et al. (2005) report that independent VCs and corporate investors add value to their portfolio companies along different dimensions. Their findings highlight venues for potential collaboration between the two investor groups. Dushnitsky and Shapira (2004) find persistent differences in the structure of venture capital syndicates that involve a corporate investor, compared to those that consist solely of independent VCs.

At the macro level, there are many opportunities to explore the relationship between CVC investment and industry and national level factors. The historical patterns of corporate venture capital in the US suggest that technological ferment and active financial markets are important drivers of each investment wave. Industry-level analysis (Dushnitsky and Lenox, 2005b) and cross-country evidence points at these factors as well as the strength of the legal regime. The fifth avenue for future research should aim to expand on this work. A comprehensive study of technological capabilities, legal regime, capital market, and competition levels may shed more light on the absolute, as well as relative, role these factors play in stimulating corporate venture capital. The analysis should go beyond the general categories; for example, within the broad legal regime definition we may find that the effect of rule-of-law or anti-directors'-rights differs from that of strong intellectual property rights. Finally, scholars should also distinguish between those factors that are driving firms' investment behaviour (i.e. originating CVC), and those that attract corporate venture capital (i.e. receiving CVC).

Relatedly, the impact of corporate venture capital on economy-wide issues is under-explored. While the dollar value of corporate venture capital activity is significantly lower than overall corporate R&D, there are reasons to believe its macroeconomic impact would exceed its relative share of innovative efforts. Corporate investors possess complementary assets and commercialization capabilities which, combined with entrepreneurs' innovative technologies, are likely to translate into industry growth, productivity increases, and technological advancement. Moreover, a corporation may syndicate investments with other firms in its own industry or beyond it as a vehicle to promote standards (e.g. the Linux company, Red Hat, received funding from Compaq, IBM, Intel, Novell, Oracle, and SAP). Therefore, future work might study the impact of CVC on growth rates in the focal industry and related industries. The effect on technological trajectory and incumbent persistence should also be explored.

Finally, institutional changes are reshaping the market for entrepreneurial financing. The literature has long recognized the rule of property right protection in facilitating and governing entrepreneurial activities (for an excellent review, see Fogel, Hawk, Morck and Yeung in Chapter 20 of this Handbook). As noted above, CVCs' relationships with entrepreneurial ventures, and indirectly IVCs, are particularly sensitive to the strength of the property right institution (i.e. the legal environment affecting an entrepreneur's ability to protect her rights to the invention or business idea). As a result, one may expect relatively more corporate-backed deals under institutional environments that secure strong property rights. Future work should explore the impact of different property right regimes on the relationships between entrepreneurs, corporate and independent investors.

Another notable institutional change is the Sarbanes-Oxley Act of 2002 (hereafter SOX). The act is intended to protect shareholders from accounting errors and fraudulent practices in the enterprise world. Experts predict that the impact of the SOX on the venture capital market will equal that of the 'Prudent Man' Act of 1979. First, there are substantial compliance requirements for going public (see Section 404 of the SOA), which pushes back the average 'IPO-able' age for venture-backed companies and may make an exit through an IPO less attractive altogether (Ernst & Young, 2002). Secondly, stricter requirements for board-independence imply that top talent can no longer sit on multiple boards and that companies cannot offer option-based compensation to attract industry experts (Ernst & Young, 2004).[38] Both trends might result in a greater role for corporate investors. As more and more entrepreneurial ventures go through expansion and late stages as private companies, they may seek corporate venture capital which offers not only funding but also access to corporate complementary assets, laboratories, and distribution channels that are crucial at the expansion and late stages. Moreover, as the availability of top talent is constrained, corporate venture capital may be an effective way to secure high-quality industry, marketing, and managerial advice. Future research may play an important role in charting the opportunities, and threats, these changes pose to corporate investors.

[38] The implications of stricter requirements for board-independence are two-fold. First, firms have less flexibility in offering option-based compensation to board members. This significantly diminishes the ability of a cash-constrained venture to recruit prominent personal and industry experts (Ernst & Young, 2002, 2004). Second, National Association of Directors' best practice requires that a professional director will not serve on more than six boards. This, in turn, may constrain venture capitalists' abilities to sit on portfolio companies' boards and provide them with advice.

References

Acs Z. J., R. Morck, J. M. Shaver and B. Yeung (1997). 'The Internationalization of Small and Medium-sized Enterprises: A Policy Perspective'. *Small Business Economics*, 9: 7–20.

Birkinshaw, J., G. Murray, and R. van Basten-Batenburg (2002). *Corporate Venturing: The State of the Art and the Prospects for the Future.* London: London Business School.

Block, Z. and I. MacMillan (1993). *Corporate Venturing: Creating New Business Within the Firm.* Boston: Harvard Business School Press.

—— and O. A. Ornati (1987). 'Compensating Corporate Venture Managers'. *Journal of Business Venturing*, 2: 41–52.

Bottazzi, L., M. DaRin and T. Hellmann (2004). 'The Changing Face of the European Venture Capital Industry: Facts and Analysis'. *Journal of Private Equity*, 7(2): 26–53.

Brandenburger, A. and B. Nalebuff (1996). *Co-opetition.* Harvard Business Press.

Bygrave, W. D. (1989). 'The Entrepreneurship Paradigm (II): Chaos and Catastrophes Among Quantum Jumps?' *Entrepreneurship: Theory and Practice*, 14(2): 7–30.

Chesbrough, H. W. (2002). 'Making Sense of Corporate Venture Capital'. *Harvard Business Review*, 80(3) (March).

—— and C. Tucci (2004). 'Corporate venture capital in the context of corporate innovation'. Paper presented at the DRUID Conference.

Djankov, S., R. La Porta, F. López-de-Silanes and A. Shleifer (2002). 'The Regulation of Entry'. *Quarterly Journal of Economics*, 117(1): 1–37.

Dushnitsky, G. (2004). 'Limitations to inter-organizational knowledge acquisition: The paradox of corporate venture capital'. Best Paper Proceedings of the 2004 Academy of Management Conference. New Orleans, LA.

—— and M. J. Lenox (2005a). 'Corporate Venture Capital and Incumbent Firm Innovation Rate'. *Research Policy*, 34(5): 615–39.

—— and —— (2005b). 'When do Firms Undertake R&D by Investing in New Ventures?' *Strategic Management Journal*, 26(10): 947–65.

—— and —— (2005c). 'When Does Corporate Venture Capital Investment Create Firm Value?' *Journal of Business Venturing*, 21(6): 753–772.

—— and Z. Shapira (2004). 'Decisions under uncertainty and corporate venture capital Syndication'. The Wharton School Working Paper.

Ernst & Young (2002). Corporate Venture Capital Report.

—— (2004). *IPO Insights 2003: The Seventh Annual IPO Transformation.*

Fast, N. D. (1978) *The Rise and Fall of Corporate New Venture Divisions.* Ann Arbor, MI: UMI Research Press.

Furman, J. L., M. Porter and S. Stern (2002). 'The Determinants of National Innovative Capacity'. *Research Policy*, 31: 899–933.

Gompers, P. (1995). 'Optimal Investment, Monitoring and the Staging of Venture Capital'. *Journal of Finance*, 50: 1461–89.

—— (2002). 'Corporations and the Financing of Innovation: The Corporate Venturing Experience'. *Economic Review – Federal Reserve Bank of Atlanta*, 87(4): 1–17.

—— J. Lerner (1998). 'The determinants of corporate venture capital success: organizational structure, incentives and complementarities'. NBER Working Paper #6725.

—— —— and D. Scharfstein (2004). 'Entrepreneurial Spawning: Public Corporations and the Genesis of New Ventures', 1986–99. *Journal of Finance*, 60(2): 577–614.

Guth, W. and A. Ginsberg (1990). 'Guest Editor's Introduction: Corporate Entrepreneurship'. *Strategic Management Journal* (SI)11: 5–15.

Hall, B., A. Jaffe and M. Trajtenberg (2001). 'The NBER Patent Citation Data File: Lessons, Insights and Methodological Tools.' NBER Working Paper 8498.

Hardymon, G., M. DeNino and S. Malcolm (1983). 'When Corporate Venture Capital Doesn't Work'. *Harvard Business Review*, 61: 114–120.

Hill, S. A., J. M. Birkinshaw and G. Murray (2004). 'Corporate venture unit structure and performance: Adoption of venture capital models to the corporate context'. Working Paper. London: London Business School.

Hoetker, G. and R. Agarwal (2004). 'Death hurts, but it isn't fatal: The post-exit diffusion of knowledge created by innovative companies'. UIUC Working Paper.

Jeng, L. A. and P. Wells (2000). 'The Determinants of Venture Capital Funding: Evidence across Countries'. *Journal of Corporate Finance*, 6: 241–89.

Kann, A. (2000). Strategic venture capital investing by corporations: A framework for structuring and valuing corporate venture capital programs. (Unpublished Dissertation). Stanford University.

Keil, T. (2002). *External Corporate Venturing: Strategic Renewal in Rapidly Changing Industries.* Quorum Books.

Kelly, M. J., J. L. Schaan and H. Joncas (2000). 'Collaboration between technology entrepreneurs and large corporations: Key design and management issues'. University of Ottawa Working Paper.

Klepper, S (2001). 'Employee Startups in High-Tech Industries'. *Industrial and Corporate Change*, 10(3): 639–74.

La Porta, R., F. López- de-Silanes, A. Shleifer and R. Vishny (1998). 'Law and Finance'. *Journal of Political Economy*, 106(6): 1113–56.

Maula, M. V. J (2001). 'Corporate Venture Capital and the Value-added for Technology-based New Firms.' Doctoral dissertation, Helsinki University of Technology.

—— and G. Murray (2001). 'Corporate Venture Capital and the Creation of US Public Companies', in Hitt, Amit, Lucier and Nixon (eds) *Creating value: Winners in the New Business Environment.* Oxford: Blackwell.

—— E. Autio and G. Murray (2005). 'Corporate Venture Capitalists and Independent Venture Capitalists: What Do They Know, Who Do They Know, and Should Entrepreneurs Care?' *Venture Capital: An International Journal of Entrepreneurial Finance*, 7(1): 3–19.

McGrath, R. (1999). 'Falling Forward: Real Options Reasoning and Entrepreneurial Failure'. *Academy of Management Review*, 24(1): 13–30.

McNally, K. (1997). *Corporate Venture Capital: Bridging the Equity Gap in the Small Business Sector.* London: Routledge.

Pisano, G. (1991). 'The Governance of Innovation: Vertical Integration and Collaborative Arrangements in the Biotechnology Industry'. *Research Policy*, 20: 237–49.

Prowse, D. S. (1998). 'The economics of the private equity market'. Federal Reserve Bank of Dallas , 3rd quarter.

Rind, K. W. (1981). 'The Role of Venture Capital in Corporate Development'. *Strategic Management Journal*, 2: 169–80.

Rosenstein, J., A. V. Bruno, W. D. Bygrave and H. T. Taylor (1993). 'The CEO, Venture Capitalists, and the Board'. *Journal of Business Venturing*, 8: 99–113.

Schildt, H. A., M. V. J. Maula and T. Keil (2004). 'Explorative and Exploitative Learning from External Corporate Ventures'. *Entrepreneurship Theory & Practice.* (SI on Entrepreneurial Learning) 29(4): 493–515.

Siegel, R., E. Siegel and I. MacMillan (1988). 'Corporate Venture Capitalists: Autonomy, Obstacles and Performance'. *Journal of Business Venturing*, 3: 233–47.

Sorenson, O. and T. E. Stuart (2001). 'Syndication Networks and the Spatial Distribution of Venture Capital Investments'. *American Journal of Sociology*, 6: 1546–88.

Stuart, T. E., H. Hoang and R. C. Hybels (1999). 'Interorganizational Endorsements and the Performance of Entrepreneurial Ventures'. *Administrative Science Quarterly*, 44: 315–49.

Sykes, H. (1986). 'The Anatomy of a Corporate Venturing Program'. *Journal of Business Venturing*, 1: 275–93.

—— (1990). 'Corporate Venture Capital: Strategies for Success'. *Journal of Business Venturing*, 5(1): 37–47.

—— (1992). 'Incentive Compensation for Corporate Venture Personnel'. *Journal of Business Venturing*, 7: 253–65.

Teece, D. J. (1986). 'Profiting from Technological Innovation: Implications for Integration, Collaboration, Licensing and Public Policy'. *Research Policy*, 15: 285–305.

Thornhill, S. and R. Amit (2001). 'A Dynamic Perspective of Internal Fit in Corporate Venturing'. *Journal of Business Venturing*, 16: 25–50.

Timmons, J. A (1994). *New Venture Creation*, 4th edn. Homewood, IL: Richard D. Irwin.

Winters and Murfin (1988). 'Venture Capital Investing for Corporate Development Objectives'. *Journal of Business Venturing*, 3: 207–22.

PART V

EMPLOYMENT, SELF-EMPLOYMENT AND BUY-OUTS

CHAPTER 16

ENTREPRENEURSHIP, SELF-EMPLOYMENT AND THE LABOUR MARKET[1]

SIMON C. PARKER

16.1 Introduction

This chapter surveys the entrepreneurship literature as it relates to the labour market. The purpose of this chapter is to describe, from a mainly but not exclusively economic perspective, the principal theoretical methods and empirical findings in the field.

It has been recognized at least since the time of Knight (1921) that entrepreneurs are engaged not only in product markets, but also in labour markets. As Knight pointed out:

> The labourer asks what he thinks the entrepreneur will be able to pay, and in any case will not accept less than he can get from some other entrepreneur, or by turning entrepreneur himself. In the same way the entrepreneur offers to any labourer what he thinks he must in order to secure his services. (Knight, 1921: 273)

[1] This research was funded by ESRC grant RES-000-22-0020. The author is grateful to an anonymous referee for helpful comments on the first draft, while absolving them of any responsibility for the contents.

This quotation identifies two ways that entrepreneurs engage in labour markets: via occupational choice (participation in entrepreneurship); and by hiring employees. These two topics will be discussed in sections 2 and 5 of this chapter respectively, which summarize insights and empirical findings from recent research in these areas.

Entrepreneurship intersects with labour markets in several other ways, too. For example, human capital theory can be used to help explain entrepreneurs' business performance; and labour supply models can be used to help understand their work effort patterns. Both topics attract policy interest, because policy-makers frequently express interest in promoting successful enterprises, and fostering an 'enterprise culture' in which hard work is encouraged and rewarded. The literatures on these topics are reviewed in sections 3 and 4 of the chapter, respectively.

Policy-makers also promote entrepreneurship because they believe it creates employment growth and reduces unemployment. By turning entrepreneur, an unemployed person not only removes him or herself from the official unemployment register, but might also remove others who would otherwise remain unemployed. I will discuss this issue in section 6.

Much of the empirical literature cited in this chapter derives from studies that apply to samples of entrepreneurs' models originally developed and tested for employees. Mostly, the literature in this area defines entrepreneurship as self-employment (Aronson, 1991; Parker, 2004). This definition follows fairly naturally from Knight's description of entrepreneurship quoted above. Also, this definition makes for great empirical convenience. For example, self-employment is a labour market categorization that is widely used and implemented in large-scale data sets (Katz, 1990). Moreover, the OECD and numerous statistical agencies regularly publish data on the share of self-employed in the workforce. I shall follow this practice and so will treat self-employment as a working definition of entrepreneurship in this chapter.

It is notable that published self-employment rates vary quite widely between different countries. In the OECD alone, non-agricultural self-employment rates range from about 6 percent in Sweden and the USA, to about 19 percent in Italy (Parker and Robson, 2004). There is an even greater dispersion of self-employment rates in developing countries (Acs et al., 1994; Parker, 2004: ch. 1.4). These findings point to systematic and pronounced differences in the labour market structures of different nations. To date, research has not identified robust sources of these cross-country variations. Acs et al (1994) emphasized macroeconomic factors, but subsequently Parker and Robson (2004) reported that the inclusion of taxes and benefits rendered macroeconomic variables insignificant, exerting strong negative effects and so implying that large government is bad for entrepreneurship.

Despite its convenience, one must nevertheless recognize that self-employment is not an uncontroversial measure of entrepreneurship. For example, some workers classified as self-employed with apparent autonomy over their work hours are effectively employees, being 'peripheral' workers subordinated to the demands of one client firm (Pollert, 1988; Harvey, 1995). Examples of workers in the 'grey area' between self-employment and paid employment include commission salespersons, freelancers, home-workers, tele-workers, workers contracted through employment agencies and franchisees (Felstead, 1992). Furthermore, some authors point out that many self-employed businesses are part-time and motivated by a hobby interest, so they are not truly 'entrepreneurial' (Reynolds, 1997). In fact, there is still a lack of general agreement over what precisely entrepreneurship is. Different authors tend to pick different definitions depending on their purpose, subject discipline, or ideology. This caveat should be borne in mind throughout the current chapter.

A second caveat is that space constraints necessarily limit the depth and breadth of my discussion. I am unable to cover several other related topics of academic and policy interest, including discrimination against entrepreneurs in the labour market, and geographical and social mobility of entrepreneurs. For treatments of these topics, see Moore (1983), Sowell (1981), and Mark Casson in Ch. 1 of this Handbook. Also, space constraints have led me to concentrate my own labour effort on two aspects of labour market issues in entrepreneurship about which we seem to know the least. I have done this in order to highlight and clarify the scope for further research on these issues: the labour supply and labour demand choices of entrepreneurs.

16.2 Self-employment as an Occupational Choice in the Labour Market

There are now many theories of entrepreneurship, whose contributions, limitations and interconnections have been exhaustively discussed in the entrepreneurship literature to date (see, for example Ch. 2 by Martin Ricketts in this Handbook). I will not recap this literature but will instead proceed directly from Knight's concept of entrepreneurship, quoted in the Introduction, as an occupational choice.

Economists have developed Knight's basic idea by utilising the framework of expected utility theory. The following gives a flavour of the approach. Let $U(.)$ be a utility function, whose argument is income, y. Income y equals the product of work hours and the hourly wage: $y = h.w$, where $h>0$, $w>0$. If the wage rate in self-employment is uncertain, depending in part on the (stochastic) state of nature θ, with distribution function $F(\theta)$, then the expected utility in self-employment is

$$E(U) = \int U[h.w(\theta)]dF(\theta) \tag{1}$$

Suppose the utility in paid employment (or unemployment) is V. Then an individual only becomes self-employed if $E(U)$ in (1) exceeds V. Otherwise, they select employee or unemployed status. This simple framework can be applied to explore which of a set of heterogeneous agents becomes self-employed. Suppose that x denotes some characteristic that increases utility in entrepreneurship, such that $E(U) = U(x)$, with $U'(x)>0$, where a prime denotes the first derivative. The distribution function of x is $G(x)$. An individual $\hat{x}$ is indifferent between the two occupations when $E[U(\hat{x})] = V$. Those with $x \geq \hat{x}$ [i.e. a total of $1-G(\hat{x})$ individuals] become entrepreneurs and the rest [a total of $G(\hat{x})$ individuals] become employees. This framework can be extended naturally to allow the payoff in paid employment to also vary with x, i.e. $V = V(x)$ (see Parker, 2003a).

This approach has been applied to enhance our understanding of several aspects of entrepreneurship. One strand of analysis has introduced non-pecuniary benefits into entrepreneurship to analyse the optimal income taxation of entrepreneurs (Boadway et al., 1991; Parker, 1999, 2001). The idea here is that entrepreneurship might provide workers with greater autonomy and independence than paid employment, with individuals who value these job prospects being the most likely to self-select into it (this might explain, for example, why the self-employed are observed to be happier on average than employees are: see Blanchflower and Oswald, 1998; Blanchflower, 2004; and Ajayi-obe and Parker, 2005). Another development introduces occupational switching costs to analyse dynamic occupational choices (Dixit and Rob, 1994; Parker, 1996, 1997). A third introduces heterogeneous risk aversion or ability in entrepreneurship (Lucas, 1978; Kihlstrom and Laffont, 1979); and a fourth analyzes occupational choice in the presence of borrowing constraints (Evans and Jovanovic, 1989; Parker, 2000). Theoretical results that have emerged from this research programme include:

- The least risk-averse and most managerially able individuals are most likely to be entrepreneurs and to run firms that are relatively large, in terms of the number of employees.
- Individuals trade off risks and returns when choosing to become entrepreneurs. Higher average returns, and/or lower income risk in entrepreneurship, increases the propensity for individuals to choose entrepreneurship instead of paid employment, all else equal.
- Uncertainty and switching costs can explain why some individuals wait before switching occupation, even when it would seem profitable to switch immediately. The greater the uncertainty in the economy as a whole, the more it pays to wait. This

can help explain the common empirical finding of relatively low switching rates (3 percent per annum or less) into self-employment (e.g. Evans and Leighton, 1989).

- Borrowing constraints might prevent individuals from reaching their optimal firm size. If individuals anticipate this possibility, it can act as a deterrent to becoming an entrepreneur in the first place.

The theoretical analysis that has been built around (1) has also been operationalized empirically. To see this, define the difference in utility payoff between self-employment and paid employment as

$$Z^* = E(U) - V. \tag{2}$$

If $E(U)$ and V are both linear functions of a vector of characteristics, X, one can write

$$Z^* = X'\beta + v, \tag{3}$$

where β is a vector of unknown reduced form parameters and v is a mean-zero disturbance term with distribution function Φ (.) and a unit variance.

While the researcher does not observe the Z_i^* value of an individual i, he or she does observe their actual occupational choice. This is either self-employment ($Z_i = 1$) or paid employment ($Z_i = 0$). It is natural to think of $Z_i = 1$ arising for individuals with $Z_i^* \geq 0$ and $Z_i = 0$ arising for individuals with $Z_i^* < 0$. Then

$$\Pr[Z_i = 1] = \Pr[Z_i^* \geq 0] = \Phi(X'\beta) \tag{4a}$$

If the researcher observes the employment status of an individual, Z_i, and specifies a set of explanatory variables X, then (4a) can be estimated using a non-linear logit or probit estimator. To date, scores of studies have followed this approach, and have estimated the factors associated with becoming or being self-employed (see Parker, 2004, for a recent overview). The most robust covariates of self-employment status, all with positive effects unless stated otherwise, are observed to be

- Age, with a ∩-shaped effect, with those in their mid- to late-30s most likely to be entering or engaged in self-employment
- Personal wealth
- Being married, especially to a working spouse
- Having a self-employed parent
- Previous labour market experience, especially in self-employment
- Education (especially years of schooling)

Most, though not all, studies in the empirical literature use cross-section data. Even though cross-section logit/probit estimation based on (4a) sometimes lacks predictive power (e.g. Reynolds, 1997), it still remains the most popular vehicle among applied researchers in the field. Predictive power can in any case usually be improved substantially if one uses panel data and controls for unobserved heterogeneity and state dependence (Henley, 2004). That involves replacing (4a) with

$$\Pr[Z_i = 1] = \Pr[Z_{i^*} \geq 0] = \Phi(X'_{it}\beta + \alpha_i + \rho Z_{it-1}) \tag{4b}$$

where t denotes time, α_i are individual fixed effects, and ρ is a parameter.

One interesting aspect of heterogeneity that relates to human capital is the diversity of individuals' skill sets. Lazear (2002, 2004) has proposed that entrepreneurs are 'jacks of all trades', so that individuals with balanced skill sets are the best placed to master the disparate and ever-changing demands of running a business. Wagner (2003) has found support for this theory using a large-scale representative sample of German adults. Wagner reported that self-employment rates were significantly higher for individuals with a large number of different post-school professional training experiences, and for those who had changed their profession frequently. Both variables serve as proxies for 'jack-of-all-trade' attributes.

Another, and perhaps more obvious, extension of (4a) is to include a relative pay differential between self-employment and paid employment. This differential measures the financial incentive to become self-employed. It is necessary to estimate the differential because individuals are typically only observed in one occupation at any one time. Details of how a model of this kind can be estimated appear in Rees and Shah (1986), Dolton and Makepeace (1990), Taylor (1996) and Parker (2003b). A sensitivity analysis in the last of these studies indicated that pecuniary factors do not robustly explain self-employment choices in practice, and therefore that the scope for income tax cuts to stimulate self-employment are likely to be limited. Instead, non-pecuniary factors and the personal characteristics listed above seem to play a greater role in explaining participation in self-employment.

Finally, multinomial logit (ML) is another useful empirical model of occupational choice, though it has not been much used in entrepreneurship. ML can used to explain behaviour when there are more than two occupations to choose from. For example, Earle and Sakova (2000) used this technique to explain participation in own-account self-employment relative to each of employer self-employment, paid employment, and unemployment.

16.3 Human Capital and Entrepreneurs' Performance

What are the financial rates of return to education and other dimensions of human capital? This question has received extensive treatment in the labour economics literature on employees. In contrast, entrepreneurs' rates of return have received much less attention. This is unfortunate, because the productivity of human capital in entrepreneurship might help inform government policy in several ways. For example, if rates of returns to schooling are relatively high in entrepreneurship, there might be a case for changing the balance of career advice to give greater weight to opportunities in entrepreneurship. That in turn might inform enterprise education programmes being devised for use in schools and universities. Below, I briefly review the available evidence on entrepreneurs' rates of return, before considering a different aspect of entrepreneurs' performance, namely survival.

16.3.1 Measuring performance as profit

A useful tool in the labour economist's toolbox is the 'earnings function', originally popularized by Mincer (1974). An earnings function explains the natural logarithm of an individual's wage, ln *w*, in terms of their number of years of schooling, *s*, experience *t* and its square, and other control variables, *X*:

$$\ln w_i = \beta_0 + \beta_1 s_i + \beta_2 t_i + \beta_3 t_i 2 + X_i' \gamma + u_i \qquad (5)$$

Of particular interest in (5) is β_1, which measures the rate of return to an extra year of education. It is interesting to ask whether the magnitudes of estimated rates of return received by entrepreneurs are comparable with those estimated for employees.

The answer on the whole tends to be negative. According to Van der Sluis et al.'s (2003) review of 21 international studies, entrepreneurs receive lower rates of return from education than employees do. These rates average around 6.1 percent in the US and less than 6 percent in Europe. That compares with an average rate of return of 6.6 percent for employees (Ashenfelter et al., 1999).

What explains this result? One possibility is that entrepreneurial success depends on numerous factors other than formal education, implying a lower β_1 for entrepreneurs than for employees. In fact, formal education might even inculcate attitudes that are antithetical to entrepreneurship (Casson, 2003). Another possibility is that part of employees' rate of return to education includes the value to employers of education as a screening device. Entrepreneurs are their own bosses and so do not receive this benefit (Wolpin, 1977). In fact, this second argument is contentious, because individuals do not always know they will become entrepreneurs when they are at school and so might acquire education as a hedge. Also, in some cases, customers and credit providers screen entrepreneurs where education generally signals positive attributes.

In fact, previous estimates of entrepreneurs' rates of return to education should be treated with some caution. There are four principal reasons for this. First, there is no single unambiguous measure of the self-employed 'wage'. The most common empirical approach measures it as business profit divided by work hours;

but reported profits are often subject to under-reporting biases in survey data (Pissarides and Weber, 1989). Secondly, estimates of the parameters in (5) might be susceptible to selection bias, if the self-employed have unmeasured characteristics that systematically affect both occupational choice and performance. Thirdly, schooling is not homogeneous. Presumably, higher quality schooling generates higher rates of return (Henley, 2004). Fourthly, education in (5) might actually be an endogenous variable, leading to biased estimation of β_1.

The first three of these problems have been variously addressed in the literature to date (see Parker, 2004: ch. 1.5). The last of them, however, has been relatively neglected. An exception is the recent article by Parker and Van Praag (2004) which proposed an Instrumental Variables (IV) estimator that replaces s_i in (5) with predicted educational outcomes that are conditioned on exogenous determinants. In contrast to OLS, IV produces consistent estimates of the parameters in the presence of endogeneity. Parker and Van Praag reported a substantially higher rate of return under IV than under OLS: 12.7 percent, compared with 6.9 percent, respectively. Taking a similar approach based on American PSID data, Van der Sluis et al. (2004) reported comparable findings, with the additional insight that entrepreneurs receive a higher rate of return to education than employees do. These results suggest that entrepreneurship might offer a very productive outlet for educational skills after all.

Of course, education is not the only form of human capital. Other forms that might also enhance performance in entrepreneurship include age and experience. For example, experience gained in entrepreneurship or elsewhere might increase productivity by enabling the entrepreneur to better exploit scarce resources and to innovate new productive resource combinations. On the other hand, as entrepreneurs age, their ability to compete with their younger counterparts might diminish, perhaps through greater physical frailty or an unwillingness to work as hard as they used to. Also, self-employed earnings–age profiles might be flatter than those of employees because the self-employed often acquire less on-the-job training than employees do (Kawaguchi, 2003), and they are not confronted with steep age–earnings profiles used by employers to elicit greater work effort (Lazear and Moore, 1984).

These last arguments suggest that the earnings–age relationship will be weaker for self-employed workers than for employees. The evidence broadly bears this prediction out (Parker, 2004). In many empirical investigations, estimates of β_2 and β_3 in (5) are insignificantly different from zero. In fact, it is sometimes quite difficult to explain entrepreneurs' wages in terms of experience or person-specific control variables. Experience for entrepreneurs can be measured in many different ways, for example in terms of the number of years previously self-employed, or in terms of the total number of years in the labour market. It should be remembered however that self-employment experience is often hard to measure, especially if it is punctuated by periods of unemployment and paid employment. And experience in paid employment might not be as helpful for subsequent spells in self-employment as previous spells in self-employment (Evans and Leighton, 1989; Quadrini, 1999; Lin et al., 2000). Some researchers have addressed this issue by focusing on experience in the same industry, or from helping in a parent's business. The latter is often a very important determinant of business ownership as well as performance therein (Lentz and Laband, 1990).

16.3.2 Measuring performance as business survival

The distinction between the different dimensions of human capital seems to be especially important when trying to explain entrepreneurs' performance in terms of business survival. A common approach used to explain business survival defines the dependent variable as a binary variable, taking the value 1 if entrepreneur *i*'s business has survived until the present date, and 0 if not. Using a probit or logit estimator, significant covariates of survival can then be identified. Another common approach estimates business survival using a hazard function. For both approaches, the corpus of empirical results broadly tells the following story:

- Greater experience is associated with significantly greater probabilities of venture survival (Holmes and Schmitz, 1996; Quadrini, 1999; Taylor, 1999).
- Survival rates are higher for middle-aged than for younger or older entrepreneurs (Bates, 1990; Holtz-Eakin et al., 1994).
- Formal education qualifications have mixed effects on business survival rates (Quadrini, 1999; and Kangasharju and Pekkala, 2002).
- Smaller and newer ventures have significantly higher probabilities of failure (Storey, 1994; Audretsch and Mahmood, 1995).
- Ventures with greater access to capital have higher survival rates (Bates, 1997; Taylor, 1999).

The survival prospects of entrepreneurs' ventures are also affected by the state of the labour market. Evidence suggests that businesses and individuals that start up in conditions of high unemployment have worse survival prospects than firms that start up in more favourable economic circumstances (Audretsch and Mahmood, 1995; Taylor, 1999). Also, individuals who were unemployed prior to entering self-employment appear to have substantially and significantly higher failure rates than those who previously worked in paid employment (Carrasco, 1999; Pfeiffer and Reize, 2000). The previously unemployed are more likely to have rusty human capital, lower quality information about business opportunities, and possibly also lower motivation.

I have discussed above two measures of entrepreneurs' performance, namely income and continuation in entrepreneurship. These do not exhaust the number of ways that one might measure performance. Another is the size of entrepreneurs' ventures, for example the number of employees that entrepreneurs hire. This topic is treated in section 5.

16.4 Labour supply and retirement of the self-employed

Labour economists have long been familiar with the difficulties involved in measuring work effort. Ideally, the quality of effort should be distinguished from the quantity of effort. The latter is often proxied by work hours. Because reliable data on work quality is hard to come by, most researchers content themselves with analysing work hours, which I will simply call 'labour supply' hereafter.

A distinction that is sometimes made in the labour supply analysis of employees, especially of females, is between participation in some kind of work, and work hours conditional on participation. In the context of the self-employed, the valid distinction is between participation in self-employment (rather than paid employment or unemployment) and the number of work hours conditional on being self-employed. The participation issue has already been discussed, in section 2. I now discuss work hours themselves.

The stylized facts are stark. Compared with employees, the self-employed work relatively long average hours for relatively low average hourly wages. This outcome—which has been observed in both the US and the UK—appears to be robust to whether or not annual or weekly hours are used in the comparisons (Aronson, 1991; Hamilton, 2000; Ajayi-obe and Parker, 2005; Carrington et al., 1996) provides historical confirmation of this phenomenon, which appears to be more pronounced for full-time than for part-time workers.

Previous analyses of self-employed work effort fall into two broad categories. One strand of research describes how entrepreneurs allocate their time between various tasks involved in running a venture (see e.g. McCarthy et al., 1990; and Cooper et al., 1997). The other applies the tools of labour economics to explain the chosen quantity of work hours. Section 16.4.1 below reviews studies of this kind.

In section 16.4.2, I briefly consider aspects of the retirement of entrepreneurs. Governments are increasingly concerned about growing public pension commitments, as their populations age and enjoy extended longevity. At the same time, governments often seek to promote entrepreneurship. The intersection of these two agendas emerges in the forum of 'Third Age Entrepreneurship', namely, entrepreneurship among the over-50s (Curran and Blackburn, 2001).

16.4.1 Explaining the labour supply of the self-employed

Early contributions to the empirical labour supply literature estimated 'static' work-hours equations, of the form

$$\ln h_i = \varsigma_0 + \varsigma_1 \ln w_i + X_i' \gamma + u_i \tag{6}$$

where h is work hours and w and X are as before, except that X now usually includes some measure of investment income. This is called a 'static' equation because it is derived from an underlying model of constrained static optimization, in which workers consider the implications of their labour decisions only within the current time period.

In the last 25 years, more sophisticated 'dynamic' models of workers' labour supply have been developed. These models recognize that labour supply decisions affect workers' prosperity—and thereby their future utility-generating opportunities—as well as their current utility. Life-cycle models of this kind have been widely estimated for employees, but not for entrepreneurs. Virtually all estimated labour supply specifications for entrepreneurs are static ones as in (6), that have utilized samples of self-employed workers. The main studies of this type include Wales (1973), Camerer et al. (1997) and Thornton (1998) for the US; and Rees and Shah (1994) and Ajayi-obe and Parker (2005) for the UK. These studies have generally found that the coefficient ς_1 in (6) is numerically small, and is sometimes negative. This means that if the work hours of the self-employed respond to changes in the wage rate at all, fewer hours will be worked in response to a higher wage.

This kind of wage response can be understood in terms of income and substitution effects. The substitution effect describes how individuals substitute work for leisure hours when the returns to work increase, holding their current income constant. It implies a positive relationship between hours and wages. In contrast, the income effect describes how individuals respond to becoming better-off from a wage increase: if leisure is a normal good, they will consume more leisure and work fewer hours. The income effect implies a negative relationship between hours and wages. Workers' total response is the sum of income and substitution effects, which being the sum of positive and negative components is ambiguously signed in general. Negative values of ς_1 suggest that the income effect dominates, while zero values implies that they cancel each other out.

Wage changes can be induced in several economically interesting ways, including changes in general productivity-related market remuneration and changes in income taxation. From a policy perspective, the above findings regarding ς_1 appear to offer little empirical support for the notion that the work effort of entrepreneurs can be stimulated by income tax cuts.

An instructive investigation by Camerer *et al.* (1997) studied the work hours of New York taxicab drivers. Their estimates of ς_1 averaged around -1 and were generally significantly different from zero. Camerer et al. proposed a different interpretation of their results than one based on a dominant income effect, suggesting instead that cab drivers cease driving when they hit some person-specific target income—which occurs sooner on 'high-wage' days. Cab drivers appear to ignore the intertemporal substitution possibilities of working harder when demand is high, and taking more leisure when wages are low. It is as if they 'take one day at a time'.

I have already alluded to problems of measuring the self-employed 'wage'. Camerer *et al.* (1997) measured the wage as revenue divided by hours, and used IV to estimate (6). They used as instruments summary statistics from the distribution of hourly wages of other workers who drove on the same day and shift. In contrast, Ajayi-obe and Parker (2005) used as instruments for the wage age and its square, education qualifications, and the length of current employment spell. Using British Household Panel Survey (BHPS) data on working-age males, Ajayi-obe and Parker also reported significant negative values of ς_1, of -0.0363 for the self-employed, compared with -0.0586 for employees. However, these estimated elasticities are too small to explain the size of the wage and hours gap between the occupations (which are around 7 percent in both cases). According to these estimates, increasing the self-employed wage (or decreasing the employee wage) by 7 percent to gain parity with the average employee wage would only decrease self-employed work hours (or increase employee work hours) by 0.12 hours (0.18 hours) on average, compared with the observed average difference of 2.95 hours per week.

While larger effects can be obtained using Camerer et al.'s estimated work hours elasticity of -1, this estimate is very large in absolute value and has not been corroborated by any other estimates to this author's knowledge. It seems plausible that some other explanation is needed to explain why the self-employed work longer hours on average for lower average wages. One possibility is that the self-employed face greater risk than employees do, and so increase their work hours to self-insure against that risk. Indeed, if random shocks impact additively on income, that is to say, if

$$E(U) = \int U[(h.w) + \theta]dF(\theta), \tag{7}$$

then this kind of response is optimal (Parker et al., 2005). However, theoretical results become ambiguous if, as in (1), shocks affect incomes multiplicatively. Parker et al. (2005) find some evidence using American PSID data that American male self-employed workers significantly and substantially increase their work hours in response to increases in the variance of their past wages—a direct measure of income risk. This effect was found to render the previously significant work hours–wage elasticity insignificant, implying that risk is the main reason for relatively long self-employed work hours.

16.4.2 Retirement

A disproportionately high fraction of active workers over 65 is self-employed. The figure is around 30 percent in the US, compared with less than 10 percent of all individuals under 65 and of working age (Iams, 1987; Bruce et al., 2000). Partial retirement and bridge jobs can account for part of this phenomenon, but not it seems all of it. According to Iams (1987), most self-employed Americans over 65 have been self-employed for many years rather than having recently switched into it from paid employment.

The body of theory that attempts to explain retirement by entrepreneurs is patchy. Singh and DeNoble (2003) discuss possible scenarios in which early retirees from any job either remain retired or return to the workforce, possibly in self-employment. Formal life-cycle modelling by Parker and Rougier (2004) identified income and substitution effects similar to those that impact on hours of work decisions. Using British data, Parker and Rougier found that the self-employed who faced substantial current earnings opportunities were significantly less likely to retire, all else equal. Strikingly, neither lifetime wealth, gender, nor ill health, were significant determinants of retirement by the self-employed.

Parker and Rougier also found some evidence that self-employment was being used as a bridge job as workers approached retirement, though this interpretation is open to challenge. Many of the employees who switched into self-employment in later life were more notable for low incomes and multiple previous job spells than for signs of purposeful life and career progression via a final period of self-employment. This suggests that self-employment might be used as an occupation of last resort by marginal and impoverished employees.

Evidently, more research is needed into the factors that induce retiring employees to switch into self-employment, with particular reference to the obstacles faced by older individuals for starting up enterprises. That would better inform policy-makers interested in promoting 'Third Age' entrepreneurship.

16.5 Labour demand and employment creation

Despite the attention given by policy-makers to the employment-creation potential of entrepreneurship, only limited evidence supports the notion that entrepreneurs create many jobs. In the US, Canada and the UK, only a minority of self-employed individuals employs any other workers. The proportion of the self-employed doing so is about 20–30 percent in these countries, a rate which seems if anything to have declined in the 1990s (see Carroll et al., 2000; Kuhn and Schuetze, 2001; and Moralee, 1998, respectively). A higher proportion of self-employed people employ others in some of the countries of continental Europe, being 46 percent in Denmark and 51 percent in Germany, for example (Cowling, 2003).

Transition rates from own account self-employment or paid employment into employer status also tend to be low. Both Carroll et al. (2000) for the US and Cowling et al. (2004) for the UK observed that only about 7–8 percent of self-employed sole traders hire any other workers over a 3–4 year period.

The theoretical literature on labour demand by entrepreneurs is sparse. To the best of my knowledge, only Jefferson (1997) and Carroll et al. (2000) have analyzed the labour demand choices of entrepreneurs in a theoretical framework. Jefferson proposed a rather unusual credit-rationing model in which individuals become entrepreneurs if they are non-rationed, and would like to lend to, and work for entrepreneurs if they are not entrepreneurs. But rationed individuals lack wealth so they cannot lend, and so are unable to verify the values of projects run by entrepreneurs. Because entrepreneurs can always claim to have poor projects, they will optimally offer a zero return to those agents. Consequently, rationed individuals will choose to become unemployed rather than work for them.

While this model claims to explain why only a small minority of the self-employed hire outside labour, its results do appear to be very model-specific. A richer specification of the production set and labour market than was analyzed by Jefferson is probably needed to fully understand the phenomenon of labour demand by entrepreneurs. Carroll et al. (2000) attempted this, although these authors were primarily concerned with analysing the effects of income tax reforms on entrepreneurs' hiring decisions. Carroll et al. distinguished between two margins: an entrepreneur becoming an employer, and the number of workers hired conditional on the entrepreneur being an employer. Let c_h and c_n denote consumption and e_h and e_n denote effort, where the h and n subscripts denote 'hiring' and 'non-hiring' status of an entrepreneur, respectively. Also, let $\pi(w,e_h)$ denotes the indirect profit function of employers, where w is the wage paid to employees. And let $B\dot{e}_n$ denote the profits from sole proprietors, where $B > 0$ is a constant. With a marginal tax rate of τ, consumption possibilities for both types of entrepreneur are

$$c_h = (1 - \tau)\pi(w,e_h) \text{ and } c_n = (1 - \tau)^b e_n$$

respectively. Letting l denote the number of hired workers, the indirect profit function π^* is obtained by solving the first order condition $\partial F/\partial l - w = 0$ from the profit function $\pi = F(e,l) - wL$ to get the labour demand function $l^* = l(e,w)$, which is put back into π to obtain $\pi^* = \pi(w,e)$.

If the utility function is separable in consumption and leisure, one can write

$$V_h = u(c_h) - v(e_h) - \mu \text{ and } V_n = u(c_n) - v(e_n)$$

where $\mu > 0$ is a fixed cost of hiring workers. Then using the envelope theorem, it follows directly that

$$\frac{\partial(V_h - V_n)}{\partial(1-\tau)} = u'(C_h)\pi(w,e_h) - u'(C_n)e_nB \tag{8}$$

Equation (8) can be expanded in a Taylor series around e_n to obtain

$$\frac{\partial(V_h - V_n)}{\partial(1-\tau)} = u'(C_n)[\pi(w,e_n) - e_nB] + u'(c_n)(1+\varepsilon)[\mathrm{e_h} - e_n]\frac{\partial F[e,l(e)]}{\partial e}\Big|_{e=e_n} \tag{9}$$

where ε is the elasticity of the marginal utility of consumption. The first term on the RHS of (9) is the utility of additional net income of being an employer relative to a sole trader, holding effort constant over the two modes. The second term captures the fact that because effort is generally different in the two modes there are effects on consumption and its marginal utility.

To sign (9), assume that effort is more productive in the employer mode than in the sole trader mode. Then $\pi(w,e_h) - e_nB > 0$ and also $e_h - e_n > 0$. So it follows directly that if $\varepsilon > -1$, then (9) is positive. So cutting income taxes would increase the propensity of entrepreneurs to hire labour.

This is precisely what Carroll et al. found empirically using US IRS data from 1985 and 1988, which span the 'tax cutting' Tax Reform Act (TRA) of 1986. Using data on sole-trader and employer entrepreneurs, Carroll et al. estimated the probit equation

$$\Pr[l_{88} > 0] = \Phi(\xi_0 + \xi_1\Delta\ln(1-\tau) + \xi_2[\mathrm{L}_{85}\Delta\ln(1-\tau)] + \xi_3\mathrm{L}_{85} + X'\delta). \tag{10}$$

The dependent variable in (10) is the probability that a given entrepreneur is an employer in 1988; $\Delta\ln(1-\tau) \equiv \ln(1-\tau_{88}) - \ln(1-\tau_{85})$ is the change in the log marginal tax rate resulting from the 1986 TRA; and l_{85} is a dummy variable taking the value one if the entrepreneur employed labour in 1985 and zero otherwise. The interaction term allows the response to changes in taxes to vary by employer status. Carroll et al.'s estimates of $\xi 1$ and $\xi 2$ suggested that decreasing an entrepreneur's marginal income tax rate by 10 percent increases the mean probability of hiring by about 12 percent. The implied elasticity of 1.2 suggests that general income tax reductions might be a powerful way of stimulating employment creation—in marked contrast to its apparent limited effects on stimulating participation in self-employment (section 2) or work hours by the self-employed (section 4).

An alternative theoretical approach to Carroll et al.'s might estimate a labour demand function $l^* = l(e,w)$ directly. That can be done if one utilizes some simple functional forms for the production and utility functions (Hamermesh, 1993). For example, Van Praag and Cramer (2001) and Cowling et al. (2004) both assumed a Cobb-Douglas production function of the form

$$F(K,l) = \delta \dot{K}^{\alpha}(1+1)^{\beta} \quad \alpha,\beta > 0 \tag{11}$$

where $\delta > 0$ is a measure of human capital (see Section 3). Cowling *et al* (2004) argued that 'job creators', that is, those self-employed for whom $l^* > 0$, will have greater human capital δ on average than self-employed sole traders for whom $l^* = 0$. This will hold if entrepreneurial employers are small relative to established firms in the labour market, and even as a group cannot move the wage themselves. However, it does not follow for the market as a whole, as can be seen by minimizing the cost function subject to (11), deriving the labour demand function using Shepherd's Lemma, and differentiating to obtain

$$\frac{\partial(1+1^*)}{\partial\delta} = -\left(\frac{\alpha+\alpha\beta}{\alpha+\beta}\right)\frac{1\dot{+}1^*}{\delta} < 0 \tag{12}$$

This shows that if entrepreneurs as a group can move the wage, then the demand for labour must be a decreasing function of human capital (and if, as Cowling et al. assume, human capital affects Cobb-Douglas output multiplicatively), for all self-employed. This is also true of job creators relative to sole traders, as can be seen by evaluating (12) at $l^* = 0$. The reason is that the entrepreneur's greater human capital increases the marginal productivity of hired labour, and hence its wage, so reducing labour demand.

I conclude my theoretical treatment by noting that future research should utilize more flexible production functions than the Cobb-Douglas. The latter is restrictive, forcing the elasticity of substitution between capital and labour to be unity. Also, (11) assumes an infinite elasticity of substitution between own labour supply and outside labour, since the total labour input is $1 + l$. These assumptions are very strong. In addition, future research should seek to explain the number of employees hired by job creators, and in the process try to measure capital inputs properly.

The empirical research that exists on labour demand by entrepreneurs is also rather limited. Van Praag and Cramer (2001) found that Dutch self-employees with higher levels of education, who are male, and with a father who was self-employed or a manager were the most likely to hire employees. Similar findings were reported by Cowling et al. (2004), who used British BHPS data from 1995. Cowling et al. found that job creators were predominantly wealthy, older, indigenous males, who were likely to hold vocational qualifications but extremely unlikely to hold higher degrees of any type. Formal academic achievements actually played little role in predicting who becomes a job creator. The deep reasons why so few self-employed people become employers remain unclear, though the fact that sole traders are more likely to become employers than wage employees or unemployed workers might point to the importance of general experience in running a business (Cowling et al., 2004).

There is a much larger empirical literature on job creation by small firms. This literature was sparked by the Birch Report in 1979. To the extent that small firm ownership can be equated with entrepreneurship, this literature would also seem pertinent to the theme of the chapter.

Birch (1979) claimed that between 1969 and 1976, small firms employing fewer than 20 workers generated 66 percent of all new US jobs, while firms with less than 100 employees accounted for 82 percent of net job gains. The implication of this research was that the small firm sector is the primary engine of job creation. Despite claims by Davis et al. (1996) that 'conventional wisdom about the job-creating powers of small businesses rests on statistical fallacies and misleading interpretations of the data' (p. 57), subsequent researchers for example, the Small Business Administration, have confirmed these findings for the US and other countries (SBA, 2001). The OECD (1998) claimed that there is now 'general agreement' that the share of jobs accounted for by small firms has steadily increased since the early 1970s in most developed economies. This is borne out by Acs and Audretsch (1993), who highlighted a distinct and continuous shift away from employment in large firms and towards small enterprises in the 1980s in every major western economy.

However, there is some evidence that the jobs created by new start-ups are of lower average quality than those created by larger firms. Small firms tend to employ more part-time workers, freelancers, and home-workers. Furthermore, their employees tend to be less well educated on average, receiving lower wages, fewer fringe benefits, lower levels of training, and working longer hours with a greater risk of major injury (Storey, 1994)—while enjoying lower job tenure than their counterparts in larger firms (Brown et al., 1990). Brown et al. (1990) in particular reported a substantial 'size-wage' premium, with workers in large companies earning over 30 percent more on average than their counterparts in small firms. This finding appears to hold across industries and countries too. Another consideration that should be borne in mind is that new and small enterprises have much higher failure rates than their older and larger counterparts.

To conclude, the evidence suggests that while small firms might be an important engine of employment growth, relatively few self-employed people hire outside workers, and the majority of created jobs are concentrated in a few exceptionally dynamic, fast-growing firms. Storey (1994) calls these the 'ten percenters', reflecting their minority status in the constellation of small firms; they are also called 'gazelles'. Relatively little research has been conducted on these particular firms either, which seems like another area that is ripe for further research.

16.6 Unemployment and Entrepreneurship

Previous researchers have suggested that unemployment affects the self-employment rate in two ways: via 'recession-push' and 'prosperity-pull' effects. According to the 'recession-push' hypothesis, unemployment reduces the opportunities of gaining paid employment and the expected gains from job search, which 'pushes' people into self-employment. This suggests a positive relationship between the unemployment rate and the self-employment rate. According to the 'prosperity-pull' hypothesis, at times of high unemployment the products and services of the self-employed face a lower market demand. This reduces self-employment incomes and possibly also the availability of capital, while increasing the risk of bankruptcy. Thus individuals are 'pulled' out of self-employment. At the same time, self-employment may become riskier because if the venture fails, it is less likely that the self-employed worker can fall back on a job in paid employment. This suggests a negative relationship between unemployment and the self-employment rate.

Empirical estimates of the self-employment–unemployment relationship invariably confound the above two effects, capturing a 'net' effect. Nevertheless, the size and direction of the net effect is still of policy interest. There are two broad approaches to measuring the relationship. At the disaggregated level, cross-section studies estimate the propensity of self-employed individuals to be located in areas with high unemployment rates (e.g. Moore and Mueller, 2002), while at the aggregated level, cross-sections of aggregate self-employment and unemployment rates across countries are compared (e.g. Blanchflower, 2000). In both cases, regional variations identify the parameters of interest. Time-series studies are all based at the aggregate level and regress aggregate self-employment rates on aggregate unemployment rates (e.g. Parker, 1996). Here temporal variation is used to identify the parameters of interest.

There are now numerous empirical studies that estimate the relationship between the unemployment rate and the self-employment rate. Rather than review them all here, I will simply summarize the key results that emerge from the literature.

- Econometric estimates generate conflicting estimates of the sign of the relationship, with cross-section studies more likely to find a negative relationship, and time-series studies more likely to find a positive relationship (Parker, 2004: ch. 3.3).
- Most entrants to self-employment switch from paid employment rather than from unemployment (Evans and Leighton, 1989; Kuhn and Schuetze, 2001). This mainly reflects the greater number of employees to unemployed people in the

workforce. A higher proportion of unemployed individuals to employees switch into self-employment at any time.

- From year to year only a small proportion of unemployed people become self-employed (Reynolds, 1997; Cowling and Taylor, 2001), with individuals who lost their jobs in the previous three years actually being less likely than average to enter self-employment subsequently (Cowling and Mitchell, 1997; Farber, 1999).
- Individuals with more unstable work histories, including those with prior spells of unemployment, are significantly more likely to be found in self-employment (Evans and Leighton, 1989; Uusitalo, 2001).

The overall conclusion is that there is no unambiguous empirical relationship between self-employment and unemployment rates. That need not be surprising if one bears in mind that for many people unemployment is a temporary phenomenon. Losing one's job is not a pre-condition for starting a venture, as the evidence cited above makes clear. This is not to deny the possibility that programmes designed to attract the unemployed into self-employment might be valuable and successful. But in the light of the findings discussed in section 3 regarding the performance of new ventures, one wonders about the viability and longevity of many of the start-ups initiated by the formerly unemployed. Indeed, evidence from evaluation studies of unemployment to self-employment schemes largely bear out this scepticism. I now turn to this evidence.

Governments in several countries have set up schemes to encourage the unemployed to become self-employed. The largest schemes have been implemented in the UK, France, Spain, Germany and Denmark; and 10 states in the US now have self-employment assistance programmes (Bruce and Schuetze, 2004). Details about the non-US schemes and their operation can be found in Meager (1994). For example, in the UK, the Enterprise Allowance Scheme (EAS) was established in 1982, offering income support of £40 per week to unemployed people with £1000 to invest in a new business for up to the whole of the first year in self-employment. The idea was to partially compensate individuals for the loss of state benefits entailed by becoming self-employed. Individuals were offered advice on running a small business, but were not screened for eligibility to join the scheme. At its peak in 1987/88, 106,000 people were on the EAS, with take-up rates declining continuously thereafter before the scheme was transferred to the Training & Enterprise Councils in 1991–92. Subsequently, start-up support to unemployed people in the UK has become fragmented, with a range of programmes and delivery agencies motivated by different objectives (Metcalf and Benson, 2000).

Most evaluations of unemployment to self-employment schemes suggest that they generate modest net benefits. For example, according to Bendick and Egan (1987), 50 percent of UK EAS-sponsored businesses would have started anyway. Fifty percent of those that did start displaced other businesses; about 50 percent of the assisted firms survived for less than three years; and those that did survive created a fraction of one job in addition to the job of the proprietor. Storey (1994), taking account of deadweight costs, displacement effects and the cost of administering the scheme relative to the benefits generated by the new start-ups, estimated that after taking account of the fact that the government would have paid unemployment benefits anyway, the EAS was at least cost-effective. Its effects on job creation and unemployment reduction were slight, with all non-proprietor jobs created by 20 percent of surviving firms (Bendick and Egan, 1987). More than 60 percent of the jobs created in surviving firms after three years under the EAS were in 4 percent of the businesses originally created (Storey, 1994).

Finally, I briefly consider the effects on entrepreneurs of a different policy that is often credited with causing unemployment: employment protection legislation (EPL). At any one time, there is usually a variety of EPL policies in place, that variously restrict employers' freedom to hire, fire, and set working conditions and other terms of employment. Applied researchers find it convenient to devise aggregate national measures of EPL that combine diverse manifestations of it into a single index. Several such measures of EPL are now publicly available, which enable researchers to test whether countries with relatively high levels of EPL have significantly higher self-employment rates than the average. A positive relationship of this sort might be expected if, for example, employers seek to circumvent EPL by contracting out work to self-employed contractors. Robson (2003) tested this possibility by regressing self-employment rates from 13 OECD countries on various measures of EPL and a set of control variables. Robson failed to detect a robust significant relationship between self-employment rates and EPL indexes. This contrasts with previous studies that have used simplistic bivariate correlations to assert a relationship between them. It also provides a salutary reminder of the importance of using appropriate econometric methodologies to test hypotheses of this sort.

16.7 Conclusion

Entrepreneurs interact with the labour market in several ways. They make occupational choices in the labour market, put their human capital to work in order to generate profits, and supply their labour while possibly also hiring employees in the process. At the more aggregate level, the activities of entrepreneurs help determine wages as well as prices; and their combined effects impinge on the unemployment rate and possibly also the growth rate of economies (Carree and Thurik, 2003).

Although research in this area is increasing, several serious gaps in our knowledge remain. More research is needed into several specific aspects of entrepreneurship and labour markets. One is the labour supply of entrepreneurs and the retirement behaviour of current and potential entrepreneurs, including the nature and extent of dynamic switches into and out of self-employment in later life. A second relates to labour demand by entrepreneurs, and the factors helping and hindering their ability to grow their ventures by increasing the number of employees. A third is the relationship between entrepreneurial performance, labour supply and labour demand—three factors that are obviously interrelated if one thinks in terms of a conventional production function.

In my view, the unemployment–self-employment nexus is not the best place to direct future research effort. This topic has now received extensive treatment by researchers, and it is not clear what further research could usefully add. Ongoing policy interest in devising ways of keeping unemployment rates low and promoting entrepreneurship is, however, likely to keep the topic near the top of policy-makers' agenda. This is not to deny that unemployment can be a route into self-employment, a possibility that many governments have naturally been eager to explore. But the scope for successful policy intervention in this regard appears to be limited, and diminishing marginal returns to government-backed programmes might well have set in—especially in low-unemployment economies like the UK (though for some contrary evidence from Germany, see Almus, 2004). Perhaps the best overall prospect is for governments to promote labour market flexibility more generally. That is probably a more reliable way of enhancing economic performance than targeting entry into self-employment specifically.

Finally, by focusing on the three topics alluded to above, researchers might try to redirect government attention to the quality rather than the quantity of new enterprises. There may after all be little point in encouraging entry into entrepreneurship if the ventures turn out to be of low quality and fail to survive. Perhaps it is time to redress the balance from promoting business entry in favour of business survival. A sound understanding of how entrepreneurship interfaces with labour markets is almost certainly a prerequisite for devising appropriate policies along these lines.

References

Acs, Z. J. and D. B. Audretsch (1993). *Small Firms and Entrepreneurship: An East–West Perspective.* Cambridge: Cambridge University Press.

—— —— and D. S. Evans (1994). 'Why does the self-employment rate vary across countries and over time?' Discussion Paper No. 871, London: CEPR.

Ajayi-obe, O. and S. C. Parker (2005). 'The Changing Nature of Work among the Self-employed in the 1990s: Evidence from Britain'. *Journal of Labor Research*, 26: 501–17.

Almus, M. (2004). 'Job Creation through Public Start-up Assistance?' *Applied Economics*, 36: 2015–24.

Aronson, R. L. (1991). *Self Employment: A Labour Market Perspective.* Ithaca, NY: ILR Press.

Ashenfelter, O., C. Harmon and H. Oosterbeck (1999). 'A Review of the Schooling/Earnings Relationship with Tests for Publication Bias'. *Labor Economics*, 6: 453–70.

Audretsch, D. B. and T. Mahmood (1995). 'New Firm Survival: New Results Using a Hazard Function'. *Review of Economics & Statistics*, 77: 97–103.

Bates, T. (1990). 'Entrepreneur Human Capital Inputs and Small Business Longevity'. *Review of Economics & Statistics*, 72: 551–59.

—— (1997). *Race, Self-employment and Upward Mobility: An Illusive American Dream.* Baltimore: Johns Hopkins University Press.

Bendick, M. and M. L. Egan (1987). 'Transfer Payment Diversion for Small Business Development: British and French Experience'. *Industrial & Labor Relations Review*, 40: 528–42.

Birch, D. L. (1979). *The Job Generation Process.* Cambridge, MA: MIT Programme on Neighbourhood and Regional Change.

Blanchflower, D. G. (2000). 'Self-employment in OECD Countries'. *Labor Economics*, 7: 471–505.

—— (2004). 'Self-employment: More May Not Be Better'. *Swedish Economic Policy Review*, 11: 15–74.

—— and A. Oswald (1998). 'What Makes an Entrepreneur?' *Journal of Labor Economics*, 16: 26–60.

Boadway, R., M. Marchand and P. Pestieau (1991). 'Optimal Linear Income Taxation in Models with Occupational Choice'. *Journal of Public Economics*, 46: 133–62.

Brown, C., J. Hamilton and J. Medoff (1990). *Employers Large and Small.* Cambridge, MA: Harvard University Press.

Bruce, D. and H. J. Schuetze (2004). 'The Labour Market Consequences of Experience in Self-employment'. *Labor Economics*, 11: 575–98.

—— D. Holtz-Eakin and J. Quinn (2000). 'Self-employment and labour market transitions at older ages'. Working Paper CRR WP 2000–13. Boston College, Boston, MA.

Camerer, C., L. Babcock, G. Loewenstein and R. Thaler (1997). 'Labour Supply of New York City Cabdrivers: One Day at a Time'. *Quarterly Journal of Economics*, 112: 407–41.

Carrasco, R. (1999). 'Transitions To and From Self-employment in Spain: An Empirical Analysis'. *Oxford Bulletin of Economics & Statistics*, 61: 315–41.

Carree, M. A. and A. R. Thurik (2003). *The impact of entrepreneurship on economic growth, in Handbook of Entrepreneurship Research: An Interdisciplinary Survey and Introduction* (eds. Z. J. Acs and D. B. Audretsch). Boston, MA: Kluwer.

Carrington, W. J., K. McCue and B. Pierce (1996). 'The Role of Employer/Employee Interactions in Labour Market Cycles: Evidence from the Self-employed'. *Journal of Labor Economics*, 14: 571–602.

Carroll, R., D. Holtz-Eakin, M. Rider and H. S. Rosen (2000). 'Income Taxes and Entrepreneurs' Use of Labour'. *Journal of Labor Economics*, 18: 324–51.

Casson, M. (2003). *The Entrepreneur: An Economic Theory*, 2nd edn. Cheltenham: Edward Elgar.

Cooper, A. C., M. Ramachandran and D. Schoorman (1997). 'Time Allocation Patterns of Craftsmen and Administrative Entrepreneurs: Implications for Financial Performance'. *Entrepreneurship Theory & Practice*, 22: 123–36.

Cowling, M. (2003). 'The contribution of the self-employed to employment in the EU'. Report to the Small Business Service, URN 03/539. Available at http://www.sbs.gov.uk/content/research/ContributionSelf-Emp.pdf

—— and P. Mitchell (1997). 'The Evolution of UK Self-employment: A Study of Government Policy and the Role of the Macroeconomy'. *Manchester School*, 65: 427–42.

—— and M. Taylor (2001). 'Entrepreneurial Women and Men: Two Different Species?' *Small Business Economics*, 16: 167–75.

—— P. Mitchell and M. Taylor (2004). 'Job Creators'. *Manchester School*, 62: 601–17.

Curran, J. and R. A. Blackburn (2001). 'Older People and the Enterprise Society: Age and self-employment propensities'. *Work Employment & Society*, 15: 889–902.

Davis, S. J., J. C. Haltiwanger and S. Schuh (1996). *Job Creation and Destruction.* Cambridge, MA: MIT Press.

Dixit, A. and R. Rob (1994). 'Switching Costs and Sectoral Adjustments in General Equilibrium with Uninsured Risk'. *Journal of Economic Theory*, 62: 48–69.

Dolton, P. J. and G. H. Makepeace (1990). 'Self-employment Among Graduates'. *Bulletin of Economic Research*, 42: 35–53.

Earle, J. S. and Z. Sakova (2000). 'Business Start-ups or Disguised Unemployment? Evidence on the Character of Self-employment from Transition Economies'. *Labor Economics*, 7: 575–601.

Evans, D. S. and B. Jovanovic (1989). 'An Estimated Model of Entrepreneurial Choice under Liquidity Constraints'. *Journal of Political Economy*, 97: 808–27.

—— and L. S. Leighton (1989). 'Some Empirical Aspects of Entrepreneurship'. *American Economic Review*, 79: 519–35.

Farber, H. S. (1999). 'Alternative and Part-time Employment Arrangements as a Response to Job Loss'. *Journal of Labor Economics*, 17: S142–S169.

Felstead, A. (1992). 'Franchising, self-employment and the "enterprise culture": A UK perspective', in P. Leighton and A. Felstead (eds) *The New Entrepreneurs: Self-employment and Small Business in Europe.* London: Kogan Page.

Hamermesh, D. S. (1993). *Labor Demand.* Princeton: Princeton University Press.

Hamilton, B. H. (2000). 'Does Entrepreneurship Pay? An Empirical Analysis of the Returns to Self-employment', *Journal of Political Economy*, 108: 604–31.

Harvey, M. (1995). *Towards the Insecurity Society: The tax trap of self-employment.* London: The Institute of Employment Rights.

Henley, A. (2004). 'Self-employment Status: The role of state dependence and initial circumstances'. *Small Business Economics*, 22: 67–82.

Holmes, T. J. and J. A. Schmitz (1996). 'Managerial Tenure, Business Age, and Small Business Turnover'. *Journal of Labor Economics*, 14: 79–99.

Holtz-Eakin, D., D. Joulfaian and H. S. Rosen (1994). 'Sticking It Out: Entrepreneurial Survival and Liquidity Constraints'. *Journal of Political Economy*, 102: 53–75.

Iams, H. M. (1987). 'Jobs of Persons Working after Receiving Retired Worker Benefits'. *Social Security Bulletin*, 50: 4–19.

Jefferson, P. N. (1997). 'Unemployment and Financial Constraints Faced by Small Firms'. *Economic Inquiry*, 35: 108–19.

Kangasharju, A. and S. Pekkala (2002). 'The Role of Education in Self-employment Success in Finland'. *Growth and Change*, 33: 216–37.

Katz, J. A. (1990). 'Longitudinal Analysis of Self-employment Follow-through', *Entrepreneurship & Regional Development*, 2: 15–25.

Kawaguchi, D. (2003). 'Human Capital Accumulation of Salaried and Self-employed Workers'. *Labor Economics*, 10: 55–71.

Kihlstrom, R. E. and J. J. Laffont (1979). 'A General Equilibrium Entrepreneurial Theory of Firm Formation Based on Risk Aversion'. *Journal of Political Economy*, 87: 719–49.

Knight, F. H. (1921). *Risk, Uncertainty and Profit.* New York: Houghton-Mifflin.

Kuhn, P. J. and H. J. Schuetze (2001). 'Self-employment Dynamics and Self-employment Trends: A Study of Canadian men and women, 1982–1998'. *Canadian Journal of Economics*, 34: 760–84.

Lazear, E. P. (2002). 'Entrepreneurship', Working Paper No. 9109. Cambridge, MA: NBER .

—— (2004). 'Balanced Skills and Entrepreneurship'. *American Economic Review Papers and Proceedings*, 94: 208–11.

—— and R. L. Moore (1984). 'Incentives, Productivity, and Labour Contracts'. *Quarterly Journal of Economics*, 99: 275–96.

Lentz, B. F. and D. N. Laband (1990). 'Entrepreneurial Success and Occupational Inheritance Among Proprietors'. *Canadian Journal of Economics*, 23: 563–79.

Lin, Z., G. Picot and J. Compton (2000). 'The Entry and Exit Dynamics of Self-employment in Canada'. *Small Business Economics*, 15: 105–25.

Lucas, R. E. (1978). 'On the Size Distribution of Business Firms'. *Bell Journal of Economics*, 9: 508–23.

McCarthy, A. M., D. A. Krueger and T. S. Schoenecker (1990). 'Changes in the Time Allocation Patterns of Entrepreneurs'. *Entrepreneurship Theory & Practice*, 15: 7–18.

Meager, N. (1994). 'Self-employment Schemes for the Unemployed in the European Community', in G. Schmid (ed.) *Labour Market Institutions in Europe.* New York: M. E. Sharpe.

Metcalf, H. and R. Benson (2000). 'From Unemployment to Self-employment: Developing an effective structure of micro-finance support'. *National Institute of Economic and Social Research.* Discussion Paper No. 170. London: NIESR.

Mincer, J. (1974). *Schooling, Education and Earnings.* Cambridge, MA: NBER.

Moore, R. L. (1983). 'Employer Discrimination: Evidence from self-employed workers'. *Review of Economics & Statistics*, 65: 496–501.

Moore, C. S. and R. E. Mueller (2002). 'The Transition from Paid to Self-employment in Canada: The importance of push factors'. *Applied Economics*, 34: 791–801.

Moralee, L. (1998). 'Self-employment in the 1990s'. *Labor Market Trends*, 106: 121–30.

OECD (1998). *Fostering Entrepreneurship.* Paris: OECD.

Parker, S. C. (1996). 'A Time Series Model of Self-employment under Uncertainty'. *Economica*, 63: 459–75.

—— (1997). 'The Effects of Risk on Self-employment'. *Small Business Economics*, 9: 515–22.

—— (1999). 'The Optimal Linear Taxation of Employment and Self-employment Incomes'. *Journal of Public Economics*, 73: 107–23.

—— (2000). 'Saving to Overcome Borrowing Constraints: Implications for small business entry and exit'. *Small Business Economics*, 15: 223–32.

—— (2001). 'Risk, Self-employment and Differential Taxation'. *Manchester School* 69: 1–15.

—— (2003a). 'Asymmetric Information, Occupational Choice and Government Policy'. *Economic Journal*, 113: 861–82.

—— (2003b). 'Does Tax Evasion Affect Occupational Choice?' *Oxford Bulletin of Economics & Statistics*, 65: 379–94.

PARKER, S. C. (2004). *The Economics of Self-employment and Entrepreneurship*. Cambridge: Cambridge University Press.

—— and M. T. ROBSON (2004). 'Explaining International Variations in Self-employment: Evidence from a panel of OECD countries'. *Southern Economic Journal*, 71: 287–301.

—— and J. ROUGIER (2004). 'Explaining the Retirement Behaviour of the Self-employed'. Paper presented to the European Society of Population Economics. Bergen, Norway.

—— and C. M. VAN PRAAG (2004). 'Schooling, Capital Constraints and Entrepreneurial Performance: The Endogenous Triangle'. Paper presented at the Babson-Kaufman Entrepreneurship Research Conference. University of Strathclyde, (June).

—— T. BARMBY and Y. BELGHITAR (2005). 'Income Uncertainty and the Labour Supply of Self-employed Workers'. *Economic Journal*, 115: C190–C207.

PFEIFFER, F. and F. REIZE (2000). 'Business Start-ups by the Unemployed: An conometric analysis based on firm data'. *Labor Economics*, 7: 629–63.

PISSARIDES, C. A. and G. WEBER (1989). 'An Expenditure-based Estimate of Britain's Black Economy'. *Journal of Public Economics*, 39: 17–32.

POLLERT, A. (1988). 'The "Flexible Firm": Fixation or fact?' *Work, Employment and Society*, 2: 281–316.

QUADRINI, V. (1999). 'The Importance of Entrepreneurship for Wealth Concentration and Mobility'. *Review of Income & Wealth*, 45: 1–19.

REES, H. and A. SHAH (1986). 'The Characteristics of the Self-employed: The supply of labour', in J. Atkinson and D. J. Storey (eds) *Employment, the Small Firm and the Labour Market*. London: Routledge.

—— and—— (1994). 'An empirical Analysis of Self-employment in the UK'. *Journal of Applied Econometrics*, 1: 95–108.

REYNOLDS, P. D. (1997). 'Who Starts New Firms? Preliminary explorations of firms-in-gestation'. *Small Business Economics*, 9: 449–62.

ROBSON, M. T. (2003). 'Does Stricter Employment Protection Legislation Promote Self-Employment?' *Small Business Economics*, 21: 309–319.

SINGH, G. and A. DENOBLE (2003). 'Early Retirees as the Next Generation of Entrepreneurs'. *Entrepreneurship Theory & Practice*, 28: 207–26.

SMALL BUSINESS ADMINISTRATION (2001). *The State of Small Business*. Washington, DC: Office of Advocacy.

SOWELL, T. (1981). *Markets and Minorities*. New York: Basic Books.

STOREY, D. J. (1994). *Understanding the Small Business Sector*. London: Routledge.

TAYLOR, M. P. (1996). 'Earnings, Independence or Unemployment: Why become self-employed?' *Oxford Bulletin of Economics & Statistics*, 58: 253–66.

—— (1999). 'Survival of the Fittest? An analysis of self-employment duration in Britain'. *Economic Journal*, 109: C140-C155.

THORNTON, J. (1998). 'The Labour Supply Behaviour of Self-employed Solo Practice Physicians'. *Applied Economics*, 30: 85–94.

UUSITALO, R. (2001). 'Homo Entreprenaurus?' *Applied Economics*, 33: 1631–38.

VAN DER SLUIS, J., C. M. VAN PRAAG and W. VIJVERBERG (2003). 'Entrepreneurship selection and performance: a meta-analysis of the impact of education in industrialised countries'. Discussion Paper. Tinbergen Institute, University of Amsterdam.

—— —— and A. WITTELOOSTUIJN (2004). 'The returns to education: a comparative study between entrepreneurs and employees'. Paper presented to the BKERC Conference. University of Strathclyde, June.

Van Praag, C. M. and J. S. Cramer (2001). 'The Roots of Entrepreneurship and Labour Demand: Individual ability and low risk aversion'. *Economica* 68: 45–62.

Wagner, J. (2003). 'Testing Lazear's Jack-of-all-trades View of Entrepreneurship with German Micro Data'. *Applied Economics Letters*, 10: 687–89.

Wales, T. J. (1973). 'Estimation of a Labour Supply Curve for Self-employed Business Proprietors'. *International Economic Review*, 14: 69–80.

Wolpin, K. I. (1977). 'Education and Screening'. *American Economic Review*, 67: 949–58.

CHAPTER 17

HABITUAL ENTREPRENEURS

DENIZ UCBASARAN, PAUL WESTHEAD AND MIKE WRIGHT

17.1 Introduction

Entrepreneurial behaviour is increasingly recognized as being heterogeneous. One notable source of heterogeneity is variations in the level and nature of entrepreneurs' experience. This has led to the distinction between experienced ('habitual') entrepreneurs and first-time ('novice') entrepreneurs. A number of high profile entrepreneurs have successfully owned several businesses (e.g. Sir Richard Branson in a variety of sectors, biotech entrepreneur Sir Chris Evans, Dr Herman Hauser of Acorn Computers and Arm Holdings, and Stelios Haji-Ioannou of easyGroup) (Wheatley, 2004). These individuals are known as habitual entrepreneurs, to reflect their ownership in more than one business, either sequentially (i.e. serial entrepreneurs) or concurrently (i.e. portfolio entrepreneurs).

Although habitual entrepreneurs are widespread and have received media attention, there has been limited conceptual and theoretical understanding of this group. In this chapter we seek to address this void by utilizing human capital theory to provide a framework for studying habitual entrepreneurs. Due to their ownership of multiple businesses, habitual entrepreneurs may have had an opportunity to develop additional knowledge and skills resulting in potentially more diverse human capital (Becker, 1975) than novice entrepreneurs. With only one experience, novice entrepreneurs are unable to move down the experience curve with respect to the problems and processes of identifying and exploiting entrepreneurial opportunities (i.e. to start or purchase a business) (MacMillan, 1986). These views led MacMillan to argue that to really learn about entrepreneurship, there is a need to study habitual entrepreneurship. As a result of their experience and associated human capital, habitual entrepreneurs need to be considered as an important sub-group of entrepreneurs who have the potential to make a fundamental contribution to the process of wealth creation in society (Rosa, 1998) and aid our understanding of entrepreneurship.

To assume that all habitual entrepreneurs will out-perform novice entrepreneurs because of their experience may, however, be too simplistic (Ucbasaran et al., 2003a). In the context of habitual entrepreneurs, there is an understanding that business ownership experience (one component of human capital) may result in the acquisition of assets and liabilities (Starr and Bygrave, 1991). While business ownership experience can result in the acquisition of human capital-enhancing assets such as additional managerial and entrepreneurial experience, an enhanced reputation (if successful) and access to additional resources (such as networks and finance), it may also lead to the acquisition of several liabilities. These liabilities can include hubris and staleness, whereby the entrepreneur becomes either over-confident and/or relies on routines that appeared to work well in his/her previous venture even though the circumstances may have changed (Starr and Bygrave, 1991; Wright et al., 1997). Further, some of the more traditional views on the value of entrepreneurial experience (e.g. Jovanovic, 1982) are based on the assumption that experience is associated with learning. While individuals generally adjust their judgement by learning from feedback based on experience, due to delays in feedback, individuals may be prone to errors and biases (Bazerman, 1990).

The possibility of business ownership experience being associated with both assets and liabilities suggests that we should not blindly assume that habitual entrepreneurs will report superior entrepreneur and firm performance than novice entrepreneurs. Although habitual entrepreneurs are increasingly considered to be important (Westhead and Wright, 1998a, 1999; Westhead et al., 2003a), there is a need to better understand the characteristics, behaviours and performance of novice and habitual entrepreneurs. In this chapter we examine theory and evidence relating to different types of entrepreneurs based on the level and nature of business ownership experience. In the next section, we propose a categorization of entrepreneurs based on their experience and offer definitions for each type.

17.2 Defining Novice, Habitual, Serial and Portfolio Entrepreneurs

Debate continues to surround the notion of entrepreneurs and entrepreneurship. In this section, we operationalize the categories of entrepreneurs explored in this review. We define entrepreneurs based on three well-established criteria: (i) business ownership; (ii) a decision-making role; and (iii) an ability to identify and exploit opportunities. Business ownership is recognized as an important dimension of entrepreneurship (Hawley, 1907). Further, given the prevalence of team-based entrepreneurship (Birley and Stockley, 2000; Ucbasaran et al., 2003), this ownership may involve minority or majority equity stakes. Emphasizing the importance of ownership, Fama and Jensen (1983) argue that classic entrepreneurial firms are those that combine residual risk bearers and decision-makers in the same individuals. The decision-making role of the entrepreneur is also deemed important (Marshall, 1920). Finally, some entrepreneurship scholars suggest that entrepreneurship involves the identification and exploitation of at least one business opportunity (Shane and Venkataraman, 2000; Ardichvili et al., 2003). A business opportunity can relate to new firm formation or the purchase of an existing private firm (Cooper and Dunkelberg, 1986). We, therefore, define entrepreneurs as having a minority or majority ownership stake in at least one business which they have either created or purchased, within which they are a key decision-maker.

A categorization of the nature of entrepreneurship by type of entrepreneur is summarized in Table 17.1. The entrepreneurs covered by cells 1, 2 and 3 are involved

Table 17.1 Types of entrepreneurs by independent business ownership experience

	Single activity	Multiple activity	
Nature of entrepreneurship	Novice entrepreneurs	Habitual entrepreneurs	
		Sequential	Simultaneous
		Serial entrepreneurs	Portfolio entrepreneurs
Involving new businesses	Novice founders 1	Serial founders 2	Portfolio founders 3
Involving existing business	Novice acquirers 4	Serial acquirers 5	Portfolio acquirers 6

in the founding of a new independent business. Novice founders (cell 1) have only founded one business, while serial founders (cell 2) and portfolio founders (cell 3) have founded more than one business sequentially or concurrently/simultaneously, respectively. The entrepreneurs in cells 4, 5 and 6 have acquired an ownership stake in an established independent business. The term 'acquirer' is used to reflect the fact that ownership in the existing business is acquired even though this may take a variety of forms. Acquirers include individuals from outside, who undertake a straight purchase or a management buy-in (MBI), and individuals from inside the firm who undertake a management buy-out (MBO). While novice acquirers (cell 4) may have only acquired a single business, serial acquirers (cell 5) and portfolio acquirers (cell 6) purchase more than one business sequentially or simultaneously, respectively. Some acquirers may initially buy the firm (i.e. buy-in or buy-out), sell it but remain as an employee and then repurchase it at a later date. The latter acquirers can be labelled serial MBO/MBI entrepreneurs.

Westhead et al. (2003a, b) have operationalized the following definitions of novice, serial and portfolio entrepreneurs. Novice entrepreneurs are individuals with no prior minority or majority business ownership experience either as a business founder, an inheritor or a purchaser of an independent business but who currently own a minority or majority equity stake in an independent business that is either new or purchased. Habitual entrepreneurs are individuals with prior business ownership experience. Two types of habitual entrepreneurs have been identified. Serial entrepreneurs are individuals who have sold/closed a business in which they had a minority or majority ownership stake, and they currently have a minority or majority ownership stake in a single independent business that is either new, purchased or inherited. Portfolio entrepreneurs are individuals who currently have minority and/or majority ownership stakes in two or more independent businesses that are either new, purchased and/or inherited.

17.3 Incidence of Habitual Entrepreneurship

Irrespective of the definition operationalized, evidence generally suggests that habitual entrepreneurs are a widespread phenomenon. The proportion of habitual entrepreneurs detected in the UK studies ranges from 12 percent (Cross, 1981) to 52 percent (Ucbasaran, 2004b). High proportions of habitual entrepreneurs have also been detected in the United States (51% to 63%) (Ronstadt, 1986; Schollhammer, 1991); Australia (49%) (Taylor, 1999); Malaysia (38%) (Taylor, 1999); and Norway

(34%) (Kolvereid and BullvÅg, 1993). Definitional differences, however, hamper discussion surrounding the scale of habitual entrepreneurship. Also, a focus on different samples of firms collected using a variety of methodologies inevitably leads to diverging assessments. Studies generally detecting the lower incidence of habitual entrepreneurs solely focus on new firm founders, while higher incidence studies focus on founder and acquirer entrepreneurs. These latter studies consider those who have a majority, or minority, equity stakes in the private ventures they own.

17.4 The case for distinguishing between different types of entrepreneurs

Once an initial opportunity has been exploited, an entrepreneur may choose to engage in a subsequent venture. Just as managerial work experience is seen as a key empirical indicator of managerial human capital (Castanias and Helfat, 2001), business ownership experience can be viewed as a significant contributor to entrepreneurial human capital (Gimeno et al., 1997). Business ownership experience may provide entrepreneurs with a variety of resources that can be utilized in identifying and exploiting subsequent ventures, such as direct entrepreneurial experience; additional managerial experience; an enhanced reputation; better access to and understanding of the requirements of finance institutions; and access to broader social and business networks (Shane and Khurana, 2003). As a result of these benefits accruing from business ownership experience, the development of subsequent businesses owned by habitual entrepreneurs can be enhanced by overcoming the liabilities of newness and attaining developmental milestones quicker (Starr and Bygrave, 1991). Habitual entrepreneurs can obtain financial resources for their subsequent ventures from a variety of sources such as banks, venture capitalists and informal investors and possibly on better terms (Wright et al., 1997). This discussion suggests that business ownership experience can lead to the accumulation/development of human capital as well as other types of capital (e.g. social and financial capital). It follows, that habitual entrepreneurs who may have more diverse human capital and access to other resources need to be distinguished from novice entrepreneurs.

Alvarez and Busenitz (2001) argue that entrepreneurs' human capital should include an understanding of their cognitive characteristics. As a result of their business ownership experience, habitual entrepreneurs may display different cognitive characteristics (i.e. in terms of how they think, process information and learn) to novice entrepreneurs. Experience provides a framework for processing information and can allow experienced entrepreneurs with diverse skills and competencies (i.e. networks, knowledge, etc.) to foresee and take advantage of disequilibrium profit opportunities that they proactively or reactively identify (Kaish and Gilad, 1991). Habitual entrepreneurs, who have multiple experiences to draw from, may be more likely to rely on information processing based on heuristics[1] than their novice counterparts (Ucbasaran et al., 2003a). Novice entrepreneurs may have fewer experience-related benchmarks or mental short-cuts to draw upon.

The expertise literature also offers a potential theoretical basis for distinguishing between novice and habitual entrepreneurs. Expert information processing literature suggests that there are differences in the cognition of novices and 'experts'. A large body of this research attributes differences between novices and experts to the quantity and organization of knowledge gained through experience (Shanteau, 1992). Experts are viewed as being able to manipulate incoming information into recognizable patterns, and then match the information to appropriate actions (Lord and Maher, 1990). This capacity reduces the burden of cognitive processing, which can allow the 'expert' to concentrate on novel or unique material (Hillerbrand, 1989). It is possible that entrepreneurs who have the benefit of additional entrepreneurial experience (i.e. habitual entrepreneurs) are more reliant on information processing resembling that of an expert's.

The above discussion suggests that there may be a theoretical case for distinguishing between habitual and novice entrepreneurs on the grounds that they think differently. As highlighted above, habitual entrepreneurs themselves can also be heterogeneous. A distinction has been made between serial, and portfolio, entrepreneurs. Schein (1978) found that self-employed individuals fell into one of two career anchors. A career anchor is defined as 'the pattern of self-perceived talents, motives, and values [which] serves to guide, constrain, stabilize and integrate the person's career' (Schein, 1978: 127). The first anchor is that of autonomy/independence, which represents a desire for freedom from rules and the control of others. The second is the entrepreneurship anchor, which focuses on the creation of something new, involving the motivation to overcome obstacles, the willingness to run risks, and the desire for personal prominence (Schein, 1978). The autonomy-oriented individual is more likely to be driven by the desire to have freedom from control by others and is likely to be involved in ventures one at a time (Katz, 1994). Serial entrepreneurs are largely motivated by autonomy, independence and an interest in gaining and maintaining control. To maintain

[1] Heuristics are simplifying strategies that individuals use to make strategic decisions especially in complex situations where incomplete information is available.

a position of control, serial entrepreneurs may feel a greater need for information and, therefore, be less reliant on heuristic based thinking. In contrast, those with an entrepreneurship anchor are driven by the opportunity recognition process and/or wealth creation (Katz, 1994). These entrepreneurs tend to be involved in multiple ventures simultaneously. These characteristics resemble more closely those of portfolio entrepreneurs. The fact that they are involved in multiple ventures suggests that they do not require complete information to the same extent as serial entrepreneurs. Portfolio entrepreneurs may be more strongly associated with a heuristic mode of cognition.

The above discussion suggests that scholars may benefit from distinguishing between novice and experienced habitual entrepreneurs on the grounds that their human capital and cognitive profiles are different, which in turn may explain differences in behaviour and performance. Furthermore, it is suggested that among habitual entrepreneurs, there are differences in the mindset, attitudes and motives of serial entrepreneurs and portfolio entrepreneurs.

17.5 Empirical evidence

Though the empirical evidence is limited, several studies have found differences between novice, serial and portfolio entrepreneurs in terms of their demographic and background characteristics (e.g. age, education, gender, parental background) and motivations (Alsos and Kolvereid, 1998; Birley and Westhead, 1993; Kolvereid and BullvÅg, 1993; Westhead and Wright, 1998a). The empirical evidence reported below is based on two groups of more recent research. The first group represents work based on a representative sample of private independent businesses owned by Scottish entrepreneurs. A valid sample of 354 entrepreneurs was used to conduct univariate analysis on the differences between novice, serial and portfolio entrepreneurs. Only statistically significant relationships at the 5 percent level or better are reported (see Westhead et al., 2003a, b; 2006 for a complete set of results). The second group of studies also relate to a representative sample of private independent businesses, but in Great Britain. The evidence relates to 631 valid respondents and is based on multivariate analysis including ordinary least squares ordered logit regression. Only statistically significant relationships at the 5 percent level or better are reported (see Ucbasaran, 2004b; Ucbasaran et al., 2005). We organize the discussion of this evidence in terms of three key themes: human capital characteristics; behaviour; and performance.

17.5.1 Human capital-based differences

While traditional measures of human capital have included education and training (Becker, 1975), the term human capital has been broadened to include achieved attributes, accumulated work and habits, and cognitive characteristics that may have a positive or negative effect on productivity (Becker, 1993; Alvarez and Busenitz, 2001). We adopt this boarder definition of human capital to review evidence relating to differences in the human capital of novice, serial and portfolio entrepreneurs.

17.5.1.1 *Education and managerial human capital*

Earlier evidence provided by Kolvereid and BullvÅg (1993) suggested that habitual entrepreneurs were more likely to report higher educational qualifications. Westhead and Wright (1998b) reported that while there was no difference in the education level of novice entrepreneurs and serial entrepreneurs, portfolio entrepreneurs reported higher levels of education than the other two groups of entrepreneurs. More recently, Westhead et al. (2006) found no significant difference in the education levels of novice, serial and portfolio entrepreneurs. Despite minimal variation in terms of education, portfolio and serial entrepreneurs reported higher levels of managerial human capital (as measured in terms of the number of organizations worked for and their highest job status) than novice entrepreneurs.

17.5.1.2 *Perceived capabilities*

Recent work on capabilities suggests the need to supplement the stock-based view of capital/resources with a more process-oriented view (Teece et al., 1997). It has been suggested that the entrepreneur must demonstrate capabilities in three functional areas: namely, entrepreneurial, managerial and technical (Penrose, 1959; Chandler and Jansen, 1992). One way of assessing these capabilities is to rely on self-assessment. Self-assessed capabilities have been found to correlate highly with actual competencies (Gist, 1987). Westhead et al. (2006) find that portfolio entrepreneurs reported significantly higher levels of perceived entrepreneurial capability than novice entrepreneurs. In particular, portfolio entrepreneurs were significantly more likely to report that 'one of my greatest strengths is my ability to seize high quality business opportunities', 'I have a special alertness or sensitivity towards spotting opportunities', and 'I can usually spot a real opportunity better than professional researchers/analysts'. Portfolio entrepreneurs reported significantly higher scores than serial entrepreneurs for the last statement. Serial entrepreneurs were significantly more likely than novice entrepreneurs to report 'I accurately perceive unmet customer needs'. Portfolio entrepreneurs also reported higher levels of perceived managerial capability. They were significantly more likely than novice entrepreneurs to report that 'one of my greatest strengths is organizing resources and coordinating tasks', 'one of my greatest strengths is my ability to supervise, influence, and lead people', and 'one of my greatest strengths is my ability to delegate effectively'. Portfolio entrepreneurs were more likely than both novice and serial entrepreneurs to report 'one of my greatest strengths is achieving results by organizing and motivating people'. Finally, with regard to technical capabilities, serial entrepreneurs were more likely than portfolio entrepreneurs to report that 'one of my greatest strengths is my expertise in a technical or functional area'.

Controlling for other dimensions of human capital, Ucbasaran (2004b) found habitual entrepreneurs to be associated with lower levels of perceived technical capability than novice entrepreneurs. Further, portfolio entrepreneurs were associated with significantly higher levels of managerial capability than serial entrepreneurs.

17.5.1.3 *Motivations*

Gimeno et al. (1997) suggest that the motivations for embarking on an entrepreneurial venture are a key component of venture-specific human capital. Motivations may have an impact on the behaviours and strategies selected by entrepreneurs. Evidence reveals that the motivations of serial and portfolio entrepreneurs are consistent with the two career anchors discussed earlier. Ucbasaran (2004b) found that serial entrepreneurs reported independence to be a significantly more important motive than portfolio entrepreneurs. Westhead et al. (2006) found that portfolio entrepreneurs appear to be particularly motivated by financial reasons and personal development. Specifically, serial entrepreneurs were more likely to be motivated by controlling their own time than novice entrepreneurs, while portfolio entrepreneurs were more motivated by having greater flexibility than novice entrepreneurs. Novice entrepreneurs were more likely to be motivated by welfare considerations such as wanting to continue a family tradition than serial entrepreneurs. Finally, novice entrepreneurs were more likely than both serial and portfolio entrepreneurs to cite reactive reasons, in particular unemployment, as a key driver.

17.5.2 Behavioural differences

17.5.2.1 *Acquisition of resources*

17.5.2.1.1 *Finance*

An entrepreneur's previous business ownership experience can have a profound influence on the amounts of initial capital, and types of finance used during the launch period of a subsequent new, acquired or inherited business. Successful habitual entrepreneurs may be expected to have larger amounts of personal capital, and greater access to external sources of funds than novice entrepreneurs. Funds from private business sales may be used by serial (and portfolio) entrepreneurs to invest in subsequent ventures. There is some evidence that serial urban founders are significantly more likely than novice and portfolio urban founders to have used funds received on exiting from their last venture to fund the next (Westhead and Wright, 1998b). However, a reluctance to be involved in projects which may undermine their standing among the financial and business community, and a desire to invest a smaller proportion of their personal wealth the second time around (Wright et al., 1997) may mean that some habitual entrepreneurs become risk averse over time.

Habitual entrepreneurs with successful track records are more credible than those who have failed first time around, and can thus lever their prior business ownership experience to obtain external financial resources from banks and venture capitalists for their subsequent ventures (Wright et al., 1997). Venture capitalists make their investment decisions with regard to an individual's previous business ownership experience, and their motivation and ability to succeed the next time around (Wright et al., 1997). Portfolio entrepreneurs who have not exited from a venture(s) they have an ownership stake(s) in may be able to leverage the internal financial resources from their existing business(es) (Alsos and Kolvereid, 1998), and may make use of finance from existing customers and suppliers. Novice entrepreneurs lacking an established track record, may have to rely upon internal sources of initial capital, including personal savings and family and friends, to obtain an ownership stake.

Westhead et al. (2003a) find support for some of these views. In particular, both serial and portfolio entrepreneurs invested more initial capital in the surveyed business than novice entrepreneurs. Further, portfolio entrepreneurs reported a significantly higher proportion of initial capital being provided by external sources (from bank loans in particular) than novice and serial entrepreneurs.

17.5.2.1.2 *Information*

Information represents a potentially valuable resource for entrepreneurs, particularly with regard to opportunity identification and exploitation (Casson, 1982; Kaish and Gilad, 1991; Shane, 2000). An individual's prior experience can influence information search behaviour (Cooper et al., 1995; Fiet, 2002). Individuals with no prior business ownership experience have fewer benchmarks to assess whether the information they have collected is appropriate to identify and exploit a business opportunity. Cooper et al. (1995) suggested that novice entrepreneurs would search for less information, due to their limited understanding of what is needed. Contrary to expectation, Cooper et al. (1995) detected that novice entrepreneurs, on average, sought more information than habitual entrepreneurs. Fiet (2002) suggest that habitual entrepreneurs may be less likely to engage in extensive search strategies because they can concentrate on searching within a more specific domain of venture ideas based on routines that worked well in the past. Habitual entrepreneurs may also acquire contacts that provide them with a flow of information relating to business opportunities (Kaish and Gilad, 1991; Rosa, 1998), implying that they may need to be less proactive in the search for opportunities and information.

Despite these expectations, Westhead et al. (2006) found that both serial and portfolio entrepreneurs utilized a greater number of information sources than novice entrepreneurs. A higher proportion of habitual entrepreneurs rather than novice entrepreneurs had used personal friends, financiers, employees and technical literature as a source of information. Further, a larger proportion of portfolio rather than novice entrepreneurs, indicated that they had used information from magazines/newspapers, trade publications, consultants, local enterprise and development agencies, and national government sources. A higher proportion of serial entrepreneurs than novice entrepreneurs had used customers and clients as a source of information. A higher proportion of serial entrepreneurs than both novice and portfolio entrepreneurs had used other business owners as a source of information.

It is notable, however, that when various dimensions of human capital were controlled for in a multivariate framework, Ucbasaran et al. (2005) did not find a significant association between the number of information sources utilized or information search intensity and business ownership experience.

17.5.2.2 *Opportunity identification and exploitation*

Information can be seen as a necessary though insufficient condition for the identification of business opportunities. However, the nature of the information used and the ability to utilize information are likely to influence the likelihood of identifying an opportunity. Certain types of information may be more useful and valuable than other types. Fiet et al. (2003) argues that information specific to an opportunity (e.g. knowledge of people, local conditions and special circumstances) is more valuable. Ucbasaran et al. (2005) find that personal rather than professional information sources were significantly associated with the number of opportunities identified in a given period. As a result of their experience, habitual entrepreneurs may have access to more personal and specific information sources. Having earned a reputation as a successful entrepreneur, financiers, advisers, other entrepreneurs and business contacts may present valuable information and even business proposals to some habitual entrepreneurs (Wright et al., 1997).

The ability to utilize information is at least as important, if not more so, than the information itself. Even if a person possesses the information necessary to identify an opportunity, he or she may fail to do so because of an inability to see new means-ends relationships (Shane and Venkataraman, 2000). Gaglio and Katz (2001) have argued that Kirzner's alertness theory relates to one extreme of an alertness continuum, but does not explore the possibility of other points on the continuum. Prior business ownership experience may allow habitual entrepreneurs to be more alert to opportunities than inexperienced novice entrepreneurs. Experience-based knowledge can direct an individual's attention, expectations, and interpretations of market stimuli, thus facilitating the generation of ideas (Gaglio, 1997). Habitual entrepreneurs may leverage their business ownership experience to 'see' business opportunities that are ignored or not recognized by novice entrepreneurs.

In support of these views, Westhead et al. (2006) find that habitual entrepreneurs identified more opportunities for purchasing or creating a business than their novice counterparts. In particular, portfolio entrepreneurs identified significantly more opportunities than novice and serial entrepreneurs. Controlling for various dimensions of human capital, Ucbasaran et al. (2005) also find support for these findings.

In many studies, there is an implicit assumption that identified opportunities will be automatically exploited. This is not necessarily the case. Even though there is no conclusive empirical evidence, casual observation suggests that not all identified opportunities are brought into fruition (Shane and Venkataraman, 2000). Because the number of opportunities exploited is the basis for our definitions of novice and habitual entrepreneurs, examining the relationship between business ownership experience and the number of opportunities exploited would be tautological. An alternative is to examine a stage between opportunity identification and exploitation, which is termed the pursuit stage. In deciding whether to exploit an opportunity, the expected value of the return from the opportunity must exceed the opportunity cost of alternatives, but also offers the individual with a premium for bearing uncertainty (Kirzner 1973, Schumpeter 1934). The pursuit stage involves time and resource commitments to evaluate the costs and benefits of exploiting the opportunity idea.

The extent to which an individual invests time and resources into evaluating (i.e. pursuing) an opportunity is likely to be a function (at least partly) of the individual's human capital characteristics. The transferability of information from business ownership experience to the opportunity (Carroll and Mosakowski, 1987) can increase the probability of pursuit, because experience and learning can reduce the costs of exploitation (Shane and Venkataraman, 2000). Individuals with prior experience may expect to receive a higher return on their investment (i.e. time and resources invested during the pursuit stage), thereby increasing the likelihood of pursuit. If habitual entrepreneurs have a broader knowledge base and access to further resources, they may feel better prepared to exploit an opportunity once it has passed the evaluation (i.e. pursuit) stage. Consequently, if habitual entrepreneurs are more likely to have the ability and resources to exploit an opportunity, they may be more likely to pursue it. Moreover, due to their business ownership experience, habitual entrepreneurs may identify better quality opportunities (or at least hold the belief that they have identified better quality opportunities), in turn increasing the likelihood of pursuing them.

Supporting these views, Westhead et al. (2006) find that a significantly higher proportion of portfolio entrepreneurs than novice and serial entrepreneurs in particular pursued two or more opportunities in a five-year period. This is supported by Ucbasaran et al. (2005) who found a significant positive association between whether an entrepreneur was a habitual entrepreneur (and in particular a portfolio entrepreneur) and the proportion of identified opportunities that were pursued.

17.5.2.3 *Organizational strategies*

The organizational practices adopted by novice, serial and portfolio entrepreneurs may offer some insight into the way in which these entrepreneurs exploit opportunities. Westhead et al. (2003a) found that habitual entrepreneurs (in particular portfolio entrepreneurs) were significantly more likely to emphasize innovation and growth. Despite some similarities between serial and portfolio entrepreneurs, the evidence suggests that portfolio entrepreneurs were more likely to exhibit several competencies that provide greater understanding surrounding why and how they own several businesses at the same time. The fact that portfolio entrepreneurs own more than one business may explain their greater focus on managerial competence and human capital resources, than serial or novice entrepreneurs. At the start of the surveyed business, they had significantly more equity partners than novice or serial entrepreneurs. Portfolio entrepreneurs also gave greater importance than novice or serial entrepreneurs to the following organizational capabilities: innovation, cost reduction, product/service differentiation and business growth. They emphasized the importance of investing heavily in R&D; increasing employee and operations productivity and efficiency; strict quality control; using novel marketing techniques; and growth through acquisitions. Moreover, portfolio entrepreneurs may develop synergistic relationships between the ventures they own to gain competitive advantages for individual ventures (Rosa, 1998). Portfolio entrepreneurs can utilize this distinct advantage to ensure the survival and development of ventures they own.

17.5.3 Performance

Stuart and Abetti (1990) explored the relationship between an entrepreneur's entrepreneurial experience (i.e. number of previous ventures and the role played in them), and business profitability and growth. They detected that the composite measure of entrepreneurial experience was the only factor that significantly explained variations in the selected performance indicators. However, neither Kolvereid and BullvÅg (1993), nor Birley and Westhead (1993) nor Westhead and Wright (1998b) were able to detect performance (with regard to employment growth, sales revenue, sales revenue growth and the ability to own profitable businesses) differences between novice and habitual entrepreneurs. Based on a representative sample of Scottish entrepreneurs, Westhead et al. (2003a) found that a larger proportion of serial than novice entrepreneurs reported that their current profit performance was above average relative to their competitors. In addition, portfolio entrepreneurs, on average, reported higher percentage full-time and total employee growth in their businesses over the 1996 to 2001 period than those owned by novice and serial entrepreneurs. Additional analysis revealed that the top 4 percent of the fastest growing businesses owned by portfolio entrepreneurs generated 55 percent of gross new jobs created, while the comparable sub-sample of firms owned by novice and serial entrepreneurs generated 44 percent and 38 percent of gross new jobs, respectively. Evidence suggests with reference to the surveyed firms alone that leading 'winning entrepreneurs' within the portfolio entrepreneur category accounted for more absolute employment growth than leading 'winning entrepreneurs' in other entrepreneur categories.

Ucbasaran (2004b) extended the sample to Great Britain and controlled for other aspects of entrepreneurs' human capital, the environment and organizational characteristics, but failed to detect any performance differences between novice and habitual entrepreneurs.

17.6 Policy implications

Policy-makers and practitioners need to more fully appreciate the resources, needs, behaviour and contributions of various types of entrepreneurs when they are formulating policies (Westhead and Wright, 1999). The evidence reviewed above offers some guidance to policy-makers on how to tailor their support to meet the specific needs and requirements of novice, serial and portfolio entrepreneurs. Rather than 'blanket support' available to all entrepreneurs, irrespective of their need or ability, there is a case to target entrepreneurs with potential who face barriers to business development that can be addressed by appropriate and sensitive 'soft' support (e.g. in the form of information, training, advice etc.) (Bridge et al., 1998; OECD, 1998). While existing evidence offers only weak support for the view that generic training (i.e. a form of soft support) improves small firm performance (Storey, 2004), it has been argued that the targeted assistance allows the better tailoring of services to needs (OECD, 1998). Therefore, a greater understanding of the needs of different types of entrepreneurs may benefit those involved in the design of policy initiatives.

A key issue in policy development and implementation relates to the identification of the objectives of a particular policy initiative (Storey, 2003). In the absence of clearly specified objectives, the appropriate policy initiative and its subsequent evaluation cannot be established. If the objective of policy-makers is to maximize the returns to their investment (Bridge et al., 1998), they may benefit from targeting their financial resources to 'winning businesses' (Storey, 1994) or 'winning entrepreneurs'. Given the conflicting evidence on the performance contributions of novice and habitual entrepreneurs, it is difficult to identify a group of 'winning entrepreneurs'.

The evidence reviewed above does, however, suggest that habitual entrepreneurs (portfolio entrepreneurs in particular) identify more opportunities in a given period than novice entrepreneurs. This former group of entrepreneurs may be particularly important to policy-makers interested in promoting an 'enterprise culture'. Rather than focusing on encouraging the formation of new businesses, many of which have a low probability of long-term survival, opportunity identification may be used as an indictor of entrepreneurial intensity. In the short term, novice entrepreneurs are restricted in their ability to acquire business ownership experience, which has been found to facilitate opportunity identification. However, Ucbasaran et al. (2005) identify additional factors favourably associated with opportunity identification intensity. Higher levels of education, managerial capability, entrepreneurial capability and information search intensity were associated with the identification of a greater number of opportunities. If one of the difficulties faced by novice and serial entrepreneurs is in terms of identifying opportunities, policy initiatives to improve various aspects of their human capital identified above may be introduced. Further, improving access to information by novice and serial entrepreneurs may facilitate greater opportunity identification.

Alongside the quantity of information, the nature of the information acquired may also be important. Additional research is warranted to explore whether individual external agencies provide or can provide appropriate information (i.e. depth and quality) to entrepreneurs in need of information to identify opportunities. Furthermore, given the importance of personal information sources, entrepreneurs may benefit from additional network initiatives. Habitual entrepreneurs (especially portfolio entrepreneurs) may be able to work in collaboration with novice entrepreneurs to facilitate business opportunity identification.

There is a continuing debate surrounding the issue of failure among entrepreneurs. Ricketts, in Ch.2 of this Handbook, notes that failure may reduce human capital and hence restrict the entrepreneur's ability to raise funds for future projects. However, this may be an unduly negative view of failure (McGrath,

1999). Some have argued that as an alternative to many European models there is a need to consider the US model where government intervention is minimal, and business failure is an acceptable part of life (Storey, 2004). Indeed, Sitkin (1992) argues that in an effort to understand its causes, failure forces individuals to identify aspects of their thinking and behaviour that need to be modified. Based on such views, policy initiatives, such as the Enterprise Act (2002) in the UK, have attempted to make bankruptcy laws more lenient to make it easier for entrepreneurs who have failed to start businesses again. However, 'hard' financial incentives through changes in tax regimes and bankruptcy laws may not be the best use of resources. Policy-makers should carefully consider the wider implications of policy initiatives, such as relaxing bankruptcy laws. Gropp et al. (1997) found that in states where bankruptcy laws were more generous, entrepreneurs faced greater difficulties in raising funds.

Policy-makers require further information to establish if failure is as valuable as some groups think. Experience (positive or negative) may not be the best teacher. Indeed, the basic premise of attribution theory (Zuckerman, 1979) is that individuals have a tendency to attribute successes to themselves and failures to external effects, inhibiting unbiased learning. Further, Shepherd (2003) argues that the loss of a business through failure can cause the feeling of grief. This leads to a negative emotional response interfering with the ability to learn from the events surrounding that loss. To overcome biases associated with learning from experience (especially failure), entrepreneurs may require guidance. Even Sitkin (1992) distinguished between failure and 'intelligent failure'. Shepherd (2004) offers a number of suggestions and methods for helping 'students' effectively manage their response to failure. These methods may be deployed by various bodies focusing on the training and skills development of entrepreneurs.

17.7 Future research

The evidence reviewed has been largely based on data collected from cross-sectional surveys. The extant empirical evidence does not address endogeneity and selection-bias issues. Further, while surveys offer a number of advantages, they can be limited in terms of their ability to capture details relating to the 'why' and 'how' aspects of a phenomenon. Future studies may benefit from the use of in-depth case studies (Ucbasaran et al., 2003b). Case studies can be used to examine each business owned by an entrepreneur and identify the motivations, opportunity identification process and performance relating to each business. Case studies may provide insights into the extent to which learning takes place between ventures owned by habitual entrepreneurs.

Longitudinal studies (using case studies or longitudinal datasets) offer the advantage of being able to establish causal relationships between human capital, entrepreneurial behaviour and performance. Longitudinal studies monitoring the 'stock' of skills and experience of each type of entrepreneur, and the 'flows' across the entrepreneur categories would provide rich process and contextual evidence. They could, for example, explore the characteristics and skills associated with novice entrepreneurs who are able to transform into serial or portfolio entrepreneurs. Also, studies might focus on the initiation processes leading to the ownership of subsequent ventures by experienced entrepreneurs, and why they accept or reject particular types of deals. Similarly, there is a need to understand how serial and portfolio entrepreneurs learn from their previous business ownership experiences. For the purposes of understanding wealth creation, there is a need to analyze the 'quality', rather than just the 'quantity' of prior business ownership experience. In addition, there is a need for research that analyses the total economic contribution of portfolio, serial and novice entrepreneurs to local and national economies. Evidence reported above suffers from the limitation of focusing on a single business owned by each type of entrepreneur.

While certain groups of entrepreneurs (i.e. habitual entrepreneurs and in particular portfolio entrepreneurs) may identify a greater number of opportunities in a given period, this offers minimal insight as to the nature and value of identified opportunities. This constitutes a limitation of the literature reviewed above but offers opportunities for future research. There is considerable debate surrounding how the value of an opportunity can be assessed. Singh (2001) argues that most definitions of opportunities represent a post-hoc view, based on criteria stipulating profitability as a requirement for entrepreneurial opportunities. Such post-hoc approaches do not always control for confounding factors (e.g. environment, mode of exploitation, managerial expertise etc.), which can influence the performance of the venture. Instead, ways of assessing the opportunity *exante* may need to be used. Fiet et al. (2003) used a panel to rank ideas based on their assessment of whether the opportunity represents a concept that could create and sustain a competitive advantage. On the downside, this approach can be time-consuming and costly, and is based on the panel's subjective opinion. Identifying approaches for assessing the value of opportunities represents an important area for future research.

Business ownership experience has been viewed as one aspect of human capital specific to entrepreneurship. Future researchers may benefit from examining the extent to which business ownership experience is a substitute, or a complement to other dimensions of human capital. For example, experience may amplify the effects of other aspects of human capital, such as managerial human capital and education. The use of interaction variables between business ownership experience and other human capital characteristics may prove useful. By exploring the extent to which business ownership experience acts as a moderator or mediator variable, possible substitutes for business ownership experience may be identified. Studies such as that by Chandler and Hanks (1998), where the substitutability of human capital and financial capital were examined, may act as a useful guide.

Habitual entrepreneur behaviour and performance as has already been reported (see above) reported may be sensitive to the definitions adopted. Alternative typologies of entrepreneurs should be considered and empirically operationalized. Taxonomies of entrepreneurs should be developed to ascertain whether novice, serial and portfolio entrepreneurs actually exist in distinct groups. As an alternative typology, Ucbasaran (2004a) distinguishes between 'experienced' and 'expert' habitual entrepreneurs and between 'pure' and 'transient' novice entrepreneurs. 'Expert' habitual entrepreneurs possess cognitive characteristics which allow them to learn effectively from their experiences. In contrast 'experienced' habitual entrepreneurs may be subject to cognitive biases and limitations. While some novice entrepreneurs have no intention of becoming a habitual entrepreneur, others do. Ucbasaran (2004b) found that only 22 percent of novice entrepreneurs reported that they intended to establish or purchase a business in the future. Accordingly, while 'pure' novice entrepreneurs represent the group of novice entrepreneurs that will remain one-time entrepreneurs, 'transient' novice entrepreneurs will at least attempt to become habitual entrepreneurs. These two types of novice entrepreneurs may display different cognitive characteristics.

There is also the need to examine habitual and especially portfolio entrepreneurship within institutional and regulatory contexts. In particular, there is a need to distinguish between whether the creation and ownership of multiple businesses is determined by incentives, such as social security and taxation regimes relating to business size, rather than the identification and pursuit of distinct opportunities. The policy and research implications of these two determinants of portfolio entrepreneurship may be quite distinct. Since we do not observe that large proportions of entrepreneurs create and own multiple enterprises simultaneously, it would appear that perverse taxation and other regulatory incentives are not the only determinant of portfolio entrepreneurship.

Alongside the institutional and regulatory environment, the relationship between the industry context and habitual entrepreneurship warrants further research. Evidence suggests that entrepreneurship is more widespread in certain industries than others (Shane, 2003). It is not yet known, however, if portfolio and/or serial entrepreneurship is more likely in certain industry contexts than others. In highly dynamic and uncertain environments, entrepreneurs may be faced with a higher risk of failure or shorter life cycles for businesses. In such industries, serial entrepreneurship may be more widespread. In this kind of environment, entrepreneurship may be viewed as a form of experimentation. Further, to spread risk, some entrepreneurs may choose to own multiple businesses and become portfolio entrepreneurs. The industrial distribution of habitual entrepreneurship represents an area for future research.

To conclude, this chapter has sought to increase our understanding of habitual entrepreneurship. Until recently, those subscribing to Jovanovic's views on entrepreneurial learning have assumed that habitual entrepreneurs are likely to outperform their novice counterparts. This is based on Jovanovic's (1982) argument that those who enter entrepreneurship gradually learn about their abilities by engaging in the actual running of a business and observing how well they do. Experience provides feedback that allows individuals to assess their true entrepreneurial ability (see Cressy, in Ch.7 of this Handbook). As they learn about their abilities, their estimates of their own ability may change. Those who revise their estimates of their ability upwards (due to success) expand output (i.e. continue their entrepreneurial career), while those revising their estimates downwards (due to failure) contract output (possibly exiting from an entrepreneurial career). Unfortunately, this approach assumes that individuals are equally able to learn from their experience and, therefore, fails to explain why habitual entrepreneurs do not necessarily outperform novice entrepreneurs. Further, it fails to explain why some entrepreneurs who have failed choose to try again. In this chapter, we have argued that traditional views on the role of experience need to be supplemented with more dynamic perspectives that draw upon the concepts of human capital and cognition. Future research might fruitfully explore this issue in more detail.

References

Alsos, G. A. and L. Kolvereid (1998). 'The Business Gestation Process of Novice, Serial and Parallel Business Founders'. *Entrepreneurship Theory and Practice*, 22: 101–14.

Alvarez, S. and L. Busenitz (2001). 'The Entrepreneurship of Resource-Based Theory'. *Journal of Management*, 27: 755–76.

Ardichvili, A., R. Cardozo and S. Ray (2003). 'A Theory of Entrepreneurial Opportunity Identification and Development'. *Journal of Business Venturing*, 18: 105–23.

Bazerman, M. H. (1990). *Judgement in Managerial Decision Making*, 2nd edn. New York: John Wiley and Sons.

Becker, G. S. (1975). *Human Capital.* New York: National Bureau of Economic Research.

—— (1993). 'Nobel Lecture: The Economic Way of Looking at Behavior'. *The Journal of Political Economy*, 101: 385–409.

Birley, S. and S. Stockley (2000). 'Entrepreneurial Teams and Venture Growth', in D. L. Sexton and H. Landström (eds) *The Blackwell Handbook of Entrepreneurship.* Oxford: Blackwell.

—— and P. Westhead (1993). 'A Comparison of New Businesses Established by 'Novice' and 'Habitual' Founders in Great Britain'. *International Small Business Journal*, 12: 38–60.

Birley, S. and P. Westhead (1994). 'A Taxonomy of Business Start-Up Reasons and their Impact on Firm Growth and Size'. *Journal of Business Venturing*, 9: 7–31.

Bridge, S., K. O'Neill and S. Cromie (1998). *Understanding Enterprise, Entrepreneurship & Small Business*. Basingstoke: Macmillan Press Ltd.

Busenitz, L. W. and J. B. Barney (1997). 'Differences Between Entrepreneurs and Managers in Large Organisations: Biases and heuristics in strategic decision-making'. *Journal of Business Venturing*, 12: 9–30.

Carroll, G. and E. Moskowski (1987). 'The Career Dynamics of Self-Employment'. *Administrative Science Quarterly*, 32: 570–89.

Casson, M. (1982). *The Entrepreneur: An Economic Theory*. Oxford: Martin Robertson.

Castanias, R. P and C. E. Helfat (2001). 'The Managerial Rents Model: Theory and Empirical Analysis'. *Journal of Management*, 27: 661–78.

Chandler, G. N. and S. H. Hanks (1998). 'An Examination of the Substitutability of Founders Human and Financial Capital in Emerging Business Ventures'. *Journal of Business Venturing*, 13: 353–69.

—— and E. Jansen (1992). 'The Founder's Self-Assessed Competence and Venture Performance'. *Journal of Business Venturing*, 7: 223–36.

Cooper, A. C. and Dunkelberg, W. C. (1986). 'Entrepreneurship and Paths to Business Ownership'. *Strategic Management Journal*, 7: 53–68.

—— T. B. Folta and C. Woo (1995). 'Entrepreneurial Information Search'. *Journal of Business Venturing*, 10: 107–120.

Cross, M. (1981). *New Firm Formation and Regional Development*. London: Gower.

Enterprise Act (2002). Available at www.dti.gov.uk/enterpriseact.

Fama, E. and M. Jensen (1983). 'Separation of Ownership and Control'. *Journal of Law and Economics*, 26(2): 301–25.

Fiet, J. O. (2002). *The Systematic Search for Entrepreneurial Discoveries*. Westport, CN: Quorum Books.

—— M. Gupta and W. I. Norton (2003). 'Evaluating the Wealth Creating Potential of Venture Ideas'. Paper presented at the Babson Kauffman Entrepreneurship Research Conference, Babson College, MA: Wellesley.

Gaglio, C. M. (1997). 'Opportunity Identification: Review, Critique and Suggested Research Directions', in J. A. Katz (ed) *Advances in Entrepreneurship, Firm Emergence and Growth*, vol. 3, Greenwich, CA: JAI Press.

—— and J. A. Katz (2001). 'The Psychological Basis of Opportunity Identification: Entrepreneurial Alertness'. *Small Business Economics*, 16(2): 95–111.

Gimeno, J., T. B. Folta, A. C. Cooper and C. Y. Woo (1997). 'Survival of the Fittest? Entrepreneurial Human Capital and the Persistence of Underperforming Firms'. *Administrative Science Quarterly*, 42: 750–83.

Gist, M. E. (1987). 'Self-Efficacy: Implications for Organizational Behavior and Human Resource Management'. *Academy of Management Review*, 12(3): 472–86.

Gropp, R., J. K. Scholtz and M. J. White (1997). 'Personal Bankruptcy and Credit Supply and Demand'. *Quarterly Journal of Economics*, 112: 217–51.

Hawley, F. B. (1907). *Enterprise and the Productive Process*. New York: G. P. Putnam's Sons.

Hillerbrand, E. (1989). 'Cognitive Differences Between Experts and Novices: Implications for Group Supervision'. *Journal of Counselling and Development*, 67: 293–6.

Jovanovic, B. (1982). 'Selection and the Evolution of Industry'. *Econometrica*, 50(3): 649–70.

KAISH, S. and B. GILAD (1991). 'Characteristics of Opportunities Search of Entrepreneurs Versus Executives: Sources, Interests, General Alertness'. *Journal of Business Venturing*, 6: 45–61.

KATZ, J. A. (1994). 'Modelling Entrepreneurial Career Progressions: Concepts and Considerations'. *Entrepreneurship Theory and Practice*, 19: 23–39.

KIRZNER, I. M. (1973). *Competition and Entrepreneurship*. Chicago: University of Chicago Press.

KOLVEREID, L. and E. BULLVÅG (1993). 'Novices Versus Experienced Founders: An Exploratory Investigation', in S. Birley, I. MacMillan and S. Subramony (eds) *Entrepreneurship Research: Global Perspectives*. pp. 275–85. Amsterdam: Elsevier Science Publishers.

LORD, R. G. and K. J. MAHER (1990). 'Alternative Information-Processing Models and Their Implications for Theory, Research, and Practice'. *Academy of Management Review*, 15(1): 9–28.

MACMILLAN, I. C. (1986). 'To Really Learn About Entrepreneurship, Let's Study Habitual Entrepreneurs'. *Journal of Business Venturing*, 1: 241–3.

MARSHALL, A. (1920). *Principles of Economics*, 8th edn, reset 1949. London: Macmillan.

MCGRATH, R. G. (1999). 'Falling Forward: Real Options Reasoning and Entrepreneurial Failure'. *Academy of Management Review*, 24: 13–30.

Organisation for Economic Co-Operation and Development (OECD) (1998). *Fostering Entrepreneurship*. Paris: Organisation for Economic Co-Operation and Development.

PENROSE, E. T. (1959). *The Theory of Growth of the Firm*. Oxford: Oxford University Press.

RONSTADT (1986). 'Exit, Stage Left: Why Entrepreneurs End their Entrepreneurial Careers Before Retirement'. *Journal of Business Venturing*, 1(3): 323–38.

ROSA, P. (1998). 'Entrepreneurial Processes of Business Cluster Formation and Growth by "Habitual" Entrepreneurs'. *Entrepreneurship Theory and Practice*, 22: 43–61.

SCHEIN, E. H. (1978). *Career Dynamics: Matching Individual and Organizational Needs*. Reading, MA: Addison-Wesley.

SCHOLLHAMMER, H. (1991). 'Incidence and Determinants of Multiple Entrepreneurship', in N. C. Churchill, W. D. Bygrave, J. G. Covin et al. (eds) *Frontiers of Entrepreneurship Research*. Wellesley, Massachusetts: Babson College.

SCHUMPETER, J. A. (1934). 'The Theory of Economic Development'. *Harvard Economic Studies*. Cambridge: Harvard University.

SHANE, S. (2000). 'Prior Knowledge and the Discovery of Entrepreneurial Opportunities'. *Organization Science*, 11(4): 448–69.

—— (2003). *A General Theory of Entrepreneurship: The Individual-Opportunity Nexus*. Edward Elgar, MA: Northampton.

—— and S. VENKATARAMAN (2000). 'The Promise of Entrepreneurship as a Field of Research'. *Academy of Management Review* 25: 217–26.

—— and K. KHURANA (2003). 'Career Experience and Firm Founding'. *Industrial and Corporate Change*, 12(3): 519–44.

SHANTEAU, J. (1992). 'Competence in Experts: The Role of Task Characteristics'. *Organizational Behavior and Human Decision Processes*, 53(2): 252–66.

SHEPHERD, D. A. (2003). 'Learning from Business Failure: Propositions of Grief Recovery for the Self-Employed'. *Academy of Management Review*, 28(2): 318–29.

SHEPHERD, D. A. (2004). 'Educating Entrepreneurship Students About Emotion and Learning from Failure'. *Academy of Management Learning and Education* 3(3): 274–87.

Singh, R. P. (2001). 'A Comment on developing the Field of Entrepreneurship through the Study of Opportunity Recognition and Exploitation'. *Academy of Management Review*, 26(1): 10–12.

Sitkin, S. B. (1992). 'Learning Through Failure: The Strategy of Small Losses'. *Research in Organizational Behavior*, 14: 231–66.

Starr, J. and W. Bygrave (1991). 'The Assets and Liabilities of Prior Start-Up Experience: An Exploratory Study of Multiple Venture Entrepreneurs', in N. C. Churchill, W. D. Bygrave, J. G. Covin et al. (eds) *Frontiers of Entrepreneurship Research*. pp. 213–27. Wellesley, Massachusetts: Babson College.

Storey, D. J. (1994). *Understanding the Small Business Sector*. London: Routledge.

—— (2003). 'Entrepreneurship, Small and Medium Sized Enterprises and Public Policies', in Z. J. Acs and D. B. Audretsch (eds) *Handbook of Entrepreneurship Research: An Interdisciplinary Survey and Introduction*. Dordrecht, The Netherlands: Kluwer.

—— (2004). 'Exploring the Link, among Small Firms, between Management Training and Firm Performance: A Comparison between the UK and other OECD Countries'. *International Journal of Human Resource Management*, 14: 112–30.

Stuart, R. W. and P. A. Abetti (1990). 'Impact of Entrepreneurial and Management Experience on Early Performance'. *Journal of Business Venturing*, 5: 151–162.

Taylor, R. (1999). 'The Small Firm as a Temporary Coalition'. *Entrepreneurship and Regional Development*, 11: 1–19.

Teece, D. J., G. Pisano and A. Shuen (1997). 'Dynamic Capabilities and Strategic Management'. *Strategic Management Journal*, 18: 509–33.

Ucbasaran, D. (2004a). 'Opportunity Identification Behavior by Different Types of Entrepreneurs', in Butler, J. (ed.), *Opportunity Identification and Entrepreneurial Behavior*. Research in Entrepreneurship and Management Series, IAP.

—— (2004b). 'Business Ownership Experience, Entrepreneurial Behavior and Performance: Novice, Serial and Portfolio Entrepreneurs'. Unpublished Doctoral Thesis, Nottingham University Business School.

—— A. Lockett, M. Wright and P. Westhead (2003). 'Entrepreneurial Founder Teams: Factors Associated with Team Member Entry and Exit'. *Entrepreneurship Theory and Practice*, 28: 107–28.

—— M. Wright, P. Westhead and L. Busenitz (2003a). 'The Impact of Entrepreneurial Experience on Opportunity Identification and Exploitation: Habitual and Novice Entrepreneurs', in J. A. Katz and D. A. Shepherd (eds) *Cognitive Approaches to Entrepreneurship*. Advances in Entrepreneurship, Firm Emergence and Growth, 6: 231–63.

—— —— and P. Westhead (2003b). 'A Longitudinal Study of Habitual Entrepreneurs: Starters and Acquirers'. *Entrepreneurship and Regional Development*, 15: 207–28.

—— P. Westhead and M. Wright (2005). 'Business Ownership Experience, Information Search and Opportunity Identification'. Working Paper, Nottingham University Business School.

Westhead, P. and M. Wright (1998a). 'Novice, Portfolio and Serial Founders: Are They Different?' *Journal of Business Venturing*, 13: 173–204.

—— and —— (1998b). 'Novice, Portfolio and Serial Founders in Rural and Urban Areas'. *Entrepreneurship Theory and Practice*, 22: 63–100.

—— and —— (1999). 'Contributions of Novice, Portfolio and Serial Founders in Rural and Urban Areas'. *Regional Studies*, 33: 157–73.

WESTHEAD, P., D. UCBASARAN and M. WRIGHT (2003a). 'Differences Between Private Firms Owned by Novice, Serial and Portfolio Entrepreneurs: Implications for Policy-Makers and Practitioners'. *Regional Studies*, 37(2): 187–200.

—— —— —— and F. MARTIN (2003b). *Habitual Entrepreneurs in Scotland: Characteristics, Search Processes, Learning and Performance – Summary Report.* Glasgow: Scottish Enterprise. Available at www.scottish-enterprise.com

—— —— —— and M. BINKS (2006). 'Policy Toward Novice, Serial and Portfolio Entrepreneurs'. *Small Business Economics*, 21.

WHEATLEY, C. (2004). 'Cover Story: Portrait of a Serial Entrepreneur'. *Real Business.* (October). Available at http://www.realbusiness.co.uk/showdetail.asp? Article ID=2804.

WOO, C. Y., A. C. COOPER and W. C. DUNKELBERG (1991). 'The Development and Interpretation of Entrepreneurial Typologies'. *Journal of Business Venturing*, 6: 93–114.

WRIGHT, M., K. ROBBIE and C. ENNEW (1997). 'Venture Capitalists and Serial Entrepreneurs'. *Journal of Business Venturing*, 12(3): 227–49.

ZUCKERMAN, M. (1979). 'Attribution of Success and Failure Revisited, or: The Motivational Bias is Alive and Well in Attribution Theory'. *Journal of Personality*, 47: 245–87.

CHAPTER 18

ENTREPRENEURSHIP AND MANAGEMENT BUY-OUTS

MIKE WRIGHT AND ANDREW BURROWS

18.1 Introduction

Leveraged (LBO) and management buy-outs (MBO), where a group of individuals or investors attains significant equity ownership in an enterprise, have become a global phenomenon. These buy-outs have typically been associated with the taking private of listed firms in industries with mature products and stable cash flows. They have attracted interest because of the expected performance benefits to be derived from reducing agency costs through the incentive effects of concentrated ownership, the discipline of debt and effective monitoring by active investors (Jensen, 1989; 1993). This view of buy-outs as a phenomenon that is restricted to a small subset of firms (Rappaport, 1990) is at some considerable variance with the scope of transactions taking place in buy-out markets worldwide. Buy-outs occur in a wide range of sectors and involve a range of vendor sources. They may also involve enterprises with substantial growth prospects that are funded by modest amounts of leverage (CMBOR, 2004).

This chapter therefore takes a broader perspective that encompasses both traditional agency-based explanations of buy-outs as well as recognizing the buy-out phenomenon as a vehicle for entrepreneurial innovation. Although early studies by Bull (1989) and Malone (1989) suggested that buy-outs involved both agency cost reduction and entrepreneurial aspects, they did not formally conceptualize these two approaches. The agency theory approach conceptualizes buy-outs as a tool that facilitates cost efficiencies. The entrepreneurial perspective sees buy-outs as a means for implementing new innovations and strategic change that enable fuller exploitation of firm resources that may have been blocked by prior ownership arrangements, such as being part of a large diversified firm or a privately-owned firm with leadership succession problems.

We first elaborate the definitions and sources of buy-outs. Secondly, we review theoretical perspectives relating to buy-outs, notably the agency approach and an entrepreneurial perspective which draws on the theory of entrepreneurial cognition. The third main section reviews a model to explain different types of buy-out drawing on these two perspectives. The fourth section reviews studies of the effects of buy-outs, identifying evidence consistent with agency and entrepreneurial views of buy-outs. The final section provides discussion and conclusions.

18.2 Definitions and Sources

In general, the generic term buy-out involves the acquisition of an enterprise by a group of individual managers and investors (Wright, Robbie, Chiplin and Albrighton, 2000). This form of acquisition contrasts with the purchase of an enterprise by a corporate group. This broad categorization includes a number of variants. The typical leveraged buy-out (LBO) concerns the purchase of a business by a specialist financier, a leveraged buy-out association or private equity firm that initiates the transaction, and whose executives taking a leading role in the board of the company. The transaction is financed by substantial amounts of debt, hence the term leveraged buy-out. In a strict LBO, incumbent management may be replaced, or may obtain very modest equity stakes. In a management buy-out (MBO), incumbent senior management members initiate the transaction and become the main non-institutional equity holders. By contrast, in a management buy-in (MBI) the transaction is initiated by a group of external individual entrepreneurs. Both MBOs and MBIs tend to be financed by moderate amounts of leverage, with private equity and venture capital firms providing significant amounts of equity and quasi-equity. If management initiate a transaction that is funded by substantial amounts of leverage, the term 'leveraged management buy-out' is used. Where the

Table 18.1a UK buy-out/buy-in deal structures, less than £10m financing

Type of finance (Average %)	1999	2000	2001	2002	2003	2004
Equity	40.4	54.4	41.1	30.4	43.1	41.1
Mezzanine	3.2	4.6	1.8	1.7	0.6	1.0
Debt	48.2	35.0	46.6	48.9	47.8	44.8
Loan note	3.3	3.6	2.8	10.5	3.0	7.1
Other finance	8.2	3.0	7.5	8.5	5.6	6.0
Total financing (£m)	385	331	402	290	223	228
Vendor contribution	4.0	2.7	4.1	6.6	2.8	7.2
Management contribution	11.7	6.3	5.0	7.6	3.5	8.6
Proportion of equity held by management	69.6	63.7	61.8	78.4	66.8	61.8

Source: CMBOR/Barclays Private Equity/Deloitte.

transaction is initiated by a private equity firm, which may introduce external managers as equity holders and finance the deal with modest amounts of debt, an investor-led buy-out (IBO) is created. In some cases, a management employee buy-out (MEBO) occurs in which both senior management and the wider body of employees become significant equity holders.

Table 18.1b UK buy-out/buy-in deal structures, £10m or more financing

Type of finance (Average %)	1999	2000	2001	2002	2003	2004
Equity	42.8	43.3	37.2	37.6	41.6	39.9
Mezzanine	3.7	4.7	5.0	4.6	3.6	5.2
Debt	46.2	46.4	46.6	50.2	49.3	50.7
Loan note	2.5	1.7	4.0	3.2	2.8	1.9
Other finance	5.8	3.8	7.3	4.4	2.7	2.3
Total financing (£m)	11,727	13,339	13,614	9,934	10,922	11,463
Vendor contribution	3.3	2.3	4.3	3.4	1.2	2.9
Management contribution	5.6	5.3	2.1	2.0	3.1	2.7
Proportion of equity held by management	35.6	32.1	36.8	35.7	27.7	33.0

Source: CMBORee/Barclays Private Equity/Deloitte.

In buy-outs, management typically obtain larger equity stakes than could be expected through stock options in listed corporations (Jensen, 1989). UK evidence suggests that for smaller buy-outs and buy-ins, defined as those with a transaction value of below £10 million, management obtained a mean equity stake of about 70 percent over the period 1999–2004 (See Table 18.1a and CMBOR, 2003). Reflecting the heavy reliance on raising external funds, management's contribution to the total purchase price of these deals was a mean of about 8 percent. For larger transactions above £10 million deal value, management obtained a mean equity stake of about 32 percent for a mean contribution to the purchase price of 3 percent over the same period (See Table 18.1b).

Much research attention has focused on leveraged buy-outs of listed corporations in the US. However, while these transactions tend to be relatively large, they account for only a small proportion of buy-outs even in the US (Table 18.2). The nature of buy-out markets varies according to various factors related to the supply and demand for deals, financial and legal infrastructures and prospects for realization of investments (Wright, et al., 1992; Wright, Kissane and Burrows, 2004; Wright, et al., 2005). Table 18.2 presents evidence on the shares of selected buy-out markets accounted for by different vendor sources. Irrespective of the institutional context, the largest shares of buy-out markets are typically provided by divestments of divisions of large corporations and the transfer of private family firms to incumbent management. Whole firm buy-outs of listed corporations are present in all markets but to varying degrees. In what follows, we focus on understanding the factors explaining these main sources of buy-out.

Table 18.2 Selected international sources of buy-outs (2000–03)

Country	Divisional (%)	Whole firm private (%)	Whole firm listed (%)	Other (%)	Base for % (no. of deals)
France	35.9	28.3	4.3	31.5	515
Germany	62.6	11.4	3.6	22.4	361
Netherlands	63.0	12.6	1.8	22.6	270
Sweden	66.1	15.3	4.2	14.4	118
UK	43.2	27.4	5.6	23.8	2,570
US	48.0	34.4	17.0	0.6	1,291
Japan	65.5	6.5	10.0	18.0	139

Source: CMBOR/Barclays Private Equity/Deloitte; Thomson Financial.

18.3 Theoretical perspectives

18.3.1 Agency theory

Agency theory suggests that managers who own small equity stakes in listed corporations may pursue their own interests to the detriment of shareholders as principals. The absence of active investors to monitor management may exacerbate the problem (Jensen, 1989). These governance problems may also be present in divisions of large over-diversified corporations who are unable to control activities that are distant from the parent geographically, or in terms of the product markets in which they operate (Wright and Thompson, 1987).

Agency problems may be particularly evident where firms in mature industries generate substantial cash flows but have few investment opportunities with a positive net present value. Leveraged buy-outs (LBOs) which introduce stricter governance, through active specialist buy-out investors and the commitment to service high leverage, and significant managerial equity incentives, may mitigate the downside problems relating to over-diversification by weakly monitored managers in such firms (Jensen, 1989). Management equity ownership provides an incentive to reduce waste and only invest in projects that create firm value (Jensen and Meckling, 1976).

However, from an agency theory perspective, greater managerial ownership may decrease firm value due to entrenchment and managerial risk aversion, arising from under-diversified wealth portfolios and an absence of product and managerial labour market competition (Morck, Shleifer and Vishny, 1988). Accordingly, managers may be concerned with wealth preservation and may reject projects of higher risk with higher profit potential. As such, a buy-out may help in overcoming this problem by facilitating strategic change to create upside opportunity. High financial leverage may create agency cost of debt problems since the potential downside loss to managers owning small proportions of the firm's equity from choosing very risky projects is relatively small. This problem may be mitigated through close monitoring by an active investor or through the use of loan covenants (Citron, Robbie and Wright, 1997).

These issues suggest that a major limitation of the agency perspective concerns its ability to address the entrepreneurial, or upside potential of buy-outs. We turn to an entrepreneurial cognition perspective to help in more fully explaining buy-out related phenomena.

18.3.2 Entrepreneurial cognition

Differences in the way managers think and make decisions may give rise to different opportunities for buy-outs. Derived from cognitive psychology, entrepreneurial cognition (Busenitz and Lau, 1996) indicates that strategic decisions are significantly influenced by individual heuristics (see Wadeson, in Ch. 4 and Ucbasaran in Ch. 17 of this Handbook, this, for further discussion of cognitive aspects). The term 'heuristics' refers to simplifying strategies that individuals use to make strategic decisions (see also Ch. 17, fn. 1). A distinction can be made between entrepreneurial and managerial cognition. 'Entrepreneurial cognition' refers to the more extensive use of heuristics and individual beliefs that impact decision-making. 'Managerial cognition' refers to more systematic decision-making where management uses accountability and compensation schemes, the structural coordination of business activities across various units, and justify future developments using quantifiable budgets.

In contrast to managers operating in established markets, entrepreneurs in innovative situations typically operate under conditions of greater decision uncertainty and decision complexity. In such conditions, the pursuit of new opportunities becomes too overwhelming and costly for those decision-makers who seek a more factual base. In contrast, heuristics enable entrepreneurs to make timely decisions without the elaborate policies, procedural routines and structural mechanisms common to established organizations (Tversky and Kahneman, 1974). Further, the more extensive use of heuristic-based decision-making may enable faster learning as decision-makers can incorporate pieces of new information and make inferences encompassing the development of new innovations (Daft and Weick, 1984; Lei et al., 1996).

18.3.3 Buy-out types

Wright et al. (2000, 2001a, b, 2003) build on the agency and entrepreneurial cognition perspectives to develop a framework for understanding why different buy-out attributes have emerged globally and how to manage them better. This section reviews the elements of this framework which is summarized in Table 18.3.

18.3.4 Efficiency-oriented buy-outs (Quadrant 1)

Buy-outs in this quadrant are largely focused on reducing agency cost problems associated with over-diversification, over-investment, and insufficient accountability that result from the misalignment of management incentives and weak monitoring in listed corporations in mature industries with substantial free cash flows. Insiders leading the buy-out with a managerial (versus entrepreneurial) cognition are likely to respond favourably to the enhanced monetary incentives introduced.

Buy-out firms (LBO associations) provide active monitoring that was absent under previous ownership. A central aspect of monitoring is the requirement for

Table 18.3 Individual mindsets and buy-out types

Context, incentive, and governance for fostering efficencies	Individual mindset	
	Managerial mindset	Entrepreneurial mindset
	Quadrant 1: Efficiency buy-out	Quadrant 4: Buy-out failure
Pre-buy-out context and decision mindset	Agency problems; low risk. Decisions based primarily on systematic data and financial criteria	Mismatch of mindset, incentives and governance
Incentives	Ownership and management combined to align incentives in buy-outs in need of efficiency gains	Managers with entrepreneurial cognition and innovation skills are mismatched with financial incentives that reward efficiency gains
Governance	LBO association; financial control systems	LBO association; financial control systems
Context, incentive, and governance for fostering innovation	Quadrant 2: Revitalization buy-out	Quadrant 3: Entrepreneurial buy-out
Pre-buy-out context and decision mindset	Bureaucratic procedures stifle innovation and investment needed to be competitive; moderate risk.	Bureaucratic procedures stifle radical innovations associated with uncertainty and limited information; or technology-based businesses headed in the wrong direction; high risk.
	Decisions to renew competitive capabilities via innovations are based on their already proven success among key competitors	
		Heuristic-based logic can lead to strategic innovations and efficient decision making
Incentives	Long-term incentives usually equity and flexibly leverage to encourage process/incremental innovation and some managerial discretion	Long-term incentives usually equity and flexible leverage. Such incentives allow discretion to owner managers with an entrepreneurial mind-set to undertake strategic innovation
Governance	Venture capital firm/LBO Association; financial control systems	Venture capital/LBO associations provide financial monitoring and technical skills

Source: adapted from Wright et al. (2000, 2001a).

managers to provide regular detailed financial reports and to meet financial targets. The need to service high leverage means places pressure on managers not to indulge in wasteful investment projects and to reduce over-diversification. Buy-outs in this quadrant are likely to involve whole firm listed corporations and divisions of listed corporations where control problems are acknowledged.

A further possibility arises in mature private family firms where growth opportunities have essentially been exhausted and where founders may become somewhat detached from the running of the business as they begin to pursue other interests (Howorth, et al., 2004). In these situations, second-tier management may possess greater information about the running of the business and possess the managerial skills to introduce requisite professional management, but not be in a position to take appropriate decisions. A management buy-out may be a means of effecting succession to professional management. This may be acceptable to the founder as the best way to preserve their psychic income through maintaining the company's independent identity and culture, as well as continuing to be involved in the business. In such businesses, it is typical that dominant founders do not develop strong second-tier management who could become owner-managers. If this is the case, a management buy-in may be needed (Robbie and Wright, 1996).

18.3.5 Revitalization buy-outs (Quadrant 2)

Firms often need some level of innovation and change for survival. However, innovation may be problematic in large integrated organizations which use bureaucratic measures to ensure performance that restrict experimentation and initiative (Francis and Smith, 1995). Structure can help create the higher powered incentives for innovation through the substitution of debt for equity in a moderately leveraged buy-out.

As bureaucratic measures of performance are likely to screen out innovative personalities, buy-outs of this type are likely to involve leaders with 'managerial cognition'. Such managers tend to be comfortable with systematically evaluating and implementing incremental, though non-entrepreneurial, improvements and innovations. To balance the managerial mindset of the business leaders, there is a need for LBO associations to acquire more technical skills beyond their traditional financial monitoring skills and to exert influence on investment decisions through their board positions. As high leverage may frustrate the ability of managers who are incentivized to engage in incremental innovations, a moderate degree of leverage may be required to provide sufficient flexibility to allow investment to occur. The focus on incumbents with a managerial mindset, suggests buy-outs in this quadrant are likely to involve management buy-outs (MBOs) and management-led employee buy-outs (MEBOs) of divisions of a publicly listed corporation and state-owned enterprises.

18.3.6 Entrepreneurial buy-outs (Quadrant 3)

Managers with more traditional managerial cognition orientations may be unable to take advantage of innovation opportunities, even with enhanced incentives. Rather, high-powered ownership incentives encourage risk-taking; and long-term rewards, in combination with heuristic-based logic, nurture the innovation process.

Opportunities for entrepreneurial buy-outs are most likely to arise in businesses with misalignments of incentives and managerial frustrations prior to a buy-out and where technology-based businesses run into substantial problems. In the first case, termed entrepreneurial release buy-outs, divisions with profitable and innovative investment opportunities may be disadvantaged if their division is not regarded as strategically central to the parent organization, and if corporate control mechanisms emphasize divisional competition on short-term efficiency indicators in internal capital markets (Wright, 1988).

In this context, managers with entrepreneurial skills are likely to become frustrated with a bureaucratic corporate structure where proposals for new ventures are rejected by corporate management because of the lack of hard information that fits into organization-level investment appraisal systems. The possibility of divestment may present a window of opportunity to managers with an entrepreneurial mindset.

In contrast to the previous two types, venture capital firms may have an important role to play in supporting entrepreneurial buy-outs, as financiers are needed who are able to understand the technology sufficiently to be able to assess the investment initially and to monitor it subsequently. Lower levels of debt and higher levels of equity may be necessary to provide greater managerial equity incentives and to fund the investment required to implement identified opportunities for strategic innovation.

Buy-out managers have often perceived the opportunities for innovation but are generally unsuccessful in realizing them under the previous ownership regime (Wright and Coyne, 1985). Entrepreneurial buy-out managers have expanded discretion to fund those creative ideas that they perceive and to do so in a more speedy manner than would otherwise have been possible.

An increasing number of buy-outs are now emerging in technology-based industries involving the divestment of non-core businesses where the parent did not understand, or have the capability to manage, the technology involved (Wright, Robbie and Albrighton, 1999). When the possibility exists for new innovations to reap substantial economic rewards, and when incumbent divisional and corporate management are either unable to see, process relevant information, or act upon such opportunities, an opening exists for outside investors to purchase the division. Capitalizing on entrepreneurial opportunities not seen by incumbent divisional and corporate management, investor-led buy-outs have emerged as a growth opportunity (Wright and Robbie, 1996).

In the second type of entrepreneurial buy-out, busted tech, or turnaround buy-outs owner-managers may already have the skillset and the incentives to pursue strategic innovations. However, little monitoring may have been exercised over management. The opportunity for a buy-out may arise when the firm encounters difficulties, either through liquidity problems or poor execution of the business plan due to a lack of technological expertise. In this case, a buy-out can be a means of bringing better governance expertise, both financial and technological, to an innovative opportunity.

Dominant founders in such situations, with their unique decision-making style may pose problems to advancing the business (Wright et al., 2001b). This is a familiar problem in venture capital investments (Fiet et al., 1997). The decision-making approach relevant for early innovative stages may be problematical in later growth stages. Many founders are unable to adjust their decision-making style in order to accommodate the more systematic needs of the maturing business. Other founders of private firms may become overly conservative in an attempt to preserve the wealth they have generated, which may be detrimental to the longer-term growth and even survival of the firm. Hence succession in the leadership of the firm may be necessary for continued growth. Replacement of the founder through an IBO or MBI may be appropriate as it brings in outsiders with the entrepreneurial mindset necessary to effect innovations but who also is more amenable to the control mechanisms likely to be brought in by investors. The demands of turning the firm around and the identification of a new entrepreneurial strategy generally suggest lower leverage than in either Quadrant 1 or 2.

18.3.7 Buy-out failures (Quadrant 4)

In some buy-out situations there may be a mismatch between the appropriate control and incentive mechanism and the entrepreneurial mindset. In some cases, management seeks to undertake an efficiency buy-out but has the mindset to pursue entrepreneurial innovations. These buy-outs will be subject to an efficiency orientation regime that conflicts with managers with an entrepreneurial mindset. Managers seeing entrepreneurial opportunities may need lower leverage and a buy-out firm or a venture capital partner that understands the firm's innovation processes, in contrast to the strong financial control and high leverage regime likely to be put in place. Buy-out failure may occur as entrepreneurial managers become frustrated with, and override financial control mechanisms. The solution is to attempt actions either to replace entrepreneurial managers with those with a managerial mindset and to introduce closer monitoring, that is, move towards Quadrant 1; or to refinance the company with lower leverage and/or bring in new investors that have the requisite skills to understand more innovative processes, that is, move towards Quadrant 3.

This type of buy-out raises the important need for flexibility in the buy-out arrangement to enable adaptation to be made in a timely and appropriate manner when it becomes clear that a mismatch has arisen. Secondary buy-outs may be a means of effecting this adaptation (Wright, et al., 2000).

18.3.8 Institutional context

The prevalence of these different forms of buy-out may depend on the institutional context. Wright, Kitamura and Hoskisson (2003) extend this conceptual framework developed in respect of Western economies to the Japanese context. They argue that pressures in Japan are more likely to give rise to buy-outs involving the revitalization of activities through incremental investment and process innovation and entrepreneurial buy-outs involving radical innovation than buy-outs focusing solely on efficiency improvements. The need to restructure *keiretsu* groups to increase their competitiveness has meant that keiretsu-affiliated companies are increasing their mobility and flexibility by divesting unprofitable and non-core units. In some contrast to the development of the buy-out market in the West, where transactions focused on under-performing divisions that provided opportunities to make efficiency gains, buy-outs in Japan are seen to be of particular relevance in the spinning-off of underperforming divisions where management's opportunities for growth are frustrated by bureaucratic internal control systems, creating opportunities for revitalization and entrepreneurial buy-outs. Independence from the parent company or *keiretsu* group may facilitate revitalization and entrepreneurship. Japanese firms have typically been highly effective in producing process innovation rather than product innovation, and in adapting and improving on existing technology rather than creating new technology. Hence, Japanese managers who perceive radical entrepreneurial opportunities are likely to be frustrated within large firms with networked relationships. The emergence of the buy-out concept in Japan means that managers have another avenue to realize entrepreneurial opportunities and there is some evidence that this is occurring.

18.4 Empirical evidence

In this section we review evidence relating to the impact of buy-outs in terms of the antecedents and stock market responses to buy-outs; the effects of buy-outs on performance, productivity and employment; the longer-term effects of buy-outs, including failure; the influence of governance mechanisms; and the impact of buy-outs on strategy, entrepreneurial orientation and control systems.

18.4.1 Antecedents and stock market responses

There is widespread evidence (see Jensen, 1993; Thompson and Wright, 1995 for a review) that whole firms going private through buy-outs generate large abnormal gain for the target's shareholders. These gains reflect the anticipated benefits from the change in ownership and governance regime but do not identify sources of these gains. Stock market studies of divestments by buy-outs find contrasting evidence depending on whether they relate to the US or the UK. Hite and Vetsuypens (1989) find small positive effects while Saadouni, Briston, Mallin and Robbie (1996) find negative effects. Existing owners returns are greater when competitive bids are received (Easterwood et al., 1994).

Despite these significant gains, there is the possibility of significant under-pricing in buy-outs with significant insider participation. Evidence from buy-out attempts that are announced and then withdrawn show some evidence that managers simply exploit asset prices which appear (to them) to be too low (DeAngelo et al., 1984; Marais et al., 1989). Smith (1990) finds no evidence of deliberate misrepresentation or concealment by management of insider information. However, the stock market response appears to depend substantially on whether or not a subsequent bid occurs (Lee, 1992). Evidence of 'earnings management' prior to a management bid is somewhat contradictory: DeAngelo (1986) reports none while Perry and Williams (1994) find evidence of consistent falls in the last complete financial year prior to an announcement.

US studies of the role of free cash flow in the decision to go private have produced mixed results. Some studies report that firms going private have greater free cash flow than firms remaining public (Lehn and Poulsen, 1989; Singh, 1990), while others possibly using more robust methods (Kieschnick, 1998; Opler and Titman, 1993; Halpern et al., 1999) find no evidence that this is the case. In contrast, a study of the governance structures associated with whether a firm is taken private in a management buy-out in the UK found that firms that go private through a buy-out are more likely to have higher CEO ownership, higher institutional ownership and more duality of CEO and chairman (Weir, Laing and Wright, 2005). These firms did not have excess free cash flows or face a greater threat of hostile acquisition but they did have lower growth opportunities. These findings are consistent with the incentive and monitoring hypotheses for buy-outs.

18.4.2 Performance, productivity and employment

Research on US LBOs indicates substantial mean improvements in profitability and cash flow measures between one year prior to buy-out and two or three years afterwards. These studies, using various estimation procedures, report mean gains in the operating cash flow/sales ratio of between 11.9 and 55 percent (Thompson and Wright, 1995). UK evidence (Wright, et al., 1996) of the impact of full firm MBOs on accounting profits finds that MBOs generated significantly higher increases in return on assets than comparable firms that did not experience an MBO over a period from two to five years after buy-out.

Both US and UK samples show that total factor productivity (TFP) improves significantly after buy-out. For the US, Lichtenberg and Siegel (1990) found that total factor productivity for plants involved in buy-outs, rose from 2 percent above its industry control, to 8.3 percent above over the first three years after buy-out. Wright, et al. (1996) and Amess (2003) find for the UK that management buy-outs also had significantly greater TFP following the change in ownership. In the largest and most robust buy-out study to date, Harris, et al. (2005) assess TFP of buy-out and non-buy-out plants and find using plant-level data that in contrast to the US evidence, buy-outs were approximately two percent less productive than comparable plants before the transfer of ownership, but experienced a substantial increase in productivity of approximately 90 percent after buy-out.

The evidence on the effects of buy-out on employment is mixed. While some US studies report small increases in total firm employment following a buy-out, more robust studies that adjust for industry effects find that buy-outs fail to expand their employment in line with industry averages (Kaplan, 1989; and Smith, 1990). UK studies suggest that job losses occur most substantially at the time of the change in ownership but subsequently increase (Wright et al., 1992). These reductions in employment appear to contribute significantly to increases in TFP (Harris et al., 2004).

18.4.3 Longer term performance and failure

Kaplan (1991) and Wright et al. (1994), covering both the US and the UK, indicate that the longevity of buy-out structures is heterogeneous. Though the majority of buy-out structures may be relatively long-lived, a substantial proportion, particularly larger firms, either return to quoted status or are sold to third parties within a relatively short period. This raises questions as to whether these changes lead to the removal of the buy-out governance structure and discretion for management. Holthausen and Larcker (1996) find that while leverage and management equity falls post-IPO, they remain high, relative to comparable listed corporations that have not undergone a buy-out. Pre-IPO, buy-outs' accounting performance is significantly higher than the median for the buy-outs' sector. Following the IPO, accounting performance remains significantly above the firms' sector for four years but declines during this period. Consistent with other studies, they find that the change is positively related to changes in insider ownership but not to leverage.

UK evidence shows that IPOs of buy-outs results in positive and highly statistically significant initial premiums. However, in contrast to evidence from UK IPOs generally, there is no evidence of a significant under-performance in the long run (Jelic, et al., 2005). Venture backed MBOs tend to IPO earlier than their non-venture backed counterparts. There is some evidence that they are more underpriced than MBOs without venture capital backing but not that they perform better than their non-VC backed counterparts in the long run. In contrast to the grandstanding hypothesis, private to public MBOs backed by more reputable VCs in the UK tend to exit earlier and these MBOs performed better than those backed by less prestigious VCs.

With respect to failure, higher leverage in buy-outs may mean that financial distress is signalled earlier than if an enterprise were funded substantially by equity, thus providing greater scope to restructure the firm successfully. The payment of excessive premia to acquire the buy-out may result in higher amounts of debt and an increased probability of failure (Kaplan and Stein, 1993). Notwithstanding the degree of leverage, greater restructuring undertaken expeditiously at the time of buy-out is associated with a greater probability of survival (Wright, Wilson, Robbie and Ennew, 1996). Interestingly, while direct investor monitoring is not found to be significantly associated with avoiding failure, positive managerial motives for buy-out were associated with reducing the probability of subsequent failure. Variables relating to the proportion of equity held by management and initiative being taken by management were weakly significant. These findings are consistent with the control function of high levels of debt which place pressure on management to restructure. At the same time, they are also consistent with the entrepreneurial opportunity recognition and behaviour of management.

18.4.4 Governance and performance

Phan and Hill (1995) find that in US buy-outs, managerial equity stakes had a much stronger effect on buy-out performance than debt levels for periods of three and five years following the transfer of ownership. Thompson et al. (1992) find that the management team shareholding size had by far the largest impact on relative performance in UK MBOs. Leveraged recapitalizations, which simply substitute debt for equity in quoted companies, have been shown to raise shareholder value (Denis and Denis, 1993) but they do not appear to have the same performance impact as buy-outs, which also involve managerial ownership and institutional involvement (Denis, 1994).

Similarly to venture capital investments (Kaplan and Strömberg, 2001), buy-outs also involve important contractual provisions that allow the private equity investor to separately allocate cash-flow right, voting rights, board rights and other control rights. These rights are frequently found to be contingent on observable measures of financial and non-financial performance. Voting and control rights tend to be allocated such that if an investee performs poorly, the private equity firm obtains control. If an investee's performance improves, the entrepreneur is likely to obtain increased control, while if the investee does very well the private equity firm is likely to get cash-flow rights but reduced control rights. Thompson, et al. (1991) find that control devices in buy-outs are substitutes for greater managerial equity holdings. These control devices involved both contractual devices such as performance contingent equity stakes for management (so-called equity ratchets) and board representation.

There are similarities but also differences in active investor governance in buy-outs and buy-ins. Sahlman (1990) notes that executives in LBO financiers may typically assume control of the board of directors but are generally less likely than venture capitalists to assume operational control (see Wright, et al., 2003, for a review of the venture capital evidence). UK evidence in buy-outs and buy-ins shows that board representation is the most popular method of monitoring investee companies with venture capitalists also requiring regular provision of accounts (Robbie, et al., 1992). However, there appears to be a greater degree of control exercised by institutions over management buy-ins than for buy-outs in terms of more regular financial reporting and greater use of performance contingent contracts.

Evidence from buy-outs and buy-ins emphasizes the importance of keeping the venture capitalists informed of developments through building a partnership and regular contact (Hatherly et al., 1994). In larger buy-outs and buy-ins, there is evidence of extensive active monitoring, especially where problems arise (Wright et al., 1994). However, in smaller transactions, the disproportionately high cost of monitoring may mean that these relationships do not develop (Robbie and Wright, 1995). Further, in small buy-outs and buy-ins, management may own the vast majority of the equity and a very small group of managers may carry out the major functions. It may thus be difficult to remove under-performing management or enforce a trade sale.

18.4.5 Strategy, entrepreneurial orientation and control

Improvements in performance have been identified as being associated with better working capital management, lower cost structures and to a lesser extent asset sales (Wright et al., 1992). Further, performance may be improved through pursuing strategies focused on more related businesses (Seth and Easterwood, 1993; Phan and Hill, 1995).

Increased leverage may be expected to put pressure on management to reduce CAPEX and R&D. US evidence shows that capital investment falls immediately following the LBO (Kaplan, 1989; Smith 1990). In the UK, however, Wright et al., 1992) report that asset sales are offset by new capital investment, particularly in plant and equipment. Several US studies report that buy-outs reduce R&D spending, but that LBOs are very largely in low R&D industries, such that the overall effect is unsubstantial. However, Zahra (1995) finds in his sample of US buy-outs that R&D expenditure is used more effectively. Both Wright et al. (1992) and Zahra (1995) find that buy-outs are followed by significant increases in new product development and other aspects of corporate entrepreneurship.

In their study of changes following buy-out, Bruining and Wright (2002) analyze how buy-outs improve their entrepreneurial orientation following the change in ownership and how private equity firms contribute to this process through the development of post-investment relationships. They show that buy-outs do occur where entrepreneurial opportunities exist and provide support for Wright et al. (2000) who argue that buy-outs do not simply involve improving efficiency in companies in mature sectors. They identify entrepreneurial decisions and practices that add value to the business through new product/new market development in their companies that were frustrated by the parent prior to MBO and show that the firms act more entrepreneurially than pre-MBO. Private equity firms' enhancement of entrepreneurial orientation in MBOs appears to occur where they: intervene in integrating the contributions of specialists in top management decision-making; influence leadership style of the CEO; keep value added strategy on track; approve bonuses for top management; assist in new ventures (consortia)/new acquisitions; and broaden market focus; and where they put effort into reviewing and monitoring the quality of R&D investment plans, budgets and marketing plans. Sometimes the private equity firm needs to invest in management information systems necessary to modernize management in order to control entrepreneurial decisions better. The private equity firm uses its network to reduce the negative impact of competition and to select key figures as CFOs and new CEOs.

The heterogeneity of buy-out types has implications for the development of management control systems. Jones (1992) focusing on efficiency buy-outs, reports increases in the quality of information used for operational control, an intensification of formal controls, more disaggregated feedback to increase operational efficiency and fulfil profit standards and a more positive attitude of employees towards accounting control systems to facilitate participation following buy-out. Jones also reports an increase of perceived importance of accounting control systems, indicating a change in the way the established management accounting techniques were applied. Jones concluded that the independence gained by the MBO firm improved the matching between accounting control systems and contextual variables. These findings signal pressures to improve efficiency after MBO and an increased reliance upon accounting control systems.

Bruining, et al. (2004) suggest that the control needs of manager-owners in revitalization and entrepreneurial MBOs requiring product development or innovation go beyond the use of the accounting control system to achieve the financial targets agreed between management and investors. Adopting Simons' (1995) framework of levers of control, they propose on the basis of qualitative analysis of a revitalization and an entrepreneurial buy-out that to implement changes in strategy after an MBO effectively, top management needs more than what the classical accounting control system provides. They suggest that in entrepreneurial buy-outs there is a need for management to be more proactive in taking the initiative to effect changes in culture rather than relying on accounting control systems and that this action has to pervade the organization. In addition, while there may be an increased emphasis upon planning in efficiency buy-outs to improve the match with the organizational context, in more entrepreneurial buy-outs there needs to be a dynamic search process of development rather than a once-for-all shift. Diagnostic control systems may develop following all types of buy-outs, but in entrepreneurial buy-outs this is also a dynamic process since the entrepreneurial search for profitable new markets takes place in an environment of great uncertainty. Private equity investors may play an important role in guiding management to underpin their more entrepreneurial belief and interaction systems. This can be achieved with appropriate diagnostic control systems that keep the buy-out on track to meet agreed targets for the realization of capital gains. In efficiency buy-outs, the planning system develops to provide additional information concerning the interface between external environments and internal operations. In more entrepreneurial buy-outs, interactive control systems develop with both the financial investor and external actors as an important part of a dynamic process of search and learning, to access insights and information that would be valuable in creating a competitive advantage in a changing market environment.

5 Discussion and Conclusions

This chapter has examined the explanations for different types of buy-outs by adopting a broad perspective that encompasses both the traditional agency cost view and an entrepreneurial cognition view. The agency cost-based approach has focused mainly on limiting managerial discretion and increasing managerial incentives. The scope for buy-outs may be extended considerably by developing understanding of the rationales for buy-outs that expand managerial discretion to foster entrepreneurial opportunity. A central point that emerges is that increasing managerial incentives and control devices is insufficient for entrepreneurial opportunities to be identified and exploited. Rather, there is a need for business leaders to have an entrepreneurial mindset.

Our review of what is now a substantial empirical literature relating to buy-outs identified considerable evidence consistent with both agency cost and entrepreneurial perspectives relating to buy-outs. There is evidence of significant performance improvements following buy-out and that these changes are associated with efficiency enhancing and cost reduction behaviour resulting from the introduction of the buy-out governance structure. However, there are also some recent doubts about the robustness of the free cash flow explanation for buy-outs. It is also possible that suggestions of the use of insider information by managers may reflect their private perception of potential entrepreneurial opportunities. Interestingly, research relating to the relative importance of different incentive and governance mechanisms in buy-outs also suggests that it is managerial equity ownership that is typically most significant rather than the control aspects. Similarly, buy-out failure is less likely when management have embarked upon the buy-out because they have identified upside opportunities. Evidence of entrepreneurial aspects is provided in relation to the extent of corporate entrepreneurship and new product development following buy-out, enhancement to entrepreneurial orientation, and the development of control systems that allow for new opportunity recognition and exploitation. These findings point to the heterogeneity of buy-outs and suggest limitations in the use of agency theory to explain management buy-outs.

Further research is required that is specifically designed to compare efficiency, revitalization and entrepreneurial buy-outs. In particular, examination that compares the performance of buy-outs in the different quadrants identified here is required, which also links this to a buy-out manager's cognitive orientation. Busenitz and Barney (1997) have developed measures to distinguish entrepreneurial and managerial mindsets involving both scales and vignettes. Buy-out financiers and management need to consider when heuristic-based decision-making leads to competitive advantage and disadvantage. In addition, they may need to identify particular types of incentives with particular buy-out attributes and decision modes associated with each quadrant. This further research might also examine whether there are significant differences in the financing and governance structures of the buy-outs in the four quadrants.

It is also evident that the vast bulk of empirical research has been related to the US and to a lesser extent, to the UK. Our evidence suggests some difference in the nature of buy-outs between the UK and US. If this is the case between two countries typically closely linked in terms of a stock market-based Anglo-American governance regime, other major differences may be apparent concerning countries with more bank-oriented or network-based systems. As buy-outs become a global phenomenon, there is therefore scope to extend this analysis to different institutional contexts. This chapter has shown, through the illustration of the Japanese context, that the nature of buy-outs may depend on the institutional context. Such analysis might also be extended to other countries of Europe and Asia where buy-outs are beginning to develop. For example, buy-out markets are developing in the transition economies of central and eastern Europe and China and it would be interesting to examine the relative importance of efficiency versus entrepreneurial aspects in these countries where financial institutions have been weak and entrepreneurship is beginning to emerge from a period when it was, officially at least, suppressed.

The analysis in this chapter has implications for understanding the returns to buy-out financiers. After several years where buy-outs have yielded high returns for investors, private equity firms are increasingly noting the difficulties in generating superior returns on their investment portfolios. The raising of massive amounts of funds from the late 1990s onwards is also contributing to an increase in competition among private equity houses for good deals. Our analysis suggests that financiers might find it attractive to move into buy-outs that provide returns not just through efficiency gains, but also through growth by identifying innovative market niches. Adopting this strategic direction may require that private equity firms acquire human capital skills to monitor and assist the development of entrepreneurial buy-outs that they do not generally possess (Lockett, Murray and Wright, 2002). Resolution of this problem may involve strategic alliances between classic LBO associations and venture capitalists. Further research might probe more carefully the ways in which private equity firms add value to buy-outs.

Our analysis links to a number of theoretical perspectives on entrepreneurship (Casson et al. in the Introduction to this Handbook; Ricketts in Ch. 2 of this Handbook). The notions of efficiency and revitalization buy-outs resonates with the Marshallian perspective of evolutionary change instituted by business management, or low-level entrepreneurship (See Casson et al. in this Handbook). Entrepreneurial buy-outs link to a Schumpeterian notion of revolutionary innovation which may not be confined to new firms. We also see the role of the entrepreneur as someone who is alert to currently unexploited opportunities in an uncertain environment. For MBO managers, these opportunities can only be realized through the change of ownership which enables action to be taken that was not possible previously. This importance of ownership also chimes with Fama and Jensen's (1983) view that classic entrepreneurial firms are associated with owners (i.e. principals) that combine residual risk bearing (i.e. ownership), and decision-making (i.e. control). Indeed, Hawley (1927) argued that ownership rights are crucial for undertaking entrepreneurship, because they allow the entrepreneur to make decisions about the coordination of resources to gain entrepreneurial rents, in return for absorbing the uncertainty of owning those resources. The contribution of funds by management teams in buy-outs and the risk of failure emphasizes the risk-bearing aspect of entrepreneurship. However, while we take a broad view of entrepreneurship to include established firms, our perspective is that economic agents vary in their ability to identify and interpret the information relating to unexploited opportunities.

Finally, the analysis in this chapter also links to issues regarding the nature of the market for entrepreneurial finance. There is some debate about the crowding out of early stage venture capital by management buy-outs (Lockett, et al., 2002). Concern centres around the notion that venture capital firms will be more willing to invest in management buy-outs of established firms in mature sectors as these offer lower risk than early-stage new ventures. An entrepreneurial perspective suggests that buy-outs can contribute economically through the identification and exploitation of opportunities for growth rather than only improving economic efficiency from cost cutting. Our illustration of buy-outs in the Japanese context also suggests that sole focus on early stage start-ups as the repository of entrepreneurial talent may be misplaced in those institutional environments that provide little incentive and scope for creative initiative taking. There may be economic benefits, therefore, from developing an entrepreneurial culture (della Guista and King, Ch. 24 in this Handbook) that stresses that entrepreneurship may be possible in established businesses. Entrepreneurial finance and taxation incentives might then be targeted at facilitating the buy-out of activities with significant growth opportunities, but which are constrained under their present ownership regime.

References

Amess, K. (2003). 'The Effect of Management Buy-outs on Firm-level Technical Efficiency: Evidence from a Panel of U.K. Machinery and Equipment Manufacturers'. *Journal of Industrial Economics*, 51: 35–44.

Bruining, H. and M. Wright (2002). 'Entrepreneurial Orientation in Management Buy-outs and the Contribution of Venture Capital'. *Venture Capital*, 4(2): 147–68.

—— M. Bonnet and M. Wright (2004). 'Management Control Systems and Strategy Change in Buy-outs'. *Management Accounting Research*, 15: 155–77.

Bull, I. (1989). 'Financial Performance of Leveraged Buy-outs: An Empirical Analysis'. *Journal of Business Venturing*, 4(4): 263–79.

Busenitz, L. and J. Barney (1997). 'Differences Between Entrepreneurs and Managers in Large Organizations: Biases and Heuristics in Strategic Decision-making'. *Journal of Business Venturing*, 12: 9–30.

—— and C. Lau (1996). 'A Cross-cultural Cognitive Model of New Venture Creation'. *Entrepreneurship Theory and Practice*, 20(4): 25–39.

Citron, D., K. Robbie and M. Wright (1997). 'Loan Covenants and MBO Lending'. *Accounting and Business Research*, 27(4): 277–96.

CMBOR (2003). 'Management Buyouts Deal Structures'. *Management Buy-outs: Quarterly Review* from CMBOR (Autumn), Tables A28 and A29, pp. 94–5.

CMBOR (2004). 'European Management Buy-outs'. *Centre for Management Buy-out Research*. University of Nottingham.

DAFT, R. and K. WEICK (1984). 'Toward a Model of Organizations as Interpretation Systems'. *Academy of Management Review*, 9(2): 284–95.

DEANGELO, L. (1986). 'Accounting Numbers as Market Valuation Substitutes: A Study of the Management Buy-outs of Public Stockholders'. *Accounting Review*, 61: 400–20.

—— L. DEANGELO and E. RICE (1984). 'Shareholder Wealth and Going Private'. *Journal of Law and Economics*, 27: 367–402.

DENIS, D. J. (1994). 'Organizational Form and the Consequences of Highly Leveraged Transactions: Kroger's Recapitalization and Safeway's LBO'. *Journal of Financial Economics*, 36(2): 193–224.

—— and D. DENIS (1993). 'Managerial Discretion, Organizational Structure and Corporate Performance'. *Journal of Accounting and Economics*, 16: 209–36.

EASTERWOOD, J. C., R. F. SINGER, A. SETH and D. F. LANG (1994). 'Controlling the Conflict of Interest in Management buy-outs'. *Review of Economics and Statistics*, 76: 512–22.

FAMA, E. and M. JENSEN (1983). 'Separation of Ownership and Control'. *Journal of Law and Economics*, 26(2): 301–25.

FIET, J., L. BUSENITZ, D. MOESEL, and J. BARNEY (1997). 'Complementary Theoretical Perspectives on the Dismissal of New Venture Team Members'. *Journal of Business Venturing*, 12: 347–66.

FRANCIS, J. and A. SMITH (1995). 'Agency Costs and Innovation: Some Empirical Evidence', *Journal of Accounting and Economics*, 19: 383–409.

HALPERN, P., R. KIESCHNICK and W. ROTENBERG (1999). 'On the Heterogeneity of Leveraged Going Private Transactions'. *The Review of Financial Studies*, 12: 281–309.

HARRIS, R., D. SIEGEL and M. WRIGHT (2005). 'Assessing the Impact of Management Buy-outs on Economic Efficiency: Plant-Level Evidence from the United Kingdom'. *Review of Economics and Statistics*, 87(1): 148–53.

HATHERLY, D. et al. (1994). 'An Exploration of the MBO-Financier Relationship'. *Corporate Governance*, 2(1): 20–9.

HAWLEY, F. (1927). 'The Orientation of Economics on Enterprise'. *American Economic Review*, 17: 409–28.

HITE, G. L. and M. R. VETSUYPENS (1989). 'Management Buy-outs of Divisions and Shareholder Wealth'. *Journal of Finance*, 44: 953–70.

HOLTHAUSEN, D. and D. LARCKER (1996). 'The Financial Performance of Reverse Leverage Buyouts'. *Journal of Financial Economics*, 42: 293–332.

HOWORTH, C., P. WESTHEAD and M. WRIGHT (2004). 'Buy-outs, Information Asymmetry and the Family-management Dyad'. *Journal of Business Venturing*, 19(4): 509–34.

JELIC, R., SAADOUNI, B. and M. WRIGHT (2005). 'Performance of Private to Public MBOs: The Role of Venture Capital'. *Journal of Business Finance and Accounting*, 32(3/4): 643–82.

JENSEN, M. (1989). 'Eclipse of the Public Corporation'. *Harvard Business Review*, 67(5): 61–74.

—— (1993). 'The Modern Industrial Revolution: Exit, and the Failure of Internal Control Systems'. *Journal of Finance*, 48: 831–80.

—— and W. MECKLING (1976). 'Theory of the Firm: Managerial Behavior, Agency Costs and Ownership Structure'. *Journal of Financial Economics*, 3(4): 305–60.

JONES, C. (1992). 'The Attitude of Owner Managers Towards Accounting Control Systems Following Management Buyout'. *Accounting Organizations and Society*, 17(2): 151–68.

Kaplan, S. N. (1989). 'The Effects of Management Buy-outs on Operations and Value'. *Journal of Financial Economics*, 24: 217–54.

—— (1991). 'The Staying Power of Leveraged buy-outs'. *Journal of Financial Economics*, 29: 287–313.

—— and J. C. Stein (1993). 'The Evolution of Buy-out Pricing in the 1980s'. *Quarterly Journal of Economics*, 108: 313–57.

—— and P. Strömberg (2001). 'Venture Capitalists as Principals: Contracting, Screening and Monitoring'. *American Economic Review*, 91(2): 426–30.

Kieschnick, R. (1998). 'Free Cash Flow and Stockholder Gains in Going Private Transaction Revisited', *Journal of Business Finance and Accounting*, 25: 187–202.

Lee, D. S. (1992). 'Management Buy-out Proposals and Inside Information'. *Journal of Finance*, 47: 1061–79.

Lehn, K. and A. Poulsen (1989). 'Free Cash Flow and Stockholder Gains in Going Private Transactions'. *Journal of Finance*, 44: 771–88.

Lei, D., M. A. Hitt and R. Bettis, (1996). 'Dynamic Core Competences through Meta-learning and Strategic Context'. *Journal of Management*, 22(4): 549–69.

Lichtenberg, F. and D. Siegel (1990). 'The Effects of Leveraged Buy-outs on Productivity and Related Aspects of Firm Behavior'. *Journal of Financial Economics*, 27(1): 165–94.

Lockett, A., G. Murray and M. Wright (2002). 'Do UK Venture Capitalists Still Have a Bias Against Technology Investments?' *Research Policy*, 31: 1009–30.

Malone, S. (1989). 'Characteristics of Smaller Company Leveraged Buy-outs'. *Journal of Business Venturing*, 4(5): 345–59.

Marais, L, K. Schipper and A. Smith (1989). 'Wealth Effects of Going Private on Senior Securities'. *Journal of Financial Economics*, 23: 155–91.

Morck, R., A. Shleifer and R. Vishny (1988). 'Management Ownership and Market Valuation: An Empirical Analysis'. *Journal of Financial Economics*, 20: 293–315.

Ofek, E. (1994). 'Efficiency Gains in Unsuccessful Management Buy-outs', *Journal of Finance*, 49: 637–54.

Opler, T. C. (1992). 'Operating Performance in Leveraged Buy-outs', *Financial Management*, 21: 27–34.

—— and Titman, S. (1993). 'The Determinants of Leveraged Buyout Activity–Free Cash Flow vs Financial Distress Costs'. *Journal of Finance*, 45(5): 1985–99.

Perry, S. E. and T. M. Williams (1994). 'Earnings Management Preceding Management Buy-out Offers'. *Journal of Accounting and Economics*, 18: 152–179.

Phan, P. and C. Hill (1995). 'Organizational Restructuring and Economic Performance in Leveraged Buy-outs: An Ex Post Study'. *Academy of Management Journal*, 38(3): 704–39.

Rappaport, A. (1990). 'The Staying Power of the Public Corporation'. *Harvard Business Review*, 68: 96–104.

Robbie, K. and M. Wright (1995). 'Managerial and Ownership Succession and Corporate Restructuring: The Case of Management Buy-ins'. *Journal of Management Studies*, 32(4): 527–50.

—— and —— (1996). *Management Buy-ins: Entrepreneurs, Active Investors and Corporate Restructuring. Studies in Finance*. Manchester: Manchester University Press.

—— —— and S. Thompson (1992). 'Management Buy-ins in the UK'. *Omega*, 20: 445–56.

SAADOUNI. B., R. BRISTON, C. MALLIN and K. ROBBIE (1996). 'Security Price Reaction to Divestments by Healthy and Financially Distressed Firms: The Case of MBOs'. *Applied Financial Economics*, 6(1): 85–90.

SAHLMAN, W. (1990). 'The Structure and Governance of Venture-Capital Organizations'. *Journal of Financial Economics*, 27: 473–521.

SETH, A. and J. EASTERWOOD (1993). 'Strategic Redirection in Large Management Buy-outs: The Evidence from Post Buy-out Restructuring Activity'. *Strategic Management Journal*, 14(4): 251–73.

SIMONS, R. L. (1995). *Levers of Control: How Managers Use Innovative Control Systems to Drive Strategic Renewal.* Cambridge: Harvard Business School.

SINGH, H. (1990). 'Management Buy-outs and Shareholder Value'. *Strategic Management Journal*, 11(SI): 111–29.

SMITH, A. (1990). 'Corporate Ownership Structure and Performance: The Case of Management Buy-outs'. *Journal of Financial Economics*, 27(1): 143–64.

THOMPSON, S. and M. WRIGHT (1991). 'UK Management Buy-outs: Debt, Equity and Agency Cost Implications'. *Managerial and Decision Economics*, 12(1): 15–26.

—— and—— (1995). 'Corporate Governance: The Role of Restructuring Transactions'. *Economic Journal*, 105(430): 690–703.

—— —— and K. ROBBIE (1992). 'Management Equity Ownership, Debt and Performance: Some Evidence from U.K. Management Buy-outs'. *Scottish Journal of Political Economy*, 39(4): 413–30.

TVERSKY, A. and D. KAHNEMAN (1974). 'Judgment Under Uncertainty: Heuristics and Biases'. *Science*, 185: 1124–31.

WEIR, C., D. LAING and M. WRIGHT (2005). 'Incentive Effects, Monitoring Mechanisms and the Threat from the Market for Corporate Control: An Analysis of the Factors Affecting Public to Private Transactions in the UK'. *Journal of Business Finance and Accounting*, 32(5, 6): 909–44.

WRIGHT, M. (1988). 'Redrawing the Boundaries of the Firm', in S. Thompson and M. Wright (eds) *Internal Organization, Efficiency and Profit.* Deddington: Philip Allan.

—— and COYNE, J. (1985). *Management Buy-outs.* Beckenham: Croom-Helm.

—— R. HOSKISSON, L. BUSENITZ and J. DIAL (2000). 'Entrepreneurial Growth Through Privatization: The Upside of Management Buy-outs'. *Academy of Management Review*, 25(3): 591–601.

—— —— and —— (2001a). 'Firm Rebirth: Buy-outs as Facilitators of Strategic Growth and Entrepreneurship'. *Academy of Management Executive*, 15(1): 111–25.

—— —— —— and J. DIAL (2001b). 'Finance and Management Buy-outs: Agency versus Entrepreneurship perspectives'. *Venture Capital*, 3(3): 239–62.

—— M. KITAMURA and R. HOSKISSON (2003). 'Management buy-outs and Restructuring Japanese Corporations'. *Long Range Planning*, 36(4): 355–74.

—— —— and A. BURROWS (2005). 'Management Buy-outs: From Europe to Japan'. *Journal of Restructuring Finance*, 2(1): 39–54.

—— J. KISSANE and A. BURROWS (2004). 'Private Equity in EU Accession Countries of Central and Eastern Europe'. *Journal of Private Equity*, 7(3): 32–46.

—— and K. ROBBIE (1996). 'Investor-led Buy-outs: A New Strategic Option'. *Long Range Planning*, 29(5): 691–702.

—— and —— (1998). 'Venture Capital and Private Equity: A Review and Synthesis'. *Journal of Business Finance and Accounting*, 25(5/6): 521–70.

Wright, M., K. Robbie and M. Albrighton (1999). 'High-technology Buy-outs'. *Venture Capital – an International Journal of Entrepreneurial Finance*, 1(3): 219–40.

—— —— and—— (2000). 'Secondary Management buy-outs and Buy-ins'. *International Journal of Entrepreneurial Behaviour & Research*, 6(1): 221–40.

—— —— B. Chiplin and M. Albrighton (2000). 'The Development of an Organizational Innovation: Management Buy-outs in the UK, 1980–1997'. *Business History*, 42(4): 137–84.

—— H. Sapienza and L. Busenitz (eds) (2003). *Venture Capital Vols I–III*. Cheltenham: Edward Elgar.

—— and S. Thompson (1987). 'Divestment and the Control of Divisionalized Firms'. *Accounting and Business Research*, 17: 259–68.

—— —— and K. Robbie, (1992). 'Venture Capital and Management-led Leveraged Buy--outs: European Evidence'. *Journal of Business Venturing*, 7(1): 47–71.

—— K. Robbie, S. Thompson and K. Starkey (1994). 'Longevity and the Life Cycle of MBOs'. *Strategic Management Journal*, 15: 215–27.

—— N. Wilson and K. Robbie (1996). 'The Longer Term Effects of Management-led Buy-outs'. *Journal of Entrepreneurial and Small Business Finance*, 5: 213–34.

—— —— —— and C. Ennew (1996). 'An Analysis of Failure in UK Buy-outs and Buy-ins'. *Managerial and Decision Economics*, 17(1): 57–70.

Zahra, S. (1995). 'Corporate Entrepreneurship and Financial Performance: The Case of Management Leveraged Buy-outs'. *Journal of Business Venturing*, 10(3): 225–47.

PART VI

SOCIAL AND CULTURAL ASPECTS

CHAPTER 19

THE SOCIAL DIMENSIONS OF ENTREPRENEURSHIP

AMIR N. LICHT AND JORDAN I. SIEGEL[1]

19.1 Introduction

In a pioneering book chapter whose title foreshadowed the present chapter's theme, Shapero and Sokol (1982: 83) averred that '[t]he social and cultural factors that enter into the formation of entrepreneurial events are most felt through the formation of individual value systems. More specifically, in a social system that places a high value on the formation of new ventures, more individuals will choose that path .... More diffusely, a social system that places a high value on innovation, risk-taking, and independence is more likely to produce entrepreneurial events than a system with contrasting values.' Subsequent research reviewed in this chapter has largely vindicated Shapero and Sokol's proposition, although the interrelations between entrepreneurship and various social dimensions now seem more complex.

[1] Amir Licht—Interdisciplinary Center Herzliya, Kanfe Nesharim St., Herzliya 46150, Israel, alicht@idc.ac.il; Jordan Siegel—Harvard Business School, Morgan Hall 231, Soldiers Field, Boston, MA 02163, USA, jsiegel@hbs.edu. For helpful comments we thank participants at the World Bank Workshop on Entry and three anonymous referees.

Research on social dimensions of entrepreneurship has made considerable progress since Shapero and Sokol (1982). While these scholars drew primarily on sociology and anthropology (focusing especially on studies of minority and immigrant communities), current research employs a variety of disciplinary approaches. The predominant analytical framework has been Hofstede's (1980, 2001) psychological theory and dataset on cultural value dimensions (Hayton et al., 2002). Recent years have witnessed an emergence of entrepreneurship research in mainstream economics, some of which relates to legal institutions. The current literature exhibits considerable methodological disarray, however. There is no agreed definition for entrepreneurship—for example, whether innovation is a necessary element or does self-employment suffice, or whether self-employment and ownership of a small business firm are equally entrepreneurial (see Ulijn and Brown, 2003). Likewise, there is often no clear definition of, and distinction among, various social institutions. This makes it difficult to compare and even relate studies to one another.

We adopt an institutional economics approach as the basic analytical framework for this chapter. Social institutions are thus defined as the written and unwritten 'rules of the game': laws, norms, beliefs, and so forth (North, 1990). This framework is enriched primarily with insights from cross-cultural psychology, the discipline that specializes in cross-national comparisons of culture. Where possible, we draw connections to other disciplines, although we are influenced by both expertise limitations and a space constraint to focus on the teachings of economics and social psychology. The reader is referred to other chapters in this volume that focus in great depth on these other perspectives.

Although this chapter is dedicated to social dimensions of entrepreneurship, we begin with a discussion of entrepreneurial motivations conducted at the individual level of analysis. Social institutions (especially culture and norms) affect the way individuals perceive the social role of the entrepreneur and how much individuals desire to become one. The documented richness of entrepreneurial motivations suggests that entrepreneurial behaviour responds to a rich set of cues from the social environment.

To organize the discussion of social institutions we draw on Williamson's (2000) framework for institutional analysis. This model distinguishes four levels of analysis. 'Level 1' consists of informal institutions. This is where norms, customs, mores, and traditions are located and where religion plays a role. More generally, this is the level of culture. Level 2 consists of formal legal rules and regulations, comprising constitutions, statutes, property rights, and so on. Informal institutions exist in the shared subjective knowledge of societal members. Formal institutions are relatively more objectively verifiable through formal documents. Institutions at both Levels 1 and 2 usually apply generally to all societal members. Minority sub-groups may develop different informal institutions, however, and local authorities may promulgate locally-applicable regulations.[2] Level 3 deals with aligning governance structures with transactions. Such structures comprise contracts, firms, and also networks. Level 4 deals with marginal analysis of prices and resource allocation. This level is of less concern here because strictly speaking, it is not an institution.

The core assumption underlying this model is that in the long run, elements located in adjacent levels should be compatible with one another as should specific institutions within each level. Thus, laws adopted organically (as opposed to forced transplantation) at Level 2 would reflect general cultural orientations, shared assumptions and beliefs from Level 1. Parties to economic transactions would structure their interaction at Level 3 in light of the strengths and weaknesses of the institutional backdrop of Levels 1 and 2. Feedback channels may reinforce institutions at lower levels. Sections 3–5 below demonstrate how specific aspects of entrepreneurship relate to social institutions at various levels.

19.2 The Entrepreneur: An Individual Portrait

Some 70 years ago, Schumpeter (1934: 93–4), the patron saint of all entrepreneurs, depicted the motives of the entrepreneur as follows:

> First of all there is the dream and the will to found a private kingdom, usually, though not necessarily, also a dynasty. ... Then there is the will to conquer: the impulse to fight, to prove oneself superior to others, to succeed for the sake, not of the fruits of success, but of success itself. From this aspect, economic action becomes akin to sport... The financial result is a secondary consideration, or, at all events, mainly valued as an index of success and as a symptom of victory, the displaying of which very often is more important as a motive of large expenditure than the wish for the consumers' goods themselves.... Finally, there is the joy of creating, of getting things done, or simply of exercising one's energy and ingenuity.... Our type seeks out difficulties, changes in order to change, delights in ventures.

Romantic as it may seem at first glance, Schumpeter's portrait of entrepreneurial motives captures essential facets of entrepreneurship that mainstream economics still grapples with. Schumpeter's core contention, that entrepreneurs do not seek greater wealth for the sake of increasing consumption seems at odds with conventional depictions of economic agents. This seeming contradiction is all the more

[2] This chapter concentrates on country- or nation-level societies. Entrepreneurship among subcultures such as immigrants and minority groups is discussed in Basu (Ch. 21 of this Handbook).

evident when one considers the alleged motives of 'the joy of creating ... delights in venturing', which, one should bear in mind, are related to economic activity in the market, not recreation and leisure.

Recent evidence suggests, however, that Schumpeter might be right. First, entrepreneurs may not be motivated primarily by pecuniary incentives. Hamilton (2000) finds that in the United States, median entrepreneurs' earnings after 10 years in business are 35 percent less than the predicted alternative wage on a paid job of the same duration. Hamilton's use of a self-selection model shows that it is not the case that low-ability workers become entrepreneurs; if anything, the evidence shows that higher-ability workers are more likely to enter into self-employment. Moskowitz and Vissing-Jørgensen (2002) and F. Kerins et al. (2004) provide evidence that entrepreneurs forgo financial benefits in order to engage in entrepreneurship. Amit et al. (2001) compared Canadian entrepreneurs with senior managers who decided not to start ventures in the high-technology sector. They found that for entrepreneurs, in their decision to start a new venture, wealth attainment was a significantly less important dimension relative to an aggregate of ten other decision dimensions (specifically: vision, stability, power, lifestyle, leadership, innovation, independence, ego, contribution and challenge).

The leading explanation for these results is based on non-pecuniary benefits from entrepreneurial activity. A further sociologically-based explanation is that high-ability individuals are culturally encouraged to start firms where family members can be employed and share directly in the profits. Further work is needed to test this hypothesis. Using Swedish data, Giannetti and Simonov (2003) do argue that social norms may drive people into entrepreneurship notwithstanding lower individual profits. In any event, one would be wrong to interpret either Schumpeter or the evidence mentioned above as suggesting that entrepreneurs are agnostic or oblivious to financial considerations. Studies conducted in several countries show that individuals are sensitive to capital constraints in their decision to take entrepreneurial positions—in particular, self-employment.[3]

Secondly, among the non-pecuniary motivations that guide entrepreneurs, autonomy, or independence, stands out as a first-order consideration. Hamilton's (2000) evidence strongly suggests that self-employment offers substantial non-pecuniary benefits, such as 'being your own boss'. Several studies hold that entrepreneurs find special importance in their independence (Blanchflower and Oswald, 1998; Blanchflower, 2000; Blanchflower et al., 2001; Hundley, 2001). Frey and Benz (2003), using survey data from the United Kingdom, Germany, and Switzerland, argue that the greater independence and autonomy of self-employed persons is largely responsible for their particular job satisfaction. Frey and Benz (2003), in a sample of 23 countries that include non-Western countries, find that the

[3] See Evans and Jovanovic (1989); Evans and Leighton (1989); Holtz-Eakin et al. (1994a, b); Van Praag and Van Ophem (1995); Lindh and Ohlsson (1996); Blanchflower and Oswald (1998); Dunn and Holtz-Eakin (2000); Van Praag (2003).

self-employed are substantially more satisfied with their work than employed persons. A series of recent studies on OECD-member nations further shows that people most often move into self-employment when they are dissatisfied with their life, and that the very act of creating their own business tends to make them more satisfied than the average person in their country (Hofstede, 1998; Noorderhaven et al., 1999, 2003; Hofstede et al., 2004). Falter (2002) holds that the greater job satisfaction exhibited by the self-employed in Switzerland stems rather from their job characteristics than from income. Falter notes that this may be due to individual over-optimism in addition to greater freedom.

Taken together, the above evidence suggests that entrepreneurs are relatively more willing to forgo income and to bear costs, including through increased risk levels, in order to engage in independent ventures. These studies may have some methodological weaknesses, however. To be able to confirm that entrepreneurs have alternative options with higher income, one would need to replicate the exercise in Stern (2004), who collected data on scientists who give up more lucrative job offers to do real science at lower pay. However, while the literature's lack of measurement on alternative options is a weak point, the preponderance of survey evidence from the entrepreneurship literature does still at least suggest that entrepreneurs often had more lucrative alternatives inside established firms (see Amit et al., 2001).

Thirdly, the special preference for autonomy found among entrepreneurs is not the only special characteristic that they exhibit in comparison to average population. Several studies maintain that entrepreneurs are more over-confident than regular people are and appear to be driven by wishful thinking (Bernardo and Welch, 2001; Arabsheibani et al., 2000; Cooper et al., 1988). Compared with non-entrepreneurs, entrepreneurs behave as if they understand the present fairly well but have rather special views regarding the future. A pilot survey comparing Russian entrepreneurs and non-entrepreneurs finds several characteristics distinguishing the former from the latter (Djankov et al., 2004). Specifically, that entrepreneurs move more frequently from one occupation to another—consistent with having a broader set of skills, greater confidence, and a greater tendency to explore new avenues.

The image of the entrepreneur reflected in these studies is still very fragmented. To gain a better understanding of these entrepreneurial motivations, we draw on insights from the psychology literature. While the literature on entrepreneurship and individual-level psychology is voluminous and lies beyond the present scope,[4] here we note briefly that entrepreneurs' risk propensity has been found to be non-distinguishable from that of non-entrepreneurs. Rather, entrepreneurs differ in their risk (under-) assessment, consistent with their general over-optimism (e.g. Palich and Bagby, 1995; Sarasvathy et al., 1998).

Researchers have developed a multi-dimensional construct of entrepreneurial orientation with three sub-dimensions: innovation, proactiveness, and risk-taking,

[4] For a review see Rauch and Frese (2000). Wadeson (Ch. 4 in this Handbook) reviews the cognitive aspects of entrepreneurship concerning decision-making and attitudes to risk.

and established its validity in several national samples (Miller, 1983; Covin and Slevin, 1989, 1991; Lumpkin and Dess, 1996; Kreiser et al., 2001). These dimensions capture more elements of entrepreneurial motivations and behaviour than other models do, thus bringing us closer to the model suggested by Schumpeter and other classic scholars (Knight, 1921; Kirzner, 1973). Importantly, these constructs lend themselves to examining the impact of national culture on entrepreneurship (Kreiser et al., 2001).

A notable feature of this branch of literature, however, is the paucity of studies on the role of personal values in differentiating entrepreneurs from salary earners. Values are conceptions of the desirable—a motivational construct. They represent broad goals that apply across contexts and time (Rokeach, 1973; Schwartz and Bilsky, 1987, 1990). Personal value emphases have been systematically related to individuals' behaviour (e.g. Bardi and Schwartz, 2003). Drawing on Rokeach's (1973) theory of values, Bird (1988) and Sarasvathy (2001) proposed that entrepreneurs' personal value emphases may distinguish them from other people (see also Djankov et al., 2004). Having searched the business, economics, and finance sections of the JSTOR database and internet resources more limitedly, we are not aware of studies that tested this proposition empirically.

The Schwartz (1992) model of individual values defines ten broad values according to the motivation that underlies each of them (specifically: power, achievement, hedonism, stimulation, self-direction, universalism, benevolence, conformity, tradition, and security). These values are presumed to encompass the range of motivationally distinct values recognized across cultures. These values can further be organized along two bipolar dimensions: self-enhancement versus self-transcendence and conservation versus openness to change. This model appears to hold promise for a more systematic analysis of entrepreneurial orientations. The Schwartz (1992) model can be used to investigate reliably whether entrepreneurs indeed possess a distinct set of motivational preferences relative to their non-entrepreneur peers, as Schumpeter conjectured. We propose, without elaboration, that a plausible hypothesis in this respect would be that entrepreneurs' value priorities will emphasize self-enhancement and openness to change over self-transcendence and conservation, respectively.

19.3 Culture and Entrepreneurship

It is now virtually undisputed in the entrepreneurship literature that culture bears a profound impact on all facets of entrepreneurship in societies (George and Zahra, 2002). This scholastic consensus is consistent with the general importance accorded to culture in management studies but is not necessarily shared by some branches in economics. Hayton et al. (2002) provide a comprehensive review of empirical studies that have examined the association between national culture and entrepreneurship. A careful reading of these studies reveals, however, that this literature has some conceptual and methodological obstacles still to overcome. Instead of recounting Hayton et al. (2002) review we concentrate on these basic issues and supplement this analysis with more recent evidence.

What is culture? Defined in subjective terms, culture refers to the complex of meanings, symbols, and assumptions about what is good or bad, legitimate or illegitimate that underlies the prevailing practices and norms in a society (Bourdieu, 1972; Markus and Kitayama, 1994). Often, culture is defined as a set of shared values and beliefs (Hofstede, 1980; 2001). A common postulate in cross-cultural psychology is that all societies confront similar basic issues or problems when they come to regulate human activity (Kluckhohn and Strodtbeck, 1961). A society's culture reflects its response to these issues in certain cultural orientations. Such cultural orientations represent general societal stances that are deeply ingrained in the functioning of major societal institutions, in widespread practices, in symbols and traditions, and, through adaptation and socialization, in the values of individuals (Kluckhohn, 1951; Hofstede, 1980; Schwartz, 1999). Cultural orientations are also associated with certain (personal) cognitive styles, leading scholars to consider cultures as 'systems of thought' (Nisbett et al., 2001; Peng et al., 2001).

A basic yet crucial point for understanding the social dimensions of entrepreneurship is that culture is a society-level phenomenon. The so-called 'ecological fallacy' occurs when one fails to acknowledge the distinction between the individual and societal levels of analysis (Hofstede, 1980, 2001). To see the level-of-analysis distinction in the present context, consider two iconic scholars: Weber (1904) and Schumpeter (1934). Weber's theory on the Protestant ethic related economic development to certain societal orientations, which Weber associated with Calvinism and Puritanism in particular. Among other things, these ethics emphasized the role of the individual in this world as a free soul seeking material wealth as evidence for being one of the chosen. Although Weber is often associated with entrepreneurship (e.g. Thomas and Mueller, 2000), his theory was not explicitly directed toward entrepreneurship (Brouwer, 2002). Crucially, Weber was interested in societal values, not in the individual entrepreneur's motivations. In contrast, Schumpeter's theory of entrepreneurial motivations, cited above, was about individual motivations and did not postulate a societal ethic. The two theories apply to different levels of analysis. An important inference from this distinction is that individuals with entrepreneurial characteristics will be found in every society, as part of the general distribution. Societies may differ, however, in the institutions that could affect the relative portion of the entrepreneurial sub-group and which facilitate or hinder entrepreneurial activity. Hence, Schumpeter (1934) cannot be considered 'a refutation of Weber's theory' (cf. Brouwer, 2002: 85).

Studies avoiding the ecological fallacy have examined the proposition that certain individual features consistent with Schumpeterian-like entrepreneurship may be more common in certain national cultures. This is a plausible proposition, which essentially seeks to find traces of cultural orientations in personal traits. Virtually without exception, researchers used Hofstede's original four cultural value dimensions of individualism/collectivism, power distance, uncertainty avoidance, and masculinity/femininity.[5] Thus, Meuller and Thomas (2001) show that innovativeness and internal locus of control were more likely to be found among students coming from cultures high in individualism and low in uncertainty avoidance (see also Thomas and Mueller, 2000).

According to Hofstede, low uncertainty avoidance 'implies a greater willingness to enter into unknown ventures' (2001: 164). Hayton et al. (2002) maintain that high individualism, high masculinity, low uncertainty avoidance, and low power distance are conducive to entrepreneurship. Nevertheless, the evidence is mixed. Using patent filings as a proxy for the level of entrepreneurship in countries, Shane (1993) argues for the realized validity of most of the hypothesized correlations. Morris et al. (1993), however, argue for a curvilinear relation between individualism/collectivism and corporate entrepreneurship. Other studies find that business ownership correlates positively with uncertainty avoidance and with power distance, but not with individualism. In support of Hofstede et al.'s (2004) theory, these empirical findings underline the idea that a climate of high uncertainty avoidance in large organizations pushes enterprising individuals to go out and create their own businesses (Wennekers et al., 2002; Noorderhaven et al., 2002, 2003).[6]

These studies and earlier ones in a similar spirit (e.g. Shane (1994, 1995)) have associated entrepreneurship with a particular cultural profile—in particular, high individualism and low uncertainty avoidance. At present, we do not believe it is possible to reach such a conclusion, given the lack of agreement on what constitutes a valid dependent variable (number of registered entrepreneurial ventures, patent filings, or something else) as well as a need for more precise econometric identification in the entrepreneurship literature. As a broad generalization,

[5] Hofstede's theory and the usefulness of his dataset, especially for contemporary empirical studies, have been criticized on various grounds, which we cannot address in the present scope. In our view, the Hofstede framework largely withstands the criticisms levelled against it. A later addition to Hofstede's (1980) theory is a cultural dimension derived from Chinese Culture Connection (1987) that was dubbed Confucian dynamism or long-term orientation. See Hofstede (2001); see also Schwartz (2004).

[6] See also Uhlaner and Thurik (2004) and Hunt and Levie (2003) for discussions using Inglehart's (1997) materialism/post-materialism value dimension.

researchers have also tended to use individual-level constructs and instruments that were developed in the United States (Kreiser et al., 2001). More work is needed to establish these elements' universality, as has been done more recently with the Schwartz (1992) model of personal values or the 'Big Five' personality attributes (see Ciavarella et al., 2004; on cognition see Mitchell et al., 2000).

In the meanwhile, one cannot dismiss the notion that current studies may miss the value-creation function of certain personal traits not highlighted in the Schumpeterian template and of other combinations of cultural orientations (profiles). Entrepreneurship à la Schumpeter and Kirzner involves motivation, cognition, and action, with possible mediators like intention (Krueger, Reilly and Carsrud 2000). The entrepreneur acts on what he or she perceives as a valuable opportunity, driven by his or her special motivations. The Schumpeterian entrepreneur is usually portrayed as a quintessential model of Western agency: an autonomous individual striving against the mainstream to take advantage of his or her uniqueness.[7] A growing literature now proposes that the Western notion of individual agency may not similarly apply in other cultures. Recent authors in social psychology have argued that cultures known to value embeddedness over autonomy are also more highly populated by individuals with a greater distaste on average for autonomous action (Menon et al., 1999; Markus and Kitayama, 2003; J. G. Miller, 2003).

Importantly, however, variations in cultural beliefs regarding individual autonomy do not by necessity preclude nor diminish entrepreneurship in non-Western societies. At the societal level, stronger collectivist orientations may not be detrimental to entrepreneurship if cultural emphases in the society on other dimensions support entrepreneurial action. Particularly relevant in this regard are cultural values that emphasize change or certain time-preferences. It therefore may be possible for Chinese and other entrepreneurs coming from Confucian-influenced societies to succeed in a highly collectivist environment while drawing legitimacy for their conduct from a cultural emphasis on active change.

Thus, the literature is currently in a state of flux. Causal explanations relying on cultural differences remain provocative at present and more work is needed to verify their robustness (see Morse et al., 1999; Mitchell et al., 2000; Begley and Tan, 2001). The studies mentioned above are premised on the assumption of conceptual compatibility among social institutions that also underlies the institutional economics approach (North, 1990; Williamson, 2000). This premise, however, does not imply that only a unique cultural profile can support entrepreneurship, particularly when broad proxies like self-employment and business ownership serve to gauge it. Culture is the set of societal responses to general issues societies face. It is not impossible to assume that different cultures could achieve roughly

[7] 'Agency' here means 'being agentic' as used in psychology. It should not connote the 'agency problem' known in economics.

equivalent levels of entrepreneurship, vaguely defined. Ulijn and Weggeman (2001) indeed argue to that effect with regard to Hofstede's model.

Yet there is still a more disconcerting alternative to this 'cultural-relativism' hypothesis. In this view, the variable for entrepreneurship used by many studies—namely, self-employment and/or ownership of a small business—could be misleading. At the individual level of analysis, the more entrepreneurial individuals in any society indeed routinely start their own ventures on a small scale. However, at the societal level of analysis, some cultural environments may be more conducive to firm growth. Consequently, these societies will come to be populated by a distribution of enterprises that includes many large firms (cf. Desai et al., 2003). This is consistent with the fact that in developing countries—which tend to rank higher on collectivism, power distance, and (less systematically) uncertainty avoidance (Hofstede, 2001)—the firm size distribution is heavily populated by very small firms (Tybout, 2000; Cabral and Mata, 2003). These findings may still underestimate the scope of the problem when one recalls that entrepreneurship in the unofficial economy is often unaccounted for and is likely to be concentrated in low-size firms.

Culture may exert its effect on levels and formats of entrepreneurial activity through numerous mediating channels. We have already considered the potential effect of culture on some personal traits relevant to entrepreneurship; now we will look at culture and widespread social norms or the law. The latter institutions are located either at the same level or at adjacent levels in Williamson's (2000) model. One is more likely to observe systematic relations with culture in these levels than between culture and higher-level phenomena, including specific facets of entrepreneurship, because mediating and/or additional (non-cultural) factors may obscure the link to the cultural environment—obscure, but not eradicate.

Beyond data availability limitations, the continuing use of Hofstede's dataset, notwithstanding the fact that it originates in the late 1960s, reflects a broad consensus in the literature that culture is relatively stable. The main concern relates to the interaction between culture and economic development. Hofstede (2001) indeed argues that greater development increases individualism, and Inglehart's (1997) theory on post-materialistic values is predicated on economic progress. Nevertheless, the little evidence regarding historical trends in national culture suggests that absent severe external shocks, cultural change is very slow (Schwartz et al., 2000; Inglehart and Baker, 2000). Among the factors contributing to this effect is the fact that cultural value priorities are imparted to individuals at very young ages (Goodnow, 1997).

The entrepreneurship literature is largely consistent with this view, although little direct attention has been paid thus far to potential effects on entrepreneurship of such dynamic processes. McGrath et al. (1992) surveyed entrepreneurs from the United States, mainland China, and Taiwan with items related to Hofstede's dimensions. These researchers conclude that on the individualism/collectivism dimension, 'fifty years of exposure to very different ideologies have done little to break down the traditional collectivist Chinese culture' among the Chinese and the Taiwanese. McGrath et al. do find evidence suggesting value change on the power distance and uncertainty avoidance dimensions. Schmitt-Rodermund and Vondracek (2002) and Schmitt-Rodermund (forthcoming) present evidence on interrelations between parenting style, personality traits, entrepreneurial orientation, and entrepreneurial career prospects among German subjects, consistent with Goodnow (1997). These results are consistent with the view that cultural values may induce path dependence in entrepreneurial activity (see also Woodruff, 1999). More indirectly, Della-Giusta and King (Ch. 24 in this Handbook) describe what they consider a failed attempt to establish an 'enterprise culture' in the United Kingdom by the Thatcher government. This may have implications for how transitional economies can better encourage entrepreneurship (see Estrin, Meyer, and Bytchkova, Ch. 27 in this Handbook).

19.4 General social institutions

'The two most important "core" institutions for encouraging entrepreneurship are well-defined property rights and the rule of law', aver Boettke and Coyne (2003: 77), echoing the current broad consensus that these social institutions are key for a thriving economy (Rodrik, Subramanian and Trebbi, 2002; Acemoglu and Johnson, 2003; Easterly and Levine, 2003). The linking of these institutions to entrepreneurship follows the same logic underlying institutional analyses of economic development: that is to say, widespread respect for well-defined legal entitlements and absence of arbitrary rent-seeking by power-holders (bribe-taking) reduce idiosyncratic risk and lower transaction costs. Entrepreneurs, being the prime agents of economic change, are especially sensitive to these factors (cf. Baumol, 1990; Harper, 1998).[8]

The institutions discussed in this section apply to the general society—usually, a nation. These institutions are more issue-specific than cultural orientations but are still generally applicable in comparison to norms and rules prevailing in subgroups such as local communities, corporate employees, or industry professionals. We first consider entrepreneurship and informal institutions—specifically, the rule

[8] Busenitz et al. (2000) define 'country institutional profile' more capaciously than the conventional definitions in the economic literature, covering also what they call 'cognitive dimension' and 'normative dimension'.

of law and corruption. It should be noted that some studies of institutions and development fail to distinguish conceptually or in their empirical specification between security of property rights, the rule of law, and corruption. Although such distinctions could be made, the fact that these informal institutions share conceptual elements as modes of wielding power, leads Licht, Goldschmidt and Schwartz (2004) to analyze them collectively as social norms of governance.

On examining the emergence of new firms in five formerly-Soviet countries, Johnson, McMillan and Woodruff (1999, 2000, 2002) find that insecure property rights—defined as frequent need to make extra-legal payments (bribes), protection, or inefficient courts—were more inhibiting to entrepreneurship than inadequate finance. Desai, Gompers and Lerner (2003), using a measure that intertwines both formal delineation and actual protection of property rights, find that in the emerging markets of Europe, greater fairness and greater property rights protection increase entry rates, reduce exit rates, and lower skewness in firm-size distributions. Further discussion and comprehensive background on institutions and entrepreneurship in transition economies is provided in Chapter 27 in this Handbook (see also Ovaska and Sobel, 2003).

Theory and evidence are not limited to transition economies, however. Laeven and Woodruff (2004) find that in Mexico, states with more effective legal systems have larger firms, suggesting that a rule-of-law state enables entrepreneurial firms to grow by reducing idiosyncratic risk. Cumming and colleagues use a measure of legality subsuming various indices of formal and informal legal protections and corruption to find that this measure predicts numerous beneficial features in venture capital transactions (Cumming, Schmidt and Walz, 2004; Cumming and Fleming, 2003). Perotti and Volpin (2004) recently advanced a political economy model in which evidence suggests that lack of political (democratic) accountability and economic inequality hinder entry.

The literature is currently unsettled as to the antecedents of informal social institutions. Some authors have noted a correlation between the mode of colonialization and the quality of governance institutions (Acemoglu and Johnson, 2003; Treisman, 2000). On the other hand, underlying cultural beliefs seem to be even more highly correlated with the quality of governance (Treisman, 2000; Husted, 1999; Hofstede, 2001; Tonoyan, 2004). Drawing on Schwartz's (1999) cultural dimension theory, Licht, Goldschmidt and Schwartz (2004) argue for robust correlations between cultural orientations and perceived legality, corruption, and democratic accountability. Consistent with the preceding discussion, this evidence suggests that cultural orientation may impact entrepreneurship through their links with informal governance institutions. More work is needed to identify the precise mechanisms by which culture and formal laws interact in influencing the quality of governance in a society.

We turn now to formal legal rules and their relations to entrepreneurship, and in the first place note that every piece of legislation that affects business also bears on entrepreneurs. Entrepreneurs, it turns out, complain first about taxes when asked about obstacles to entrepreneurship (Estrin et al., Ch. 27 in this Handbook). Beyond obvious issues like credit regulation and taxes, the list of relevant laws spans the gamut from regulation of entry, measured by the steps required to establish a firm (Djankov et al., 2002), to investors' legal rights (La Porta et al., 1998) to procedural rules in commercial courts (Djankov et al., 2003). Thus, Klapper, Laeven and Rajan (2004) document a correlation between more intensive entry regulation and lower firm growth as well as lower entry in less corrupt countries. This literature generally holds that greater protection of economic interests ('property rights' broadly defined) and nimble courts lead to beneficial outcomes. Needless to say, the effectiveness of formal legal rules hinges on a widespread social norm of legality (Berkovitz, Pistor and Richard, 2003), which, in turn, is strongly linked to national culture (Licht, Goldschmidt and Schwartz, 2004).

Note in this respect that many countries have a substantial unofficial sector (black market). Well-known measurement problems with regard to this sector also make it difficult to assess institutional antecedents of entrepreneurship in these economies. Johnson et al. (2000) find that in five post-communist countries, the size of hidden 'unofficial' activity (of 'official' firms) rises with effective tax rates, corruption, greater incidence of mafia protection, and less faith in the court system. Klapper et al.'s (2004) finding that regulatory entry barriers have no adverse effect on entry in corrupt countries, should thus be interpreted with the understanding that entry into the official economy is already strongly deterred by systemic institutional weaknesses noted above.

Here we highlight one issue that has stirred considerable interest among entrepreneurship scholars, namely, the factors that facilitated the remarkable success of the high-tech industry in Silicon Valley. Saxenian (1996) pointed out Silicon Valley's culture of openness, independence, democratic ('flat') corporate structure, and the Valley's 'pioneer' entrepreneurial spirit as such factors. Saxenian further contrasted Silicon Valley's culture with Route 128's culture of secrecy, corporate hierarchy, and general Yankee conservatism. The Valley's 'high-velocity labour market' enabled skilled employees to switch firms frequently or start new firms as entrepreneurs (Hyde, 1998). Gilson (1999) responds that the different regional cultures are the consequence—not the antecedent—of the two regions' legal rules concerning the enforceability of covenants not to compete. While Massachusetts enforces such covenants within limits on employees, the California courts interpret its employment law as flatly banning these covenants—according to Gilson (2003), due to an historical accident that cannot be duplicated elsewhere.

This case is noteworthy for several reasons. First, although Saxenian's analysis applied to the regional level, one can identify in it the major features found in cross-cultural comparisons of countries that employ Hofstede's dimensions. Compared with Massachusetts, California is depicted as higher on individualism and lower on power distance and uncertainty avoidance—a 'frontier culture'. But as Hofstede (2001) relentlessly notes, such comparisons are always relative. The alleged rigidity of Route 128's culture relative to that of Silicon Valley very likely pales in comparison to other institutional environments (see Schwartz, 2004). Secondly, in the long run, formal legal rules and the surrounding culture should be conceptually compatible with one another (Williamson, 2000; Licht et al., 2005). While the legal precedents interpreting California's law as banning covenants not to compete preceded the emergence of Silicon Valley, these precedents have been adopted and not overruled since, because they were compatible with their contemporary 'pioneer' culture. Finally, the Silicon Valley case indicates the limits of the clearer-and-better-protected-property-rights thesis. What is highlighted as the key to the Valley's success—be it legal or cultural—is a norm that essentially eroded existing firms' intellectual property. California thus managed to achieve an optimal blend of a high-quality institutional environment with the right dose of Schumpeterian 'creative destruction' of property rights. Whether countries can mimic California's precedent is debatable on positive and normative grounds.

19.5 Networks, Reputational Bonding and Social Capital

Networks are an organizational form distinct from both market exchange and firms (Granovetter, 1973). In the entrepreneurship context, networks may serve a variety of social purposes for facilitating entrepreneurship. McCann (Ch. 25 in this Handbook) reviews the role of networks in facilitating clusters, industrial districts and regional development. Several recent studies point to social networks as information dissemination mechanisms that facilitate entrepreneurship (Saxenian, 2002; Djankov et al., 2004; Guiso and Schivardi, 2005; Gompers et al., 2005). Here, we focus on social networks as a structural response to the social environment of governance institutions—namely, to the formal and informal institutions at deeper levels. Responding efficiently to the institutional environment is essential, and more difficult, where governance institutions are weak. However, social networks also prove valuable where these institutions are generally stronger but cannot address problems that entrepreneurs face in certain industries or at early stages of projects.

One of the main challenges for entrepreneurs around the world, but particularly for entrepreneurs in emerging and transition economies, is how to navigate around weak governance institutions at the country and regional level. Without strong governance institutions, especially without a strong legal system, outside investors go unprotected and are less likely to want to invest in a new entrepreneurial venture. The lack of strong governance institutions, therefore, stifles the broad sharing of technological and financial resources and capabilities across firm boundaries. Numerous studies, for example, have shown that firm-level development suffers from the lack of an effective rule of law (Demirgüc-Kunt and Maksimovic, 1998; Levine, 1999; Morck et al., 2000; Wurgler, 2000). Without sufficient rule of law, only some privileged networks of entrepreneurs will possess the enforcement mechanisms necessary to make joint investments, and the economy will see fewer large firms and more concentrated and entrenched ownership (He et al., 2003). Lower political accountability likewise hinders new entry (Perotti and Volpin, 2004). Because both cultural and legal institutions are difficult to change (Milhaupt, 1998; Roe, 1996; Bebchuk and Roe, 1999), firms in emerging economies select institutional strategies so that they can at least individually gain long-term access to outside resources and capabilities.

In all environments, entrepreneurs must build reputation-enhancing relationships with outside resource providers who are willing to share valuable information, technology and finance. At the earliest stages of a firm's existence, entrepreneurs require social contacts who can share the best leads on suppliers and customers. They also require financial investors willing to share scarce finance on an early-stage idea. Studies have shown that in emerging economies, credit constraints are one of the leading causes of small business failure (Fredland and Morris, 1976; Peterson and Shulman, 1987). Moreover, in most emerging economies, even just registering the firm and getting a business licence is a long and cumbersome process (Djankov et al., 2002). Finding both talented and trustworthy employees is also difficult without help from reliable network contacts.

The challenge for the entrepreneur is how to gain the confidence of these network contacts so that they will trust the entrepreneur with their valuable time, technology, and finance. This trust is not easy to create. Transactions built on social capital are typically not written down on paper and are rarely enforceable in court. Instead, as Portes (1998:4) comments, these transactions based on social capital 'tend to be characterized by unspecified obligations, uncertain time horizons, and the possible violation of reciprocity expectations'.

In order to ameliorate the uncertainty and risk inherent in such transactions based on social capital, the entrepreneur can pursue what is termed a strategy of reputational bonding (Siegel, 2005). A reputational bonding strategy is an effort by the entrepreneurs to reduce their own incentive and manoeuverability for later expropriation of outside resource providers. The idea is to bond oneself by embedding oneself in a dense social network where the entrepreneur's future access to suppliers and customers is determined by an ongoing record of trustworthy business dealings. Much as in Greif's (1993) description of the Maghribi traders, entrepreneurs often seek out outside resource providers who share a common cultural bond. These cultural bonds are a major step towards building shared systems of fealty and honest business conduct.

Beyond drawing on shared historical relations, entrepreneurs must often go one step further in creating ongoing social systems of mutual investment and non-legal enforcement. As told in Siegel (2006), Korean entrepreneurs actively embed themselves in high school networks of elites. Just as for the Maghribi traders, Koreans share a collectivist culture based on shared identity and historical experience. While culture no doubt helps to facilitate resource sharing, culture is aided by ongoing firm-specific investments in network development and governance. These networks often take on the role of prosecutor, judge and jury in Korean society. Formal courts are costly and slow in operation. Members of the same network monitor each other and share information on each other's behaviour with other members. When one member is alleged to cheat on one another, ongoing norms of community enforcement help to spread news of the transgression and to build legitimacy for a joint punishment. Only those who have most strongly embedded themselves in the network structure, and who have gone on to obey the social norms of conduct within the network, enjoy the largest benefits in terms of receiving large-scale investment from network members.

The concept of reputational bonding follows a long line of studies in the entrepreneurship literature on the 'network success' hypothesis. The seminal study in this tradition was that of Aldrich and Zimmer (1986), who noted that entrepreneurs are highly social actors who actively embed themselves in a social context. During the past decade, it has become an accepted theory in the global entrepreneurship literature that 'those entrepreneurs who can refer to a broad and diverse social network and who receive much support from their network are more successful (network success hypothesis)' (Brüderal and Preisendörfer, 1998).

Reputational bonding is not just a successful strategy for firms in countries with weak legal institutions: it is also an essential strategy for firms in advanced knowledge-driven industries around the world where the rules of competition are in play, the value of an inventor's new technology is uncertain to outside investors and cannot easily be described and paid for through an *ex ante* contract, the important sources of knowledge are disperse and held by a large number of decentralized actors, and where the inventors must rely heavily on outside investors and collaborators for key complementary resources and skills. As illustrated in Powell (1996), biotechnology companies in the US were often started by scientists without managerial experience, access to finance, or access to product distribution channels. As a result, these biotech entrepreneurs used outside collaborators to share in the task of management, marketing, and the attraction of financial resources.

In any knowledge-driven industry, because so many projects cannot be directly contracted on *ex ante*, an entrepreneur's reputation is key to gaining access to outside complementary resources through networks of potential collaborators. In more recent work, Powell et al. (2005) show that the biotechnology industry is characterized by frequent changes in the entrepreneur's need for specific outside complements, and by a kind of dynamism where an external collaborator's knowledge is essential today, not needed tomorrow, but then might become essential at some point in the future. It is precisely in this kind of environment of uncertainty that a firm must learn how to enter and exit partnerships while maintaining a near-pristine reputation for fair dealing.

In order to understand how social capital helps entrepreneurs to gain the trust of outside resource providers, it is worthwhile to examine the mechanisms by which social capital leads to trust. Portes and Sensenbrenner (1993) compellingly describe the four sources of social capital. The first source, value introjection, is based on identity from birth with a group, and leads the individual to behave in altruistic ways specifically towards members of that group. The second source, reciprocity exchanges, leads individuals to act generously to others in a defined group based on an established norm of reciprocity. The third source of social capital, bounded solidarity, comes from having experienced a common event or set of events during the course of life with a defined group of people. The final source of social capital, enforceable trust, comes from an expectation that a defined group would punish any individual who treats another member of the group inappropriately. Of these four sources of social capital, the global entrepreneurship literature has placed emphasis on reciprocity transactions and enforceable trust, the two sources that are motivated primarily by rational utility maximization. The other two sources, value introjection and bounded solidarity, have been seriously understudied within the entrepreneurship literature. It is time that further attention be given to their theoretical importance since even the rational game-theoretical view of community enforcement often relies on an underlying cultural foundation based on common historical identity.

Prior studies measure the importance of social capital through a well-accepted set of measures. The main approach of the literature looks at the personal network of the entrepreneurs and explores the effects of the network size and depth on business performance. The following variables are all thought to be positive indicators of social capital: network size, network density, network diversity, the preponderance of strong or weak ties, and network redundancy (Brüderal and Preisendörfer, 1998). Strong ties are here defined based on the intensity of the relationship between two actors. Where intensity is high, the ties are labelled as being strong. This typically includes family members and close friends. Where intensity is low, but yet ongoing social contact is at least possible, the ties are characterized as weak. Granovetter (1974) found that network diversity through weak ties is most essential to gaining non-redundant information about the labour market. Burt (1982) further argued that entrepreneurs seeking information and market leverage should pursue bridging weak ties between otherwise disconnected economic actors.

While weak ties may be most useful for accessing information and leveraging, strong ties are believed most essential for building the trust necessary for joint investment and collaboration. Coleman (1990) argued using a rational choice logic that strong ties are most helpful to those economic actors who require a social community that can enforce norms and good behaviour. Coleman's (1990) concept of closure is the most important in understanding the importance of strong ties for reputational bonding. Closure means the existence of a sufficient density of ties among a group of people to guarantee the faithful observance of norms. With a higher degree of mutual interaction, it becomes possible to have non-legal/extra-legal social enforcement of informal obligations. With enforcement comes trust and increases in joint investment for entrepreneurial ventures. The rational choice explanation, however, is mostly not by itself sufficient to explain why dense ties lead to trust. Rational enforcement is potentially bolstered also through the process of value introjection and bounded solidarity cited above on p. 527. With dense ties comes the potential for joint experiences within a densely connected group. The dense ties not only bring a greater probability of shared experience, but also allow for the cultural lessons and values drawn on those experiences to be more easily taught and positively reinforced within the shared community.

The conclusion of this literature is not that investment in one type of social ties is uniformly better than another, especially given the fact that these ties bring different types of resources to the entrepreneur. Strong ties can bring in resources that depend on non-legal enforcement of obligations. These resources can include finance, technology and human capital. Weak ties, in contrast, can help the entrepreneur with accessing the diverse market information necessary to evaluate alternative managerial choices, to negotiate better terms with suppliers and customers, and to think of new solutions to business problems not already solved within the entrepreneur's existing network.

Prior studies measuring investments in both strong and weak ties had some serious flaws, and without empirical remedies, the literature is left without a clear idea of how these ties are created and what their actual returns to the entrepreneurial venture are. One set of studies focused on the opportunity structure by asking how many social contacts an entrepreneur might conceivably be able to approach for support (Aldrich and Zimmer, 1986). This strategy did not go further to ask what investments entrepreneurs actually had made in trying to access this social structure. A second set of studies took the latter approach to trying to isolate the actual investment in social capital (Aldrich et al., 1987; Aldrich et al., 1989), and it is not surprising that these latter studies produce the most convincing findings about positive returns to investment in social capital (Brüderal and Preisendörfer, 1998).

The other main challenge for this literature is about achieving more careful econometric identification of social capital as distinct from unobserved firm quality and other parts of the error term. In fact, without clear identification, many studies have failed to find any positive benefits from social capital. Aldrich et al. (1987) could not find significant positive effects of six social capital measures on business profitability. Also, without more careful econometric identification, numerous studies have found evidence suggesting that the decision to invest in social capital is really just an artifact of having weak resource endowments and a high probability of failure based on market performance (Bates, 1994; Waldinger et al., 1990; Light and Bhachu, 1993). Without finding instruments that isolate the decision to invest in social capital, these studies leave many open questions about whether social capital is actually of first-order importance when compared to unobserved human capital quality and other resource endowments inside the firm. It could be the case the 'network success' hypothesis should be replaced with the 'network compensation' hypothesis, by which weak firms compensate their weakness with social support (Brüderal and Preisendörfer, 1998). But we will not know a more definite answer to this debate unless future studies solve these challenges of identification.

The empirical solution is to adopt greater use of instruments and exogenous shift variables to better identify the returns to investments in social capital and reputational bonding. Most models in the global entrepreneurship literature have focused on cross-sectional samples in which firm quality is proxied by recent sales growth. As Davidsson and Honig (2003) point out, such cross-sectional analysis cannot be used to determine at what stages of the entrepreneurial process the investment in social capital is important. As Hoang and Antoncic (2003) appropriately argue, entrepreneurial studies should be longitudinal and show how network content, governance and structure emerge over time. This is true, but even when work is focused on a certain stage of an entrepreneurial venture, no analysis that uses observables like sale growth as the only effort to control for unobserved quality will lead to clear identification. The problem is that even with an observable variable like sales growth, there is still a high potential for the unobserved portion of firm quality in the error term to be correlated with the coefficient on network investments.

There are solutions to this core methodological problem in the literature, and one example comes from a neighbouring literature on overall social network effects. Bertrand et al. (2000) wanted to test the theory in social science that poverty reinforces itself through social networks. The problem with demonstrating the economic importance of networks is that network effects may be highly correlated with unobserved individual, group and societal characteristics. In asking whether an individual was more likely to apply for social welfare if they lived next to other people on social welfare, Bertrand et al. devised a clever empirical design to deal with the unobserved factors. They focused on the fact that individuals who speak a non-English language at home tend to interact mainly with others who speak that language. Bertrand et al. could insert fixed effects both for the neighbourhood and for the language groups present in the neighborhood. With the fixed effects, they could soak up the unobserved factors. By then focusing on the interaction between language group and welfare use, they could show clear identification of strong network effects on welfare use.

While this empirical strategy of finding an instrument (in this case non-English language groups interacted with welfare use) for network connections is highly useful, few studies in the global entrepreneurship literature have tried to come up with instruments. It is, nevertheless, possible to find instruments in various countries that can be used to cleanly identify the returns to entrepreneurial investment in social capital and reputation. One example is the study on investments in Korean social capital by Siegel (2006). That study exploited two facts common to Korean society: (1) South Korean elites tend to favour members of the same high school network because high schools are the channel by which elites from politically hostile regions form personal alliances; and (2) South Korea has undergone a series of political shocks the main effect of which has been to remove one high school network from political power and to replace it with another. By focusing on the choice of an entrepreneur to hire a CEO or other senior executive from one rival network or another, and then by measuring the returns to these connections through their interaction with multiple political shocks, Siegel (2006) was able to identify the importance of social networks for Korean entrepreneurs in gaining access to outside resources.

The challenge for future empirical work in this literature is to look for instruments that determine investments in certain types of social capital, or else exogenous shocks that only affect entrepreneurs who have made certain investments. Without clear identification strategies, it is difficult to differentiate the 'network success' hypothesis from rival hypotheses focusing on the unobserved quality of individual entrepreneurs. The literature has made enormous strides in doing more careful longitudinal analysis, but more work on the process of entrepreneurship and the concurrent process of reputation building is needed.

19.6 Conclusion

This chapter has given a broad overview of what the social dimensions of entrepreneurship are, and how scholars have studied entrepreneurial attempts to build social advantage and reputation in the face of weak macro-level institutions for resource sharing. It is precisely in environments of weak resource-sharing institutions that reputation becomes both a scarce and economically more valuable asset. To build reputation, entrepreneurs must bond themselves by affiliating with a social network. Theory has predicted that entrepreneurs who invest the most in social capital will enjoy the highest overall financial returns. Yet empirical work testing this hypothesis has been inconclusive. Improved identification strategies are needed to better delineate the mechanism by which investments in social capital lead to sustainable competitive advantage.

References

ACEMOGLU, D. and JOHNSON, S. H. (2003). 'Unbundling Institutions'. NBER Working Paper No. 9934. Cambridge, MA: NBER.

ALDRICH, H. E., REESE, P. R. and DUBINI, P. (1989). 'Women on the Verge of a Breakthrough? Networking Among Entrepreneurs in the United States and Italy'. *Entrepreneurship and Regional Development*, 1: 339–56.

—— B. ROSEN and W. WOODWARD (1987). 'The Impact of Social Networks on Business Foundings and Profit: A Longitudinal Study', in N. Churchill, J. Hornaday, O. J. Krasner and K. Vesper (eds) *Frontiers of Entrepreneurship Research*. Wellesley, MA: Babson College.

—— and C. ZIMMER (1986). 'Entrepreneurship Through Social Networks', in D. Sexton and R. Smiler (eds) *The Art and Science of Entrepreneurship*. New York, NY: Ballinger.

AMIT, R. K., R. MACCRIMMON, C. ZIETSMA and M. J. OESCH (2001). 'Does Money Matter? Wealth Attainment as the motive for initiating growth-oriented ventures'. *Journal of Business Venturing*, 16: 119–43.

ARABSHEIBANI, G., D. DE MEZA, J. MALONEY and B. PEARSON (2000). 'And a Vision Appeared Unto Them of a Great Profit: Evidence of Self-Deception Among the Self-Employed'. *Economics Letters*, 67: 35–41.

BARDI, A. and S. H. SCHWARTZ (2003). 'Values and Behavior: Strength and Structure of Relations'. *Personality and Social Psychology Bulletin*, 29: 1207–20.

BATES, T. (1994). 'Social Resources Generated by Group Support Networks May Not Be Beneficial to Asian Immigrant-Owned Small Businesses'. *Social Forces*, 72: 671–89.

BAUMOL, W. J. (1990). 'Entrepreneurship: Productive, Unproductive, and Destructive'. *Journal of Political Economy*, 98: 893–921.

BEBCHUK, L. and M. ROE (1999). 'A Theory of Path Dependence in Corporate Governance and Ownership'. *Stanford Law Review*, 52: 127–70.

BEGLEY, T. and W. L. TAN (2001). 'The Socio-Cultural Environment for Entrepreneurship: A Comparison between East Asian and Anglo Countries'. *Journal of International Business Studies*, 32: 537–54.

BENZ, M. and B. S. FREY (2003). 'The Value of Autonomy: Evidence from the Self-Employed in 23 Countries'. IEER Working Paper No. 173.

BERKOWITZ, D., K. PISTOR and J.-F. RICHARD (2003). 'Economic Development, Legality and the Transplant Effect'. *European Economic Review*, 47: 165–95.

BERNARDO, A. and I. WELCH (2001). 'On the Evolution of Overconfidence of Entrepreneurs'. *Journal of Economics and Management Strategy*, 10: 301–30.

Bertrand, M., E. F. P. Luttmer and S. Mullainathan (2000). 'Network Effects and Welfare Cultures'. *Quarterly Journal of Economics*, 115: 1019–55.

Bird, B. (1988). 'Implementing entrepreneurial ideas: The case of intention'. *Academy of Management Review*, 13: 442–53.

Blanchflower, D. G. (2000). 'Self-Employment in OECD Countries'. *Labour Economics*, 7: 471–505.

—— and A. J. Oswald (1998). 'What Makes an Entrepreneur?' *Journal of Labor Economics*, 16: 26–60.

—— A. J. Oswald and A. Stutzer (2001). 'Latent Entrepreneurship Across Nations'. *European Economic Review*, 45: 680–91.

Boettke, P. J. and C. J. Coyne (2003). 'Entrepreneurship and Development: Cause or Consequence?' *Advances in Austrian Economics*, 6: 67–88.

Bourdieu, P. (1972). *Outline of a Theory of Practice*. Cambridge: Cambridge University Press.

Bradley, D. E. and J. A. Roberts (2004). 'Self-Employment and Job Satisfaction: Investigating the Role of Self-Efficacy, Depression, and Seniority'. *Journal of Small Business Management*, 42: 37–58.

Brouwer, M. T. (2002). 'Weber, Schumpeter and Knight on Entrepreneurship and Economic Development'. *Journal of Evolutionary Economics*, 12: 83–105.

Brüderal, J. and P. Preisendörfer (1998). 'Network Support and the Success of Newly Founded Businesses'. *Small Business Economics*, 10: 213–25.

Burt, R. S. (1982). *Structural Holes: The Social Structure of Competition*. Cambridge, MA: Harvard University Press.

Busenitz, L., C. Gomez and J. W. Spencer (2000). 'Country Institutional Profiles: Unlocking Entrepreneurial Phenomena'. *Academy of Management Journal*, 43: 994–1003.

Cabral, L. M. B. and J. Mata (2003). 'On the Evolution of the Firm Size Distribution'. *American Economic Review*, 93: 1075–90.

Chinese Culture Connection (1987). 'Chinese Values and the Search for Culture-Free Dimensions of Culture', *Journal of Cross-Cultural Psychology*, 18: 143–64.

Ciavarella, M. A., A. K. Buchholtz, C. M. Riordan et al. (2004). 'The Big Five and Venture Survival: Is There a Linkage?' *Journal of Business Venturing*, 19: 465–83.

Coleman, J. S. (1990). *Foundations of Social Theory*. Cambridge, MA: Harvard University Press.

Cooper, A., C. Woo and W. Dunkelberg (1988). 'Entrepreneurs' Perceived Chances for Success'. *Journal of Business Venturing*, 3: 97–108.

Covin, J. (1991). 'A Conceptual Model of Entrepreneurship as Firm Behavior'. *Entrepreneurship Theory and Practice*.

—— and Slevin, D. (1989). 'Strategic Management of Small Firms in Hostile and Benign Environments'. *Strategic Management Journal*, 10: 75–87.

Cumming, D. J. and G. Fleming (2003). 'The Impact of Legality on Private Equity Markets: Evidence from the Asia-Pacific'. Working paper. University of Alberta and Australian National University.

—— Schmidt, D. and U. Walz (2004). 'Legality and Venture Governance Around the World'. RICAFE Working Paper No. 10. London: London School of Economics.

Davidsson, P. and B. Honig, (2003). 'The Role of Social and Human Capital among Nascent Entrepreneurs'. *Journal of Business Venturing*, 301–31.

Demirguc-Kunt, A. and V. Maksimovic (1998). 'Law, Finance, and Firm Growth'. *Journal of Finance*, 53: 2107–39.

Desai, M., P. Gompers and J. Lerner (2003). 'Institutions, Capital Constraints and Entrepreneurial Firm Dynamics: Evidence from Europe'. NBER Working Papers No. 10165. Cambridge, MA: NBER.

Djankov, S., R. La Porta F. López- De-Silanes and A. Shleifer (2002). 'The Regulation of Entry'. *Quarterly Journal of Economics*, —— (2003). 'Courts: The Lex Mundi Project'. *Quarterly Journal of Economics*, pp. 453–517.

—— E. Miguel, Y. Qian, G. Roland and E. V. Zhuravskaya (2004). 'Entrepreneurship: First Results from Russia'. Working paper.

Dunn, T. and D. Holtz-Eakin (2000). 'Financial Capital, Human Capital, and the Transition to Self-Employment: Evidence from Intergenerational Links'. *Journal of Labor Economics*.

Easterly, W. and R. Levine (2003). 'Tropics, Germs, and Crops: How Endowments Influence Economic Development'. *Journal of Monetary Economics*, 50: 3–39.

Evans, D. S. and B. Jovanovic (1989). 'An Estimated Model of Entrepreneurial Choice under Liquidity Constraints'. *Journal of Political Economy*, 97: 808–27.

—— and L. Leighton (1989). 'Some Empirical Aspects of Entrepreneurship'. *American Economic Review*, 79: 519–35.

Falter, J. M. (2002). 'Are Self-Employed Happier at Work?' Working Paper. University of Geneva.

Fredland, E. and C. Morris (1976). 'A Cross Section Analysis of Small Business Failure'. *American Journal of Business*, 1: 7–17.

Frey, B. S. and M. Benz (2003). 'Being Independent is a Great Thing: Subjective Evaluations of Self-Employment and Hierarchy'. CESifo Working Paper No. 959.

George, G. and A. S. Zahra (2002). 'National Culture and Entrepreneurship: A Review of Behavioral Research.' *Entrepreneurship: Theory and Practice*, 26: 33–49.

Giannetti, M. and A. Simonov (2003). 'Does Prestige Matter More than Profits? Evidence from Entrepreneurial Choice'. Working paper. Stockholm: Stockholm School of Economics.

Gilson, R. J. (1999). 'The Legal Infrastructure of High Technology Industrial Districts: Silicon Valley, Route 128, and Covenants not to Compete'. *New York University Law Review*, 74: 575–629.

—— (2003). 'Engineering a Venture Capital Market: Lessons from the American Experience'. *Stanford Law Review*, 55: 1067–103.

Gompers, P., J. Lerner and D. Scharfstein (2005). 'Entrepreneurial Spawning: Public Corporations and the Formation of New Ventures, 1986–99'. *Journal of Finance* (April) 60(2): 577–614.

Goodnow, J. J. (1997). 'Parenting and the Transmission and Internalization of Values: From Social-Cultural Perspectives to Within-Family Analyses', in J. E. Grusec and L. Kuczynski (eds) *Parenting and Children's Internalization of Values: A Handbook of Contemporary Theory*. New York: Wiley.

Granovetter, M. S. (1973) 'The Strength of Weak Ties.' *American Journal of Sociology*, 78: 1360–89.

—— (1974). *Getting a Job*. Cambridge: Harvard University Press.

Greif, A. (1993). 'Contract Enforceability and Economic Institutions in Early Trade: The Maghribi Traders' Coalition'. *American Economic Review*, 83: 525–48.

Guiso, L. and F. Schivardi (2005). 'Learning to be an Entrepreneur'. CEPR Discussion Paper, no. 5290.

Hamilton, B. H. (2000). 'Does Entrepreneurship Pay? An Empirical Analysis of the Returns to Self-Employment'. *Journal of Political Economy*, 108: 604–31.

Harper, D. A. (1998). 'Institutional Conditions for Entrepreneurship', in P. J. Boettke, I. M. Kirzner and M. J. Rizzo (eds), *Advances in Austrian Economics*, vol. 5, pp. 241–75. Connecticut: JAI Press Inc.

Hayton, J., G. George and A. S. Zahra (2002). 'National Culture and entrepreneruship: A Review of Behavioral Research'. *Entrepreneurship Theory and Practice*, 26: 33–49.

He, K., R. Morck and B. Yeung (2003). 'Corporate Stability and Economic Growth'. Working paper. Edmonton, Alberta and New York, New York: University of Alberta and New York University.

Hoang, H. and B. Antoncic (2003). 'Network-Based Research in Entrepreneurship: A Critical Review'. *Journal of Business Venturing*, 18: 165–87.

Hofstede, G. H. (1980). *Culture's Consequences: International Differences in Work-Related Values*. Thousand Oaks, CA: Sage.

—— (1998). *Entrepreneurship in Europe*. Schuman Lecture 1998, Studium Generale Maastricht/House of Europe.

—— (2001). *Culture's Consequences: Comparing Values, Behaviors, Institutions, and Organizations Across Nations*, 2nd edn. Thousand Oaks, CA: Sage.

—— N. G. Noorderhaven, A. R. Thurik et al. (2004). 'Culture's Role in Entrepreneurship: Self-Employment out of Dissatisfaction', in J. Ulijn and T. Brown (eds) *Innovation, Entrepreneurship and Culture: The Interaction between Technology, Progress and Economic Growth*. Cheltenham: Edward Elgar.

Holtz-Eakin, D., D. Joulfaian and H. S. Rosen (1994*a*). 'Sticking It Out: Entrepreneurial Survival and Liquidity Constraints'. *Journal of Political Economy*, 334–47.

—— —— and —— (1994*b*). 'Entrepreneurial Decisions and Liquidity Constraints'. *Rand Journal of Economics*, 25: 334–47.

Hundley, G. (2001). 'Why and When Are the Self-Employed More Satisfied With Their Work?' *Industrial Relations*.

Hunt, S. and J. Levie (2003). 'Culture as a Predictor of Entrepreneurial Activity', in Bygrave et al. (eds) *Frontiers of Entrepreneurship Research 2003*. Wellesley, MA: Babson College.

Husted, B. W. (1999). 'Wealth, Culture and Corruption'. *Journal of International Business Studies*, 30: 339–60.

Hyde, A. (1998). 'Silicon Valley's High-Velocity Labor Market'. *Journal of Applied Corporate Finance*, 11: 28–37.

Inglehart, R. (1997). *Modernization and Post Modernization: Culture, Economic and Political Change in 43 Societies*. Princeton, NJ: Princeton University Press.

—— and W. Baker (2000). 'Modernization, Cultural Change, and the Persistance of Traditional Values'. *American Sociology Review* 65: 19–51.

Johnson, S. (2000). 'Entrepreneurs and the Ordering of Institutional Reform: Poland, Slovakia, Romania, Russia and the Ukraine Compared'. *Economics of Transition* 8: 1–36.

—— (2002). 'Property Rights and Finance and Entrepreneurship'. *American Economic Review* 92: 1335–56.

—— J. McMillan and Woodruff C. (1999). 'Property Rights, Finance, and Entrepreneurship'. Working Paper.

Johnson, S., D. Kaufmann, J. McMillan and Woodruff, C. (2000). 'Why Do Firms Hide? Bribes and unofficial activity after communism'. *Journal of Public Economics*, 76: 495–520.

Kerins, F., J. K. Smith and R. Smith (2004). 'Opportunity Cost of Capital for Venture Capital Investors and Entrepreneurs'. *Journal of Financial and Quantitative Analysis*, 39: 385–406.

Kirzner, I. M. (1973). *Competition and Entrepreneurship*. Chicago: University of Chicago Press.

Klapper, L., L. Laeven and R. G. Rajan (2004). 'Barriers to entrepreneurship'. Working Paper. The World Bank.

Kluckhohn, C. (1951). 'Value and Value Orientations in the Theory of Action', in Parsons, T. and E. Shils (eds) *Toward a General Theory of Action*. Cambridge, MA: Harvard University Press.

Kluckhohn, F. and Strodtbeck, F. (1961). *Variations in Value Orientations*. Evanston, IL: Row Petersen.

Knight, F. H. (1921). *Risk, Uncertainty and Profit*. Chicago, IL: University of Chicago Press.

Kogut, B. and H. Singh (1988). 'The Effect of National Culture on the Choice of Entry Mode'. *Journal of International Business Studies*, 20: 411–32.

Kreiser, P. M., L. Marino and K. M. Weaver (2001). 'Assessing the Psychometric Properties of the Entrepreneurial Orientation Scale: A Multi-Country Analysis'. *Entrepreneurship: Theory and Practice*, 26: 71–94.

Krueger, N. F. (Jr), M. D. Reilly and A. L. Carsud (2000). 'Competing Models of Entrepreneurial Intentions'. *Journal of Business Venturing*, 15: 411–32.

La Porta, R., F. Lópes-de-Silanes, A. Shleifer and R. Vishny (1998). 'Law and Finance'. *Journal of Political Economy*, 106: 1113–55.

Laeven, L. A. and C. Woodruff (2004). 'The Quality of the Legal System and Firm Size'. Working paper. The World Bank.

Levine, R. (1999). 'Law, Finance, and Economic Growth'. *Journal of Financial Intermediation*, 8: 8–35.

Licht, A. N., C. Goldschmidt and S. H. Schwartz (2004). 'Culture Rules: The Foundations of the Rule of Law and Other Norms of Governance'. Working paper. Herzliya: Interdisciplinary Center Herzliya.

—— —— and —— (2005). 'Culture, Law, and Corporate Governance'. *International Review of Law and Economics*.

Light, I. and P. Bhachu (eds) (1993). *Immigration and Entrepreneurship*. New Brunswick, NJ: Transaction.

Lindh, T. and H. Ohlsson (1996). 'Self-Employment and Windfall Gains: Evidence from the Swedish Lottery'. *The Economic Journal*, 106: 1515–26.

Lumpkin, G. T. and G. G. Dess (1996). 'Clarifying the Entrepreneurial Orientation Construct and Linking it to Performance'. *Academy of Management Review*, 21: 135–72.

Markus, H. R. (2003). 'Models of Agency: Sociocultural Diversity in the Construction of Action', in V. Murphy-Berman and J. J. Berman (eds) *Nebraska Symposium on Motivation: Cross-cultural differences in perspectives on the self*, 49: 1–57. Lincoln: University of Nebraska Press.

—— and S. Kitayama (1994). 'A Collective Fear of the Collective: Implications for Selves and Theories of Selves'. *Personality and Social Psychology Bulletin*, 20: 568–79.

McGrath, R. G., I. C. MacMillan, E. A. Yang and W. Tsai (1992). 'Does Culture Endure, or is it Malleable? Issues for Entrepreneurial Economic Development'. *Journal of Business Venturing*, 7: 441–58.

Menon, T., M. W. Morris, C-y Chiu and Y-y Hong (1999). 'Culture and the Construal of Agency: Attribution to Individuals Versus Group Dispositions'. *Journal of Personality and Social Psychology*, 76: 701–17.

Milhaupt, C. (1998). 'Property Rights in Firms'. *Virginia Law Review*, 84: 1145–95.

Miller, D. (1983). 'The Correlates of Entrepreneurship in Three Types of Firms'. *Management Science*, 29: 770–91.

Miller, J. G. (2003). 'Culture and Agency: Implications for Psychological Theories of Motivation and Social Development', in V. Murphy-Berman and J. J. Berman (eds) *Nebraska Symposium on Motivation: Cross-cultural differences in perspectives on the self*, 49: 1–57. Lincoln: University of Nebraska Press.

Mitchell, R. K., B. Smith, K. W. Seawright and E. A. Morse (2000). 'Cross-cultural Cognitions and Venture Creation'. *Academy of Management Journal*, 43: 974–93.

Morck, R., B. Yeung and W. Yu (2000). 'The Information Content of Stock Markets: Why do Emerging Markets have Synchronous Price Movements?'. *Journal of Financial Economics*, 58: 215–60.

Morris, M. H., R. A. Avila and J. Allen (1993). 'Individualism and the Modern Corporation: Implications for Innovation and Entrepreneurship'. *Journal of Management*, 19: 595–12.

Morse, E. A., R. K. Mitchell, J. B. Smith and K. W. Seawright (1999). 'Cultural Values and Venture Cognitions on the Pacific Rim'. *Global Focus*, 11: 135–53.

Moskowitz, T. J. and Vissing-Jùrgensen, A. (2002). 'The Returns to Entrepreneurial Investment: A Private Equity Premium Puzzle?' *American Economic Review* 92: 745–78.

Mueller, S. L. and A. S. Thomas (2001). 'Culture and Entrepreneurial Potential: A Nine Country Study of Locus of Control and Innovativeness'. *Journal of Business Venturing*, 16: 51–75.

Nisbett, R. E., K. Peng, I. Choi and A. Norenzayan (2001). 'Culture and Systems of Thought: Holistic versus Analytic Cognition'. *Psychological Review*, 108: 291–310.

Noorderhaven, N. G., S. Wennekers, G. H. Hofstede, et al. (1999). 'Self-Employment out of Dissatisfaction: An International Study'. Working paper. Tinbergen: Tinbergem Institute.

—— A. R. Thurik, S. Wennekers and A. van Stel (2003). 'Self-Employment Across 15 European Countries: The Role of Dissatisfaction'. Working Paper. Rotterdam: Rotterdam School of Economics.

North, D. C. (1990). *Institutions, Institutional Change and Economic Performance*. Cambridge, UK: Cambridge University Press.

Ovaska, T. and R. S. Sobel (2003). 'Entrepreneurship in Post-Socialist Economies'. Working Paper. Morgantown, WV: West Virginia University.

Palich, L. E. and D. R. Bagby (1995). 'Using cognitive theory to explain entrepreneurial risk taking: Challenging conventional wisdom'. *Journal of Business Venturing*, 10: 425–38.

Peng, K., D. R. Ames and E. Knowles (2001). 'Culture and Human Inference', in D. Matsumoto (ed.) *Handbook of Culture and Psychology*. Oxford and New York: Oxford University Press.

Peterson, R. and J. Shulman (1987). 'Entrepreneurs and Bank Lending in Canada'. *Journal of Small Business and Entrepreneurship*, 5: 41–5.

PEROTTI, E. C. and P. F. VOLPIN (2004). 'Lobbying on Entry'. Working Paper. London: London School of Economics.

PORTES, A. (1998). 'Social Capital: Its Origins and Applications in Modern Sociology'. *Annual Review of Sociology*, 24: 1–24.

—— and J. SENSENBRENNER (1993). 'Embeddedness and Immigration: Notes on the Social Determinants of Economic Action'. *American Journal of Sociology* 98: 1320–50.

POWELL, W. W. (1996). 'Inter-Organizational Collaboration in the Biotechnology Industry.' *Journal of Institutional and Theoretical Economics* 152: 197–215.

—— WHITE, D. R., K. W. KOPUT and J. OWEN-SMITH (2005). 'Network Dynamics and Field Evolution: The Growth of Inter-organizational Collaboration in the Life Sciences'. *American Journal of Sociology*, 110: 901–75.

RAUCH, A. and M. FRESE (2000). 'Psychological Approaches to Entrepreneurial Success. A General Model and an Overview of Findings', in C. L. Cooper and I. T. Robertson (eds) *International Review of Industrial and Organizational Psychology*. Chichester: Wiley. 101–42.

RODRIK, D., A. SUBRAMANIAN and F. TREBBI (2002). 'Institutions Rule: The Primacy of Institutions over Geography and Integration in Economic Development'. NBER Working Paper No. 9305. Cambridge, MA: NBER.

ROE, M. (1996). 'Chaos and Evolution in Law and Economics'. *Harvard Law Review*, 109: 641–69.

ROKEACH, M. (1973). *The Nature of Human Values*. New York: The Free Press.

SARASVATHY, S. D. (2001). 'Causation and Effectuation: Toward a Theoretical Shift from Economic Inevitability to Entrepreneurial Contingency'. *Academy of Management Review*, 26: 243–63.

SARASVATHY, D. K., H. A. SIMON and L. LAVE (1998). 'Perceiving and Managing Business Risks: Differences Between Entrepreneurs and Bankers'. *Journal of Economic Behavior and Organization*, 33: 207–26.

SAXENIAN, A. (1996). *Regional Advantage: Culture and Competition in Silicon Valley and Route 128*, 2nd edn. Cambridge, MA: Harvard University Press.

—— (2002). Local and Global Networks of Immigrants in Silicon Valley. San Francisco: Public Policy Institute of California.

SCHMITT-RODERMUND, E. (forthcoming). 'Pathways to Successful Entrepreneurship: Parenting, Personality, Competence, and Interests'. *Journal of Vocational Behavior*, 65: 498–518.

—— and F. W. VONDRACEK (2002). 'Occupational Dreams, Choices, and Aspirations: Adolescents' Entrepreneurial Prospects and Orientations'. *Journal of Adolescence*, 25: 65–78.

SCHUMPETER, J. A. (1934). *The Theory of Economic Development* (trans R. Opie). Cambridge, MA: Harvard University Press.

SCHWARTZ, S. H. (1992). 'Universals in the Content and Structure of Values: Theoretical Advances and Empirical Tests in 20 Countries', in M. P. Zanna (ed.) *Advances in Experimental Social Psychology*, 25: 1–65.

—— (1999). 'Cultural Value Differences: Some Implications for Work'. *Applied Psychology International Review*, 48: 23–47.

—— (2004). 'Mapping and Interpreting Cultural Differences around the World', in Vinken, H., J. Soeters and P. Ester (eds) *Comparing Cultures: Dimensions of Culture in a Comparative Perspective*. Leiden: Brill Academic Publishers.

Schwartz, S. H. and W. Bilsky (1987). 'Toward a Universal Psychological Structure of Human Values'. *Journal of Personality and Social Psychology*, 53: 550–62.

—— and —— (1990). 'Toward a Theory of the Universal Content and Structure of Values: Extensions and Cross-Cultural Replications'. *Journal of Personality and Social Psychology*, 58: 878–91.

—— A. Bardi and G. Bianchi (2000). 'Value Adaptation to the Imposition and Collapse of Communist Regimes in East-Central Europe', in S. A. Renshon and J. Duckitt (eds) *Political Psychology: Cultural and Cross-Cultural Foundations*. New York: New York University Press.

—— G. Melech, A. Lehmann et al. (2001). 'Extending the Cross-Cultural Validity of the Theory of Basic Human Values with a Different Method of Measurement'. *Journal of Cross-Cultural Psychology*, 32: 519–42.

Shane, S. (1993). 'Cultural Influences on National Rates of Innovation'. *Journal of Business Venturing*, 8: 59–73.

—— (1994). 'Cultural Values and the Championing Process'. *Entrepreneurship: Theory and Practice*, 18: 25–41.

—— (1995). 'Uncertainty Avoidance and the Preference for Innovation Championing Roles'. *Journal of International Business Studies*, 26: 47–68.

Shapero, A. and L. Sokol (1982). 'The Social Dimensions of Entrepreneurship', in C. Kent, D. Sexton and K. H. Vesper (eds) *The Encyclopedia of Entrepreneurship*. Englewood Cliffs, NJ: Prentice-Hall.

Siegel, J. I. (2006). 'Contingent Political Capital and International Alliances: Evidence from South Korea' Working Paper. Boston: Harvard Business School.

—— (2005). 'Can Foreign Firms Bond Themselves Effectively by Renting U.S. Securities Laws?' *Journal of Financial Economics*, 73: 319–59.

Stern, S. (2004). 'Do Scientists Pay to Be Scientists?' *Management Science*, 50: 835–53.

Thomas, A. S., and S. L. Mueller (2000). 'A Case for Comparative Entrepreneurship: Assessing the Relevance of Culture'. *Journal of International Business Studies*, 31: 287–301.

Tonoyan, V. (2004). 'The Bright and Dark Sides of Trust: Corruption and Entrepreneurship' in H.-H. Hönmann and F. Welter (eds) *Trust and Entrepreneurship: A West-East-Perspective*. Cheltenham: Edward Elgar.

Treisman, D. (2000). 'The Causes of Corruption: A Cross-National Study'. *Journal of Public Economics*, 76: 399–457.

Tybout, J. R. (2000). 'Manufacturing Firms in Developing Countries: How Well They Do, and Why?' *Journal of Economic Literature*, 38: 11–44.

Uhlaner, L. and R. Thurik (2004). 'Post-Materialism: A Cultural Factor Influencing Total Entrepreneurial Activity Across Nations'. Working Paper. Jena: Max Planck Institute for Research into Economic Systems.

Ulijn, J. and T. E. Brown. (2003). 'Innovation, Entrepreneurship and Culture: A Matter of Interaction between Technology, Progress and Economic Growth? An Introduction', in T. Brown and J. Ulijn (eds) *Innovation, Entrepreneurship and Culture: The Interaction between Technology, Progress and Economic Growth*. Cheltenham, UK: Edward Elgar.

—— and M. Weggeman (2001). 'Towards an Innovation Culture: What are its National, Corporate, Marketing, and Engineering Aspects, Some Experimental Evidence', in C. Cooper, S. Cartwright and C. Early (eds) *International Handbook of Organizational Culture and Climate*. London: Wiley.

Van Praag, M. (2003). 'Initial Capital Constraints Hinder Entrepreneurial Venture Performance: An Empirical Analysis'. CESifo Working Paper No. 887. Münich: CESifo.

—— and van Ophem, J. (1995). 'Determinants of Willingness and Opportunity to Start as an Entrepreneur'. *Kyklos*, 48: 513–40.

Waldinger, R., H. E. Aldrich and R. Ward (1990). *Ethnic Entrepreneurs*. Newbury Park, CA: Sage.

Weber, M. (1904). *The Protestant Ethic and the Spirit of Capitalism* (1930 English translation). New York: Scribner; London: Allen and Unwin.

Wennekers, S., R. Thurik, A. van Stel and N. Noorderhaven (2002). 'Uncertainty Avoidance and the Rate of Business Ownership across 22 OECD Countries, 1976–2000'. Working Paper. Tinbergen: Tinbergem Institute.

Williamson, O. E. (2000). 'The New Institutional Economics: Taking Stock, Looking Ahead'. *Journal of Economic Literature*, 38: 595–613.

Woodruff, C. (1999). 'Can Any Small Firm Grow Up? Entrepreneurship and Family Background in Mexico'. Working Paper. La Jolla, CA: University of California, San Diego.

Wurgler, J. (2000). 'Financial Markets and the Allocation of Capital'. *Journal of Financial Economics*, 58: 187–214.

CHAPTER 20

INSTITUTIONAL OBSTACLES TO ENTREPRENEURSHIP

KATHY FOGEL, ASHTON HAWK, RANDALL MORCK AND BERNARD YEUNG

20.1 Introduction

This chapter focuses on institutional obstacles to entrepreneurship. Entrepreneurs carry out a highly complicated composite act. They need intelligence to collect and digest information about business opportunities. They need foresight about the possibilities new technologies and other developments create. They need judgement and leadership skills to found a company and guide its growth. They need communication skills to enthuse financiers to back their vision. The number of active entrepreneurs therefore depends on how many individuals possess these skills. But skills are not endowments. Individuals decide to develop those skills that advance their well being and to forgo developing those that do not.

The prospects of a career as an entrepreneur depend on the economic environment, which can be facilitative or detrimental. A multitude of factors determine this environment: rules and regulations, the quality of government, the availability of education, and the ambient culture. Many of these factors fall under the heading of 'institutions', by which we mean the constraints on behaviour imposed by the state or societal norms that shape economic interactions. This is the often cited definition in North (1990). At its most general, an institution is any predictable pattern of behaviour, including 'culture'.

Of particular importance in determining the abundance of entrepreneurs are the following:

1 Rules, regulations, and property rights, and their enforcement matter because they affect what we call *transactional trust*: the degree of trust the parties to a business transaction place in each other. Entrepreneurship requires long term transactions, such as skilled employees or financial backers investing their time and money now for rewards in the distant future. If they typically cannot trust the entrepreneur to fulfil his or her obligations, their time and money are not proffered, and the entrepreneurial venture is unviable. Property rights matter, for example, because De Soto (2000) shows that home mortgages are a key source of entrepreneurial financing in much of the world. More complicated financial dealings also require well enforced property rights. For example, stock markets require legal protection of investors' property rights over their investments.

2 Government matters because it establishes and enforces rules, regulations, and property rights. Good government raises transactional trust and so facilitates entrepreneurship. Insufficient government fails to protect the rights of the weak, and this discourages entrepreneurship. What impoverished entrepreneur would work day and night to build a new firm knowing that robber barons will seize it at the first signs of profit? But excessive government can be just as bad. Cumbersome regulations and burdensome rules can raise the costs of running a new business to the point where acquiring the skills needed to be an entrepreneur seems pointless. Moreover, governments of any size can follow bad policies: subsidies to ill-governed firms run by cronies can crowd out private investments and volatile macroeconomic policies can create uncertainties that make long term investments unnecessarily risky.

3 The distribution of control over corporate assets matters because elites with concentrated control of large swaths of the large corporate sector have political influence. Those on top most appreciate the status quo, of which entrepreneurship is innately disruptive. Established elites can preserve the status quo by, for example, lobbying for policies that check the financial system's ability to back upstart firms. Rules and regulations with high compliance costs also disproportionately burden small, new firms, as do high tax rates with complicated loopholes.

4 Culture matters, for the literature shows that authoritarian and hierarchical societies fail to honour self-made success, and social status is surely part of the pay-off to entrepreneurs.

5 Very basic institutions matter profoundly. Universal basic education lets latent entrepreneurs realize that opportunities exist. Openness to the outside world lets in foreign ideas and opportunities along with foreign goods and capital. Diversity also matters because it opens minds to new ideas. These factors all affect entrepreneurship because they stimulate information exchange. New ideas are a necessary condition for successful entrepreneurship.

These institutional constraints may seem almost trivial to the inhabitants of some developed economies, but they are largely lacking in many poorer countries and regions and are surprisingly limited even in many otherwise developed economies. All are fundamentally important, and a deficit in any can impede entrepreneurship throughout a region, a country, or a civilization. To clarify this, we first explore the economics of entrepreneurship more deeply and then provide some preliminary empirical investigation of the validity of these arguments.

20.2 What is an Entrepreneurial Act?

A common perception of an entrepreneur is as an innovator, who starts and operates a thriving upstart business. Many well-known entrepreneurs are innovators, or successful business persons who commercialize innovations. But entrepreneurship encompasses more than invention.

Schumpeter (1912: 1934) suggests that an entrepreneur is not a pure inventor; and need not even be an inventor at all. Often, an entrepreneur adopts new inventions devised by others, or merely creates new combinations of old activities to fulfill familiar economic purposes more efficiently and effectively. Similarly, Hayek (1937) and Kirzner (1973) view an entrepreneur as an arbitrageur: a middleman who recombines productive activities to produce more valuable outputs and/or use cheaper inputs. An entrepreneur collects and digests information and makes a judgement about the payoffs from using a new combination of activities, instead of an old one. This act of creativity requires uncommon foresight and judgement, as well as more mundane skills. Hayek (1948) points out that this form of arbitrage drives increasing economic efficiency, which can intuitively, but essentially correctly, be defined as 'always producing the most valuable outputs from the cheapest possible inputs'.

In addition, an entrepreneur directs work processes and resource allocation, which Coase (1937) refers to as entrepreneurial coordination. Hence, an entrepreneur can be distinguished as having the managerial skills and insights to devise and implement new work processes or procedures, or to apply old ones in new businesses. Henry Ford I was a hugely successful entrepreneur, whose assembly-line production process revolutionized the automobile industry and many others. Sam Walton, the founder of Walmart, was another, who revolutionized retailing on a global scale. Arora et al. (2004) document that, in the US, new industry leaders were often highly concentrated geographically, and spawned other successful firms, typically in the same region, that become leaders in related industries. For example, the TV receiver industry developed from the radio industry in this way.

Another facet of entrepreneurial activities is risk-taking. To implement an entrepreneurship, an entrepreneur has to accept the risk that her investment of money, time and energy may not pay off. Cantillon (1755) emphasizes that an entrepreneur is a specialist in taking on risks. Much new work confirms that entrepreneurs are less risk-averse than others. Gentry and Hubbard (2004) show that entrepreneurs have poorly diversified portfolios. Moskowitz and Vissing-Jorgensen (2002) show that entrepreneurs bear high risks. Evans and Leighton (1989) show that entrepreneurs typically believe their firms' performance largely depends on their own actions. Puri and Robinson (2004) use US survey data to show that entrepreneurs are unusually risk-loving and optimistic.

That entrepreneurs seldom start out independently wealthy, and so need financial support to break through market entry barriers is long recognized since Schumpeter (1942). Recent work confirms that liquidity constraints limit entrepreneurship and financial market development facilitates it. For example, Evans and Jovanovic (1989) show that individuals founding new businesses typically faced liquidity constraints and had to accumulate personal wealth first. Holtz-Eakin, Joulfaian, and Rosen (1994b) show that individuals with inherited wealth are more likely to become sole business proprietors. Holtz-Eakin, Joulfaian, and Rosen (1994a) show that inheritance-induced relaxation in liquidity constraints raises entrepreneurs' business survival and performance rates.

In summary, an entrepreneurial act is composite in nature. To conduct a Schumpeterian entrepreneurial 'recombination', entrepreneurs must be a risk-takers. Yet, they cannot be foolhardy. They need information, including information about technological innovations and new business practices. They need the foresight to see where these might lead, and the judgement to get there. They need the business skills to found a firm and manage its market entry. And they needs the skills to persuade capitalists to back their venture. All of these traits are, in part at least, skills that individuals must develop. An economy's institutional environment can either encourage or discourage this, and so determines, in part at least, its level of entrepreneurial activity. Of special importance are institutions that permit *transactional trust*; that is, trust between the parties of a transaction whose outlay and return are far separated geographically or temporally.

20.3 Institutions Affect Entrepreneurship

Before investigating the role of institutions further, we need to clarify the term. North (1990: 3) defines institutions as 'the rules of the game in a society or, more formally, ... the humanly devised constraints that shape human interaction.' A government is an 'institution' because it is normally responsible for setting up and enforcing 'the rules of the game'. This technical definition is not far off the standard dictionary definition of an institution as 'an organized pattern of group behaviour, established and generally accepted'. Both include the subject matter above: laws, rules, regulations, and cultural constraints on behaviour, like religions. Hence, 'institution' is a succinct term for 'the rules of the game', 'government', and 'organized patterns of behaviour' which includes culture, religions, and even 'markets.'

The incidence of entrepreneurial acts, shown above to be composite in nature, depends not just on the incidence of capable individuals, but also on a variety of institutional factors that may facilitate or hinder entrepreneurship. For example, institutional features that impede information flow, raise information costs, and erode the gains from information, limit entrepreneurial activity. These can include lax accounting standards and disclosure requirements, weak property rights protection, an inefficient judiciary, and ambient corruption. Besides their direct negative impact on the information-seeking aspect of entrepreneurial activity, these institutional deficiencies also retard capital market development, which further dampens entrepreneurial activity. They render markets less competitive, diversified, and developed, and this also reduces economic pressures on established firms to explore new opportunities, like innovatively entering vertically related lines of business.

Many institutional features that influence entrepreneurship, like laws and regulations, are directly controlled by the state and hence by those who influence it. Others, such as law enforcement and judicial efficiency, are heavily influenced by the state. Yet others, such as culture and religion, probably lie outside the control of the state, except perhaps in the very long run. This may explain why some emerging economies, like China and Poland seem more entrepreneurial than others.

Systematic investigation of these matters is difficult within the confines of a single economy because these factors, once established, usually change very slowly. Recent years have produced a surge of cross-country studies relating economic development to institutions, especially those affecting capital market development and functionality.[1] This attention arose as formerly socialist command economies

[1] The literature grows almost exponentially. A good starting point would be La Porta et al. (1997, 1998), King and Levine (1993a, b), and the recent surveys in Levine (1997), Durnev et al. (2004) and Beck and Levine (2005).

sought to develop market economies. Their experiences exposed how limited economists' knowledge was about the formation and functionality of markets. Economic theories based on mature and highly-developed economies were quickly proved inadequate guides, for they implicitly assumed institutional constraints that had to be constructed in most transition economies.

As researchers grappled with a new appreciation of the critical role of institutions, their fundamental connection to entrepreneurship grew apparent. Different transition economies quickly came to display vastly different levels of entrepreneurship (e.g. McMillan and Woodruff, 2002). Even among developed economies, the variation is non-trivial and statistically related to the institutional environment (e.g. Desai, Gompers and Lerner, 2003). A growing literature sheds light on this relationship.

There are two ways we could organize our discussion. We might organize the literature along 'functional' lines following the entrepreneurial process: information acquisition, economic foresight, risk tolerance, property rights, financing, and market entry. This would let us consider how institutional factors affect each function. However, each institutional feature typically affects all the components of this chain. We therefore take the more succinct (and less repetitious) approach of exploring how each relevant institutional feature affects the composite chain of entrepreneurial activity.

20.3.1 Two general comments

20.3.1.1 *The type of government*

Practically all economies have a government charged with laying down rules, laws, and regulations, and with administering a judicial system to enforce them. By these activities, the government fosters the development of markets and shapes economic behavioural norms. The government also directly affects resource allocation and market behaviour through its tax, fiscal, monetary, and other economic policies.

Frye and Shleifer (1997) conceptually sort governments into three basic styles, characterized by an invisible hand, a helping hand, or a grabbing hand.

> Under the invisible hand model, the government is well-organized, generally uncorrupted, and relatively benevolent. It restricts itself to providing basic public goods, such as contract enforcement, law and order, and some regulations, and it leaves most allocative decisions to the private sector.
> Under the helping-hand model, bureaucrats are intimately involved in promoting private economic activities, they support some firms and kills off others, pursue industrial policy, and often have close economic and family ties to entrepreneurs. ... Bureaucrats are corrupt, but corruption is relatively limited and organized.

In the final, grabbing-hand, model, government is just as interventionist, but much less organized, than in the helping-hand model. The government consists of a large number of substantially independent bureaucrats pursuing their own agendas, including taking bribes. (p. 354)

The three styles articulate a continuum of possible stances for the government—from setting up rules and regulations to facilitating economic transactions through meddling more than necessary, and to blatantly corrupt politicians and bureaucrats treating the economy as prey. Our theme in this chapter is how the costs and benefits prospective entrepreneurs envision shifts as they move from invisible hand, to helping hand and to grabbing hand governments. It seems that entrepreneurship is most viable if the government offers an invisible hand and least viable if the state reaches out with a grabbing hand.

A deep question at the intersection of economics and political science is why the hands of different states take different forms, and how these can be changed. Recent work uses political economy frameworks to analyze the determinants of governments' hands and their enthusiasm for different sorts of institutional development (see Morck, Wolfenzon, and Yeung (2005) and Perotti and Volpin (2004)). Much more work along these lines is needed.

20.3.2 Stages of development

Which institutional factors most significantly affect entrepreneurship probably depends on an economy's stages of development. For example, state-of-the-art accounting disclosure rules are of little use in an economy where most of the population is illiterate or judges are irredeemably corrupt.

Entrepreneurial activity in low-income developing countries often entails an individual setting-up a small business to earn a living. At this stage, the state can promote entrepreneurial activity by offering entrepreneurs secure ownership of their businesses, legal enforcement of business contracts they enter, basic communication and transportation infrastructure, and an educated population from which to hire.

This can ignite economic growth as small business owners and employees develop business skills and the broader society comes to appreciate their achievements. Individuals who succeed in these endeavours save from their earnings and invest further in the human capital of their children, in their own businesses or more broadly. The last creates opportunities for developing a financial system, which extends entrepreneurial career opportunities to people lacking personal or family wealth. This sows the seed for the next stage of development and for more intense entrepreneurial activity.

A typical entrepreneur now starts a business hoping to build a successful enterprise with a national or even global market share. Accounting disclosure standards, bank regulation, and corporate governance now take prominence as entrepreneurs' needs for large-scale capital grow. The quality of local universities, constraints due to labour laws, and the attractiveness of the country to foreign experts now also all acquire importance as entrepreneurs seek ever higher quality human capital.

While the above dichotomization is artificial, empirical results corroborate with it, for developed and developing countries differ starkly in the institutional factors that predict firm entry (Desai, Gompers, and Lerner, 2003) and firm turnover (Fogel, Morck, and Yeung, 2004). Detailed empirical work in this area is difficult, and hindered by a lack of reliable and publicly available data, especially for developing nations.

20.3.2 Specific considerations

We now turn to more specific institutional features that affect entrepreneur supply.

20.3.2.1 *Rules, regulations, property rights, and the legal environment*

Entrepreneurial activity relies on individuals taking advantage of arbitrage opportunities, bearing risks, raising capital, and entering markets. Entrepreneurs need to be able to trust their sources of information. They also need to be able to earn the trust of their financiers, and build trusting business relationships with transacting partners. That is, entrepreneurship critically relies on the ability to secure transactional trust.

These sorts of trust do not come easily. Successful entrepreneurship requires intangible skills and effort. Intangibles like information processing skills, foresight about changing markets, insight about the viability of new combinations of production processes, risk assessment, and managerial skills are difficult for others to verify *ex ante*. This difficulty is exacerbated by the very long term nature of the contracts and commitments involved in building a business. The support of entrepreneurs requires the committing of resources now, and hoping for returns in the far distant future. These long delays unavoidably create uncertainty and give cheaters cover to behave opportunistically. Long term transactions based on information-based skills are often untenable because information asymmetry, moral hazard, adverse selection and agency problems undermine transactional trust.

Entrepreneurs find it difficult to be trusting, too. Stand-alone entrepreneurs are often inexperienced market entrants with limited recourses to punish people or organizations who cheat on them or discriminate against them. This is particularly the case if the offenders are bureaucrats, powerful financiers or dominant established suppliers or distributors. Well-enforced rules and regulations strengthen transactional trust. Clearly laying out what is acceptable and what is punishable gives transacting parties stronger property rights by letting them more readily detect and punish cheating. More importantly, it lets people commit to 'verifiable honesty' and thus enables long term transactions. Examples of these rules and regulations include mandatory disclosure requirements, specified investor and creditor rights, definitions for performance clauses in trade contracts, and the like. Well-enforced rules and regulations of these sorts facilitate the use of legal contracts to create transactional trust.

The absence of transactional trust advantages individuals who can overcome the resulting institutional deficiencies. For example, an absence of transactional trust weakens the financial system, giving an advantage to individuals who can raise money from family members. A family member who cheats relatives can be punished by the family in many ways, up to and including ostracization. Repeated interactions can also create transactional trust because an accumulated reputation for honesty is a valuable asset for future transactions, and even minor cheating greatly dissipates its value. This explains why, in many developing economies, a 'relationship' must precede any substantial business dealings. High profile demonstrations of choosing honesty over opportunistic behaviour also help build valuable reputations. Fulfilling unfavourable contractual obligations may cost money in the short term, but it builds a reputation that serves as a durable asset.

If the cost of a damaged reputation outweighs the gain from cheating, people do not cheat. But much business involves one-time incidental transactions between strangers, where cheating has no real reputation cost. Moreover, these methods of overcoming low ambient levels of transactional trust are not available to most people. Individuals from small and poor families cannot amass enough family wealth to start a business. Transactional trust based on long-term relationships or demonstrations of honesty is an advantage to the established, but a barrier to upstarts. For these reasons, formal and freely accessible mechanisms that engender transactional trust can spur entrepreneurship. Without them, entrepreneurs emerge only from the privileged and established. (See also Johnson, et al., 2002a.)

Entrepreneurial activity also depends on how well entrepreneurs' property rights are protected from the grabbing hands of bureaucrats and from established elites with political influence. Any one of the following scenarios discourages entrepreneurship. Consider a business venture that is about to become eminently successful, thanks to the founding entrepreneur's insight, skills, and years of hard work. The business can lose its value overnight if the government suddenly requires a hitherto unneeded operating licence. A corrupt bureaucrat can demand a bribe of anything up to the value of the business for granting the licence. Or, the corrupt bureaucrat can grant an operating licence to a relative, friend, or even himself; and the licence holder can then buy the entrepreneur out at a sure fire sale price, force a joint venture upon her, or bankrupt the entrepreneur and then set up a copy cat operation. In these ways, bureaucrats or parties with political influence can grab the lion's share of the gain the entrepreneur would otherwise have earned. A rational prospective entrepreneur, foreseeing this, would opt for another career—perhaps as a bureaucrat. Even if she did not, rational technology experts and investors would doubt her ability to pay high returns in the future and withhold their time and money. This sort of corruption certainly also occurs in developed economies, but it is tragically commonplace in much of the developing world and the former Eastern Bloc. The consequence of these failures to safeguard entrepreneurs' property rights is a paucity of entrepreneurship.

The laws and regulations that deter such behaviour and thereby permit transactional trust must be enforced to have a real effect on entrepreneurship. Obviously, an honest, independent, and efficient judicial system is needed. Several considerations merit note.[2]

First, law enforcement is a government's job. Generally, a more constrained government is less attractive to corrupt bureaucrats and less useful to powerful elites. As the bank robber Willy Horton replied when asked why he robbed banks, 'That's where the money is.' Constrained governments with smaller budgets and fewer regulatory powers are therefore likely to be less corrupt and better at administering an efficient and effective court system. The constraints can stem from a strong constitution, mass media created social transparency, a well-educated populace, or plain social culture and values.

Secondly, the origin of a country's legal system may matter. La Porta et al. (1998) show that a legal system derived from British common law best protects property rights protection and promotes judicial efficiency. The reasons for this are unclear. Common law legal systems may well coincide with other less tangible institutions derived from a British colonial heritage. Or, common law may actually better protect weak outsiders from powerful insiders. Further work is needed to illuminate these issues.

Thus, limited and well-defined rules and regulations, well-protected property rights, good government, and an efficient and effective judicial system all promote entrepreneurship. The empirical literature offers support for all of these links.

Desai, et al. (2003) gauge entrepreneurship in European Union members and Central and Eastern European countries using entry rates, average firm size, average firm age, and the skewness of the firm size distribution. They regard higher entry rates, a smaller average firm size, a greater average firm age, and a more symmetric size distribution as evidence of more active entrepreneurs. They report, through the use of these measures, that there is more entrepreneurship in the less corrupt countries, and in those countries that better protect private property rights. They also show a less consistent link between less interventionist courts and more entrepreneurial activity.

[2] The literature is long; interested readers should consult, e.g. Morck et al. (2004, section VII).

All of these linkages are far less statistically significant in developed countries than in transition economies. This means either that these institutional features are more important in developing countries or that exceeding a threshold level of institutional development is very important, but further refinement is less critical. Morck, et al. (2000) find evidence of such a threshold effect in the impact of property rights protection on asset price informativeness.

Johnson, et al. (2002b) use a 1997 survey of recently formed and relatively small manufacturing firms in Poland, Slovakia, Romania, Russia, and Ukraine. They infer the lack of property rights by respondents' answers about the need to make 'extra-legal payments' for government services (e.g. fire and sanitary services, registration renewal) and licences, and to pay exorbitant 'protection' fees. Their survey also asks how effective the courts are at resolving commercial disputes. They find that established firms earn significantly higher after-tax profits in countries with weak property rights and ineffective courts. Since high profits should be eroded by the entry of new competitors, they conclude that these institutional deficits discourage entry. They also report that weak property rights and lack of faith in the courts discourage firms from re-investing their profits, even if potentially profitable reinvestment opportunities exist.

As of about 1997, Johnson, et al. (2000) also measure these same countries' market infrastructure by using (i) firms' typical sales outside their immediate localities, (ii) the extent to which private firms do not depend on state-owned enterprises as suppliers or customers, and (iii) the importance of wholesale traders. They report that countries' rankings in these metrics correspond well to their rankings in measures of government quality, including the legal system's effectiveness, the rule of law, the absence of corruption, and the general level of economic freedom. They report Poland leading other transition economies in both the development of its legal and regulatory environment, and its market infrastructure. Slovakia follows closely and Ukraine tends to guard the rear. They conclude that the control of corruption is an essential institutional reform if entrepreneurship is to develop.

20.3.2.2 *Regulatory burden*

Not all well-enforced laws and regulations facilitate entrepreneurship. 'Invisible hand' governments impose and enforce laws and regulations to define property rights and create transactional trust, and might err on the side of too little regulation. 'Helping hand' and especially 'grabbing hand' governments impose economically inefficient regulations that burden entrants to protect incumbents with political influence or to extort bribes. Overall, empirical work suggests excessive laws and regulations are the more general problem. Countries with higher regulatory burden support less entrepreneurship.

De Soto (1990) painstakingly documents every detail about the bribes, delays, and regulatory headaches confronted by anyone without political influence attempting to establish a legal small business in Peru.

Djankov et al. (2002) document the number of regulatory hurdles on the path to establishing a small business in 85 countries. The number of required procedures range from 2 in Canada to 21 in the Dominican Republic, and the average is 10. They also show that the minimum time required to meet these hurdles ranges from 2 days (Australia and Canada) to 152 days (Madagascar), with a world average of 47 days. More burdensome entry regulations correlate with more corruption, but not with higher goods quality, less pollution or better health outcome. Controlling for per capita income, countries with more closely-held political power, fewer political rights, and fewer constraints on their executives have more burdensome entry regulations. This is consistent with grabbing hands imposing excessive regulatory burden in much of the world.

Desai et al. (2003) report that these same 'regulatory burdens' data correlate positively with higher average firm sizes in European countries, indicating that the burdens probably protect large incumbents' market shares. 'Regulatory burdens' are positively correlated with entry in Central and Eastern European countries, but this may be a statistical artifact of an unusual negative correlation between regulatory burden and corruption in those countries.

Fogel et al. (2005) examine the staying power of dominant firms from 1975 to 1996 across different countries. They find that higher regulatory burdens correlate with lower turnover of top firms, particularly in high income countries.

20.3.2.3 *Crowding out*

'Helping hand' governments proactively manage their economies to advance social and economic development. These governments typically have large budgets and direct many state controlled enterprises. While these activities are probably covers for 'grabbing hand' politics in some countries, they reflect genuinely benevolent government in others. Even so, 'helping hand' governments impose costs upon the economy. Their activities bid up factor costs, including capital costs, and crowd out private investment. This is particularly unfavourable to upstarts.

Generally, direct government activism favours large established corporations. Högfeldt (2005) describes in detail how Sweden's social democratic governments forged de facto partnerships with large established corporate groups, essentially offering protection from competitors in return for cooperation in implementing new social policies. Politicians quite understandably find dealing with the controlling owners of a few large corporate groups simpler and more predictable than dealing with the managers of many smaller independent firms. To the extent that this preference leads to government favouritism towards large established corporations, it adversely affects entrepreneurship. Fogel et al. (2005) present evidence consistent with Högfeldt's hypothesis across a broad cross-section of countries.

However, governments can and do allocate direct subsidies, loan guarantees, and the like to small businesses and even to businesses in the process of formation. Gompers and Lerner (1999) describe a variety of such schemes in the US and elsewhere and conclude that most are surprisingly ineffective, but that there are occasional qualified successes. For example, small firms backed by the US Small Business Innovation Research grew faster than otherwise similar businesses. The qualification here is that this must be balanced against the drag on the economy due to the higher taxes and government debt the programme required. This sort of counterfactual analysis is very uncertain.

Gompers and Lerner (1999), after an extensive and detailed analysis of such programmes, offer relatively simple advice to policy-makers: Keep public funds out of overheated 'chic' sectors already flush with private money. Instead, fund out-of-fashion but promising ventures. Overall, they conclude that venture capital financing is best accomplished by specialized funds with accumulated technological and managerial expertise. Governments (and large established corporations) have great difficulty matching such funds' ability to distinguish sound from unsound ventures early on, and to reallocate capital swiftly.

Finally, government subsidy programmes of any sort are tempting targets for political lobbying. Stigler (1986), Krueger (1993) and others present plausible arguments about how self-interested civil servants can slowly change 'helping hand' bureaucracies into 'grabbing hands' and much empirical evidence now supports this view. These transformations do not require corrupt civil servants, only a degree of self-interest similar to that of everyone else.

20.3.2.4 *Economic stability*

Entrepreneurship entails inter-temporal exchange—investing time, effort, and money now for returns in the distant future. Such exchanges are more tenable if the future is more 'predictable.' A fundamental internal contradiction arises here in that entrepreneurship disrupts the status quo, making the future less predictable. Entrepreneurial activity thus ought to be self-regulating: entrepreneurship that disrupts the economy sufficiently discourages further entrepreneurship until things settle down.

But entrepreneurship is not the only source of unpredictability—especially at the macroeconomic level. Ill-conceived or erratic macroeconomic policies make foreign exchange rates, tax rates, interest rates, and inflation rates unnecessarily unpredictable. These risks make promised future payments less valuable to entrepreneurs, their prospective financial backers, and technology experts they might otherwise compensate with future claims, like stock options.[3] Large, established

[3] A rigorous treatment of the problem in a general equilibrium framework is available in Angeletos and Calvet (2006). They build a neo-classical growth economy with idiosyncratic production risk and incomplete markets where each agent is an entrepreneur operating his or her own neo-classical technology with his or her own capital stock. They show that idiosyncratic production shocks,

firms are less likely to be damaged by this uncertainty than upstarts, for their ongoing earnings let them deal in cash, rather than promises in the distant future.

Macroeconomic volatility thus discourages entrepreneurship. Financial backing becomes more expensive, for even highly sophisticated investors using financial hedging instruments cannot escape such risks entirely. No analogous techniques let the entrepreneur or his/her technology experts evade the risks in their undiversified investments of time and effort. Also, such risks impede transactional trust. McMillan and Woodruff (2002) propose that macroeconomic volatility makes it harder to decipher whether or not transaction partners behave honestly. This discourages the long-term contracts and relationships necessary for successful entrepreneurship. While the well-known empirical link between high macroeconomic volatility and low growth (consistent with low entrepreneurial activity) supports this contention, we are unaware of empirical work linking macroeconomic volatility directly to entrepreneurship.

Macroeconomic volatility is, however, linked to 'grabbing hand' government. Acemoglu et al. (2003) find greater macroeconomic volatility in countries that place fewer constraints on politicians. Controlling for the constraints imposed on politicians' freedom of action in standard regressions explaining growth with macroeconomic volatility actually renders the latter insignificant.[4]

20.3.2.5 *Financial development*

Schumpeter (1912: 1934) proposed that a well-developed financial system is a prerequisite for widespread entrepreneurship because most potential entrepreneurs lack extensive personal or family wealth. Levine (2004) reviews a substantial body of empirical work confirming this, and Perotti and Volpin (2004) explicitly link financial development to the entry of new, entrepreneurial firms.

The law and finance literature, pioneered by La Porta et al. (1997a and 1998), argues that institutions—property rights honouring government, investor and creditor rights, and efficient judicial enforcement—are critical to capital market development. Morck et al. (2000), Wurgler (2000), Durnev et al. (2004) and many others add to a growing empirical literature demonstrating that sound political institutions, as well as sound financial regulation, are important to the efficient functioning of financial markets.

Research into entrepreneurship, most notably Gompers and Lerner (1999, 2000, 2001) pay special attention to venture capital funds. These financial intermediaries accumulate rare combinations of technological and managerial expertise that gives

which we link here with macroeconomic volatility, introduce a risk premium on private equity and reduce investment. The steady state is characterized by a lower capital stock.

[4] In Acemoglu et al. (2003) macroeconomic volatility is measured with government spending, inflation, and exchange rates.

them an advantage in screening prospective entrepreneurs and monitoring entrepreneurial ventures. In essence, venture capital funds specialize in bridging gaps in transactional trust between entrepreneurs and investors. Of course, they also provide their investors more mundane financial services, like diversification into syndicated offerings by other venture capital funds. But these are secondary to their primary advantage: distinguishing technologically and financially sound undertakings from unsound ones. This requires in-house pools of scientific and managerial talent not available elsewhere.

Venture capital activities are highly geographically concentrated. This does not seem driven by financial development, for hotbeds of venture capital activity, like California and Massachusetts, do not correspond to financial centres, like New York. However, Gompers and Lerner (1999) suggest that considerations involving human capital, rather than financial capital, are key. Highly skilled individuals prefer to locate amid many possible employers so if one firm fails, other openings are available without the costs of moving. Clusters of universities and research foundations created these pools of employers in a few specific localities. Entrepreneurial start-ups exploiting new technology require highly skilled employees, and so prefer to locate where such pools of skill already exist. Venture capital funds, needing such experts too, also locate in these labour markets.

20.3.2.6 *Concentrated corporate governance*

In recent years, the literature offers another relevant perspective, surveyed in Morck, Wolfenzon, and Yeung (2005). Most large American and British corporations are owned by multitudes of small shareholders, and lack controlling owners; but elsewhere, most large firms do have controlling owners—often extremely wealthy families (La Porta et al., 1999). These families typically use pyramidal ownership structures, in which a family firm controls many listed firms, each of which controls yet more listed firms, and so on *ad valorem infinitum*. Super voting shares and crossholdings let many such families leverage substantial family wealth into control over vast swathes of their countries' large corporate sectors.

Khanna and Palepu (2000) and others show that firms belonging to such business groups often out-perform independent firms in developing economies. This may be because business groups substitute for missing institutions in these economies. If group firms can obtain credit from each other, the absence of a sound financial system actually becomes a competitive advantage for them. Inefficient managerial or technical labour markets are likewise not a problem if group firms hire from each other as needed. But business groups do become a problem if the elite families who control them use their political influence to stymie financial development to preserve these advantages. Of course, a paucity of sound arm's-length investments in countries with weak financial systems might also deter these families from selling control, as suggested by Casson (1999) and Burkart et al.

(2003). Quite plausibly, both directions of causality combine to lock-in weak institutions that impede financial development.

Pyramidal business groups plausibly contribute to both microeconomic and macroeconomic inefficiency. At the firm level, group firms are mostly controlled, but not directly owned by wealthy families. The actual financial investment of wealthy families in the indirectly controlled members of their pyramidal groups can often be surprisingly trivial (Bebchuk et al. 2000). This creates agency problems of the sort described in Jensen and Meckling (1976).

Macroeconomic inefficiency results because economies whose large corporate sectors are controlled by a handful of wealthy families suffer from strong political lobbying and weak competition. Morck and Yeung (2004), and Morck et al. (2005) argue that families controlling numerous large listed companies have extremely low lobbying costs because they can use the resources of firms they control, but in which their actual investment is small, to lobby for policies that benefit firms in which their investment is large.

Morck and Yeung (2004) argue that such families also have a direct interest in suppressing technological change that would disrupt the status quo. Schumpeter (1912: 1934) argues that entrepreneurship is a process of creative destruction. A stand-alone entrepreneurial entrant treats the destruction of stagnant firms with obsolete assets as an ignorable externality. But an elite, whose wealth is tied up in the assets of established firms, cannot ignore such costs. Innovation that adds value to one firm, but destroys value in another is of problematic value to a family that owns both firms. Consistent with this, Morck et al. (2000) report spending on innovation to be lower in countries where inherited billionaire family wealth is a large fraction of GDP.

If weak institutions retard financial development in these countries, entrepreneurs without ties to leading families are thwarted by transactional trust problems. Of course, entrepreneurship backed by wealthy families is possible, and Khanna and Palepu (2005) document the involvement of one old moneyed Indian family, the Tatas, in that country's software boom. But such cases are remarkable for their rarity. Moreover, family members and associates may not be the best people to run such entrepreneurial ventures. Almeida and Wolfenzon (2005a, b) argue that intragroup financing arrangements of the sort Khanna and Palepu (2000, 2005) document can be quite inefficient because projects by business group companies are over-funded and projects by outsiders are under-funded.

Elites with concentrated corporate control over their economy's large corporate sector also plausibly have capital market power (Morck et al., 2000). By virtue of the sheer volume of corporate earnings they control, such elites face a downward sloping demand curve for the capital they may bring to the capital market. Likewise, by virtue of the sheer volume of corporate investment projects they can bring to the market, elites have market power as a user of external capital. The market power leads to preferential capital access for units inside the groups controlled by these elites. Understandably, such elites may be disinclined to finance upstarts that would erode their capital market dominance. After all, if too many successful entrants grow wealthy, capital markets naturally grow more competitive. Morck et al. (2000) show that firms controlled by old money families enjoy preferential access to capital.

In practical terms, this capital market power could arise in several ways. First, weak investor property rights keep small players out of equity markets. The low ambient level of transactional trust raises the cost of equity capital, as only the very wealthy supply capital. Upstarts are negatively affected.

Secondly, rich families could directly own banks, the other major financing alternative. Examining the ten largest banks in 44 countries in 2001, Caprio, Laeven and Levine (2003) find most to have controlling owners and most of these to be wealthy families. Wealthy families can use their banks to channel capital to the corporations they own. La Porta et al. (2003) show that such related lending accounts for 20 percent of Mexican commercial loans, that related borrowers pay lower interest rates than unrelated borrowers, but nonetheless are more likely to default. Such abuses understandably induce governments to oversee bank lending more overtly. But Beck et al. (2005) show that empowering official supervisory agencies to monitor, discipline, and influence banks engenders corruption.

Thirdly, elites can plausibly use their formidable political influence to forestall capital market reforms, or even reverse them (Rajan and Zingales, 2004). Their means include directly seeking public office, financing politicians or parties, controlling the mass media, and bribing public policy decision-makers, and so on (see Acemoglu et al. (2005), and Morck et al., 2005).

20.3.2.7 *Culture and values*

Entrepreneurs are different from ordinary people. They are often well connected in social networks. They are able to see opportunities others can not. They take risks others shun. They are optimistic while others are conservative. They think outside the box, challenge orthodoxy, and make profits doing so.

Mark Casson (1993), in defining entrepreneurship, wrote:[5]

> The supply of entrepreneurs depends not only on reward and status, but also on personality, culture, and life experience. An entrepreneur will often find that his opinion is in conflict with the majority view. He needs the self-confidence that, even though in a minority, he is right. ... In identifying profitable opportunities the entrepreneur needs to synthesize information from different sources.

The population of entrepreneurs is higher in some societies than in others. Political and economic environments affect people's tendency to be entrepreneurial. For

[5] See http://www.econlib.org/library/Enc/Entrepreneurship.html

example, the Chinese in the 2000s are more commercially entrepreneurial than the Chinese in the pre-reform 1970s. Allegedly, Americans in the Silicon Valley area are more entrepreneurial than Americans in New England (*The Economist*, 20 February 1999, 'Silicon Envy'). Possibly, the 'entrepreneurial spirit' is a part of a collective 'personality trait' and determined by social 'culture' and 'values'. Casson (1993) continues:

> The culture of a community may be an important influence on the level of entrepreneurship. A community that accords the highest status to those at the top of hierarchical organizations encourages "pyramid climbing", while awarding high status to professional expertise may encourage premature educational specialization. Both of these are inimical to entrepreneurship. The first directs ambition away from innovation (rocking the boat), while the second leads to the neglect of relevant information generated outside the limited boundaries of the profession. According high status to the "self-made" man or woman is more likely to encourage entrepreneurship.

Casson articulates the societal factors most likely to affect entrepreneurship. Dominance by hierarchical organizations that demand docile respect for status and ladder climbing discourage the values demanded for entrepreneurship. Such societies encourage theological orthodoxy and rhetorical elegance rather than commercially oriented innovation. But societies that emphasize meritocracy and reward 'self-made' success encourage entrepreneurship. Unsurprisingly, societies more dominated by hierarchical religious organization are shown to have lower levels of ambient trust and less developed capital markets (La Porta et al., 1997b and Stulz and Williamson, 2003). At present, whether sparse rewards for innovators or low transactional trust (or something else) best explains the lack of entrepreneurship in societies with hierarchical religions remains unclear.

Another factor that could affect behavioural norms is the mass media. The media can vigorously expose opportunistic behaviour by the political and business elite, or uncritically sing their praises. The former discourages dishonesty in government and big business. By contributing to social transparency, it raises people's willingness to challenge established elites. This gives rise to patterns of thought that stimulate entrepreneurial discovery and lock in a meritocracy (Dyck and Zingales, 2003).

20.3.2.8 *Other factors: Education, diversity and openness*

A country's education institutions contribute to entrepreneurship both indirectly and directly. Given that entrepreneurial discovery involves 're-combination' of ideas and practices, entrepreneurship is affected by the education level of the populace and the diversity of ideas they can entertain. Higher general levels of education make a greater fraction of the population available as entrepreneurs or as the skilled technology experts they often need.

In addition, institutions of higher education in particular can contribute more directly to entrepreneurship. America's high technology clusters of entrepreneurial firms correspond to clusters of leading research universities. Since other top research universities lack accompanying clusters of entrepreneurial firms, the particular characteristics of the universities that spawn them are of interest. Intellectual property rights policies seem critical here. Most universities claim intellectual property rights ownership of any ideas developed by their researchers. Researchers at such universities reap meagre rewards from commercialized innovations, so few ensue (Di Gregorio et al., 2003). Universities surrounded by high technology clusters tend to let individual researchers retain ownership of their innovations and grant them freedom to contract with any external parties to develop those innovations. At present, it is unclear if the latter universities come out ahead because of gifts and bequests from their wealthy alumni entrepreneurs. Certainly, a strong case can be made that their intellectual property rights policies better advance social welfare.

Education is but one way to promote diversity in thinking. Jacobs (1985) shows that cities with industrially diversified economies are better able to sustain prosperity over the very long term. She argues that a diverse mixture of businesses give the local economy more resilience against industry shocks, but also stresses that a diverse cross-section of industries lets ideas from one cross-pollinate others. Glaeser et al. (1992) provide econometric evidence on US cities showing that she is probably right.

Finally, by easing cross border exchanges of ideas and best practices, openness in the form of international trade and investment stimulates competition and entrepreneurship[6]. (Caves, 1996).

20.4 A TENTATIVE EMPIRICAL EFFORT

This section undertakes a preliminary empirical investigation of the above thoughts. We gauge entrepreneurial activity by firm entry rates in a cross-section of 34 European countries. Then proxies for each institutional factor are introduced. By examining how these institutional variables correlate with entrepreneurship, we can test the basic plausibility of the ideas we have already raised. We emphasize that

[6] We note here that openness is itself a policy variable which is affected by constraints on government, distribution of economic power, and possible other concerns. Admitting the possible, we include openness here as an economic environment variable.

our intention is to explore correlations, not to conduct an exhaustive empirical investigation that would overcome intrinsic statistical problems like endogeneity.

20.4.1 Entrepreneurship

Our entry rates are based on the Amadeus dataset of European corporate activity.[7] Amadeus, produced by the Bureau van Dijk, covers nearly 7 million companies, both public and private. Because of the variety of information sources and disclosure requirements across countries and over time, data coverage varies in depth and completeness. To create comparable samples across countries, we remove countries with fewer than 100 firms and firms with fewer than 20 employees, following Desai, Gompers and Lerner (2003). We also remove all firms that are inactive (bankrupt or merged) as of 1995.

We define 'entry' in year *t* as 'active' firms that are not in the database at time *t-1* but present at *t*. Some newly included firms in period *t* have an incorporation date from an earlier year. Some others are included even if they are inactive due to bankruptcies or mergers. Their inclusion merely reflects a change in database coverage, so we exclude them from our entry calculation.

An entry by a firm with only one or two employees is not the same as an entry by a firm with, say, 50 employees. We therefore construct two entry measures: equally weighted and labour weighted. The equally weighted entry rate in period *t* is defined as the total number of entries in *t* over the total number of firms in *t-1*. The labour weighted entry rate of period *t* is the total number of employees of new entrants in *t* over the total number of employees of existing firms in *t-1*.

We calculate an entry rate for every two consecutive years starting in 1996. We thus have biannual entry rates ending in 1997 through 2001 for every country. Entry rates in some countries vary widely from period to period, possibly due to changes in disclosure requirements that result in widening of data coverage. For example, the equally weighted entry rates of Austria range from 5.1 percent in 2001 to 23.6 percent in 1999. We use the median entry rate from 1997 to 2001 to remove such swings. Using average entry rates for each period yields similar results to those shown below.

Table 20.1, Panel A lists E_V, the labour weighted entry rate, and E_E, the equally weighted entry rate, for each of our 34 countries. The two indices are, unsurprisingly, highly significantly correlated ($\rho = 0.76$). Table 20.1, Panel B shows the usual summary statistics.

[7] Comprehensive global entry data are unfortunately not yet available.

Table 20.1a Entry rates

	E_V	E_E		E_V	E_E
Austria	0.055	0.134	Luxembourg	0.000	0.000
Belgium	0.012	0.017	Macedonia	0.001	0.006
Bosnia and Herzeg.	0.000	0.000	Malta	0.011	0.017
Bulgaria	0.008	0.011	Netherlands	0.027	0.017
Croatia	0.013	0.016	Norway	0.055	0.060
Czech Republic	0.024	0.042	Poland	0.007	0.015
Denmark	0.048	0.053	Portugal	0.005	0.014
Estonia	0.047	0.054	Romania	0.041	0.053
Finland	0.059	0.032	Russia	0.012	0.043
France	0.008	0.024	Serbia and Montenegro	0.000	0.000
Germany	0.059	0.039	Slovak	0.000	0.000
Greece	0.019	0.036	Slovenia	0.000	0.000
Hungary	0.011	0.017	Spain	0.032	0.038
Ireland	0.009	0.012	Sweden	0.021	0.027
Italy	0.009	0.006	Switzerland	0.007	0.022
Latvia	0.023	0.043	Ukraine	0.013	0.013
Lithuania	0.017	0.043	United Kingdom	0.033	0.031

Table 20.1b Summary statistics

	Mean	Median	Std. Dev.	Min.	Max.
Entry rate, labour-weighed E_V	.0202	.0122	.0188	.000	.0589
Entry rate, equally-weighted E_E	.0275	.0194	.0258	.000	.134
Log of 1996 per capita GDP ln(*y*)	9.44	9.51	.587	8.39	10.5

Note: Table 1 lists median entry rates of 1997 to 2001, weighted by firms' employees, E_V, and median entry rates of the same period, equally weighted, E_E. Entry rates are calculated based on Amadeus data on every two consecutive years from 1996 to 2001. *Entry* in year *t* is defined as active firms that are not in the database in year *t-1*, that enter the database in year *t* and have year of incorporation no earlier than year *t*-1. Equal-weight entry rate of year *t* is the number of entry in year *t* over the total number of firms in *t-1*. Labour-weighted entry rate of year *t* is defined as the total number of employees of entry firms in year *t* over the total number of employees of firms in *t-1*.

20.4.2 Institutional variables

Our institutional variables can be divided into sub-categories: 'rules, property rights, and legal regime', 'government quality and actions', 'distribution of control of corporations', 'culture', and 'education, market diversity, and openness'.

20.4.2.1 *Rules, property rights and legal regime*

These variables proxy for the institutional features conducive to sound property rights and transactional trust. 'Respect for the rule of law' is a comprehensive index estimated by Kaufmann et al. (2003), a higher value indicating more widespread law and order. 'Judicial efficiency', produced by the country risk rating agency Business International Corp, is an assessment of the 'efficiency and integrity of the legal environment as it affects business, particularly foreign firms'. These data are from La Porta et al. (1998). 'Property rights protection' is a survey result from Freedom House, a higher value indicating better perceived protection for private property rights. 'Absence of Bribery' comes from a survey by the Global Competitiveness Report 1997, a higher value indicating fewer incidents of bribery. This variable differs from government corruption because bribery can affect dealings between businesses as well as between businesses and the government. However, the two are very highly correlated ($\rho = 0.84$).

We also include 'French legal origin'—an indicator variable set to one for legal systems descending from that of France, and to zero for all other legal origins. We incorporate this variable because the law and finance literature (e.g. La Porta et al., 1997, 1998) indicates that countries with a French legal origin have the least developed property rights protection and the lowest levels of transactional trust.

Well-defined regulations, efficient judicial systems, and clean governments that respect property rights are all institutional features critical for the development of transactional trust. Countries with these features should support more entrepreneurial activity. French legal systems are associated with weaker property rights and lower ambient trust, so these countries should exhibit less entrepreneurial activity.

20.4.2.2 *Government quality and actions*

The quality of government can be divided into sub-categories. One dimension of government quality is its respect for property rights (e.g. lack of corruption) and effectiveness. A second reflects its regulatory stances. A third concerns government activism. A fourth gauges the volatility of government macroeconomics policies. Some of these variables potentially double as measures of the quality of the legal system. This seems unavoidable.

20.4.2.2.1 *Quality of government*

We use 'government accountability', 'government effectiveness', and 'control of corruption' to gauge the quality of government. All three indices are from Kaufmann et al. (2003), who use statistical methods to aggregate a large collection of governance indicators from various international organizations, think tanks, political and business risk-rating agencies, and non-governmental organizations. 'Government accountability' measures citizens' political rights in selecting their governments. 'Government effectiveness' speaks of the ability of governments to produce and implement policies independently and competently. 'Control of corruption' measures the limits on politicians' freedom to use of public power for private gains. For all these indices, a higher value indicates better outcomes, that is more representative, autonomous, effective, honest, and property rights respecting governments.

We expect these variables to be positively associated with entrepreneurship.

20.4.2.2.2 *Regulatory stances*

'Regulatory quality' is also from Kaufmann, Kraay, and Mastruzzi (2002). A high value indicates fewer anti-market policies, such as price controls, and lighter regulatory burdens on trade and commerce. We obtain from the World Competitiveness Report (1997) our 'absence of bureaucratic hindrance to business' variable. This assumes a higher value for lighter bureaucratic burdens on businesses. From the World Bank's Doing Business Report we obtain the variable 'rigid employment laws', which gauges the difficulty firms encounter in hiring and firing employees and the rigidity of working hours. A higher value indicates more rigid employment regulation.

The first two of these variables plausibly lower costs to entrepreneurs and the last raises them. We expect 'regulatory quality' and 'absence of bureaucratic hindrance to business' to be positively associated with entrepreneurship, and 'rigid employment laws' to be negatively correlated with entrepreneurship.

20.4.2.2.3 *Government activism*

We capture government activism in several ways. First, we use the 'size of government', the average of government spending over GDP from 1991 to 1996. This variable is from the Penn World Tables 6.1 (see Appendix 20.1). Our second measure is 'government ownership of banks', the fraction of the country's top ten banks owned by the government. The variable is from La Porta et al. (2000). We expect both variables to be negatively related to entrepreneurship.

Thirdly, we use 'absence of price control', an inverse index of government intervention in imposing price control from the Fraser Institute. We expect this index to be associated with more entrepreneur entry.

'Successful subsidy targets' assumes a higher value if government subsidies are awarded to commercial winners. Similarly, 'openness in awarding public contracts' takes a higher value if public contracts are open to foreign bidders. The last two variables are from the Global Competitiveness Report and plausibly indicate whether or not government subsidies are granted based on competence and merits. We expect these indices to be positively related to entrepreneurship.

20.4.2.2.4 *Volatility of economic policies*

We use 'average inflation' and the 'variance of inflation' to capture the volatility of monetary policies, and the 'variance of government spending' to capture the volatility of fiscal policies. The inflation rate we use is the GDP deflator from the

World Development Indicators. Both the average and the variance of inflation are calculated for the years 1994 to 1997. The variance of government spending is calculated using the government share of real per capita GDP in 1996 constant prices from the Penn World Tables 6.1 (see App. 20.1). Volatile government macroeconomic policies by themselves raise investment risks and also make it difficult to identify opportunistic transactional behaviour. Thus, volatile macroeconomic policies may be negatively related to entrepreneurship.

20.4.2.3 *Concentration of corporate governance*

We use two measures of the distribution of corporate control rights. 'Oligarch family control' is the fraction of top ten corporate groups majority controlled by a wealthy family in 1996, from Fogel (2006). This measures the extent to which wealthy families control the large corporate sector of each country. 'Firm size Herfindahl' is the median from 1991 to 1996 of the employee-based Herfindahl Index of all firms included in the Amadeus database for each country. It measures the skewness of the firm size distribution in each country. A higher Herfindahl index means that large firms are more dominant.

The above arguments suggest that both variables reflect conditions unconducive to upstart firms and so out to correlate negatively with entrepreneurship.

20.4.2.4 *Culture and the influence of mass media*

We follow Stulz and Williamson (2003) and use the dominant religion of a country to proxy for cultural influence. Our data are from the CIA World Factbook.[8] We define a 'hierarchical religion' indicator variable set to 1 if a country's dominant religion is Roman Catholic, Muslim, or Eastern Orthodox, and to 0 otherwise. The literature suggests that hierarchical religions encourage respect for traditional ideas and impair ambient trust, so the indicator should correlate negatively with entrepreneurship.

We follow Dyck and Zingales (2003) and use 'newspapers per capita' to measure the influence of the mass media. Our raw data are the total average circulations, or copies printed, of daily newspapers per thousand inhabitants in each country in 1997, and are from the online statistical section of UNESCO. Dividing that number by 1000 gives us the per capita figure. The above discussion suggests that social transparency directly stimulates entrepreneurial discovery and also fosters transactional norms conducive to entrepreneurship. We therefore expect entrepreneurship to be positively related to 'newspapers per capita'.

Of course, this measure is an imperfect proxy for a genuinely free press because newspapers could be controlled by the state or rich tycoons. If so, the mass media

[8] http://www.cia.gov/cia/publications/factbook/

might laud the achievements of the elite, rather than criticize its foibles. Thus, newspaper circulation in countries controlled by such elites might actually be negatively related to genuine social transparency.

20.4.2.5 *Education, market diversity and openness*

We use 'education attainment', the logarithm of the average years of education for people aged 25 or over, to proxy for the initial stock of human capital in each country. These data are for 1990 and are from Barro and Lee (2000). Higher levels of education attainment should be related to more entrepreneurship.

We measure 'market diversity' by counting the total number of three-digit SIC codes in each country in the Amadeus dataset. To side-step potential problems caused by changes in database coverage over time, we use the median of the SIC counts from 1991 to 1996.

We capture product market openness by 'trade openness', imports plus exports as fraction of GDP in 1996. The effects of trade openness on entry are two-fold. On the one hand, since trade openness expands markets, constrains local monopolists, and introduces new ideas, it should encourage entrepreneurship. On the other hand, intense competition from abroad may increases the capability requirement for entrepreneurship and could have a negative effect.

We measure capital market openness by '*capital restrictions*', the number of types of capital flow restrictions (out of a maximum of 12) each country had in 1997. Capital restrictions apply to both cross-border portfolio flows and direct investment. Capital account openness allows local prospective entrepreneurs access to a broader array of investors, and thus should correlate positively with entrepreneurship. Foreign direct investment especially should stimulate entrepreneurship more directly by undermining domestic market power and by introducing foreign technologies and management ideas. We therefore also measure capital market openness by '*Gross FDI flows*', the gross foreign direct investments as a fraction of GDP in 1996. We expect entrepreneurship to be negative related to *capital restrictions* but positively related to *gross FDI flows*.

Appendix 20.1 summarizes the description, data year, and data source of each variable.

20.4.3 Method and results

We first present simple correlation between entry and our institutional variables. To capture central tendencies, we use each country's median entry rate in 1997 through 2001. Our institutional variables are all dated before 1997, except the 'rigid employment laws' indicator, for which we cannot find early data.

The institutional variables could easily proxy for basic economic development. For example, entrepreneurship might simply be more evident in richer countries. Hence, simple correlations between the institutional variables and entrepreneurship could be spurious. To address this, we regress entry on the various institutional variables one at a time, but including initial per capital GDP (1996 data) as a control.

We reiterate that the results that follow are illustrative only. We hope to stimulate future more systematic efforts as better data become available.

20.4.3.1 *Results on rules, property rights and legal regime*

The left columns of Table 20.2 show the simple correlation coefficients of labour-weighted and equally-weighted entry rates with our institutional variables. The correlation coefficients between labour-weighted entry rates and variables measuring 'respect for the rule of law', 'judiciary efficiency', 'property rights protection', and 'the absence of bribery' are all positive and highly significant. This is consistent

Table 20.2 Entry rate and institutions for transactional trust

	A: simple correlation		B: regression of entry on institutions controlling for 1996 per capita GDP	
	E_V	E_E	E_V	E_E
Institutions for Transactional Trust:				
Respect for the rule of law	**0.436**	0.287	**.0203**	.0198
	(.01)	(.11)	**(.01)**	(.12)
Judiciary efficiency	**0.452**	0.255	.00712	.00468
	(.08)	(.34)	(.18)	(.61)
Property rights protection	**0.378**	0.211	**.0121**	.0144
	(.04)	(.26)	**(.04)**	(.11)
Absence of bribery	**0.629**	0.300	**.00800**	.00300
	(.00)	(.19)	**(.08)**	(.72)
French legal origin	−0.237	−0.231	**−0.0152**	−0.0199
	(.18)	(.20)	**(.04)**	(.08)

Notes: (i) Panel A presents simple correlation coefficients between median entry rates, labour-weighted, E_V, and equally-weighted, E_E, from 1997 to 2001 and variables measuring institutions for transactional trust. Panel B presents regressions of the form: entry rates $= \beta0+\beta1^{*}$ institutional variables $+\beta2^{*} \ln(y) + \varepsilon$. Only coefficient estimates on institutional variables ($\beta1$) are shown.
(ii) Numbers in parentheses are probability levels for rejecting the null hypothesis of zero correlation coefficients or regression coefficients.

with better institutions, which nurture transactional trust, encouraging entrepreneurial entries. Equally-weighted entry rates are also positively related to respect for the rule of law, judiciary efficiency, and property rights, but the correlation coefficients are less significant.

The right columns of Table 20.2 present regressions of entry on institutions controlling for initial GDP per capita. Only the regression coefficients for the institutional variables are shown. The coefficient for 'respect for the rule of law' is .0203 and is highly statistically significant at 1 percent. The coefficient on 'property rights protection' and 'absence of bribery' are also positive and significant. However, the coefficient for the judicial efficiency variable is insignificant, albeit positive.

Legal origin seems to matter. The simple correlation coefficient of entry with the 'French legal origin' dummy is negative and insignificant. However, the indicator becomes significant once we control for initial per capita GDP.

In summary, Table 20.2 supports institutions conducive to the development of transactional trust facilitating entrepreneurship. In particular, countries in which the rule of law is more respected, property rights better protected, and bribery less commonplace have more entrepreneurship. Also, countries whose legal systems descend from that of France seem less conducive to entrepreneurship.

20.4.3.2 *Results on government quality and actions*

The top panel of Table 20.3 shows that higher entry rates are associated with higher quality government, characterized by greater accountability, greater effectiveness, and less corruption. All three measures are highly statistically significantly related to the labour-weighted entry rate in simple correlations, and the regression coefficients on the corruption and effectiveness measures remain significant after controlling for 1996 per capita GDP. Simple correlation and regression coefficients of the equal-weighted entry rates tell a similar story, albeit less significant statistically.

The next panel relates entry rates to regulatory stances of the government. The positive and significant correlations indicate that higher regulatory quality promotes entrepreneurship. Similarly, the absence of bureaucratic hindrance to business encourages start-ups. Employment laws that impose strict restrictions on hiring and firing workers and on working hours hinder entrepreneurship. These laws plausibly raise both the entry and exit costs of offering employment, and thus discourage start-ups.

The third panel of Table 20.3 correlates government activism with entry. An interesting and complicated picture emerges. First, both government spending/GDP and government ownership of banks are negatively related to entrepreneurship, but the relationship is utterly insignificant. This is inconsistent with the crowding-out effect discussed on p. 551 above. Secondly, less governmental interference in setting prices ('absence of price control') appears to encourage

Table 20.3 Entry rate and government quality

	A: Simple correlation		B: Regression of entry on institutions controlling for 1996 per capita GDP	
	E_V	E_E	E_V	E_E
Government Quality:				
Government accountability	**0.395**	0.268	.0147	.00902
	(.03)	(.14)	(.19)	(.59)
Government effectiveness	**0.339**	0.192	**.0230**	.0191
	(.06)	(.30)	**(.06)**	(.31)
Control of corruption	**0.370**	0.176	**.0152**	.00712
	(.04)	(.34)	**(.06)**	(.56)
Regulatory Stances:				
Regulatory quality	**0.464**	**0.337**	**.0224**	.0214
	(.01)	**(.06)**	**(.02)**	(.15)
Absence of bureaucracy hindrance to business	**0.592**	0.159	**.00659**	.000783
	(.01)	(.52)	**(.02)**	(.89)
Rigid employment laws	**−0.386**	**−0.369**	−.000405	**−.000751**
	(.04)	**(.04)**	(.14)	**(.08)**
Government Activism:				
Size of government	−0.280	−0.188	−5.05E-04	−6.99E-04
	(.13)	(.31)	(.31)	(.35)
Government ownership of banks	−0.190	−0.010	−0.002	0.020
	(.38)	(.96)	(.93)	(.47)
Absence of price controls	**0.581**	0.306	**.00488**	.00458
	(.00)	(.12)	**(.02)**	(.19)
Successful government subsidy targets	**0.350**	0.185	**.00969**	.00516
	(.10)	(.40)	**(.06)**	(.54)
Openness in awarding public contracts	**0.551**	0.268	**.01362**	.00907
	(.01)	(.22)	**(.03)**	(.38)
Volatility of Government Policies:				
Average inflation	−0.161	−0.116	−1.28E-05	−3.62E-05
	(.38)	(.53)	(.80)	(.63)
Variance of inflation	−0.158	−0.162	−3.41E-08	−9.09E-08
	(.39)	(.38)	(.67)	(.45)
Variance of government spending	−0.127	−0.029	−5.28E-05	−4.27E-06
	(.49)	(.88)	(.69)	(.98)

Notes: (i) Panel A presents simple correlation coefficients between median entry rates, labor weighted, E_V, and equally weighted, E_E, from 1997 to 2001 and variables measuring government quality. Panel B presents regressions of the form: entry rates $= \beta0+\beta1^*$ government quality variables $+\beta2^* \ln(y) + \varepsilon$. Only coefficient estimates on government quality ($\beta1$) are shown.

(ii) Numbers in parentheses are probability levels for rejecting the null hypothesis of zero correlation coefficients or regression coefficients.

entrepreneurship. This suggests that direct government interference with market price mechanisms discourages entrepreneurship, which is itself a market mechanism. Thirdly, government incentives might still encourage entrepreneurship if public subsidies are granted for competence and merit. Entrepreneurship is more evident if the government is more impartial when choosing subsidy recipients and contractors for public contracts (ref: the last two rows in the panel—'successful government subsidy targets' and 'openness in awarding public contracts'). Again, these effects remain after controlling for initial per capita GDP.

The last panel of Table 20.3 relates the volatilities of government macroeconomic policies to entry rates. Higher inflation rates, more variable inflation rates, and more variable government budgets are all negatively, but insignificantly, related to entry. At first glance, unstable macroeconomic policies do not seem to be of first order importance in retarding entrepreneurship.

Overall, the results in Table 20.3 suggest that an effective, uncorrupt, and transparent government that avoids direct interference with market mechanisms encourages entrepreneurship. But burdensome regulations on business, and rigid employment laws discourage entrepreneurs from forming new businesses. Government subsidies might encourage entrepreneurship if granted based on merit and competence. The volatility of government policies does not appear to have any significant effect on the rates of entry.

20.4.3.3 *Results on the concentration of corporate control*

The top panel of Table 20.4 relates the distribution of corporate control to entry rates. *Oligarchic family control*, the fraction of top ten conglomerates controlled by wealthy families, is negatively and significantly related to labour-weighted entry rates. The variable, however, becomes insignificant in regressions controlling for initial GDP per capita. A negative relationship also exists between the firm size Herfindahl index, measuring the relative importance of large firms, and entry. This relationship grows more significant after initial per capita GDP is included as a control. These results support the argument that large established businesses use their market power and/or political power to impede entrepreneurship.

20.4.3.4 *Result on culture and mass media*

The next panel in Table 20.4 relates new firm entry rates to variables reflecting national cultural differences. The results show that entrepreneurs thrive in countries with extensive mass media, as indicated by the highly significant relationship between newspaper circulation and both of entry rate measures, even after controlling for per capita GDP. This is consistent with social transparency, sharpened by an energetic press, creating a better social and economic environment for entrepreneurs. A vigorous free press also places significant constraints on

Table 20.4 Entry rate and other institutions

	A: simple correlation		B: regression of entry on institutions controlling for 1996 per capita GDP	
	E_V	E_E	E_V	E_E
Distribution of Corporate Control:				
Oligarchic family control	**−0.466**	−.0422	−.0206	.0182
	(.07)	(.88)	(.39)	(.65)
Firm size Herfindahl	−0.246	−0.226	**−0.117**	−0.142
	(.17)	(.21)	**(.05)**	(.12)
Culture and Mass Media:				
Hierarchical religion	**−0.491**	−0.173	**−.0188**	−.0113
	(.00)	(.34)	**(.01)**	(.31)
Newspaper per capita	**0.597**	**0.351**	**.0937**	.0760
	(.00)	**(.07)**	**(.00)**	(.14)
Education:				
Education attainment	**0.439**	0.145	.0266	.00249
	(.09)	(.59)	(.30)	(.95)
Market Diversity:				
Industry diversification	**0.464**	**0.325**	**9.93E-05**	1.07E-04
	(.01)	**(.07)**	**(.02)**	(.11)
Openness:				
Number of capital flow restrictions	**−0.371**	−0.208	−.00142	−.00142
	(.08)	(.34)	(.46)	(.65)
Gross FDI	0.233	.0505	.000308	−.000942
	(.21)	(.79)	(.80)	(.62)
Trade	−0.267	−.2416	−.0000955	−.000145
	(.13)	(.18)	(.23)	(.22)

Notes: (i) Panel A presents simple correlation coefficients between median entry rates, labour-weighted, E_V, and equally weighted, E_E, from 1997 to 2001 and political economy variables. Panel B presents regressions of the form: entry rates $= \beta0+\beta1^*$ political economy variables $+\beta2^* \ln(y) + \varepsilon$. Only coefficient estimates on political economy variables ($\beta1$) are shown.
(ii) Numbers in parentheses are probability levels for rejecting the null hypothesis of zero correlation coefficients or regression coefficients.

government misbehaviour, reducing corruption and other opportunistic behaviour. This is consistent with a better political environment for entrepreneurs. Finally, a dynamic mass media might also directly stimulate information processing and entrepreneurial discovery.

20.4.3.5 *Results on education, market diversity and openness*

Other factors, such as education, market diversity, and capital and trade openness, appear in the bottom panels of Table 20.4. Better educated adults are associated with more entrepreneurship. Market diversity, measured by the number of different three-digit SIC industries in a country's corporate sector, is positively and significantly associated with both entry rate measures. Tighter capital flow restrictions are associated with less entrepreneurial formation. This is consistent with binding capital market restrictions blocking entrepreneurs' access to capital. Interestingly, and contrary to our expectation, openness to neither foreign direct investment flows nor trade is significantly related to entrepreneurship.

20.4.3.6 *Summary*

The results in this section support the thesis that better institutions promote entrepreneurship.

- New firm entry rates are higher in countries where the rule of law and private property rights are respected, and where the government is honest and effective. Entry rates are depressed in countries that inherited the French Civil Codes and with inefficient judicial systems. Thus, institutional factors that preserve property rights and facilitate the development of transactional trust do seem critical for entrepreneurship.
- Entry rates are also higher where regulations are more business-friendly, less burdensome, and interfere less with market mechanisms. Entry is also higher in countries with fewer restrictions on foreign capital flow. Thus, features normally associated with good government appear to promote entrepreneurship.
- Entry rates are higher in countries with more industrially diversified economies. This supports the thesis of Jacobs (1985) that entrepreneurs often use ideas from one industry to rejuvenate another.
- Entry rates lower in countries whose corporate sectors are more dominated by a few large firms. This is consistent with entrenched insiders using their political influence to protect the status quo.
- Countries with more educated people, more egalitarian religions, and more dynamic mass media have higher entry rates of new firms. This is consistent with these cultural factors being conducive to the development of entrepreneurial capabilities and ambitions.

Intriguingly, some conventional wisdom is not borne out. We find no evidence that (i) government spending crowds out start-ups; (ii) volatile macroeconomic policies discourage entrepreneurship; or (iii) trade and foreign direct investment barriers affect entrepreneurship. Finally, government subsidies might promote entrepreneurship if based on merit.

We repeated our empirical analyses splitting our sample into developed and developing countries. The pattern of correlations is broadly preserved, though the significance levels are substantially reduced because of the smaller sample sizes—especially for the developing country sub-sample. We thus unfortunately cannot investigate how these institutional factors relate to entrepreneurship in countries at different stages of economic development.

20.5 Conclusions

Entrepreneurship is a composite act, consisting of information gathering and processing, the identification of arbitrage opportunities, risk-taking, managing upstarts and market entry, and soliciting financial backing, technological expertise, and other inputs. These activities are substantially inter-temporal in nature—time and money are invested now in hopes of returns in the distant future. Success depends on intangibles embodied in an entrepreneur—the information and capabilities he/she has and the effort he/she puts forth—which are difficult to observe. Upstarts are also vulnerable to entry deterrence by incumbents, to the rent-extraction or outright asset grabbing by established dominant corporations or government officials.

Entrepreneurship, therefore, fundamentally depends on property rights being well defined and transactional trust existing between entrepreneurs and their investors and skilled employees. The development of transactional trust critically depends on the institutional environment, especially on well-enforced laws and regulations that define and protect property rights and that constrain opportunistic behaviour. The enactment and enforcement of such laws is the charge of the government. Hence, entrepreneurship also required an honest, property rights respecting and effective government.

Entrepreneurship has other determinants that are also affected by institutional factors. Entry barriers deter entrepreneurship. An interventionist government imposing burdensome rules and market regulations can stifle incentives to be entrepreneurial. Entry barriers can be subtly imposed by dominant economic powers to lock-in the status quo. In an economy where the control of corporations is concentrated in the hands of a few rich families, entrepreneur supply suffers. These economically dominant elites may, and do, translate their economic power into political influence to protect the status quo in numerous ways. Concentrated control over the large corporate sector could be the result of poor institutional environments as well as the cause, for it is a solution to weak property rights and inefficient markets.

Entrepreneurship is related to the market environment and culture. In an industrially diverse economy with a highly-educated workforce, entrepreneurial discovery proceeds apace. A society with high volume of news flows is also conducive to entrepreneurship. Social transparency can induce meritocracy, which contributes to the development of entrepreneurial spirit. Likewise, a society with a culture that rewards self-made success rather than submission to hierarchical authority is more likely to breed entrepreneurs.

Based on 1997 to 2001 entry data from 34 European countries, we generate preliminary empirical evidence supportive of these ideas. However, this work, both from a theoretical and empirical perspective, is preliminary. Entrepreneurship is a basic process fueling economic growth. The subject matter deserves further serious research effort. Several issues deserve particular attention.

First, entrepreneurship plausibly takes different forms at different stages of a country's development. Entrepreneurship in an African village is probably not the same as entrepreneurship in Silicon Valley in the US. Their institutional requirements are more likely vastly different. Empirical verification of these differences awaits better data, especially comprehensive cross-country panel of entry rates. Understanding the interactive dynamic relationship between entrepreneurship and stages of development, and the associated evolution of institutions, remains a challenging and deep topic.

Secondly, the relationship between entrepreneurship and institutional development deserves serious research attention per se. While this chapter treats institutions as exogenous, this is almost certainly an oversimplification. Recent work, including Acemoglu et al. (2005), Morck et al. (2005), and Perotti and Volpin (2004) treats government officials as endogenous decision-makers, who alter the institutional environment based on political pressures and self-interest. Institutions, like social economic conditions, or the distribution of economic and political power, all come into play in such exercises; and all affect entrepreneurship and are affected by past entrepreneurial activity. For example, as entrepreneurs become more active, politicians may see greater benefits in improving property rights laws because the gains from this are now greater. More subtly, but perhaps also more importantly in the long run, ongoing successful entrepreneurship changes behavioural norms, social values, and culture, and more likely promotes future entrepreneurship. All these are challenging and interesting topics that beg serious cross-disciplinary research.

APPENDIX

Table 20.A1 Variable description

Variable	Data year	Description	Source
Entrepreneurship Rate:			
Median entry rate, labour-weighted	Median of 1997–2001	The number of entry in current year over the total number of firms in previous year.	Authors' own calculation based on Amadeus data
Median entry rate, equally-weighted	Median of 1997–2001	The total number of employees of entry firms in current year over the total number of employees of firms in previous year.	Authors' own calculation based on Amadeus data
Institutions for Transactional Trust:			
Respect for the rule of law	1996	Index ranges from -2.5 to 2.5, with higher value indicating more abidance by the rules of law.	Kaufmann, Kraay and Mastruzzi (2003)
Judiciary efficiency	Average of 1980–83	Index ranges from zero to ten, with higher value indicating more efficient judiciary system.	La Porta, et al. (1998)
Property rights protection	1996	Index ranges from one to five, with higher value indicating more protection of private property.	Freedom House
Absence of bribery	1996	Index ranges from zero to ten, with higher value indicating less. incidences of bribery.	World Competitiveness Report, 1997
French legal origin	Historical	Dummy set to one for French Civil Code legal systems, and zero otherwise.	La Porta, et al. (1998)
Government Quality:			
Government accountability	1996	Index ranges from −2.5 to 2.5, with higher value indicating more civil liberty and political rights.	Kaufmann, Kraay and Mastruzzi (2003)
Government effectiveness	1996	Index ranges from −2.5 to 2.5, with higher value indicating more effective, competent, and independent civil service.	Kaufmann, Kraay and Mastruzzi (2003)
Control of corruption	1996	Index ranges from −2.5 to 2.5, with higher value indicating less corruption.	Kaufmann, Kraay and Mastruzzi (2003)

(*contd.*)

Table 20.A1 Variable description (*contd.*)

Variable	Data year	Description	Source
Regulatory Stances:			
Regulatory quality	1996	Index ranges from -2.5 to 2.5, with higher value indicating fewer incidences of market unfriendly regulations and excessive regulatory burdens.	Kaufmann, Kraay and Mastruzzi (2003)
Absence of bureaucracy hindrance to business	1996	Index ranges from one to seven, with higher value indicating less bureaucratic barrier to business.	World Competitiveness Report 1997
Rigid Employment Laws	2003	Index ranges from zero to one hundred, with higher value indicating more rigid labor regulation.	World Bank Doing Business
Government Activism:			
Size of government	Average of 1991–96	Government share of real GDP per capita in 1996 constant prices.	Penn World Tables 6.1.
Government ownership of banks	1995	Percentage of top ten banks owned by government.	La Porta, et al. (2000)
Absence of price controls	1995	Index ranges form zero to ten, with higher value indicating more freedom for businesses to set their own prices.	Fraser Institute
Successful subsidy targets	1997	Index ranges from one to seven, with higher value indicating government subsidies are likely to direct towards future winners.	World Competitiveness Report 1998
Openness in awarding public contracts	1997	Index ranges from one to seven, with higher value indicating public sector contracts are more open to foreign bidders.	World Competitiveness Report 1998
Volatility of Government Policies:			
Average inflation	1994–97	Average rate of inflation based on GDP deflator.	Authors' own calculation based on World Development Indicators
Volatility of inflation	1994–97	Variance of inflation based on GDP deflator.	Authors' own calculation based on World Development Indicators

(*contd.*)

Table 20.A1 Variable description (*contd.*)

Variable	Data year	Description	Source
Volatility of government spending	1991–96	Variance of government share of real per capita GDP.	Authors' own calculation based on Penn World Tables 6.1
Distribution of Corporate Control:			
Oligarchic family control	1996	The proportion of largest ten corporate groups controlled by very wealthy business families, weighted by group employees.	Fogel (2006)
Firm size Herfindahl	Median of 1991–96	Country level employee-based Herfindahl index of all firms included in the Amadeus database.	Authors' own calculation based on Amadeus data
Culture and Mass Media:			
Hierarchical religion	Current	Dummy variable that sets to one for hierarchical religions such as Roman Catholic, Muslim, East Orthodox, and to zero for all other religions.	CIA World Fact Book Online
Newspaper per capita	1997	Total average circulation (or copies printed) of daily newspaper per inhabitant.	UNESCO Statistics http://stats.uis.unesco.org
Education:			
Education attainment	1990	Log of the average years of education for people aged 25 or over.	Barro and Lee (2000)
Market Diversity:			
Industry diversification	Median of 1991–96	Total number of primary 3-digit SIC codes in each country.	Authors' own calculation from Amadeus dataset
Openness:			
Trade	1996	Trade (import plus export) as a percentage of GDP.	World Development Indicators
Capital restrictions	1997	Index ranges from 0 to 12 to measure how many capital control restrictions a country has, out of twelve types of restrictions.	Global Competitiveness Report 1998
Gross FDI flows	1996	Gross foreign direct investment flows as a percentage of GDP.	World Development Indicators

References

Acemoglu, D., S. Johnson, J. Robinson and Y. Thaicharoen (2003). 'Institutional Causes, Macroeconomic Symptoms: Volatility, Crises, and Growth', *Journal of Monetary Economics* (January): 50 49–123.

—— —— and —— (2005). 'Institutions as the Fundamental Cause of Long-run Growth', NBER WP 10481, in the *Handbook of Economic Growth.* North Holland: Elsevier.

Almeida, H. and D. Wolfenzon (2005a). 'A Theory of Pyramidal Ownership and Family Business Groups', Stern NYU Working paper. *Journal of Finance.*

—— and —— (2005b). 'Should Business Groups Be Dismantled? The Equilibrium Costs of Inefficient Internal Capital Markets'. *Journal of Financial Economics*, 79: 99–144.

Angeletos, G-M. and L-E. Calvet (2006). 'Idiosyncratic Production Risk, Growth and the Business Cycle.' NBER WP. 9764. *Journal of Monetary Economics* (Forthcoming).

Arora, A., A. Gambardella, S. Klepper (2004). 'Organizational Capabilities and the Rise of the Software Industry in the Emerging Economies: Lessons from the History of Some US Industries', Mimeo. Carnegie Mellon University.

Barro, R. and J-W. Lee (2000). 'International Data on Educational Attainment: Updates and Implications'. Manuscript, Harvard University.

Barth, J., R., G. Caprio, Jr. and R. Levine (2004). 'Bank Regulation and Supervision: What Works Best?' *Journal of Financial Intermediation*, 13: 205–48.

Bebchuk, L., R. Kraakman and G. Triantis (2002). 'Stock Pyramids, Cross-ownership, and Dual Class Equity: The Mechanisms and Agency Costs of Separating Control from Cash-flow Rights', in *Concentrated Corporate Ownership.* Randall Morck (ed.) National Bureau of Economic Research Conference Volume. University of Chicago Press. [Also Circulated as National Bureau of Economic Research Working Paper 6951].

Beck, T., A. Demirgüç-Kunt and R. Levine (2005). 'Bank Supervision and Corruption in Lending'. Mimeo. University of Minnesota.

—— and R. Levine (2005). 'Legal Institutions and Financial Development', in C. Menard and M. M. Shirley (eds) *Handbook for New Institutional Economics.* Norwell, MA: Kluwer Academic Publishers.

Burkart, M., F. Panunzi and A. Shleifer (2003). 'Family Firms'. *Journal of Finance*, 58: 5: 2167–201.

Cantillon, R. (1755). *Essai sur la nature du commerce en generale* (ed. Henry Higgs). London: Macmillan, 1931.

Caprio, G., L. Laeven and R. Levine (2003). 'Governance and Bank Valuation'. NBER wp. 10158 (August).

Casson, M. (1993). 'Entrepreneurship', in D. R. Henderson (ed.) *The Fortune Encyclopaedia of Economics* New York: Warner Books.

—— (1999). 'The Economics of the Family Firm'. *Scandinavian Economic History Review*, 47(1): 10–23.

Caves, R. E. (1996). *Multinational Enterprise and Economic Analysis*, 2nd edn. Cambridge: Cambridge University Press.

Coase, R. (1937). 'The Nature of the Firm'. *Economica* (November) 4(16): 386–405.

De Soto, H. (1990). *The Other Path.* New York, NY: Harper and Row.

—— (2000). *The Mystery of Capital: Why Capitalism Triumphs in the West and Fails Everywhere Else.* New York: Basic books.

Di Gregorio, D. and S. Shane (2003). 'Why do Some Universities Generate More Start-ups Than Others?' *Research Policy*, 32(2): 209–27.

Djankov, S. R. La Porta, F. López-de-Silanes and A. Shleifer (2002). 'The Regulation of Entry'. *Quarterly Journal of Economics* (February) 67(1): 1–37.

Desai, M. P. Gompers and J. Lerner (2003). 'Institutions, Capital Constraints and Entrepreneurial Firm Dynamics: Evidence from Europe'. NBER Working Paper No. 10165.

Durnev, A. K. Li, R. Morck and B. Yeung (2004). 'Capital Markets and Capital Allocation: Implications for Economies in Transition'. *Economics of Transition*, 12(4): 593–634.

Dyck, A. and L. Zingales (2003). 'Private Benefits of Control: An International Comparison'. *Journal of Finance* (April) 59(2): 537–600.

Evans, D. S. and B. Jovanovic (1989). 'An Estimated Model of Entrepreneurial Choice under Liquidity Constraints'. *Journal of Political Economy* (August) 97(4): 808–27.

—— and L. S. Leighton (1989). 'Some Empirical Aspects of Entrepreneurship'. *American Economic Review*, 79: 519–35.

Fogel, K. (2006). 'Oligarchic Family Control and the Quality of Government'. *Journal of International Business Studies* (forthcoming).

—— R. Morck and B. Yeung (2005). 'Corporate Stability and Economic Growth: 'Is What's Good for General Motors Good for America?' Paper presented at American Finance Association 2005 meetings.

Frye, T. and A. Shleifer (1997). 'The Invisible Hand and the Grabbing Hand'. *American Economic Review*, 87(2): 354–8.

Gentry, W. and G. Hubbard (2004). 'Entrepreneurship and Household Saving'. *Advances in Economic Analysis & Policy*. Berkeley Electronic Press, 4(1): art. 8. (Previous version: National Bureau of Economic Research, Working Paper No. 7894, September, 2002.)

Glaeser, E., H. Kallal, J. Scheinkman, and A. Schleifer (1992). 'Growth in Cities'. *Journal of Political Economy* (December) 100(6): 1126–52.

Gompers, P. and J. Lerner (1999). *The Venture Capital Cycle*. MIT Press.

—— and —— (2000). 'The Determinants of Corporate Venture Capital Success: Organizational Structure, Incentives, and Complementarities', in R. Morck (ed.) *Concentrated Corporate Control*. Chicago: University of Chicago Press.

—— and —— (2001). 'The Venture Capital Revolution'. *Journal of Economics Perspectives* (Spring) 15(2): 145–168.

Hayek, F. A. von (1937). 'Economics and Knowledge'. *Economica* (February) 4: 33–54.

—— (1945). 'The Use of Knowledge in Society'. *American Economic Review* (September) 35(4): 519–30.

—— (1948). *Individualism and Economic Order*. London: Routledge and Kegan Paul.

Högfeldt, P. (2005). 'The History and Politics of Corporate Ownership in Sweden', in R. Morck (ed.) *The History of Corporate Governance around the World: Family Business Groups to Professional Managers*. Chicago: University of Chicago Press.

Holtz-Eakin, D., D. Joulfaian and H. S. Rosen (1994a). 'Sticking It Out: Entrepreneurial Survival and Liquidity Constraints'. *Journal of Political Economy*, 102: 53–75.

Holtz-Eakin, D., D. Joulfaian and H. S. Rosen (1994b). 'Entrepreneurial Decisions and Liquidity Constraints'. *Rand Journal of Economics*, 25: 334–47.

Jacobs, J. (1985). *Cities and the Wealth of Nations: Principles of Economic Life*. New York: Vintage Books, Random House.

Jensen, M. and W. Meckling (1976). 'The Theory of Firm: Mangerial behavior, agency costs and ownership structure'. *Journal of Financial Economics*, 3: 305–60.

JOHNSON, S., J. MCMILLAN and C. WOODRUFF (2000). 'Entrepreneurs and the Ordering of Institutional Reform: Poland, Slovakia, Romania, Russia and Ukraine Compared'. *Economics of Transition*, 8(1): 1–36.

—— —— and —— (2002a). 'Courts and Relational Contracts'. *Journal of Law, Economics, and Organization*, 18(1): 221–77.

—— —— and —— (2002b). 'Property Rights and Finance'. *American Economic Review*, 92: 1335–56.

KAUFMANN, D., A. KRAAY and M. MASTRUZZI (2003). 'Governance Matters III: Governance Indicators for 1996–2002'. World Bank Working Paper.

KHANNA, T. and K. PALEPU (2000). 'Is Group Affiliation Profitable in Emerging Markets? An analysis of Diversified Indian Business Groups'. *Journal of Finance* (April) 55(2): 867–93.

—— and —— (2005). 'The Evolution of Concentrated Ownership in India: Broad Patterns and a History of the Indian Software Industry', in R. Morck (ed.) *History of Corporate Governance around the world: Family Business Groups to Professional Managers.* Chicago: University of Chicago Press.

KING, R., G and R. LEVINE (1993a). 'Finance, Entrepreneurship, and Growth: Theory and Evidence', *Journal of Monetary Economics* (December) 32(3): 513–42.

—— and —— (1993b). 'Finance and Growth: Schumpeter Might Be Right'. *Quarterly Journal of Economics* (August) 153: 717–38.

KIRZNER, I. M. (1973). *Competition and Entrepreneurship.* Chicago: University of Chicago Press.

—— (1997). 'Entrepreneurial Discovery and the Competitive Market Process: an Austrian Approach'. *Journal of Economics Literature* (March) 35(1): 60–85.

KRUEGER, A. O. (1993). 'Virtuous and Vicious Circles in Economic Development', *American Economic Review* (May) 83(2): 351–5.

LA PORTA, R., F. LÓPEZ-DE-SILANES, A. SHLEIFER and R. VISHNY. (1997a). 'Legal Determinants of External Finance'. *Journal of Finance*, 52(3):1 1131–50.

—— —— —— and —— (1997b). 'Trust in Large Organizations'. *American Economic Review Papers and Proceedings*, (May) 97(2): 333–9.

—— —— —— and—— (1998). 'Law and Finance'. *Journal of Political Economy*, 106 1113–55.

—— —— —— and—— (1999). 'Corporate Ownership around the World'. *Journal of Finance*, 54(2): 471–517.

—— —— —— and —— (2000). 'Government Ownership of Banks'. National Bureau of Economic Research Working Paper 7620.

—— —— and GUILLERMO ZAMARRIPA (2003). 'Related Lending'. *Quarterly Journal of Economics*, 118(1): 231–68.

LANDES, DAVID. (1949). 'French Entrepreneurship and Industrial Growth in the Nineteenth Century'. *Journal of Economic History*, 9: 45–61.

LEVINE, R. (2005). 'Finance and Growth: Theory and Evidence', in P. Aghion and S. Durlanf (eds) *Handbook of Economic* Growth. The Netherlands: Elsevier Science.

MCMILLAN, J. and C. WOODRUFF (1999). 'Interfirm Relationships and Informal Credit in Vietnam'. *Quarterly Journal of Economics* (November) 114(4): 1285–320..

—— and —— (2002). 'The Central Role of Entrepreneurs in Transition Economies'. *Journal of Economic Perspectives* (Summer) 16(3): 153–70.

Morck, R., D. Stangeland and B. Yeung (2000). 'Inherited Wealth, Corporate Control, and Economic Growth', in. Randall Morck (ed.) *Concentrated Corporate Ownership* University of Chicago Press, pp. 319–69. (NBER Working Paper, #6814 1998.)

—— D. Wolfenzon and B. Yeung (2005). 'Corporate Governance, Economic Entrenchment and Growth'. *Journal of Economics Literature* (September) 43: 657–722.

—— B. Yeung and W. Yu (2000). 'The Information Content of Stock Markets: Why Do Emerging Markets Have Synchronous Stock Price Movements?' *Journal of Financial Economics* (October) 59(1 and 2): 215–60..

Moskowitz, T. and A. Vissing-Jorgensen (2002). 'The Returns to Entrepreneurial Investment: A Private Equity Premium Puzzle?' *American Economic Review*, 92: 745–78.

North, D. C. (1990). *Institutions, Institutional Change, and Economic Performance.* New York: Cambridge University Press.

Perotti, E. and P. Volpin (2004). 'Lobbying on Entry'. Paper presented at the World Bank-Stern 'Entry Workshop' January 2005.

Puri, M. and D. T. Robinson (2004). 'Optimism, Work/Life Choices, and Entrepreneurship'. Paper presented at the Worldbank-Stern-NYU Entrepreneurship Workshop, World Bank, 10 January 2005.

Rajan, R. and L. Zingales. (2004). *Saving Capitalism from the Capitalists: Unleashing the Power of Financial Markets to Create Wealth and Spread Opportunity.* Princeton: Princeton University Press.

Schumpeter, J. (1912: 1934). *Theorie der Wirtschaftlichen Entwichlung.* Leipzig: Dunker and Humbolt. (trans. Redvers Opie 1934). *The Theory of Economic Development.* Cambridge, MA: Harvard University Press.

—— (1942). *Capitalism, Socialism and Democracy*, 3rd edn. New York: Harper & Bros.

Stigler, G. (1986). *The Organization of Industry.* Chicago: University of Chicago Press.

Stulz, R. and R. Williamson. (2003). 'Culture, Openness and Finance'. *Journal of Finance*, 70(3): 313–49.

Wurgler J. (2000). 'Financial markets and the allocation of capital'. *Journal of Financial Economics*, 58: 187–214.

CHAPTER 21

ETHNIC MINORITY ENTREPRENEURSHIP

ANURADHA BASU

21.1 Introduction

Ethnic entrepreneurship has attracted the attention of an increasing number of scholars from a range of different disciplines in recent years. This is attributable to three main factors. First, there is growing evidence that ethnic minorities tend to have high self-employment rates and own a significant proportion of businesses in most western industrialized countries. In the UK, average self-employment rates among ethnic minority groups are at least 2 percent higher than the 11 percent rate among the White population (UK Office of National Statistics (ONS), 2004). In the US, minorities owned just over 3 million businesses or nearly 15 percent of all US firms in 1997, compared with 7 percent in 1982. Of the 3 million ethnic minority-owned businesses, 615,222 had paid employees and, on aggregate, generated more than US$591 billion in revenues, created over 4.5 million jobs, and provided about US$96 billion in payroll to their workers (U.S. Department of Commerce, 2001). The significant economic contribution made by minority-owned businesses has led western policy-makers to regard self-employment as a promising route for ethnic minorities to create employment, achieve economic and social advancement, and also be accepted by the majority community.

At the same time, there is growing concern about the heterogeneity in the economic performance of ethnic groups, and the need for policy to address the differential rates of self-employment and economic success among different groups, since ethnic entrepreneurship is a viable response from ethnic minorities to economic restructuring. In the UK, for instance, the self-employment rate among the

Chinese and Pakistanis is around 20 percent, compared with 12–13 percent among Bangladeshis and Indians, and 6–7 percent among the Black African and Caribbean population (ONS, UK, 2004). In Germany, ethnic minorities generally display low self-employment rates, the only exception being the Turkish population which shows a high propensity toward self-employment (Constant et al., 2003). Asians own a disproportionate share of all US companies. While they comprise 4 percent of the US population, they own 4.4 percent of all US companies (US Census Bureau 2001). In contrast, Blacks and Hispanics account for 12 percent and 13 percent of the population but own 4 percent and 5.8 percent, respectively, of all businesses. Moreover, Asian businesses are larger, with average annual revenues of $336,200 compared with $155,200 for Hispanic companies and $86,500 for Black-owned companies. Asians, including Chinese, Indians and Pacific Islanders, have started nearly 600,000 businesses in the US during the wave of immigration in the last two decades. There are 10,561 Asian-owned companies in the US for every 100,000 adults, which is nearly twice the rate for Hispanics, and more than thrice the rate for Blacks.

Thirdly, it is possible to argue that with the increasing globalization of the world economy, entrepreneurial ethnic groups are likely to assume greater significance in the years ahead, as they become more mobile, build global networks that are strengthened by faster and cheaper communications technology, and conduct global business and trade among themselves.

Despite these trends that highlight the growing significance of ethnic minority entrepreneurs, the exact concept of ethnic entrepreneurship and the factors that stimulate it and influence its survival and success remain controversial. This may be due, in part, to the fact that empirical studies have focused on the experience of specific groups, rather than a comparison among different minority groups.

This chapter reviews the existing theoretical and empirical literature on ethnic entrepreneurship. It primarily focuses on the empirical research conducted in Britain and the United States. It examines the definition of ethnic entrepreneurship and evaluates the forces affecting the entry into ethnic entrepreneurship, entrepreneurial survival and success, as well as the factors underlying the heterogeneity in entrepreneurial behaviour and performance among ethnic minority groups.

21.2 Definitions of Ethnic Entrepreneurship

Given its very nature, ethnic entrepreneurship has been studied from several different perspectives. These include cultural anthropology, sociology, geography, politics, and strategic management, as well as economics. Nevertheless, the exact definition of 'ethnic entrepreneurship' remains open to interpretation by scholars since there is no universal agreement on the concepts of 'ethnic' or 'entrepreneurship'.

The concept of ethnicity has been explored in the sociological literature and refers to a sense of kinship, group solidarity, common culture, and self-identification with an ethnic group (Hutchinson and Smith, 1996). An ethnic group has been defined as 'a collectivity within a larger society having real or putative common ancestry, memories of a shared historical past, and a cultural focus on one or more symbolic elements defined as the epitome of their peoplehood. Examples of such symbolic elements are: kinship patterns, physical contiguity, regional affiliation, language ... nationality ... or any combination of these' (Schermerhorn 1978: 12). In the context of ethnic entrepreneurship, 'ethnic' refers to 'a set of connections and regular patterns of interaction among people sharing common national background or migration experiences' (Waldinger et al., 1990: 33).

The notions of ethnic entrepreneurship, minority entrepreneurship, and immigrant entrepreneurship, are frequently used interchangeably in the literature. However, Chaganti and Greene (2002) point out that there are subtle differences between ethnic entrepreneurs, using the concept of 'ethnic' as defined above, and immigrant or minority entrepreneurs. Immigrants are recent arrivals in a country, who often enter business as a means of economic survival. They may or may not be part of a network linking migrants, former migrants, and non-migrants with a common origin and destination (see Chaganti and Greene, 2002). Minority entrepreneurs are business owners who do not belong to the majority population. The US government identifies the following as minorities: Black, Hispanic, Asian, Pacific Islander, American Indian, or Alaska Native descent. Women are also occasionally included as a minority group. Thus, a minority entrepreneur may not be an immigrant and may not share a strong sense of group solidarity with an ethnic group, in terms of a shared history, religion, or language. An immigrant entrepreneur of Caucasian descent would not be considered an ethnic minority entrepreneur in the western world. Likewise, an ethnic entrepreneur may or may not be an immigrant, but is likely to belong to a minority community. As indicated by its title, this chapter focuses on ethnic minority entrepreneurs, that is, entrepreneurs who belong to a minority ethnic community.

In the ethnic entrepreneurship literature, 'entrepreneurship' tends to be equated with self-employment. Many researchers define ethnic entrepreneurship as the ownership of a business, small or medium-sized, by an individual belonging to a specific socio-cultural or ethnic background (see, e.g. Masurel et al., 2002). In most cases, the businesses owned are very small and unpromising in terms of their employment or growth prospects. The extant literature on ethnic entrepreneurship generally neglects to draw a distinction between the self-employed who have employees, and the self-employed without employees, or between the ownership of small businesses versus entrepreneurial ventures that are scalable and likely to achieve high growth. This may be one of the reasons why there is disagreement among scholars and empirical studies regarding the motives for, and nature of, ethnic entrepreneurship—as will be discussed in the next section. Moreover, while entrepreneurship is generally regarded as an individual endeavour by economic theory, it is usually a family endeavour in the context of ethnic minorities as observed by empirical studies (Baines and Wheelock, 1998; Basu and Altinay, 2003).

21.3 Factors influencing business entry

One of the main issues addressed in the context of ethnic entrepreneurship is the role of macro conditions and micro motives in stimulating business entry. Economic explanations of ethnic minority business entry usually focus on the impact of prevailing labour market conditions. Theories of ethnic entrepreneurship focus on how the ethnicity or outsider (immigrant or minority) status of an individual has an effect on his or her decision to enter business. It is possible to distinguish between four main sets of explanations for business entry by an individual belonging to an ethnic minority group. These are economic disadvantage, cultural preferences, contextual factors, and opportunity recognition.

21.3.1 Economic disadvantage: 'Push' factors

One set of explanations emphasizes the role of economic disadvantage, stemming from racial discrimination in the labour market, in pushing ethnic minorities into self-employment. According to this view, if racial prejudice reduces the rewards of paid employment, minorities are more likely to search for alternatives to it, as emphasized by models of self-employment (de Wit, 1993; Clark and Drinkwater, 1998). The argument advanced in the context of the UK is that the contracting jobs market of the 1970s exacerbated problems among ethnic minorities and immigrants, who were forced to opt for self-employment as a 'damage limitation' exercise, to avoid unemployment (Jones et al., 1994). Empirical research on the factors affecting self-employment in Britain between 1973 and 1995 supports the view that 'discrimination contributes to ethnic minority self-employment in Britain' (Clark and Drinkwater, 1998: 402). Many members of ethnic minority groups are economically disadvantaged when compared with their counterparts from the majority community and have been compelled to create their own jobs, especially, during economic downturns.

This explanation of necessity-driven ethnic entrepreneurship suffers from several limitations and cannot fully explain the ethnic minority business entry decision. First, as Clark and Drinkwater (1998) acknowledge, not all ethnic minorities who face discrimination opt for self-employment, which suggests that there may be additional factors that attract certain groups more than others, toward self-employment. Secondly, the economic disadvantage explanation implicitly implies that starting up one's own business is an 'easy' option or an easier option than finding a job, which is a naïve generalization. While the ability to find employment is likely to be related to educational qualifications, skills, and fluency in the host country language as well as macroeconomic conditions, and conditions in the specific industry, the ability to enter self-employment requires some sort of expertise or knowledge, access to finance, favourable contextual factors including low barriers to entry, as well as the drive to execute.

To say that all ethnic minority entrepreneurs started their own businesses because they were economically disadvantaged, is too simplistic an explanation. It does not distinguish between those who were unable to find a job, perhaps because they were educationally disadvantaged, and those who secured jobs, but spotted an opportunity or felt that they had reached a glass ceiling beyond which they could not progress as employees. For instance, several Indian entrepreneurs who established high-tech businesses in Silicon Valley, California, in the late 1970s and early 1980s, said in interviews with the author that it was very difficult for Indians to progress beyond technical management positions in those days. The widely-held belief among American employers at the time was that Indian engineers made excellent technical managers but did not have the ability or skills to be general managers or CEOs. On the other hand, many of those who started new ventures in Silicon Valley in the 1990s did so not because they lacked employment opportunities but because they hit upon a new business idea or were influenced by the role models of successful Indian entrepreneurs that they saw in their midst.

Thus, economic disadvantage may play a role in pushing ethnic minorities into entrepreneurship, but higher ambition or advancement may also be a motive for taking the leap into entrepreneurship.

21.3.2 Cultural predisposition: Pull factors

A second set of explanations may be labelled under the head of cultural theories. This holds that ethnic minorities choose entrepreneurship because of a cultural predilection toward self-employment in favour of working for someone else. Here, culture refers to the shared beliefs, values, and norms of the ethnic minority group. Early proponents of the link between entrepreneurship and culture in the form of religious beliefs include Sombart (1951), who emphasized the role of Jewish rationalism in stimulating Jewish entrepreneurialism, and Weber (1976) who asserted that the Protestant work ethic, with its emphasis on individualism, achievement, rational conduct, asceticism, and self-reliance, rewarded capital accumulation and self-employment and, hence, encouraged entrepreneurship. In a similar vein, it can be argued that ethnic groups like the Gujarati Lohanas, Ismailis, and Marwaris, have a tradition of business and trading, and value entrepreneurship far more than paid employment (Dobbin, 1996). The cultural norms of these communities encourage hard work, self-sufficiency, thrift, and helping each other by way of informal credit institutions, and predispose members towards entrepreneurship.

While cultural factors may explain the propensity toward entrepreneurship among certain minority groups like the East African Gujaratis and Ismailis in the UK, these are unsatisfactory as a general explanation of entrepreneurial entry among all ethnic minority groups. This is because the ethnic communities that are regarded as entrepreneurial in one country do not always have a tradition of entrepreneurship in other countries, or in their home countries. For instance, Pakistanis in the UK display high self-employment rates and are regarded as entrepreneurial (Werbner, 1990); however, they are not as well known for their entrepreneurial propensity in other countries. Similarly, Cubans and Koreans have an impressive record of entrepreneurship in the US but do not have a history of entrepreneurship elsewhere in the world (Light and Rosenstein, 1995). Likewise, the highly-educated, technically trained Indians in Silicon Valley in the US display much higher levels of entrepreneurship than reflected by the history of entrepreneurial activity among technically qualified Indians in India and in other countries. This suggests the importance of contextual factors in influencing entrepreneurial propensities among different groups. The fact that minorities tend to display higher self-employment rates than non-minority or majority groups, implies the need to look beyond cultural theories to historical and other contextual factors for an understanding of the factors stimulating ethnic minority entrepreneurship.

21.3.3 Contextual factors

A third set of explanations highlights the influence of historical factors, geographical clusters, market conditions, and institutional structures in shaping ethnic minorities' decision to enter entrepreneurship. Historical factors, such as the trading background of minority communities like the Kutchhi Lohana, Ismailis, Jews, Marwaris, and Sindhis, can explain why these groups continue to display high rates of entrepreneurship, which is a family tradition (Tripathi, 1984).

The residential clustering of members of the same ethnic community in a neighbourhood, known as an 'ethnic enclave', can create entrepreneurial opportunities, as captured by the so-called theory of ethnic enclaves. Ethnic enclaves create niche market opportunities for serving the local ethnic population. They offer a 'protected market' and 'captive prices' for ethnic goods and services (Aldrich and Waldinger, 1990). Thus, ethnic enclaves make it easier to start some types of businesses such as those that cater to the specific needs and tastes of the local ethnic population, or those that require critical support in the form of finance or labour from within the ethnic enclave. The role of these resources is discussed in greater depth in the next section.

Waldinger et al. (1990) argue that opportunities may also arise outside the ethnic enclave, in the mainstream market, usually in markets that have low barriers to entry or that are 'under-served or abandoned' by non-ethnic entrepreneurs because they regard them as unattractive. For instance, ethnic minorities own taxi services in several large cities, like New York and London, which can be explained by the low entry barriers to running a taxi business. Similarly, most of the small groceries or 'corner shops' in Britain were started by ethnic minorities who were prepared to work the long hours entailed by the business for relatively low returns.

Recent research on ethnic minority entrepreneurship in the Netherlands tries to synthesize previously advanced notions of ethnic disadvantage, ethnic resources and opportunities, class resources and ethnic enclaves. It suggests that ethnic minority entrepreneurship depends on the 'mixed embeddedness' or interaction between socio-economic and ethno-social characteristics of the immigrant group (Kloosterman et al., 1999; Kloosterman and Rath, 2001). It argues that limited socio-economic resources push immigrants towards entrepreneurship at the lower end of the opportunity structure in traditional sectors (retailing, wholesale and restaurants) where informal production could give them a competitive advantage over their competitors. At the same time, immigrant entrepreneurs tend to set up businesses within their co-ethnic neighbourhoods, so as to access their family or co-ethnic networks for information, capital and labour.

The opportunities described, whether arising from within the ethnic enclave, or outside it in markets with low entry barriers, implicitly assume that ethnic minority entrepreneurs possess very limited technical skills and few ideas to start a business other than one that satisfies existing demand in the ethnic (or mainstream) market in the low technology sector. This appears to underestimate the creative talents and technical competency of many ethnic minority entrepreneurs.

Furthermore, the concept of ethnic enclaves does not capture a situation in which members of the same ethnic community are dispersed across a city or region, but remain connected with each other via social networks. The influence of geographically wider ethnic social networks, which extend beyond ethnic enclaves, on entrepreneurial entry by members of the same minority group has been discussed by Saxenian (2000) but has yet to be systematically analyzed in the literature.

Empirical research suggests that entrepreneurs invariably use their social networks to search for ideas and gather information regarding new venture opportunities (Singh et al., 1999). For minority entrepreneurs, exploratory research undertaken by the author suggests that ethnically defined social networks can be a powerful source of support, providing access to information, mentoring, and start-up finance, for entrepreneurial entry. Research by Carter et al. (2002), comparing the reasons for entrepreneurship among minority and non-minority nascent entrepreneurs in the US shows that while the motives of the two groups are fairly similar, family roles and tradition as well as recognition within the community matter more to minorities than to non-minorities regardless of whether or not they are nascent entrepreneurs.

The characteristics of formal institutions, which include government policies and regulations both in respect of immigration and in granting permission to ethnic minorities and immigrants to start, own, and raise funds for new ventures have an impact on business entry decisions and the nature of the businesses started. For instance, Saxenian (2000) discusses the impact of changes in the US immigration system between 1965 and 1990, which increasingly favoured the immigration of engineers and other skilled individuals, on the ethnicity of the Silicon Valley technology labour force. A large number of the immigrant engineers in the Valley were of Chinese and Indian origin and eventually started their own hi-technology businesses, many of which grew to become highly successful companies.

The characteristics and structure of the local environment that more broadly affect all entrepreneurs are also likely to affect entrepreneurial decisions made by ethnic minorities. It has been argued, for instance, that a region predominated by small companies is more likely to foster ethnic (as well as non-ethnic) start-ups than a region where large companies predominate (Rekers and van Kempen, 2000). These broader institutional characteristics may help to explain, at least in part, why many more ethnic minority hi-tech businesses have been started in Silicon Valley than in other parts of the United States. The other factor contributing to this trend is the large population of Chinese and Indian engineers in the Valley, as noted by Saxenian (2000).

21.3.4 Opportunity recognition

A form of market opportunity, not considered by Waldinger et al. (1990) and neglected by most of the ethnic entrepreneurship literature, is that arising from ethnic minorities' involvement in dual cultures and countries. It can be argued that involvement in dual or multiple cultures produces a duality of personality and culture, of nearness and distance, in an individual (Dobbin, 1996). Such an individual may be more creative in business and, hence, closer in character to a

Schumpetarian entrepreneur. Such an individual is also likely to be more alert and sensitive to his or her environment and hence, possess Kirzner's attribute of economic alertness, or 'the ability to notice—without search—opportunities that have hitherto been overlooked' (Kirzner, 1979: 48). Theories of entrepreneurship have recognized the role of informational asymmetries (Kirzner, 1979) and prior knowledge and experience (Shane, 2000; Shane and Venkatraman, 2000) in discovering new entrepreneurial opportunities. Prior knowledge and experience of different countries and cultures are likely to have a significant impact on the business entry decision of ethnic minority immigrant entrepreneurs, especially those who have maintained their ties with their home countries.

It is also necessary to draw a distinction between the traditional ethnic entrepreneur—who tends to be less educated and inward looking—and the more modern, better-educated ethnic entrepreneur, who often possesses skills that are highly prized and scarce in the host country. The latter entrepreneur is more likely to spot opportunities overlooked by her or his native counterparts.

21.3.5 Business survival and success

There is no single indicator of entrepreneurial success, but in the case of ethnic minority businesses it is generally associated with economic survival, that is, making a profit and generating sales that allow the business to become sustainable. While a large proportion of ethnic entrepreneurs operate on the economic fringes of society, a small proportion have succeeded in building viable businesses that have expanded over time. It is possible to distinguish between two main views among academic scholars regarding the factors influencing ethnic entrepreneurial success. One holds that entrepreneurial survival or success achieved by ethnic minorities is attributable to their unique access to, or exploitation of, ethnic resources and opportunities, which cannot be accessed by non-members. A second set of explanations attributes ethnic entrepreneurial success to economic resources that are not exclusively accessible by ethnic minority entrepreneurs. It also holds that in order to become successful, ethnic entrepreneurs need to adopt strategies that look beyond leveraging their own local co-ethnic community. These explanations, which need not be mutually exclusive, are discussed in the two sections that follow.

21.3.6 Role of ethnic resources

Ethnic resources refer to the resources available to the entrepreneur by virtue of belonging to an ethnic minority group. These resources enable the ethnic minority entrepreneur to compete and survive in the host country. Ethnic resources include access to relatively inexpensive, reliable, trustworthy labour; access to finance from within the ethnic community—the trading experience of many migrant communities—and cultural features such as strong family structures (Mars and Ward, 1984; Waldinger et al., 1990). More broadly, ethnic resources include intangible resources such as access to information and advice from other community members.

It has been argued that ethnic community members are willing to extend labour or financial support as a goodwill gesture and in the interests of reciprocity, with the thought that they might be able to 'call in the favour' at a later date (Basu and Parker, 2001). They may also be willing to offer advice and share information, experience and contacts with each other because of a sense of solidarity and trust among them.

The concept of ethnic resources is closely related to the elements of social capital identified by Portes (1995) as being relevant to ethnic entrepreneurs. These include shared cultural values that induce people to behave in ways other than those motivated by sheer greed, reciprocity transactions based on previous good deeds, bounded solidarity emerging from a situation in which a class of people face common adversities and, finally, enforceable trust flowing from group membership. Conventional wisdom suggests that closer or stronger relationships would generate higher levels of social capital and facilitate business growth. By mutually supporting each other, ethnic entrepreneurs lower transaction costs among community members and increase their own chances of survival and success.

However, the existence of ethnic social networks does not necessarily mean that these networks will be valuable to entrepreneurship under all circumstances. For instance, shared values among community and family members may encourage them to be less greedy but may simultaneously promote 'groupthink', risk aversion and a lack of innovativeness in the family business. Similarly, bounded solidarity may result in entrepreneurs being unduly partial to their family member or co-ethnic employee compared with non-family employees in the workplace. Community members may be eager to offer advice, but if their own experience and knowledge base are limited, their advice may not be particularly valuable to the entrepreneur. In fact, relying exclusively on co-ethnic community members' advice may prove detrimental to the entrepreneur's survival. Granovetter (1995) suggests that distant relationships or 'weaker ties' are a more valuable source of information for people since the information received is more diverse and therefore more likely to generate new ideas. Social capital generated by co-ethnic community networks may, therefore, have advantages as well as drawbacks for entrepreneurship.

Empirical studies of ethnic minority businesses generally emphasize the positive effects of community networks in providing access to a pool of inexpensive and reliable labour (Metcalf et al., 1996; Werbner, 1990). On the other hand, some studies suggest that the excessive reliance on family labour might be detrimental to the business. This is one of the conclusions drawn by Ram (1994) in his case studies of small businesses in Birmingham, England. In a similar vein, Bates (1994), in a study of Asian immigrant-owned businesses in the US, finds that the less successful, failure-prone businessmen rely most heavily on co-ethnic community networks for customers, employees, and finance. Other studies, like Basu and Goswami (1999) find that while family and co-ethnic networks can play a crucial role at business start-up, they become less significant for business growth. Moreover, the value of co-ethnic and family networks depends on the resources possessed by members and the depth and diversity of their experience, knowledge, and contacts (Basu and Altinay, 2003).

Ethnic resources and ethnic social networks, which stem from the entrepreneur's ethnic identity, can be defined narrowly or broadly. If defined narrowly, the entrepreneur's network may be restricted to his or her extended family members, or sub-caste, or geographically proximate community members. In the existing literature, ethnic resources are perceived very much as geographically proximate, local resources. The nature and quantity of these resources therefore vary not only by ethnic group but also with the particular environment. For instance, New York's Chinatown is different from that in San Francisco; Detroit's black community differs from that in Atlanta (Light and Gold, 2000). Similarly, the Gujarati Vaniks (a small caste-based community) in London are a narrowly defined, close-knit social group.

On the other hand, such a narrow conception of ethnic resources ignores today's economic realities of globalization and increasingly interconnected markets. Many of today's ethnic minority entrepreneurs have family, friends and community members spread across the globe. Modern communication has made it possible to nurture global ethnic networks. Global ethnic networks can, in fact, be extremely valuable in offering ethnic entrepreneurs a competitive edge over their rivals in the domestic market. This is evident from recent examples of ethnic minority entrepreneurs who have started dual-location global ventures, with operations in their adopted country and home country. For instance, ethnic social networks like Silicon Valley-based TiE (The Indus Entrepreneurs) are more broadly defined to include all those of Indian or South Asian origin. TiE is now a global network with 42 chapters in 9 countries around the world (www.tie.org). Thus, the access to cross-national or global community networks increases the chances of gaining a competitive advantage. This is not to deny the value of going beyond co-ethnic networks and belonging to ethnic, as well as non-ethnic, networks, since the access to multiple networks is believed to increase the chances of innovation (Ruef, 2002). However, the notion and measures of social capital remain vague. Consequently, the precise causal effects of social capital on entrepreneurial entry and effectiveness continue to remain ambiguous. (See Ch. 19 by Licht and Seigel in this Handbook for a further exploration of these issues).

21.3.7 Role of socio-economic resources

An important aspect neglected by the ethnic resources perspective is the role of socio-economic resources like education and the class background of migrants, as emphasized by Light (1984) in stimulating entrepreneurial entry and facilitating survival. Educational attainment is likely to positively affect the entrepreneur's knowledge base and ability to evaluate opportunities and replicate business models, as well as his or her ability to communicate with customers, banks, and other stakeholders. Ethnic entrepreneurs are likely to find it easier to negotiate their position in an alien environment if they are educated and possess business or technical skills. In addition, work experience in the host country prior to business entry contributes towards enhancing the ethnic minority entrepreneur's human capital and knowledge of the host country environment, lowering the information costs of operating in the host country, and improving the chances of starting a viable business. Education and prior work experience in the host country not only enhance human capital, but also provide access to wider social networks beyond the entrepreneur's own ethnic community. The access to multiple networks or greater social capital together with the educated and experienced entrepreneur's improved communication and negotiation skills increase the chances of access to financial capital from outside the entrepreneur's own ethnic community.

Empirical research supports the argument regarding the positive impact of education on entrepreneurship. Research on the factors influencing the survival and growth of ethnic entrepreneurs in the UK suggests that higher education consistently has a positive relationship with business growth (Basu and Goswami, 1999; Basu and Altinay, 2002). The advantages of education on business survival are also noticeable in the case of ethnic minorities in the US. For instance, Bates (1994) finds that survival and success among Asian immigrant-owned small businesses can be traced to the owners' impressive educational backgrounds and capital investments at start-up. Similarly, Silicon Valley's successful Chinese and Indian entrepreneurs are mostly engineers by training (Saxenian, 2000).

Ethnic and class resources are closely intertwined. Thus, the access to community finance depends not only on mutual trust and solidarity but also on the economic ability of community members to offer such support. Entrepreneurs belonging to less well-off minority groups are less likely to have access to this type of finance. Similarly, the ability of ethnic community members to offer valuable advice and information would depend on the breadth and depth of their knowledge and business experience or, in other words, their class resources.

21.3.8 Role of strategy

While ethnic entrepreneurs have a baggage of resources, both ethnic as well as non-ethnic, they have to make conscious decisions regarding what resources to draw on and what market(s) to address. Their survival depends not only on their starting resources, but also on the characteristics of their business and the strategies they adopt. Studies of business survival in the ethnic entrepreneurship literature have tended to underplay the role of proactive strategy formulation, and how and why strategies might shift over time.

Ethnic entrepreneurship theory (Mars and Ward, 1984; Waldinger et al., 1990) explains the survival of ethnic minority entrepreneurs in the context of ethnic resources (as already discussed), and opportunities created by an enclave economy. Business opportunities are generated by the emergence of niche markets to satisfy the demand of co-ethnic community members for ethnic products and services and by the shift of business interests among the majority community to more prosperous business locations. In this scenario, opportunities for business expansion are severely constrained by the size of the ethnic enclave community and the competition for markets and resources.

According to Waldinger et al. (1990), the ethnic entrepreneur has two main options for branching out of the ethnic enclave economy. One option is to adopt a middleman minority strategy of providing goods and services to the wider, majority community while continuing to rely on co-ethnic labour and community networks. An alternative strategy is economic assimilation, by offering goods and services typical of an indigenous majority-owned business and running the business in the same way as the majority community.

Although both the above alternatives are realistic and observable in practice, they ignore the existence of further strategic alternatives that may be available to ethnic minority entrepreneurs equipped with higher levels of education, a wider knowledge base, multiple or wider social networks, more information, and greater imagination.

A few recent studies have distinguished between alternative strategies that ethnic entrepreneurs can pursue, in terms of focusing on ethnic products and ethnic (local or global) markets, or mainstream products and mainstream (local or global) markets, or some combination among these alternative categories of products and markets (Jones et al., 2000; Basu, 2003). While a niche market strategy targeting local, ethnic customers may be logical at start-up, ethnic entrepreneurs who want to ensure survival and success need to broaden their customer base by serving global or mainstream markets.

Empirical research supports the above theory. In the case of ethnic minority entrepreneurs in the UK, an exploratory analysis of business performance by product–market strategy of 356 entrepreneurs shows that ethnic entrepreneurs whose businesses have experienced positive sales growth at constant prices since

Table 21.1 Alternative product–market strategies of ethnic entrepreneurs

Market: product:	Local ethnic	Local non-ethnic	Non-local ethnic	Non-local non-ethnic
Ethnic product	Stereotypical ethnic niche (A)	Local ethnic product niche (C)	National/global ethnic niche (E)	National/global ethnic product niche (G)
Non-ethnic product	Local ethnic client niche (B)	Local mainstream (D)	National/global ethnic client niche (F)	Mainstream mass market development (H)

start-up, display a higher propensity compared with their less successful couterparts (that have recorded zero or negative growth) to supply mainstream, non-ethnic products in national or international markets (strategies F and H in Table 1 above) (Basu, 2003). Although the strategy of supplying ethnic products to non-local, majority community customers (strategy G) is by far the most common strategy among the sample studied, the reliance on ethnic products, whether supplied to local, national or international markets (strategies A, C and G) is higher among the less successful businesses. Thus, the evidence indicates that more successful ethnic entrepreneurs aim to serve the wider community and have either broken out of, or stayed out of, co-ethnic niche markets.

21.4 Disparities among Ethnic Minority Entrepreneurs

Until the 1990s, studies of ethnic minority entrepreneurs either focused on a single community, like the Gujarati Patels (Lyon, 1972), the Pakistanis in Manchester (Werbner, 1990), and the Koreans in Los Angeles (Light and Bonacich, 1988), or treated some categories like 'Asians' in Britain as a single homogeneous group (Aldrich et al., 1981). More recent studies have compared the entrepreneurial behaviour of two or more different ethnic groups in the UK. (Rafiq, 1992; Metcalf et al., 1996; Basu, 1998; Basu and Goswami, 1999; Borooah and Hart, 1999; Basu and Altinay, 2002) and the US (Fairlie, 2004). It is imperative to do so since not all groups display the same rate of self-employment or are equally successful in entrepreneurship, even though they may suffer the same level of discrimination in their adopted country. From a policy perspective, it is important to recognize the heterogeneity among ethnic minority groups, in terms of culture, language, and socio-economic position, in order to understand what causes disparities among them, and institute policies that assist those groups that most deserve such assistance.

Several alternative explanations have been advanced to account for disparities in rates of entrepreneurship among different ethnic minority groups. One explanation is that these differences stem from cultural differences between communities. In other words, it is argued that certain ethnic groups are inherently more entrepreneurial than others due to their family tradition of being in business. For those of Indian origin, this cultural tradition is associated with the caste system; people belonging to business or trading castes are more likely to be self-employed. The validity of this explanation is supported by recent empirical evidence which shows that children whose parents owned businesses are much more likely to become self-employed themselves than those whose parents were not business owners (Dunn and Holtz-Eakin, 2000). Thus, a culture or tradition of business ownership among certain ethnic minority communities may explain their relatively higher propensity towards, and success in, entrepreneurship. Entrepreneurs who have a family tradition of business ownership have the added advantage of access to community and family resources, in the form of cheap and trustworthy labour, finance available at competitive rates, and advice, information and mentoring from other family and community members. Such resources may create further disparities between ethnic minorities since access to those resources are peculiar to ethnic communities that have a tradition in business and are not available to minorities who do not belong to a business community. For instance, a comparison of self-employment rates between Indians and Black Caribbean men in Great Britain indicates that differences can be attributed to family formation and individual characteristics (Borooah and Hart, 1999). A comparative study of Bangladeshi, Indian, East African, Pakistani, Turkish, and Turkish Cypriot entrepreneurs shows that a family tradition in business and strong family ties have a significant impact on business entry motives, as well as on sources of start-up finance, the choice of business, and women's participation in business (Basu and Altinay, 2002). The study found the sharpest contrast to be between East African entrepreneurs, who chose self-employment because of a family background in trade and relied on family finance at start-up, and Turkish Cypriots, comparatively few of whom had fathers in business or relied on family finance, but who chose self-employment as a means of economic advancement.

A further, related explanation points to differences in the historical reasons for, and patterns of, migration of different ethnic minority groups. For instance, the Asians who migrated to Britain from Kenya and Uganda in the early 1970s (they were expelled from Uganda in 1972) belonged to a business and trading background and established businesses, many in retail and wholesale trade, in the UK. On the other hand, the Afro-Caribbean, Indian, and Pakistani people who migrated to the UK in the 1950s and 1960s came to fill the post-war labour shortage in Britain's factories. Most of them had been blue-collar workers and were not highly educated. The early African migrants to the US were taken as slave labour and denied an education for many years even after living in the US. It can be argued that years of slavery had an effect on the African psyche and made it more difficult for them to have the self-confidence to start their own businesses. A similar argument is advanced in the case of the Afro-Caribbean migrants to the UK: their history of oppression destroyed their self-esteem, resulted in weak family and community ties, poor individual motivation, and insufficient personal resources (Barrett et al., 1996). This may explain the divergent entrepreneurial experience of Asians and Afro-Caribbeans in the UK. In contrast, the South Asians who migrated to the US in the 1970s and after were highly educated and went to gain further educational qualifications. Many of them established fast growing, innovative, technology-based businesses in Silicon Valley, California and other parts of the US.

The role of education in contributing to higher rates of entrepreneurship and economic advancement is discussed in theory in the previous section and substantiated by available empirical evidence. Light and Gold's (2000) analysis of US census data showed that nearly 30 percent of Hispanic business owner-employers were college graduates compared with less than 9 percent of the Hispanic adult population. This implies that educated ethnic minorities are more likely to become business owners than those who are less educated. Recent empirical research for the United States indicates that the growth of self-employment among Blacks during the 1980s and 1990s, and the narrowing of the gap between Black and White self-employment rates can be traced to increasing educational levels among Black men (Fairlie, 2004). The study shows that in contrast, the widening gap in self-employment rates between Hispanics and Whites over the same period (1979–98) is associated with no corresponding improvement in the educational attainment of Hispanic men. Furthermore, Fairlie (2004) concludes that the increase in the number of business owners among different racial groups in the US during the 1980s and 1990s can be largely explained by demographic forces such as the growth of the labour force in these groups. The picture is more ambiguous for the UK. For instance, even though the Chinese and Indians in Britain display high rates of educational attainment, self-employment rates among the Chinese are much higher than among the Indian population. On the other hand, Pakistanis have lower educational levels compared with most other ethnic minority groups in the UK, but are the most likely to be self-employed (UK ONS 2004). The reasons for these disparities among communities in Britain and in the pattern observed in the UK and US merit further investigation.

21.5 Conclusion: Policy implications and future research

This chapter has attempted to provide a summary of the issues of interest to academics studying ethnic minority entrepreneurship. The foregoing analysis suggests that ethnic minority entrepreneurship needs to be defined more carefully to clarify the ethnic, minority, and migration characteristics of the group being discussed, as well as their economic characteristics, whether as self-employed individuals without employees, self-employed employers, micro- or small-business owners, or owners of fast-growth businesses.

Ethnic minorities' entry into entrepreneurship is attributable to a complex set of factors or triggers. These include push factors like economic disadvantage and racial prejudice as well as pull factors like cultural norms and values, and contextual factors like a family background in entrepreneurship, role models of successful co-ethnic entrepreneurs, and close-knit community networks enjoyed by ethnic minorities. Pull factors could also include spotting an opportunity not noticed by others by virtue of the ethnic entrepreneur's involvement in two countries and cultures, which afford her or him informational advantages. These advantages are especially afforded to those entrepreneurs who have established ties with members of the majority community but have maintained their ties with their home country. The latter are more likely to be prevalent in the case of recent immigrants, but not restricted to them in today's global world. Empirical analyses indicate the difficulty of identifying one, overriding factor as being a trigger for ethnic minorities' entry into entrepreneurship. Thus, the decision to start one's own business in an environment where one is part of a minority community, usually stems from push and pull factors created by the interaction of micro-motives and macro, environmental conditions.

Ethnic entrepreneurial success is attributable to a combination of ethnic and economic resources and entrepreneurs' strategic business decisions. In particular, both theory and empirical research highlight the crucial role of higher education in providing the ethnic entrepreneur with the analytical and communications skills necessary for lowering barriers to business entry, widening their access to information and social networks as well as formal sources of finance, and contributing towards business success.

The persistence of disparities in the rates of business ownership and economic advancement among different ethnic communities implies the need for direct policy intervention that is targeted towards the relatively disadvantaged groups. The intervention could take the form of helping to raise the education levels of those groups, generating awareness and enthusiasm among them about entrepreneurship as a career option, offering access to advice, information, and mentoring services, and equipping entrepreneurs with the skills necessary to operate their own businesses and access financial resources. Support agencies could try to identify successful entrepreneur role models for each ethnic minority community to encourage others to follow their example. They could encourage entrepreneurs to form, or join, both co-ethnic and non-ethnic business networks and associations. Since ethnic minority entrepreneurs are often stuck in marginal businesses, support agencies could help them to review their business strategies and find ways to break out of these businesses that have low entry barriers into more promising industries and markets.

While many reasons for disparities in rates of entrepreneurship across different ethnic communities have been identified, future research needs to look more closely at comparing different communities in the same country and the same ethnic community across different countries. In fact, there are hardly any cross-country comparisons of ethnic minority entrepreneurship in the existing literature. This points to the need for further research in that direction.

Another area that merits further research is the inter-generational life-cycle of ethnic entrepreneurs. Despite the fact that ethnic minorities frequently operate family-run businesses, there is hardly any empirical evidence on the impact of factors such as changing educational attainment, the nature of business, and perceptions of payback from it, on business succession from one generation to the next among ethnic minority entrepreneurs.

References

Aldrich, H. and R. Waldinger (1990). 'Ethnicity and Entrepreneurship'. *Annual Review of Sociology*, 16: 111–135.

—— J. C. Cater, T. P. Jones and D. McEvoy (1981). 'Business Development and Self-Segregation: Asian Enterprise in Three British Cities', in C. Peach, V. Robinson and S. Smith (eds) *Ethnic Segregation in Cities*. London: CroomHelm.

Baines, S. and J. Wheelock (1998). 'Working for Each Other: Gender, the household and micro-business survival and growth'. *International Small Business Journal*, 5(2): 179–98.

Barrett, A. G., T. P. Jones and D. McEvoy (1996). 'Ethnic Minority Business: Theoretical Discourse in Britain and North America'. *Urban Studies*, 33(4–5): 783–809.

Basu, A. (1998). 'An exploration of entrepreneurial activity among Asian small businesses in Britain'. *Small Business Economics*, 10(4): 313–26.

—— (2003). 'Overcoming market barriers: successful "break out" strategies of immigrant entrepreneurs'. Paper presented at the 17th Annual UIC Research Symposium on Marketing and Entrepreneurship, Chicago, August.

—— and A. Goswami (1999). 'Determinants of South Asian Entrepreneurial Growth in Britain: A Multivariate Analysis'. *Small Business Economics*, 13(1): 313–26.

—— and S. Parker (2001). 'Family Finance and New Business Start-ups'. *Oxford Bulletin of Economics and Statistics*, 63(3): 333–58.

Basu, A. and E. Altinay (2002). 'The Interaction Between Culture and Entrepreneurship in London's Immigrant Businesses'. *International Small Business Journal*, 20(4): 371–92.

—— and —— (2003). *Family and Work in Minority Ethnic Businesses.* Brsitol: The Policy Press.

Bates, T. (1994). 'Social Resources Generated by Group Support Networks May Not Be Beneficial to Asian Immigrant-owned Small Businesses'. *Social Forces*, 72(3): 671–89.

Borooah, V. K and M. Hart (1999). 'Factors Affecting Self-employment Among Indian and Black Caribbean Men in Britain'. *Small Business Economics*, 13(2): 111–19.

Carter, N. M., W. B. Gartner and P. G. Greene (2002). 'The Career Reasons of Minority Nascent Entrepreneurs'. *Academy of Management Proceedings*, ENT D1-D6.

Chaganti, R. and P. Greene (2002). 'Who Are Ethnic Entrepreneurs? A Study of Entrepreneurs'. Ethnic Involvement and Business Characteristics. *Journal of Small Business Management*, 40(2): 126–43.

Clark, K. and S. Drinkwater (1998). 'Ethnicity and Self-employment in Britain'. *Oxford Bulletin of Economics and Statistics*, 60(3): 383–407.

Constant, A., Y. Shachmurove and K. F. Zimmerman (2003). What makes an entrepreneur and does it pay? Native men, Turks and other migrants in Germany. IZA Discussion Paper No. 940, Institute for the Study of Labour, Bonn, November.

de Wit, G. (1993). 'Models of Self-Employment in a Competitive Market'. *Journal of Economic Surveys*, 7(4): 367–97.

Dobbin, C. (1996). *Asian Entrepreneurial Minorities: Conjoint Communities in the Making of the World Economy, 1570–1940.* Richmond: Curzon Press.

Dunn, Thomas A. and D. J. Holtz-Eakin (2000). 'Financial Capital, Human Capital, and the Transition to Self-employment: Evidence from intergenerational links'. *Journal of Labour Economics*, 18(2): 282–305.

Fairlie, R. W. (2004). 'Recent Trends in Ethnic and Racial Business Ownership'. *Small Business Economics*, 23(3): 203–18.

Flap, H., A. Kumcu and B. Bulder (2000). 'The Social Capital of Ethnic Entrepreneurs and their Business Success', in J. Rath (ed.) *Immigrant Businesses: The Economic, Political and Social Environment.* London: Macmillan.

Granovetter, M. (1995). 'The Economic Sociology of Firms and Entrepreneurs', in A. Portes (ed.) *The Economic Sociology of Immigration: Essays on Networks, Ethnicity, and Entrepreneurship.* New York: Russell Sage Foundation.

Hutchinson, J. and A. D. Smith (1996). *Ethnicity.* Oxford: Oxford University Press.

Jones, T., G. Barrett and D. McEvoy (2000). 'Market Potential as a Decisive Influence on the Performance of Ethnic Minority Business', in J. Rath (ed.) *Immigrant Businesses: The Economic, Political and Social Environment.* London: Macmillan .

—— D. McEvoy and G. Barrett (1994). 'Labour Intensive Practices in the Ethnic Minority Firm', in J. Atkinson and D. Storey (eds) *Employment, the Small Firm and the Labour Market.* London: Routledge.

Kirzner, I. M. (1979). *Perception, Opportunity and Profit: Studies in the Theory of Entrepreneurship.* Chicago: University of Chicago Press.

Kloosterman, R., J. Van Der Leun and J. Rath (1999). 'Mixed Embeddedness: In (Economic Activities and Immigrant Businesses in the Netherlands'. *International Journal of Urban and Regional Research*, 23(2): 252–67.

Kloosterman, R. and J. Rath (2001). 'Immigrant Entrepreneurs in Advanced Economies: Mixed Embeddedness further explored'. Special Issue on Immigrant Entrepreneurship, *Journal of Ethnic and Migration Studies*, 27(2): 189–202.

Light, I. (1984). 'Immigrant and ethnic enterprise in North America'. *Ethnic and Racial Studies*, 7: 195–216.

—— and E. Bonacich (1988). *Immigrant Entrepreneurs: Koreans in Los Angeles 1965–82*. Berkeley: University of California Press.

—— and C. Rosenstein (1995). *Race, Ethnicity and Entrepreneurship in Urban America*. New York: Aldine de Gruyter.

—— and S. J. Gold (2000). *Ethnic Economies*. San Diego: Academic Press.

Lyon, M. (1972). 'Ethnicity in Britain: The Gujarati Tradition'. *New Community*, 21(1): 1–12.

Mars, G. and R. Ward (1984). 'Ethnic Business Development in Britain: Opportunities and Resources', in R. Ward and R. Jenkins (eds) *Ethnic Communities in Business*. Cambridge: Cambridge University Press.

Masurel, E., P. Nijkamp, M. Tastan and G. Vindigni (2002). 'Motivations and Performance Conditions for Ethnic Entrepreneurship'. *Growth and Change*, 33(2): 238–60.

Metcalf, H., T. Modood and S. Virdee (1996). *Asian Self-Employment: The Interaction of Culture and Economics in England*. London: Policy Studies Institute.

Portes, A. (1995). 'Economic Sociology and the Sociology of Immigration: A Conceptual Overview', A. Portes (ed.) *The Economic Sociology of Immigration: Essays on Networks, Ethnicity, and Entrepreneurship*. New York: Russell Sage Foundation.

Rafiq, M. (1992). 'Ethnicity and Enterprise: A Comparison of Muslim and-Muslim Owned Asian Businesses in Britain'. *New Community*, 19(1): 43–60.

Ram, M. (1994). *Managing to Survive: Working Lives in Small Firms*. Oxford: Blackwell.

Rekers, A. and R. van Kempen (2000). 'Location Matters: Ethnic entrepreneurs and the spatial context', in J. Rath (ed.) *Immigrant Business: The Economic, Political and Social Environment*. London: Macmillan.

Reuf, M. (2002). 'Strong Ties, Weak Ties and Islands: Structural and cultural predictors of organizational innovation'. *Industrial and Corporate Change*, 11(3): 427–49.

Saxenian, A. (2000). 'Networks of Immigrant Entrepreneurs', in C. M. Lee, W. F. Miller, M. G. Hancock and H. S. Rowen (eds) *The Silicon Valley Edge*. Stanford: Stanford University Press.

Schermerhorn, R. A. (1978). *Comparative Ethnic Relations: A Framework for Theory and Research*. Chicago: University of Chicago Press.

Shane, S. (2000). 'Prior Knowledge and the Discovery of Entrepreneurial Opportunities'. *Organization Science*, 11(4): 448–69.

Shane, S. and S. Venkatraman (2000). 'The Promise of Entrepreneurship as a Field of Research'. *Academy of Management Review*, 25(1): 217–26.

Singh, R. P., G. E. Hills, R. C. Hybel and G. T. Lumpkin (1999). 'Opportunity Recognition Through Social Network Characteristics of Entrepreneurs', in P. D. Reynolds (ed.) *Frontiers of Entrepreneurship Research*. Wellesley, MA: Babson College.

Sombart, W. (1951). *The Jews and Modern Capitalism*. Glencoe, IL: Free Press.

Tripathi, D. (1984). *Business Communities of India*. Delhi: Manohar.

UK Office of National Statistics (ONS) (2004). Ethnicity and Identity: National statistics on employment patterns Available at http://www.statistics.gov.uk/cci/nugget.asp?id=463 and education Available at http://www.statistics.gov.uk/cci/nugget.asp?id=461.

US Department of Commerce (2001). *The State of Minority Business: 1997 Survey of Minority-owned Business Enterprises.* Washington, DC: Minority Business Development Agency.

US Census Bureau (2001). Available at www.census.gov

Waldinger, R., H. Aldrich, R. Ward and Associates (1990). *Ethnic Entrepreneurs: Immigrant Business in Industrial Societies.* London: Sage.

Weber, M. (1976). *The Protestant Ethic and the Spirit of Capitalism*, 2nd edn. London: George Allen and Unwin.

Werbner, P. (1990). 'Renewing an Industrial Past: British Pakistani entrepreneurship in Manchester'. *Migration*, 8: 17–41.

CHAPTER 22

MIGRATION OF ENTREPRENEURS

ANDREW GODLEY

In the classical and neoclassical economists' development of the theory of entrepreneurship, little role was allocated to one of the more obvious empirical observations of entrepreneurial behaviour: entrepreneurs have always been highly mobile individuals. This omission may of course have been because the focus of so much attention among nineteenth century economists was on the dramatic events then unfolding in the industrializing regions of Britain and the United States, before then spreading further afield. Smith, Ricardo, Mill, Marx and Marshall were therefore more concerned with explaining the development of industrial activities in specific locations than the movement of key individuals (see Ricketts in Ch. 2 of this Handbook). Even Schumpeter and Knight in heralding the modern theory of entrepreneurship, were more taken by the newly emerging corporate structures (Casson and Godley, 2005). But the sheer extent of geographic mobility among entrepreneurs needs to be underlined before any theoretical explanation is offered. This chapter therefore reviews the literature on immigrant entrepreneurship, focusing especially on recently published investigations of historic cases, before making some theoretical observations and suggesting areas for further research.

Nathan Mayer Rothschild is widely recognised as having been the most successful entrepreneur in history and so might be a plausible candidate for the most prominent immigrant entrepreneur ever (Ferguson, 1998). He was born in 1777, in the Jewish ghetto in Frankfurt, Germany, and he arrived in England in 1808 or 1809. After a few years as a textile merchant in Manchester, he rose spectacularly to become the dominant figure in British and then global finance from the 1820s, almost single-handedly creating the modern bond market. However, the far less well-known Armenian merchant, Khwaja Wajid, may well run Nathan Mayer Rothschild close. Wajid moved to Bengal and experienced no less a spectacular rise as Rothschild, becoming the monopoly supplier of the entire saltpetre (a critical component then for the manufacturing of gunpowder) and salt monopolies in the North East India sub-continent. While Rothschild's career has been covered in Ferguson's majesterial family history, Wajid, born in Patna, the son of an influential Armenian immigrant merchant in Kashmir (Choudhury, 2005) remains yet a shadowy figure.

The Armenian entrepreneurial Diaspora was a demographic by-product of the raw silk produced on the shores of the Caspian Sea. In early modern times most European silk came from the Caspian, Caucasus and Iran. As European demand grew, Iran became ever more the dominant producer, but in fact several dozen Armenian families dominated its distribution and sale. The privileged position of the most prominent Armenian merchants in the global silk trade was cemented after winning the auction for the Shah's silk monopoly of 1617 (Baghdiantz McCabe, 2005).

Early modern Iran was an autocratic feudal state, with the Shah visciously competing with regional lords for power. The granting of such a profitable monopoly to outsiders was a convenient solution to ensuring that no other faction at court would gain additional power and so become more of a threat. But the Armenians, while aware of the greater power politics at stake, were nevertheless willing to pay more for the silk monopoly than any other competitor because they alone could generate more profit.

The leading families of Armenian merchants had developed extensive trading networks with the principal European and Asian markets over several generations. (Curtin, 1984, Braudel, 1984). During the seventeenth century these trading networks expanded, as silk exports increased. The Armenian trading networks were based on extended family units. Family members dispersed as far away as Amsterdam to Surat in Indonesia were able to act as global silk merchants, managing transactions efficiently across a vast geographical range. They were eager to diversify into other areas, maximizing profits on their market-making skills. In consequence, they prospered.

In the late seventeenth and early eighteenth centuries, the fastest growing market in the world was not north-western Europe—the Industrial revolution came later—but northeast India. Several Armenian families immigrated to Bengal to follow this market (Baghdiantz McCabe, 1999). Wajid was a scion of one of these Armenian immigrant merchant families. While the contours of Wajid's early career are unclear, his family background in Persia would have given him a good grounding in business and an especial appreciation of the profitability of royal monopolies. This must have been useful because the Bengali court exercised a jurisdiction over key trades similar to the Shah.

Wajid entered the Bengali Royal Court in 1741. Evidently his personality enabled him to extend his influence at court rapidly. By the late 1740s he had gained 'virtual control of the economy of Bihar' and its famed saltpetre production (Chaudhuri, 2005: 6). By 1753, he had gained monopoly control of the entire saltpetre trade and was master of the Bengali defence industry. Furthermore Wajid also went on to win the contract for the Bengali salt monopoly, which was profitably farmed by him from 1752 onwards (salt was hugely valuable in the sweaty tropical and sub-tropical climates). With further diversification into shipping, banking and opium, at his peak Wajid could easily have been the richest man in the world. His business empire was based on privileged access to the centre of political and economic authority in these feudal economies. While he exploited the traditional Armenian trading networks and his own extended family to ensure the profitability of his monopolies, his prosperity was dependent on the incumbent regime both remaining on good terms with him, and staying in power. After the British victory at the Battle of Plessey in 1757, Wajid's days were numbered. The British, under the auspices of the East India Company, were in no mood to tolerate their long time competitor in the region. Company servants simply seized control of the salt and saltpetre monopolies. Robert Clive ensured Wajid's downfall and he apparently poisoned himself in jail in 1759.

This close association between an ethnic minority, like Wajid's Armenian immigrant mercantile families in India, and the successful exploitation of one specific niche within a large political unit, like the Persian or Bengali empires, was repeated among other Diaspora groups. In the Ancient world, the Phoenicians built trading networks from Spain to Babylon, and the Assyrians governed vast movements of international trade and farmed out monopolies. In medieval times, the banking dynasties in Italy and South Germany similarly developed vast trading networks, benefiting from access to monopolies of some kind or other. Venetian merchants were renowned throughout Asia. Carmel Vassalo (2005) has recently shown how Maltese traders in sixteenth-century Spain benefited from their island's close association with the Catholic Order of St John. This religious association opened up the Spanish Empire to Maltese traders, who exploited their geographic position to become intermediaries between the Catholic Spanish and the Muslim Ottoman empires, and eventually were given the privileged status of carrying the valuable cotton transhipment trade.

Greek merchants also benefited from their geographical position on the western fringe of the Ottoman Empire. Indeed the Greeks, in contrast to the Maltese, were actually Ottoman subjects. Because they were the most European of his subjects, Greek shipping families became the Caliph's *dragoman*, or representatives to the European courts, enabling them to develop, and almost monopolize, the Ottoman European trading axis from the sixteenth century onwards (Fusaro, 2005).

By the nineteenth century, the leading Greek merchant families were able to control the Black Sea grain trade and, ultimately, to develop into the leading entrepreneurs in the global shipping industry (Harlaftis, 1996). And in the train of these examples of relatively powerful outsider families exploiting some privileged position, several dozen more families were able to develop more minor international business links, as lesser (though still very significant) traders in the nineteenth and twentieth centuries.

From ancient to modern times, whether it was Jewish immigrants such as Rothschild, Armenians such as Wajid, or Maltese or Greeks, there has been a strong correspondence between migration and entrepreneurship. Perhaps the best way of understanding the disposition for entrepreneurs to migrate is to apply the conventional international labour market model to the migration of entrepreneurs as is used to explain the international migration of unskilled labour (Hatton and Williamson, 1998). Here the critical determinant of the rate of migration is the relative reward between home and host economies. Applications of the model invariably use relative wages, but in order to explain the international migration of entrepreneurs, attention would need to focus on relative profits. The migration of men like Rothschild, Wajid and others then becomes easier to understand. Whether it was to Manchester in the 1800s or Calcutta in the 1740s, the booming local economies attracted men on the make.

But the evidence of entrepreneurs clustering in areas of rapid economic change from before the industrial revolution to the present simply suggests that there is a correlation between profits and entrepreneurs. Such an observation doesn't particularly assist us to gain a greater theoretical hold on the subject. Simply applying any of Knight's focus on uncertainty, or Kirzner's concern for entrepreneurial alertness, or Casson's definition of the entrepreneur as a judgemental decision-maker, or even Schumpeter's dramatic notion of creative destruction, will not particularly assist us further in understanding the greater tendency for entrepreneurs to migrate. A clearer understanding of the concept is needed first. For immigrant entrepreneurship as a concept is surely about more than those exceptional immigrants with the Midas touch.

Any survey of the conceptual literature is hardly assisted by a conflation between the terms ethnic entrepreneurship and immigrant entrepreneurship. But any survey of immigrant entrepreneurship through history would, for example, be unlikely to include examples like Andrew Carnegie (the Scottish-born founder of US Steel) and Cecil Rhodes (the plunderer of southern Africa, Ferguson 2003), for while Carnegie in the United States and the rapacious Rhodes in pre-colonial Africa were immigrants, and were spectacularly successful fortune-hunters, they should not be included as immigrant entrepreneurs, because to do so would render the concept meaningless. The interest of the concept is surely that immigrants have overcome some degree of adversity through their entrepreneurial endeavours. Bonacich (1973), for example, in a classic statement on ethnic entrepreneurship, emphasized that for migrant entrepreneurs to be included in her model of middlemen minorities, they needed to face some hostility from the host community.

Consider two recent examples of entrepreneurial minorities, the East African Asians in Britain and the offshore Chinese in Malaysia and Indonesia. In 1972 President Idi Amin expelled the Asian population of Uganda, the acme of a more substantial departure of Asians disenchanted with post-colonial East Africa; 155,000 arrived in the UK (Panayi 1999). Out of a total population of over 1 million immigrants from India, Pakistan and Bangladesh, they consist of only a relatively small percentage of the total. But they have had a disproportionate impact on entrepreneurship and entrepreneurial success among the Asians in Britain (Basu, 1998).

These East African Asian immigrants in Britain are in fact third-or fourth-generation migrant population, with the majority of population originating from Gujarat, especially the Kutch region, and emigrating to British East Africa in the final quarter of the nineteenth century. They emigrated because they were encouraged by the British imperial government to go and provide commercial infrastructure, which was largely absent then in East Africa. After two generations of small-scale retailing and commerce, the British withdrew from East Africa, and the Asian population suddenly became vulnerable to post-colonial nationalistic forces. Many left to settle in Canada, the United States and, of course, Britain, where they went on to reconstitute business and meet with disproportionate success. The important observation to make is that Gujarati Hindu immigrant entrepreneurs in Africa were offering entrepreneurial services in an economic region where the indigenous population was largely unwilling to offer entrepreneurship.

A similar conclusion can be drawn about the offshore Chinese entrepreneurs, who have experienced such success in South East Asia since the 1960s. In total the ethnic Chinese in South East Asia remain a tiny minority, perhaps only 3 percent of the total population there. But they dominate South East Asian business. In Indonesia, for example, Chinese business represents 73 percent of the Indonesian corporate sector, by market capitalization (Brown, 2000). Unlike those in Taiwan and Hong Kong, the overwhelming majority of Chinese families in Singapore, Malaysia, Indonesia, Thailand and the rest of South East Asia, left China, not in response to the Communist Revolution, but earlier during the period from roughly 1870 to 1920. Moreover the offshore Chinese in South East Asia were economic rather than political migrants, and came mostly from Guangdong and Fujian provinces and Hainan Island, on the south-eastern corner of China.

They were economic migrants because in the final quarter of the nineteenth century, economic conditions in southeastern China were relatively poor. And the barriers to moving to tin mines, rubber plantations to, say, in Malaysia, were just as considerable as moving to the Mandarin-speaking north and west. Analysis of the dialects spoken by these offshore Chinese suggests a very strong propensity for chain migration, with prominent dialects among the Chinese population in certain regions of South East Asia coming from only very small regions of southeastern

China. *Hokkien*, for example, is a dialect originating from the south of the Fujian province. It is the dominant ancestral dialect of the Singaporean and Filipino Chinese and prominent among the Malay Chinese. *Teochin*, to take another example, originates from the Shantou area of northern Guangdong. Perhaps 80 percent of Thai Chinese population are *Teochin* speakers (Bachman and Butler, 2003). By contrast, Cantonese, which is the dominant dialect in Hong Kong (which became known for entrepreneurial exceptionalism only after the Communist revolution) is otherwise much less prominent outside small Chinese communities in Kuala Lumpur and Saigon.

These Chinese entrepreneurs participated fully in the boom years of South East Asian globalization, from the 1880s to the 1920s, and then suffered in the years of global depression, war and reconstruction (Brown, 2000). But the move to post-colonial independence in South East Asia had just as powerful an effect on Chinese entrepreneurs there as it did with the Indian entrepreneurs in East Africa, but this time mostly positive. For in contrast to East Africa, newly appointed governments in independent Malaysia and Indonesia depended increasingly on Chinese entrepreneurs, especially in nationalistic attempts to exclude western capital in the 1960s.

It follows that the entrepreneurial activities of the East African Asians in Britain, the offshore Chinese in South East Asia, just like the island Greek, and Maltese traders, and Armenian merchants (also the Lebanese and Syrian traders and others) are all examples of geographically mobile entrepreneurial minorities. These immigrants have offered entrepreneurial services in regions where the indigenous population was either reluctant or unable to do so.

The legion of examples of successful immigrant entrepreneurs in the past could be expanded, but for the purposes of surveying entrepreneurial mobility of ethnic minorities in western nations today, the relevance of these historic examples needs to be drawn out. Entrepreneurial minorities were after all very common in the past, but typically in economic regions where the indigenous population were either unwilling or unable to supply entrepreneurship themselves. This was sometime for religious or socio-cultural reasons.

In the Middle Ages, a ban on usury in Christian communities allowed Jewish money lenders to corner private banking. Seventeenth-century Persian Shahs were so suspicious of their rivals that Armenian Christian merchants were given valuable trading opportunities. Timur Kuran's thesis on Islamic economic retardation emphasizes the link between the sense of the Koran being the complete and final revelation form God and entrepreneurial inertia (Kuran, 1997). This allowed non-Muslims in the Ottoman empire to prosper, like the Greeks, Lebanese, and other Christian and Jewish minorities. The prominence of the Baghdadi Jews in the Persian empire may have owed similar origins (Plüss, 2005).

The historic prominence of certain entrepreneurial minorities therefore appears to be strongly associated with political constraints imposed on entrepreneurial activities among the indigenous population. While this might have been a profitable niche for entrepreneurial ethnic minorities to pursue in the past, it clearly does not represent an optimal political environment for promoting economic development more generally. Ultimately competition between political systems has mostly led to successful systems in the main, replacing the less successful ones (Jones, 2003). Almost all political restrictions on indigenous participation in entrepreneurial activities are no longer in force. In consequence, however, the scope for entrepreneurial minorities to pursue their previously profitable niches free from competition has substantially diminished (see Rubinstein, 2000 for a similar argument focusing on modern corporate structures).

Moreover, where ethnic minorities continue to pursue profitable entrepreneurial niches in open economies, the explanation is more typically found to lie in skills or attributes specific to that minority population. Two apparently successful immigrant communities in the United States in recent times are illustrative here.

By the 1970s, the Cuban émigré community was renowned already for its colour and verve but research identified what was previously unknown: that a high proportion of the Cuban immigrants had become successful entrepreneurs (Portes and Bach, 1985). Their route into the market was often via competitive immigrant sectors. But unlike other Hispanic immigrant communities in the United States, the Cubans had very high rates of self-employment and enjoyed very significant income gains. Portes's explanation emphasized the role of Cuban self-help and cultural values operating effectively within what he described as ethnic enclaves. And so, according to Portes, with sufficiently strong initial conditions, particularly associated with strong communal or cultural values (what has since been termed as 'social capital'), the Cuban émigrés were able to build businesses and industries.

Further evidence of other successful entrepreneurship strategies emerged after Portes's seminal contribution. In particular, it became clear that Korean immigrants in the United States, since the late 1960s, had been able to develop successful retail operations. Once these were investigated further, it appeared that Korean entrepreneurs also benefited disproportionately from communal services, with revolving credit societies being only the most well-known example.

The focus of attention on the role played by strong cultures in developing these self-help solutions to immigrant mobility led to the identification of the value of strong ties within the tightly bound networks in immigrant communities. Thus the two contemporary examples of Cuban and Korean ethnic entrepreneurs appeared to confirm that policy initiatives ought to be targeted at stimulating self-employment among all immigrant groups.

More recent research on the 'ethnic enclave' route to upward mobility and assimilation has, however, been more equivocal in the advantages generated from this route to assimilation, with 'evidence for the advantages and disadvantages of participating in co-ethnic economies as opposed to mainstream primary and secondary sectors has been far from conclusive' (Morawska 1990: 203). The Cuban, and Korean routes remain exceptional. The reason for this is two-fold: First, the hypothesis that strong ties in immigrant network economies were responsible for success, does not hold with the generally accepted model that successful networks tend to be based on 'weak ties' not strong ones.

Secondly, and more importantly, the interpretation of Cuban and Korean 'entrepreneurial success' is, as recent research has shown, actually better interpreted as 'failure'. This is because both the Cuban refugees and the Korean immigrants were populations disproportionately composed of professionals and entrepreneurs in their home countries (Morawska, 1990, Waldinger, Aldrich and Ward, 1990). With such strong advantages in terms of their skills background and knowledge on arrival, it is less surprising that they have proven to be relatively successful in the years since. Indeed from the perspective of the actors themselves, arriving from professional or established business backgrounds in Cuba and Korea, their self-perception is typically more of status-loss and of relative failure (Morawska, 1990).

Any survey of immigration and entrepreneurship is likely to be overwhelmed by the sheer abundance of evidence, and while this summary has, at the margin, preferred to emphasize the less well-known cases over the more famous, the general conclusions remain the same. Historically, there has been a strong association between ethnic minority entrepreneurship and political restrictions on the indigenous populations. These restrictions may have arisen for political or for cultural and religious reasons (Jones, 2003; Kuran, 1997). But the resulting distribution of knowledge about merchanting skills and opportunities has exaggerated any unevenness. And so the experience of different ethnic minorities in recent years in nations like the United States and the United Kingdom has been for those immigrant populations with relatively advantaged human capital endowments to prosper, and those without to suffer.

This is where the greatest impact of further research would be felt. For while there are now many micro-studies of ethnic minority experience in Britain and America and elsewhere few are comparative, and few have incorporated any understanding of the ethnic minority human capital endowments (although see good examples in Altinay, 2005; Rath, 2002).

References

Altinay, E. (2005). 'Ethnic Minority Entrepreneurship: Factors Influencing Business Growth: A study of Turkish Community Businesses in London: A Multivariate Analysis'. Unpublished Ph.D. thesis, University of Reading.

Baghdiantz McCabe, I. (1999). *The Shah's Silk for Europe's Silver: The Eurasian Silk trade of the Julfan Armenians in Safavid Iran and India (1590–1750.)* Atlanta: Scholar's Press.

Baghdiantz McCabe, I. (2005). 'Global trading Ambitions in Diaspora: The Armenians and their Eurasian Silk Trade, 1530–1750', in Baghdiantz McCabe, Harlaftis and Minoglou (eds) *Diaspora Entrepreneurial Networks: Four Centuries of History.* Oxford: Berg.

—— G. Harlaftis and I. Pepelasis Minoglou (eds) (2005). *Diaspora Entrepreneurial Networks: Four Centuries of History.* Oxford: Berg.

Backman, M. and C. Butler (2003). *Big in Asia: 25 Strategies for Business Success.* Basingstoke: Palgrave.

Basu, A. (1998). 'An Exploration of Entrepreneurial Activity among Asian Small Businesses in Britain'. *Small Business Economics,* 10(4): 58–81.

Bonacich, E. (1973). 'A Theory of Middlemen Minorities'. *American Sociological Review,* pp. 583–94.

Braudel, F. (1984). *Civilization and Capitalism.* New York: Collins, Fontana.

Brown, R. (2000). *Chinese Big Business and the Wealth of Nations.* Basingstoke: Macmillan.

Casson, M. and A. Godley (2005). 'Historical Perspectives on Entrepreneurship and Vertical Integration'. Paper presented at the Conference on Entrepreneurship, Ohio State University, Columbus, Ohio.

Chaudhuri, S. (2005). 'Trading Networks in a Traditional Diaspora: Armenians in India', in Baghdiantz McCabe, Harlaftis and Minoglou (eds) *Diaspora Entrepreneurial Networks: Four Centuries of History.* Oxford: Berg.

Curtin, P. (1984). *Cross-Cultural Trade in World History.* Cambridge: Cambridge University Press.

Ferguson, N. (1998). *The World's Banker: The History of the House of Rothschild.* London: Weidenfeld and Nicholson.

—— (2003). *Empire: How Britain Made the Modern World.* London: Allen Lane.

Fusaro, M. (2005). 'Coping with Transition: greek Merchants and Shipowners between Venice and England in the Late Sixteenth Century', in I. Baghdiantz McCabe, G. Harlaftis and P. Minoglou (eds) *Diaspora Entrepreneurial Networks: Four Centuries of History.* Oxford: Berg.

Harlaftis, G. (1996). *A History of Greek Owned Shipping: The Making of an International Tramp Fleet, 1830 to the Present Day.* London: Routledge.

—— (2005). 'Mapping the Greek Maritime Diaspora from the Early Eighteenth to the Late Twentieth Centuries', in I. Baghdiantz McCabe, G. Harlaftis and P. Minoglou (eds) *Diaspora Entrepreneurial Networks: Four Centuries of History.* Oxford: Berg.

Hatton, T. and J. Williamson (1998). *The Age of Mass Migration.* Oxford: Oxford University Press.

Jones, E. (2003). *The European Miracle: Environments, Economies and geopolitics in the History of Europe and Asia.,* 3rd edn. Cambridge: Cambridge University Press.

Kuran, T. (1997). 'Islam and Underdevelopment: An Old Puzzle revisited'. *Journal of Institutional and Theoretical Economics,* 153: 41–79.

Morawska, E. (1990). 'The Sociology and Historiography of Immigration', in *Immigration Reconsidered: History, Sociology and Politics* V. Yans-McLaughlin (ed.). New York: Oxford University Press.

Panayi, P. (1999). *The Impact of Immigration.* Manchester: Manchester University Press.

Plüss, C. (2005). 'Globalizing Ethnicity with Multi-local Identifications: The Parsee, Indian Muslim and Sephardic Trade Diasporas in Hong Kong', in I. Baghdiantz McCabe, G. Harlaftis and P. Minoglou (eds) *Diaspora Entrepreneurial Networks: Four Centuries of History.* Oxford: Berg.

PORTES, A. and R. BACH (1985). *Latin Journey: Cuban and Mexican Immigrants in the United States.* Berkeley: University of California Press.

RATH, J. (ed.) (2002). *Unravelling the Rag Trade: Immigrant Entrepreneurship in Seven World Cities.* Oxford: Berg.

RUBINSTEIN, W. (2000). 'Entrepreneurial Minorities: A Typology', in M. Casson and A. Godley (eds) *Cultural Factors in Economic Growth.* Berlin: Springer.

VASSAL, C. (2005). 'Maltese Entrepreneurial Networks', in I. Baghdiantz McCabe, G. Harlaftis and P. Minoglou (eds) *Diaspora Entrepreneurial Networks: Four Centuries of History* Oxford: Berg.

WALDINGER, R., H. ALDRICH and R. WARD (1990). *Ethnic Entrepreneurs: Immigrant Business in Industrial Societies.* Newbury Park, CA: Sage.

CHAPTER 23

WOMEN ENTREPRENEURS: A RESEARCH OVERVIEW

CANDIDA G. BRUSH[1]

23.1 Introduction

Entrepreneurship was historically defined as a 'man's domain'. Early characterizations of entrepreneurs included the 'captain of industry' (Schumpeter, 1934), the 'hero who perceives gaps and connects markets' (Liebenstein, 1968), the 'enterprising man' (Collins and Moore, 1964), 'key man' (Hebert and Link, 1982) and the 'man who organizes the firm (business unit) and/or increases its productive capacity' (McClelland, 1961: 205). The emphasis on male entrepreneurs in early literature is not at all surprising since men were primary participants in entrepreneurship world wide. History shows us that men were those most active in self-employment, business creation and business ownership for decades (Hebert and Link, 1982).

More recent definitions are less gendered, suggesting entrepreneurs carry out a series of activities to create something new of value under different conditions (Acs and Audretsch, 1993: Shane and Venkataraman, 2000). Specifically, entrepreneurs are defined as those who:

[1] The author is most grateful to Nancy Carter, Patricia Greene, Elizabeth Gatewood and Myra Hart for their contributions and ideas for this chapter.

- pursue opportunities without regard to resources they control (Stevenson and Jarillo, 1990)
- create innovative economic organizations for the purpose of gain or growth under conditions of risk and uncertainty (Low and MacMillan, 1988)
- discover, evaluate and exploit opportunities to introduce new goods and services, ways of organizing markets, processes and raw materials through organizing efforts that did not previously exist (Shane and Venkatarman, 2000).

Despite the proliferation of research, the population of women entrepreneurs is vastly understudied. This is surprising considering women are one of the fastest rising populations of entrepreneurs, and contribute significantly to innovation, job creation and economies around the world. Why are women entrepreneurs comparatively understudied? What have we learned about women entrepreneurs in the past few decades? What are future research directions? This chapter addresses these questions. We begin with a brief overview on the extent of research on women's entrepreneurship and consider reasons why they are under-studied. The next section explores empirical findings in terms of similarities and differences between men and women entrepreneurs, then we conclude with suggestions for future research.

23.2 Extent of research on women's entrepreneurship

The first notable article on women's entrepreneurship appeared in the mid-1970s. Eleanor Brantley Schwartz's (1976) pioneering article, 'Entrepreneurship, a New Female Frontier' included measures from Collins and Moore (1964) and compared these to the characteristics, motivations and attitudes of women. She found that similarly to men, women were motivated by the need to achieve, job satisfaction and independence. Schwartz (1976) was followed by, Hisrich and Brush (1983, 1984, 1985, 1986, 1987) who described characteristics of women entrepreneurs and their businesses and considered factors leading to success in the first and largest longitudinal study in the US. Their conclusion was that women were similar in motivations to men, but were less often business educated, faced barriers to capital access, and grew businesses more slowly than men. Watkins and Watkins (1983) examined biases against women in the UK finding different educational and work patterns. Holmquist and Sundin (1988) used Hisrich and Brush's survey in Sweden finding similarities in motives, but gender differences in business goals. Following these early works, the study of women's entrepreneurship gained momentum in the 1990s.

Several reviews considered the extent of research on women entrepreneurs. The earliest reviewed 57 academic articles and categorized these within an existing framework (Brush, 1992). This analysis concluded that even with the rising numbers of women entrepreneurs, academic studies were comparatively scarce. At the time, the majority of studies were descriptive, and focused primarily on characteristics of women entrepreneurs. A subsequent review by Baker et al. (1997) examining all management journals found that about 7 percent of articles published between 1969 and 1994 included or focused on women business owners. Brush and Edelman (2000) covered two years of journals and found 6 percent of articles studied women business owners. More recently, the Diana Project[2] reviewed the 7 main entrepreneurship journals for all years since their inception and found an average of 3.5 percent of all articles published included or focused on women entrepreneurs (Gatewood et al., 2003). Terjesen (2004) replicated Brush's 1992 study considering 108 articles coming to a similar conclusion. All of these reviews show that only a tiny proportion of articles focuses on, or includes women entrepreneurs. This is surprising considering the participation and contributions of women entrepreneurs.

23.3 Women's entrepreneurship: the phenomenon

In 1977, there were approximately 700,000 women-owned businesses in the US generating US$41.5 million in revenues ('The Bottom Line', 1978). According to the Bureau of Census, in 1972 only 4.6 percent of all US businesses were women-owned. However, those numbers soon began to increase. A Bureau of Labor report showed that the number of self-employed women increased from 1.5 million in 1972 to 2.1 million in 1979 and climbed to 3.5 million in 1984 (Hisrich and Brush, 1986).

From 1997 to 2002, women formed new businesses at twice the national rate (Center for Women's Business Research, 2002). As a result, women are recognized as a driving force in the US economy, whether measured by the number of

[2] The Diana Project is a multi-year, research programme focused on women business owners and entrepreneurs. Though it covers a wide range of topics, its primary emphasis is on financing and growth strategies for women-led enterprizes in the United States. Collaborators are Dr Candida Brush, Dr Nancy Carter, Dr Elizabeth Gatewood, Dr Patricia Greene and Dr Myra Hart.

businesses owned, the revenues generated, or the number of people employed. Of the privately-held majority-owned firms in the US, 10.6 million of the approximately 22 million firms in the US are 50 percent owned by women.[3] These women-owned firms contribute US$2.5 trillion in sales and employ 19.1 million employees (Center for Women's Business Research, 2005). Female entrepreneurs are increasingly prominent as employers, customers, suppliers, and competitors in the US and in the global community.

Other reports show women are important drivers of growth in many of the world's economies (Minniti, Arenius and Langowitz, 2005). Recent statistics from the Global Entrepreneurship Monitor (GEM) study estimate that women-owned businesses comprise 25–33 percent of all businesses in the formal economy, and a greater percentage in the informal sector. There is wide variation in women's participation as entrepreneurs depending on country income level, but, either way, there is significant interest in their contributions to jobs and revenues. Peru reflects the highest rate of total entrepreneurial activity (TEA) at 39 percent while Japan is the lowest at 1.2 percent. In Australia, women's participation in entrepreneurship is comparatively high at 33 percent and women's total entrepreneurial activity rate is increasing. In Denmark, women account for 30 percent of new enterprises that are established and 25 percent of all self-employed (Neergaard, 2006). In Finland, nearly 33 percent of all women are self-employed (Kovalainen and Arenius, 2006). In nearly all countries, women entrepreneurs are a significant presence in the world economy, the population is growing and they contribute to jobs and revenues. However, regardless of women's participation and contributions to economies, research has not kept pace.

23.4 Why are women entrepreneurs under-studied?

Considering that the phenomenon of women's entrepreneurship has grown significantly, why is there such a disparity in the contributions and participation of women entrepreneurs and the amount of research? There are three possible explanations:

[3] In 2000 the US Census Department changed the way that women-owned firms were classified to include two definitions. Of those firms 51% majority owned privately held firms, women comprised 6.7 million and of those 50% owned by women, 10.6 million were women-led. (Center for Women's Business Research 2005).

1 Women's entrepreneurship is a new phenomenon. As already noted, until the 1980s, men were the primary population of business owners and their ventures, big and small. In the US, growth in the population of women entrepreneurs occurred in the late 1980s shortly after the US government passed the Equal Credit Opportunity Act (1975) prohibiting banks from discriminating against women in lending. Prior to this, women often needed co-signers to obtain bank financing. The first comprehensive report on US women business owners, 'The Bottom Line' was published in 1978. The Women's Business Ownership Act was enacted in 1988, creating a commission to encourage women's economic development. These legislative and political factors were followed by significant programmes to encourage and support women's business development. At the same time, the OECD published a landmark book documenting women's entrepreneurship in developed countries (1992). A series of OECD conferences raised the awareness of women's entrepreneurship (Ducheneaut, 1997) and programmes for women entrepreneurs followed. In sum, the growth of women's entrepreneurship is most evident over the past 25 years.

2 The assumption that there are no differences between men and women entrepreneurs. Early research focused primarily on male entrepreneurs and developed general theory about entrepreneurial behaviour (Knight, 1921; Schumpeter, 1934; McClelland, 1961). Empirical research testing these theories focused almost exclusively on male populations. Some argued that studying women separately was not important to understanding entrepreneurship and that general theories of entrepreneurship should apply to all populations (Churchill and Hornaday, 1987). As a result, the study of entrepreneurship emerged with measures and theories developed primarily on men due to an assumption that general theory would guide behaviour (Hurley, 1991).

3 The study of women's entrepreneurship lacks legitimacy, institutional support and funding. This idea stems from two perspectives. First, there is a general stereotype that women entrepreneurs are less qualified, less capable and therefore less entrepreneurial (Brush et al., 2004). The notion that women are more likely to start 'hobby-type businesses' that are not fast growth oriented, creates the impression that they are less worth of study. Secondly, reward systems in colleges and universities typically favoured research on large firms, that were publicly traded and owned by men (Baker et al., 1997). At the same time, few foundations, research centres and institutions offered financial support for research on women-owned firms which were often smaller and service based, while journal editors and members of editorial review boards were comprised of an extremely small percentage of women researchers generally, and specifically those studying women's entrepreneurship (Hurley, 1991).

To some degree, all three of these explanations are true. It is true that academic research on women's entrepreneurship is comparatively new, and that large scale government sponsored studies including and analyzing businesses by sex were done only within the past 10 years (Boden and Nucci, 1997; Lin et al., 2000). Further, the assumption that all entrepreneurs were the same led to continued theoretical and methodological research that focused primarily on economic dimensions (e.g. decision-making, labour, capital and pursuit of profit (Kirzner, 1985; Baumol, 1993) with less attention to social and cultural dimensions (Hurley, 1998; Ahl 2004). Finally, there is some evidence that women are more likely to be present in service and retailing, even though the past decade shows dramatic increases of women founding and growing technology-based firms (Center for Women's Business Research, 2002; Brush et al., 2004). However, these explanations for the scarcity of study do not necessarily justify a continued lack of research on this sizeable and growing population. Even though there is a comparative paucity of studies, the research to date does provide some important findings.

23.5 What have we learned about women entrepreneurs from academic research?

23.5.1 Evolution of theory, methods and samples

It is argued that research about women's entrepreneurship can be divided into two distinct eras: the 1980s where gender was considered a variable; and the 1990s where gender was used as a lens (Brush, Greene and Gatewood, 2006). Early research sought to answer two questions: *Who is the woman entrepreneur?* and *Do theory / measures developed on men apply to women?* Research considered several units of analysis—women founders, their teams, their ventures and their communities. At the individual level, studies focused on demographic information identifying characteristics of women entrepreneurs, their personal goals, as well as their reasons for selecting business ownership over wage and salary work (Hagan et al., 1989; Brush, 1992). Theories used were often rooted in psychology (Sexton and Bowman, 1986) or sociology (Aldrich, 1989), samples were frequently small and convenient (Brush, 1992), and the most popular method was survey. For the most part, sampling, methods and theories paralleled research in entrepreneurship generally (Sexton and Kasarda, 1992). Instead of direct tests of theory, gender (sex) was used as a sampling or analytical variable only.

By the 1990s, general research in entrepreneurship gained popular attention with broad political/economic changes, increased availability of equity funding and vast demands for entrepreneurship education (Hart, 2003; Bhide, 2000; Mason and Harrison, 1999; Brush et al., 2003). Research on women increased and became more rigorous. Studies attempted to answer three basic questions: *What influences women's choices for entrepreneurship?, What affects growth and development of women-owned businesses?* and *What is the effect of country context on women's entrepreneurship?* Similarly to the 1980s, research continued to focus on the entrepreneur, but more attention to the business venture, management practices and community aspects were apparent. A greater emphasis on theory testing emerged, where researchers drew from human capital, social network, resource-based view, labour economics, career, finance, economic geography, sociology, cognitive psychology and a host of others. More rigorous attention to sample selection, control variables and statistical analysis is present. Application and development of feminist theory suggested gender is a lens with which to examine venture creation and entrepreneurship (Bird and Brush, 2002; Ahl, 2004; Greer and Greene, 2004).

Importantly, large scale federal studies emerged. For instance, Dolinsky et al. (1993) and Dolinsky and Caputo (1994) used longitudinal census data from the National Longitudinal Survey of Labor Market Experience to discover the importance of self-employment to social and economic mobility. They focused on specific effects of entrepreneurship on the improvement of the status of less-educated and economically-disadvantaged individuals. The flow of people in and out of self-employment was also studied using the Revenue Canada Longitudinal data from Survey of Labor and Income Dynamics (Lin et al., 2000), while research about youth self-employment in the US and Australia utilized the National Survey of Income and Program Participation (Blanchflower and Meyer, 1992). Finally, the Panel Study of Entrepreneurial Dynamics (PSED), a national household study of nascent entrepreneurs, examined start-up behaviours (Gartner et al., 2004). This research was replicated in a number of countries (Delmar and Shane, 1994).

Throughout the history of this research, a central question has to do with similarities and differences between men and women entrepreneurs, and their ventures. The next two sections will highlight the major areas of similarity and difference.

23.5.2 Similarities

Research comparing men and women entrepreneurs finds similarities in three main categories: demographics, motivations and business practices.

Demographics. Comparisons of men and women based on demographic variables show that age, education and birth order are often the same (Hisrich and Brush, 1984). Evans and Leighton (1989) using the Current Population survey found similarities by age and motivators for self-employment (1989). International studies in Sweden and Ireland reflected the same conclusions (Klofsten and Jones-Evans, 2000). Dolinsky et al. (1993) and Dolinsky and Caputo (1994) used longitudinal census data from the National Longitudinal Survey of Labor Market Experience to discover the importance of self-employment to social and economic mobility. They found racial differences in education and economics were more prevalent than gender differences. Capital stocks and flows were also studied using the Panel Study of Income Dynamics (PSID). The data revealed that the presence of a self-employed husband enabled intra-family flows of financial and human capital and encouraged females to become self-employed (Bruce, 1999). Another analysis using PSID data showed that the number of men and women making the transition to self-employment was almost equal but that men were more likely to move upward in earnings distribution (Holtz-Eakin et al., 2000).

Motivations. The earliest studies examining reasons why women choose entrepreneurship found that independence, achievement and personal satisfaction were typical motives, similar to those of males (Hisrich and Brush, 1984). In Norway, women had the same motivations as men (Ljunggren and Kolvereid, 1996), while in Pakistan, women desired freedom, security and satisfaction, similarly to their male counterparts (Shabbir and Di Gregorio, 1996).

Business practices. Several studies examined problems of women entrepreneurs and found that many challenges were similar to those that all entrepreneurs encountered in the process of growing a venture (Pellegrino and Reece, 1982; Hisrich and Brush, 1986). A Canadian study analyzed the effects of personal characteristics, industry, and organizational structure on survival and found women-owned businesses were no less likely to survive than their male counterparts (Kalleberg and Leicht, 1991). Later work shows that men and women business owners of larger and established businesses are quite similar in terms of personal and business structure characteristics (Swift and Riding, 1998; McKechnie et al., 1998).

23.5.3 Differences

Major differences between men and women entrepreneurs are found in representation in the business sector, entrepreneurial process, and access to resources, especially growth capital.

Business sector. 'The Bottom Line' (1978), and work by Hisrich and Brush (1984) showed most US women were clustered in service and retail sectors. Early in the UK and Italy, studies found women were more likely to start ventures in traditional sectors (Watkins and Watkins, 1983; Aldrich et al., 1989; Rosa and Hamilton, 1994). One study argued women had lower self-efficacy in non-traditional sectors which explained their choice of industry selection (Anna et al., 2000). Relatedly, in an Australian study, Barrett found men were more likely to choose a business with a female 'image' than women choosing businesses with a male 'image'. The choice of business sector is arguably strategic, and Carter et al. (1997) found that women-owned firms were at higher risk of discontinuing because of their prevalence in highly competitive retail and service sectors. Business positioning in less profitable industries was studied by several scholars, who concluded that choice of sector resulted in lower sales, profits and inability to secure government contracts (Loscocco and Robinson, 1991; Loscocco et al., 1991).

Entrepreneurial process. Boden (1996) used the Characteristics of Business Owners (CBO) to show that gender inequality in wage and salary earnings may positively influence some women's decision to leave wage employment for self-employment. Boden and Nucci (1997) used both the CPS and the CPO for 1982–1987 to compare sex, age, education, marital status, percent income from self-employment, industry, and region. Gender was found to be a major explanatory variable for differing rates of self-employment (Boden and Nucci, 1997). And finally, Boden and Nucci (2000) used census data to examine the relationship between owner and business characteristics and business survival for the years 1982 and 1987. When considering only sole proprietorships in retail and service industries, survival rates were affected by owner experience for both males and females, but the survival rate for male-owned businesses was higher by six percent. The authors concluded that women were disadvantaged in terms of previous managerial experiences and wage opportunities and, therefore, had less human and financial capital for business ownership. Studies about business strategies found women were more likely to emphasize product/service quality rather than customization and cost efficiency (Chaganti and Parasuraman, 1996). Relatedly, they tend to adopt more flexible and conservative start-up strategies than their than men (Verheul and Thurik, 2001). Cliff (1998) studied personal and economic considerations of Canadian female and male entrepreneurs. She found women were more likely to establish maximum sizes that were smaller than their male counterparts, even though they were just as likely to desire growth, they had more concerns with risk and therefore adopted a slower and steadier growth rate.

Research on social roles and support finds that role models, self-assurance and marriage were positively related to supply of women entrepreneurs (Schiller and Crewson, 1997). On the other hand, men receive more social support from their spouses than women do (Birley et al., 1986; Biggart, 1988; Baines and Wheelock, 1998).

Access to resources. Initial start-up resources were considered by several authors. One study showed men used more debt but concluded that this was due to women being more risk-averse (Sherr et al., 1993). Research into Dutch entrepreneurs reported that women founded ventures with smaller amounts of capital, but there were no differences in the proportion of debt to equity (Verheul and Thurik, 2001). A later study found women and men did not differ in choice of debt or equity financing (Chaganti et al. 1995) but other work from the UK shows men use larger amounts of capital at start-up (Carter and Rosa, 1998). While women and men do not differ in choice of debt, Coleman (2000) using bank data found that lenders did discriminate on the basis of firm size, preferring to lend to larger and more established firms rather than smaller, and often female-owned firms. She also found women were often charged higher interest rates and had higher collateral requirements.

Several studies examine women's access to capital. During the 1980s research showed obtaining start-up capital (bank loans, informal loans) were challenges (Hisrich and Brush, 1986). Studies examining gender stereotypes found lenders did not perceive women as possessing characteristics necessary for successful entrepreneurship (Buttner and Rosen, 1988). Several studies show women are less likely to receive capital from individual investors and are less likely to use commercial credit (Carter and Rosa, 1998).

Social networks are argued to be central to resource acquisition (Aldrich, 1999). Studies show there are variations in men's and women's networks, where women have more women in their networks and men have more mixed networks (Aldrich et al., 1989). Another large data set, the General Social Survey, was used to analyze differences in human and social capital of women business owners (Greene and Johnson, 1995) as well as the incidence of social networking and the differences in the level of networking between women entrepreneurs, male entrepreneurs, and female salaried managers (Katz and Williams, 1997). This study allowed for a secondary analysis of weak-tie network linkage in formal organizations and concluded that entrepreneurs' weak-tie network efforts are lower than those of managers, and that female entrepreneurs engage in less weak-tie networking than salaried male managers (Katz and Williams, 1997).

Growth aspirations were studied by several researchers. Carter and Allen (1997) explored whether women-led businesses were smaller due to the owner's lifestyle intentions and choices, or due to the level of resources controlled. They found strong evidence that access to resources had stronger effects on growth than did intention or choice. A study of African and Latin American ventures shows that male-run enterprises were much more likely to grow than female-owned firms, even after controlling for effects of other variables (Liedholm, 2002). Finally, The

Diana Project studied women's access to equity capital in the US. From 30 years of data on investments by venture capitalists in US businesses, they found that women received only 4.1 percent of all investments (Greene, Brush, Hart and Saparito, 2001).

Overall, these differences raise important questions for which there is no single answer, although they do suggest future research directions and implications.

23.6 Conclusions and Implications

This analysis suggests that key differences between men and women entrepreneurs fall into three areas: representation in the business sector, entrepreneurial process, and access to resources—especially growth capital. There are two major explanations for these differences. First, liberal feminism would argue that social structures such as occupational segregation limit women's ability to gain experience in certain sectors (Fischer et al., 1993; Carter and Williams, 2004; Greer and Greene, 2004). This suggests that the uneven participation of women in traditional male-dominated and often high-technology sectors is due to structural factors in the economy that prevent women from gaining experience, access to markets, or resources. For example, emerging work in transition economies finds women comprised significant portions of the illiterate society, thereby limiting their ability to become self-employed (Welter and Smallbone, 2005). This extends to the glass ceiling where women are often denied the chance to gain high level managerial decision-making experience which could be beneficial in an entrepreneurial start-up. Organizational hierarchies are frequently male-dominated limiting the chance for women to gain this experience (Brush et al., 2004). These limitations also can influence their ability to assemble start-up resources, in that they often come from lower-paying jobs (Verheul and Thurik, 2001). Similarly, women are left out of certain networks, especially financial. Research by the Diana Project found less than 10 percent of all people in the venture capital industry were female, and that during the burst of venture capital financing, 1995–2000, their numbers did not increase accordingly (Brush et al, 2004). Since most would argue that venture capital financing is based on connections and networks, the lack of women in the networks could be viewed as a structural barrier.

Alternatively, social feminism would argue socialization of women creates different perspectives, goals and choices for women. Instead of being denied opportunities in certain sectors, they instead choose to move into retail and/or services where they have stronger self-confidence, and the businesses may be more in keeping with their social values. This choice to pursue businesses in traditionally female service sectors also limits start-up resources and perspectives on future growth. Studies of social roles and social learning support this view. For example, women's levels of self-efficacy and expectations were lower, showing less preference for entrepreneurship (Matthews and Moser, 1996). Relatedly, research in sociology shows the relationship between family and work is stronger for women finding examples of women integrating more compassion and support into their ventures (Holliday and Letherby, 1993). At the same time, it is arguable that aspirations for growth are personal, and that women may choose to keep their ventures small and manageable in order to care for families (Brush et al., 2004).

Because research on women's entrepreneurship is so sparse, it is not possible to draw significant conclusions as to whether a theory of female entrepreneurship is needed, or whether gender should be introduced into current theory. Instead, there is a need to abandon the assumption that men and women entrepreneurs are the same in all respects, and instead, explore where theory applies and where it does not. In other words, general theory needs to be tested to see if it applies on populations and samples of women entrepreneurs.

The two perspectives, liberal and social feminism, suggest future directions for research. Most theories of entrepreneurship (venture creation, self-employment, performance of new ventures) assume that differences among entrepreneurs will be based on factors such as confidence, reputation, and cognitive ability. But, it is not expected that variation could be systematically gendered. While the theoretical explanations from feminist literature above suggest that indeed there might be systematic variations by sex, no formal testing has been done. Future research might address the following questions:

- Do structural factors such as inheritance laws differentially affect male and females, thereby influencing the amount of start-up resources they bring to an entrepreneurial venture?
- Do occupational structures and mobility differentially affect males and females, thereby influencing the experience base with which they start entrepreneurial ventures?
- Does variation in social networks of male and female entrepreneurs influence ability to acquire resources for venture start-up and growth?
- What is the influence of self-confidence on the likelihood of male and female entrepreneurial start-up and growth?
- Do men and women perceive opportunities in the same way, and what, if any, variations are their in implementation of venture creation?

In sum, women's entrepreneurship is a significant and growing phenomenon worldwide, yet research has not kept pace. In many countries, women comprise one-third of the population of entrepreneurs, but we know little about them. By including this population in our research, we will effectively know more about entrepreneurship in general.

References

Acs, Z. and D. B. Audretsch (1993). 'Innovation and Technological Change: The new Learning', in G. D. Libecap (ed.) *Advances in the Study of Entrepreneurship, Innovation and Economic Growth.* Greenwich, CT: JAI Press, 109–42.

Ahl, H. (2004). *The Scientific Reproduction of Gender Inequality: A Discourse Analysis of Research Texts on Women's Entrepreneurship.* Liber: Copenhagen Business School Press.

Aldrich, H. (1989). 'Networking Among Women Entrepreneurs', in O. Hagan, C. Rivchun, and D. Sexton (eds) *Women-owned businesses*, pp. 103–32. New York: Praeger.

—— (1999). *Organizations Evolving.* Thousand Oaks, CA: Sage Publications.

—— P. R. Reese, P. Dubini, et al. (1989). 'Women on the Verge of a Breakthrough? Networking among entrepreneurs in the United States and Italy', in R. H. Brockhaus, Sr., N. C. Churchill, J. A. Katz, et al. (eds) *Frontiers of Entrepreneurial Research*, pp. 560–74. Boston, MA: Babson College.

Anna, A. L., G. N. Chandler, E. Jansen and N. P. Mero (2000). 'Women Business Owners in traditional and Non-traditional Industries'. *Journal of Business Venturing*, 15(3): 279–303.

Baines, S. and J. Wheelock (1998). 'Working for each other: Gender, the household, and micro-business survival and growth'. *International Small Business Journal*, 17(1): 16–36.

Baker, T., H. E. Aldrich and N. Liou (1997). 'Invisible Entrepreneurs: The neglect of women business owners by mass media and scholarly journals in the U.S.A.'. *Entrepreneurship and Regional Development*, 9: 221–38.

Barrett, M. (1995). 'Feminist Perspectives on Learning for Entrepreneurship: The view from small business', in W. D. Bygrave, B. J, Bird, S. Birley et al. (eds) *Frontiers of Entrepreneurship Research.* Boston, MA: Babson College.

Baumol, W. (1993). 'Formal Entrepreneurship Theory in Economics: Existence and bounds'. *Journal of Business Venturing*, 8(3): 197–210.

Bhide, A. (2000). *The Origin and Evolution of New Businesses.* New York: Oxford University Press.

Biggart, N. (1988). *Charismatic Capitalism.* Chicago: University of Chicago Press.

Bird, B. J. and C. G. Brush (2002). 'A Gendered Perspective on Organizational Creation'. *Entrepreneurship Theory and Practice*, 26(3): 41–65.

Birley, S., C. Moss and P. Saunders (1986). 'Do Women Entrepreneurs Require Different Training?' *American Journal of Small Business*, 12(1): 27–35.

Blanchflower, D. and B. Meyer (1992). 'A Longitudinal Analysis of the Young Self-Employed in Australia and the United States'. *Small Business Economics*, 6(1): 1–20.

Boden, R. J. (1996). 'Gender and Self-employment Selection: An empirical assessment'. *Journal of Socio-Economics*, 25(6): 671–82.

—— (1999a). 'Gender Inequality in Wage Earnings and Female Self-employment Selection'. *Journal of Socio-Economics*, 28(3): 351–64.

—— (1999b). 'Flexible Working Hours, Family Responsibilities, and Female Self-employment: Gender differences in self-employment selection'. *American Journal of Economics and Sociology*, 58(1): 71–84.

—— and A. R. Nucci (1997). 'Counting the Self-employed Using Household and Business Sample Data'. *Small Business Economics*, 9(5): 427–36.

—— and —— (2000). 'On the survival prospects of men's and women's new business ventures'. *Journal of Business Venturing*, 15(4): 347–62.

BRUCE, D. (1999). 'Do Husbands Matter? Married women entering self-employment'. *Small Business Economics*, 13(4): 317–29.

BRUSH, C. G. (1990). 'Women and Enterprise Creation: Barriers and opportunities', in S. Gould and J. Parzen (eds) *Enterprising Women: Local Initiatives for Job Creation*. Paris: OECD, pp. 37–58.

—— (1992). 'Research on Women Business Owners: Past trends, a new perspective and future directions'. *Entrepreneurship Theory and Practice*, 16(4): 5–30.

—— (1997). 'Women-owned Businesses: Obstacles and opportunities'. *Journal of Developmental Entrepreneurship*, 2(1): 1–24.

—— and L. EDELMAN (2000). 'Women Entrepreneurs Opportunities for Database Research', in J. Katz (ed.) *Databases for the Study of Entrepreneurship*. New York: JAI.

—— and R. D. HISRICH (1991). 'Antecedent Influences on Women-owned Businesses'. *Journal of Managerial Psychology*, 6(2): 9–16.

—— I. DUHAIME, W. GARTNER et al. (2003). 'Task Force Report on Doctoral Education in Entrepreneurship'. *Journal of Management*, 29(3): 309–31.

—— CARTER, N., GATEWOOD, E. et al. (2004). *Clearing the Hurdles: Women Building High Growth Businesses*. New York: Prentice Hall Financial Times.

—— and P. G. GREENE and E. J. GATEWOOD (2006). 'Perspectives on Women Entrepreneurs: Past findings and new directions', in M. Minniti (ed.) *Praeger Perspectives Series: The Entrepreneurial Process*, vol. 1. Westport, CA: Praeger Publishing.

BUCAR, B. and R. D. HISRICH (2001). 'Ethics of Business Managers vs. Entrepreneurs'. *Journal of Developmental Entrepreneurship*, 6(1): 59–82.

BUTTNER, E. H. (1993). 'Female Entrepreneurs: How far have they come?'. *Business Horizons*, 36(2): 59–65.

—— (2001). 'Examining Female Entrepreneurs' Management Style: An application of a relational frame'. *Journal of Business Ethics*, 29(3): 253–70.

—— and B. ROSEN (1988). 'Bank Loan Officers' Perceptions of Characteristics of Men, Women and Successful Entrepreneurs'. *Journal of Business Venturing*, 3(3): 249–58.

—— and B. ROSEN (1989). 'Funding New Business Ventures: Are decision makers biased against women entrepreneurs?' *Journal of Business Venturing*, 4(4): 249–61.

CARTER, N. M. and K. R. ALLEN (1997). 'Size-determinants of Women-owned Businesses: Choice or barriers to resources'. *Entrepreneurship and Regional Development*, 9(3): 211–20.

—— and M. WILLIAMS (2004). 'Comparing Social Feminism and Liberal Feminism', in J. Butler (ed.) *New Perspectives on Women Entrepreneurs*. Greenwich, CT: Information Age Publishing.

—— —— and P. D. REYNOLDS (1997). 'Discontinuance Among New Firms in Retail: The influence of initial resources, strategy and gender'. *Journal of Business Venturing*, 12(2): 125–45.

CARTER, S. and P. ROSA (1998). 'The Financing of Male and Female Owned-business'. *Entrepreneurship and Regional Development*, 10(3): 225–41.

Center for Women's Business Research (2002). *New Analysis Documents Employment and Revenue Distribution of Women-Owned Firms in 2002* (August 27). Available at www.womensbusinessresearch.org.

—— (2005). *Key Facts About Women-Owned Businesses* (August) Available at www.womensbusinessresearch.org.

CHAGANTI, R. (1986). 'Management in Women-owned Enterprises'. *Journal of Small Business Management*, 24(4): 18–29.

CHAGANTI, R., D. DECAROLIS and D. DEEDS (1995). 'Predictors of Capital Structure in Small Ventures'. *Entrepreneurship Theory and Practice*, 20(2): 7–18.

—— and S. PARASURAMAN (1996). 'A Study of the Impact of Gender on Business Performance and Management Patterns in Small Businesses'. *Entrepreneurship Theory and Practice*, 21(2): 73–5.

CHURCHILL, N. and J. HORNADAY (1987). 'Current Trends in Entrepreneurial Research', in N. Churchill, J. Hornaday, B. Kirchhoff et al. (eds) *Frontiers of Entrepreneurship Research*, pp. 1–22. Babson Park: Babson College.

CLIFF, J. E. (1998). 'Does One Size Fit All? Exploring the relationship between attitudes towards growth, gender, and business size'. *Journal of Business Venturing*, 13(6): 523–42.

COLEMAN, S. (2000). 'Access to Capital and Terms of Credit: A comparison of men- and women-owned small businesses'. *Journal of Small Business Management*, 38(3): 37–52.

COLLINS, O. F. and D. G. MOORE (1964). *The Enterprising Man*. East Lansing: Bureau of Business and Economic Research, Graduate School of Business Administration, Michigan State University.

DELMAR, F. and S. SHANE (2004). 'Legitimizing First: Organizing activities and the survival of new ventures'. *Journal of Business Venturing*, 19: 385–410.

DOLINSKY, A. L., R. K. CAPUTO, K. PASUMARTY and H. QUAZI (1993). 'The Effects of Education on Business Ownership: A longitudinal study of women'. *Entrepreneurship Theory and Practice*, 18(1): 43–53.

—— and R. K. CAPUTO (1994). 'Long-term Entrepreneurship Patterns: A national study of black and white female entry and stayer status differences'. *Journal of Small Business Management*, 32(1): 18–26.

DUCHENEAUT, B. (1997). *Women Entrepreneurs in SME's: A Report Prepared for the OECD Conference on Women Entrepreneurs in Small and Medium Enterprises: A Major Force for Innovation and Job Creation*. Paris: OECD.

EVANS, E. and L. LEIGHTON (1989). 'The Determinants of Changes in U.S. Self-employment, 1968–1987'. *Small Business Economics*: 1: 111–19.

FISCHER, E. M., A. R. REUBER and L. S. DYKE (1993). 'A Theoretical Overview and Extension of Research on Sex, Gender, and Entrepreneurship'. *Journal of Business Venturing*, 8(2): 151–68.

GADENNE, D. (1998). 'Critical Success Factors for Small Business: An inter-industry comparison'. *International Small Business Journal*, 17(1): 36–57.

GARTNER, W., K. SHAVER, N. CARTER and P. REYNOLDS (eds) (2004). *The Handbook of Entrepreneurial Dynamics: The Process of Organization Creation*. Newbury Park, CA: Sage Series.

GATEWOOD, E. J., K. G. SHAVER and W. B. GARTNER (1995). 'A Longitudinal Study of Cognitive Factors Influencing Start-up Behaviors and Success at Venture Creation'. *Journal of Business Venturing*, 10(5): 371–91.

—— N. M. CARTER, C. G. BRUSH et al. (2003). *Women Entrepreneurs, Their Ventures, and the Venture Capital Industry: An Annotated Bibliography*. Stockholm: ESBRI.

GREENE, P. G. and M. JOHNSON (1995). 'Middleman Minority Theory. A theoretical consideration of self-employed women'. *The National Journal of Sociology*, 9(1): 59–84.

—— C. G. BRUSH, M. M. HART and P. SAPARITO (2001). 'Patterns of Venture Capital Funding: Is gender a factor?' *Venture Capital: An International Journal of Entrepreneurial Finance*, 3(1): 63–83.

Greer, M. A. and P. G. Greene, (2004). 'Feminist Theory and the Study of Entrepreneurship', in J. E. Butler (ed.) *New Perspectives on Women Entrepreneurs.* London. Information Age Publishing.

Hagan, O., C. Rivchun and D. Sexton (eds) (1989). *Women-Owned Businesses.* New York: Praeger Publishing.

Hart, D. (2003). *The Emergence of Entrepreneurship Policy.* Cambridge: Cambridge University Press.

Hebert, R. F. and A. N. Link (1982). *The Entrepreneur: Mainstream Views and Radical Critiques.* New York: Praeger Publishing.

Hisrich, R. D. and C. Brush (1983). 'The Woman Entrepreneur: Implications of family educational, and occupational experience', in J. A. Hornaday, J. A. Timmons and K. H. Vesper (eds) *Frontiers of Entrepreneurial Research,* pp. 255–70. Boston, MA: Babson College.

—— and —— (1984). 'The Woman Entrepreneur: Management skills and business problems'. *Journal of Small Business Management,* 22(1): 30–7.

—— and —— (1985). 'Women and Minority Entrepreneurs: A comparative analysis', in J. A. Hornaday, E. B. Shils, J. A. Timmons and K. H. Vesper (eds) *Frontiers of Entrepreneurial Research. Boston, MA: Babson College.*

—— and —— (1986). *The Woman Entrepreneur: Starting, Managing, and Financing a Successful New Business.* Lexington, MA: Lexington Books.

—— and —— (1987). 'Women Entrepreneurs: A longitudinal study', in N. N. Churchill, J. A. Hornaday, B. A. Kirchhoff, et al. (eds) *Frontiers of Entrepreneurial Research.* Boston, MA: Babson College.

Holliday, R. and G. Letherby (1993). 'Happy Families or Poor Relations? An exploration of familial analogies in the small firm'. *International Small Business Journal,* 11:(2): 54–63.

Holmquist, C. and E. Sundin (1988). 'Women as Entrepreneurs in Sweden: Conclusions from a survey'. *Frontiers of Entrepreneurship Research,* pp. 626–42.

—— and E. Sundin (1990). 'What's Special about Highly Educated Women Entrepreneurs?' *Entrepreneurship and Regional Development,* 2: 181–93.

Holtz-Eakin, D., H. S. Rosen and R. Weathers (2000). 'Horatio Alger Meets the Mobility Tables'. *Small Business Economics,* 14(4): 243–74.

Hurley, A. E. (1991). 'Incorporating Feminist Theories into Sociological Theories of Entrepreneurship.' Paper presented at the Annual Meetings of the Academy of Management, Miami, FL, August.

—— (1998). 'Incorporating Feminist Theories into Sociological Theories of Entrepreneurship'. *Women in Management Review,* ISSN: 0964–9425, (March 1999), 14(2): 54–62.

Kalleberg, A. L. and K. T. Leicht (1991). 'Gender and Organizational Performance: Determinants of small business survival and success'. *Academy of Management Journal,* 34(1): 136–161.

Katz, J. A. and P. M. Williams (1997). 'Gender, Self Employment and Weak-tie Networking Through Formal Organizations—A secondary analysis approach'. *Entrepreneurship and Regional Development,* 9(3): 183–97.

Kirzner, I. (1985). *Discovery and the Capitalist Process.* Chicago: University of Chicago Press.

Klofsten, M. and D. Jones-Evans (2000). 'Comparing Academic Entrepreneurship in Europe: The case of Sweden and Ireland'. *Small Business Economics,* 14(4): 299–309.

Knight, F. (1921). *Risk, Uncertainty and Profits.* New York: Houghton Mifflin.

KOLVALAINEN, A. and P. ARENIUS (2006). Country Report on Finland, in C. Brush, N. Carter, E. Gatewood et al. (eds) *The Diana Project International: Growth Oriented Women Entrepreneurs and their Businesses: A Global Research Perspective (New Horizons in Entrepreneurship).* London: Elgar.

LIEBENSTEIN, H. (1968). 'Entrepreneurship and Development'. *American Economic Review* (May) 58.

LIEDHOLM, C. (2002). 'Small Firm Dynamics: Evidence from Africa and Latin America'. *Small Business Economics,* 18(1–3): 227–42.

LIN, Z., G. PICOT and J. COMPTON (2000). 'The Entry and Exit Dynamics of Self-employment in Canada'. *Small Business Economics,* 15(2): 105–25.

LJUNGGREN, E. and L. KOLVEREID (1996). 'New Business Formation: Does gender make a difference?' *Women in Management Review,* 11(4): 3–12.

LOSCOCCO, K. A. and J. ROBINSON (1991). 'Barriers to Women's Small-business Success in the United States'. *Gender & Society,* 5: 511–32.

—— —— R. H. HALL and J. K. ALLEN (1991). 'Gender and Small Business Success: An inquiry into women's relative disadvantage'. *Social Forces,* 70(1): 65–85.

LOW, M. and I. MACMILLAN (1988). 'Entrepreneurship: Past research and future challenges'. *Journal of Management,* 14(2): 139–61.

MASON, C. and R. HARRISON (1999). 'Venture Capital: Rationale, Aims and Scope'. *Venture Capital,* 1(1): 1–46.

MASTERS, R. and R. MEIER (1988). 'Sex Differences and Risk-taking Propensity of Entrepreneurs'. *Journal of Small Business Management,* 26(1): 31–5.

MATHEWS, C. H. and S. B. MOSER (1996). 'A Longitudinal Investigation of the Impact of Family Background and Gender on Interest in Small Firm Ownership'. *Journal of Small Business Management,* 34(2): 29–43.

MCCLELLAND, D. (1961). *The Achieving Society.* New York: The Free Press.

MCKECHNIE, S. A., C. T. ENNEW and L. H. READ (1998). 'The Nature of the Banking Relationship: A comparison of the experiences of male and female small business owners'. *International Small Business Journal* (April–June) 16(3): 39–55.

MINNITI, M., P. ARENIUS and N. LANGOWITZ (2005). *Global Entrepreneurship Monitor: 2004 Report on Women and Entrepreneurship.* Babson Park, MA London: Babson College London Business School.

NEERGAARD, H. (2006). Country Report on Denmark, in C. Brush, N. Carter, E. Gatewood et al. (eds) *The Diana Project International: Growth Oriented Women Entrepreneurs and their Businesses: A Global Research Perspective (New Horizons in Entrepreneurship).* London: Elgar.

PELLEGRINO, E. T. and B. L. REECE (1982). 'Perceived Formative and Operational Problems Encountered by Female Entrepreneurs in Retail and Service Firms'. *Journal of Small Business Management,* 20(2): 15–25.

REYNOLDS, P. D., M. HAY, W. BYGRAVE et al. (2000). Global Entrepreneurship Monitor, Executive Report, Kauffman Center for Entrepreneurial Leadership.

RIDING, A. L. and C. S. SWIFT (1990). 'Women Business Owners and Terms of Dredit: Some empirical findings of the Canadian experience'. *Journal of Business Venturing,* 5(5): 327–40.

ROSA, P. and HAMILTON, D. (1994). 'Gender and Ownership in U.K. Small Firms'. *Entrepreneurship: Theory and Practice,* 18(3): 11–27.

ROSA, P., S. CARTER and D. HAMILTON (1996). 'Gender as a Determinant of Small Business Performance: Insights from a British study'. *Small Business Economics*, 8(4): 463–78.

SCHERR, F. C., T. F. SUGRUE and J. B. WARD (1993). 'Financing the Small Firm Start-up: Determinants of debt use'. *Journal of Small Business Finance*, 3(1): 17–36.

SCHILLER, B. R. and P. E. CREWSON (1997). 'Entrepreneurial Origins: A longitudinal inquiry'. *Economic Inquiry*, 35(3): 523–31.

SCHUMPETER, J. (1934). *The Theory of Economic Development*. Cambridge, MA: Harvard University Press.

SCHWARTZ, E. (1976). 'Entrepreneurship: A new female frontier'. *Journal of Contemporary Business*, 5(1): 47–76.

SEXTON, D. L., and N. B. BOWMAN (1986). 'Validation of a Personality Index: Comparative psychological characteristics analysis of female entrepreneurs, managers, entrepreneurship students and business students', in R. Ronstadt, J. A. Hornaday, R. Peterson and K. H. Vesper (eds) *Frontiers of Entrepreneurship Research*, pp. 40–51. Boston, MA: Babson College.

—— and —— (1990). 'Female and Male Entrepreneurs: Psychological characteristics and their role in gender related discrimination'. *Journal of Business Venturing*, 5(1): 29–36.

—— and J. KASARDA (1992). *The State of the Art of Entrepreneurship*. Boston: PWS Kent.

SHABBIR, A. and DI GREGORIO, S. (1996). 'An Examination of the Relationship Between Women's Personal Goals and Structural Factors Influencing their Decisions to Start a Business: The case of Pakistan'. *Journal of Business Venturing*, 11(6): 507–29.

SHANE, S. and S. VENKATARAMAN (2000). 'The Promise of Entrepreneurship as a Field of Research'. *Academy of Management Review*, 25: 217–26.

SMITH, N. R., G. MCCAIN and A. WARREN (1982). 'Women Entrepreneurs Really are Different: A comparison of constructed ideal types of male and female entrepreneurs', in K. H. Vesper (ed.) *Frontiers of Entrepreneurship Research*. Boston, MA: Babson College.

STEVENSON, H. and J. JARILLO (1990). 'A Paradigm of Entrepreneurship: Entrepreneurial management'. *Strategic Management Journal* (Summer) 11: 17–27.

TERJESEN, S. (2004). 'Female Business Owners: A Review of the Last Decade of Research'. Presentation at the annual Academy of Management Meetings.

'The Bottom Line: Unequal Enterprise in America'. (1978). *Report of the President's Interagency Task Force on Women Business Owners*. Washington, DC: Government Printing Office.

U.S. Bureau of Census (2001). 'Women Owned Business'. 1997 Economic Census. U.S., Department of Commerce.

VERHEUL, I. and R. THURIK (2001). 'Start-up Capital: Does gender matter?' *Small Business Economics*, 16(4): 329–45.

WATKINS, J. M. and D. S. WATKINS (1983). 'The Female Entrepreneur: Her background and determinants of business choice: Some British data', in J. A. Hornaday, J. A. Timmons, and K. H. Vesper (eds.) *Frontiers of Entrepreneurship Research*. Boston, MA: Babson College.

WELTER, F., D. SMALLBONE and N. ISAKOVA (eds) April 2006. *Women in Transition Economies*. Ashgate Pub. Co.

ZAPALSKA, A. M. (1997). 'A Profile of Women Entrepreneurs and Enterprises in Poland'. *Journal of Small Business Management*, 35(4): 76–82.

CHAPTER 24

ENTERPRISE CULTURE

MARINA DELLA-GIUSTA AND ZELLA KING[1]

'I want this government to be the champion of entrepreneurs. We need society as a whole to applaud you - you are the front-line troops of Britain's new economy' (Blair, speaking to an audience of venture capitalists in 1999)

'Of course, we need to do more to create an enterprise culture, where people feel success is admired, new business ideas flourish and the entrepreneurial spirit more widely spread'. (Blair speaking to the CBI, 5 November 2001)

24.1 WHAT IS ENTERPRISE CULTURE?

Over the past decades the need to promote entrepreneurship through a revitalized 'enterprise culture' has become a central focus of policy-making in several European countries (HM Treasury, 2004). In this chapter, we examine the intentions

[1] We are very grateful for the comments of Mark Casson, David Storey and other colleagues at the Oxford Handbook of Entrepreneurship Authors' conferences, University of Reading, April 2005.

underlying attempts by governments to promote 'enterprise culture', and review the evidence for the success of such initiatives in the UK.

We begin our discussion by defining what we mean by enterprise culture. Both 'enterprise' and 'culture' have been the focus of much scholarly enquiry, and both terms are analytically vague, complex and multifaceted. In simple, neutral terms, the term 'culture' refers to a common set of values and beliefs shared by a social group. The group could be as small as a few people, or as large as a nation state. The term 'enterprise culture' can be considered to refer to values and beliefs shared by a social group that endorse, and are conducive to, entrepreneurial behaviour.

Efforts to promote an 'enterprise culture' have been adopted since the 1970s by several European governments in a response to economic volatility associated with global sources of competition, and are perhaps most commonly associated with Thatcher's Britain. The term 'enterprise culture' is often used to describe a perceived failing. For example, in a 1999 speech on Britain's 'enterprise culture', Tony Blair noted that historically both the Conservative elite and the traditional Labour Party in Britain 'showed a certain snobbery towards people who had an idea, developed it and went out and made money'. In this context, the United States is often mentioned as a laudable comparator, and in many public policy discussions it is simply assumed that somehow the US naturally has an entrepreneurial culture.

As a result, the term 'enterprise culture' has become associated with an ideological programme of reform intended to promote entrepreneurial values among citizens, businesses and in the welfare state (Heelas and Morris, 1992). As du Gay (1996: 56) defines it:

> an enterprise culture is one in which certain enterprising qualities—such as self-reliance, personal responsibility, boldness and a willingness to take risks in the pursuit of goals—are regarded as human virtues and promoted as such...

When using the term 'enterprise culture' in this chapter, we adopt a neutral stance, referring to a set of shared values that are conducive to entrepreneurial behaviour. The 'culture' (i.e. the shared values) of a given team, firm, community or nation state may or may not be conducive to entrepreneurial behaviour. We use the UK as a case study illustrating the unfolding of what we refer to as the 'enterprise culture project'—the set of policies initiated by Thatcher, and maintained by subsequent governments, that is intended to revitalize British entrepreneurial attitudes and behaviour.

In the remainder of the chapter, we first revisit the rationale for adopting an 'enterprise culture project', with specific reference to the case of Britain over the years from the 1980s to the present. We then consider how efforts to promote enterprise culture might be evaluated, and examine some of the evidence about the impact of enterprise policies in Britain on entrepreneurial attitudes and behaviour. We then review some of the academic literature on 'enterprise culture' policy and ideology, with a wider discussion of enterprise projects and their implications.

24.2 The 'enterprise project' as an attempt to promote enterprise culture in Britain

At this point it is important to make an analytical distinction between socio-political 'enterprise culture' projects and the neo-liberalist economic policies that they are often associated with. In the 1970s, Britain was in the grip of economic decline. As the 'golden' age of post-WWII productivity was coming to end, oil prices were rising and new sources of global competition were increasingly apparent, Western governments realized that something had to be done to address ailing productivity. In the wake of a visit from the International Monetary Fund (IMF) in 1976, neo-liberalist macro-economic stabilization policies were adopted by the Labour Government. The fiscal austerity agenda implemented by the government was not compatible with Britain's very rigid labour market, on which the unions held a tight grip. When the Conservative Government came to power in 1979, Margaret Thatcher introduced a range of policies intended to render the labour market more flexible by weakening the power of the unions and enhancing the rewards of work relative to unemployment (for more details, see Blanchflower and Freeman, 1994; and for details of industrial relations reform, Millward et al., 2002).

The 'enterprise project' can be seen as a set of policies initiated by the Thatcher government that are distinguishable from, although closely associated with, this wider macroeconomic policy context. Deflationary economic policy had the effect of creating a large reserve army of unemployed, which in turn risked engendering a culture of dependency on state support. To avoid this, the government pursued a series of initiatives intended to transform Britain's economy and education by encouraging the unemployed into self-employment and entrepreneurship.

Lord Young (formerly Chairman of the Manpower Services Commission and Secretary of State for Employment from 1985 to 1987) is the person most closely identified with promoting an enterprise culture in Britain (MacDonald and Coffield, 1991; see also Lord Young, 1992). Lord Young blamed the British lack of enterprise on four 'culprits': Britain's education system, which had no regard for industry or vocational skills, its financial system, which had little concern for small business, a protectionist industrial system and confrontational industrial relations. The following quote from Lord Young encapsulates the ideology of the Conservative Government of the 1980s:

> The problems of our economy have largely stemmed from a lack of enterprise. But don't pick on the managers in British industry today. At least, they made the choice to go into industry and commerce, they took on the challenge of producing goods and services and they are fighting to create wealth and jobs. The real culprits are bedded deep in our national history and culture. (Lord Young, 1986: 25; quoted in MacDonald and Coffield, 1991: 19)

Table 24.1 Enterprise culture initiatives introduced by the Thatcher government during the 1980s

Initiative	Intended purpose
Technical and Vocational Education Initiative (TVEI)	To enrich the curriculum to help 14- to 18-year-olds prepare for the world of work. Introduced in 1982.
Mini Enterprise in Schools Project (MESP)	To give schoolchildren the opportunity to run a small business. Every participating school given £40 grant and the option of a £50 loan. Introduced in 1985.
Enterprise in YTS	To develop an enterprise culture among young people. The Manpower Services Commission offered a range of enterprise training to young people on Youth Training Schemes (YTS). Launched in 1986.
Training for Enterprise Programme (TFE)	To equip potential and existing entrepreneurs with the skills and knowledge to launch, manage and develop a small business. Began in 1977 with 32 trainees and grew to over 115,000 in 1987–88
Enterprise Allowance Scheme (EAS)	To help unemployed people who wanted to work for themselves by paying them £40 a week in addition to what they earned from their business. Introduced in 1983 with 25,000 places and expanded rapidly to over 329,000 in 1988.
Enterprise and Education White Paper	To encourage employers to contribute to the development of the curriculum, the management of schools and the promotion of enterprise activities within schools. Government targets were set to (a) involve 10% of teachers in industrial placements (b) provide all secondary pupils with two or more weeks of work experience and (c) communicate employer needs to trainee teachers. White paper issued in 1988. An Enterprise Awareness in Teacher Education (EATE) project was launched in 1989.
Enterprise in Higher Education (EHE)	To assist higher education institutions to develop, in partnership with employers, competencies and aptitude relevant to enterprise in all graduates. Launched through the Training Agency in 1987.
Local Enterprise Agencies	To provide free, confidential business advice service for unemployed people. Private sector led. Over 400 by 1990.
Training and Enterprise Councils (TECs)	To develop training and enterprise in a given locality, as independent companies entering into a commercial contract with the Secretary of State for Employment.

Source: Adapted from MacDonald and Coffield (1991).

To tackle this perceived deficit of entrepreneurial attitudes, a wide range of programmes intended to promote enterprise culture by tackling education, training and employment was introduced in the 1980s. An extensive review of these schemes, courses, agencies and publications is offered in MacDonald and Coffield's

(1991) ethnographic study of enterprise culture policies and their impact on young people in Cleveland. These included the Enterprise in Education initiative, intended to promote enterprise values and employment involvement within the curriculum of schools, colleges and universities, the establishment of employer-led Training and Enterprise Councils (TECs) set up to develop and deliver training to young people, and the Enterprise Allowance Scheme (EAS), which offered unemployed people £40 per week to help them work for themselves.

Table 24.1 lists some of the initiatives that were introduced in England and Wales, although the list is by no means exhaustive. In reviewing this list of initiatives, MacDonald and Coffield concluded that:

> A brave new world of enterprise has been brought into being and its influence is spreading in so many different directions simultaneously that few people are likely to escape whether they are children in primary school, students in university, unemployed miners or redundant executives. (MacDonald and Coffield, 1991: 25)

Many of the initiatives listed in Table 24.1 were targeted at the unemployed, trainees and school and university students. The enterprise project, as it emerged in the 1980s, was also very much concerned with addressing a perceived malaise in work organizations, particularly small businesses. For example, the Private Enterprise Programme (part of Training For Enterprise) offered training for managers in existing businesses in an effort to make them more entrepreneurial and innovative. Over that period the perception that work organizations were ailing became apparent in both the US and Europe in response to new global sources of competition, particularly from Japan. Management consultants and 'gurus' such as Tom Peters and Rosabeth Moss Kanter argued that work organizations could become flexible and innovative through a focus on 'excellence' (Peters and Waterman, 1982; see also Ouchi, 1980; Kanter, 1989). 'Excellence' required restructuring, changes in work design and 'culture change' programmes that promoted enterprise values and 'intrapreneurship' by employees. Thus alongside harsh measures to curb union control, the perceived lack of enterprise was to be addressed by adopting new organizational forms that promoted and harnessed enterprising behaviour among the individuals within them, 'encouraging them to conduct themselves with boldness and vigour, to calculate for their own advantage, to drive themselves hard and to accept risk in the pursuit of goals' (Rose, 1992: 146).

Alongside the promotion of enterprise in education, training and employment, and the use of enterprise schemes to reduce unemployment and state dependency, a wider programme of reform espousing free market values, and the behaviour associated with them, was adopted in the late 1980s and 1990s by the Conservative Government. Swathes of state institutions were privatized, and the discipline and rigour of the market were imposed on national institutions that remained in government ownership, such as health and education. In hospitals, for example, the idea was that those running hospitals would not simply provide treatment, but would also be accountable for what it cost (Heelas and Morris, 1992). People who had been relying on state provision were encouraged to take a more active role, for example by buying their council house or investing in private pensions and health insurance.

Under Blair's New Labour Government, British enterprise policies are remarkably similar to those initiated by Thatcher (Dodd and Anderson, 2001; Curran, 2000), as regards both small business and entrepreneurship. New Labour's policies are characterized by a participatory ethos and a strong emphasis on choice and self-responsibility. This is illustrated by the eschewal of welfarism (as in 'Welfare to Work' or 'Helping people to help themselves') and a rebranding of benefits as targeted support, such as the 'working families' tax credits'. In addition, New Labour has presided over a proliferation of government agencies intended to promote enterprise, many of which are explicitly focused on making small businesses more enterprising (such as the Small Business Service or Business Link). Each of these agencies has its own logo and slogan, creating an impression of participation and modernization of government, although many continue to operate as they did when they were part of the same government ministries.

In 2003, the Small Business Service launched its 'Government Action Plan for Small Business' which is 'intended to make the UK the best place in the world to start and grow a business' (SBS, 2003b). It is based around seven themes which have been identified as 'key drivers of economic growth, improved productivity and enterprise for all' (for more details see Storey in Ch. 10 of this Handbook). One of these key drivers is 'building an enterprise culture', which in turn is suggested to lead to other key drivers 'more dynamic start-up markets' and 'building the capability for small business growth' (SBS, 2003b). The SBS notes that enterprise needs to be seen as a positive and worthwhile activity, advocating that Government can play a role in spreading information about enterprise activities, providing access to support, and providing opportunities for people to experience enterprise at key points in their lives. The SBS comments:

> What would an enterprise culture look like? The government's vision is of a nation in which all sections of society are better equipped to respond positively to change and new opportunities, to create and implement new ideas and ways of working, and make reasonable assessments of risks and rewards and act upon them. The spread of these skills will enable all to manage a flexible career, and help create a business environment supportive to becoming involved in enterprise. (SBS, 2003b: 14)

In late 2004, an implementation review (SBS, 2004) noted some of the initiatives intended to promote an enterprise culture, and these are listed in Table 24.2. These include some long-running programmes, such as Young Enterprise (a charity that runs enterprise and education programmes) and Shell LiveWire (a programme to help 16–30-year-olds set up their own business), as well as a number of new ideas such as the Queen's Award for Enterprise Promotion. Elsewhere in government, there are numerous other initiatives to promote enterprise in schools, colleges, universities, and the NHS as well as industry.

Table 24.2 Enterprise culture initiatives introduced by the Blair government during the 2000s

Initiative	Intended purpose
Enterprise Insight	To help develop a culture of enterprise in the UK by running a national campaign promoting the spirit of enterprise to young people and those who influence them. Ei's Board is made up of the Chief Executives of the UK's main business representative organisations, and membership includes the UK's main delivery organisations for enterprise education, training, mentoring and support. Initiatives to date include a discussion paper (Ei/SBS/DTI, 2004), a website aimed at young people www.starttalkingideas and 'Enterprise Week' in 2004.
Shell Livewire	To help 16–30-year-olds start and develop their own business, and to promote awareness of enterprise among young people and those who work with them. A long-running programme, initiated by Shell UK plc in 1982 and now supported by the Small Business Service. Recent innovations include a national awards competition where entrants can win over £10,000 and the title "Shell LiveWIRE Young Entrepreneur Of The Year', and online mentoring scheme, providing prospective entrepreneurs with expert advice from peers who are business owners.
Young Enterprise	To inspire and equip young people to learn and succeed through enterprise. A later variant of the MESP (see Table 24.1), now running programmes for school children to set up companies and do business projects, master classes for potential entrepreneurs in schools and higher education, team courses for young people with learning difficulties and/or disabilities
Davies' Review on Enterprise and the Economy in Education	To consider how to promote better understanding of business, the economy and enterprise throughout the school and further education systems. Howard Davies, Chair of Financial Services Authority, recommended that the Government commit annual funding of £54m to enable every pupil to experience enterprise activity at some point during the school career, together with enterprise learning in the curriculum.
Enterprise Promotion Fund	To encourage creativity in promoting enterprise awareness across all sections of society, by supporting projects that are intended to 'test out new ways to show people what enterprise is all about and give them the understanding and enthusiasm to try out enterprise for themselves'. Launched in 2003, with 19 projects funded in 2004.
Enterprise Education Schemes	To raise levels of small business involvement in enterprise awareness, asking real entrepreneurs to volunteer their time as speakers, role models and mentors in the hope of raising young people's aspirations and broadening their awareness of the options available to them

(contd.)

Table 24.2 Enterprise culture initiatives introduced by the Blair Government during the 2000s (*contd.*)

Initiative	Intended purpose
Enterprising Britain	A national competition to find the town, city or place in the country that is best improving economic prospects and encouraging enterprise. Aims to help raise awareness of enterprise activities and celebrate success. Launched in 2004.
Queen's Award for Enterprise Promotion	To recognise individuals who have made an outstanding contribution to building an enterprise culture. 10 awards made each year. Launched in 2004.
Other awareness-raising initiatives	To encourage people into enterprise activities by signposting support available to potential entrepreneurs, enhancing awareness of immigration schemes to attract entrepreneurs to the UK, promoting enterprise amongst minority groups.

Source: SBS (2005) Implementation Review on Building an Enterprise Culture, and programme websites.

In much recent government documentation, there is a sense of aspiration rather than attainment, giving the impression that, despite the raft of enterprise initiatives that have gone before in the 1980s and 1990s, an enterprise culture still eludes Britain. Indeed, in comparing Tables 24.1 and 24.2, it is striking how many of the Blair initiatives seem remarkably similar to those of their predecessors. Although operating under new logos (the Skills Councils replacing the TECs for example), the underlying philosophies seem broadly the same. In his review of enterprise in education, Davies (2002: 7) notes that although attitudes to entrepreneurship and business are positive, young people 'lack the skills and confidence to turn positive attitudes in action'. Successful entrepreneurs are fêted as role models, attitudes to entrepreneurship are optimistic in Britain, but nonetheless an 'enterprise gap' remains (Ei/SBS/HMT, 2004).

24.3 How should we evaluate the impact of enterprise culture project? Criteria and evidence

Having established what enterprise projects purport to achieve in broad terms, we now consider how we might evaluate their impact on Britain. As Storey notes in

Chapter 10 of this Handbook, the Labour Government's strategic thinking on enterprise policy has taken time to come to fruition, and given the recency of many of the initiatives in Table 24.2, it will be some time before evaluation is feasible. For that reason, our focus in the remainder of this chapter is concerned with the legacy of Thatcher's enterprise culture project.

As we described above, the enterprise project in Thatcher's Britain had several stated objectives, all broadly connected to the idea of achieving economic growth through cultural re-engineering. International competitiveness was to be achieved through greater productivity, achieved in part through labour market flexibility, but also by innovation and entrepreneurship producing higher value-added economic activity. If these goals had been achieved, then over the period of the project we might expect to see improvements in rates of firm founding, extent of value-added activities and higher levels of innovation in the British economy exhibited by higher GDP per capita.

At the organizational level, the infusion of enterprising values within work organizations might be expected to have led to new and growing enterprises generating jobs, and becoming more innovative through the entrepreneurial actions not only of founders but also of employees. Through the adoption of organizational forms that promote entrepreneurial behaviour, and the advent of participative employment relations, we might expect to find that both large corporations and small firms are more innovative than they used to be. Since even those employees who would not consider themselves as 'entrepreneurs' would have the opportunity to take greater initiative at work, and to gain greater emotional as well as material rewards from their employment, we might also expect to find that workplaces have become happier as well as more productive and efficient.

Evaluating the achievements of the enterprise project in these terms is a very significant and ambitious task. Perhaps for that reason, there have been few attempts at a holistic evaluation (although see Hetzner, 1999 for an appraisal of Thatcher's enterprise policies, and Blanchflower and Freeman, 1994, for an assessment of the impact of her reforms on British labour market performance), and the evaluation of specific programmes is a wide and complex area that is just beginning to develop (see Greene and Storey, 2004; and Storey, Ch. 10, in this Handbook). Within the scope of this chapter, we review some of the available evidence to give a sense of the achievements and limitations of the enterprise project.

It is important at this point to refer back to the distinction we drew at the beginning, between neo-liberal macroeconomic policies and enterprise culture initiatives. As far as the UK is concerned, policies of labour market flexibility appear to have paid off in terms of economic growth, at least in the 1990s. The outcome of Thatcher's labour market reforms was certainly to decrease the power of the unions and their negative impact on economic growth, and increase the incentive to work (Blanchflower et al., 1991; Blanchflower and Freeman, 1994). The

UK now has record high levels of employment, and productivity calculated as GDP per worker has improved significantly over the 1990s. However, this does not mean that productivity levels have caught up with those of other G5 countries.[2]

Moveover, there are concerns that labour market flexibility has created some adverse incentives in terms of investment in workforce skills, and more broadly in privately funded R&D (Keep and Payne, 2002). There is little evidence to suggest that British workplaces have become more enterprising and innovative, with greater levels of entrepreneurial activity by employees. Evidence from successive workplace industrial relations surveys (WIRS) indicates that union impact on wage levels evaporated during the period 1980 to 1998, industrial action disappeared after 1990, and unions lost their hold over joint consultative committees and health and safety representation. The Labour Government has not sought to restore collective representation. In its place, management-initiated methods of communicating with employees and involving employees in problem-solving have grown during the 1990s (Millward et al., 2002). The general consensus from WIRS surveys, however, is that almost half of British workplaces, and probably a majority in the private sector, persist in adopting a 'low-road' low-skill approach, eschewing both collective representation and progressive management practices (Guest, 2001).

Indeed, British workplaces might be becoming worse places to work in, rather than better. Taylor's (2002) analysis of the 'Working in Britain 2000' survey indicates that since 1992 there has been a significant decline in satisfaction with working hours, and that this in turn is associated with a greater intensity of work. Evidence from other surveys (e.g. Guest and Conway, 2002; Cully et al., 1999) indicates that at least half of the British workforce, or possibly as many as three-quarters are satisfied with their work, although there does appear to be a long-term decline in job satisfaction, particularly in the public sector (Guest and Conway, 2002). However, there is little evidence, despite numerous protestations to the contrary, that increasing labour market flexibility is causing a decline in perceptions of job security and job tenure. If anything, perceptions of job security and tenure are becoming more positive (Taylor, 2002) and at the very least they are consistent with macroeconomic trends (Green, 2004).

More important for our purposes, is the question of what outcomes might be indicative of the success of the 'enterprise' project as a means to promote

[2] A typical performance comparison of high versus low enterprise environments is that between the US economy and Euroland. The US's higher GDP growth performance is usually explained in terms of higher productivity levels and productivity growth. Daly (2004) shows however that by analysing GDP per head as the product of productivity and labour utilization (average hours worked by the employment rate by proportion of the population that is of working age), it is possible to account for the superior performance of the US through the low rate of labour utilization (low employment rates and low average hours worked) of Euroland, rather than productivity. He also argues that Euroland's higher profitability (return on equity) should in fact be linked to this theoretical prediction that the rate of return on capital should be higher in countries where productivity growth is faster (Daly, 2004).

entrepreneurial attitudes and behaviour. Measuring entrepreneurship is inevitably contentious (Dale, 1991), especially where looking for evidence over time. The Global Entrepreneurship Monitor looks at variation in the level of entreprenurial activity between countries. In terms of the proportion of the labour force actively involved in starting or managing a new business, Britain scores well ahead of G7 comparators France, Germany and Japan, although significantly behind the US and Canada. However, in terms of attitudes to entrepreneurship and risk-taking, Britain is well behind France, Germany and even Italy, which has a rigid labour market and has not engaged in enterprise culture projects of the kind described here (DTI, 2003). A discussion paper by the Enterprise Initiative (Ei/SBS/HMT, 2004) refers to an 'enterprise gap', and a recent Small Business survey of attitudes to entrepreneurship, found that 76 percent of the adult population in Britain are 'avoiders'—that is, they are not currently engaged in entrepreneurship, nor thinking of doing so (SBS, 2003a).

Business start-up rates are commonly used as an indication of entrepreneurship, as they 'demonstrate the entrepreneurial dynamism of the economy as a whole and its capacity to transform and adjust itself to new market opportunities' (DTI, 2003: 70). More people are becoming self-employed (with 3.4m in self-employment in 2004, the highest since 1991), and numbers of small businesses are rising (with 200,000 more small businesses in 2004 than in 1994) (Ei/SBS/HMT, 2004). However, it is contentious whether business start-up rates, especially taken in isolation from data on enterprise survival and growth, necessarily indicates that entrepreneurship is flourishing in the UK. Using such data as indicators of entrepreneurship can be misleading, because growth in the number of SMEs could be an outcome of industrial restructuring rather than entrepreneurship (Dodd & Andersen, 2001).

Blanchflower and Oswald (1990) conducted an econometric analysis of self-employment and its links with enterprise culture using the British Social Attitudes survey. They investigated whether the remarkable growth in numbers of self-employed over the 1980s (from 8 to 12 percent of all those in work) could be attributed to some other factor—a growing entrepreneurial culture, perhaps—after the economic characteristics of those in the labour market and the economic recovery over that period are taken into account. They found that when unemployment is low, people are more likely to enter self-employment. There was no change in the demographic characteristics of people entering self-employment over the 1980s: through that period, people running their own businesses tended to be male, older and working in construction and retailing. Despite the range of initiatives targeting young people in the 1980s (see Table 24.1), there is little evidence that more young people entered self-employment. If there was a renaissance in entrepreneurial spirit in Britain in the late 1980s, this was due to macroeconomic factors. Other research by the same authors also supports the idea that entrepreneurial behaviour is determined by economic factors. Using various US microeconomic datasets, Blanchflower and Oswald (1998) find that it is the availability of capital, rather than psychological traits, which plays a role in determining entrepreneurship.

Dodd and Anderson (2001) question the effectiveness of government-sponsored enterprise initiatives, arguing that no more than 7–10 percent of SMEs use them. They explain this by highlighting a misfit between the imposed enterprise culture and the reality of the small business world. Small business creators and owners operate in a world that is evolutionary, adaptive and pragmatic, in sharp contrast to the contrived, manufactured and universalist viewpoint of the enterprise culture policy-makers. The diversity of the SME population compounds this problem: the provision of generic solutions to a very diverse group of businesses has meant that enterprise initiatives are viewed with little credibility and some suspicion by small business owners (Curran and Blackburn, 1999).

Dodd and Anderson's analysis, which is based on drawing conceptual contrasts between different cultural paradigms, suggests that enterprise culture policies are misconstrued. Empirical assessments of policy initiatives support this view (although, as Storey notes in Ch. 10 of this Handbook, the 'science' of policy evaluation is still evolving; see also Greene and Storey, 2004). Greene et al. (2004), for example, adopt a 'policy-on, policy-off' design to evaluate the impact of enterprise policy in Cleveland/Tees Valley area of North East England. Cleveland had the lowest rates of new firm formation in the UK, and had therefore been a target for enterprise policy in the 1980s. They find that although businesses in the region were more numerous in the 1980s than in the 1970s and 1990s, they were of lower quality as measured by their human capital attributes, their survival rate, and their performance. In contrast to prevailing policy 'wisdom', incentives to increase rates of new firm formation in the 1980s had little impact on economic growth because increases in the number of new firms led to a fall in the quality of firms.

MacDonald and Coffield (1991) report a detailed evaluation of enterprise policy in the same part of England, drawing on survey and interview data with professionals working in the 'enterprise' industry, and qualitative interviews with 100 young people in the late 1980s. They examined how the concept and philosophy of enterprise was translated from theory and initiatives at national level (such as those in Table 24.1) into practice. They found that alongside the 'pull' of entrepreneurship (being your own boss, achieving independence and control), equally important was the fact that unemployment 'pushed' many young people into self-employment. Most of their businesses were under-capitalised, and long hours, low pay, insecurity, isolation, loneliness, stress and financial concerns were common. The picture painted is far from the glossy image of 'enterprise' promoted by Government. Moreover, one unintended consequence of the promotion of enterprise culture was the provision of jobs for a new tier of bureaucrats and enterprise trainers, rather than for the unemployed. New schemes kept emerging in a flurry of 'policy on the hoof', with little or no continuity:

In short, large sums of public money were used to underwrite a sprawling industry which promoted an incoherent and uncoordinated set of initiatives and activities. (MacDonald and Coffield, 1991: 230).

In overall terms, then, we find some evidence of improvements in productivity and business start-up rates, but little evidence of a step-change in levels of innovation and entrepreneurship in Britain. At best, evaluative evidence suggests that policies have a mixed effect. In the following section, we review a wider academic literature on 'enterprise culture'. Unlike the empirical evidence reviewed above, some of this literature is conceptual in nature, targeted at the philosophical and socio-cultural underpinning of enterprise projects. That literature extends well beyond this chapter's focus on outcomes related to entrepreneurship and innovation. There are many much wider and more profound critiques levelled at the broad range of programmes associated with enterprise culture, including their role in increasing inequality, eroding welfare provision, impoverishing quality of life and, at the most fundamental level, its prioritization of competitive, self-interested aspects of human nature versus community and cooperation. For further reading on the critiques of the enterprise culture projects, see Dodd and Anderson (2001), Heelas and Morris (1992), Hetzner (1999), and Keat and Abercrombie (1991).

24.4 Academic critiques of 'enterprise culture' policy and ideology

Enterprise projects (particularly the British ones) have been the focus of scholarly interests from a range of disciplines, including sociology, politics, economics, and critical theory. Our review of the literature has identified three levels at which these enterprise projects are suggested to play out: societal-political, organizational, and individual. Each level is implicated within the others, since economic policy initiatives by politicians create, but are also constrained by, the institutional context within which business takes place. Similarly, action by individuals (as business owners, managers, entrepreneurs, employees and citizens) determines, but is also constrained by, the organizational and institutional context in which they operate (Burrows, 1991).[3] It is this interconnection that makes the notion of 'enterprise culture' a powerful ideological tool. Rose (1992) argues that enterprise is a very

[3] The ideas expressed in this paragraph are consistent with sociological notions of structuration and enactment. For a discussion of such concepts see Giddens, 1991; Reich, 1995.

potent language for expressing a political ideology because it has the power to connect general political ideology with very specific programmes of action in many different social locales. Thus, a political ideology of 'enterprise', supported by a raft of schemes and programmes such as those initiated in Cleveland in the 1980s (see MacDonald and Coffield, 1991) might be interpreted as a smokescreen behind which to mask labour market policies that are unpalatable to the electorate.

Most academics who offer critical appraisals contend that, in Britain at least, the enterprise project has largely failed to achieve its objectives in promoting the values of economic modernization and rationalization (e.g. Hetzner, 1999). There are several possible explanations for this, some of which we explore further in this section. One is that British culture is simply not conducive to entrepreneurialism (Saxenian, 1989; Hetzner, 1999), and that anti-business and risk-averse values cannot be changed through political reform. As Dodd and Anderson (2001) observe, cultural meaning systems are contested and non-universal, so that attempting to impose a particular set of values on an entire nation is an improbable task.

Another reason for the failure of enterprise culture initiatives is an economic contingency argument. Keep and Payne (2002) argue that the key to delivering high productivity and a higher-value added economy is patient, long-term job redesign to ensure the optimal use of skills. Britain does not have a culture of work participation, as this tends to require social partnership between unions and employers, as well as government support, and the historical antagonism between these actors has prevented it from happening. Furthermore, with a flexible labour market there is little incentive for individual employers to invest in people's skills and technology. For these reasons, the project's vision of the creation of 'excellent', enterprising workplaces is largely detached from economic reality.

Indeed, rather than creating 'excellent' workplaces, much recent commentary suggests that British workplaces have become increasingly unpleasant places to be. Bunting (2004) uses anecdotal evidence combined with statistics to allude to workplace stress, longer working hours, high insecurity and exhaustion (see also Hutton, 1996; Sennett, 1998). The changing nature of work in Britain, and indeed in all western capitalist countries, has been widely discussed and debated by academics and popular commentators alike (e.g. Osterman, 1996; Cappelli, 1999; Andresky, 2001; Donkin, 2001; Reich, 2001). Many base their arguments on the demise of organizational hierarchies, a perceived decline in traditional, predictable career paths and increasing levels of flexibility, and individualization in employment relations. The extent to which such changes are actually borne out in reality may be overstated (see for example, TUC, 2000; White et al., 2004), especially since job tenure and job security statistics do not support them (Taylor, 2002; Green 2004).

Nonetheless, accounts such as Bunting's (2004) seem to chime with public opinion, which does suggest that, despite the statistics, people think their work is becoming more intense and less secure. Keep and Payne (2002) argue that both high-and low-skilled ends of the labour market are being required to work harder: the elite because long-standing British cultural beliefs aver that there are relatively few of them, and the majority because of the low value and low productivity of their labour. Public sector workers, subjected to rounds of initiatives promoting emphasis on productivity and accountability, have not fared any better, with declining job satisfaction and a culture of suspicion among civil servants. Public sector reform under both Conservative and Labour governments was strongly influenced by 'enterprise culture' thinking: competition between service providers, performance measures and above all redefining the client as a customer (Osborne & Gaebler, 1992). Even if the years since enterprise culture initiatives began have seen higher incomes for most (alongside higher inequality), Bunting (2004) suggests a high price has been paid, in terms of long hours and diminished quality of life. Employee cynicism and negative reactions to increasing work intensity are perhaps one of the key reasons why enterprise culture initiatives have failed to deliver the entrepreneurial workplaces that were envisaged.

Sociologists and critical theorists of organization, such as Grey (1994), du Gay (1991, 1996), Hall (1988b), and Rose (1992), argue that embedded within the enterprise project lies a profound conception of a regulated self. Building on Foucauldian analysis, they argue that, because the market has come to define the sort of relation an individual should have with him herself, and the 'habits of action' she/he should acquire and exhibit, the self is now seen as an 'enterprise project' in its own right (du Gay, 1996: 56). Contemporary individuals are incited to live as if making a project of themselves: they are to work on their relations with employment and to make provisions for the preservation and reproduction of their human capital as part of the continuous business of living (Gordon, 1991; Rose, 1992). A variety of mechanisms or 'technologies of regulation', including performance appraisals, psychometric testing, attitude surveys, and self-directed training, and the use of psychologically trained experts to oversee these processes, are suggested to help senior managers normalize this self-regulating behaviour at all levels of the organization (Grey, 1994; du Gay, 1996).

Critics also argue that the use of such technologies has the effect of blurring distinctions between work and consumption identities (du Gay, 1996). Work is seen as a locale for investment in one's career capital, rather than the exchange of one's labour, and a raft of popular self-help guides and academic texts have emerged which prescribe how this should be done (e.g. Bridges, 1997; Inkson and Arthur, 2001). Work is construed as the site of emotional, as well as material rewards (Bunting, 2004). Moreover, the project of the enterprising self extends outside employment, as individuals are expected to work on their emotional world, their domestic and conjugal arrangements, their techniques of sexual pleasure and to develop a style of living that will maximise the worth of their existence to themselves (Rose, 1992: 149; du Gay, 1996: 69).

24.5 What can we conclude about enterprise culture?

Attempts at cultural engineering can make enterprise seem a natural and laudable objective. The expectation that Britain, and other western European countries such as France and Germany, need to become more enterprising is taken for granted in many walks of life. As we have seen in this chapter, the central objective of the 'enterprise culture' project is the liberation of entrepreneurial tendencies in all citizens. The project takes as its basis the assumption that people are born with entrepreneurial characteristics, which can either be unleashed through appropriate market mechanisms (Lord Young, 1992), or fostered into entrepreneurial action through exposure to enterprise in education (Davies, 2002).

Britain has weathered several recessions to deliver significant economic growth in the years since enterprise policies were initiated in 1979. In the mid-2000s, self-employment growth rates are high, and numbers of small business are increasing. Successful entrepreneurs are now celebrated in the media and by government as popular heroes. However, the extent to which Britain's economic outcomes can be attributed to enterprise policies, as opposed to the wider macroeconomic context, is a moot point. In this chapter, we have indicated a series of possible expected outcomes and reviewed evidence to suggest that top-down enterprise policies are at best only indirectly effective, and at worst have no economic impact at all.

Indeed even the notion of enterprise itself is fraught with ambiguity, being widely used, much abused and poorly understood, as MacDonald and Coffield note:

> We are not dealing with a tightly defined, agreed and unitary concept but with a farrago of 'hurrah' words like 'creativity', 'initiative' and 'leadership' ... Part of the confusion stems from the fact that the word 'enterprise' is used in different ways, sometimes referring to an individual ability considered amenable to improvement and at other times to a form of economic activity, usually in small businesses. (MacDonald and Coffield, 1991: 29)

These difficulties have been compounded by a wider failure to recognize the complexity of different characterizations of 'entrepreneur' (Dale, 1991). The corporate executive has a very different set of characteristics, motivations and objectives than the small business owner, or the self-employed person. Thus, Lord Young's notion that the entire population is composed of would-be entrepreneurs is perhaps misguided. Dodd and Anderson (2001) for example, argue that there is no evidence of unique enterprising traits waiting to be unleashed in all citizens, and no evidence that business creation is necessarily the natural outlet for initiative, drive and creativity.

How, then, can we account for the enduring popularity of the enterprise culture model in Britain, and the apparent continuity of policy between Conservative and

Labour governments? One answer lies in the tractable nature of the term 'enterprise', being at once progressive, industrious and innovative, and connoting both individualist endeavour and collective outcomes. As such, the term offers a malleable political tool. Politicians need rhetorics that give meaning to the past and hope for the future (Dodd and Anderson, 2001: 23). For Thatcher, some critics argue that the notion of 'enterprise' masked economic policy intended to increase profits at the expense of wages. For Blair, 'enterprise' promises a revitalized Britain and a dynamic, bright, inclusive future.

By examining Britain's attempts to manufacture an enterprise culture, our discussion touches on issues and debates that extend well beyond the British context and tie-in to to some of the themes addressed elsewhere in this Handbook, as well as themes which could usefully be addressed elsewhere. Can government policy impose entrepreneurial values among citizens? What are knock-on effects of attempting to do so on individuals, families and organizations? What are the outcomes in terms of economic performance in the short and long term? In essence, what is the relationship between cultural value systems and socio-economic systems?

References

Andresky, J. (2001). *White-Collar Sweatshop: The Deterioration of Work and its Rewards in Corporate America.* W. W. Norton.

Blanchflower, D. and A. Oswald (1990). 'Self-employment and the Enterprise Culture', in R. Jowell, S. Witherspoon and L. Brook (eds) *British Social Attitudes: The 1990 Report.* Gower.

—— N. Millward and A. Oswald (1991). 'Unionism and Employment Behavior'. *Economic Journal*, 101(407): 815–834.

—— and R. Freeman (1994). 'Did the Thatcher reforms change British labour market performance?', in R. Barrell (ed.) *The UK Labour Market: Comparative Aspects and Institutional Developments.* Cambridge: Cambridge University Press.

—— and A. J. Oswald (1998). 'What Makes an Entrepreneur?' *Journal of Labor Economics*, 16(1): 26–60.

Bridges, W. (1997). *Creating You and Co.* London: Brealey.

Bunting, M. (2004). *Willing Slaves: How the Overwork Culture is Ruling our Lives.* London: HarperCollins.

Burrows, R. (1991). 'Introduction: Entrepreneurship, petty capitalism and the restructuring of Britain', in R. Keat and N. Abercrombie (eds) *Enterprise Culture.* London: Routledge.

Cappelli, P. (1999). *The New Deal at Work: Managing the Market-Driven Workforce.* Harvard, MA: Harvard Business School Press.

Cully, M., A. O'Reilly, S. Woodland and G. Dix (1999), *Britain at Work: As Depicted by the 1998 Workplace Employee Relations Survey.* London: Routledge.

Curran, J. (2000). 'What is Small Business Policy in the UK For? Evaluation and assessing small business policies'. *International Small Business Journal*, 18(3): 36–51.

—— and R. A. Blackburn (1999). 'Panacea or White Elephant? A critical examination of the proposed new small business service and response to the DTI consultancy paper'. *Regional Studies*, 34(2): 181–206.

Dale, A. (1991). 'Self-employment and Entrepreneurship: Notes on two problematic concepts', in R. Keat and N. Abercrombie (eds) *Enterprise Culture*. London: Routledge.

Daly, K. (2004). 'Has Euroland Performed that Badly?' *The Business Economist*, 35(1): 35–52.

Davies, H. (2002). *Review of Enterprise and the Economy in Education*. London: HM Treasury.

Dodd, S. D. and A. R. Anderson (2001). 'Understanding the Enterprise Culture: Paradigm, paradox and policy'. *Entrepreneurship and Innovation*.

Donkin, R. (2001). *Blood, Sweat and Tears: The Evolution of Work*. Texere.

DTI (2003). *UK Competitiveness Indicators*. London: Department of Trade and Industry.

du Gay, P. (1991). 'Enterprise Culture and the Ideology of Excellence'. *New Formations*, 13: 45–61.

—— (1996). *Consumption and Identity at work*. London: Sage.

Gordon, C. (1991). 'Governmental Rationality: An introduction', in G. Burchell, C. Gordon and P. Miller (eds) *The Foucault Effect: Studies in Governmentality*. Brighton: Harvester Wheatsheaf.

Green, F. (2004). *Under Pressure–Measuring the Quality of Working Life*. Princeton, NJ: Princeton University Press.

Greene, F. J., K. F. Mole and D. J. Storey (2004). 'Does More Mean Worse? Three decades of enterprise policy in the Tees Valley', *Urban Studies*, 41(7): 1207–28.

—— and D. J. Storey (2004). 'An Assessment of a Venture Creation Programme: The case of Shell LiveWIRE'. *Entrepreneurship and Regional Development*, 16(2): 145–59.

Grey, C. (1994). 'Career as a Project of the Self and Labour Process Discipline'. *Sociology*, 28(2): 479–97.

Guest, D. (2001). 'Industrial Relations and Human Resource Management', in J. Storey (ed.) *Human Resource Management: A Critical Text*, 2nd edn. London: Thompson Learning.

—— and N. Conway (2002). *Pressure of Work and the Psychological Contract*. London: Chartered Institute of Personnel and Development.

Hall, S. (1988b). *The Hard Road to Renewal: Thatcherism and the Crisis of the Left*. London: Verso.

Heelas P. and P. Morris (eds) (1992). *The Values of the Enterprise Culture*. London: Routledge.

Hetzner, C. (1999). *The Unfinished Business of Thatcherism: The Values of the Enterprise Culture*. New York: Peter Lang.

HM Treasury (2004). *Towards an Enterprising Europe: A paper by the French, German and UK Governments*. London: HM Treasury.

Hutton, W. (1996). *The State We're In: Why Britain is in Crisis and How to Overcome It*. London: Vintage.

Inkson, K. and M. B. Arthur (2001). 'How to be a Successful Career Capitalist'. *Organizational Dynamics*, 30(1): 48–61.

Kanter, R. M. (1989). *When Giants Learn to Dance: Mastering the Challenges of Strategy, Management and Careers in the 1990s*. New York: Basic Books.

Keat, R. and N. Abercombie (eds) (1991). *Enterprise Culture*. London: Routledge.

Keep, E. and J. Payne (2002). 'What can the UK learn from the Norwegian and Finnish Experience of Attempts at Work Reorganisation?', SKOPE research paper no. 41.

Lord Young of Graffham (1992). 'Enterprise regained', in P. Heelas and P. Morris (eds) *Enterprise culture: its values and value*. London: Routledge.

MacDonald, R. and R. Coffield (1991). *Risky Business: Youth and the Enterprise Culture*. London: Routledge.

Millward, N., A. Bryson and J. Forth (2002). *All Change at Work: British Employment Relations 1980–1998, as Portrayed by the Workplace Industrial Relations Survey series*. London: Routledge.

Osborne, D. and T. Gaebler (1992). *Reinventing Government: How the Entrepreneurial Spirit is Transforming the Public Sector*. London: Perseus.

Osterman, P. (ed.) (1996). *Broken Ladders: Managerial Careers in the New Economy*. Oxford: Oxford University Press.

Ouchi, W. G. (1980). 'Markets, Bureaucracies and Clans', *Administrative Science Quarterly*, 25: 129–41.

Peters, T. and R. Waterman (1982). *In Search of Excellence*. New York: Harper & Row.

Reich, R. B. (2001). *The Future of Success*. New York: Alfred A. Knopf.

Rose, N. (1992). 'Governing the Enterprising Self', in P. Heelas and P. Morris (eds.) *Enterprise culture: its values and value*. London: Routledge.

Saxenian, A. (1989). 'The Cheshire Cat's Grin: Innovation, Regional Development and the Cambridge Case'. *Economy and Society*, 18(4).

SBS (2003a). *Government Action Plan for Small Business*. London: Small Business Service.

SBS (2003b). *Household Survey of Entrepreneurship*. London: Small Business Service.

SBS (2004). Government Action Plan for Small Business: Implementation Review. Available at http://www.sbs.gov.uk/7-strategies/strategy-1.php

Sennett, R. (1998). *The Corrosion of Character: The Personal Consequences of Work in the New Capitalism*. New York: W. W. Norton.

Taylor, R. (2002). *Britain's World of Work–Myths and Realities*. Swindon: Economic and Social Research Council.

TUC (2000). *The Future of Work*. London: TUC.

White, M., S. Hill, C. Mills and D. Smeaton (2004). *Managing to Change? British Workplaces and the Future of Work*. Palgrave: Macmillian.

PART VII

SPATIAL AND INTERNATIONAL DIMENSIONS

CHAPTER 25

REGIONAL DEVELOPMENT: CLUSTERS AND DISTRICTS

PHILIP McCANN

25.1 Introduction to Clusters, Industrial Districts and Regional Development

The relationship between industrial clustering and regional development is a topic which has received a great deal of interest over recent years. Much of the recent growth in interest in this issue has arisen in part out of a generally renewed interest in agglomeration economies, on the part of both economists (Krugman, 1991) and business analysts (Porter 1990). Following Porter's (1990) initial application of his principles of competitive advantage to regions and nations, discussions of the potential advantages of clusters as locations for dynamic investment, risk-taking, entrepreneurship and innovation are now widespread. The resulting research agenda has therefore attempted to understand not only the ways in which clustering may encourage individuals and firms to be entrepreneurial and innovative, but also the relationship between the development of such clusters and regional development.

Recent theoretical developments in economics (Krugman, 1991) and management science (Porter, 1990, 1998) have highlighted the role that geographical clustering in industrial districts may play in encouraging consistent variations in the spatial patterns of new firm foundations, new product developments and new process innovations. Questions concerning the relationship between entrepreneurship, innovation and regional development have tended to focus on the role played by agglomeration economies in fostering localized learning processes within the economy (Glaeser, 1999). In these literatures, it is argued that variations in local information externalities (Jaffe et al., 1993), labour hysteresis effects (Simpson, 1992; Audretsch and Feldman, 1996), and location-specific input sources, can generate conditions under which such economic developments emerge and then tend to remain localized. The resulting outcomes of these localized learning processes are assumed to include the genesis of new products and processes, the initial development of which is perceived to be facilitated by geographical proximity (Saxenian, 1994).

Such theoretical arguments have also been bolstered by observations of certain key industrial clusters, or so-called 'new industrial areas' (Scott, 1988), which do appear to spawn a high degree of industrial innovations, such as Silicon Valley (Saxenian, 1994; Larsen and Rogers, 1984; Scott, 1988), the Southern California electronics industry (Scott, 1993), the Emilio-Romagna region of Italy (Scott, 1988; Castells and Hall, 1994), and the science-based industrial cluster around Cambridge, England (Castells and Hall, 1994). These industrial districts appear to be characterized primarily by a large number of small-to medium-sized firms, which generate a range of new products and services whose product life cycles tend to be short Vernon, (1966). Smallness is argued to provide flexibility in a firm's relations with other firms (Saxenian, 1994), thereby maximizing the firm's ability to make the appropriate alliances for the duration of a project. Anecdotal evidence suggests that clustered firms appear to form ever-changing inter-firm alliances and coalitions in order to successfully innovate, depending on the information currently available within the cluster. Entrepreneurship, innovation and industrial clustering therefore all appear to be related, and these are the central elements in Porter's (1990) concept of national and regional advantage.

From the perspective of public policy-makers, economic geographers and regional planners, these arguments have naturally lead to new discussions concerning the potential impacts of regional planning policies in the fostering of localized innovation and growth. However, in this paper it is argued that employing the notion of clusters and industrial districts in order to motivate discussions of the entrepreneurship, innovation and regional development is not at all as straightforward as it may at first appear. This is because many of the issues linking entrepreneurship, innovation and regional development depend on the educational, social and psychological backgrounds of the individual persons concerned. In addition to this, however, the development of new products, processes and services is also clearly related to the levels and types of market information available locally, and the nature of the barriers to entry into the local markets. Therefore, when discussing the relationship between clustering, innovation, entrepreneurship and regional development, it is necessary for us to ask whether there are certain aspects of the regional social, industrial, or institutional fabric which generally tend to encourage or discourage such dynamic behaviour. In other words, we need to ask whether there are any features of the regional economic system, over and above the individual personal characteristics, which provide for the requisite flows of information and market entry possibilities necessary for local innovation and entrepreneurship to flourish. Moreover, we need to ask whether public policy can better effect the local provision of such beneficial features than simply a competitive market environment.

The paper is organized as follows. In the next section (25.2), we make some clarifications regarding the terminology we use and assumptions we make, simply for expositional purposes. In section 25.3 we outline the basic tenets of the concept of agglomeration and industrial districts, highlighting the mechanisms by which the spatial grouping of activities and the generation of localized economies of scale may be related. In section 25.4 we review the various hypotheses which are evident in the literature concerning the relationship between the spatial organization of industrial activity and the spatial patterns of innovation. In section 25.5 we explain the current trends in thought about these relationships, pointing out the recent popularity of the concept of a cluster. Section 25.6 then investigates the various notions of clusters and industrial districts from a transactions costs perspective, and section 25.7 provides an assessment of the insights generated from these cluster arguments. Our conclusions as to the usefulness or otherwise of these concepts will focus on the need to consider the opportunity costs and benefits to the firm of having local information spillovers, and to relate these issues to the regional sectoral and industrial structure.

25.2 Terminology and Methodology

A problem with investigating the dynamic relationship between issues such as clusters, innovation, entrepreneurship and regional development, is that not only is the terminology employed often rather ambiguous, but also there are assumed to be particular types of ideal relationships between these phenomena.

On the first point for example, many authors use the terms 'innovation' and 'entrepreneurship' more or less interchangeably to mean generally the development of new products, processes or services, particularly within small firms. On the other hand, within some areas of the literature there has emerged a broad implicit distinction, in that 'entrepreneurship' tends to be associated with individuals or very small firms, whereas 'innovation' is generally used to discuss such phenomena within medium-sized and large firms (Simmie 1998).[1] While this distinction is not clear-cut, it is useful for our purposes here to consider entrepreneurship and innovation as representing something of a continuum which relates the development of the new products or services to the size of the firm in which it originates. Essentially, the same phenomena take place under either heading, except that the distribution of the risk-bearing differs depending on the size of the firm. In very small enterprises, all of the risk is borne by a tiny number of individuals, whereas in large enterprises the risk is spread over a wide range of people. This is the terminology that we will adopt for purposes of clarity and consistency in this paper.

On a second point, we make no qualitative judgement a priori, as to what is the most preferable structural arrangement for fostering the links between issues such as clusters, innovation, entrepreneurship and regional development. In other words, from the point of view of regional development, we assume that it does not really matter whether the new product or service is developed by a very small firm, a medium-sized firm or within a large firm. For our purposes, from a regional perspective, all that concerns us here is the relationship between the location of where the new product or service originates, and the location of where it is implemented. This is important because our intention here is to examine whether there is any evidence in favour of any particular structural–regional relationships.

It is important for us to clarify this point here, because there is a large body of literature which does make an implicit (and in some cases explicit) judgement as to the importance of the structural origins of the innovations, in particular assuming that new products and services developed within very small firms provide preferable outcomes for local regional development than those developed within large firms. This literature has emerged as a combination of the output on industrial 'clusters',[2] plus the economic geography literature on 'new industrial areas' (Scott, 1988; Saxenian, 1994). Although the origins of these two sets of literatures are quite different, in that the clusters literature emerged from management science (Porter, 1990) whereas the new industrial spaces literature emerged from economic geography (Scott, 1988), they have subsequently overlapped enormously, to the point that in many people's writings they have largely merged. As such, terminology from both strands are nowadays often used interchangeably, and particularly in

[1] The reason for this distinction is that while we may talk about single person or a small firm as being 'innovative', we rarely would describe a large multinational firm as being 'entrepreneurial'.

[2] Porter (1990) himself is largely neutral on the issue of firm size, although many of the proponents of regional cluster theories argue strongly in favour of SMEs rather than large firms.

discussions concerning the relationship between innovation and regional development. Therefore, in the rest of this paper for expositional simplicity we will employ the term 'new industrial clusters' to mean this general body of clusters literature which has emerged as a fusion of these two originally distinct strands of literature.

Finally, our analytical approach in this paper is that, rather than engaging in the various details of many of the contemporary debates on clusters, in section 6 we simply distil a wide variety of current literature according to one particular set of themes; namely the transactions-costs assumptions of these cluster models. As such, we are not developing any theories or critiques of clusters, nor are we questioning how well these concepts translate from aspatial to spatial settings. Rather, we aim only to clarify the transactions-costs assumptions embedded in the various cluster concepts. It is our aim to demonstrate that the conditions under which such 'new industrial clusters' theories or arguments can be sustained are actually very restrictive indeed, and that simple generalizations are not tenable. The reason for this is that the cluster concepts themselves cut across a range of different (transactions-costs) approaches to the analysis of institutions and market behaviour, each of which has very different implications for regional development. Our argument therefore calls into question much of the assumed applicability of these models, both as a means of explanation of observations, or as a model of regional development.

25.3 Agglomeration and Local Regional Growth

The observation that economic activities and people are generally clustered together in space, in spite of the appreciation of local land and labour prices, suggests that economies of scale can be place-specific. Such location-specific economies of scale are generally known as agglomeration economies, and it was Alfred Marshall who is generally credited[3] with first providing a detailed description of the sources of these economies of scale associated with industrial districts. In Marshall's (1920) discussion these economies are generally understood to be external economies,

[3] In particular by Krugman (1991). However, the language and nature of Marshall's discussion of 'industrial districts' suggests that he was almost certainly aware of the 1951 British Parliamentary Inquiry into the expansion of the railway system to Manchester (British Parliamentary Papers, 1845, 39, No. 225, 311–13). This documents in detail the advantages of 'manufacturing districts' in a manner which is strikingly similar to Marshall's later textbook description.

which are independent of a single firm, but which accrue to all of the firms located in the same area. Marshall provided three reasons why such localized economies of scale might exist: namely, information spillovers, local non-traded inputs, and a local skilled labour pool.

First, if many firms in the same industry are grouped together in the same location, it implies that the employees of any one particular firm have relatively easy access to employees from other local firms. This easy access allows for frequent direct informal face-to-face contact between individuals, which may allow for tacit knowledge to be shared between the individuals. Tacit knowledge is knowledge that is incomplete and is shared on a non-market basis. This process of the mutual informal trading of knowledge allows each of the local market participants to build up a more coherent picture of the overall market environment, thereby improving their ability to compete in the market, relative to those competitors in other locations. The advantage of spatial clustering in this case is therefore that proximity maximizes the mutual accessibility of all individuals within the cluster, thereby improving the information spillovers available to all local participants.

Secondly, in situations where many firms in the same industry are grouped together in the same area, there will also be possibilities for certain specialist inputs to be provided to the group, in a more efficient manner than would be the case if all of the firms were dispersed. In many cases, the costs of providing such services would normally be prohibitive to most market participants. However, the fact that a large number of potential customer firms within the same sector are also located at the same place allows the costs to be spread across the group, and the costs of the input to each firm within the group will fall as more firms join the group.

Thirdly, the spatial grouping of firms provides for the creation of a local specialized labour pool, thereby allowing all firms within the group to reduce their labour acquisition costs. There are two aspects to these cost reductions: (i) a local skill-base reduces the general hiring and re-training costs incurred by the local firm that are associated with any job-changes within the group. Labour can move between firms relatively easily and the firms are also able to employ new workers relatively easily; (ii) this ease of local labour adjustment also acts as a risk reduction mechanism on the part of both the firm and the labour in the face of demand fluctuations.

For identification and empirical evaluation purposes, these three Marshallian sources of agglomeration economies have subsequently been re-classified on a sectoral basis (Ohlin, 1933; Hoover, 1937, 1948) into localization, and urbanization economies. If the ensuing agglomeration benefits accrue to activities in the same sector located at the same place, these are termed localization economies, whereas if the benefits accrue to a range of local sectors, they are termed urbanization economies (Jacobs 1960). However, each of Marshall's sources of agglomeration can contribute to the development of either localization economies or urbanization economies.

The discussion so far has focused on a rather static notion of industrial districts and agglomeration, in that agglomerations are perceived to represent location-specific economies scale. While these assumptions are useful from an analytical point of view, it is also possible, however, to introduce dynamic elements into the discussion of cities. This is achieved by incorporating notions of learning and the evolution in information within the standard spillovers-type framework. In order to do this, it is necessary to consider the role played by cities, clusters and industrial districts in the process of information generation, entrepreneurship, innovation and firm creation.

25.4 Hypotheses about the Geography of Innovation and Entrepreneurship

In the regional development field there have emerged really two quite distinct strands of literature which are generally used to consider issues such as entrepreneurship, innovation and regional development. The first strand is the well-known 'product-cycle' literature, and the second strand derives from the broad new industrial clusters literature. From these two strands of literature, there have been developed four principal hypotheses (Gordon and McCann, 2005a,b) and to account for the widely observed uneven spatial distribution of innovative behaviour (Sternberg, 1996). The first two hypotheses derive from the product-cycle literature, and the second two derive from the new industrial clusters literature. Following Gordon and McCann (2005a,b), these four principal hypotheses are:

Hypothesis 1: *The contemporary geography of innovation is essentially a geography of the currently more innovative sectors of the economy*

This hypothesis derives from the observation that at any particular time period there will be some sectors of the economy which will be more involved in the innovation of products or processes than others. This may be due to the particular phase which has been reached in the life cycle of their particular product set, or because some activities with very short product cycles are more or less permanently locked into the innovative phase. If each of these industries exhibits rather different location behaviour because of the nature of their production or input–output technologies, it may then be possible to reduce the geography of innovation simply to a geography of industrial location. With activities remaining in the same broad locations through all of the phases of the product cycle, places which they dominate will also appear to move through that cycle, except for the homes of the permanent innovators, which would remain continuing sites of innovation.

Hypothesis 2: *The contemporary geography of innovation is essentially a result of spatial differences in the phases of product- or profit-cycles*

This second interpretation of product-cycle geography focuses on the types of shifts in locational requirements between the phases of an industry's product- or profit-cycle (Markusen, 1985). From this perspective, during the early innovative phases of the product-cycle, neither the scale of production nor the certainty of growth are sufficient for firms to attempt self-sufficiency either in production or training, while design uncertainties also militate against reliance on either distant suppliers or semi-skilled labour. As such, the early phases of the cycle emphasize the role played by agglomeration economies during the innovative phases of an industry's product-cycle, in which access to appropriate skills and sub-contractors are a crucial condition for successful innovation and the management of uncertainties. In the later mature phases of the cycle in which sufficient output scale has been achieved, production methods have been routinized, and cost factors have become increasingly important; both the simple geographical dispersal to lower cost locations and the spatial division of labour will become increasingly relevant.

Both the first and the second hypotheses are developed on the basis of the product-cycle model, associated primarily with the work of Vernon (1960, 1966). Although the insights of this work originated within the context of urban and regional development (Vernon, 1960), these insights have been used for the most part, to discuss the spatial investment behaviour of large multi-plant and multinational firms. The spatial aspects of the product-cycle literature within the regional development field (Markusen, 1985) imply that within corporate organizational hierarchies, new ideas, products and processes will generally tend to emerge from the parts of the organization that are located in key information centres such as major cities in advanced regions. Products and processes of a more mature vintage will tend to be those that are being produced and operated in more geographically peripheral lower-wage regions. The outcome of this is that there will tend to emerge a clear core–periphery structure to the geography of corporate innovation, with products in the early stages of their life cycle in the core locations, and more mature vintages in the peripheral areas. The actual relationship between geography, innovation and entrepreneurship depends on the relationship between geography and the corporate organizational characteristics of the firms. On this point, there is a fundamental difference between these two hypotheses. The first hypothesis assumes that as innovation takes place, the innovating firms are primarily static in terms of their location behaviour, such that different phases of the product-cycle are not reflected in changing industrial geographies. On the other hand, the second hypothesis works on the assumption that the innovating firms are largely dynamic in terms of their location behaviour, so that the different phases of the product-cycles are indeed reflected in terms of evolving industrial geographies.

Hypothesis 3: *The contemporary geography of innovation is essentially the outcome of variations in the characteristics between different places which lead to differences in the geography of creativity and entrepreneurship.*

The third approach to understanding the distribution of innovative activity focuses on the geography of creativity and entrepreneurship, in the sense that particular local area characteristics may relatively favour the development and commercial launching of new or improved products, either through established or new business organizations. In other words, the emphasis here is on the specifically local characteristics that stimulate and enable novel developments while also facilitating the selection of those with real competitive potential. The three key sets of factors generally argued to underlie this hypothesis involve (Gordon and McCann, 2000) first, a rich 'soup' of skills, ideas, technologies, and cultures within which new compounds and forms of life can emerge; secondly, a permissive environment enabling unconventional initiatives to be brought to the marketplace; and thirdly, vigorously competitive and critical arenas operating selection criteria which anticipate and shape those of wider future markets.

In some circumstances, particularly when the driver has patentable scientific knowledge which can be profitably produced and exploited in-house, the relevant environment may be primarily that of a global business corporation. More typically, it is likely to be a place with the 'unique buzz, unique fizz (and) special kind of energy' coupled with discretionary spending power (Hall, 1999).[4]

In terms of these arguments, therefore, what is generally significant about the geography of innovative activities is not the distribution of creative or inventive potential, but the production conditions which allow infant firms and industries to survive and thrive in a nursery environment, until they acquire the scale and experience to strike out on their own. Duranton and Puga (2001) in their life cycle model emphasize diversity as the key requirement of nursery environments in which firms introducing new products have access to an array of models of production processes to borrow and try out, before routinizing and relocating to more specialized cities. However, while there is a line of argument going back to Schumpeter (1934, 1942) which has pointed to the crucial role of big firms' R&D, in his classic comparison of New York and Pittsburgh, Chinitz (1961) argued that the ability of new enterprises to combine relevant technical and market expertise is generally limited in an urban economy dominated by large bureaucratic businesses, which tend to limit local market entry. Porter (1990) also highlights some of these issues relating to local industrial structure, arguing for the importance of both local competitive rivalry as well as a discriminating local market among local producers, as spurs to quality improvements in their goods or services. Under this third hypothesis, the extent of innovation and entrepreneurship is therefore perceived to depend primarily on the levels of local competition, market entry and variety.

[4] p. 963

Hypothesis 4: *The contemporary geography of innovation is essentially a result of the fact that innovation is most likely to occur in small and medium-sized enterprises, whose spatial patterns happen to be uneven.*

A fourth approach to explaining the uneven geographical patterns of innovation also picks up the theme of market entry. In common with the previous approach, this approach rests on the perception that innovation is most likely to occur in highly competitive local markets dominated by small- and medium-sized enterprises, which have neither the scale nor the risk-bearing capacity to provide all of the key inputs on their own account. However, this fourth approach involves another type of 'milieu' (Aydalot and Keeble, 1988) argument which instead of focusing on competition, emphasizes the geography of cooperation, and the development of 'trust' relations between firms. The foundations of this approach come from the social network model (Granovetter, 1973, 1985, 1991 and 1992) which highlights the role of social, as well as purely instrumental, business links. Observations of industrial districts such as Silicon Valley (Scott, 1988; Saxenian, 1994) and the Emilio-Romagna region of Italy (Scott, 1988; Castells and Hall, 1994) have suggested that the geographical proximity of SMEs may be a necessary criterion for the development of mutual trust relations based on a shared experience and interaction of decision-making agents in different firms.

25.5 Contemporary Thinking about Innovation and Geography

Over recent years within the regional development field, the insights of the product-cycle literature accounted for by hypotheses 1 and 2 have been largely superseded by the second composite 'new industrial clusters' strand of literature, which broadly accounts for hypotheses 3 and 4. One major reason why this composite 'new industrial clusters' literature has tended to dominate the older product cycle literature is because of the assumed increasing role played by smaller firms in innovation and entrepreneurship. Indeed, there is much evidence to suggest that during the last two decades, small firms have played a major role in the generation of economic growth (Barkham et al., 1996). As such, small firms are regarded nowadays by many commentators (Keeble and Wilkinson, 1999) as the major source of many new ideas, products and processes. The result has been that the new industrial clusters literature has been used extensively during the last decade or so to discuss the growth behaviour of certain dynamic regions dominated by SMEs, with a particular focus on high-technology firms (Scott, 1988; Saxenian, 1994; Castells and Hall, 1994; Porter, 1990). On the other hand, because the product-cycle literature tended to focus primarily on large organizational hierarchies, to many commentators it has become somewhat inappropriate for discussing modern groupings of highly dynamic small firms. As such, the influence of the product-cycle hypotheses appears to have waned, in favour of the new industrial clusters literature.

An unfortunate aspect of these changes in the emphases of academic thinking, however, is that as this new industrial clusters strand of literature has gained progressively more influence in contemporary thinking about entrepreneurship, innovation and regional development, in many cases it has now come to be presented not only as a positive analysis of regional development, but also as something of a normative one (Saxenian, 1994). In particular, many commentators argue that the spatial clustering of small firms, and in particular those engaged in high technology activities, provides the optimal spatial–industrial structure for twenty-first century regional development (Castells and Hall, 1994), because such spatial organizational groupings best allow for the flexible rearrangement of inter-firm ties and alliances (Aydalot and Keeble, 1988; Saxenian, 1994). The major characteristics of this idealized type of industrial cluster are that there are many small member firms engaging in mutual inter-firm information exchanges of both an informal and formal nature, the result of which is a high degree of flexibility in their inter-firm alliances. Proponents of this view argue that this particular form of industrial organization provides the optimal environment for localized entrepreneurship, innovation and growth.

While there is no generalizable robust empirical evidence for this assertion, it is a belief that has become widely adopted in a variety of circles. The result of this is that in both academic research and public policy-making, the focus of debate has tended be on the issues raised by the two hypotheses associated with new industrial clusters literature, and much less so on those issues raised by the product-cycle literature. Yet, it is important to note here that the hypotheses outlined in the previous section are exactly that; they are hypotheses that require testing and validation or refutation. However, a problem with much of this intertwined new industrial clusters literature is that, as the material is currently specified, there is no real null hypothesis to be tested (McCann and Sheppard, 2003), nor is there anything that can be generalized. Part of the reason for this is that the underlying assumptions embedded in these arguments are very rarely specified. Therefore, in order to make this material amenable to some sort of hypothesis testing it is necessary to consider explicitly the implicit underlying bases of these hypotheses. Therefore, in order to make our analysis of the interrelationships between industrial clustering, entrepreneurship and innovation more general, it is necessary to explain the various assumptions behind various notions of economic geography, and then relate them to different contexts and situations.

25.6 A TRANSACTIONS COSTS APPROACH TO DEFINING INDUSTRIAL CLUSTERS

Market mechanisms are mediated via a range of different types of institutions, which can be of an economic, political or legal nature. From the perspective of innovation and entrepreneurship, situations where such transactions costs are significant can lead to missing markets and an absence of new dynamic and entrepreneurial developments. On the other hand, cases in which the institutional arrangements lead to low transactions-costs may facilitate innovation and entrepreneurship.[5] Therefore, where institutional environments differ between locations, the (non-trivial) transactions-costs involved in overcoming such local market barriers to entry and information access may vary significantly. Variations in institutional environments could therefore be a possible explanation as to why some regions appear to foster entrepreneurship and innovation while other regions do not appear to do so to the same extent.

One way of investigating whether this is so is to consider the types of institutional arrangements which exist within a region, and to identify whether such arrangements affect the level of information flows and market entry possibilities required to reward entrepreneurial behaviour. The most appropriate analytical approach we can employ to discuss these institutional issues is a transactions-costs model (Williamson, 1975). However, because such models are essentially aspatial, it is therefore necessary for us to frame a transactions costs model within an explicitly geographical setting.

In order to see this we can adopt a transactions-costs perspective to define three distinct types of industrial clusters which exist in the regional development literature. These three stylized types of industrial clusters are defined according to the assumed nature of the firms and agents within the cluster, the nature of their relations, and nature of the transactions which take place within the cluster (Simmie and Sennet, 1999; Gordon and McCann, 2000; McCann, 2001; McCann and Sheppard, 2003, McCann and Shefer, 2004). These three clusters types are not in themselves theories, nor are they an invented theoretical construct. Rather, they simply represent the implicit (and in some cases explicit) assumptions embedded in the various existing models of industrial clustering. Our reason for discussing them here is to make such transactions-costs assumptions explicit in all cases of clustering, and in particular to highlight the assumptions underlying the 'new industrial clusters' models.

[5] By 'institutional arrangements', we mean here specifically the types of inter-firm relations which exist, the types of local barriers to entry which prevail, and the types of information flows which are available.

Table 25.1 Industrial clusters: A transactions costs approach

Characteristics	Pure agglomeration	Industrial complex	Social network
Firm size	Atomistic	Some firms are large	Variable
Characteristics of relations	Non-identifiable, fragmented, unstable	Identifiable stable trading	Trust, loyalty, joint lobbying, joint ventures, non-opportunistic
Membership access to cluster	Open rental payments, location necessary	Closed internal investment, location necessary	Partially open history experience, location necessary but not sufficient
Space outcomes	Rent appreciation	No effect on rents	Partial rental capitalization
Notion of space	Urban	Local but not urban	Local but not urban
Example of cluster	Competitive urban economy	Steel or chemicals production complex	New industrial areas
Analytical approaches	Models of pure agglomeration	Location-production theory, input-output analysis	Social network theory (Granovetter)

The three distinct types of industrial clusters are: (i) the *pure agglomeration*; (ii) the *industrial complex*; and (iii) the *social network*. The characteristics of each of the cluster types are listed in Table 25.1, where we can see that the three stylized ideal types of cluster are all quite different.

In the model of pure agglomeration, inter-firm relations are inherently transient. Firms are essentially atomistic, in the sense of having no market power, and they will continuously change their relations with other firms and customers in response to market arbitrage opportunities, thereby leading to intense local competition. As such, there is no loyalty between firms, nor are any particular relations long-term. The external benefits of clustering accrue to all local firms simply by reason of their local presence. The cost of membership of this cluster is simply the local real estate market rent. There are no free riders, access to the cluster is open, and consequently it is the growth in the local real estate rents which is the indicator of the cluster's performance. This idealized type is best represented by the Marshall (1920) model of agglomeration described in section 3, and is the notion of clustering underlying models of new economic geography (Krugman, 1991; Fujita et al., 1999). The notion of space in these models is essentially urban space in that this type of clustering only exists within individual cities.

The industrial complex is characterized primarily by long-term stable and predictable relations between the firms in the cluster. This type of cluster is most commonly observed in industries such as steel and chemicals, and is the type of spatial cluster typically discussed by classical (Weber, 1909) and neo-classical (Moses, 1958) location–production models, representing a fusion of locational analysis with input–output analysis (Isard and Kuenne, 1953). Component firms within the spatial grouping each undertake significant long term investments, particularly in terms of physical capital and local real estate, in order to become part of the grouping. Access to the group is therefore severely restricted both by high entry and exit costs; and the rationale for spatial clustering in these types of industries is that proximity is required primarily in order to minimize inter-firm transport transactions costs. Rental appreciation is not a feature of the cluster, because the land which has already been purchased by the firms is not for sale. The notion of space in the industrial complex is local, but not necessarily urban, in that these types of complexes can exist either within or outside of an individual city. This complex model is actually the single explicitly spatial element in the transactions costs approach of Williamson (1975), where the focus is on the types of flow-process scale economies which firms can realize by being part of vertically-integrated production complexes. This type of thinking has often been the basis of policies aimed at the fostering of industrial enclaves, particularly in developing economies (Isard and Vietorisz, 1955).

The third type of spatial industrial cluster is the social network model. This is associated primarily with the work of Granovetter (1973), and is a response to the hierarchies model of Williamson (1975). The social network model argues that mutual trust relations between key decision-making agents in different organizations may be at least as important as decision-making hierarchies within individual organizations. These trust relations will be manifested by a variety of features, such as joint lobbying, joint ventures, informal alliances, and reciprocal arrangements regarding trading relationships. However, the key feature of such trust relations is an absence of opportunism, in that individual firms will not fear reprisals after any reorganization of inter-firm relations. Inter-firm cooperative relations may therefore differ significantly from the organizational boundaries associated with individual firms, and these relations may be continually reconstituted. All of these behavioural features rely on a common culture of mutual trust, the development of which depends largely on a shared history and experience of the decision-making agents. This social network model is essentially aspatial, but from the point of view of geography, it can be argued that in some cases, spatial proximity will tend to foster such trust relations, thereby leading to a local business environment of confidence, risk-taking and cooperation. Spatial proximity is therefore necessary but not sufficient to acquire access to the network. As such, membership of the network is only partially open, in that local rental payments will not guarantee access, although they will improve the chances of access.

Importantly, for our purposes, the geographical manifestation of the social network is the so-called 'new industrial areas' model (Scott, 1988), which has been used to describe the characteristics and performance of areas such as the Emilio-Romagna region of Italy (Piore and Sabel, 1984; Scott, 1988; Castells and Hall, 1994) and Silicon Valley (Scott, 1988; Saxenian, 1994; Castells and Hall, 1994). In this model, space is once again local, but not necessarily urban.

In reality, all spatial clusters will contain characteristics of one or more of these ideal types, although one type will tend to be dominant in each cluster at a particular time period. Therefore, in order to understand the advantages to the dynamic, innovative and entrepreneurial firm of being located in any particular cluster, it is first necessary to determine which of the ideal types of industrial cluster, described in Table 25.1, most accurately reflects the overall characteristics and behaviour of the firms in the cluster. With this knowledge, we can then consider how the organizational characteristics and objectives of our innovative firm or agent relate to the characteristics and behaviour of the other clustered firms.

25.7 Discussion

From all of the arguments covered in sections 25.4 to 25.6, we see that understanding the relationship between entrepreneurship, innovation and regional development, requires an institutional understanding of the types of inter-firm relations which exist locally, the types of local barriers to market entry which prevail, and the types of information flows which are available to local economic agents.[6] As we saw in section 25.6, this is because there are strong (transactions-costs) grounds for arguing that different types of clusters will have different advantages for different types of innovation, risk-taking and entrepreneurial behaviour. Such a mode of analysis allows us to distinguish which types of firms will benefit from which particular type of cluster, on the basis of a consideration of the associated organizational, information and institutional issues.

In the pure agglomeration model, a monopolistically competitive market structure is characterized by a large number of firms, each with a relatively small market share and profits. Thus, such firms would appear to have little to lose from knowledge outflows and more to gain from inflows stemming from a strong clustered location, so that the public good aspect of knowledge may predominate

[6] This approach to analysis, whereby the decision-making and organizational characteristics of the firm are considered explicitly with respect to the firm's technology and environment, is a standard methodological approach in industrial organisational research (Caves, 1982; Aliber, 1993).

and knowledge outflows are viewed as being positive overall (Jaffe et al., 1993; Saxenian, 1994). This public-good feature of local knowledge may also encourage additional inward mobile investment from businesses seeking a conducive environment for an innovation-based growth strategy.

On the other hand, in an oligopolistic industry structure, such oligopolistic firms realize that knowledge outflows to industry rivals can be extremely costly in terms of lost competitive advantage, because in these circumstances the private good aspect of knowledge is generally the dominant consideration. In situations where any information outflows from a firm are more valuable to a firm's competitors than any potential information outflows from these competitors to the firm, the overall effect of the knowledge outflows is perceived to be negative. This information spillover argument therefore provides a powerful counter-argument to the simple new industrial clusters logic, because if we apply the Akerlof (1970) market-for-lemons model, industrial clusters which include large oligopolistic competitors will be plagued by adverse selection and should either fail to form, or become concentrations of mediocrity,[7] unless the cluster exhibits the characteristics of an industrial complex. This will lead the firm to decide not to locate in clusters characterized by pure agglomeration, although, depending on the transportation costs, they may consider locating in complexes characterized by stable, planned, and long-term inter-firm relationships. The only other possible reason why such a firm would locate in a cluster characterized by either pure agglomeration or a social network, would simply be as a means of facilitating the hiring of specialist labour in situations where more orthodox hiring arrangements are for some reason not possible.

As we have seen in section 6 above, the treatment of knowledge and information flows within the new industrial clustering literature is quite different to those evident in the pure agglomeration and industrial complex models, and is based on a very specific set of assumptions regarding the nature of the inter-firm transactions, information flows and organizational arrangements. This alternative description of localized growth within new industrial clusters literature assumes that modern dynamic industrial clustering depends to a large extent on the Granovetter assumptions of inter-firm trust. However, a problem with this argument is that spatial clustering is neither a necessary nor a sufficient criterion for the development of trust relations. For innovation, key features of trust relations are a confidence in the competence of collaborators to operate in an innovative environment, and absence of fear of reprisals after any reorganization of inter-firm relations. It is true that co-location and a shared history may contribute to the development of such local trust. However, trust of this kind also requires a

[7] This counter-argument to the Porter logic appears to explain the empirical finding that many of the largest firms do not co-locate their knowledge creation activities with those of their competitive rivals (Cantwell and Santangelo, 1999; Simmie, 1998).

combination of inside information about competences and dispositions, about whose capacities can be relied on or not, and about the forms of social control which penalize breaches of a community's business norms. Inside information and social control will tend to be maximised in rather conservative, static activities and regional economies, and such tight forms of social control are likely to be inimical to innovation (Rodriguez-Pose, 1999). As such, there is something of a tension between these requirements and those highlighted by the clusters-trust approach. Not all trust relations therefore are supportive of innovation, and thus, the relationship between innovation and trust relations appears rather ill-defined. Unfortunately, however, rather than making these issues part of the research question, the idealized spatial-organizational arrangements assumed by the new industrial clusters literature are treated as being exogenously given, because of the assumed (unsubstantiated) nature of modern technology (Saxenian, 1994). Unsurprisingly, the result of this new industrial clusters literature, whereby spatial and organizational arrangements are simply assumed away, is that the relationships between clustering, innovation, entrepreneurship and regional development are still little understood.

25.8 Conclusions

By analyzing the nature of the inter-firm relations and transactions, we see that there is no inherent reason why the relationship between geography and industrial organization assumed by the new industrial clusters literature, should be systematically superior to alternative spatial-industrial arrangements in promoting innovation and entrepreneurship. The reason is that alternative forms of spatial and institutional arrangements are appropriate for different environments, and attempts at characterizing an idealized typology of firm–industry–geography organization which maximizes innovation would appear to misunderstand the inherent features of innovation itself. It is quite possible that for many of those sectors where clustering is perceived to aid innovation, this particular spatial pattern had already emerged to a large extent for other rather different reasons. Simple cluster and industrial districts assumptions may therefore only be applicable to certain types of situations and certain types of industrial structures, and may therefore be rather limited in their applicability for regional development issues in general. More importantly, analysts need to consider the types of firms and organizations already within a region, the costs and benefits to these firms of local knowledge inflows and outflows, the relationships between information requirements and the organizational boundaries of these firms, and the nature and stability of their local transactions. An analysis of these complex intertwined issues is required in order to understand the relationship between clusters, industrial districts, innovation, entrepreneurship and regional development.

References

ACS, Z. (2002). *Innovation and the Growth of Cities.* Edward Elgar: Cheltenham.

Akerlof, G. A. (1970). 'The Market for "Lemons": Quality uncertainty and the market mechanism'. *Quarterly Journal of Economics*, 84(3): 488–500.

Aliber, R. Z. (1993). *The Multinational Paradigm.* Cambridge, MA: MIT Press.

Audrestch, D. B. and M. P. Feldman (1996). 'R&D Spillovers and the Geography of Innovation and Production'. *American Economic Review*, 86(3): 630–40.

Aydalot, P. and D. Keeble (1988). *Milieux innovateurs en Europe.* Paris: GREMI.

Barkham, R., G. Gudgin, M. Hart and E. Hanvey (1996). *The Determinants of Small Firm Growth.* London: Jessica Kingsley.

Caniels, M. C. J. (1999). *Knowledge Spillovers and Economic Growth.* Cheltenhan: Edward Elgar.

Cantwell, J. A. and G. D. Santangelo (1999). 'The Frontier of International Technology Networks: Sourcing abroad the most highly tacit capabilities', *Information Economics and Policy*, 11: 101–23.

Castells, M. and P. Hall (1994). *Technopoles of the World: The Making of the 21st Century Industrial Complexes.* New York: Routledge.

Caves, R. E. (1982). *Multinational Enterprise and Economic Analysis.* Cambridge: Cambridge University Press.

Chinitz, B. (1961). 'Contrasts in Agglomeration: New York and Pittsburgh'. *American Economic Review*, 51: 279–89.

Duranton, G. and D. Puga (2001). 'Nursery Cities: Urban Diversity, Process Innovation, and the Life Cycle of Products'. *American Economic Review*, 91(5): 1454–77.

Fujita, M., P. Krugman and A. J. Venables (1999). *The Spatial Economy: Cities, Regions and International Trade.* Cambridge, MA: MIT Press.

Glaeser, E. L. (1998). 'Are Cities Dying?' *Journal of Economic Perspectives*, 12(2): 139–60.

—— (1999). 'Learning in Cities'. *Journal of Urban Economics*, 46: 254–77.

—— H. D. Kallal, J. A. Schinkmann and A. Shleifer (1992). 'Growth in Cities'. *Journal of Political Economy*, 100: 1126–52.

Granovetter, M. (1973). 'The Strength of Weak Ties'. *American Journal of Sociology*, 78: 1360–89

—— (1985). 'Economic Action and Social Structure: The Problem of Embeddedness'. *American Journal of Sociology*, 91: 481–510.

—— (1991). 'The Social Construction of Economic Institutions', in A. Etzoni and R. Lawrence (eds) *Socio-economics: Towards a New Synthesis*, pp. 75–81. New York: Armonk.

—— (1992). 'Problems of Explanation in Economic Sociology', in N. Nohria and R. Eccles (eds) *Networks and Organisations: Form and Action*, pp. 25–56. Cambridge, MA: Harvard Business School Press.

GORDON, I. R. and P. MCCANN (2005a). 'Innovation, Agglomeration and Regional Development'. *Journal of Economic Geography*, 5(5): 523–43.

—— and —— (2005b). 'Clusters, Innovation and Regional Development: An Analysis of Current Theories and Evidence', in B. Johansson, C. Karlsson and R. Stough (eds) *Entrepreneurship, Spatial Industrial Clusters and Inter-Firm Networks.* Cheltenham: Edward Elgar.

HALL, P. G. (1998). *Cities in Civilization: Culture, Innovation and the Urban Order.* London: Weidenfeld and Nicolson.

HENDERSON, J. V., A. KUNCORO and M. TURNER (1995). 'Industrial Development in Cities'. *Journal of Political Economy*, 103: 1067–85.

HOOVER, E. M. (1937). 'Location Theory and the Shoe and Leather Industries'. Cambridge, MA: Harvard University Press.

—— (1948). *The Location of Economic Activity.* New York: McGraw-Hill.

ISARD, W. and R. E. KUENNE (1953). 'The Impact of Steel upon the Greater New York–Philadelphia Industrial Region'. *Review of Economics and Statistics*, 35: 289–301.

—— and T. VIETORISZ (1955). 'Industrial Complex Analysis, and Regional Development with Particular Reference to Puerto Rico'. *Papers and Proceedings of the Regional Science Association*, 1: 229–47.

JACOBS, J. (1960). *The Economy of Cities.* New York: Random House.

JAFFE, A. B., M. TRAJTENBERG and R. HENDERSON (1993). 'Geographic Localization of Knowledge Spillovers as Evidenced by Patent Citations'. *Quarterly Journal of Economics*, 108: 577–98.

KEEBLE, D. and F. WILKINSON (1999). 'Collective Learning and Knowledge Development in the Evolution of High Technology SMEs in Europe'. *Regional Studies*, 33(4): 295–303.

KRUGMAN, P. (1991). *Geography and Trade.* Cambridge, MA: MIT Press.

—— (1998). 'Space: The final frontier'. *Journal of Economic Perspectives*, 12: 161–74.

LARSEN, J. K. and E. M. ROGERS (1984). *Silicon Valley Fever.* London: George Allen and Unwin.

MARKUSEN, A. (1985). *Profit Cycles, Oligopoly and Regional Development.* Cambridge, MA: MIT Press.

MARSHALL, A. (1920). *Principles of Economics*, 8th edn. London: Macmillan.

MCCANN, P. (2001). *Urban and Regional Economics.* Oxford: Oxford University Press.

—— and S. C. SHEPPARD (2003). 'The Rise, Fall and Rise Again of Industrial Location Theory'. *Regional Studies*, 37(6–7): 649–63.

—— and D. SHEFER (2004). 'Location, Agglomeration and Infrastructure'. *Papers in Regional Science*, 83(1): 177–96

MOSES, L. (1958). 'Location and the Theory of Production'. *Quarterly Journal of Economics*, 78: 259–72.

OHLIN, B. (1933). *Interregional and International Trade.* Cambridge, MA: Harvard University Press.

PIORE, M. J. and C. F. SABEL (1984). *The Second Industrial Divide: Possibilities for Prosperity.* New York: Basic Books.

PORTER, M. (1990). *The Competitive Advantage of Nations.* New York: The Free Press.

—— (1998). 'Clusters and the New Economics of Competition'. *Harvard Business Review*, 76(6): 77–90.

RODRIGUEZ-POSE, A. (1999). 'Innovation Prone and Innovation Averse Societies: Economic performance in Europe'. *Growth and Change*, 30: 75–105.

SAXENIAN, A. (1994). *Regional Advantage.* Cambridge, MA: Harvard University Press.

SCHUMPETER, J. A. (1934). *The Theory of Economic Development.* Cambridge, MA: Harvard University Press.

—— (1942). *Capitalism, Socialism, and Democracy.* New York: Harper and Brothers.

SCOTT, A. J. (1988). *New Industrial Spaces.* London: Pion.

—— (1993). *Technopolis: High-technology Industry and Regional Development in Southern California.* Los Angeles: University of California Press.

SIMMIE, J. (1998). 'Reasons for the Development of "Islands of Innovation": Evidence from Hertfordshire'. *Urban Studies,* 35(8): 1261–89.

—— (2002). (ed). *Innovative Cities.* London: Spon.

SIMPSON, W. (1992). *Urban Structure and the Labour Market: Workers Mobility, Commuting and Underemployment in Cities.* Oxford: Clarendon Press.

STERNBERG, R. (1996). 'Reasons for the Genesis of High-tech Regions–theoretical Explanation and Empirical Evidence. *Geoforum,* 27(2): 205–23.

VERNON, R. (1960). *Metropolis 1985.* Cambridge, MA: Harvard University Press.

—— (1966). 'International Investment and International Trade in the Product Cycle'. *Quarterly Journal of Economics,* 80(2): 190–207.

WEBER, A. (1909). *Uber den Standort der Industrien* (trans. C. J. Friedrich, 1929) *Alfred Weber's Theory of the Location of Industries.* Chicago: University of Chicago. Press.

WILLIAMSON, O. E. (1975). *Markets and Hierarchies.* New York: The Free Press.

CHAPTER 26

INTERNATIONAL EXPANSION: FOREIGN DIRECT INVESTMENT BY SMALL- AND MEDIUM-SIZED ENTERPRISES[1]

PETER J. BUCKLEY[2]

26.1 Introduction

International expansion by small- and medium-sized enterprises has long been a subject of research. The fact that internationalization begins earlier in a firm's life cycle has attracted attention to international new ventures (defined by Oviatt and McDougall 1994: 46) as 'a business organization that, from inception, seeks to derive significant competitive advantage from the use of resources and the sale of outputs in multiple countries), 'early internationalizers' and 'born global firms'. This chapter analyzes the internationalization of SMEs and examines the role of entrepreneurship in the literature. McDougall and Oviatt (2000: 903) define international

[1] This paper draws on earlier papers Buckley (1997), Buckley and Casson (2001), Buckley, et al., (2002) and Buckley and Frecknall Hughes (2005).

[2] I would like to thank Mark Casson, Bernard Yeung and Nigel Wadeson for comments on earlier versions.

entrepreneurship as 'a combination of innovative proactive and risk-seeking behaviour that crosses national borders and is intended to create value in organizations'. As we shall see, this definition provides a wide scope for research but also poses problems in terms of the level of the analysis and difficulties with respect to outcomes that are so far unresolved. This creates a rich, but unfulfilled agenda. (Dana, 2004).

26.2 The role of entrepreneurship in internationalization

In what sense is an internationalization move more 'entrepreneurial' when it is carried out by a small firm rather than a large one? First, the degree of risk is higher in that the proportion of resources of the firm as a whole is likely to be greater. This is true of financial resources but it is even more true of management and informational resources as foreign ventures are intensive in these scare resources. It is important to distinguish small firm foreign investment and foreign investment by inexperienced naive firms (that may be large), particularly those of first-time investors, where information costs, and time, may weigh heavily (Buckley et al., 1988). Secondly, entrepreneurship involves innovation and overcoming barriers. The first move abroad represents innovation and any move abroad has to overcome barriers of unfamiliarity of location and culture. Thirdly, entrepreneurship involves the utilization of decision-making capacity (Casson 1982, 2000b) and certainly foreign ventures require high degrees of attention to a set of dimensions either in a new context (choice of products and production techniques) or from a new perspective (cultural adaptation in production marketing and management). Finally, the early perception of an opportunity requires entrepreneurial skill.

26.3 Theoretical approaches to internationalization by SMEs

In a previous paper (Buckley, 1989), I reviewed the analysis of the internationalization of SMEs under four generic headings: the economics of the firm's growth; internationalization and evolutionary approaches to growth; the 'gambler's earnings hypothesis'; and the corporate decision-making approach. There is no point in reviewing each of these in detail again; instead, this paper attempts to synthesize the key issues and update the arguments.

Several key arguments can be abstracted from the literature. First, there is an important relationship between the firm and the market. There is a crucial relationship between the firm's size and overall market size. In one polar case, we can envisage a small firm attempting to grow (internationalize) in a 'big-firm' industry, that is, an industry where optimal scale is large in relation to market size. This poses problems in terms of resource acquisition, notably capital and management skills. In the other extreme case, there are industries with few economies of scale where many small firms prosper. Industries requiring a wide range of specialist intermediate inputs, in particular, present a small firm in equilibrium with a small market. Thus we can make a distinction between absolute smallness and relative smallness. The role of small firms in filling a niche market has been noted as a key attribute of Third World multinationals whose key competitive advantage is their skill as versatile users of flexible equipment (Wells, 1983). There is a case to be made that the current 'downsizing' and moves towards 'lean production' and 'outsourcing' mean greater opportunities for smaller firms to fill new supply niches.

Secondly, there are several important constraints on the international activities of SMEs. Perhaps the most important of these are internal constraints. Two key issues here are shortages of capital and of managerial skill. In raising capital, a small firm faces a 'catch-22' problem—how to raise finance without disclosing its competitive advantages (in particular its proprietary technology). These institutional difficulties of capitalizing knowledge are compounded by the necessity to retain (family) control. The shortage of skilled management in SMEs is often a more serious problem. Small firms, typically, do not have specialist executives to manage their international operations, nor do they possess a hierarchy of mangers through which complex decisions can be filtred. Decision-making is likely to be personalized, involving ad hoc, short-term reckoning based on individual perception and prejudice (this is not unknown in large multinationals). A shortage of management time leads to the firm taking short cuts without a proper evaluation of alternatives. Information costs bear heavily on small firms, and attempts to avoid or reduce these costs—for instance by making no serious attempt to evaluate a potential agent to joint venture partner—can be disastrous. The horizons of small firms are limited by managerial constraints and there is little 'global scanning' of opportunities. Therefore, when an opportunity presents itself, it is often seized without proper evaluation. Given this problem, why does the firm not recruit management from outside the firm? One problem is the desire of family-owned companies to retain control inside the family circle; the other is the difficulty in obtaining specialist knowledge of how to evaluate outsiders. Lack of these crucial evaluation skills constrains recruitment and renders endemic the burden on management. Consequently, small firms with inexperienced mangers can behave in a naive fashion, particularly outside their normal cultural milieu. They can be politically naive because they lack public relations skills, lobbying power and the sheer economic muscle of larger firms.

The role of risk and uncertainty is an important one in determining SME internationalization patterns. It is likely that the proportion of resources committed to a foreign direct investment will be greater than for a large, diversified multinational. Failure is thus more costly. This can interact with information costs in a negative way, in that costly information collection will not be undertaken. Thus 'shortcuts' or spurning of opportunities can result. Alternatively, owner-mangers often act on impulse and are often greater risk-takers than more 'managerialist' entrepreneurs. The rather erratic financial behaviour of SMEs may also be explained by these factors. The 'gambler's earnings hypothesis' highlights an important empirical phenomenon—a small initial foreign investment eventually leading to a large payback of profit in the form of dividends. An explanation is given by analogy with ploughing and harvesting. A period of ploughing may be set by the firm (say 5 to 7 years). In this time the foreign subsidiary is given a great deal of freedom of action. After that, the foreign subsidiary either generates a stream of income for the next project (the next ploughing) or it is sold off to obtain a return on the capital. The short decision-making horizon arises because of the restricted capital and management capacity. Thus a target rate of return and/or payback period are discovered by trial and error.

Fourthly, we need to pay attention to the dynamics of growth in the industry. Large multinational firms often have highly sector-specific expansion routes. This leaves niche markets or 'interstices' for SMEs to exploit. These niches are often in 'small firms industries' or exist as a fringe in 'large firm industries'. SMEs may thus be 'pulled' into foreign markets by large firms requiring suppliers, or 'pushed' abroad by increasing competition in home markets. The flexibility of SMEs in adjusting to external conditions needs to be set against their vulnerability to radical change in technological, political, institutional and competitive conditions. The role of SMEs will vary over the life cycle of an industry. In the early stages, numbers of small firms will vie for position. As the industry matures, economies of scale become prevalent and only a few will survive. In the decline phase, established competitors will face a threat from new entrepreneurial, innovating SMEs (Vernon, 1966, 1974, 1979).

The influence of networks of firms is therefore very significant (Casson, 2005) for the internationalization process of SMEs (Corviello and Munro, 1997). Models of globalization and vertical structure and of market thickness effects (McLaren, 2000), and of the impact of the extent of the market (Stigler, 1951) could be used with good effect in extending this research area and giving more rigour to the analysis. What is clear is that the trajectories of expansion of MNEs are co-evolutionary with those of SMEs. These elements need to be factored into the analyses of the globalization and internationalization of SMEs. Networks represent an asset (resource) for SMEs (Chen, 2003) when they are included, but we should also remember the potentially negative effects of networks on SMEs—through exclusion (Buckley and Casson, 1988) or through the exercise of the excessive power of larger network members as purchasers, suppliers or partners. Network effects need careful (case-by-case and longitudinal) analysis—they should not always be assumed to be benign (Welch and Welch, 1996).

26.4 Internationalization, globalization and SMEs

The motivation for SMEs to make foreign direct investments is remarkably orthodox. The three key motives which we observe for multinational companies—market seeking, resource seeking, and efficiency (low cost) seeking investments—are all present in the list of motivations for SMEs as they are for multinationals (Buckley, 1979). It is possible to contrast internationalization with globalization. Internationalization is the term normally used for the gradual, sequential incremental approach described in Scandinavian literature (Johanson and Wiedersheim-Paul, 1975; Johanson and Vahlne, 1977) and by the studies carried out at Bradford (Buckley et al., 1988; Buckley et al., 1983). In contrast, the globalization approach suggests that firms can reach foreign markets in a simultaneous fashion—by a 'big bang'.

Casson (1994) has attempted to synthesize these approaches by examining internationalization as a corporate learning process. He posits a model where the cost of acquisition of information about a market generates a set-up cost of entry. The sequential approach to entry hinges on the exploitation of systematic similarities between markets. Because of such similarities, experience acquired in one foreign market is of potential relevance to another. If foreign markets were all totally different from one another, then nothing learned in one market would have any significance for another. However if markets are very similar, then a globalization pattern—a single discrete simultaneous entry into all markets—becomes feasible.

In a sequential approach, decisions about entering the second market are deferred until the first has been entered because this provides an option value which strengthens the case of sequential entry when some markets are only marginally profitable. However, this model assumes that each market is investigated before the local marketing strategy is determined. This can be contrasted with purely experimental learning where the market is entered without systematic investigation, and learning results from responding to mistakes. The decision to learn by experience, Casson suggests, depends 'first and foremost on the confidence of the management, and on the costliness of mistakes, and only peripherally on the issue of sequential entry' (1994: 15). Thus there is a key trade-off between exploiting economies of scope in knowledge (maximized by a sequential strategy), and the gains from exploiting profitable market opportunities without delay (a simultaneous entry globalization strategy).

Casson's piece is also illuminating on the issue of uncertainty. He suggests that there are two varieties of uncertainty facing the internationalizing firm: uncertainty about the state of the market (how similar it is to the home market and other previously entered markets); and the cost of collecting information to overcome this problem. The cost of collection depends on the type of market which is not known in advance. The cost of 'mistaken entry' may well be below that of systematic investigation; thus, making mistakes may be a rational way of expansion.

26.5 Managerial processes in small firms and technology transfer

Chen and Hambrick (1995) found (in a study of airlines) that the small firms tended to be more active than the large ones in initiating competitive moves; but in contrast, large firms seemed to be more responsive when attacked. This is consistent with the flexibility and rapidity in strategy often ascribed to small firms. With regard to action visibility, small firms were more likely to be more low-key and even secretive. The authors characterize actions as follows: 'it appears that small airlines tend to hold their fire, calculating well-developed, visible responses; large airlines act quickly but in rather straightforward, unexciting ways' (p. 474). Hence the title of the paper: 'Speed, stealth and selective attack: how small firms, differ from large firms in competitive behaviour'.

This stereotype of small firms as fast-moving opportunists may not be generalizable across industries or across cultures, Steinmann, Kumar and Wasner (1981) found that German medium-sized firms in the USA followed a rather cautious, managerialist approach to internationalization. Briemann (1989) found that smaller British firms invested in search of new markets, whereas German firms were more concerned with securing existing market positions.

The multinational research project on the international transfer of technology by small- and medium-sized enterprises (Buckley et al., 1997) found that industry, national host and source country factors influenced the form and nature of technology transfer but that idiosyncratic management influences were strong in SMEs.

Scandinavian literature on the internationalization strategy of the firm emphasizes the incremental and sequential nature of both the export process and the foreign direct investment process (see for example, Johanson and Wiedersheim-Paul, 1975; Johanson and Vahlne, 1977; Strandskov, 1993). Firms acquire experience of one foreign market before entering the next: they do not enter all major markets at the outset. In this way they benefit from the lessons learned in the early stages of expansion and avoid making too many big mistakes. There are two other theories, however—namely, internalization and globalization—which seem to imply that, on the contrary, firms will internationalize in a single discrete step involving simultaneous entry into all markets. This conflict between the theories is more apparent than real, however. This paper shows that the theory of organizational learning implicit in the Scandinavian approach in fact complements these other approaches, by highlighting factors which they omit. A formal model is presented which clarifies these complementarities and so enriches all three areas of theory. This chapter attempts to show the relevance of the real option analysis in the internationalization process.

It turns out that this model includes, as a special case, an international analogue (Penrose, 1959) of theory of the growth of the firm. This is because it embodies, in addition to Scandinavian insights, one of Penrose's key ideas, namely that it is prohibitively costly for any team of managers to diversify in several directions at once. It touches on an even more fundamental issue too: the scope of the rational actor model in analyzing managerial behaviour. It is widely believed that rational action implies that managers do not make mistakes. It is claimed that, in consequence, behavioural models of learning may provide a better account of managerial behaviour than does the rational action approach.

This argument ignores the possibility that rational managers will take account of information costs, however. The model presented here shows that, when information is costly, rational managers will make mistakes because the optimal frequency of mistakes is greater than zero. Because the model assumes rationality it can actually predict the kind of mistakes that will be made and the frequency with which they will occur. It shows that the entire internationalization strategy of the firm can be interpreted as a strategy designed to reduce, but not eliminate, the incidence of mistakes in individual market entry strategies. This illustrates one of the main strengths of the rational action approach: the facilitation of simple mathematical modelling, which not only captures existing insights in parsimonious terms, but deepens these insights and reveals new ones as well.

26.6 Collecting information

It is often suggested that uncertainty is a basic fact of life, but this is not quite correct. Uncertainty can be dispelled by collecting information. Even if it cannot be dispelled entirely, its impact can be reduced by narrowing down the margin for error. It is therefore irrational to always passively accept uncertainty.

But how is it possible to know how much information is worth collecting? Rational action modelling provides an answer to this question. All that is required is that the decision-maker can estimate the cost of collecting relevant items of information, and attach subjective probabilities to what the results of investigation will turn out to be. This allows the decision-maker to estimate both the costs and the benefits of collecting information, and therefore to arrive at a rational information strategy (Casson, 2000a).

Decision-making becomes a two-stage procedure: in the first stage the decision-maker decides how much information to collect, and in the second stage uses the information collected to take the decision. These two stages are interdependent, and the rational decision-maker arrives at a strategy by considering them in reverse order. He or she knows that it would be a waste of time collecting information that would not influence their decision. Therefore there is a need to determine in advance how any item of information would be used if it were to hand. If it were not to be used, whatever it turned out to be, then it would be a waste of time collecting it. Only once the decision-maker has decided how he or she would use it are they in a position to decide whether they want to collect it or not. (See Table 26.1).

Table 26.1 Information gathering versus investment deferral decisions

	Do not defer commit resource time t	Defer commitment of resource 'Real options'
Do not collect information (Measure things you would otherwise not know).	1 Gung-ho investor	3 Cautious but uninformed investor
Do collect information research prudentially	2 Informed risk-taker	4 Sophisticated investor

26.6.1 Using decision trees

The fundamental point about research is that it alters the information set available to the decision-maker at the time of the decision. Without research, the decision-maker acts first and the true situation reveals itself later, whereas with research the situation is revealed before the decision-maker acts.

A complete description of a research strategy involves specifying not only what information will be collected but also what the decision-maker will do with the information once it has been collected.

The gist of this discussion so far may be summarized as follows:

(1) Research strategies enlarge the information set available to the decision-maker and thereby reduce the risk of error;
(2) Research strategies involve rules for using the information that has been collected in the course of the research; and
(3) As new strategies are introduced, new critical points are introduced at which switching between strategies occurs.

26.6.2 Deferring decisions: Real options

Research is not the only way of augmenting the information set. If a decision-maker waits long enough, the information they require may reveal itself anyway. Deferring a decision may save the cost of collecting the information at the outset. The reason why firms do not delay decisions is because there is a cost involved. For example, if market entry is to be profitable right away, profits will be lost if entry is deferred. Furthermore, there is a risk that another firm may enter the market and pre-empt the profit opportunity. Comparing deferment with research, therefore, there is a trade-off between saving information costs on the one hand, and losing revenue on the other.

If market entry decisions were fully reversible then there would be no need to defer a decision at all. A provisional decision would be made on the basis of the information that was freely available at the outset, and when additional information became available this decision would be changed as appropriate. The revenue stream would therefore commence immediately, and the cost of information would be avoided altogether. The only losses would relate to errors made at the outset, and corrected later.

In practice, of course, most decisions are not reversible. If the firm invests in a foreign production plant, for example, it will not be able to sell it off for as much as it cost to build. The 'illiquidity' of the plant means that the firm incurs a capital loss. Similarly, if the firm adapts the plant to some alternative use, then adjustment costs will be incurred. Some investments are more readily reversed than others. Strategies that involve reversible investments afford more flexibility than those which do not. High levels of uncertainty favour the selection of flexible strategies, since mistakes are easier to put right (Buckley and Casson, 1998b).

26.7 Evaluation of the Uppsala Approach

The preceding analysis has immediate relevance to the evaluation of alternative theories of the firm. To begin with, the analysis highlights the importance of subjective beliefs about the similarity and dissimilarity of different markets. It shows that the advantage of a sequential approach to expansion is greatest when foreign markets are believed to be different from the home one, but are likely to be similar to each other. Given that they are indeed similar, the sequential approach maximizes the economies of scope that the first investigation affords. Conversely, the advantage of the simultaneous strategy is greatest when the foreign markets are believed to be similar to the home one, and, if different, to be different in their own particular way. This means that experience gained from any particular market will be of little relevance elsewhere.

The strategic management literature advocating globalization (Porter, 1986) clearly adopts this latter view. The markets of different industrialized countries are claimed to be basically similar—at least so far as the preferences of young high-income consumers are concerned—and any variation tends to be imputed to local factors peculiar to each market. Globalization therefore appears in the present model as a specific response to a particular configuration of the international market system.

Internalization theory is often alleged to favour a rather similar strategy. This is because of the theory's emphasis on the public good properties of knowledge developed in the domestic market, and the advantage of exploiting these properties internally through expansion of the firm. In fact, however, most authors in this tradition have been very aware of the 'psychic costs' to the firm of entering foreign markets (Buckley and Casson, 1976). Internalization theorists have tended to assume that all markets are different, so that there is always a cost of entry. Because all markets are different, the scope economies of accrued experience of market entry have not been emphasized in the same way as in the Scandinavian literature. The internalization view has supported the simultaneous approach simply because there is little point in deferring entry if the costs cannot be reduced using experience gained in other markets first. Simultaneous entry is also promoted by the fact that, where technological knowledge is concerned, patents expire and trade secrets leak out, so that early entry into all markets is advisable before the potential monopoly rents are dissipated. Internalization theory, in other words, highlights a particular kind of pre-emptive advantage.

Where internalization theorists have argued for sequential entry it has generally been in terms of the 'Penrose' effect—that simultaneous internationalization of the firm will overstretch its managerial resources. The Penrose argument is, however, quite distinct from the argument for sequential internationalization based on economies of scope available from the learning process. The two approaches are, in principle, rival explanations of the sequential expansion of the firm, although they can be regarded as complementary and mutually reinforcing within a synthetic view. While this chapter is committed to elaborating the learning approach, it has been useful, from the standpoint of practical application, to have incorporated the Penrose theory within the model as a special case.

The difference between the internalization approach and the globalization approach lies not, therefore, in the recommended internationalization strategy but rather in the perceived profitability of internationalization per se. Because internalization theory recognizes psychic costs that globalization theory discounts, it more often favours the null strategy of remaining at home and licensing the technology to other firms overseas. Licensing to foreign firms with local knowledge of market conditions is an important element of internalization theory precisely because the psychic costs of foreign market entry are fully recognized. (See Table 26.2.)

It can be seen that, by elimination, the Uppsala approach focuses on those situations where foreign markets are unlike the home market but very similar to each other. The older literature associated with the Uppsala school emphasizes the need to expand in stages in a manner reminiscent of (but not coincident with) the product cycle model (Vernon, 1979). The more recent literature, on the other hand,

Table 26.2 Classification of theoretical approaches to internationalization

Foreign markets	Home and foreign markets Same	Different
Same	Globalization	Uppsala
Different	–	Internalization

Note: Because globalization assumes that foreign markets are essentially the same as the home market, it follows that differences between foreign markets must be small. But in so far as these small differences are idiosyncratic to each market, the logic of simultaneous internationalization will be more secure.

emphasizes the importance of speeding up the learning process by improving communication between foreign subsidiaries.

Recall that the net advantage of the sequential approach depends on, among other things, the excess of the cost of investigation over the cost of communication between subsidiaries. To encourage subsidiaries to learn from each other, it is desirable not only to improve headquarters—subsidiary communication but to encourage subsidiaries to communicate directly with each other. Organizational learning needs to be decentralized, in other words. This is an important aspect of the thinking underlying the 'heterarchy' or the 'network' firm (Hedlund, 1986; Chesnais, 1988). While the discussion of the heterarchies tends to focus on the organizational restructuring of the mature multinational enterprise, the present model emphasizes the more general advantage to the firm of building up the heterarchy in stepwise fashion from the very start of the internationalization process.

As indicated earlier, learning by doing is a satisfactory alternative to systematic investigation if the costs of making a mistake are not too great. To control these costs, firms will tend to make small commitments to begin with, and only increase their commitments once experience has been gained. Thus sequential entry into markets is accompanied by incremental expansion in these markets over time. Because systematic investigation reduces the likelihood of mistakes (in the model above it eliminates it altogether—which is clearly a very extreme case) it supports a greater initial commitment. Thus sequential expansion will be associated with different degrees of initial commitment according to the way that knowledge of markets is acquired. This coincides with the general thrust of the Uppsala approach.

Insights from these models can be used to construct 'dynamic' versions of existing static theories. The real option perspective can be applied to standard IB theories, including classic theories such as the Product Cycle model and its variants (Vernon, 1966, 1974, 1979). The real option perspective can provide a formal analysis of the leads and lags in the internationalization process which is missing from many orthodox accounts of the subject.

26.8 Early Internationalization

There is a general presumption that firms are internationalizing earlier—both in real time (from birth—hence 'born globals'), Madsen and Servais, 1997; Gabrielsson and Kirpalani, 2004) and in size. This is the result of a number of factors including downsizing, outsourcing and offshoring by large firms, the encouragement of buy-outs and buy-ins by managers and groups of managers (increasingly encouraged by the financial markets), the rise of the internet which reduces the fixed costs of marketing and the set-up costs of e-commerce based firms. (Carter 2006, see Ch. 5 in this Handbook). Global marketing and e-procurement allows firms, including SMEs, to develop global supply chains. Such chains reduce costs for large firms and may also include other SMEs in different roles. Government policy, too, may encourage early internationalization—subsidies encourage SMEs to export and thus start moves which may lead to outward FDI, and subsidies to inward investors will encourage SMEs to undertake FDI.

Recently, there have been a number of articles that attempt to synthesize and codify the research on international entrepreneurship: see Jones and Coviello (2005), Dimitratos and Jones (2005), a Special Issue of *International Business Review* 14(2) (2005) including Rialp et al. (2005). There are difficulties in attempting both to analyze entrepreneurship as a behavioural process and to evaluate performance outcomes while holding environmental conditions constant. Efforts to hold this together with 'multi theoretical perspectives' (Jones and Corviello, 2005: 299) are unconvincing. Far better to specify the research programme of international entrepreneurship as a number of distinct issues, each with its own combination of theory, method and objective. This avoids the confusion of levels of

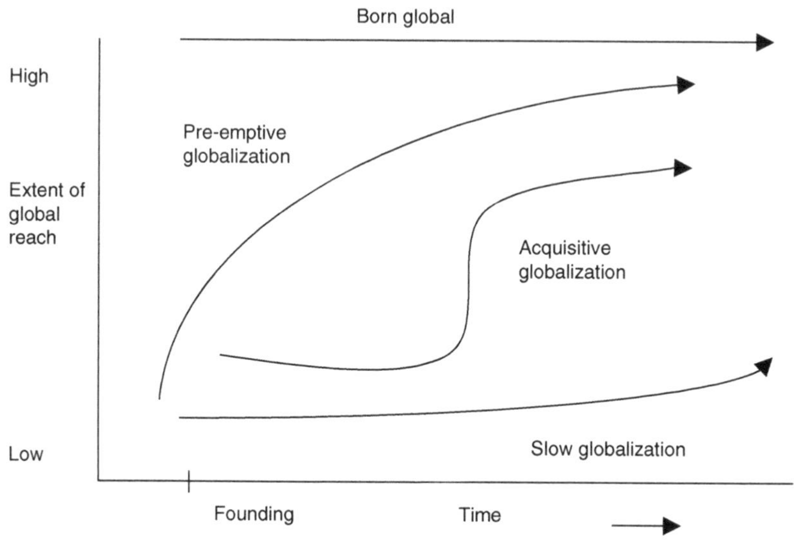

Figure 26.1 Strategies of newly-formed companies' global expansion

Source: Gupta and Govindarajan (2004 p. 175)

analysis time perspective and *ceteris paribus* assumptions that currently cloud some potentially fascinating work.

The dilemma is shown in Figure 26.1. This shows alternative strategies for global expansion by newly formed firms. The difficulty is to specify which of these alternative paths is the optimal one for the firm under consideration. More precisely, it is necessary to specify the particular conditions under which a particular path is most appropriate. As much of the modern literature makes no attempt to measure outcome (unlike some of the early material such as Buckley et al. (1988), Buckley et al. (1993) which tried to measure 'success'), then it is difficult to go beyond description (see Autio et al. 2000; Cooper, 1993; Lu and Beamish, 2001; Lumpkin and Dess, 1996). At the level of the case study there are attempts to use longitudinal methods to specify outcome (McGaughey, 2004) but generalization is difficult.

This research area, of course, is plagued by a lack of data. In 1997, the OECD pointed out that statistics on international SME activity was unavailable in the vast majority of countries. Data on small firms in general is problematic—the problem is far more acute in internationalization studies and researchers have to generate their own datasets—hence problems of non-comparability arise and generalization is hampered.

26.9 'Born globals' and 'e-commerce'

26.9.1 'Born globals'

A recent strand of literature has suggested that firms do not take incremental steps into foreign markets but are established *ab initio* with the intention of selling goods and services to foreign or indeed global markets. Effectively, these firms are set up with no preferential treatment for a 'home market'. It should be noted that this is not a new phenomenon—it mirrors the establishment of trading companies—such as the East India company (Keay, 1994). The difference from such venerable institutions is the rapidity with which overseas contacts are developed and exploited (Jones, 1999).

Oviatt and McDougall (1994), consider such firms as international new ventures which are born global. They operate typically in markets which are worldwide and dynamic where rapid change and product obsolescence are common. Madsen and Servais (1997) concur with this. To begin with, though, an idea for immediate international development means that an opportunity for business must have been identified for speedy exploitation. Coviello and Munro (1997), looking at the development of small software firms, suggest that networking and forming partnerships with larger organizations speed up development. Of the four firms they examined, all had an initial domestic focus, but clear intentions to internationalize right from the time of the firm's inception, which was achieved within three years of set-up. Coviello and Munro suggest three stages to internationalization in the context of these small software firms (i) foreign market intention, (ii) initial relationship with a larger firm for product development—a 'piggybacking' arrangement, which lead in turn to (iii) more complex entry modes into markets round the world, usually facilitated by the initial relationship, with a network of formal and informal contacts being developed.

Increased success in these arenas leads to a desire for greater autonomy with three possible further developments—diversification from core products, proactive pursuit of new markets and/or establishment of sales and marketing offices independent of network partners. As the small firm visibility increases it may become the target for acquisition by a larger firm—often associated with the network of operations. However, the initial network partner may retain sufficient control to limit activities and inhibit development other than within the existing network relationships.

This model is almost a reverse of the incremental/stages models. The small firm enters contracts, which may or may not be encapsulated in legal agreements, to become part of a larger organization in order to access international markets as per its original intention. While it may possibly become independent in due course, it could equally remain under the larger organization's control; effectively functioning as a subsidiary. It is as though having begun to mature, it has now not exactly shrunk, but its independent development has been curtailed. The small firm which does break out of network dependency would appear to exhibit subsequent autonomous development though the focus of business might still be on networks.

It is significant to stress here again the type of businesses examined: all software firms, which would be expected to be at the cutting edge of new technology. It should not surprise us that firms such as these have displayed a slightly different model of development. They would be accustomed to an environment in which rapid change is the norm. It would be expected that their business would use the latest developments in the products they themselves develop. The in-built possibility of obsolescence in product design means that speed is a feature of business. Rewards will go to the first business which successfully develops the next generation of software ahead of rivals. It is not the same as, say, car manufacture, which is slower in design and development and where differentiation of products is part of the business: not everyone wants to have the same model of car, but everyone might need the same sort of software to allow one business to interact with another.

Coviello and Munro (1997) also cite other studies which do not validate the incremental step approach into overseas markets: Chang and Grub (1992) identify stages of competitive strategy in the same firm internationalization process, but (importantly) no linear relationships between these stages and the internationalization mechanisms; and Lindquist (1988) and Bell (1995) challenge the traditional view of incremental internationalization. They also remark that the process of incremental commitment for smaller firms may be different from that displayed by larger firms, citing Lau (1992), though this is still perceived as an incremental process. If one moves away from the fixed idea of a step-by-step structure and accepts the idea of a network, then these studies show different ways in which this might be achieved. The notion of structure playing an active part in overseas development is becoming redundant.

26.9.2 The 'e-commerce model'

In the above models, it seems clear that business is moving away from the idea of becoming global or international by means of incremental steps forward into new markets, based on experience, trial and error, market evaluation, and so forth. A further, natural development from networks based on agreement in the earlier model and the 'born global' model is inherent in the possibilities that exist now because of the Internet and the World Wide Web enabling business to be carried out by electronic means. While this might be termed more accurately an 'instant global' model, we use the term 'e-commerce' model to preclude any confusion between this and the similarly named 'born global' model. A firm set up to do business over the Internet (an e-company) is in concept a very different entity from a traditional 'bricks and mortar' firm, which can frequently have, as the above models have demonstrated, physical presences in one or more geographical locations. 'The e-company is potentially multinational from genesis: it can operate internationally without the physical constraint of geographical boundaries, sometimes without even a physical presence.' (Frecknall Hughes and Glaister, 2002).

It very much depends on the type of business under consideration as to how exactly an e-commerce model would deal with it. If a company deals in products which can be delivered electronically (such as computer programs or games, digitally deliverable music, etc.), then all business can be done electronically. There will be a need for a physical presence in some country to deal with a certain amount of administration, to develop new products (research and development) and for tax purposes, but this is minimal. Obviously there will be companies which produce and deliver a physical product, so it is the selling and administration for such businesses which will be dealt with electronically: factories will still be needed to produce goods as, even if production is computerized, a physical location in which to carry this out is still needed. Businesses that currently produce physical products, and are converting to use of the Internet for business, will find that doing business this way requires a fundamental re-evaluation of all their systems. It is essential that all the 'backroom technology' be in place to work without the slightest glitch, as problems could be very costly in terms of lost sales, lost reputation and getting the hitches sorted out. It will be far more difficult to convert an existing business to use the Internet than to set up one from first principles, because it requires a completely different appreciation of how business functions interact. It is envisaged though, that doing business electronically will transform all aspects of the way business is done, 'from internal chain management to running the business and the management of its relationships ... it can increase revenues, cut costs, improve customer service and make product/service production and delivery faster. It may also facilitate the development of new business models and ventures that may be entirely or substantially based around the Internet' (Frecknall Hughes and Glaister, 2002).

At present, Internet-based business is in its infancy. However, all one theoretically needs as a customer to buy goods or services, is a PC and access to the World Wide Web. It does not matter where in the world that customer and the PC are located: it is possible to place an order from anywhere if these basics are in place. There is no longer the same need for an overseas export agent or a sales subsidiary to facilitate business. Inevitably this means that other business features such as delivery and distribution will change too.

26.10 Small and Large Firms in the Global Economy

It is important to end this review as we began—by examining the relationship between small and large firms, which remains a key determinant of expansion paths by SMEs. The interstices, as revealed by Penrose (1959) between the operations of large firms are arguably increasing as large MNEs redefine their core business and more strategies include offshoring and outsourcing. The traditional strengths of small firms—their flexibility, nimbleness, and ability to seek new openings—are still to the fore. As shown above, electronic communication has opened new areas for small firms to fill in completing the networks of the MNE's 'global factory' (Buckley, 2004). Thus, in many cases, SMEs should not be considered as 'stand alone' firms but as part of a symbiotic network with large firms (Acs et al., 1997). Indeed, large firms are often the conduits for the diffusion of SME innovations. The market servicing strategies of SMEs (exporting, licensing, joint ventures or wholly-owned foreign subsidiaries) are often co-determined by their interactions with MNEs. SMEs can thus be pushed from their home base or 'pulled' to a new foreign market by decisions of large firm suppliers, customers or co-producers.

26.11 Conclusion

Opportunities for small firms are often global but the means to achieve profitability from these opportunities are not always immediately available. This makes international expansion problematic and the firm faced with such a challenge is often vulnerable. Cautious step-by-step incremental development is often derided in the current literature in favour of rapid (sometimes incautious) internationalization. Difficulties of expanding the managing team, matching production and distribution to need, research for a stream of new products and controlling geographically separated activities are huge problems for SMEs and the balance of opportunity and risk must be evaluated at all stages of international development.

A real weakness of the current literature on early internationalizers, be they called 'born global' or not, is the lack of a link to performance. It is often assumed that internationalization per se is a good thing for small firms (often for MNEs, too). It is necessary to establish when (in what environmental and internal conditions) internationalization benefits the firm and when caution is required. Careful experimental design will be necessary to provide definitive results (see also Zahra et al., 2004 who also see performance as a critical focus of research).

The literature also suffers from a lack of focus and sometimes difficulties in establishing the appropriate unit of analysis. Research switches from the individual manager (issues of cognition) to organizational units within the firm (strategic business units, subsidiaries, divisions) to 'the firm' and to multiple firms ('networks') and without control this bedevils the results and the theorising. Some interesting attempts to examine the characteristics of individual entrepreneurs or managers (and management teams) on the performance of the firm have been made (Reuber and Fischer, 1997, 1999) and this approach is worthy of development.

It is expected that there will be considerable progress in the literature of small-firm foreign investment and internationalization in the near future. New datasets, which rise above the single case study and anecdotal evidence, are required. The meta analysis of this paper and other reviews shows that theorising is progressing, albeit at an uneven pace. Research methods need attention if progress is to be made. Decisions need to be related to outcomes and feedbacks must be specified. Results that relate entrepreneurial internationalization decisions to definite outcomes, and that specify the conditions under which success is most (and least) likely, are anticipated.

References

Acs, Z. J., R. J. M. S. Morck and B. Yeung. (1997). 'The Internationalization of Small and Medium Sized Enterprises: A policy perspective'. *Small Business Economics*, 9(1): 7–20.

Allen, L. and C. Pantzalis (1996). 'Valuation of the Operating Flexibility of Multinational Corporations'. *Journal of International Business Studies*, 27(4): 633–53.

Autio, E., H. J. Sapienza and T. G. Almeida (2000). 'Effects of Age of Entry, Knowledge Intensity and Imitability on International Growth'. *Academy of Management Journal*, 43(5): 909–24.

Bell, J. (1995). 'The Internationalization of Small Computer Firms–a further challenge to 'stage' theories'. *European Journal of Marketing*, 29(8): 60–75.

Briemann, N. (1989). 'A Comparative Study of Foreign Investment Decisions by Small and Medium Sized British and German Manufacturing Companies'. Unpublished Ph.D. thesis, Manchester Business School.

Buckley, P. J. (1979). 'Foreign Investment Success for Smaller Firms'. *Multinational Business*, 5: 12–19.

—— (1989). 'Foreign Direct Investment by Small and Medium Sized Enterprises: The theoretical background'. *Small Business Economics*, (1): 89–100.

—— (1997). 'International Technology Transfer by Small and Medium-Sized Enterprises'. *Small Business Economics* (February) 9(1): 67–78.

—— (2004). 'The Role of China in the Global Strategy of Multinational Enterprises'. *Journal of Chinese Business and Economic Studies* (January) 2(1): 1–25.

—— and M. Casson (1976). *The Future of the Multinational Enterprise*. London: Macmillan.

—— and —— (1981). 'Optimal Timing of a Foreign Direct Investment'. *Economic Journal*, 91: 75–87.

—— and —— (1988). 'A Theory of Cooperation in International Business'. *Management International Review* (SI on Cooperative Strategies) 28: 19–38.

—— and —— (1998a). 'Analysing Foreign Market Entry Strategies: Extending the internalisation approach'. *Journal of International Business Studies*, 29(3): 539–61.

—— and —— (1998b). Models of the Multinational Enterprise. *Journal of International Business Studies*, 29: 21–44.

—— and —— (2001). 'Strategic Complexity in International Business', in Alan M. Rugman and Thomas L. Brewer (eds) *The Oxford Handbook of International Business*. Oxford: Oxford University Press.

—— Z. Berkova and G. D. Newbould (1993). *Direct Investment in the UK by Smaller UK Firms*. London: Macmillan.

—— J. Campos, H. Mirza and E. White (eds) (1997). *International Technology Transfer by Small and Medium Sized Enterprises*. London: Macmillan.

Buckley, P. J., G. D. Newbould and J. Thurwell (1988). *Foreign Direct Investment by Smaller UK Firms.* London: Macmillan. (Previously published in 1978 as *Going International–The Experience of Smaller Companies Overseas.* London: Associated Business Press).

—— and M. Casson and M. A. Gulamhussen (2002). 'Internationalisation–Real Options, Knowledge Management and the Uppsala Approach', in V. Havila, M. Forsgren and H. Hakansson (eds) *Critical Perspectives on Internationalisation.* Oxford: Elsevier Science.

—— and J. Frecknall-Hughes (2005). 'New Forms of Internationalisation: The global scanning and e-commerce models.' Mimeo. *Leeds University Business School.*

Casson, M. (1982). *The Entrepreneur–An Economic Theory.* Oxford: Martin Robertson.

—— (1994). 'Internationalisation as a Learning Process: A Model of Corporate Growth and Geographical Diversification', in V. N. Balasubramanyam and David Sapsford (eds) *The Economics of International Investment.* Aldershot: Edward Elgar.

—— (1995). *Organization of International Business.* Aldershot: Edward Elgar.

—— (2000a). *Economics of International Business: A New Research Agenda.* Cheltenham: Edward Elgar.

—— (2000b). *Entrepreneurship and Leadership.* Cheltenham: Edward Elgar.

—— (2005). 'Networks: A New Paradigm in Economic and Business History?' Mimeo. University of Reading.

Chang. T. L. and P. D. Grub (1992). 'Competitive Strategies of Taiwanese PC Firms in their Internationalisation Process'. *Journal of Global Marketing,* 6(3): 5–27.

Chen, M-J. and D. C. Hambrick (1995). 'Speed, Stealth and Selective Attack: How Small Firms Differ from Large Firms in Competitive Behaviour'. *Academy of Management Journal,* 38: 453–82.

Chen, T-J. (2003). 'Network resources for internationalization: the case of Taiwan's electronics firms'. *Journal of Management Studies* (July) 40(5): 1107–1130.

Chesnais, F. (1988). 'Technical Co-operation agreements between firms'. *STI Review,* (December) 4: 51–119.

Cooper, A. C. (1993). 'Challenges in predicting new firm performance'. *Journal of Business Venturing,* 8(3): 241–53.

Coviello, N. and H. Munro (1997). 'Network Relationships and the Internationalisation Process of Small Software Firms'. *International Business Review,* 6(4): 361–86.

Dana, L-P. (2004). *Handbook of Research on International Entrepreneurship.* Cheltenham: Edward Elgar.

DeMeza, D. and F. Van Der Ploeg (1987). 'Production Flexibility as a Motive for Multinationality'. *Journal of Industrial Economics,* 35(3): 343–51.

Dimitratos P. and M. V. Jones (2005). 'Future Directions for International Entrepreneurship Research'. *International Business Review,* 14(2): 119–28.

Frecknall Hughes, J. and K. W. Glaister (2002). 'E-commerce and International Taxation: A preliminary analysis', in D. Salter and A. Lymer (eds) *Contemporary Issues in Taxation Research.* Aldershot: Ashgate Publishers.

Gabrielsson, M. and V. H. Minek Kirpalani (2004). 'Born Globals: How to reach new business space rapidly'. *International Business Review* (October) 13(5): 555–71.

Graham, E. M. (1990). Exchange of Threat Between Multinational Firms as an Infinitely Repeated Game. *International Trade Journal,* 4: 259–77.

Gupta, A. K. and V. Govindarajan (2004). *Global Strategy and Organization.* Hoboken, NJ: John Wiley & Sons Inc.

Hedlund, G. (1986). 'The Hypermodern MNC–a heterarchy?'. *Human Resource Management,* 25(1): 9–35.

Hirshleifer, J. and J. G. Riley (1992). *The Analytics of Uncertainty and Information.* Cambridge: Cambridge University Press.

International Business Review (2005) (SI) 14:(2).

Johanson, J. and F. Wiedersheim-Paul (1975). 'The Internationalisation of the Firm–Four Swedish Case Studies'. *Journal of Management Studies,* 12, 305–22.

—— and J-E. Vahlne (1977). 'The Internationalisation Process of the Firm—A Model of Knowledge Development and Increasing Foreign Market Commitments', *Journal of International Business Studies,* 8: 23–32.

Jones, M. E. (1999). 'The Internationalization of Small High-technology Firms'. *Journal of International Marketing,* 7(4): 15–41.

—— and N. E. Corviello (2005). 'Internationalisation: Conceptualising an entrepreneurial process of behaviour in time'. *Journal of International Business Studies,* 36: 284–303.

Keay, J. (1994). *The Honourable Company: In History of the English East India Company.* New York: MacMillan.

Kreps, D. M. (1990). *Game Theory and Economic Modelling.* Oxford: Oxford University Press.

Lau, H. F. (1992). 'Internationalisation, Internalization, or a New Theory for Small, Law Technology Multinational Enterprise.' *European Journal of Marketing,* 26(10): 17–31.

Lindquist, M. (1988). 'Internationalisation of Small Technology-based Firms: Three illustrative case studies on Swedish firms'. Stockholm School of Economics Research Paper 88/15.

Lu, J. W. and P. W. Beamish (2001). 'The Internationalization and Performance of SMEs'. *Strategic Management Journal,* 22(6/7): 565–86.

Lumpkin, G. T. and G. G. Dess (1966). 'Clarifying the Entrepreneurial Orientation Construct and Linking it to Performance'. *Academy of Management Review,* 21(1): 135–172.

Madsen, T. K and P. Servais (1997). 'The Internationalisation of Born Globals on Evolutionary Process?' *International Business Review,* 6(6): 561–83.

McDougall, P. P. and B. M. Oviatt (2000). 'International Entrepreneurship: The intersection of two research paths'. *Academy of Management Journal,* 43(5): 902–6.

McGaughey, S. (2004). 'New descriptions and understandings of internationalisation: A tale of knowledge intensive SMEs'. Unpublished Ph.D. thesis, University of Queensland.

McLaren, J. (2000). ' "Globalization" and Vertical Structure'. *American Economic Review* (December) pp. 1239–54.

OECD (1997). *Globalisation and Small and Medium Enterprises,* vols. 1 and 2. Paris: OECD

Oviatt, B. M. and P. P. McDougall (1994). 'Towards a Theory of International New Ventures'. *International Business Studies,* 25(1): 45–64.

Penrose, E. T. (1959). *The Theory of the Growth of the Firm.* Oxford: Basil Blackwell.

Porter, M. E. (1986). *Competition in Global Industries.* Cambridge, MA: Harvard Business School Press.

—— (1991). 'Towards a Dynamic Theory of Strategy'. *Strategic Management Journal,* SI, 12: 95–117.

Reuber, A. R. and E. Fischer (1997). 'The Influence of the Management Team's International Experience in Internationalization Behavior'. *Journal of International Business Studies,* 28(4): 807–25.

Reuber, A. R. and E. Fischer (1999). 'Understanding the Consequences of the Founder's Experience'. *Journal of Small Business Management*, 37(2): 30–45.

Rialp, A., J. Rialp and G. A. Knight (2005). 'The Phenomenon of Early Internationalizing Firms: What do we know after a decade (1993–2003) of scientific enquiry?' *International Business Review*, 14(2): 147–66.

Steinmann, H., B. Kumar and A. Wasner (1981). 'Some Aspects of Managing U.S. Subsidiaries of German Medium-Sized Enterprises'. *Management International Review*, 21: 27–37.

Stigler, G. J. (1951). 'The Division of Labour is Limited by the Extent of the Market'. *The Journal of Political Economy*, 59(3): 185–93.

Strandskov, J. (1993). 'Towards a New Approach for Studying the Internationalisation Process of Firms' in P. J. Buckley and P. N . Ghauri (eds) *The Internationalisation of the Firm: A Reader*. London: Academic Press.

Vernon, R. (1966). 'International Investment and International Trade in the Product Cycle'. *Quarterly Journal of Economics*, 80: 190–207.

—— (1974). 'The Location of Economic Activity', in J. H. Dunning, (ed.) *Economic Analysis and the Multinational Enterprise*. London: George Allen and Unwin.

—— (1979). The Product Cycle Hypothesis in a New International Environment. *Oxford Bulletin of Economics and Statistics*, 41: 255–67.

Welch, D. E. and L. S. Welch (1996). 'The Internationalization Process and Networks: A strategic management perspective'. *Journal of International Marketing*, 4(3): 11–28.

Wells, L. T. (1983). *Third World Multinationals: The Rise of Foreign Investment from Developing Countries*. Cambridge, MA: MIT Press.

Zahra, S. A., P. Cloninger, J. Feng Yu and Y. Choi (2004). 'Emerging Research Issues in International Entrepreneurship', in Leo-Paul Dana (ed.) *Handbook of Research on International Entrepreneurship*. Cheltenham: Edward Elgar.

CHAPTER 27

ENTREPRENEURSHIP IN TRANSITION ECONOMIES[1]

SAUL ESTRIN, KLAUS E. MEYER AND MARIA BYTCHKOVA

27.1 Introduction

The establishment and growth of new enterprises is central to the transition process. This is because the change in the economic system from communism to capitalism implies a reallocation of resources in which new firms have to be the main actors (see e.g., Olson, 1992). Compared to other situations of major liberalization, existing firms are less well placed to be the engine of structural change because they are themselves institutions of the planning system and must also be subject to major reforms. Thus, while mainstream economists have emphasized the three pillars of the 'Washington consensus'—stabilization, liberalization and privatization (World Bank, 1996)—analysts such as Kornai (1990) and McMillan and

[1] The authors gratefully acknowledge helpful comments from Ruta Aidis, Bat Batjargal, Alberto Chilosi, Bruno Dallago, David De Meza, Modestas Gelbuda, Michael Keren, Bruce Kogut, Mike Wright, an anonymous referee and participants in the Authors' Conference for this Handbook at Reading University. Rhana Neidenbach provided excellent research assistance. Meyer thanks the Danish SSF for supporting his research on business in transition economies under grant number 24-01-0152.

Woodruff (2002) have instead argued that the creation of firms *de novo* would be the primary mechanism of the transition.

As a period of major economic and institutional change, transition throws up numerous opportunities for 'low-level' entrepreneurs (Kirzner, 1983) to transfer resources from low to high productivity uses in the new market economy. Moreover, the incentives for innovation and efficiency were notoriously weak under communism (Hayek, 1945) so reformers in the transition economies have been also greatly concerned with Schumpeterian entrepreneurship (Schumpeter, 1934). Over-centralization and inappropriate management incentives were important causes of the stagnation in the last years of communism (see e.g. Ericson, 1991) and new technologies have to be adopted to restore growth. As with all innovation, the driving force was expected to be 'high-level' entrepreneurship.

However, the transition economies started their reforms with few legal, institutional and policy structures to provide the basis for an entrepreneurial market economy (see e.g. Verheul et al., 2002; Chilosi, 2001). To the contrary, the institutional environment has created numerous new barriers to entry, some conventional and others unique to transition. These have prevented entrepreneurs from fully exploiting the opportunities opened up by transition. Moreover, the institutional environment is evolving (Murrell, 1996; Spicer, et al., 2000) and the process of reform did not always enhance rapid or fundamental change. Indeed, in many countries the chaos associated with transformational reforms instead led to an entrenchment of the former elite in a new quasi-market environment (Boycko et al., 1995). The development of the entrepreneurial sector is sensitive to the institutional environment and there is a distinction between the more market-oriented economies of Central and Eastern Europe (CEE) and the slower and more erratic pace of change in the former Soviet Union (FSU). Successful entrepreneurship depends not only on initial conditions in the transition economies but also on the speed and consistency with which the reform process has been applied.

Despite the unpropitious environment, we observe a remarkable expansion of the private sector in all transition economies. The average share of private sector output in GDP rose from virtually zero in 1989, at least in centralized economies like Czechoslovakia or the Soviet Union, to 62 percent in 2001. The transition economies therefore experienced a similar transformation to China, as Deng Xiaoping's remark about the first eight years of Chinese reform shows, 'all sorts of small enterprises boomed in the countryside, as if a strange army appeared suddenly from nowhere' (cited by McMillan and Woodruff, 2002). Table 27.1 shows that the increases occurred in every country, and were paralleled by rises in the share of private sector employment. Growth in the private sector share was caused by privatization of existing firms as well as the emergence of entirely new enterprises. Privatization has received enormous attention in the literature (Djankov and Murrell, 2002), but new firm growth was probably at least as important; we

Table 27.1 Private sector share in GDP and employment in Eastern Europe, 1989–1994

	In GDP			In Employment		
	1991	1995	2002	1991	1995	2001
Albania	24	60	75	..	74	82
Armenia	..	45	70	29	49	..
Azerbaijan	..	25	60	..	43	..
Belarus	7	15	25	2	7	..
Bosnia and Herzegovina	..	..	45	..	..	..
Bulgaria	17	50	75	10	41	81
Croatia	25	40	60	22	48	..
Czech Republic	17	70	80	19	57	70
Estonia	18	65	80	11	..	..
FYR Macedonia	..	40	60	..	..	..
Georgia	27	30	65	25	..	..
Hungary	33	60	80	...	71	...
Kazakhstan	12	25	65	5	..	75
Kyrgyz Republic	..	40	65	..	69	79
Latvia	..	55	70	12	60	73
Lithuania	15	65	75	16	...	...
Moldova	..	30	50	36	..	..
Poland	45	60	75	51	61	72
Romania	24	45	65	34	51	75
Russia	10	55	70	5	..	..
Serbia and Montenegro	..	..	45	..	..	..
Slovak Republic	..	60	80	13	60	75
Slovenia	16	50	65	18	48	..
Tajikistan	..	25	50	..	53	63
Turkmenistan	..	15	25	..	..	..
Ukraine	8	45	65	..	..	..
Uzbekistan	..	30	45	..	..	..
Means	20	44	62			

Sources: EBRD Transition Report 1999, 2003;

observe that a significant proportion of private sector development preceded privatization in most transition economies (see EBRD 1994; World Bank, 1996).

In this chapter, we examine the opportunities and constraints for entrepreneurship offered by the evolving institutional environment and the characteristics of the people who stepped up to the challenge. In the next section, we place the concept of entrepreneurship in a transition context, before identifying in the third section the unique features of entrepreneurship in transition economies. Section 4 discusses the evolving business environment, while the scale and nature of entrepreneurship in transition economies is reported in the fifth. The personal characteristics and the business strategies of entrepreneurs in the transition economies are discussed in the sixth and seventh sections respectively. Section 8 concludes by outlining directions for future work.

27.2 Entrepreneurship and Economic Transition

To what extent can definitions of entrepreneurship be transferred from mature market economies to transition economies? Defining entrepreneurship for transition economies is not made easier by the fact that definitions of entrepreneurship vary in the literature, as other chapters in this Handbook reveal. In this section, we discuss the distinctive character of entrepreneurship in transition and analyze how this might change as the transition process develops.

27.2.1 Defining entrepreneurship in a transition context

Existing definitions stress the innovative aspect of an entrepreneur, as decision-maker under uncertainty, and the role as coordinator of resources (see Ricketts, 2002). These were developed in work on Western economies but entrepreneurs face a different business environment in the transition context. They have to learn a different coping behaviour,[2] formed by their experience under communism, and they may have different personal characteristics. Baumol (1990) argues that the definition of the entrepreneur should reflect the local incentive structure. In transition economies, this encompasses the onslaught of rapid changes and the resulting uncertainty, a wide range of opportunities thrown up by the restructuring of formerly planned economies, imbalances between supply and demand, fragile or only partial market institutions and a variety of informal rules and behaviours which are remnants of the communist past. However, while many market

[2] For examples of coping behaviour with regard to resource procurement, initiative incentives and decision-making learnt under communism, see Ledeneva (1998) and Smallbone and Welter (2001).

institutions were absent, the skill level and educational attainment and in some cases investment into local technology were on a par with the developed world.

Thus, the characteristics of entrepreneurs and their economic impact cannot be assumed to be the same as those in Western countries (Smallbone and Welter, 2006). For example, entrepreneurs in transition economies can be value subtracting because of the numerous opportunities in rent-seeking. Dallago (1997) distinguishes between systemic and economic entrepreneurs, with the former introducing changes into the system of institutions and rules. Building on Wennekers and Thurik (1999), Aidis (2003) defines productive entrepreneurship as entailing 'innovative activity under uncertainty resulting in an economically productive business'. Thus, entrepreneurship does not necessarily require the establishment of a new enterprise, but includes leaders who take over state-owned enterprises and employ new combinations of resources. This definition includes the formation of new businesses as well as spin-offs from former state firms and management employee buy-outs (MEBOs), but excludes managers continuing in their role in old enterprises. We refine this definition by focusing on individuals who:

(a) perceive and create new economic opportunities through innovative activity;
(b) introduce their ideas in the market in the face of uncertainty and other obstacles;
(c) undertake efforts that result in a viable business that contributes to national economic growth and personal livelihood, and
(d) engage in this activity at opportunity cost of pursuing other occupations.

27.2.2 Entrepreneurship and stages in transition

The transition process can be divided into several stages that give rise to different kinds of entrepreneurship. In the first stage, early transition, equilibration of supply and demand, manifested in adjustment of relative prices, opens up opportunities for mainly Kirznian-type entrepreneurs. This is a period of extreme uncertainty, as there is no previous market information. Channels of resource allocation face disruption as planning is abandoned, though nomenclatura networks may provide some alleviation.

Macroeconomic stabilization, indicated by reduced inflation and a resumption of economic growth, removes extreme uncertainty and increases the incentives for Schumpeterian entrepreneurship. In this second stage, the price mechanism can be used to convey information about supply and demand and macroeconomic stability reduces business risks. This allows investments into longer-term projects and unmasks needs for new projects and technologies.

In the third stage, market institutions become more developed and provide better mechanisms for resource co-ordination, information gathering and contract enforcement. Property rights enforcement relies less on physical threat or reputation and more on courts, so resources are increasingly accessed through financial institutions and market exchange. At this stage, Schumpeterian entrepreneurship becomes more feasible.

Thus changes in environment and opportunities over time in the transition economies are likely to lead to differences in entrepreneurial endeavour, strategies and personal characteristics. One can expect the initial stage to attract a larger number of entrepreneurs but also to witness a larger failure rate. The skill set, and physical as well as social capital of initial entrepreneurs, may differ from those in later years, as will the types and strategies of businesses created by these entrepreneurs. However, one cannot assume an automatic progression from stage to stage, so the forms of entrepreneurship that emerge in the early stages may become entrenched.

27.3 The functions of entrepreneurship in economic transition

In this section, we identify the unique opportunities for entrepreneurship in transition economies. We thus discuss the heritage from planning and describe the reform process and its effect on entrepreneurship, drawing on the literature in comparative economics (see e.g. Gregory and Stuart, 1995; Ellman, 1994).

27.3.1 The heritage from planning

The emergence of a market economy from a planned one implies a major reallocation of resources: from industry to services, domestic to global production, intermediate products to final goods. Planned economies were over-industrialized—the share on industry in GDP was routinely in the 45–50 percent range as against less than 30 percent in developed market economies, and output was focused on the manufacture of intermediate products. Moreover, though most communist countries were small, they were not very open, especially to West European neighbours, as planners had concentrated trade within the communist bloc. Thus reforms opened many profitable opportunities in services, final products and international trade. One might expect this reallocation to be spearheaded by existing firms rather than entrepreneurial ones. However, existing firms were themselves institutions of planning, and therefore part of the problem rather than its solution. It was hoped that the sharper incentives and improved governance would follow privatization, but this was everywhere a major and lengthy project and new firms would also have to play a major role in restructuring.

Former state-owned firms were, however, an important breeding ground for entrepreneurs, as well as a source of fixed assets. Socialist enterprises were highly integrated vertically and these structures were often liquidated when the logic of planning was replaced by market incentives allowing their workers and managers to acquire the assets at low prices (see Johnson and Loveman, 1995). New firms, often very small, therefore spun out of the socialist enterprise and filled niches in consultancy, logistics, and business services (see Lizal and Svejnar, 2002).

The new market economy also emerged from grey- and black-market activities. Planning led to shortages of consumer goods, which created an environment in which arbitragers, black marketeers and criminals thrived. At the same time, the rigidity and inflexibility of the planning system, combined with strong incentives for managers to attain plan targets, created a class of 'middlemen', providing inputs critical to the production process. These individuals were often local party members or associated with local government or the secret police. This process of intermediation through informal networks was another important seed bed for the new entrepreneurial class, especially in the former Soviet Union (see Ledeneva, 1998) However, the distinguishing feature of this group was not their ability to spot new economic opportunities but rather their networking skills among the political and economic elites.

27.3.2 Transition policies and entrepreneurship

The transition process itself also influenced the pattern of entrepreneurship. In the early 1990s, the established order broke down and the resulting macroeconomic instability as well as some of the methods of privatization chosen by policy-makers in those crucial early years constrained entrepreneurship. Thus, the general business climate in the early years was recessionary and inflationary. Even in the least affected economies, like Poland or Hungary, GDP fell by up to 20 percent; in much of the former Soviet Union it halved using official statistics (see EBRD, 1994). There was also inflation everywhere after prices were liberalized and though, in countries like Poland and Czechoslovakia, it was fairly speedily brought under control, in most countries, it remained persistently high for the early years of transition, greatly increasing the risks faced by entrepreneurs. The chaotic business environment that existed while a legal and institutional framework was being developed also gave many opportunities for nomenclatura-based networking, and led to an increase of corruption, a failure to enforce property rights and the rise of mafias. One can discern a clear distinction between the sustained progress in business environment in Central and Eastern Europe (CEE)—perhaps as a consequence of the European Union Accession process—and the more erratic path followed in the former Soviet Union (FSU) and much of the Balkans.

Privatization policy was also crucial for entrepreneurship. The bulk of new firms in the early years was probably created by the 'small privatization'—the sale of houses, flats, shops, garages, restaurants and so on. When SOEs were either restructured for privatization, or liquidated, their assets—plant and machinery but also less expensive and more versatile capital goods such as trucks or office equipment—were sold, often at sure fire sale prices. This factor was particularly significant in the more advanced transition countries like Poland (see Belka et al., 1995; Spicer, McDermott and Kogut, 2000).

27.4 Barriers to entrepreneurship in transition

Institutions affect entrepreneurial endeavours in two ways. First, they may hinder the creation of firms, thus lowering the total number of entrants into the market. Secondly, they may create obstacles to firm performance, as measured by survival period, growth or profits. Though transition opened many opportunities for entrepreneurship, the heritage from the planned era was in many ways not favourable and many aspects of the reform process acted to make the environment even less conducive to entrepreneurs. In this section, we review the evolution of the institutional, social and cultural environment for entrepreneurs in transition economies, before considering in subsequent sections its impact on the scale and character of entrepreneurship. We commence with financial and institutional barriers, before turning to human capital and cultural factors. In this discussion, we also reflect that some institutions may have a stronger impact on firm creation while others may have more effect on firm performance.

27.4.1 Financial barriers

Entrepreneurs require financial resources in order to establish and run their new enterprises, and they must either provide this from their own (or family) saving, or borrow it from financial markets. Neither of these sources was widely available, particularly at the onset of transition. Under communism, individuals were not permitted to accumulate financial assets—almost all wealth was owned by the state—and this must have been a major constraint on the possibilities for entrepreneurship (Pissarides, 1999; Chilosi, 2001). More generally, the distribution of income and wealth may be an important determinant of the level of entrepreneurial activity. According to Banerji and Long (2001), quoted by Chilosi (2001), 'under capital market imperfections due to moral hazard, the very rich and the very poor do not undertake any risk and become passive lenders ... only individuals whose wealth lies within the medium range choose to be entrepreneurs' (p. 1). This is because poor people would not have access to risk capital, and rich people do not wish to undertake extra effort, which implies that entrepreneurs will largely come from the middle-classes. But this is precisely the group that was largely absent at the start of transition.

Financial markets were also seriously deficient and progress in this area (EBRD, 2004) has been slow. The European Bank for Reconstruction and Development (EBRD)'s annual indicators report the progress in reform of the securities market and non-bank financial institutions (EBRD, various years). By 1994, only five countries had attained a ranking of 3 for the capital market indices and the situation had not improved markedly by 2000.[3] Ten countries had not altered their category in the last five years and the situation had deteriorated in three—Russia, Slovakia and Slovenia. However, there is differentiation; Poland and Hungary have reached a ranking of 4 and the three Baltic States have also improved somewhat.

Thus financial markets in transition are often very limited and underdeveloped and the market structure is highly concentrated with banks often achieving only low levels of efficiency. The banking sector is also relatively inexperienced in private sector lending, and project finance in particular, and thus lacks organizational capabilities to finance entrepreneurial businesses (Pissarides, 1999). The evidence suggests that state-owned banks continued to favour state-owned firms and, to some extent, large privatized firms by providing soft loans (Lizal and Svejnar, 2002). However, they rarely lent to the *de novo* private sector, particularly at the start of the transition process (see Richter and Schaffer, 1996; Feakins, 2002).[4] This

[3] On a scale of 1–4, 1 represents little progress, 2 indicates a rudimentary exchange and legal framework, 3 means making some progress (securities being issued by private firms, some protection of minority shareholders and the beginnings of a regulatory framework), 4 means that countries have relatively liquid and well functioning securities markets and effective regulations and 4+ implies countries have reached the standard of advanced industrial economies.

[4] The almost complete absence of privately held savings in the communist era and state ownership of banks led to imprudent lending, followed by a bad loans crisis in several countries. As a result some

is a serious obstacle for entrepreneurship because financial development has been found to exert a disproportionately large effect on the growth of industries that are dependent on small firms (Beck et al., 2004).

Access to finance may be crucial for the growth of small businesses, but less for their initial establishment (ISEAED, 2001). It appears very high on entrepreneurs' own lists of obstacles (Fogel and Zapalska, 2001; Pissarides et al., 2003) but there is little evidence that finance has been a binding constraint on growth. For instance, Johnson et al. (2000) find that whether or not the firm had a bank loan at the early stage of their existence, has no significant effect on firm growth. They argue 'external finance matters *only after* property rights provide some minimum level of security (and assuming that there is macroeconomic stability)' (Johnson, et al., 2000).

In assessing the validity of surveys of entrepreneurs, one has to keep in mind that aspiring entrepreneurs who are rejected by banks for valid reasons—for instance because they lack a clearly defined business plan, or they are considered incapable of implementing their plans—would also complain about not having been funded. Moreover, the contrary evidence between Pissarides et al. (2003) on the one hand, and Johnson et al. (2000) on the other may arise from the fact that the former have good measures of access to finance and weak ones of other institutions, while the latter have the converse. We still await convincing evidence on the relative importance of access to finance versus general institutions and property rights for entrepreneurship in transition economies.

27.4.2 Institutional environment

The institutional argument concerning obstacles to entrepreneurial establishment and growth has been advanced in recent years by a number of economists including McMillan and Woodruff (1999, 2002); De Soto (2000); Frye and Zhuravskaya (2000); Djankov et al. (2004) and Roland and Verdier (2003). Several institutions are suggested as being likely to affect entrepreneurial endeavour: quality of commercial code, strength of legal enforcement, administrative barriers, extra-legal payments and lack of market-supporting institutions. The legal and institutional system is certainly immature, having only been introduced in many countries for the first time in the early years of transition. Most of the CEE economies had an outdated commercial code in 1989, but, even here, new laws were needed to define

countries saw privatization of domestic banks to foreign owners (Berglof and Bolton, 2002). While this may have raised efficiency of lending, these banks are still likely to favour large projects, focusing on corporate lending and avoid retail financing, as EBRD experience with foreign banks suggests (Pissarides, 1999).

the concept of a private firm, and to create procedures for entry, and bankruptcy. In the FSU, and much of the Balkans, the legal heritage for a market economy was even weaker. In the legal vacuum after the fall of communism, the difficulty of enforcing voluntary contracts was also of great importance. For example, cus-

Table 27.2 The institutional environment for entrepreneurship

	Bulgaria	Hungary	Lithuania	Poland	Russia	China	Germany	UK
Starting a business, days[a]	32	52	26	31	36	41	45	18
Starting a business, procedures[a]	11	6	8	10	9	12	9	6
Enforcing a contract, days[a]	440	365	154	1,000	330	241	184	288
Enforcing a contract, procedures[a]	34	21	17	41	29	25	26	14
Registering property, days[a]	19	79	3	204	37	32	41	21
Registering property, procedures[a]	9	4	3	7	6	3	4	2
Resolving insolvency[a]	3,3	2	1,2	1,4	1,5	2,4	1,2	1
Taxes[b]	77,9	74,5	82,2	74,4	90,6			
Financing[b]	72,5	60,0	69,8	48,0	78,8			
Policy instability[b]	70,4	57,0	50,0	55,2	84,8			
Inflation[b]	58,6	52,1	56,4	52,9	88,2			
Exchange rate[b]	47,5	16,3	29,0	40,8	72,7			
Functioning of judiciary[b]	41,3	8,3	36,3	39,1	29,8			
Corruption[b]	54,3	28,5	53,0	39,4	50,5			
Street crime[b]	57,8	25,1	53,8	40,3	50,2			
Organized crime[b]	51,2	25,0	48,4	28,5	49,8			
Infrastructure[b]	42,8	15,3	24,5	16,9	32,6			
Frequent legal changes cause costs[c]		3.51	3.67	4.12				
Important to obtain info on changes in the law[c]		4.19	4.08	4.30				
Important to obtain info on changes in regulation[c]		4.15	4.17	4.23				
Corruption perceptions index rank[d]	54	42	44	67	90	71	15	11

Sources and notes:[a] = World Bank (2004); [b]= EBRD (...): Enterprise Survey in Transition 2002 (% of respondents indicating moderate or major obstacle to the business environment in 2002); [c]= Meyer et al. (2005): five point scale from 1 = do not agree at all, to 5 = fully agree; [d]= Transparency International (2004).

tomers failed to pay for goods, or firms failed to pay wages (see Earle and Sabirianova, 1998). In many countries, especially but not exclusively in the FSU, the state also continued to be very active in enterprise affairs, putting out its 'grabbing hand' (Shleifer and Vishny, 1999) to the detriment of all firms, but especially *de novo* private ones (Belka et al., 1995). Entrepreneurs are often more affected by corruption and ineffective regulatory frameworks because they lack bargaining power vis-à-vis the public bureaucracy.

In Table 27.2, we provide an overview of the institutional environment that may affect entrepreneurs and small firms. In addition to five representative transition economies, we also consider China and two West European economies as benchmarks. In the upper part of the table, we report formal indicators based on the World Bank's interviews with experts in the respective country; in the lower part the EBRD's indicators based on entrepreneurs' assessment of major obstacles. Lastly, we report data from a recent FDI survey (Meyer et al., 2005) and Transparency International's corruption perception ranking. The different types of indicators tell different stories about the business environment, and thus highlight the importance of methodological aspects of these kinds of studies.

The World Bank data (World Bank, 2005, Djankov et al., 2004) suggest that institutional settings in CEE are largely on a par with West European counterparts, although there are major outliers. On the positive side, registering property can be done much faster in Lithuania and Bulgaria than in our benchmark countries. On the other hand, contract enforcement still takes much longer in CEE (except Lithuania) compared to the UK or Germany. Poland, often applauded for its entrepreneur-friendly environment, appears on this data to be the laggard for three of the seven indicators; Russia, with a reputation for being particularly obstinate to business, never gets the worst score; while the supposedly entrepreneurial Hungarians need to spend 52 days, the highest in our selection of countries, to set up their business. Thus, World Bank data show a pattern of diversity within the region, and overall a not particularly worse performance than in Western Europe.

The picture presented by the EBRD data is very different (EBRD, 2004; Pissarides, Singer and Svejnar, 2003). The EBRD asked entrepreneurs which, out of a list of possible obstacles, was inhibiting their business creation and growth in 2002. The findings indicate that entrepreneurs in Russia and Bulgaria experience far more obstacles than Hungary and Poland, with Lithuania taking an intermediate position. On the important issues of taxation and financing,[5] Poland appears to provide least obstacles to entrepreneurs, while Hungary performs best on several indicators including inflation, functioning of the judiciary and infrastructure.

[5] Contradictory evidence to these data emerges in a different study that also reports entrepreneurs' own views about the environment. In Fogel and Zapalska (2001), Polish entrepreneurs appear to have more problems accessing finance than their Hungarian counterparts.

The differences in these evaluations are likely to stem from differences in methodology of these surveys. The World Bank data attempt to provide objective, quantifiable measures of institutional and administrative barriers to entrepreneurship. Validity of these data, however, relies heavily on the source of information on business environments. Countries with policy implementation gaps may have advanced business law on books but reality may be different due to informal institutions. Moreover, a high number of procedures to start business may be less of a deterrent for entrepreneurs than uncertainty of the procedure's outcome, not captured by the survey. On the other hand, differences reported in subjective surveys may be either real or perceptional, a problem known in the methodology literature as 'equivalence'. This creates problems for comparison of 'real' levels of institutional development between countries. However, such surveys are still useful in analyzing entrepreneurs' willingness to engage in business activity, as these decisions are likely to be guided by perceptions of the business environment.

Both EBRD and World Bank surveys seem to correspond to the broad consensus that ascribes higher institutional development to Central European countries when compared to former Soviet republics. More interesting may be the relative importance of different obstacles across countries, and this pattern is fairly consistent. In all the transition countries, *taxes*, *financing* and *policy instability* are among the top four items mentioned (except policy instability in Lithuania) while informal institutions, such as crime, or the functioning of the judiciary, are mentioned less frequently. In their analysis, Pissarides, Singer and Svejnar (2003) find that high interest rates and obstacles to raising funding are (on average) the most highly-rated items, followed by 'suppliers unable to deliver', 'other operational issues' and 'access to land and buildings'. Taxes and price volatility are also important, but classic informal institution issues do not make the top list.

Taxes are a common complaint by entrepreneurs worldwide. However, little distinction is made between the level of taxation and the methods of tax collection and enforcement. In transition economies, the costs created by an inefficient or corrupt system of tax collection may substantially add to the costs of running an entrepreneurial business. Some support for this can be found in Aidis and Mickiewicz (2004). They find that perception of high taxes has a negative effect on the growth expectations of small firms in Lithuania. The measure of taxation is correlated with two omitted variables, 'frequent changes to tax policy' and 'ambiguity of taxes', suggesting that all aspects of the system of corporate taxation, rather than the level alone, may inhibit entrepreneurial growth. A recent study by Meyer et al. (2005) also points to instability of the rules and regulation, rather than the actual state of these variables, as a major obstacle reported by foreign investors. Even though the regulatory framework is moving towards the regulatory frameworks in other EU countries, the change process as such creates costs and uncertainties that affect businesses.

Work on the importance of legal enforcement is less conclusive. Johnson, McMillan and Woodruff (2000) find that the entrepreneur's belief in the courts' ability to enforce contracts has a negative effect on employment growth, though this effect is not significant with respect to sales growth. Djankov et al. (2004) report that in Russia, entrepreneurs seem to have less confidence than non-entrepreneurs in the efficiency of the court system. However, research in this field is plagued by methodological problems in estimating the impact of institutions on firm performance that have not yet been resolved. Thus barriers are hard to measure and entrepreneurs in the same context face the same institutional barriers, yet cross-country or even cross-regional studies capture a lot of contextual variation that cannot usually be attributed to a specific variable. In addition, the majority of studies use entrepreneurs' own perceptions as a proxy for institutions and it would be desirable to use variables that come from a different source than the performance measure.

27.4.3 Human capital and socio-economic factors

Human capital is also an important ingredient for entrepreneurship, and this is confirmed by Barberis et al. (1996), who show that new human capital was a crucial ingredient for successful new entry by small firms in Russia. The transition countries fare relatively well in terms of formal measures of education. However, the social and cultural environment is less conducive. In Table 27.3, we use the United Nations Human Development Index to address some of these issues for the same countries as Table 27.2.

The socialist regimes, including China, created extensive education and health services, which contribute to good performance in this index and CEE economies continue to invest a high proportion of GDP in education, even outperforming some West European countries. As a result literacy rates are high in transition economies and educational standards are comparable to Western Europe. Also, transition economies typically have a high proportion of students in 'hard' subjects of science, mathematics and engineering. These indicators thus suggest a good human capital basis for entrepreneurship, probably more so than pertains in developing economies.

Turning to indicators of adoption of modern technology—here mobile phone and Internet users—given the heritage from planning, it is unsurprising that the transition economies are lagging behind Western Europe. These indicators also show major variations within the region: Poland, Hungary and Lithuania are catching up, while Bulgaria and Russia are lagging quite far behind. With respect to expenditures in research and development (R&D), transition economies show

Table 27.3 Business environment in transition economies

	Bulgaria	Hungary	Lithuania	Poland	Russia	China	Germany	UK
GDP per capita (US$), 2002	1.944	6.481	3.977	4.894	2.405	989	24.051	26.444
Human Development Index, 2002	0,796	0,848	0,842	0,850	0,795	0,745	0,925	0,936
Public expenditure on education (as % of GDP), 1999–2001	...	5,8	...	5,4	3,1	2,3	4,6	4,6
Tertiary students in science, math & engineering (% of all tertiary students), 1994–97	25	32	38	...	49	53	31	29
Mobile phone subscribers (per 1,000 people), 2002	333	676	475	363	120	161	727	841
Internet users (per 1,000 people), 2002	80,0	157,6	144,4	230	40,9	46,0	411,9	423,1
Research and development expenditures (as % of GDP), 1996–2002	0,5	0,9	0,6	0,7	1,2	1,1	2,5	1,9
Population age composition: ages 0–14, 2002:	14,8	16,5	18,2	18,2	16,9	24,2	15,1	18,4

Source: United Nations: Human Development Report (2003).

considerably less investment than Western Europe; during the socialist period R&D investments used to be comparatively high but were often inefficient.

An important aspect of the human capital is also the age structure of the population as most entrepreneurs are in the age range of 30 to 45, while young customers are more likely to adopt new products and services. The demographic structure of CEE in many ways resembles that of Western Europe with relatively few young people. This in itself may be seen as an obstacle to entrepreneurship.

There is also evidence that managerial skills are in short supply. Most top directors in transition economies came from an engineering background and lacked managerial skills as well as market experience (see Estrin and Peiperl, 1998). The economy had been run bureaucratically. Its concentration of reward on plan attainment suppressed the appetite for risk and instead bred habits of obedience and 'playing it safe' (see Ellman, 1994). History also acts strongly against an entrepreneurial tradition, particularly in the FSU. Entrepreneurship in the sense of creating new private businesses had been illegal in what was the Soviet Union since 1917, and in CEE after 1945. Moreover, the culture has been strongly opposed to entrepreneurial activity—little distinction was made in the media or public perception between entrepreneurs and criminals.

27.5 The patterns of entrepreneurship

Market liberalization and the introduction of private property have paved the way for emergence of legal entrepreneurship in Central and Eastern Europe. This section provides empirical evidence on the pattern of firm creation and on strategies adopted by entrepreneurs in response to their environment.

The starting point for the transition economies in the late 1980s was an environment containing very few firms, mostly very large, and with almost no small enterprises outside agriculture or craft. Thus according to Acs and Audretch (1993), the percentage of workers employed in small enterprises in the late 1980s was only 1.4 percent in Czechoslovakia, 1.1 percent in East Germany and 10 percent in Poland. Indeed the total number of firms was very small in Central European economies, only 19,000 in Hungary and 16,000 in Czechoslovakia, compared with 200, 000 in neighbouring and comparable Austria.

The early years of transition saw a remarkable rise in the number of firms, a fundamental shift in the size distribution towards smaller enterprises, and the creation of a service sector largely comprised of numerous small enterprises. It seems likely that a significant proportion of this new firm creation represents entrepreneurship of the Kirznian sort. A few figures, tables and charts illustrate the rapid development of a new Small- and Medium-size Enterprise (SME) sector. The number of incorporated firms increased enormously. According to Eurostat, firm numbers had risen more than tenfold in parts of CEE by 1994, with 167,000 firms registered in the Czech Republic, 101 000 in Hungary and 95,000 on Poland.[6] In Table 27.4, we compare the distribution of firms in the late 1990s in a selection of (advanced) transition economies and some developed Western economies. The turnaround from the data on firm distribution size provided by Acs and Audretsch

[6] Official statistics have to be treated with caution, especially in periods of rapid change. Entrepreneurs have strong incentives not to report the full extent of their activities to minimize their tax obligations and the potential for extortion by illegal groups and the incentives magnify if institutions are rapidly changing or non-transparent. On the other hand, many registered new firms have never been operational.

Table 27.4 Firms with less than 20 employees as a percentage of total (1990s)

	Firms			Employment		
	Total Economy	Manufacturing	Services	Total economy	Manufacturing	Services
West Germany	89.6	85.3	...	25.8	16.6	...
UK	...	81.3	...	...	12.4	...
US	88.0	72.6	88.7	18.6	6.7	19.9
Slovenia	87.7	71.6	93.1	13.4	5.1	26.0
Hungary	84.4	71.1	90.8	16.0	8.8	23.6
Estonia	80.6	64.6	87.1	22.8	11.5	34.2
Latvia	87.7	87.8	87.6	24.7	26.9	24.2
Romania	90.9	77.1	95.6	12.9	4.2	31.6

Source: Bartelsmann, Haltiwanger and Scarpetta (2004).

(1993), is extraordinary. By the late 1990s, the transition countries have approximately the same share of small firms as West Germany or the United States (80–90%), though the share of employment in such enterprises is rather less, except in the Baltic economies. There is a difference between the manufacturing and the service sectors. In the latter, the share of firms, and of employment, in small enterprises is typically larger in transition economies than in the OECD countries, because the service sector had to be created from scratch. In manufacturing, however, though there has been a substantial increase since 1990 with the exception of Latvia, the share of small firms in total firm numbers remains somewhat below that observed in developed economies, and the difference is even more marked with respect to employment. Thus, the share of small enterprises in manufacturing employment in West Germany is 16.6 percent compared with only 5.1 percent in Slovenia and 4.3 percent in Romania.

The distribution for CEE had moved even closer to the EU average by 2002, according to Eurostat (2002). For the EU as a whole in manufacturing, 8.5 percent of employment is in micro firms, 32 percent in small firms and 59.5 percent in medium-sized and large firms. The comparable figures for Hungary at that date were 12.0, 25.1 and 62.9 percent respectively; for Poland 9.5, 25.9 and 64.6 percent and for the Czech Republic 11.3, 25.7 and 63.1 percent. Thus by 2002, we see convergence in CEE to the EU norms in terms of firm size distribution, even in the manufacturing sector.

Russia also experienced an upsurge in firm numbers in the early years of transition, but, according to Kontorovich (1999), the pace has not been sustained

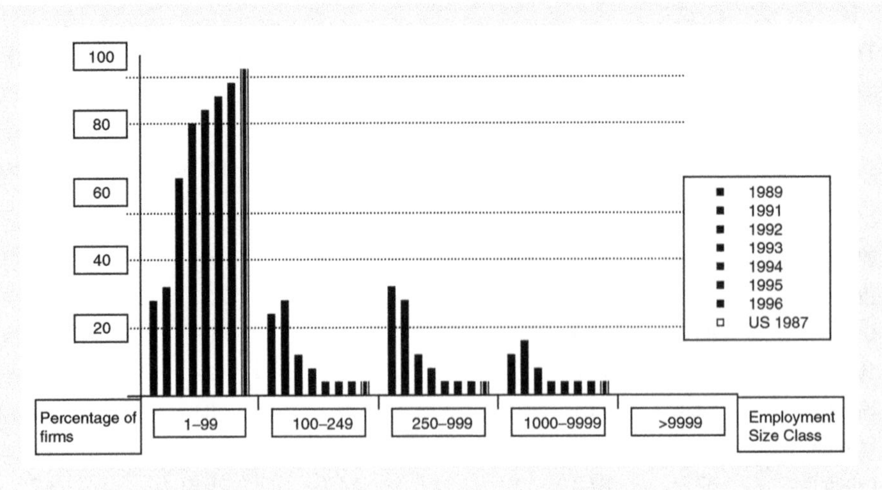

Figure 27.1 Size distribution of firms in manufacturing sectors: Russia and the United States

post-1994. Figure 27.1 reproduces a chart from Brown and Brown (1999), which reveals very rapid growth in the share of small firms from only around 25 percent in 1989 to almost 90 percent in 1996. Hence the Russian firm size distribution is converging to the American one in less than a decade. However, while the size distribution has taken a more regular shape, the numbers of firms remains quite limited. According to Desai (2005), the number of firms in Russia employing no more than 100 workers had risen by 10 percent in 2004 to 946 000, to serve a population of 140 million. Businesses of this size only generated around 10 percent of Russian GDP and provided employment to 19 percent of the labour force. The seeming discrepancy between Brown and Brown (1999) and Desai (2005) data is explained by the former examining the size distribution of firms in manufacturing and the latter looking at the output and employment count in the economy as a whole. While at least in the manufacturing sector size distribution is converging to that of US, the economy as a whole is still dominated by a few large firms, particularly in the natural resources-based industries, while SMEs contribute a modest proportion of national output. Thus 23 firms in Russia control 33 percent of output and around 16 percent of employment.

The growth of a new small firm sector, however remarkable in pace, is not necessarily evidence for an upsurge in entrepreneurship. The increase in firm numbers may also represent the incorporation of enterprises previously operating on grey or black markets, the formation of paper enterprises as an insurance against future unemployment or for shady purposes, or a state-imposed break up of former SOEs. Earle and Sabirianova (1998) analyze self-employment in six transition economies and distinguish between people who work for themselves and those that create jobs for others, a group they identify with entrepreneurs. They find the self-employment share in total employment in 1993 to be highest in Poland, at 23 percent, followed by Bulgaria, Czech Republic, Hungary and Slovakia in the range of 8–11 percent, and finally by Russia with only 4 percent. Comparable figures for Western economies are in the range of 10–15 percent. Nonetheless, these proportions had more than doubled in the transition economies since 1978, from around 11 percent in Poland, 4 percent Bulgaria and Hungary, and less than 1 percent in the more centralized planned economies—Russia and Czechoslovakia. 'Entrepreneurs' in the Earle–Sabirianova definition remain a relatively small fraction of the self-employed in each country; less than one quarter of the total in Poland and Russia but around half in Hungary and the Czech Republic.[7]

In similar vein, Blanchflower et al. (2001) use 'latent entrepreneurship', which they define as the proportion of people who say that they would prefer to be self-employed. They find a great variation in latent entrepreneurship across countries, with countries like the USA, West Germany and Switzerland having rather high proportions—more than 60 percent—while those in Denmark and Norway are rather low, less than 30 percent. Several of the transition economies are at the lower end of the spectrum, i.e. Russia at 33.2 percent and the Czech Republic at 36.8 percent. However, Slovenia, Bulgaria and Hungary are in the middle between 50 percent and 60 percent, while Poland is at the very top of the table with a score of 79.9 percent. Their study suggests no lack of potential entrepreneurs in many transition economies, though perhaps the low social esteem of entrepreneurs in Russia explains the lower aspirations to self-employment.

Entrepreneurial development has been uneven across CEE. Advanced economies of Central Europe lead over former Soviet republics, whether entrepreneurship levels are measured in number of firms per capita (Glas and Dinovsek, 2003), share of total employment or output in SMEs (World Bank, 2002) or percentage of the labour force engaged in entrepreneurial activity (Dutz et al., 2001). However, cross-country comparisons are hindered by inconsistencies of definition and different legal requirements. Small firm definitions range from companies with up to 100 employees in Russia (Goskomstat, 2001) to firms with up 50 employees in Poland (Huebner, 1997) or may be based both on employment count and total assets as in Bulgaria (Mateev, 2003). However, while these statistics preclude an exact ranking of countries in terms of small firm numbers, the low number of small firms in Russia (adjusted by population) and their contribution to national output is manifest when compared to that in Poland, particularly when one takes into account that the cut-off in the Polish definition is much lower.

[7] This measurement of entrepreneurship, however, is also not without fault, as decision to register as self-employed or employing others may be influenced by payroll taxes, which may differ from country to country.

Furthermore, consistency of findings in showing higher prevalence of entrepreneurs in Central European countries lends credibility to the notion that levels of entrepreneurship are higher in more advanced transition economies. This is also supported by results of labour surveys conducted in the second half of 1990s. Thus Dutz et al. (2001) provide further evidence by analyzing the proportion of the labour force engaged in entrepreneurial activity. Their findings show a particularly high proportion employed in entrepreneurship in Hungary (10.9%) and Poland (8.6%). In Armenia, Croatia, Kyrgyzstan and Russia entrepreneurial employment ranges between 4 and 6 percent. In Ukraine, only 1 percent of labour force is employed in entrepreneurship.

27.6 The New Entrepreneurs

Who are the people that are willing to face the risks, and chase the opportunities of setting up their own business? The entrepreneurship literature has analyzed them in terms of their motives and personal characteristics, distinguishing first and foremost between needs-based and opportunity-driven entrepreneurship. The needs-based or survival motive induces people who set up a business to earn a living or a proper income where other forms of employment (and social welfare) are scarce.

Opportunity-driven entrepreneurs follow more intrinsic motives such as to be independent, to implement an idea, a technology, or to make a contribution to society, and are more typical for developed countries.

The Global Entrepreneurship Monitor (GEM, 2003) suggests that in Eastern Europe few entrepreneurs are driven by needs-based motives. Especially compared to other middle-income economies, where setting up your own business is an important route out of poverty, few people in CEE start their own business under pressures to survive or to earn an acceptable family income. This reflects the still very extensive social security in CEE, which may inhibit new firm creation. In contrast to GEM (2003), Smallbone and Welter (2001) observe a large proportion of start-ups being motivated by push factors. This may stem from difference in survey samples as well as from the difficulty of giving empirical content to necessity versus opportunity-driven entrepreneurship.

Scase (2003) offers a different dichotomy, namely, in entrepreneurs' commitment to business growth. He argues that in transition economies, a large proportion of business owners are 'proprietors' who use profits for private consumption rather than reinvest into business. Thus even though SME numbers may be high, they do not necessarily constitute a growth engine, as their motivation is different from that of their Western European counterparts. To our knowledge, there is no conclusive empirical evidence linking motivation and economic impact.

The distinction between self-employed and those who actually grow a business and thus employ other people, used by Earle and Sabirianova (1998), provides a basis for a typology by Ronas-Tas (2002), which we reproduce in Figure 27.2. From a policy perspective, it is especially the second type of business that holds economic growth potential, while the first may substitute for employment relationships in over-regulated labour markets. Peng (2001) offers a more refined typology of four types of individuals that become entrepreneurs in transition economies, to which we add a fifth:

	The caterpillar	**The worm**
Main actor	Entrepreneur	Self-employed
Main unit	Enterprise with its own space	Household
Main goal	Accumulation	Survival/consumption
Main resource	Smart combination of factors of production	Labour
Genesis	Pull	Push
Strategy	Innovative, initiative (prospector)	Defensive, reactive, imitative
Commitment	High, full-time	Low or intermittent, part-time
Contracts	Formal, legal	Informal
Employment	Employs others	Employs only self, family, good friends
Legal form	Incorporated, limited liability	Sole proprietorship, unlimited liability
Market	Anywhere, potentially even abroad	Local
Business relationships	Supplier, subcontractor to big businesses	No substantive relations
Source of profits	Market opportunities	Self-exploitation
Business cycle	Expansion in up cycle	Expansion in down cycle
Taxes	Major source of tax revenue	Often tax evading
Policy intervention	Access to credit	Training
Growth	Likely to grow when successful	Keeps its size small even if successful

Figure 27.2 A typology of entrepreneurs in transition economies

(*Source*: Ronas-Tas 2002)

- *Individuals escaping poverty* may set up as street traders, possibly moving up to become a bazaar trader and then shopowner. These would mostly be needs-driven entrepreneurs, often earning barely enough to survive. They include individuals laid off in the public sector or in state-owned enterprises, and may hold formal education that would qualify them for professions of high qualification that are no longer well paid, such as doctors or scientists.
- *Farmers* may develop their family farm that provides employment for an extended family to expand beyond agriculture. The farm also provides initial resources to set up a business. In the transition economies, farms were usually collectivized during the communist period (except in Poland), and re-privatization provided business opportunities for new owners, although often inhibited by a lack of economies of scale.
- *Professionals*, e.g. researchers, may create their own business out of their previous organization. Typical examples might include university professors who moonlight as consultants, perhaps eventually quitting their jobs to set up their own businesses.
- *Former cadres* at the early stages of transition used their de facto control over resources; including licences, operating permits, bank credit and business networks. As we have seen, the privatization process created opportunities for insiders of firms and government authorities to exploit their position for personal benefit, using not only legal means.
- In addition, *returning expatriates* may set up new businesses, drawing on experiences gained during their years of expatriation, or building on restituted property regained upon their return. Moreover, countries like Poland permitted large numbers of workers to seek employment abroad during the 1980s and their return brought people with accumulated wealth and experiences from countries like Canada, the US and Australia. It seems likely these returnees played a disproportionate role in the early years of private sector development, and substituted for the absence of an indigenous entrepreneurial tradition under communism. Yet there is little formal evidence on entrepreneurship by returning expatriates.

Other studies have investigated empirically the personal characteristics of individuals becoming entrepreneurs. For instance, Smallbone and Welter (2001) find that entrepreneurs often have comparatively high education levels and previous management experience, though typically from SOEs. According to Szelenyi (1988), entrepreneurs under socialism often came from families with previous entrepreneurial traditions, a finding confirmed by Webster (1992). Smallbone and Welter (2001) argue that family tradition was of particular importance in countries like Poland, which permitted the continuation of small-scale private activities throughout the communist era.

Lussier and Pfeifer (2000) compare Croatian and US entrepreneurs and find that the Croatians are on average younger and have less management experience, and fewer have parents with entrepreneurial experience. They start their business with less capital, less planning and less external management advice. In other words, Croatians appear more spontaneous and less systematically prepared in setting up their own business. Similarly, evidence from Lithuania points to enthusiastic but relatively inexperienced young people coming a long way in building new businesses (Gelbuda, 2005). This would suggest some adaptation of entrepreneurial characteristics to the transition environment.

However, the personal characteristics of entrepreneurs vary greatly across transition economies. Roberts and Zhou (2000) find that CIS countries, represented by Armenia, Georgia and Ukraine, saw different entrepreneurial strategies than did advanced reformers such as Hungary, Poland and Slovakia. First, CIS entrepreneurs are more likely to start in trading and then diversify into a different field. Thus a 'generic businessman, always trading, maybe opening a restaurant one year, a taxi business the next, then maybe buying a meat-processing plant ...' (Roberts and Zhou, 2000: 194). Their Central European counterparts are more likely to create firms that exploit and enhance their specialist skills and thus develop more focused business profiles.

Second, entrepreneurs in Commonwealth of Independent States (CIS) countries are more likely to pursue entrepreneurial careers as a part-time occupation while being simultaneously employed elsewhere, often in a SOE. Another distinctive characteristic of entrepreneurship in CIS countries is the prevalence of partnerships as a legal type of business, while entrepreneurs in Central Europe are more often sole proprietors. Finally, Central European firms mostly operate in the official economy while CIS entrepreneurs conduct a significant proportion of their business in the second economy.[8]

A World Bank sponsored study is investigating the characteristics of entrepreneurs and the obstacles they face. At the time of writing, the first results from a pilot study using a matched sample of 777 entrepreneurs and non-entrepreneurs in Russia are available. Regression analysis suggests that family background and exposure to business experience are very important. A cognitive test score and a proxy for 'greed' also have positive effects, as does, perhaps surprisingly, short size. Individuals reporting positive attitudes of society and governments to entrepreneurship are more likely to become entrepreneurs, while perceived corruption has a negative effect (Djankov et al., 2004). This ongoing project can be expected to generate major insights on the determinants of entrepreneurship in transition economies, which, as this review demonstrates, are so far not well understood. Future research may moreover relate characteristics of individuals to their

[8] Differences in entrepreneurial profiles were also identified within the former Soviet Union (Ardichvili and Gaparishvili, 2003). These dissimilarities are a result of historical differences as well as a reflection on quality of existing institutions. In consequence, inferences from one country to the other should be treated with caution.

performance as entrepreneurs, possibly using the aforementioned typologies as a starting point.

27.7 Entrepreneurial strategies

How do these entrepreneurs in transition economies build their businesses in view of high uncertainty and a not very supportive institutional environment? Generally, they adopt strategies that allow them to circumvent burdensome institutions or create substitutes for missing ones. As McMillan and Woodruff (2002) argue, entrepreneurs in transition economies 'succeeded by self-help: they built for themselves substitutes for the missing institutions. Reputational incentives substituted for court enforcement of contracts. Trade credit (loans from firm to firm along the supply chain) substituted for bank credit. Reinvestment of profits substituted for outside equity'. Strategies documented in the literature include engagement in trade and diversification of activities as a means of capital accumulation and hedging against risks (Smallbone and Welter, 2001) and using network-based transactions to substitute for missing or costly markets (Stark, 1996, Batjargal, 2003).

27.7.1 Coping with risk and capital scarcity

Capital scarcity poses a problem not only for the establishment of businesses but also for their growth. Case studies suggest that engagement in trade often serves as initial capital accumulation that allows the entrepreneur to branch off into a different business (Smallbone and Welter, 2001). Portfolio entrepreneurship is another way for businesses to hedge against volatility of markets in transition. Welter and Smallbone (2003) find that entrepreneurs engaged in manufacturing and construction are more likely to have several enterprises then those operating in the services sector. They explain this phenomenon by higher volatility and unpredictability of the manufacturing and construction sectors, particularly in regard to financial flows.

The nature of enterprises also reflects the riskiness of the business environment in transition. Smallbone and Welter (2001) find that 28 percent of entrepreneurs in Ukraine, Belarus and Moldova—countries considered to lag in business environment—are engaged in other occupations. Multiple ownership may also be a consequence of greater risk. Its occurrence is higher in former Soviet republics, and thus may reflect the need for security and access to resources through networking, which is increased by attracting several owners. While these strategies may help entrepreneurs to cope with their environment, they may also preclude development of business efficiency based on specialization of production and streamlining of organizational structures.

27.7.2 Networking as a means of entrepreneurial growth

A persistently recurring issue in studies of entrepreneurs in transition economies is the importance of networks across transition economies, from China (Peng and Heath, 1996; Batjargal and Liu, 2004) and Vietnam (McMillan and Woodruff, 1999) to Hungary (Stark, 1996; Lyles, Saxton and Watson, 2004) and Russia (Batjargal, 2003). The way entrepreneurs use networks varies greatly as the practices are often culturally grounded: for example *guanxi* networks in China 'function' in a very different way than *blat* networks in Russia (Michailova and Worm, 2003). Scholars from a variety of disciplinary perspectives ranging from economics (McMillan and Woodruff, 2002), to sociology (Stark 1996; Sedaitis 1998; Batjargal, 2003), to business strategy (Peng and Heath, 1996; Puffer and McCarthy, 2001; Peng, 2001; Lyles et al., 2004) and entrepreneurship (Smallbone and Welter, 2001) have recognized the importance of the phenomenon, and have investigated its antecedents and consequences. Why are networks so important in transition economies and what are the consequences of an entrepreneurial sector that relies to a higher degree on personal relationships?

Many scholars relate the prevalence of networking to the absence of a well-functioning formal institutional framework (McMillan and Woodruff, 2002; Peng 2001). However there is also a view that sees the pattern of networking, such as *blat* in Russia, as historical and culturally embedded and thus not only as an outcome of the ways the institutional framework has developed during the period of economic transition (Vlachoutsicos, 2000; Buck, 2003).

The transactions costs argument runs as follows: under-developed formal institutions in transition economies cause extensive market failures due to information asymmetries, lack of contract enforcement, high search and negotiation costs and various other effects (Swaan, 1997). In consequence, firms either stay out of these markets or they have to create alternative means to secure themselves. Hence, they build business networks and rely on those relationships to ensure that business partners stick to their side of deals. Moreover, long-term relationships can be built to resemble a repeated game, so the anticipation of benefits from future collaboration outweighs the potential short-term profits of cheating on a partner. These business networks can extend and reinforce the effects of personal reputation. If business partners depend on reputation within a business network, they would be cautious to cheat on anyone in the network as the damaged reputation may outweigh the short-term benefits of cheating—as observed by McMillan and Woodruff (1999) in Vietnam.

Sociologists have analyzed entrepreneurs' embeddedness in their local environment (Granovetter, 1985) and thus view entrepreneurial action to a large degree as an outcome of social interactions. Businesses benefit from networking in many ways, including the circulation of ideas, sharing of knowledge and creation of inter-organizational trust. Research on CEE stimulated by sociology thus has emphasized the prevalence of networks as mechanisms of inter-personal and inter-organizational interaction, and thus as a means to access resources, but also as a source of inertia (Stark, 1996; Grabher and Stark, 1997; Kogut et al., 2000). This approach has been developed with respect to Russian entrepreneurs by Batjargal (2003). He considers systems of entrepreneurs' social relations as social capital, which has been shown to enhance entrepreneurial performance in other contexts. In Russia, where pure market transactions are subject to high transaction costs, such social capital can be expected to be particularly important. In his empirical study, Batjargal (2003) investigates various dimensions of entrepreneurial networks for the Russian context, and finds that in particular, weak ties and resource mobilization (i.e. the ability to access resources through network contacts), enhance revenue growth.

Is the widespread reliance on networks an obstacle or an advantage for entrepreneurs? Taking an institutional economics perspective, networks may first and foremost be a symptom of an inefficient formal institutional framework. However, networking-based business practices can themselves become an institution, as businesses follow certain unwritten rules about how to act within networks, and their strategic actions focus on enhancing or exploiting network relationships. As informal institutions, existing business networks, together with informal rules on how to act within networks, can create barriers to entry and cause inertia in inter-business relationships. In this way, they would inhibit flexibility and the change of industrial structures.

In view of the importance of both formal and informal institutions for entrepreneurs in transition economies, Nee (1998) raises the question of how these would combine to shape economic performance. He suggests that formal and informal norms would be mutually reinforcing, only if the formal rules were congruent with the preferences and interests of economic actors. On the other hand, if formal rules are at variance with the preferences and interests of individuals and organizations, then formal and informal rules may be decoupled, with formal rules becoming largely ceremonial, while informal rules guide day-to-day business. Such varying interactions between formal and informal institutions may explain the diversity in the assessment of network-based economic activity. Reading the literature across transition economies, one notices that scholars of Russian business tend to emphasize the negative effects (Ledeneva, 1998; Johnson et al., 2000; Puffer and McCarthy, 2001), while scholars of China are more cognizant of the positive effects (Peng, 2001; Batjargal and Liu, 2004). In part, this variation may be grounded in cultural differences in the networking practices, and perceptions about the role of networks (Michailova and Worm, 2003). In China, networks may have a higher degree of continuity and network-based practices may provide more coherent overall coordination of economic activity, while Russian networks may have experienced more disruptions during political changes, and therefore provide a less coherent coordination mechanism. In China, networks may have provided an avenue, however imperfect, to alleviate the imperfections of markets supporting institutions. The same may have applied to early stages of transition in CEE, but it is not clear that such a conclusion would also apply to contemporary Russia.

Thus, further research is required to investigate the interaction between formal and informal institutions in guiding entrepreneurs, and the changing role of these institutions at different stages of the transition process (Peng, 2003). Moreover, little research has been undertaken to establish whether networks have become institutionalized and thus create path dependencies that hinder evolution of more efficient market institutions.

27.8 Conclusions

In this chapter, we have outlined the main directions of research on entrepreneurship in the transition economies. Transition from one economic system to another has created unique opportunities for entrepreneurs to create new businesses that fill voids in the structure of industry and services. Yet, it also created unusual risks due to both macroeconomic and institutional instability. A broad consensus in the literature suggests that the specific nature of the institutional environment and of institutional change processes shapes the patterns of entrepreneurship. Multiple lines of theorizing outline how institutions might affect small businesses. However, hard evidence on alternative arguments are hard to come by; empirical results vary with the research methods used, with the performance criteria considered, with the specific proxies used to capture the institutional influence, and the study context in terms of time and location.

So which institutions or policies affect entrepreneurial development in transition? No single policy or institution can account for the rising SME contribution to employment and value added. The most crucial ingredients include economic growth and rule of law as these send a message on the success of reforms and quality of entrepreneurship. Other factors, such as political continuity or discontinuity, rapid and gradual change and state officials who are perceived to be supportive or hostile towards new enterprises can all be context for the successful development of a small firm sector. However, overall success—a critical mass of successful reforms—seems to be the answer, which may explain the growing divergence between Central Europe and the former Soviet Union.

Future research may help resolve these issues by working with more rigorous measures of institutions, beyond entrepreneurs' own perceptions, and by systematic comparative studies in multiple countries. Thus, we need more rigorous study of the characteristics of entrepreneurs and of the determinants of growth using a wider variety of potentially relevant explanatory factors. The research agenda also has to move forward. The empirical research questions addressed in the literature so far concern entrepreneurial businesses in their early stages in transition economies. As these firms mature, they face some major challenges not dissimilar to those in other emerging markets. First, entrepreneurial firms have to develop into mature business organizations, which require different organizational structures, and different leadership skills. This organizational transition from young entrepreneurial firm to mature business firm merits research attention. Secondly, SMEs from transition economies face major obstacles in accessing global markets, even if they have been successful at home. Many entrepreneurs in CEE appear to have engaged in international business relatively early (Gelbuda, 2005), yet failure rates of early internationalizing firms appear to be especially high (Lyles, Saxton and Watson, 2004). On the global stage, firms need other types of resources to obtain competitive advantages, including global brands and access to distribution channels in Europe and North America. Local business networks may be important for growth within a country, but do not help in developing an international strategy. Outward international business by entrepreneurial firms is therefore an important research issue in transition economies, and in emerging markets more generally.

References

Acs, Z. J. and Audretsch, D. (eds) (1993). *Small Firms and Entrepreneurship an East–West Perspective.* Cambridge: Cambridge University Press.

Aidis, R. (2003). *By Law and by Custom: Factors Affecting Small- and Medium-Sized Enterprises during the Transition in Lithuania.* Amsterdam: Thela Thesis.

—— (2003). 'Officially Despised yet Tolerated: Open-Air Markets and Entrepreneurship in Postsocialist Countries'. *Post-Communist Economies,* 15(3): 461–473.

AIDIS, R. and T. MICKIEWICZ (2004). 'Which Entrepreneurs Expect to Expand Their Business? Evidence from Survey Data in Lithuania'. *William Davidson Institute Working Paper* 723.

ARDICHVILI, A. and A. GAPARISHVILI (2003). 'Russian and Georgian Entrepreneurs and Non-entrepreneurs: A study of Value Differences'. *Organization Studies*, 24: 29–46.

BANERJI, S. and N. LONG (2001). 'Wealth Distribution, Entrepreneurship and Intertemporal Trade'. *Cirano Scientific Series*, pp. 2001–36.

BARBERIS, N., M. BOYCKO, A. SHLEIFER and N. TSUKANOVA (1996). 'How Does Privatization Work? Evidence from the Russian Shops'. *Journal of Political Economy*, 104(4): 764–91.

BARTELSMANN, E., J. HALTIWANGER and S. SCARPETTA (2004). 'Microeconomic Evidence of Creative Destruction in Industrial and Developing Countries'. IZA Discussion Paper, 1374.

BATJARGAL, B. (2003). 'Social Capital and Entrepreneurial Performance in Russia: A Longitudinal Study'. *Organization Studies*, 24(4): 5353–556.

—— and M. LIU (2004). 'Entrepreneurs' Access to Private Equity in China: The Role of Social Capital'. *Organization Science*, 15(2): 159–72.

BAUMOL, W. J. (1990). 'Entrepreneurship: Productive, Unproductive, and Destructive'. *Journal of Political Economy*, 98(5): 893–921.

BECK, T., A. DEMIRGUC-KUNT, L. LAEVEN and R. LEVINE (2004). 'Finance, Firm Size, and Growth', NBER Working Paper, No. 10983.

BELKA, M., S. ESTRIN, M. SCHAFFER and I. SINGH (1995). 'Enterprise Adjustment in Poland: Evidence from a Survey of 200 Private, Privatized and State-owned Firms'. *Centre of Economic Performance Discussion Paper*, 223.

BERGLOF, E. and P. BOLTON (2002). 'The Great Divide and Beyond: Financial Architecture in Transition'. *Journal of Economic Perspectives*, 16(1): 77–100.

BLANCHFLOWER, D., A. OSWALD and A. STUTZER (2001). 'Latent Entrepreneurship Across Nations'. *European Economic Review*, 45(4–6): 680–691.

BOYCKO, M., A. SHLEIFER and R. VISHNY (1995). *Privatizing Russia*. Cambridge, MA: MIT Press.

BROWN, A. and D. BROWN (1999). 'The Transition of Market Structure in Russia: Economic Lessons and Implications for Competition'. Stockholm Institute of Transition Economics Discussion Paper, 99/01.

BUCK, T. (2003). 'Modern Russian Corporate Governance: Convergent Forces or Product of Russia's History?' *Journal of World Business*, 38(4): 299–313.

CHILOSI, A. (2001). 'Entrepreneurship and Transition'. *MOCT-MOST: Economic Policy in Economic Transition*, 11: 327–57.

DALLAGO, B. (1997). 'The Economic System, Transition and Opportunities for Entrepreneurship' *Entrepreneurship and SMEs in Transition Economies*. OECD Proceedings, Visegrad Conference, OECD.

DESAI, P. (2005). 'Russian Retrospectives on Reform from Yeltsin to Putin'. *Journal of Economic Perspectives*, 19(1): 87–106.

DESOTO, H. (2000). *The Mystery of Capital: Why Capitalism Triumphs in the West and Fails Everywhere Else*. New York: Harper & Row.

DJANKOV, S. and P. MURRELL (2002). 'Enterprise Restructuring in Transition: A Quantitative Survey'. *Journal of Economic Literature*, 40(3): 739–93.

—— E. MIGUEL, Y. QIAN, G. ROLAND and E. ZHURAVSKAYA (2004). 'Who are Russia's Entrepreneurs'. Mimeo. The World Bank.

Dutz, M., C. Kaufmann, S. Najarian, P. Sanfey and R. Yemtsov (2001). 'Labour Market States, Mobility and Entrepreneurship in Transition Economies', EBRD Working Paper, No. 66.

Earle, J. and K. Sabirianova (1998). 'Understanding Wage Arrears in Russia'. Stockholm Institute of Transition Economics Working Paper, 139.

EBRD (1994–2004). *Transition Report.* London: European Bank for Reconstruction and Development.

Ellman, M. (1994). *Socialist Planning.* Cambridge: Cambridge University Press.

Ericson, R. (1991). 'The Classical Soviet-Type Economy: Nature of the System and Implications for Reform'. *Journal of Economic Perspectives*, 5(4): 11–27.

Estrin, S. and M. Peiperl (1998). 'Managerial Markets in Transition in Central and Eastern Europe: A Field Study and Implications'. *International Journal of Human Resource Management*, 9(1): 58–78.

Eurostat (2002). 'SMEs in Europe—Candidate Countries. European Commission'. Belgium: Brussels.

Feakins, M. (2002). 'Commercial Bank Lending to SMEs in Poland'. *Small Business Economics*, 23: 51–70.

Fogel, G. and A. Zapalska (2001). 'A Comparison of Small-and Medium-Size Enterprise Development in Central and Eastern Europe'. *Comparative Economic Studies*, 43(3): 35–68.

Frye, T. and E. Zhuravskaya (2000). 'Rackets, Regulation and the Rule of Law'. *Journal of Law, Economics and Organization*, 16(2): 478–502.

Gelbuda, M. (2005). 'Exploring Internationalization and Learning: Towards an Interpretive Perspective'. Doctoral Dissertation, Department of Business Studies, Aalborg University: Denmark.

GEM (2003). 'Global Entrepreneurship Monitor'. London: London Business School.

Glas, M. and M. Dinovsek (2003). 'Small Business in Slovenia: Expectations and Accomplishments', in D. Kirby and A. Watson (eds) *Small Firms and Economic Development in Developed and Transition Economies: A Reader.* Aldershot: Ashgate.

Goskomstat (2001). *Maloe Predprinimatelstvo v Rossii.* Moscow: Goskomstat.

Grabher, G. and D. Stark (1997). 'Organizing Diversity: Evolutionary Theory, Network Analysis and Postsocialism'. *Regional Studies*, 31(5): 533–44.

Granovetter, M. (1985). 'Small is Bountiful: Labor Markets and Establishment size'. *American Sociological Review*, 49(3): 323–35.

Gregory, P. and R. Stuart (1995). *Soviet Economic Structure and Performance.* New York: Harper & Row.

Hayek, F. (1945). 'The Use of Knowledge in Society'. *American Economic Review*, 32(4): 943–6.

Huebner, D. (1997). 'A Strategy of SMEs in Poland'. *Entrepreneurship and SMEs in Transition Economies.* OECD Proceedings, the Visegrad Conference: OECD.

ISEAED (2001). *Izuchenie Situazii v Sektore Malogo i Srednego Biznessa.* Moscow: ISEAED.

Johnson, S. and G. Loveman (1995). 'Starting Over: Poland After Communism'. *Harvard Business Review*, 73(2): 44–55.

—— J. McMillan and C. Woodruff (2000). 'Entrepreneurs and the Ordering of Institutional Reform'. *Economics of Transition*, 8(1): 1–36.

Kirzner, I. (1983). 'The Entrepreneur, Mainstream Views and Radical Critiques (Book Review)'. *Southern Economic Journal*, 50(2): 611–3.

Kogut, B., A. Spicer and G. McDermott (2000). 'Entrepreneurship and Privatization in Central Europe: The Tenuous Balance between Creation and Destruction'. *Academy of Management Review*, 25: 630–49.

Kontorovich, V. (1999). 'Has New Business Creation in Russia Come to a Halt?' *Journal of Business Venturing*, 14(5–6): 451–60.

Kornai, J. (1990). *Road to a Free Economy*. New York: Norton.

Ledeneva, A. (1998). *Russia's Economy of Favours: Blat, Networking and Informal Exchange*. Cambridge: Cambridge University Press.

Lizal, L. and J. Svejnar (2002). 'Investment, Credit Rationing, and the Soft Budget Constraint: Evidence from Czech Panel Data'. *The Review of Economics and Statistics*, 84(2): 353–70.

Lussier, R. and S. Pfeifer (2000). 'A Comparison of Business Success versus Failure Variables between US and Central Eastern Europe Croatian Entrepreneurs'. *Entrepreneurship: Theory and Practice*, 24(4): 59–68.

Lyles, M., T. Saxton and K. Watson (2004). 'Venture Survival in a Transition Economy'. *Journal of Management*, 30(3): 351–75.

Mateev, M. (2003). 'Entrepreneurship and SME Development in Transition Countries: The Case of Bulgaria', in D. Kirby and A. Watson (eds) *Small Firms and Economic Development and Transition Economies: A Reader*. Aldershot: Ashgate.

McMillan, J. and C. Woodruff (1999). 'Interfirm Relationships and Informal Credit in Vietnam'. *Quarterly Journal of Economics*, 114(4): 1285–320.

—— and —— (2002). 'The Central Role of Entrepreneurs in Transition Economies'. *Journal of Economic Perspectives*, 16(3): 153–70.

Meyer, K., D. Ionascu, P. Kulawczuk, A. Szczesniak, Z. Antal-Mokos, K. Tóth and V. Darskuvenie (2005). 'The Changing Patterns of Foreign Direct Investment in EU Accession Countries: Insights from a New Survey'. Working Paper. Centre for Eastern European Studies, Copenhagen Business School.

Michailova, S. and V. Worm (2003). 'Personal Networking in Russia and China: Blat and Guanxi'. *European Management Journal*, 23(4): 509–19.

Murrel, P. (1996). 'How Far Has the Transition Progressed?' *Journal of Economic Perspectives*, 10(2): 25–44.

Olson, M. (1992). 'The Hidden Path to a Successful Economy', in C. Clague and G. Rausser (eds) *The Emergence of Market Economies in Eastern Europe*. Oxford: Blackwell.

Nee, V. (1998). 'Norms and Networks in Economic and Organizational Performance'. *American Economic Review*, 88(2): 85–9.

Peng, M. W. (2001). 'How Entrepreneurs Create Wealth in Transition Economies', *Academy of Management Executive*, 15: 95–110.

—— (2003). 'Institutional Transitions and Strategic Choices'. *Academy of Management Review*, 28(2): 275–97.

—— and P. Heath (1996). 'The Growth of the Firm in Planned Economies in Transition: Institutions, Organizations, and Strategic Choices'. *Academy of Management Review*, 21(2): 492–528.

Pissarides, F. (1999). 'Is the Lack of Funds the Main Obstacle to Growth? EBRD's Experience with Small- and Medium-sized Businesses in Central and Eastern Europe'. *Journal of Business Venturing*, 14: 519–39.

—— M. Singer and J. Svejnar (2003). 'Objectives and Constraints of Entrepreneurs: Evidence from Small and Medium Size Firms in Bulgaria and Russia'. *Journal of Comparative Economics*, 31: 503–31.

Puffer, S. and D. McCarthy (2001). 'Navigating the Hostile Maze: A Framework for Russian Entrepreneurship'. *Academy of Management Executive*, 15(4): 24–36.

Richter, A. and M. Schaffer (1996). 'The Performance of De Novo Private Firms in Russian Manufacturing', in Commander, Fan and Schaffer (eds) *Enterprise Restructuring Economic Policy in Russia*. EDI/ The World Bank.

Ricketts, M. (2002). *The Economies of Business Enterprise: An Introduction to Economic Organization and the Theory of the Firm*. Cheltenham: Edward Elgar.

Roberts, K. and C. Zhou (2000). 'New Private Enterprises in Three Transitional Contexts: Central Europe, the Former Soviet Union and China'. *Post-Communist Economies*, 12(2): 187–99.

Roland, G. and T. Verdier (2003). 'Law Enforcement and Transition'. *European Economic Review*, 47(4): 669–86.

Ronas-Tas (2002). 'The Worm and the Caterpillar: The Small Private Sector in the Czech Republic, Hungary, and Slovakia', in V. Bonnell and T. Gold (eds) *The New Entrepreneurs of Europe and Asia: Patterns of Business Development in Russia, Eastern Europe, and China*. Armonk, NY: M. E. Sharpe.

Scase, R. (2003). 'Entrepreneurship and Proprietorship in Transition: Policy implications for the SME sector', in R. J. McIntyre and B. Dallago (eds) *Small and Medium Enterprises in Transitional Economies*. Basingstoke New York: Houndmills Palgrave, Macmillan.

Schumpeter, J. (1934). *The Theory of Economic Development*. Cambridge, MA: Harvard University Press.

Sedaitis, J. (1998). 'The Alliances of Spin-offs Versus Start-ups: Social Ties in the Genesis of Post-Soviet Alliances'. *Organization Science: A Journal of the Institute of Management Sciences*, 9(3): 368–82.

Shleifer, A. and R. Vishny (1999). *In The Grabbing Hand: Government Pathologies and Their Cures*. Boston, MA: Harvard University Press.

Smallbone, D. and F. Welter (2001). 'The Distinctiveness of Entrepreneurship in Transition Economies'. *Small Business Economics*, 16(4): 249–62.

—— and F. Welter (2006). 'Conceptualising Entrepreneurship in a Transition Context'. *International Journal of Entrepreneurship and Small Business*, 3(2): 190–206.

Spicer, A., G. McDermott and B. Kogut (2000). 'Entrepreneurship and Privatization in Central Europe: The Tenuous Balance between Destruction and Creation', *Academy of Management Review*, 25(3): 630–49.

Stark, D. (1996). 'Recombinant Property in East European Capitalism'. *American Journal of Sociology*, 101(4): 993–1027.

Swaan, W. (1997). 'Knowledge, Transaction Costs and the Creation of Markets in Post-socialist Economies', in P. Hare and J. Davis (eds) *Transition to the Market Economy*. London: Routledge.

Szelenyi, I. (1988). *Socialist Entrepreneurs*. Madison, WI: University of Wisconsin Press.

Verheul, I., S. Wennekers, D. Audretsch, and A. Thurik (2002). 'An Eclectic Theory of Entrepreneurship: Policies, Institutions and Culture', in D. Audretsch, A. Thurik, I. Verheul and A. Wennekers (eds) *Entrepreneurship: Determinants and Policy in a European–US Comparison.* Boston/Dordrecht: Kluwer Academic Publishers.

Vlachoutsicos, C. (2000). 'Russian Communitarianism', in D. Denison (ed.) *Managing Organizational Change in Transition Economies.* Mahway, NJ: LEA.

Webster. L. (1992). *Private Sector Manufacturing in Czech and Slovak Federal Republic: A Survey of Firms.* Industry Development Division, Industry and Energy Department, The World Bank.

—— (1992). *Private Sector Manufacturing in Hungary: A Survey of Firms.* Industry Development Division, Industry and Energy Department, The World Bank.

Welter, F. and D. Smallbone (2003). 'Entrepreneurship and Enterprise Strategies in Transition Economies: An Institutional Perspective', in D. Kirby and A. Watson (eds) *Small Firms and Economic Development in Developed and Transition Economies: A Reader.* Aldershot: Ashgate.

Wennekers, S. and R. Thurik (1999). 'Linking Entrepreneurship and Economic Growth'. *Small Business Economics,* 13: 27–55.

World Bank (1996, 2002, 2005). *World Development Report.* Washington, DC: World Bank.

Index

Lightning Source UK Ltd.
Milton Keynes UK
UKHW030335220119
335983UK00002B/4/P

9 780199 546992